SMITH'S
STORY OF THE MENNONITES

SMITH'S STORY OF THE MENNONITES

by
C. Henry Smith

Fifth Edition
Revised and Enlarged
by
Cornelius Krahn

Wipf & Stock
PUBLISHERS
Eugene, Oregon

Wipf and Stock Publishers
199 W 8th Ave, Suite 3
Eugene, OR 97401

Smith's Story of the Mennonites
Fifth Edition
By Smith, C. Henry
Copyright©1981 Herald Press
ISBN: 1-59752-026-8
Publication date 1/26/2005
Previously published by Faith and Life Press, 1981

Fifth Edition Revised and Enlarged by Cornelius Krahn

Table of Contents

Foreword · Robert Kreider ix
Preface xvii

EUROPE

I. *The Anabaptists* 3
    1. Switzerland 3
    2. South Germany 18
    3. Middle Germany 24
    4. Tyrol and Austria 31
    5. Moravia 33
    6. The Lower Rhine 41
    7. Münster 44

II. *Menno Simons* 53

III. *Switzerland* 75
    1. Continued Persecution 75
    2. Toleration Granted 94

IV. *The Netherlands* 103
    1. After Menno Simons 103
    2. Internal Divisions 109
    3. The Golden Age 115
    4. A Period of Decline 130
    5. At the Turn of the Century 137

V. *Northern Germany* 147
    1. Northwest Germany 147
    2. West Prussia and Poland 166

VI. *South Germany* 189
    1. Habsburg Crown Lands 189
    2. Bavaria 191
    3. The Palatinate 192
    4. Galicia and Volhynia 208
    5. Alsace-Lorraine and France 209
    6. The Mennonites of Germany Today 220

VII. *The Hutterites* 225

VIII. *Russia* 249
    1. The Chortitza Settlement 253

	2. The Molotschna Settlement	257
	3. Economic Progress	261
	4. Religious Life	272
	5. Migrations to America and Asia	283
	6. Era of Expansion	300
	7. World War I and After	310
	8. The Mennonites in Russia Today	341

AMERICA

IX.	*First Settlements and Expansions (1683-1800)*	359
	1. New York and Germantown	359
	2. Swiss-German Palatines	364
	3. Early Amish Settlements	371
	4. Expansion of the Pioneer Settlements	373
	5. Ontario	376
X.	*The Nineteenth Century Westward Expansion*	381
	1. Pennsylvania and Virginia Emigrants	381
	2. The New Immigrant Tide	384
XI.	*Pennsylvania German Groups*	395
	1. Mennonite Branches	395
	2. Amish Branches	409
	3. The (Old) Mennonite Church	417
XII.	*Russo-German Groups*	425
	1. The Prairie States and Provinces (1874-1884)	425
	2. Mennonites Move Westward	434
	3. Mennonites in Manitoba	435
	4. Western United States	447
	5. The General Conference Mennonite Church	459
XIII.	*In Search of Freedom of Conscience*	473
	1. Canada	473
	2. Mexico	484
	3. Paraguay	489
	4. Brazil	500
XIV.	*Theological and Cultural Developments*	507
XV.	*Witnessing in War and Peace*	535
	1. Church and State in Early America	535
	2. World War I	539
	3. World War II and After	552

Bibliography ... 561
Index ... 573

List of Maps and Illustrations

C. Henry Smith	viii
Central Europe in 1550	2
Menno Simons	54
Where Menno Simons Lived	56
Mennonites in Switzerland	74
Mennonites in the Netherlands	104
Mennonites in Northern Germany	148
Mennonites in Southern Germany	188
The Spread of Mennonites in Russia	250
Mennonite Migration from Russia 1874-1930	322
Germantown Mennonite Meetinghouse	358
The Teutonia	426
Mennonites in South America	506

C. Henry Smith (1875-1948)

Foreword

Dr. C. Henry Smith was one of the admired adults in my boyhood world in Bluffton, Ohio. When he walked downtown to the Citizens National Bank where he was president, we all knew that there went a distinguished man. He wore a Phi Beta Kappa key, often carried a cane, read the *Cleveland Plain Dealer*, and chatted in a friendly, easy manner with passersby. He wrote books, traveled to faraway places, and paused to talk with us as we played ball on a nearby vacant lot. He seemed more genial and approachable than most adults. (Once I received a postcard from him sent from Hawaii.) He and his wife, Laura, lived alone in a big Dutch Colonial house on College Drive across from the wooded campus. Their only child, a son, had died in infancy and lay buried in the Zion Mennonite cemetery three miles west of town.

We heard Smith lecture entertainingly on current events, his travels, or Mennonite history. In the mornings at the college he was a popular teacher of history; in the afternoons, a banker; and in the evenings, a writer of history books. We sensed that the Smiths were well-to-do, but they lived simply like the rest of their neighbors. I remember listening in on adult talk with Smith present. He told stories, asked lots of questions about people's family history, and conversed vividly on a wide range of subjects.

Several years later while traveling to Europe, I carried in my knapsack a paperback edition of his small book *Menno Simons—Apostle of the Nonresistant Life*. As we cycled to the historic Mennonite scenes at Witmarsum, Leeuwarden, and Amsterdam, the pages from Smith's booklet brought a 400-year-old past to life. We met Mennonite leaders in The Hague, Amsterdam, and in South Germany who knew Smith and spoke admiringly of him. Smith helped me, at age nineteen, to feel good about being a Mennonite.

After his death I received from Mrs. Smith her husband's doctoral robe and hood, which now hang in my closet. The recipient of one of the first doctorates earned by a Mennonite in America, he received his degree from the same department and the same university where I earned my degree forty-six years later.

C. Henry Smith was born into an Amish home near Metamora, Illinois, in 1875—ten years after the death of Abraham Lincoln, before the invention of the telephone, Edison's light bulb, the automobile, the airplane, and before the establishment of Rural Free Delivery. When he died in 1948 at the age of seventy-three, the Cold War had just begun, but neither the hydrogen bomb nor the pocket computer had been invented. Xerox and television had not appeared.

At his death Harold S. Bender, another leading Mennonite historian, stated:

> Dr. Smith was unquestionably the greatest of the historians produced by the Mennonites of America and the peer of any of the European Mennonite historians. With his five major works, written over a period of thirty-five years, he published more full-length historical works than any other Mennonite historian. His particular gift was that of synthesis of masses of material into well-written, interesting, integrated accounts. He was pre-eminently the general Mennonite historian who took the great sweep of our history in both Europe and America and put it into clear, easily read volumes that will remain standard works for years to come.

The last of Smith's works was *The Story of the Mennonites*, published in 1941 when Smith was sixty-six years old. This has since become the most widely read Mennonite history ever published.

Historical Works

The Story of the Mennonites was based on Smith's 1920 history, *The Mennonites: A Brief History of Their Origin and Later Development in both Europe and America*, which he expanded to double the size of the original volume. *The Mennonites*, in turn, had its roots in *Mennonites of America*, published in 1909, which grew out of his doctoral dissertation of 1907.

One of Smith's most popular books was *The Coming of the Russian Mennonites: An Episode in the Settling of the Last Frontier 1874-1884*, which resulted from a year of research as visiting professor at Bethel College in 1922-23. His best historical contribution probably was *The Mennonite Immigration to Pennsylvania in the Eighteenth Century*, which appeared in 1929, the year of the stock market crash. He wrote little during the following decade of depression as he worked to help a bank and a

INTRODUCTION

college to survive.

Among my favorites are two additional works: a slender volume, *One Hundred Years Ago*, an address delivered at the first homecoming celebration of the Old Partridge congregation near Metamora, Illinois, August 20, 1940, and *Mennonite Country Boy, The Early Years of C. Henry Smith*, published in 1962, fourteen years after his death, but written thirty-seven years earlier when he was fifty.

In addition to the fifteen books he wrote or edited, thirty-three encyclopedia articles and more than one hundred sixty articles in Mennonite periodicals bear his name. His first article appeared in 1895 in a Mennonite youth paper on the subject "Reading and Home Education." As early as 1905 he wrote eight articles on the Anabaptists. He roamed far and wide in his writing, touching such topics as the following: "Tolstoy," "The Poetry of the Bible," "Our Feathered Friends," "Christopher Dock," "The Hand of God in American History," "The Indians of Alaska," "Dwight L. Moody and War," "Keeping the Faith," "A Five Foot Shelf on Peace."

The Story of the Mennonites was the last major contribution of C. Henry Smith. It received lavish praise from Harold Bender and colleagues Ernst Correll and Robert Friedman: "a scholarly, well-written, and readable history of the Mennonites, the best, we dare say, which has been written to date in any language... a splendid work, one of whose chief excellences is its easy, readable style... (he was) a good storyteller, with an eye for the main outlines of the tale, and for the elements of permanent human interest."

Smith's *Story* drew critical fire, however, from Bender and colleagues on a number of counts: it was too pro-General Conference, too reserved in its appreciation for the "Old" Mennonites at the center of the Anabaptist heritage. He was criticized for his lack of penetration into the soul of Mennonitism (piety, ethics, theology); his neglect of Michael Sattler and Pilgram Marbeck, and his undue praise of Hans Denk; his overemphasis on individualism and underemphasis on brotherhood themes; his failure to write history as *Geistesgeschichte* (history focused on the shaping of theological and philosophical motifs); his failure to define the essence of Anabaptism, and more.

Those who seek to synthesize complex and sweeping expanses of history are easy prey for the revisionists. Undoubtedly Dr. Smith, reflecting the optimistic climate of his age, found liberation in individualism, education, and progress—all of these themes seen as ingredients in the Anabaptist legacy. Undoubtedly his memories of brittle and restrictive church controls prevented him from embracing fully the concept of the caring, affirming, binding-and-loosing fellowship of his Anabaptist heritage. Undoubtedly he could have been more discerning in theological distinctions and nuances. At times, especially in his popular articles, he seemed to accept uncritically the American mythology of progress, manifest destiny, and the superiority of American civilization. In 1940, during the first year of World War II, he reflected a less Americanized view of the future. In an address before his home congregation in Metamora, Illinois, he stated:

> At no time for centuries has religious toleration and the very existence of religious faith itself, to say nothing of democracy and peace been so challenged and threatened throughout a large part of the world as today. . . . It is not at all certain but that the true followers of Christ may again have to face the tests of discipleship as did our forefathers. God grant that this test may never come to us here; but if it does may God also grant us the same sublime courage and sustaining faith to meet the test so eminently shown by them.

The easy optimism was gone.

Despite the imperfections, C. Henry Smith remains a heroic pioneer figure. He did so much with so little. When he began his work as a historian, there were no Mennonite historical libraries and archives, only a few isolated private collections of Mennonite books. When C. Henry Smith came to teach at Goshen College, the library consisted of "only one row of books on a single shelf across the back end of one of the recitation rooms." In his autobiography he tells of how he spent his summers going from courthouse to courthouse and person to person in the East to try and reconstruct the Mennonite story. Even as late as 1940, when he submitted his manuscript on *The Story of the Mennonites* to the press, C. Henry Smith probably had not one-tenth of the books, periodicals, and documents a scholar has today in telling the same story.

For C. Henry Smith, scholarship in Mennonite studies was embued with affection. In his very first book, written in 1907 at age thirty-two, he stated in the final paragraph: "I feel that a knowledge of what the Mennonite church has stood for in the past will help us to gain a greater respect for ourselves." Like the Old Testament chroniclers he came to help his people remember how God had worked in their history so that they could return to more faithful ways. In a particular way, C. Henry Smith, the first of his Amish community to go on to college, saw in the recovery of a historical consciousness and in the establishment of Mennonite colleges a way "to save the young men and women for the old faith." And so he gave his life to writing history and establishing and teaching in four Mennonite schools—Elkhart, Goshen, Bluffton, and Witmarsum Theological Seminary.

INTRODUCTION   xiii

C. Henry Smith is remarkable because he set foot on, and occupied, virgin terrain. A lone figure, he had few scholarly comrades in his explorations. He brought with him from his university studies good scholarly tools which he used with care. But he was attractive as an historian because he wrote for the people. He went beyond conference minute books to note the songs the people sang, the meetinghouses they built, the stories they told, the games they played, the customs they practiced, the ways they taught their children. In his *One Hundred Years Ago*, the story of the Old Partridge congregation, he displayed his gift of recovering the atmosphere of times past. One travels by buggy with him from farm to meetinghouse to schoolhouse.

C. Henry Smith may not have been so skilled in systematically identifying and analyzing the theological propositions which shape a people. However, he was gifted in conveying an understanding of the multiple ways in which a people pass on their faith from parents to children. His autobiography beautifully illustrates the art and grace of a people in nurturing their faith from generation to generation. Perhaps C. Henry Smith's sensing of the interconnectedness of all the experiences of a people is every bit as important as the art of defining precisely the history of ideas of a group. One of the regrets I have for Smith was that he apprenticed so few disciples. Despite his amiable spirit, he remained a private person.

The Making of an Historian

This leads to some concluding reflections on the intriguing story of how an Amish boy in Illinois caught fire with a love of learning and an affection for his Mennonite people. The story begins with his growing up in an Amish home where he loved his parents and was loved by them. In *Mennonite Country Boy*, Smith tells of a Willie Whitmire, a schoolteacher with a contagious gift for learning, who suggested to him that he might become a schoolteacher. One Sunday in January, a Mennonite preacher from Indiana by the name of John S. Coffman preached an English sermon in which he showed himself "thoroughly at home in the fields of literature and history and other subjects.... He seemed a kindred spirit.... riding home with us, he told me ... about the stars which I had just been reading about." A few years later, J. S. Coffman would be inviting the twenty-three-year-old Henry to teach at the Elkhart Institute and to live with his family. C. Henry remembers with affection his farmer father, selected by lot at age forty-four to be bishop, reading his Bible into the night, preparing for his next sermon. He loved his father and was proud of his vigorous speaking out on such issues as the saloon. Every year until his death, C. Henry Smith returned to his family and his home community to renew his sense of worth and belonging.

To be an Amish boy, one of a peculiar people, was also a burden for the young Henry. He caught glimpses of a world beyond his Amish community which beckoned him. He was uneasy with the "wave of puritanical censorship, first sponsored by certain Indiana Mennonite evangelists" which spread through the community and transformed the recreational life of the young people. The county seat of Metamora, with its population of seven hundred, symbolized an alternative world. In the Metamora courthouse, Abraham Lincoln, and later Bob Ingersoll and the first Adlai Stevenson, had practiced law. Cass Irving, editor of the local paper, introduced him to the *Scientific American* and showed him a letter his father had once received from Lincoln.

C. Henry began to teach country school at the age of sixteen. In the summer of 1894 he traveled all the way to Elkhart to attend the newly founded Mennonite school. There he met a lively young group of volunteers working at the local Mennonite Publishing Company. For Henry this was a big, new, expanding Mennonite world. In the fall of 1896 he left teaching to enter normal school on the outskirts of Bloomington. One bright memory in two years of plodding normal school was his election as president of the local YMCA and a trip to the YMCA Conference at Lake Geneva, Wisconsin, where he heard the missionary statesman John R. Mott speak. On the train he met a young Mennonite, Noah E. Byers, then a student at Northwestern University, soon to become principal of the Elkhart Institute, and later president of Goshen College.

Bored with normal school, C. Henry dropped out of the teacher's course to go to Elkhart to take a job at forty-five dollars a month teaching physics, botany, Latin, history, pedagogy, and psychology at the new Mennonite Institute. Frugal young man that he was, he cycled along dirt roads the two hundred miles from Metamora to Elkhart. There he yearned to be a good teacher, and resolved that "the student's interest must first be aroused." He saw the best teaching to be that "which engenders an abiding enthusiasm for the fields of knowledge in question."

During his vacations at Elkhart his restless curiosity took him to the St. Louis Fair, to the Rocky Mountains, and up Pike's Peak. In the making of a Mennonite historian, the most important discovery that first summer at Elkhart was for him to find his way into the library of John F. Funk, Mennonite publisher. Here was the most complete collection in America of books and pamphlets dealing with Mennonite and Anabaptist history. Here he decided on his life work.

INTRODUCTION

In 1900 he was at Champaign attending the University of Illinois. Within three years, at the Universities of Illinois and Chicago, he had acquired his B.A. and M.A. degrees as well as a Phi Beta Kappa key. The University of Chicago was then in its first decade of development under William Rainey Harper. He studied history and government under Judson, Jameson, and Merriam; sang with a choral society; heard Caruso and Schumann-Heink at the opera; and saw Richard Mansfield, Julia Marlowe, and Ethel Barrymore at the theater. At Chicago he made another important discovery:

> One day while casually leafing through a book on Baptist history in the library of the seminary I ran across the name of Menno Simons.... I found to my surprise that all Baptist historians claimed a common spiritual origin with the Mennonites in the Anabaptist movement.... Continued reading during the winter revealed the fact, to my increasing delight, that the Congregationalists, too, credited the Dutch Mennonite artisans and religious refugees who came to southeastern England ... as the source of the ideas of religious toleration.... I had always thought of Mennonites as an obscure, peculiar people, with strange unpopular practices.... To discover, therefore, that they were pioneers in the rise of religious toleration, and that they were the spiritual forefathers of both the Baptists and the Congregationalists, as well as the earliest of all modern peace societies, was a revelation to me as surprising as pleasing. My respect for the religion of my forefathers was greatly enhanced.

In 1903 he was called to the faculty of the new Goshen College and delivered the address at the ground-breaking ceremonies. Four years later, in 1907, he received his doctorate at the University of Chicago with a dissertation on the history of the Mennonites in America. The following year he married Laura Ioder and returned to Goshen to serve as teacher of history, academic dean, librarian, and writer. In 1913 he and President N. E. Byers moved to Bluffton. There is much more to the story, but this is sufficient to suggest that the stories of C. Henry Smith will be told as long as there will be records of the people called Mennonites.

The life of C. Henry Smith embraces a rich fund of memories through three-quarters of a century of revolutionary changes in the American Mennonite experience. We need a full biography of the life and times of C. Henry Smith. One of the keepers and collectors of the Smith legacy is Cornelius Krahn, who has edited and revised this classic, *The Story of the Mennonites*. We owe so much to C. Henry Smith, to Cornelius Krahn, and to others who have helped us to remember the works of the Lord in diverse places like the Old Partridge meetinghouse near the timber, the library of John F. Funk, and a cluttered study in Bluffton, Ohio.

Robert Kreider

Preface

The Story of the Mennonites, by C. Henry Smith, is a book which has had a long and interesting history. It had its beginning at the University of Chicago, where, in 1907, C. Henry Smith wrote his Ph.D. dissertation on *The Mennonites in America*, which was published in 1909. This was followed in 1910 by *The Mennonites* in which Smith covered the total history of the European and American Mennonites. This was the forerunner of *The Story of the Mennonites* first published in 1941. It was the first Mennonite book in the English language covering the total history of the Mennonites in all countries. Smith was one of the first Mennonite scholars in this field with the gift and the intention to tell the story of the Mennonites in a popular and appealing way for both the scholar and the layman. In this he succeeded very well. A reprint edition appeared in 1945. Both were published by the Mennonite Book Concern, Berne, Indiana.

Before C. Henry Smith died on October 18, 1948, he asked me to revise and edit the *Story*, keeping in mind the great changes that had taken place during World War II in all countries in which Mennonites resided. This was done by bringing chapters dealing with contemporary questions and developments up to date. The size of the book was increased considerably, partly because of the added bibliography. This and the following edition were published by the Board of Education and Publication of the General Conference Mennonite Church, Newton, Kansas. The third edition appeared in 1950 and was reprinted in 1957. The fourth edition underwent fewer changes but was supplemented by some illustrations and charts. The present edition is thus the fifth edition of *The Story of the Mennonites*.

It would lead too far to explain all changes and additions that have been made in this edition, but they were substantial in various ways. In some cases the terminology, vocabulary, and sentence structure were slightly changed so that the present generation would better understand what was said a generation or two ago.

This was also the case in the use of some theological terms common in those days. Some chapters were enlarged, some rewritten, and some paragraphs were added to bring the developments since World War II up to date. This was particularly the case where the Mennonite population was removed from their settlements to other places during and after World War II in Russia, Germany, and South America. But even in North America there is a population shift where Mennonites leave the rural areas and move to the cities.

The great changes in the outreach programs in missions, relief work, peace and nonresistance, education, scholarly research, and publications had to be taken into consideration. The limited range of professions open to Mennonites has been widened and continues to grow.

The *Story* can easily be supplemented by making use of the bibliography at the end of the book and other printed materials now available in abundance in libraries and bookstores.

Among the many helpful suggestions that have been made in connection with the various editions of the *Story*, mention must be made that the marked copy of Maynard Shelly was used extensively to remove mistakes or misprints in order to improve the present edition. Above all, Elizabeth Yoder, general editor for the Commission on Education, has been most helpful in the total production of this edition of the *Story*.

May this revised edition be again an aid to all who read this account of witnessing, suffering, and victories in the days past and challenge us to be followers of Christ.

Cornelius Krahn

EUROPE

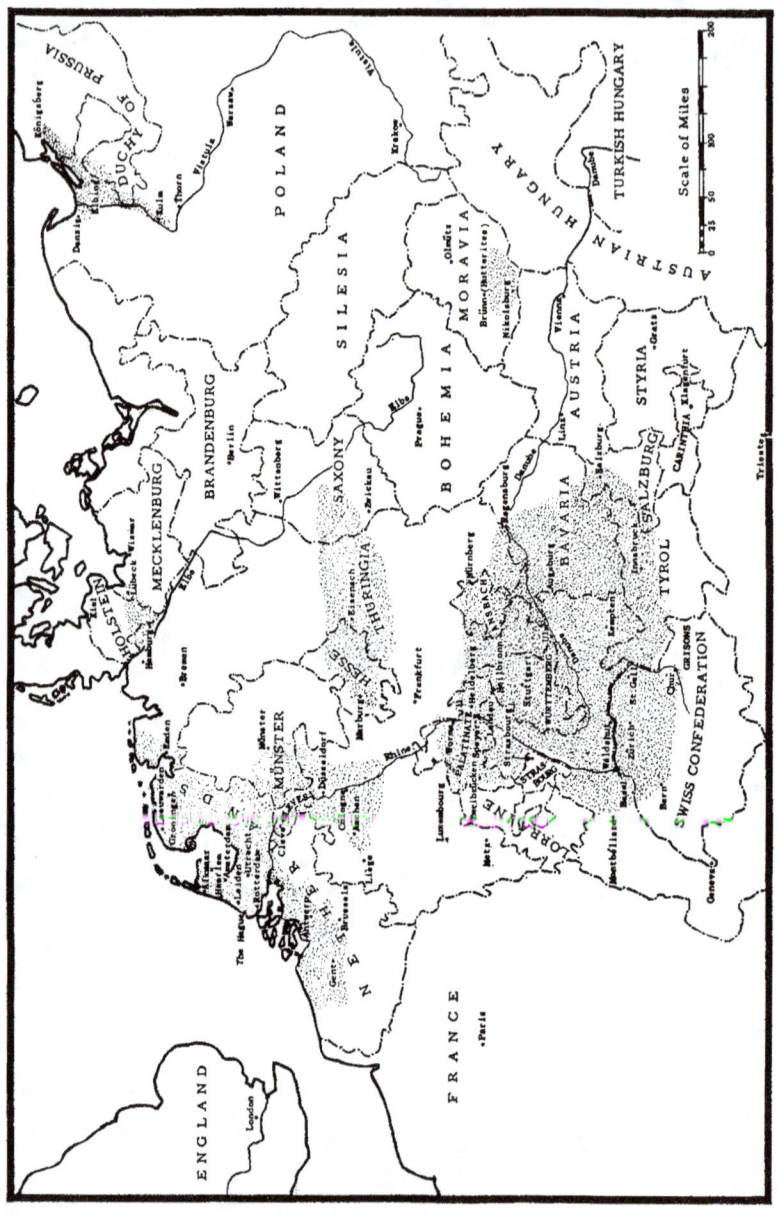

Central Europe in 1550 (Shaded areas are the chief Anabaptist areas. Only those larger political units and cities which had significant numbers of Anabaptists are shown.)

I
The Anabaptists

1. SWITZERLAND
Zwingli and the Swiss Brethren

The Anabaptists or Mennonites had their beginning in Zürich, Switzerland, as followers of Ulrich Zwingli, the founder of the Reformed Church. Zwingli was much more radical in his break with the Roman Catholic Church than Luther had been a few years before him.

As Zwingli began to preach from the open Bible in the Grossmünster Cathedral of Zürich, he soon removed the usual mediums of Catholic worship such as statues and paintings of the saints, stained glass, and even the organ. Nothing was to obstruct the direct access to the throne of grace to obtain forgiveness of sin. Luther never dared nor intended a reformation that radical.

In the early period of his reforming career, Ulrich Zwingli seemed much more inclined than in his later years to radical changes from the old order. He was very much interested in a study of the Bible, and in finding within its covers a solution for the problems of his day. Soon after his installation as the head pastor at the Grossmünster in Zürich in 1519, he preached against tithes, and spoke lightly of church fasts. Soon, too, he opposed Swiss military service in the armies of the Pope, though on social and economic rather than scriptural grounds. As an army chaplain among these mercenary troops he had had ample opportunity for observing the evil results of this foreign service, first upon the morals of the troops themselves, and later indirectly upon the Swiss communities to which they returned after service.

But radical as he was, he did not succeed in satisfying all his co-reformers. There were some who felt the cause of reform was not moving swiftly enough. In 1522 Wilhelm Reublin joined the Zürich circle as pastor in the neighboring village of Wytekon.

Driven out of Basel because of his excessive reforming zeal, he was accused of having carried a Bible in a procession instead of the usual relics, which he declared to be dead men's bones. The next year this same priest was the first of the clergy to take a wife. At the same time, Ludwig Haetzer, by training a linguist, greatly stirred up the populace with a tract against images and pictures as used in worship. In Waldshut, just across the border, Balthasar Hubmaier, a famous theologian, was beginning to deny the validity of infant baptism. Simon Stumpf, pastor at Höngg, a village just on the outskirts of Zürich, was preaching against tithes and rents.

Zwingli, although inclined to follow these friends of reform, cautioned them to move slowly, and refused to march ahead of public opinion or to inaugurate any innovations without the consent of the political authorities. Desirous of testing out the opinion of the public, he consented to a general debate in Zürich in January of 1523, in which all the parties, Catholics included, were to express themselves freely on the religious questions of the day. In this disputation Zwingli was easily the central figure, occupying a middle position between the conservative and reforming groups. He favored, among other innovations, the immediate abolition of the mass, the rejection of celibacy, the dissolution of monasteries and convents, the use of the Swiss language instead of Latin in the baptismal service, and a simplification all around of the forms of worship. But he refused to go any further.

Considerable progress having been made by the reform movement during the summer of 1523, another public discussion was held in October on the issues that now separated the different factions of the Reformation group. The Catholics were not represented at this meeting. It was in this debate that Zwingli and his radical friends parted company. When Zwingli suggested in the course of a controversy that certain irreconcilable differences between the factions should be referred to the Zürich Council for final decision, Simon Stumpf, the spokesman for the radicals on this occasion, declared, "Master Ulrich, you have no right to refer this question to the Council; the matter is already settled, the Spirit of God has decided." Here we have the very heart of what is later known as Anabaptism. Neither an ecclesiastical hierarchy, as the Catholics maintained, nor political authority, as the Zwinglians declared, has a right to dictate in matters of faith. The guidance of the Spirit of God in the brotherhood is decisive.

And so, during the two following years, while the new state church was formulating its policies and practices, the breach between the radical wing and the main body of Zwinglian

THE ANABAPTISTS

dissenters was growing ever wider. Conrad Grebel, Felix Manz, Wilhelm Reublin, and Simon Stumpf now began to insist not only upon a complete break with the Catholic establishment, but upon a new fellowship of believers based on principles and doctrines so radical that a break with the Zwinglians too seemed inevitable. What they asked for now was a "pure" church, a church composed of men and women who were not necessarily sinless, but rather sin-conscious. They wanted a church composed of adults, not children—men and women who of their own volition had formed themselves into a voluntary band of worshipers after the example of apostolic times. The small company holding these views was in the habit of meeting in the homes of various members of the group, spending their time largely in Bible study, and Zwingli had at first occasionally joined. The more they studied the New Testament, the more they were convinced that their view of the true church was the right one.

Whatever his earlier views may have been, Zwingli was by this time firmly resolved, however, against any church establishment that was not subject to the Council of Zürich. He was not yet ready for a "pure" church, nor for a separation of church and state. "What will the angels in heaven have to do on judgment day," he said, "if the tares be separated from the wheat here and now?" "The ark contained both pure and impure," said Bullinger, his successor. These and similar arguments were advanced by the state-church defenders in an attempt to find biblical authority against the radical reformers.

A pure, voluntary, church made up of those who were conscious of sin, and who were admitted upon confession of faith, of course left no room in its practice for infant baptism, if that event was regarded as an essential symbol of admission into the church. For a year or two infant baptism became a chief bone of contention in the arguments between the two groups among the Swiss reformers.

Among the first of the radicals to preach against infant baptism were Wilhelm Reublin and Balthasar Hubmaier. Early in 1524 Reublin had persuaded many of the parents in his parish of Wytekon to withhold baptism from their children. Hubmaier, as we have already seen, had an argument on the subject with Zwingli the following year. Both these men, and their followers after them, maintained that according to the New Testament baptism must be based on faith, and since children cannot have faith, their baptism has no validity. Zwingli, drawing his arguments from the same Bible, though not always from the New Testament, replied that infant baptism in the New Testament took the place of circumcision in the Old, and advanced other arguments equally farfetched. There is no place in the Bible where infant baptism is commanded, declared the Brethren. "Nor can you show where it is forbidden," replied Zwingli. So the argument continued without convincing either side; but the unbiased reader cannot help but conclude that from the standpoint of direct scriptural authority, the radicals made out the better case.

Whether Zwingli's earlier views would entitle him to be classed with the group later known as Anabaptists is debatable. That he at one time questioned the validity of infant baptism, in spite of his later defense of the practice, is, of course, known from his own confession. But he never accepted the heart of Anabaptism—a regenerate church, practicing believer's baptism and discipleship. His earlier so-called pacifism was based on expediency, and not on religious conviction. A man must be judged not only by what he says, but also by what he does. Up to 1520, Zwingli drew a papal pension as an army chaplain, and ten years later he led Swiss troops in a civil war, himself falling in battle. He never advocated believer's baptism; and his religious tolerance was limited.

The controversy over infant baptism led to another public debate on January 17, 1525. Unlike its predecessors, the purpose of this meeting, which was sponsored by both Zwingli and the council, was not to arrive at an open decision but rather to silence the opposition. The final decision by the council in favor of Zwingli's view was a foregone conclusion. The political authorities, as well as the authorities of the church, were not yet ready for a voluntary believers' church. Within a few days after this meeting, the council ordered that all children must be baptized within eight days, that the special meetings for Bible study must be discontinued, and that radical leaders of the movement who were not natives of Zürich were to be banished. This last order involved Haetzer, Castelberger, Brötli, and Reublin.

Early Leaders

It may not be out of place here to say a little more about the men who thus far had led the movement for an independent church. First among these who must be mentioned is *Conrad Grebel*, native of Zürich and son of councilman Jacob Grebel. Grebel was well educated in the schools of his time, including the universities of Paris and Vienna. He was well connected socially, belonging to one of the most prominent families in the city of Zürich; and he was a brother-in-law of Vadian of St. Gall, who was, next to Zwingli, the leading Swiss reformer. After leading a rather irregular life as a young man, Grebel finally became interested in the reform movement, associating himself closely with the Zürich leader, by whom he was called "that candid and learned youth."

By 1523, however, Grebel began to break with Zwingli. He soon assumed a leading role in the agitation against infant baptism, and finally was the first to administer baptism upon confession of faith in 1525, thus inaugurating the practice of believer's baptism. Still a young man, he died of the pest in 1526, thus undoubtedly escaping a later martyr's death. His father met his death the same year at the hands of a Zürich executioner, though not for religious unorthodoxy but on a charge of treason.

Felix Manz, son of a canon of the cathedral church, was also a native of Zürich. At first an ardent disciple of Zwingli, he followed Grebel into the opposition and became his close associate in all the later events. A most zealous witness of the believers' church, he, too, was well educated and a good Hebrew scholar. It was in his mother's home that the small circle of radicals held their Bible readings after their separation from the state church. Frequently imprisoned because he refused to obey the orders of the Zürich Council to cease preaching and baptizing, Manz was the first Anabaptist martyr. He was drowned near the head of Lake Zürich in January 1527.

Georg Blaurock of Chur, of the House of Jacob, a monastic establishment, was called *Blaurock* because of the color of his cloak, and sometimes also spoken of as "Strong Georg." Next to Felix Manz and Conrad Grebel, Blaurock was the most important leader of the new cause immediately after the debate of 1525. His most important work, however, was preaching the gospel throughout northern Switzerland and Tyrol in the years immediately following. The major part of his story, therefore, belongs to a later period. Blaurock had renounced the Catholic Church before 1523. He soon after came to Zwingli for help to solve his religious doubts; but failing to find a satisfactory answer to his questionings, he cast his lot with the Zürich Brethren. It is said that during the next four years of his short but busy life, he baptized over one thousand converts.

Wilhelm Reublin, the fiery preacher of Wytekon, was born at Rottenburg on the Neckar. One of the first advocates, as we have seen, of radical changes, he was also one of the first to get into trouble with the authorities. Reublin was banished from Basel in 1522 and imprisoned in Zürich in 1524. He was intimately associated with Grebel and Manz in all their religious pioneering, and was present at the January debate. He became an early and influential missionary to Tyrol and Moravia, and seemingly was one of the few Anabaptists who did not fall a victim to the executioner's ax because of his religious faith. He died a natural death sometime near the middle of the century.

These four men were the leaders of the radical movement up to the time of the debate on baptism in 1525, and were present at that historic event. Associated with these four were a number of other equally earnest and pious men with no less zeal, though with perhaps less ability. Among these was *Andreas Castelberger*, evidently a cripple, for he is frequently spoken of in the early records as Andreas "on crutches." He came originally from Grisons, and was known as an ardent advocate of social reform. *Heinrich Aberli*, who was one of the signers of a letter to Müntzer in 1524, must also have taken an aggressive part in the activities of the Zürich radicals, for soon after the great debate in 1525 he testified that he had already been imprisoned in the tower four times. He had furnished temporary asylum for Hubmaier, contrary to the law of the land, at the time that Hubmaier was exiled from Waldshut.

Simon Stumpf, pastor of Höngg, was as we saw, the first to challenge publicly Zwingli's right to submit religious questions to any other authority than that of the Bible. Space permits the mention here of but two more among a long list of pioneers in the struggle for freedom of conscience—*Hans Brötli*, of Zollikon, whose name after the fashion of that day sometimes appears in its Latinized form, *Paniculum*; and *Lorenz Hochrütiner* of St. Gall, banished several years before from Zürich, who became a radical leader among the working men of his adopted canton. *Balthasar Hubmaier* and *Ludwig Haetzer* identified themselves with the Anabaptist movement later on.

Introduction of Believer's Baptism

At about this time, this small group of disciples devoted to a New Testament church took the next step which logically followed their rejection of infant baptism—they introduced believer's baptism upon confession of faith. It was at one of the private meetings held for study of the Bible at which Grebel, Manz, Blaurock, and others were present that Grebel, who though not an ordained minister was no doubt recognized as a leader of the group, baptized Blaurock, who then baptized a number of others present. This act was followed by the breaking of bread. Since it was believed that baptism administered by the church regenerated the child automatically, repetition of baptism was blasphemy and unpardonable. This step—believer's baptism—completely separated them from Zwingli.

The significance of this event lies in the fact that it marked the complete break with the state church and inaugurated a new church based on the revolutionary principle of religious freedom and a church membership upon confession of faith and believer's

THE ANABAPTISTS

baptism. The Zwinglians soon spoke of the new party as *Wiedertäufer* (rebaptizers); but the latter, denying that they were rebaptized, since their first baptism as infants they considered invalid, rejected the name, calling one another *Brethren*. In Switzerland the names *Täufer*, and *Taufgesinnte*, became common; while in Holland *Doopsgezinde* was applied to those who held the same views as the Swiss Brethren. In English-speaking countries, the term *Anabaptist* gradually came into common use.

This radical departure from the religious practices of the day met with bitter opposition from both the Zürich Council, representing the temporal authorities, and Zwingli, in behalf of the state clergy. Both state and church were now determined to secure by legal force what they had been unable to accomplish by moral suasion. To the mandates already on the statute books against all those who preached against infant baptism, new and more stringent ones were added against those who preached and practiced rebaptism. Parents refusing to have their children baptized were to be fined for a first offense and exiled for repeated disobedience.

It is one thing, however, to abolish religious conviction by law, and quite another to enforce it. The Swiss Brethren did not cease their preaching and baptizing, nor did those from out of town immediately take their departure. "We must obey God rather than man," they said. And so it was not long until Grebel, Manz, Blaurock, Brötli, and others had been cast into prison to remain on a bread-and-water diet "until they rot." Prison discipline at first must have been rather lax, and collusion with jailers frequent, for the prisoners repeatedly escaped, only to be rearrested as they continued to follow their convictions rather than the orders of the council.

Felix Manz, the First Martyr

Failing to stamp out the rapidly spreading faith of the Brethren by imprisonment, the council finally decided on March 7, 1526, on more drastic measures. Leaders who refused to comply with the orders already issued were to be punished by drowning. It was not until a full year later, however, that this threat was actually carried out. The first victim was Felix Manz. On January 5, 1527, with his hands tied to his knees to prevent any possibility of escape from the water, Manz was rowed from the town hall in Zürich down the Limmat. He was accompanied by a Reformed clergyman who tried to the last to secure a recantation. His mother and brother followed along the banks, shouting words of encouragement. Just where the Limmat River leaves beautiful

Lake Zürich, reflecting the blue sky above and the deep green hills along the shore, where the upper bridge now spans the stream, Manz, uttering his last prayer, "Father, into Thy hands I commit my soul," was tossed overboard and disappeared beneath the waves, the first of a long line of martyrs who preferred to die rather than to give up their faith. On the same day, Georg Blaurock, "stripped to the waist," was whipped out of town as an alien.

The fires of persecution were now kindled. Scores of martyrs followed the fate of Manz in the same year in many lands, and thousands in the years to come. For a full century and more, not only in Switzerland, but all over South Germany, Austria, and Moravia, up and down the Rhine and the upper Danube, wherever they were found, Anabaptists had to pay the extreme price for their faith. They were left to rot in prison, broken on the rack, thrown into rivers and lakes, burned at the stake, beheaded, and buried alive.

To all this terrible butchery the churches, whether Catholic, Lutheran, or Reformed, gave their full assent and assistance. The day of religious toleration had not yet arrived. In fact, even the dawn was still a hundred years in the future. Zwingli, whose conscience perhaps troubled him somewhat, tried to justify the execution of Manz on the ground that the charges against him were political rather than religious. But the most casual acquaintance with the facts precludes any such explanation.

That Zwingli was reluctant at first to try extreme measures was to his credit. That he was not by nature disposed to cruelty, and that he acted from what he regarded as worthy motives, may well be admitted. But being thoroughly committed to the state-church idea, he had no sympathy for the separatism involved in the Anabaptist movement. For several years he tried to win the Brethren over to his views by argument and moral suasion, and in the hope of ultimate success he may even have used his influence with the Zürich Council to delay radical action. But when once convinced that the Brethren could not be won over by argument, he was ready to go the limit. From then on he worked hand-in-glove with the political authorities in every attempt to root out by the severest measures necessary what he regarded as a menace to the perpetuity of the established ecclesiastical order.

The fanatical persecuting zeal of that time must be interpreted in the light of the spirit of the age. Religious tolerance was still an unheard-of virture in the days of Luther and Zwingli. For many years to come, men and women were still born into compulsory membership in two equally all-embracing and powerful social organizations—one civil, the other ecclesiastical—the state and

THE ANABAPTISTS

the church. In neither case was there any choice in the matter. Disloyalty to the one was treason, to the other, heresy; both were punishable by death. The Anabaptist view of an independent church was, therefore, considered dangerously radical. To the ecclesiastical hierarchy—whether bishop, priest, or pastor, Catholic or Protestant—who enjoyed comfortable livings from compulsory church taxes, there would be little attraction in a religious system which would abolish the tithe and substitute for it uncertain voluntary support, and whose advocates refused to attend the prevailing church and observe the customary holy days.

It was but natural, too, that many of the unusual religious practices of the Brethren should be misunderstood and often willfully misinterpreted. The secret meetings at night, held in out-of-the-way places, were made the basis for charges of immorality. Because they refused to have their children baptized, they were called soul murderers by those who believed that baptismal water had the magic power to save. Marriage by their own ministers instead of the regular clergy made them adulterers, and branded their children as illegitimate, with no legal rights. To these charges, based on misrepresentations, were added others of a more serious nature. There was no doubt some truth in the contention of both Lutherans and Reformed that in their struggle against the Catholic Church, the defection of the Anabaptists gave considerable comfort to the common enemy. The various peasants' revolts raging throughout northern Switzerland and southern Germany just at this time, also, caused the governing authorities to regard with suspicion all mass movements among the common people, peaceful and religious as well as violent and revolutionary. Serious, also, from the standpoint of the state, was the refusal of the Brethren to take the oath, hold office, or go to war. All these charges, given wide publicity by the leaders of the state churches, aroused a widespread distrust of the Anabaptist cause wherever it appeared.

Spread of the Faith

In the meantime, Anabaptism had spread rapidly beyond the confines of the Canton of Zürich. The blood of the martyrs, it is said, is the seed of the church. So it was here. Driven on by the rod of persecution, and urged forward by a burning zeal to share their newly found freedom with their fellows, the leaders of the movement soon carried their story into neighboring lands. Within a short time after the debate of 1525, Grebel had gone to Schaffhausen; Brötli to Hallau; and Reublin to Waldshut, where he had baptized Hubmaier and his whole congregation. Anabaptist centers were soon established in all the important cities of the northern cantons. In Appenzell a flourishing congregation of fifteen hundred developed immediately; in St. Gall, under the leadership of Lorenz Hochrütiner, the new faith made almost a clean sweep, nearly emptying the Catholic churches. The people here, says Johannes Kessler, a well-known historian of that period, "ran after baptism as the Galatians after circumcision."

Under the leadership of such men as Reublin, Haetzer, Hubmaier, and others, the movement rapidly flowed over into South Germany, Tyrol, Austria, and Moravia. Before 1527 it had entered the regions of the upper Danube and the upper Rhine, and by 1530 into the Netherlands and northwestern Germany, where numerous congregations had been planted in nearly all the large cities. Sebastian Franck, an old chronicler of that day and not unsympathetic to the new faith, wrote:

> In the year 1526 a new party arose whose leaders and bishops were Hubmaier, Rink, Denk, and Haetzer. They spread so rapidly that their teachings soon covered the whole land and they secured a large following and also added to their number many good hearts who were zealous toward God.

The valleys of the Rhine and the upper Danube as far east as Vienna, however, remained the exclusive home of the new movement throughout its entire early history. Just why may be a matter of interesting speculation. Perhaps it was because within the confines of these valleys were to be found the big cities of commerce and centers of culture and intellectual life. It was these same regions to which the whole Reformation movement was largely confined; and Anabaptism was merely a radical wing of that movement. The first Anabaptist congregations were all found in the big cities. It was only after the Brethren were driven underground by persecution that they forsook the cities and found refuge in remote country places and mountain fastnesses.

This rapid, and seemingly spontaneous, spread of Anabaptism within well-defined territorial limits has led some scholars to the conclusion that Anabaptism must have had its origin largely in other evangelical groups which had existed for some time in these same regions, especially the Waldenses. Among other arguments with which the theory of Waldensian origin is supported is some similarity of the two faiths in doctrine and practice, their presence in the same cities and localities, and the disappearance of the Waldenses with the coming of the Anabaptists in these same localities. There are too many weak links in the chain of evidence that would trace the one entirely to the other. Among these is the lack of evidence of a direct connection. The first Anabaptist leaders all came directly out of the Catholic Church; and with but

THE ANABAPTISTS

one or two possible exceptions, none seem to have had any Waldensian connections. Furthermore, Waldensian congregations did not completely die out with the coming of the Reformation. In fact, some of them remain to this day.

Outlawed by Imperial Decree

The period of rapid growth, however, was of short duration. Church and state united in an effort to root out a movement which, if successful, would endanger the grip which the privileged classes held upon both the bodies and spirits of the masses. The world was not yet ready for a separation of church and state. Although the authorities never quite succeeded in completely strangling the movement, they did drive it underground, and in a few years removed all possibility of its having a large popular following. In the northern Swiss cantons, in South Germany, in Moravia, Tyrol, Austria, and wherever the Brethren had carried their faith, bishops, kings, and emperors, with but few exceptions, condemned them—men, women and children—to the executioner's block or the burning stake. In 1529 the imperial Diet of Speyer, by an edict of outlawry effective throughout the empire, practically shut off the hope of milder treatment on the part of those local rulers who personally favored a more humane policy. By 1530 the rapid advance of the movement was checked, and most of the pioneer leaders, after a few years of devoted service to the cause, had followed Manz to a martyr's grave. Grebel, as we saw, had died of the pest in 1526; Sattler was burned at the stake in Rottenburg in 1527; Hubmaier met the same fate in Vienna during that year. In 1529 Blaurock was executed in Innsbruck, and Haetzer was beheaded in Constance. Few died a natural death. Execution was frequently preceded by acts of the most horrible cruelty. Typical was the case of Michael Sattler.

Sattler, an ex-monk, was apprehended while engaged in missionary efforts in South Germany and tried in Rottenburg. The court decreed that he "shall be delivered to the executioner, who shall lead him to the place of execution and cut out his tongue, and then throw him upon a wagon, and then tear his body twice with red hot tongs, and after he has been brought within the gate he shall be pinched five times in the same manner." This order was carried out literally, and was followed by burning at the stake. The charges made against Sattler were that he preached against the real presence of the flesh and blood of Christ in the bread and wine in the Lord's Supper, infant baptism, worship of Mary and the saints, oaths, warfare, extreme unction, communion of one kind, and finally that "he had left the monastic order and married a wife."

Essentials of Anabaptism

The essentials of Anabaptism—an independent, voluntary church composed of adult members, sin-conscious, and admitted into membership by baptism upon confession of faith—have already been referred to. It remains now to discuss the system of beliefs and practices which grew out of these fundamental principles as they developed during the early years of the movement.

Since the act of baptism, shorn of all the magic power to insure eternal salvation with which the Catholic theologians had clothed it, was regarded merely as an initiatory formula signifying admittance into the church, not much weight was attached to the particular form under which it was administered. Although immersion was practiced in a few isolated cases, some form of sprinkling or pouring was the prevailing custom. Hans Brubacher of Zumikon, describing his own baptismal experiences, says he was *bespritzt* (sprinkled) by Blaurock; Hans Hottinger was admitted into membership with a "hand full of water." Hubmaier administered the rite in his congregation at Waldshut "out of a milk pail"; Fridli Schumacher met Brötli at Hirslanden in South Germany, and was baptized by him at a well. A few leaders seemingly preferred to baptize near the banks of a stream or in running water.

The spiritual life among the Brethren was decidedly a personal matter. Conversions were sudden, resulting from a deep conviction of a sinful life, followed by a strong sense of contrition. The case of Hans Brubacher, who before his baptism "fell on his knees and with bitter tears lamented his sinful state," was typical. The whole movement was thoroughly evangelical, and characterized by a strong missionary zeal. Meetings were held day and night. Bible reading, exhortation, testimonies, and singing of hymns, often of their own composition, constituted a large part of the worship. Baptism was administered to new recruits at nearly every meeting, followed usually by the breaking of bread, and occasionally by the washing of feet, after the example of the early apostolic church. Except in a few cases in the beginning like that of Hubmaier at Waldshut, and Hochrütiner at St. Gall, who were able to carry along their entire congregations into the new faith, these meetings had to be held secretly in private houses, or at night in out-of-the-way places. It was years, and in some cases centuries, before the Anabaptists had meetinghouses.

In fact, the whole movement was an attempt to restitute the apostolic church in its original purity and simplicity, and to restore Christianity once more to a basis of individual responsibility. To these reformers the Bible was the sole source of spiritual authority; the apostolic church, their model; and the Sermon on the Mount, quite literally interpreted, their social and spiritual program. In their respect for the Bible, of course, they were not altogether unique among the Reformation efforts. Luther and Zwingli also claimed a scriptural basis for their innovations. It was rather in their interpretation of what the Scriptures meant that they differed from the other reformers. And yet it must be admitted that the Anabaptists relied more exclusively and more devotedly than did the others upon the Bible as a guide in their efforts to restore the biblical church. While Lutherans and Reformed claimed the assistance of governing councils and university faculties in their interpretations, and Catholics the assistance of a highly organized hierarchy and the church fathers, the Anabaptists insisted that each individual must decide the Bible message for himself. Bible study in groups was the source of their spiritual life and living. No other people during the Reformation period knew the contents of the Bible as did the Anabaptists.

They soon accumulated a well-defined body of beliefs and practices agreed upon by congregations and conferences. To these they insisted all members of the group must subscribe, or remove themselves from the fellowship of the body. But they did not believe in the use of physical force to bring about uniformity.

They did not have a specially trained and supported ministry. Like the missionaries in the primitive church, ministers were to live by the labor of their own hands. The ministry was to be regarded as a labor of love. *Hirelings* was a term often applied to the state clergy. Benefices and fat livings were as frequently criticized as any other practice among the established institutions. Ministers were chosen by the congregation from among their own number. The first leaders, of course, were highly trained men, converts, for the most part, from the Catholic priesthood or university graduates. But after these had been killed off and the Brethren had been dispersed, there were few trained leaders.

Among the fundamental Anabaptist beliefs was nonresistance. Love, the Brethren said, must be the basis of all social relations. "Love thine enemies" and "Resist not evil" were injunctions as binding as any others in the New Testament and must be taken literally. This principle they tried to follow in all their individual, as well as group, relationships, even though its application might bring them into conflict with the ruling authorities occasionally. War they refused to sanction, and military service they rejected as unchristian. Instead of appearing in public places with daggers in their belts, as was the custom of the time, they wore short wooden staves.

In Switzerland, where military service was considered more or less obligatory at the time, and the hiring of mercenary soldiers was an important source of public revenue, this refusal to bear arms later became one of the serious charges against them on the part of the temporal rulers. In other countries, however, where universal service was not demanded, the refusal to go to war was not the leading cause of persecution.

The attitude toward the magistrate's office was also a continual source of misunderstanding. According to Anabaptist views, no Christian could hold a political office, although it was his duty to give his government implicit obedience insofar as it did not conflict with his conscience. This duty rested not only on the doctrine of nonresistance, but upon the positive New Testament injunction to be obedient to the civil authorities as well. By the same authority the Christian was enjoined to pray for his rulers. But with prayer and obedience it was thought all obligation ended. There were two kingdoms, the kingdom of God and the kingdom of the world. In the worldly kingdom, government was necessary for the purpose of protecting the good and punishing the evil. It was the duty of the worldly government, therefore, to protect the Christian; but in the kingdom of God force was not necessary—rather a naive and somewhat selfish political philosophy, one is inclined to think in this day of religious liberty and political democracy, but perfectly inevitable and logical in that day of intolerance and union of state and church. If the magistracy must enforce religious uniformity and burn men at the stake for their religious beliefs, then of course no Christian, according to the Anabaptist standard, who believed in absolute soul liberty could consistently hold office. But the Scriptures enjoin obedience to civil authority. The only possible escape from this dilemma, if one wished to reconcile heavenly with earthly citizenship, was that pointed out by the Anabaptist view above mentioned. A strong sense of otherworldliness characterized the whole life of the Anabaptists and a conviction that they were not of this world. The terrible persecutions which they suffered no doubt greatly strengthened this feeling that their citizenship was a heavenly, rather than an earthly, one.

Their refusal to take an oath, too, was generally construed as an act of rebellion against the temporal government. But in reality it had no such meaning among the Anabaptists. Although its rejection for any reason whatsoever may have been perfectly in keeping with their attitude toward the magistracy, yet opposition was primarily based on a literal interpretation of the injunction "Swear not at all."

The Christian life, pure and undefiled, was to the Anabaptists not merely a set of dogmas, but to be practiced daily. It must function in improved conduct. It is a fact well known among church historians that moral conditions among the people were not immediately bettered by the early reformers. In fact, as respect for Catholic doctrines declined and the discipline of the church grew correspondingly more lax, the general moral standards of the time were lowered rather than raised among the masses. A state church with a compulsory membership and little personal discipline beyond the insistence upon orthodox beliefs was not, at best, conducive to an improvement in morality.

The Brethren, on the other hand, insisted from the start that the new faith must bear fruit in purer living. Conrad Grebel informed an early applicant for baptism that church membership required of him that he be free from adultery, gambling, drunkenness, usury, and other vices of the day. Ludwig Haetzer undoubtedly wrote the first prohibition treatise of modern times in his tract *Evangelical Cups*. Discipline against an occasional offender was rigidly enforced among the Brethren. According to the *Schleitheim Confession* of 1527, the earliest Anabaptist confession on record, any member having fallen into gross sin, and refusing to repent after having been admonished according to Matthew 18, was to be expelled from membership. Kessler, describing the daily life of the Swiss Brethren, says of them—

> Their daily walk and deportment appears to be upright, godly, and entirely blameless. They shun costly clothes, avoid excessive eating and drinking, wear coarse clothing, and broad felt hats. They go about humbly, without weapons, neither swords nor pikes, but with a short bread knife. They seem much more concerned about living an upright life than the Papists.

The grand duke of Hesse, speaking a little later of the Anabaptists of middle Germany, declared, "I see more upright living among those that are called sects than among the Lutherans."

Both of these testimonials come from defenders of the state churches. Even their bitterest enemies could find no fault with their conduct except to call them "wolves in sheep's clothing" and ascribe their piety, and even the courage and fortitude with which they met death, to the devil. In fact Zwingli, realizing that the immorality found among some of the state clergy contributed not a little to the growth of Anabaptism, instituted a reform movement among his own clergy for more consistent living. In a synodal meeting held in Zürich in 1528, one pastor was accused by his congregation of swearing, drinking, and gambling; another was convicted of stealing. The pastor at Steinmaur was removed for adultery. The one at Bulach, who was accused of neglecting his pastoral duties for worldly gain, was ordered to pursue a further course of study at Zürich. Among frequent charges brought against various clergymen were wife beating, frequenting of taverns, gambling, excessive drinking, fighting, pride, and general neglect of duty. Unquestionably the high standards of personal sobriety and integrity maintained by the Anabaptists exerted a wholesome influence upon the personal conduct of both the clergy and laity of the state churches among whom they lived.

In the matter of private property, neither the Swiss Brethren nor their fellow Anabaptists elsewhere, with the exception of the Moravian Hutterites, were communalists, as was often charged against them. Benefices and fat livings held by the clergy, they decidedly opposed; but they did not object to private possessions of the laity. Compassion for the less fortunate, however, must constrain the possessor of an ample store of worldly goods to share his surplus liberally with the needy in case of distress. The Christian, after all, is merely a steward of his possessions, they said.

The Lord's Supper was a symbol and not a sacrament in the sense in which that term was used by the state churches. The ceremonial theory of baptism has been mentioned elsewhere. Anabaptist doctrines were inclined to be scriptural though not theologically speculative.

From the political and economic revolutionary movements and peasant revolts then sweeping over Switzerland and South Germany, the Swiss Brethren remained remarkably free. Although they incorporated in their living the principles of fair dealing and economic justice taught in the Sermon on the Mount, they remained almost exclusively a religious community disentangled from all the social and economic currents of the time. Their nonresistant principles forbade any fellowship with a movement that might require the use of force in gaining its objective, laudable though the goal might be.

2. SOUTH GERMANY

The Swiss Brethren, when driven out of their native cantons, carried their faith, almost from the start, across the border into South Germany. Within a few years, good-sized congregations had been established in all the larger cities throughout Bavaria, Baden, Württemberg, the Palatinate, Alsace, and as far north as Thuringia and Saxony. The free imperial cities, centers of an active commercial life where there was little governmental interference from local princes and kings, were especially

THE ANABAPTISTS   19

favorable to the rapid growth of the new cause. One of the earliest and largest of these congregations was begun at Augsburg in 1526.

Augsburg, the leading financial and commercial center of all South Germany, was, at this time, a city of some fifteen thousand. It espoused the Reformation cause quite early and was slow to choose between the Lutherans and Zwinglians. The city also became a favorite meeting place for the Anabaptists throughout these regions. The first of the later prominent leaders to pass through was Balthasar Hubmaier. In the summer of 1526, while on his way from Switzerland to Moravia, Hubmaier stopped long enough to baptize Hans Denk, who in turn became the organizer of the Augsburg congregation. Since the history of any movement is largely the life story of a few individuals, a short biographical sketch of this Anabaptist leader may not be out of place at this point.

Hans Denk

Hans Denk, born in Bavaria about 1495, occupies an important place among the founders of German Anabaptism. Not much is known of his early life before 1523, when we find him in Basel as a university student and printer, a friend of Oecolampadius, and other Reformation leaders. Through his friend he received the appointment of rector of a school at Nürnberg at the age of twenty-eight. Here he remained only two years; for, allying himself with a group of radical reformers who advocated many doctrines similar to those held by the Swiss Brethren, he was exiled by Osiander, the Lutheran leader in that city. At St. Gall he had his first contact with the Anabaptists, though he did not join them at that time. It was in Augsburg, where he lived from September of 1525 to October of the following year, that he was baptized by Hubmaier. Here he soon built up a large congregation and won over a number of men of local influence, including Eitelhans Langenmantel, member of a prominent family and, after Denk, the principal leader of the Augsburg group. Because of his activities in behalf of his faith, and because of his influence among the masses, Denk was ordered into exile by both the city and ecclesiastical authorities. We next find him in Strassburg, where dissenters were still tolerated. Here he met such Anabaptists as Sattler and Haetzer and such evangelical writers as Sebastian Franck and Casper Schwenckfeld, as well as such tolerant state-church reformers as Martin Bucer and Wolfgang Capito, by all of whom he was held in the highest esteem during his short stay in this city. Here he had hoped to retire from the public eye and, in collaboration with Haetzer, to translate the Old Testament prophets from the Hebrew into German. But the fight against the Anabaptists was so bitter everywhere that he could not altogether evade the responsibilities of defending their cause. So it was only after spending some time in missionary work in the general region of Strassburg—in Worms, Landau, and Bergzabern—that they were able to finish the translation which became so popular that ultimately it went through sixteen editions. In 1527 we find him in Augsburg again as chairman of the Martyrs' Synod. But his days were already numbered. Soon after this he returned to Basel, ill and heartbroken, after having been driven from one city to another. He begged his old teacher, Oecolampadius, for permission to end his days in the city where he had begun his career some years before. Not yet thirty-two years old, he died a few months later of the pest.

Hans Denk was one of the gentlest spirits of the Anabaptist groups and one of the noblest characters of the whole Reformation movement. A fine scholar, of a modest and retiring disposition, he had little taste for religious controversy. He was yet destined to become, through his voluminous writings, one of the chief defenders of the Anabaptist cause. As a disciple of Johann Tauler, he was inclined toward mysticism. Although orthodox on most of the fundamentals of his adopted faith, he laid less stress than did most of his brethren on the worth and necessity of mere outward symbols and religious ceremonies.

Denk's mysticism, capable of many interpretations, was often bitterly criticized by those not his friends. He was charged with all sorts of heresies. But a sympathetic reader of his writings finds little ground for these charges. He exerted great influence, both through his writings and by personal contact, upon his co-laborers, and no doubt his gentle mysticism served as a wholesome corrective to the literalism of his friend Michael Sattler and the fanaticism of Hans Hut, his disciple whom he baptized. That Denk was a man of fine personality and rare charm is evident. Bader calls him the "renowned Hans Denk"; Vadian speaks of him as "a most gifted youth"; Bucer refers to him as "the Anabaptist pope"; and Haller, as the "Anabaptist Apollo."

Ludwig Haetzer

Associated with Denk, both in Augsburg and especially in Strassburg, was Ludwig Haetzer, whom we already saw as a pioneer Anabaptist in South Germany soon after his expulsion from Zürich in 1525. The two were associated not only in a partnership in the translation of the Old Testament prophets, but in all their efforts in behalf of the Anabaptist cause. Both were

THE ANABAPTISTS

present at the Martyrs' Synod; but after that Haetzer's whereabouts are not so well known. He evidently was active though, for in a report from Nürnberg, January 1, 1528, he appears as "Ludwig Haetzer, an erect, lean, pale fellow, who, here in our town, baptized many secretly." He was arrested in Constance the next year and was beheaded on a charge of immorality. This charge may have been a mere pretense to cover the real cause of his execution, that of being an Anabaptist. Such misrepresentations were frequent. Haetzer wrote a number of tracts on doctrinal and practical subjects, including, as noted elsewhere, a treatise on prohibition, *Evangelical Cups*. In this treatise Haetzer pioneered in his criticism of the excessive drinking that was common in his day.

The Martyrs' Synod

The Martyrs' Synod, so called because so many of these leaders met a martyr's fate soon after, was held in Augsburg in 1527 and was attended by nearly all of the leaders of the region. It was called for the purpose of ironing out certain differences of opinion that had arisen among the Brethren of South Germany and Austria due to the millenarian views of Hans Hut, and to assign missionaries to various fields of labor in central Europe. This meeting marked the crest of Anabaptist growth in Augsburg. The congregation at the time numbered above one thousand. Soon after this the city authorities, urged on by the state-church hierarchy as well as by imperial decree, and by the example of other cities and principalities, decided upon a policy of extermination of all "sects." The Brethren were ordered to renounce their faith, and their leaders were put under arrest. Many went into exile. By 1529, it was said, there were more than one hundred Augsburg Anabaptists in Strassburg alone, where liberty of conscience was still given some consideration. Among several others, Hut decided to remain. Soon after the meeting, he was cast into prison where he died from accidental burns. But even though dead, he was tried as a heretic, condemned, and officially burned—or rather reburned—at the stake. Langenmantel, because he was a native of the city, and because he was of a prominent family, was permitted to go into exile; but he, too, the next year suffered the death of a martyr. By 1530 there were few Anabaptists left in the city, though they were still to be found in seclusion in the regions around about.

Strassburg

Important as an early Anabaptist center was the free city of Strassburg, seat of culture and home of an active evangelical life during the late medieval age. Zwinglianism and Lutheranism were still contending for supremacy at the time, though a little later the former won. Capito and Bucer, the two religious leaders of the city, both hesitated long before making their final choice in the matter. Capito, especially, was at first quite sympathetic toward the dissenters; he even doubted the validity of infant baptism himself for a time, though, like Zwingli, he never became a separatist. Under these favorable conditions, Strassburg remained an asylum for the persecuted groups during the late 1520s at a time when they were being sent into exile and to the stake almost everywhere else.

A small circle of Swiss exiles banded themselves together in Strassburg as early as 1525. Here Hubmaier had his first treatise on baptism published, though it is not likely that he actively engaged in the spreading of his views at this time. Wilhelm Reublin, who arrived in the spring of 1526, is said to have been the first Anabaptist with whom Capito came into personal contact. Beginning in 1526 and continuing for some years after, however, most of the prominent Anabaptists—Denk, Haetzer, Sattler, Reublin, Gross, Marbeck, Hofmann—made visits at one time or another for shorter or longer periods to the city on the Rhine. Sattler and Haetzer even lived in the home of Capito for a time. Even after the growing intolerance of the age and the imperial edicts demanding that the Anabaptist movement be suppressed, the Strassburg authorities hesitated to use the harsh means to secure this end that were common elsewhere. Both Capito and Bucer favored moderate treatment as long as possible, hoping that argument and mild treatment would be a more effective means of winning back the erring than banishment and the stake. As late as 1536 the city council advised that Anabaptists should be put to some useful public work, rather than to be cast into prison. Even though banishment was resorted to finally, the death penalty seemingly was never imposed in Strassburg for religious dissent. Throughout the sixteenth century the city was a favorite meeting place for Anabaptist and Mennonite general councils.

Michael Sattler

Among the influential Strassburg leaders who have not already been given extended notice elsewhere must be included Michael Sattler, a South German ex-monk who had joined the Brethren in Zürich from whence he had come to Strassburg as an exile. His brief service in behalf of his faith, like that of most of his fellow laborers, was packed full of intense activity and devoted self-sacrifice. He is credited with being the author of the first

Anabaptist confession of faith on record, the *Schleitheim Articles* of 1527. It was during this year, too, that while engaged in missionary work along the lower Neckar, he was apprehended in a little village called Horb and later executed in Rottenburg with horrible torture. The story of his execution, told elsewhere in this chapter, is recorded in the *Martyrs Mirror*. He evidently was a man of strong convictions and was a firm advocate of a rather literal interpretation of the New Testament practices. He did not hesitate to differ vigorously with Denk's mysticism, though he did not refuse to work with Denk in behalf of their common cause. Sattler must have been a man of unusual piety and humility. Even Bucer, the less tolerant of the two Strassburg reformers, refers to him as a "martyr in Christ; even though he was a leader among the Anabaptists, he was much more reasonable and honorable than some of the rest."

Pilgram Marbeck

Pilgram Marbeck was a rather unusual man. Of pious Catholic parentage, he early became an Anabaptist in Tyrol where, as a mining engineer, he held an important government position. Forced to leave his Tyrolean home, presumably because of persecution, he appeared among the Brethren first in Augsburg in 1527, then in Strassburg the following year. In the latter city he won the favor of the authorities because of his aid in building a difficult engineering project which proved of great benefit to the public. It was for this reason, no doubt, that he was dealt with more generously than most Anabaptists, for he remained an ardent Anabaptist to the end. He helped to organize new communities, and wrote extensively in behalf of his beliefs. His most important treatise, a general dissertation on baptism, the magistracy, the supper, and other distinctive Anabaptist doctrines, was written in 1542. It was in reply to this book that Schwenckfeld wrote his *Judicium*, which led to a series of controversies in which neither Schwenckfeld nor Marbeck did himself credit. According to Bucer, Marbeck and his wife were "pious people living a blameless life." "But," adds Bucer, "that is just the decoy bird with which Satan even in the days of the Apostles allured the innocent to their death." In 1532 after a public debate with Bucer, Marbeck was banished from Strassburg by order of the city council. He went to Ulm, and from this time until his death in 1556, he remained the building spirit among the scattered Anabaptist communities all along the valley of the upper Neckar. He was one of the very few of the pioneer leaders to escape martyrdom.

Strassburg, Nürnberg, Regensburg

In 1529 Melchior Hofmann visited Strassburg long enough to gain some followers for his unusual views; but since his chief field of labor was confined to the regions along the Lower Rhine, the story of his activities is told in a later section of this chapter.

Casper Schwenckfeld and Sebastian Franck, two other well-known Strassburg dissenters, though in thorough agreement in many points with the Anabaptists, were never affiliated with them, and cannot be classed as such.

Among other cities in which Anabaptism struck its roots early was Nurnberg, old center of learning, full of evangelical life, with its school of heretical painters under the famous Albrecht Dürer. It was here that Hans Denk lived before he became an Anabaptist, and here that he met many of his faith afterwards.

Regensburg also harbored a congregation by 1527. Haetzer, Hut, Denk, and Hubmaier all made this a frequent stopping place during the few years of their active service. This city, too, followed a policy toward dissenters that was much milder than the surrounding regions which were directly under the rule of the Bavarian duke.

In fact, in all the cities of South Germany—Ulm, Munich, Stuttgart, Passau, wherever the impulses of the Reformation were felt, and in some places where they were not—Anabaptist groups were likely to appear and flourish for a time when the movement was at its peak.

3. MIDDLE GERMANY

There was a vigorous growth of Anabaptism in middle Germany too, in the general region of Fulda, Erfurt, Halberstadt, and Mühlhausen—in **Hesse, Franconia, Saxony, and Thuringia**. These were the regions where the Zwickau prophets labored, and where the Peasants' Revolt broke out in 1524 and collapsed so ingloriously the following year. It was perhaps for this reason, largely, that the Anabaptist movement here developed a character of its own, somewhat apart from that of other localities already mentioned. It was tinged much more than elsewhere with a spirit of millenarianism. Although quite orthodox and sound on such fundamental doctrines as believer's baptism, nonresistance, nonparticipation in government, and insistence upon living a life of strict piety and sobriety, the Anabaptists here were much more keenly expectant of the early inauguration of the kingdom of the elect through some great cataclysm than were their more sober-minded brethren in other regions. This chiliastic tone of the movement in middle Germany was no doubt partly due to the

THE ANABAPTISTS

lingering influence in this area of Thomas Müntzer and his followers, but also in no small degree to the unhealthy millenarian ideas of a new leader, Hans Hut, who for a time had this part of Germany largely to himself as a field of labor.

Müntzer and the Peasant Revolt

Thomas Müntzer, born about 1490, was a restless, fiery spirit who had taken up the work of reform even before Luther, having formed a conspiracy against the bishop of Magdeburg in 1513. After some years of wandering, he settled down at Zwickau as a Lutheran pastor with the full approval of Luther himself. It was here that he met Nikolaus Storch, with whom he began an attack upon the avarice and corruption of the monks and priests, ending with a denunciation of many of the practices of the new, as well as the old, church. The result was exile for both of them. Two years later Müntzer turned up at Alstaedt, where he gathered together a large congregation before whom he denounced state churches as well as the temporal government, and began a crusade against pictures, statues, altars, and even church buildings on the grounds that they were not necessary for true worship. He was also a follower of the inner light. "One might read ten thousand Bibles," he said, "and yet it would not help him." He believed himself to be God's special prophet, and like many of the enthusiasts of his day, he aimed to make the primitive church, together with certain teachings of the Old Testament, the basis of his new system. He rejected infant baptism as useless, though he never practiced rebaptism.

With his radical religious views, he preached revolutionary political doctrines. The present governments, he said, must soon be destroyed:

> Those princes who would not repent and would not accept the Gospel must even as the Catholic ecclesiastics be destroyed with fire and sword. They stand not only against the true faith, but also against the natural rights of man. Consequently they must be strangled like dogs.

Rulers must govern for the good of the people and are accountable to them, he said. He seemed to favor communism and a leveling of all class distinctions. As a result of these views, Müntzer was exiled from Alstaedt by Duke George of Saxony, never to return. For a time he hovered about Mühlhausen and other points in South Germany, and finally in 1524 he made a tour through northern Switzerland, coming into brief contact with Hubmaier and perhaps several other leaders of the radical reform movement. He warmly sympathized with the peasants of these regions in their fight against the economic and social burdens to which the church and the land tenure systems of the time subjected them; and when the Peasants' Revolt broke out in South Germany, Müntzer became one of the leaders of the movement. He was captured in the battle of Frankenhausen with a number of others and was shortly afterward executed.

That the Zwickau prophets were not Anabaptists, especially not of the peaceful, nonresistant Swiss Brethren type, is apparent and needs no further proof than a mere recital of their violent, revolutionary views.

Hans Hut

Hans Hut, a native Franconian and sexton to Hans von Bibra, first attracted local attention when, about the time of the agitation by the Zwickau prophets, he was imprisoned for refusing to baptize his child. We next hear of him in Nürnberg, where he learned the trade of bookbinder. He evidently was interested quite early in religious questions and became a sort of colporteur; for, when captured with other peasants after the battle of Frankenhausen, he secured his release on the plea that he had accompanied the band of armed peasants not as a fighter but as a bookseller. Several years later, in describing him to the court officials who were on his trail, the Nürnberg Council speaks of him as a book peddler, "in person a tall, lean, boorish sort of fellow, with a little pale, yellow beard, and a closely cropped head. His clothes consist of a grey riding jacket, and sometimes black, and a wide-brimmed grey hat."

He soon added the profession of lay preacher to that of bookseller, and went about preaching the gospel as he understood it. He labored without salary, supporting himself by his book trade and carpentering. He was a man without education in the schools but thoroughly familiar with the text of the Bible. Like many teachers of his day, he was especially fascinated with the prophecies of Daniel and the ecstatic visions of Revelation. He shared with Müntzer the belief in an early coming of the millennium. Every detail in the inauguration of the cataclysmic kingdom was carefully worked out by him. In one of his tracts published on the subject he says:

> Shortly before the end of the age, all the godless will be destroyed, and that by true Christians; if the number of Christians shall be sufficient, they will go from Germany to Switzerland, or Hungary. They will pay no attention to lords and princes. When some thousands of them shall have assembled, they shall exchange their goods for money so that they may have enough of food; then, they shall wait until the Turk comes. If the Turk fails to destroy the princes, monks, priests, nobles, and knights, they then will be stricken down by the little company of true Christians. But if the

THE ANABAPTISTS

godless shall march against the Turks, then the true Christians shall remain at home, but if many of the princes and lords remain at home too, and do not march against the Turks, they shall be struck down a short time afterwards. Then it will come to pass that the true Christians will have no one but God alone, who will then be and remain their Lord.

This near justification by Hut of the use of force by the Christians in helping to usher in the kingdom of the elect was full of danger to the whole Anabaptist cause. Hut himself was not a revolutionist so far as is known, and he took no part in any attempt at violence. He still hoped that the Turk would relieve the Christians of the necessity of preparing the world for the elect by the destruction of the wicked. But his teaching that in case the Turks failed, then the Christians themselves might undertake the task at the appointed time led to disastrous consequences later on when, under more radical leaders, the conviction dawned upon them that this appointed time for participation had actually arrived.

This fear of the Turk played an important role, not only in the apocalyptic ideals of the Anabaptists of middle and northwestern Germany, but in the whole Reformation movement as well. The relief in the early coming of Christ on the earth was by no means confined to the fanatics of the time. Luther himself held that view. And it was not strange that the Turks should be regarded as the probable means of ushering in the new era, for the Turkish fear was a real fear throughout middle Europe during these times. For years they had been hovering on the eastern frontier, threatening to destroy Christian Europe, and in 1529 and several times later, they had actually laid siege to Vienna. In fact, it was the necessity of keeping back the Turks that accounted for Emperor Charles's inability to suppress the Lutheran movement during the most critical years of its history, the lifetime of Luther himself.

All of these radical views of Hut had been well developed while he was still a Lutheran, for he did not become an Anabaptist, as noted elsewhere, until the summer of 1526. Unfortunately his baptism seemingly did not greatly modify his millenarian theories, though his contact with the mild-spirited Denk at Augsburg, and the conservative Hubmaier at Nikolsburg during the following year, had a sobering influence upon him. He was destined to serve his adopted faith for hardly more than a year. But that brief period was packed full of hectic activity and devoted service. He was a fiery, eloquent speaker, especially popular with the laboring men, and he traveled extensively and continually as an itinerant preacher, baptizing many in Tyrol, Austria, and Moravia. In Moravia, he clashed with Hubmaier and was imprisoned by a fellow Anabaptist, Leonhard von Liechtenstein. In middle Germany he baptized converts by the hundreds and was the outstanding and almost sole leader of the entire movement for that brief period. He almost literally baptized on the run. Many of his converts hardly rememberd his name. While the reluctance which these often showed, when hailed before court tribunals to give testimony to their faith, to remember their baptizer by any other name than merely "Hans" may have been due to the desire to shield him from the authorities, yet it is entirely likely that they had never known him by any other. Often the restless preacher would come into a house under cover of night, deliver his message, perhaps baptize the whole household on the spur of the moment, and before morning leave for parts unknown, seeking refuge and other converts, hardly leaving behind him even his full name.

Hut was present at the Martyrs' Synod in Augsburg in 1527, where he was induced to renounce some of his radical theories. But it was already too late for him to undo the damage he had done to the cause, for soon after this he was cast into prison in this city and was accidentally burned to death in his prison cell.

Among other influential leaders who played a minor role here must be mentioned Melchior Rink (sometimes confused by contemporary writers with Melchior Hofmann), Hans Romer, and Christopher Kürschner.

Chiliastic Tendencies

Under such leadership it is small wonder that the whole Anabaptist movement of middle Germany was permeated with a strong chiliastic spirit. Most of the Anabaptists believed with Hut that the wicked would be destroyed and the new era would be ushered in by an overwhelming victory of the Turks over the armies of the worldly forces. Nürnberg, it was quite generally agreed, would be the scene of the final battle. Not all, however, were convinced that the Turks would be the chosen agents for ending the old order. At least one man whose beliefs were tested at an inquisitorial court, drawing heavily no doubt from the history of the Israelites, gave it as his opinion that the old dispensation would be wound up by a plague of grasshoppers.

That many of the Anabaptists of this region were not unfamiliar with the arguments used by both the peasants of Germany and those of other countries in their struggle against economic oppression is shown by the fact that they knew the literature of that struggle. More than once a victim of the inquisitorial courts was heard to quote in the course of the couplet well known among the English peasants in their revolts in the

THE ANABAPTISTS

thirteenth century—

> *Da Adam reute und Eva spann*
> *Wer war die Zeit ein Edelmann?*
> (When Adam delved and Eve span
> Who was then the gentleman?)

It is possible to reproduce many of the details of the distinctive religious practices common among the Anabaptists of this area. Like their brethren in other sections, they stressed sobriety and simplicity in all the activities of life, disapproving especially of excessive eating and drinking, dancing, gambling, and riotous living. Their clothes were plain and simple, usually of a dark and somber color. True to their nonresistant principles, they substituted for the sword usually worn on public occasions a short wooden staff, similar to that worn by the Swiss Brethren. This often served as a special mark of identification by which their enemies singled them out in times of persecution. A common password among them was their usual form of greeting—*Der Friede des Herrn sei mit Dir* (The peace of the Lord be with you) or *Gott grüss Dich in dem Herrn* (Greetings in the name of the Lord), and the rejoinder *Ich danke Dir in dem Herrn* (I thank you in the Lord), or simply *Amen*.

In their religious practices they unconsciously, perhaps, retained some of undoubted Catholic origin. In administering the act of baptism the form of a cross was often made on the forehead of the candidate, as the one who administered the rite uttered the formula "In the name of the Father, Son, and Holy Spirit." For a reason not known, the phrase in the Lord's Prayer "Give us our daily bread" was generally replaced by *Das wahrhaftige Brot, dein ewiges Wort, gib uns heute.* (Give us the true bread, your eternal Word.) They addressed each other as brother and sister, applying these terms to one another irrespective of relationship, and often they spoke of themselves as the "beloved of God."

Did Not Escape Persecution

The Anabaptists of Middle and South Germany, of course, did not escape persecution, although Luther himself was at first slow to sanction any interference on the part of the civil authorities. Fearing, no doubt, the effect of intolerance upon the freedom of his own followers in states that were still dominantly Catholic, he for a time advocated a spirit of toleration in matters of religious belief. But as the danger to his own followers receded, and his impatience with those who differed with him increased, he grew less inclined to tolerate dissent. By 1527 he still suggested that the civil authority had no right to interfere in matters of religious conviction. But in the same breath he invalidated all the benefits that might accrue from this fine spirit by an ingenious interpretation of the right to enforce the law against blasphemy and sedition. Blasphemy he soon interpreted as false teaching, and false teaching as any teaching contrary to the doctrines of Lutheranism. By 1530 he no longer needed to indulge in even this sort of casuistry. He was ready to admit that Anabaptism must be destroyed and willing to try any means, no matter how drastic, necessary to accomplish that end. Most of the other Lutheran theologians followed him in this policy.

But if the theologians were a bit slow in making up their minds to use extreme measures, the temporal authorities were not. Almost from the start in most of the states of middle Europe, the Anabaptists were made to feel the iron hand of persecution. The imperial edict issued at the Diet of Speyer on April 23, 1529, ordering all Anabaptists, men and women, in all the states of the empire to be destroyed with fire and sword, has already been mentioned.

Among the local rulers who practiced unusually harsh measures was the elector John the Steadfast of Saxony, in Luther's own state. He not only put men and women to death for their faith in his own duchy, but urgently insisted that his neighboring princes do likewise. The Catholic princes were the most relentless of all. In the Swabian League four companies of horsemen of one hundred each scoured the territory under their jurisdiction, literally driving the Anabaptists out of the land. The duke of Bavaria reached the limit of perfidy and cruelty perhaps in the cold-blooded order that those who recanted were to be beheaded, while those who did not were to be burned at the stake. Only Philip of Hesse refused to take extreme measures. In spite of the pressure brought to bear upon him by the elector of Saxony and the edict of Speyer, he could still boast in 1530 that up to that time he had not yet put anyone to death in his duchy because of religious faith. Ludwig V, the count of the Palatinate, although a Catholic, up to the time of the Diet of Speyer refused to resort to harsh means; but later rulers followed the intolerant spirit of the day.

Anabaptism died hard; the Brethren stuck to their faith tenaciously. In Thuringia the count of Henneberg complained that "neither godly Scripture, nor sound godly warning, nor pain has any effect on them." In the Palatinate the count of Alzey asked, "What shall I do? The more I condemn and execute, the more they increase."

But the small scattered groups of peace-loving nonresistants, whose only wish was to be left alone to worship God in their own

THE ANABAPTISTS

way, were no match for the organized forces of both state and church urged on by a relentless hatred of religious nonconformity and fear of political anarchy. Persecuting zeal grew from year to year, until by 1535 the Anabaptists who were left in middle and southern Germany were relegated to the obscure outlying districts.

4. TYROL AND AUSTRIA

The Anabaptist movement confined itself in the south to the German-speaking sections of the empire. Missionaries and refugees from Switzerland early found their way to the east across Voralberg into Tyrol and Austria, along the Inn and the Danube as far as Vienna. Large Anabaptist centers were formed at Landeck, Innsbruck, and Kitzbühel along the upper Inn; at Passau where the Inn enters the Danube; and at Steyr, Linz, and other towns farther down the Danube. Following the trade routes through the famous Brenner Pass, flourishing congregations were established around Sterzing on the north side of the pass, and others on the south side along the valleys of the Eisack, Puster, and Etch, which combine in southern Tyrol to form the Adige in Italy.

In the Tyrolean valleys alone, it was said that by 1529 Anabaptists were found in 120 localities. Just when they first appeared here is not definitely known, but it was likely soon after the dispersion at Zürich in 1525. Georg Zaunring, arrested in 1528, said that he had baptized many along the Inn. The following year Matthias Langer claimed 100 converts. The leader of the Tyroleans was Georg Blaurock, who was burned at the stake September 6, 1529. Succeeding Blaurock was Jakob Hutter, a hatter, native of the Puster Valley, who this same year was sent by his persecuted brethren to Moravia to investigate the advisability of a wholesale migration to that land of promise. Pilgram Marbeck had left for Strassburg before the heaviest persecution had set in.

Scattered groups were found in the accessible valleys of all the neighboring Habsburg provinces, Upper and Lower Austria, Salzburg, Carinthia, and Styria. It is known that Hans Hut spent some time in these sections in 1527, greatly influencing the whole movement. At Steyr he sent out a number of missionaries.

In all the Habsburg lands, which remained solidly Catholic, Anabaptist persecution was inaugurated almost from the beginning. Ferdinand, the brother of Emperor Charles, was charged with the task of protecting the crown lands against both the Turks from without and all the dissenters from within. The second task he performed well. The first victim executed at Rottenburg on the Inn January 4, 1528, was Leonhard Schiemer. Hymn 31 in the *Ausbund* is accredited to him:

> Thine holy place they have destroyed,
>   Thine altar overthrown
> And, reaching forth their bloody hands
>   Have foully slain Thine own;
>
> And we alone, a little flock,
>   The few who still remain,
> Are exiles wandering through the land
>   In sorrow and in pain.
>
> We are, alas, like scattered sheep,
>   The shepherd out of sight,
> Each far away from home and hearth
>   And, like the birds of night
> That hide away; in rocky clefts
>   We have our rocky hold,
> Yet near at hand, as for the birds,
>   There waits the hunter bold.
>
> We wander in the forests dark
>   With dogs upon our track
> And, like the captive, silent lamb,
>   Men bring us, prisoners, back.
> They point to us amid the throng
>   And with their taunts offend,
> And long to let the sharpened ax
>   On heretics descend.

Schiemer was followed by hundreds of others. In Kitzbühel, a town in the archbishopric of Salzburg, during this same year 200 Anabaptist prisoners were reported. The next year in the same district, fifty children were made orphans by the execution of their parents. No stone was left unturned by the Catholic rulers to completely root out the Anabaptist faith. Special state police were organized to search out heretics. The houses of the victims were burned down; they were sent to the galleys, beheaded, drowned, and burned at the stake. Prospective mothers were given a respite, when condemned for their faith, only until their children were born. The infants were turned over to orthodox Catholic orphanages, and the mothers were thrown into the river or burned at the stake. Most despicable of all was the sending out of secret agents, who, preying upon the simple faith of the unsuspecting Brethren, were urged by the ruling authorities to pretend conversion, submit to baptism, learn the names of their brethren in the faith, and then betray them to the authorities.

Under such determined efforts to root out their faith, the

THE ANABAPTISTS

Anabaptists were soon driven out of the larger centers and into the out-of-the-way places. Many left for Moravia.

5. MORAVIA

In pleasing contrast to the common experiences of the Anabaptists elsewhere was the welcome they received for a few years in southern Moravia. There were several reasons why Moravia, at this particular time, could offer an asylum to the persecuted sects from other regions. It was ruled by a *Markgraf* who was a vassal to the king of Bohemia. During the struggle between rival claimants to the Bohemian throne, many of the vassals of the kingdom had virtually managed their own affairs with little interference from above. In 1526 the crown fell to the lot of Archduke Ferdinand of Austria. Although the archduke was wont to rule his possessions with an iron hand, yet he did not dare to encroach too early upon the liberties of the powerful Moravian nobility. So these were left for some years with their former autonomous rights. Many of the Moravian noblemen had been sympathetic, for both economic and religious reasons, toward the dissenting groups. Owing to numerous civil wars, the population had been greatly reduced in some regions, and large estates had been devastated and made unprofitable. And so, Anabaptists, who were known to be good farmers, were often welcomed for economic reasons within the domains of local noblemen, in spite of kingly and imperial edicts to the contrary.

Among the tolerant noblemen in southern Moravia was Leonhard von Liechtenstein, whose seat of government was the ancient city of Nikolsburg, near the Austrian border. Anabaptist refugees must have come here quite early; but we know little of them before the coming of Balthasar Hubmaier in July 1526.

Balthasar Hubmaier

Balthasar Hubmaier, whom we remember as one of the early agitators against infant baptism in Switzerland, was one of the most learned of Anabaptist leaders. Born about 1480 near Augsburg, he was a university graduate and later a university professor in Ingoldstadt. He became an eloquent preacher of Catholic doctrines, both in the cathedral church in Regensburg and later in Waldshut, the latter an Austrian town just across the Swiss border. His connection both with Zwingli and with the opponents of infant baptism in Zürich has been mentioned elsewhere. Baptized by Reublin, he joined the Swiss Brethren in the spring of 1525, and afterward devoted himself wholeheartedly to the Anabaptist cause. He was immediately marked for destruction by Archduke Ferdinand, who ordered the town of Waldshut to surrender him. But Hubmaier had secured a large following, and the town authorities refused to turn him over to the archduke. The town, besieged soon after, surrendered to the Austrian troops. But in the meantime, Hubmaier had fled from the city to Zürich, where, unfortunately for himself, as an Anabaptist he was also an outlaw. Here, together with a number of others, he was imprisoned. But upon a partial recantation and a promise to leave the city, he was released. After a short stay in Constance and a brief period of activity in Augsburg, where, as we have seen, he baptized Hans Denk, he arrived in Nikolsburg in July 1526. There for one brief year he exercised a dominating influence over the rapidly growing Anabaptist movement, if indeed he was not the actual founder of it.

Rapid Growth

Anabaptism at Nikolsburg grew by leaps and bounds, capturing the leading Lutheran preachers of the city, Oswald Glaidt and Hans Spittelmaier, as well as Leonhard von Liechtenstein. Following the example of both their spiritual leaders and their temporal rulers, the people flocked to the new faith by the thousands. In fact, Anabaptism practically became the state church. It is said that by the close of the first year it numbered some six thousand; some say double that number. It is likely that the former is more nearly correct. How much of this growth was due to the efforts of Hubmaier is not known, but it is likely that he was ably assisted by other leaders. How many of the adherents were natives and how many were refugees is also a matter of conjecture, though the latter undoubtedly were far in the minority. Among the Swiss refugees, though never quite a full-fledged Anabaptist, was the Zürich publisher Christoph Froschauer. He was founder of a well-known Zürich printing firm, and was publisher during the sixteenth century of numerous editions of the famous Froschauer Bible, which was in general use among the Swiss Anabaptists for the next three centuries. Froschauer set up a printing establishment in Nikolsburg, and there Hubmaier had published during the year no less than fifteen separate pamphlets, mostly on some phase of the baptism question and all dedicated to various tolerant noblemen of Moravia.

The so-called Moravian Anabaptists were separatists, and they advocated and practiced religious toleration within certain limits. They rejected infant baptism and practiced adult baptism upon confession of faith. But on the question of the relation of church to state, they differed quite materially from the other Anabaptists.

They did not advocate or practice full nonresistance, a fundamental doctrine of the faith as taught by Grebel, Blaurock, Denk, Sattler, and even to a limited extent by Hut and Hofmann. In his treatise *On the Sword*, Hubmaier taught that the Christian might use the sword and go to war on certain occasions, and that he was permitted to be a magistrate, although no magistrate should use his power to enforce religious conformity. Baron von Liechtenstein violated this doctrine, however, when with the apparent consent of Hubmaier he imprisoned Hut, a fellow Anabaptist, because of a religious difference. Liechtenstein might have justified this action on the ground that it was impossible to maintain a stable order without the use of force. And it is undoubtedly true that nonresistant Anabaptism and temporal government are incompatible terms in a sinful world.

Factional Disputes

Unfortunately, the same spirit of freedom which in the domain of Liechtenstein guaranteed the greatest degree of religious toleration, also afforded ample opportunity for the development of those petty factional quarrels which developed so readily in the extreme individualism of the Anabaptist movement. Moravian Anabaptism evidently did not grow its rarest flowers in an atmosphere of too much freedom. It was at its worst just here where it should have been at its best.

The first cleavage appeared between the native Lutheran converts to Anabaptism under the leadership of Hubmaier, and the Swiss and Tyrolean refugees under the leadership of Hans Hut, who had also come to Nikolsburg in the fall of 1526, and Jakob Wideman, who had arrived at about the same time. Both Hut and Wideman strenuously opposed Hubmaier's halfway measures. No Christian can be a magistrate they said; neither can he take up the sword except, as Hut suggested, at the specific command of the Lord at the proper time, to help the Turk usher in the millennium. Wideman called war taxes "blood money." As a result of this controversy, Hut found himself in prison. He soon escaped, however, and went to Augsburg, where during the fall of 1527 he met his death.

Hubmaier too disappeared from the Moravian stage of activity in the summer of the same year. Ever since his radical activities at Waldshut he had been closely watched by the archduke of Austria. First at Waldshut, then at Zürich, and now again at Nikolsburg, Ferdinand demanded that he be turned over to the Austrian authorities for punishment. Baron von Liechtenstein was none too reluctant, as it seems to us now, to turn over a fellow Anabaptist to what he knew would be sure death. Likely he could not help himself. Hubmaier and his wife were both imprisoned in Vienna. On March 10, 1528, he was burned at the stake; and a few days later his devoted wife, with a stone tied about her neck, was tossed into the Danube.

The troubles in the Nikolsburg church did not cease with the disappearance of Hut and Hubmaier. Wideman continued his dispute with Hubmaier's successor, Hans Spittelmaier, in behalf of the Swiss type of the faith. But to the old subject of controversy a new one now was added—the demand that all goods be held in common. This resulted from the necessities of the poverty-stricken refugees who continually found their way into the barony. Caring for these refugees was a heavy burden on the native Anabaptists. Early in the spring of 1527, Wideman complained that the native church "does not give shelter to the pilgrims and refugees from other countries." Soon natives and exiles had separate meetings. The larger group, faithful to the teaching of Hubmaier on the sword, and mostly natives, were known as *Schwertler* (the "party of the sword"); while Wideman's smaller party, mostly exiles with Swiss views, were known as *Stäbler* (the "party of the staff").

The Community of Goods

But von Liechtenstein would permit no division within the ranks of his church. He informed Wideman that if he could not conform to the will of the majority, he would have to leave. With a small group of about two hundred, Wideman chose to do so. Now was an opportune time to adopt the communal practice. On their outward journey, the party stopped just beyond the city walls, where, electing a "minister of temporal needs," they

> laid down their cloaks, and every man threw down on it entirely of his own accord without compulsion, his earthly possessions according to the teachings of the prophets and apostles for the benefit of the needy.

Although Leonhard von Liechtenstein forced the issue which resulted in the exile of the little flock of *Stäbler* and communalists, he evidently bore them no ill will, for he accompanied them to the borders of his country, where he dismissed them with his blessing, drinking to their health and bidding them Godspeed. At the border the little party was fortunate in being met by another set of noblemen, the Barons von Kaunitz, who were as glad to receive the exiles on their devastated estates near Austerlitz as the Liechtensteins were loath to see them go. "If there were a thousand of them," said one of the Kaunitz brothers, "we would gladly receive them."

THE ANABAPTISTS

The Austerlitz settlement was founded on a communal basis. The whole community lived as one family in a group called a *Bruderhof* household. Believing to have found here the promised land, they soon sent out messengers to their persecuted brethren in the Palatinate, Swabia, Bavaria, Hesse, and especially Tyrol, urging all of them to come to Moravia where they would be welcome. Many came, including among others such leaders as Wilhelm Reublin, prominent in the Swiss beginnings a few years before, and Georg Zaunring with a number of Tyrolean followers. Soon additional households had to be established at Znaim, Brünn, Eibenschitz, and Schäckowitz, all nearby. At Rossitz a large community was founded by Gabriel Ascherham with his following from Silesia, which in a short time mounted up to twelve hundred members. To these latter was added also about this time a company of some five hundred Swabians under the leadership of Philip Blauärmel.

It would have been strange indeed if these different groups, coming as they did from various sections of middle Europe with differing customs and practices and their own strong-minded leaders, should not have had some difficulty under the stress of communal control in harmonizing their conflicting views. In Austerlitz the original household, where Jakob Wideman exercised a rather arbitrary and rigid discipline and where he guarded jealously his ministerial authority against all newcomers, there soon developed a rather unlovely controversy among both leaders and laymen. The old question of the relation of the state to the church evidently was not entirely settled by leaving Nikolsburg. Some of those from Austerlitz, citing the example of Jesus at Capernaum, insisted that the brethren should assume all the burdens of citizenship like the other inhabitants of the land; others declared this to be impossible under the nonresistant faith. Their duty was merely to obey and pray for the authorities over them.

The strict enforcement by Wideman of the communal regulations became extremely distasteful to many who had come from congregations where that style of life was unknown. Even in his own original flock Wideman found some difficulty in securing implicit obedience. His attempt to secure husbands for the marriageable sisters was especially resented by them. The sisters also complained that their taskmaster gave them difficult Scripture lessons to memorize which greatly humiliated them in case of failure. Some evidently did not share their all. These went to the markets, it was said, and buying what they pleased, brought discontent to the others. Some complained because housing quarters were crowded. The Tyroleans thought that the order of worship was not as good as theirs at home and that there was much laxness in the bringing up of the children.

These differences came to a head one day in 1530, when Reublin, who was an ordained minister, began to expound the Scriptures during the absence of Wideman. He was severely reprimanded by Wideman upon his return. Zaunring, a Tyrolean minister whose gift was not recognized by Wideman, sided with Reublin and his fellows. As a result, about one hundred fifty members under the leadership of these two left for the neighboring district of Auspitz, where on convent lands given them by the Abbess of Brünn they established a separate household.

In the meantime, Gabriel Ascherham and Philip Blauärmel had fallen out with one another at Rossitz. Philip also led his faction to Auspitz. These two groups came to be known in the records of the period as *Gabrielists* and *Philipists*.

Jakob Hutter and Communal Living

These various religious controversies seriously impaired the spiritual health of the whole Moravian Anabaptist community. Some of the more devoted adherents of the faith among all the different groups, realizing the seriousness of the situation, appealed to their Tyrolean brethren for an impartial arbitrator who might help them heal their troubles. In 1531, the Tyroleans sent them a minister who had already been in Moravia two years before and who was to play an important role among them for a few years—Jakob Hutter.

Whether Hutter promoted a community of goods while in Tyrol is not known, but at the time of his first visit to Moravia in 1529, he had freely associated with the elders of the communal congregation at Austerlitz and found himself as of "one heart and mind" with them, "in the fear and service of the Lord." Upon his return to his native land, his enthusiastic report of the freedom enjoyed in Moravia sent many of his oppressed brethren to that land of promise. Most of these, no doubt, affiliated themselves with the Austerlitz groups. Hutter himself remained to direct the work in Tyrol. How he succeeded as peacemaker between the congregations at Auspitz and Austerlitz on the occasion of his second visit in 1531 we do not know. But when he returned in 1533 to Auspitz to make that his permanent home, he came "not as to strangers," he said, "but as to dear brethren"; and according to an old chronicler, "bringing with him to the common treasury a temporal gift, a sweet offering, yes a little saving so that the loan which the Abbess of Brünn had made them could be paid off." Here Hutter was invited by his many admirers to assume equal pastoral duties with others. Although each household was already well supplied

THE ANABAPTISTS

with native pastors, he was not slow to act upon this suggestion.

Jakob Hutter evidently was a man of a strong and aggressive personality and a strict disciplinarian. Most of the other ministers were soon lined up against him. But having won the confidence of a majority of the members in the various congregations, he was able to discipline his fellow ministers with a ruthless hand. Especially insistent was he upon a rigid enforcement of the communal life. The controversy was not always carried on in the spirit of Christian humility befitting fellow sufferers for the faith. Uncomplimentary adjectives and harsh epithets were hurled back and forth without the least compunction. The Philipists were most bitter against the friends of Hutter, and the latter found fault with almost all the others. Wilhelm Reublin, who was such a credit to the early Swiss movement, was now charged with reserving twenty-four *gulden* of his own private money from the common treasury in a time of sickness, and was cast out as a "faithless, lying, malicious Ananias." Philip Blauärmel was also excommunicated by Hutter as a "liar" for saying that the people were worshiping Hutter as an idol. Bohemian David was expelled because he had engaged a company of soldiers to accompany him when he departed from Austerlitz; Zaunring was expelled for taking back his wife, who had been charged with adultery; and Schützinger, Hutter's co-laborer in his earlier visits to Moravia, for deceit. Some of these, upon proper confession of their sins, were permitted to return to the fold. Reublin, however, completely disappeared from Anabaptist history at this point.

So completely did Jakob Hutter dominate the whole Moravian situation that, according to the chronicler of these events, all the survivors of the church are called *Hutterisch* (Hutterites) to this day. That all the other ministers were sinners and Hutter alone was a saint is not likely. But be that as it may, the fact remains that all the other factions of the Moravian Anabaptist faith ultimately disappeared, and only the Hutterites survived the stress of the times. A small handful of these survivors, driven out of their native land, set their faces toward the East. In the course of the next two centuries their children's children found their way finally by way of Hungary and Walachia to Russia, and ultimately, during the latter part of the last century, to the prairies of the Dakotas and Canada.

The freedom from outside interference in affairs of religion enjoyed by the Moravian Anabaptists was too good to last. King Ferdinand, who had always hated them as "more dangerous than murderers, and enemies of the land," had withheld the iron hand of persecution only because of fear of the powerful noblemen in his newly acquired kingdom. By 1532, he had evidently won sufficient influence over these noblemen to venture upon an aggressive policy of persecution. At any rate, he succeeded in forcing through the Moravian *Landtag*, held at Znaim, an edict banishing all Anabaptists and Jews from the land. The nobles, no matter how highly they might prize the economic worth of their industrious tenants, now had no recourse but to enforce the order of the king. The households consequently were broken up, and their occupants were driven out into the open fields and under the open sky to seek a living as best they could. The inhabitants everywhere were forbidden under pain of heavy punishment to give these exiles shelter, food, or drink. The object evidently was to harry them out of the land as rapidly as possible.

All factions and parties had to go—the *Schwertler* of Nikolsburg, as well as the *Stäbler* of Austerlitz, the *Philipists*, who left with "songs on their lips," the *Gabrielists*, and the *Hutterisch*. At first the large company tried to keep together, but finding this impossible, they formed into small groups of eight or ten to seek as best they could their sustenance among an unfriendly people. The natives remained for the most part hidden in the forests and hills of their own native Moravian homeland, hoping for better times. Many of the foreign refugees found their way back to the lands from which they had originally come—the Philipists to Swabia the Gabrielists to Silesia. Jakob Hutter, with "pack on his back," turned his face toward his native Tyrol. Some sixty Swiss Brethren were apprehended near the Bavarian border, where they were imprisoned in the castle of Passau. Here they composed during the next few years a group of hymns which later formed the nucleus of the famous *Ausbund*, the hymnbook still in use, without a change, by the Old Order Amish among the hills of eastern Pennsylvania and the plains of central Kansas.

In vain Hutter pled with the Moravian authorities in behalf of his brethren:

> We do not seek to harm or injure any one, he said, not even our worst enemy. Our deeds are an open book, our words public to all. Rather than owe any man a penny, we would be robbed of a hundred gulden. Rather than harm anyone with a stroke of the hand, we would lose our lives. Our whole life ambition is to live according to God's truth and justice in peace and harmony as true followers of Christ. Those who say we have gathered in the open fields by the thousands as if to prepare for war are not telling the truth. If all the world were like-minded, all wars would cease, and all unrighteousness would have an end.

But his efforts were all to no avail. The households were not restored. The congregations were scattered.

In Tyrol, Jakob Hutter was permitted only a brief period of

THE ANABAPTISTS

further labor—all the while at the risk of great personal danger. With a price upon his head, he was a marked man. In the cellars of the houses of his friends, in the forests, in secret places among the hills, wherever he could do so without inviting detection, he gathered together his brethren and ministered unto them to the end. He was finally apprehended near his birthplace and taken to Innsbruck, where he lay in prison for some months. After undergoing a season of the most cruel torture inflicted upon him by his enemies in the hope that they might secure from him a denial of his faith and information as to the identity and whereabouts of his brethren, he was burned at the stake in the early spring of 1536, stouthearted and faithful to the very last.

6. THE LOWER RHINE

Anabaptism found its way down the Rhine River rather slowly. It took several years after its first appearance in Switzerland before there were many traces of it in the Netherlands and northwestern Germany. Here the soil had been prepared by the "Sacramentarian" movement that denied the actual presence of the flesh of Christ in the communion bread. Melchior Hofmann accepted and spread this view, applying it also to an adult believer's baptism.

Melchior Hofmann

Melchior Hofmann, a Swabian by birth, early in life learned the trade of a tanner. "That good-for-nothing fellow who dresses hides," Zwingli called him in 1523. Although he had little formal education, he was unusually familiar with the contents of the Bible and possessed of an eloquent tongue and a vivid imagination. He early became a fiery and popular lay preacher of radical Lutheran principles, for a time with the approval of Luther himself. For several years he traveled continually and extensively along the Baltic Sea coast, on both the German and Swedish sides. With such radical fellow laborers as Andreas Karlstadt and Melchior Rink, the latter a follower of Thomas Müntzer, he plied his trade while he preached to large and enthusiastic groups of followers. Sometimes this had disastrous results, as when in Stockholm he was driven from the city for inaugurating a crusade against the pictures and statues in the city churches. In 1527, he was invited by the king of Denmark to serve as a court preacher at Kiel. Here he established a printing press on which he published many of his numerous tracts explaining his radical views on many of the mysteries of the Scriptures.

Hofmann was especially attracted by the prophecies of the

Bible as they appeared in Daniel and Revelation, dangerous books in the hands of unlettered enthusiasts. Adept at an allegorical interpretation of the Scriptures, he greatly astonished and attracted the unlearned masses with his supposed insight into divine mysteries. He made much of biblical symbolism; every recurring number, especially the number seven, and every occult phrase had a significant meaning for him. Particularly dangerous were his eschatological and chiliastic views. While still in Sweden, he taught the people that Christ's kingdom, the kingdom of the elect, would soon appear on the earth. By a method of computation all his own, based on both Daniel and Revelation, he calculated that the great cataclysm would take place seven years from that time—in the year 1533. Strassburg was to be the assembling place of the one hundred forty-four thousand saints which the prophecies foretold would be the number of faithful left on the earth to inaugurate the New Jerusalem.

Like Hut, Hofmann believed that the new era, preceded by a period of great persecution, would be ushered in through the agency of the Turks. Two reincarnated messengers, Elijah and Enoch, would appear in due time to clear the way for the great event. One of these, Elijah, was already here in the person of Hofmann himself. Enoch was to follow. Hofmann, it will be observed, did not advocate the use of force in bringing in the new kingdom. Nor did he share the belief of Hut that at a later appointed time the Christian would be justified in participating in bringing about that event. Later, however, under more fanatical leadership, his theories were no less dangerous than were those of the more militant Hut.

One other peculiar view of Hofmann distinguished him at this particular time from his co-laborers—his theory of the incarnation. According to his view, Jesus at His birth owed nothing of His being to the flesh of Mary. She served merely as a medium through which Jesus came into the world, "like unto light as it passes through glass," as later disciples of his put it. Behind this unusual explanation of the incarnation in the mind of Hofmann was the necessity of keeping Jesus sinless. Hofmann could not see how sinlessness could emerge from sinful flesh. The only escape was to have Jesus born without either earthly father or mother. The latter view was especially objectionable to the Catholics, since it detracted from the adoration of Mary as the mother of Jesus.

Hofmann arrived at his Anabaptist views rather gradually. At first an ardent Lutheran, he soon leaned toward many of the doctrines of Zwingli, especially in the matter of the Lord's Supper. Finally he shared with the Anabaptists especially those views based on a literal interpretation of the Scriptures, such as those on the oath and the magistracy. He became an Anabaptist in 1529 when, it is thought, he was baptized at Strassburg, after coming in contact with such leaders as Denk, Haetzer, and Sebastian Franck.

He perhaps underwent little change of heart and mind. By his baptism he officially joined a group with whom he was already at one. In his remaining years he became an aggressive and fiery expounder and apostle of Anabaptist views as he understood them. He left immediately after his baptism for the city of Emden in East Friesland, where he introduced adult baptism in these regions. He immediately gained a great following, especially among the common people, and in 1530 after a sermon he had preached, he baptized three hundred converts in the church of Emden. This was the beginning of Anabaptism in the Low Countries.

The Netherlands

The time was ripe in the Low Countries for an aggressive leader of a new evangelical life. Neither Lutheranism nor Zwinglianism had as yet taken strong root here. The evangelical movement, influenced somewhat by earlier dissenting groups, remained unorganized, highly individualistic, and leaderless. It was Hofmann's great opportunity, and he was not slow to take advantage of it. From Emden as a center, he spent the next few years of his life in ceaseless missionary activity in behalf of the Anabaptist cause, traveling all over the provinces of northern Holland and East Friesland, preaching and baptizing, and not forgetting to prophesy the inauguration of the kingdom of the just within a few years.

The common people, especially, heard him gladly, and converts flocked to him by the thousands. Among the converts was Jan Volkertsz Trypmaker, who in 1530 was the first to introduce Anabaptism into Amsterdam. Trypmaker was an enthusiastic apostle of the new cause and was beheaded for his faith the next year at The Hague. Among the number converted and baptized by Trypmaker were two men who, because of their later connection with Anabaptist history, are of interest here: Sicke Freerks, the tailor whose execution at Leeuwarden a little later caused a Witmarsum priest named Menno Simons to study the Bible for an explanation of infant baptism; and Jan Matthijsz, a Haarlem baker, who preached a chiliastic doctrine more fanatical than Hofmann ever dreamed of. Matthijsz himself soon became an enthusiastic preacher of the new faith and an eloquent missionary of the cause, not only traveling extensively but sending out many disciples who carried his own teaching through all northern Netherlands. Among these were two who visited Friesland, Bartel de Boeckbinder and Dirck Cuper, who baptized two brothers at Leeuwarden, Obbe and Dirk Philips. The latter two won Menno Simons to the cause.

But neither church nor state approved of the religious movement so enthusiastically promoted by Hofmann and Trypmaker. Many of the converts were sent to prison; and most of the preachers, to the executioner's block as rebels and heretics. Hofmann was greatly disappointed and disillusioned by this turn of affairs. Thinking that the favor with which his message was received in Emden and the toleration granted him there were certain evidence of the approval of God and of the inauguration of His kingdom, he was puzzled and dismayed by the fierce persecution that now set in against his brethren. Perhaps after all he was mistaken as to the time. But Hofmann was not the kind of man who would long be without bibilical justification for a change of tactics, if necessary. Finding in the Old Testament that Zerubbabel had one time delayed work on the rebuilding of the temple at Jerusalem for a period of two years because of the opposition of the enemy, he now also ordered his disciples to cease baptizing for an equal period of time to avoid persecution. No doubt he hoped that by that time the new kingdom would be established. Preaching, however, continued. His adherents became known as *Melchiorites*.

Melchior Hofmann followed his visions to the end. Influenced by the prophecies of an old man that he, Hofmann, must first be imprisoned for six months in Strassburg, which was now to be the New Jerusalem, he journeyed to that city to be present among the one hundred forty-four thousand who were to gather there at the appropriate time, the year 1533. The old man's prophecies were fulfilled. Hofmann had no difficulty in getting himself imprisoned—not for six months, but for the rest of his life. Here he died some years later.

7. MÜNSTER

In the meantime another evangelical movement, entirely independent of the one just mentioned, was developing in the city of Münster, the seat of a Catholic bishopric in Westphalia. The bishop, an unusually harsh ruler, was decidedly unpopular among his subjects, a fact which greatly encouraged the demand for religious as well as political reform. By 1533, under the leadership of Bernhard Rothmann, the city had accepted the Lutheran faith. Paralleling this religious movement was one of social democracy, supported by the working men of the city and led by Bernhard Knipperdolling. Religious and social reform were thus closely intertwined here from the first. With the coming of Henric Rol, an Anabaptist of the Melchiorite party from Jülich-Cleve, the Münster agitation entered a new phase. Rothmann was persuaded to accept baptism, and many followed his example. Although the Lutheran religious forces in the city stoutly opposed this new development, the labor guilds of the town, attracted by the social message, enthusiastically supported Rothmann and Rol in their religious efforts.

The Anabaptist movement in Münster up to this time had been of the Melchiorite variety, still peaceful and largely nonresistant, and with the exception of the millenarian germ, not particularly to be feared. But with the coming of Jan Matthijsz and his disciples in the early spring of 1534, the movement entered a more dangerous phase. Nonresistance now gave way to an aggressive spirit of revolution. And with the passing of the nonresistant spirit, the Anabaptism which we have been following so far in this chapter throughout middle Europe changed in Münster in everything but name.

Jan Matthijsz

As we have seen, Jan Matthijsz preached a much more militant type of millenarianism than did his teacher, Melchior Hofmann. According to Hofmann, the Christian's part in the great drama was a passive one—merely to await the coming of the great day. But according to Matthijsz, the day was already at hand and he was the Enoch prophesied by Hofmann. It was now the duty of the faithful to take up the sword in behalf of the new kingdom to be established. Münster, instead of Strassburg, was to be the seat of the New Jerusalem.

Now that Hofmann was a prisoner in Strassburg, Matthijsz, who had already chafed under Hofmann's order to cease baptizing for two years, took control of the Anabaptist movement in these regions. He announced that the time for action had now arrived, and that baptizing might be resumed. Numerous disciples of his were sent throughout the land, broadcasting this news. Two of them, as we have just seen, entered Münster in January of 1534.

That Matthijsz did not regard himself as merely the successor to Hofmann, but that he thought himself about to inaugurate an entirely new movement, is evidenced by the fact that he insisted on rebaptizing all those who had already been initiated through the rite of baptism into the church of Rothmann and Rol, including these two leaders themselves. Within a few days, fourteen hundred were added to his group, no doubt embracing the larger part of those already Anabaptists. His followers can no longer be regarded as Anabaptists of the type of Sattler and Denk or even of Hofmann. In fact, the act of baptism was now a political rather than a religious symbol. Apostles of this Münsterite movement were sent out under the personal leadership of Matthijsz throughout the Low Countries, appearing first among the Melchiorites wherever possible, preaching the new gospel, and inviting all the faithful to gather in Münster to await the ushering in of the New Jerusalem.

In the meantime, the Catholic bishop of Münster, who had been driven from his charge some time before, was alarmed at the turn affairs had taken, and determined to crush all revolt against his authority. He gathered a small army among his followers and laid siege to the city. The movement entered its final stage when, in April of 1534, Jan Matthijsz was killed in an attempt to break through the lines, leaving Jan van Leyden in command of the misguided enthusiasts. It was under van Leyden's rule of a little more than a year that all the horrible excesses and bloody orgies, which have ever since given the whole Münster affair such an unsavory reputation in Reformation annals, took place.

While no attempt is made here to justify all that was done in the name of religion by Jan van Leyden, yet even the most disreputable and fanatical practices indulged in by the Münsterites at this time can be explained by the facts of their real situation. They were engaged in a life-and-death struggle. There was no hope of escape. Those who tried to break through the lines were taken captive and executed. Every ounce of reserve force would have to be mobilized and conserved against the danger from the outside. There could be no divided loyalty within. During a critical period of the siege, all those who wished to take the chance of escape through the lines were given an opportunity to leave the city; all others were forced to submit to baptism, an act which was no longer of particular religious significance, but was merely a covenant cementing together the entire body as a single unit in its resolve to fight together to the last ditch—a sort of a blood oath of allegiance. Strict discipline now demanded that every act of treachery must be punished. This accounts for the countless executions in cold blood upon the mere word of Jan van Leyden during the closing months of the siege. It was not because of religious fanaticism, but because of the necessity of keeping discipline within the ranks.

As the months dragged on and the situation of the Münsterites became more desperate and hopeless, van Leyden devised new schemes of control and discovered new sources of hope of

THE ANABAPTISTS   47

victory—upon Bible authority, of course, because that gave all he did religious sanction. Following Old Testament example, he now abandoned the theocratic form of government with ruling elders which had been established by Matthijsz, and set up a supreme dictatorship with himself at the head under the title of King David. From now on his word was law. Perhaps even the introduction of polygamy was the result of the emergency situation rather than a concession to the lust of King David. There were many more women than men in Münster at this period. It is entirely possible that the order compelling every woman to choose a husband was inaugurated as a measure of protection to the women themselves and in the interests of public morality. At any rate, the practice had ample Old Testament sanction. Contrary to the popular notion, there was no promiscuity or community of wives. Breaches of the marriage tie and violations of the prescribed standards were summarily punished.

Jan van Leyden

In the meantime, the apostles who had earlier been sent out to invite the oppressed to share the "New Israel" were now succeeded by envoys who were secretly sent through the lines to urge these same oppressed to come to the help of their brethren in distress. The times evidently were ripe for a wide acceptance throughout the whole north country of the Münsterite views. The hope of relief from a relentless religious persecution and economic oppression, famine and pestilence, religious fanaticism, the breaking down of inefficient local government, and even a sign in the heavens in the form of a comet—all turned many to revolt against the established religious order. In many towns and villages there were groups, varying as to size, of enthusiastic and fanatical men and women who either attempted to set up local *Münsters*, or who gathered together relief expeditions for the doomed city in Westphalia.

But none of the relief expeditions ever got far beyond their place of beginning; and nowhere were the fanatics able to gain the upper hand, although a number of cities along the Lower Rhine barely missed the fate of Münster. Some of these religious enthusiasts were perhaps recruited from the ranks of the Melchiorite party. Very few, if any, were of the peaceful, nonresistant group later known as Obbenites (followers of Obbe Philips). Many of them were pure adventurers ready for any excitement that came along. Most of them were genuine religious enthusiasts, misguided though sincere, seeking escape from religious persecution and hoping for participation in the joys of the New Israel soon to be established. These latter generally accepted rebaptism, which now had become a mere symbol of admission into a new revolutionary party and, perhaps, no longer had any real religious significance. But they are generally known by the name "Anabaptist."

The End of the "Kingdom"

The situation of the defenders of Münster became increasingly desperate in the winter of 1534 and spring of 1535. Intercourse with the outside world had been entirely cut off. Food became scarce. Famine and disease threatened early disaster. Every available foot of ground space within the walls was planted to seed. First the horses were slaughtered, then the dogs and cats, and later, mice and rats and every living thing that could be eaten. Finally the daily diet was reduced to leather, leaves, and grass. Small groups of discouraged spirits continually attempted escape through the lines, only to be captured by the army of the bishop and put to immediate death. Near the end, the population had been so reduced by famine, disease, desertion, execution, and suicide that by the time the city fell, through the treachery of one of its own defenders, there were only a few hundred of the faithful left. Those who survived the above calamities were now summarily put to the sword by the victorious besiegers. A few of the leaders were reserved for a worse fate. Rothmann disappeared, and his fate has remained a mystery. But Jan van Leyden and Bernhard Knipperdolling were taken captive together, later to be sent through some of the towns of northwestern Germany as criminal exhibits and, after severe torture, to be publicly executed as dangerous criminals. Their bodies were then placed in iron cages suspended from the towers of St. Lambert's Church of Münster, and were exposed to the public gaze until they rotted. Their bones lay bleaching in the sun for many years as an example to the passerby of what happens to those who dare oppose the established authority in church and state. The cages are hanging on the church tower to this day.

Among the lessons to be extracted from this unfortunate episode in Anabaptist history, perhaps this one is outstanding—the union of intense enthusiasm with ignorance is almost sure to bear evil fruit. The leaders of the more sober and thoroughly sane type of Anabaptism—men like Conrad Grebel, Balthasar Hubmaier, Hans Denk, Michael Sattler, and later Menno Simons—were men of solid learning, ex-monks and university graduates for the most part; the leaders of the fanatical offshoots, on the other hand, were men of little or no scholastic training. They were laboring men, intensely interested, and perhaps well posted in the contents of the Bible, but with little knowledge of the great field of learning outside their narrow world. Self-appointed lay preachers largely, they were men of unbalanced interests. Hans Hut was a carpenter, and Melchior Hofmann a tanner; Jan Matthijsz was a baker, and Jan van Leyden a tailor. Even knowledge of the Bible, if not backed up by a sane and well-balanced world view, may not be a safeguard against religious fanaticism and spiritual anarchy.

It is quite evident that the misguided, fanatical, and violently revolutionary Münsterites differ as night and day from the peaceful, sober, nonresistant Swiss Brethren, and their following in Tyrol, Moravia, and South Germany. The two groups shared but one thing in common—both were separatists, and made rebaptism a symbol of their separation from the prevailing state churches. The Münsterites, however, practically established a state church of their own. In other practices and doctrines they differed so widely that their differences were much greater than their common interest.

And so, between the Swiss and other nonresistant Anabaptists and the Münsterites, there was no spiritual kinship. But no matter how bitterly the nonresistant groups repudiated the revolutionary acts of the Münsterites, nor how insistently they complained against being classified in the same group, the authorities, both church and state, persisted in branding all separatists who practiced rebaptism under one name—the hated name of Münsterite Anabaptist. For in the stigma of that name they possessed a powerful weapon in their fight against all those who demanded freedom of conscience. The nonresistant Swiss Brethren never were able to clear themselves of the odium. And as a result, after the collapse of Münster, all groups which practiced adult baptism, irrespective of any other theories or practices, were submitted to a period of terrible persecution all over Europe which lasted for nearly another full century.

After Münster

It should be remembered, too, that the Münster influence was confined almost exclusively to northwestern Germany and the Netherlands. It never reached far southward. The Brethren of the South did not have to contend with the fanatics as did the Anabaptists of the Low Countries. In the Netherlands, too, there were many Melchiorites who were not corrupted by the Münsterites. This remnant, directed by a saner and more intelligent leadership, kept their sanity; and finding no evidence in the Scriptures of an immediate impending social cataclysm, they were convinced that the world would continue for some time to move along conventional lines, with the tares and the wheat growing up together, and sinner and saint living side by side. Sin would continue in the world, and the true Christian would have to continue the struggle to build up the kingdom of God on earth against the evil designs of the wicked. The millennium was still far away, and the end of suffering was not yet.

The leader of this group was Obbe Philips, who was aided later by his younger brother Dirk. Two devout Frisian Catholics from Leeuwarden, they had in the early thirties of the century affiliated themselves with the Melchior Hofmann Anabaptists of that region. Of the two brothers, Dirk was the better educated, being a member of the order of Franciscans. But Obbe too, a surgeon by profession, must have been a man of more than ordinary intelligence.

Although ordained an elder in the Melchior Hofmann group, Obbe Philips soon found himself at variance with the Melchiorite teaching on the early approach of the millennium. When some of the Melchiorites began to develop decided leanings toward Münster, he launched a vigorous protest against the whole Münsterite movement. Those of his members who left for Münster he expelled from membership. And in order to save his flock from contamination by the expelled Münsterites, he added another religious practice to that of expulsion—*avoidance*, which forbade all social intercourse as well as religious affiliation with an expelled member. This practice which, as we shall see later, played an important role among the controversies in the early history of the Mennonite church, was thus first inaugurated as a defensive measure guarding the church against false teaching from without.

This peaceful and soundly biblical wing of the Anabaptist movement in the Netherlands was sometimes called by the name of *Obbenites* after their chief leaders, and was the group with which Menno Simons later affiliated.

Anabaptist Divisions

In order, therefore, to be true to historic fact, as well as to be fair to a large body of humble and pious followers of Christ, one must discriminate when speaking of the people generally known during the Reformation period as Anabaptists. Although historians often fail to make this distinction, the writers of the middle of the sixteenth century did not. Heinrich Bullinger, the successor of Ulrich Zwingli, writing in 1560, recognized thirteen different groups among the Anabaptists in the course of their history to his time. Among others, he mentions the *Apostolic*, who read their Bibles literally, traveled about without staff and shoes, and carried no money; the *Holy, Sinless Baptists*, who omitted

THE ANABAPTISTS

"forgive our sins" from the Lord's Prayer because they were beyond sinning; the *Enthusiasts*; and the *Free Brethren*. The *Münsterites*, he said, differed from all the others in that while all others lived a peaceful, sober life, pious and humble, opposed to the exercise of authority, these on the other hand "aimed to dominate the world through force."

Christoph Erhard, a bitter opponent of the Hutterites, writing in 1589, lists forty separate groups. Among his Latin and German titles, foisted upon them by their enemies, of course, are the following, here freely translated into English: *Münsterites, Müntzerites, Stäbler, Austerlitzer, David Jorists, Mennonites, Silent Brethren, Hofmannites, Apostolical, Holy Brethren, Blood Thirsty, Barefooted Brethren, Priest Murderers, Adam Pastorites, Gabrielites, Swiss Brethren, Pilgram Marbeckites, Epicureans*, and *Hutterites*. Like Bullinger's list, of course, this also includes all the factions from the beginning of the movement up to the author's own day, all but three of which by this time had long since passed into history. Several of them seemingly never existed at all, at least not as Anabaptists.

Only one type of Anabaptism has survived to this present time—the nonresistant type. These are divided into three groups—the Dutch group, called *Doopsgezinde* or *Mennonites*; the Moravian *Hutterites*; and the Swiss *Brethren*, usually called *Alt-Evangelische Taufgesinnte* or *Täufer*. Their opponents called them *Wiedertäufer* (Anabaptists).

The fall of Münster, whetting as it did the appetite of the ruling authorities for persecution and intensifying the determination to root out every vestige of Anabaptism, good and bad, completely drove the movement under cover in the Low Countries, and all but exterminated the fanatical wing of the party. However the Münster spirit still lingered on for a time in a number of places. Under a new leader, Jan van Batenburg, a former burgomaster of Steenwijk, polygamy, the right of revolution, and the near approach of the New Jerusalem were upheld. Though oppressed, the Melchiorites remained for a time as strong as ever; but soon the conservative wing, the Obbenites, disagreeing with the Melchiorites in their immediate millenarian expectations, were gaining at the expense of all the others.

It now occurred to someone—just who made the first suggestion is not known, but perhaps David Joris—to call a convention of the different factions to attempt a reconciliation of their various views. The conference was held in the summer of 1536 in the Westphalian town of Bocholt near the Dutch border. None of the leaders of the various factions attended the meeting except David Joris himself, who was easily the dominating spirit. The

Batenburger, however, were present, as were also some of the Melchiorites and perhaps a few Obbenites. The chief issue under discussion was the use of the sword to bring about the new order. The Batenburger said yes; the Melchiorites and Obbenites said no. Joris, who had formerly been a Melchiorite and had been ordained as a minister by Obbe Philips, tried the part of a compromiser by suggesting that although the Batenburger were right in their contention that the Christian might use the sword, the time was not yet ripe for such action. Joris no doubt won a number to his way of thinking, for soon after this we find in the records mention of a new Anabaptist group—the David Jorists. When Batenburg heard of the results of this meeting, he was enraged at what he thought was a deliberate attempt on the part of Joris to gain a personal following. Calling Joris an Absalom, he threatened him with personal violence.

It is not likely that the Bocholt conference succeeded very far in the attempt to harmonize the views of the different factions, for as late as the middle of the century Countess Anna of East Friesland still recognized among the different parties the *Batenburger, Davidians, Obbenites,* and now also the *Mennonties*. Batenburg was executed for revolutionary teachings in 1538. Joris soon developed further unsound religious theories and was excommunicated by Obbe Philips. After a rather questionable career, he finally found his way to Basel, where under an assumed name he lived down his past and even won a place of honor by his death in 1556. In the course of time the various corrupt sects died out, and the nonresistant Obbenites, and no doubt many of the Melchiorites, were gathered together under a new leader—Menno Simons.

II
Menno Simons

Menno Simons, like his contemporary Martin Luther, was of peasant origin, having been born in 1496 in the Frisian village of Witmarsum, located a few miles inland from the North Sea coast. Of his early life we know little beyond what he himself has left us in a brief autobiographical sketch written in his later years. Evidently he was early destined for the church, for in his twenty-eighth year he assumed the duties of the priesthood in what was then his father's village, Pingjum, a mile or two seaward from his own birthplace. His preparation was not extensive, perhaps just enough to meet the simple requirements of a country priest. He knew a little Latin, less Greek, and, according to his own confession, no Scripture. Later in life, however, through wide reading he acquired not only a minute knowledge of the Bible, but a rather broad acquaintance with the general field of church history and theology as well.

Priesthood

As a priest, Menno likely lived the life of his class—an easygoing, carefree life, assuming the burdens of his office rather lightheartedly. Like his companions, he spent his days, he says, in "playing, drinking, and all manner of frivolous diversions." However, he was blessed with an open mind and a tender conscience. Such being the case, he could not remain entirely oblivious to the revolutionary religious movements that were then shaking all northern Europe to its very foundations. It is known that quite early in his ecclesiastical career he had access to the writings of Luther which were being circulated throughout the Dutch monasteries and among the Dutch priests in spite of every effort on the part of the higher state and church authorities to suppress them. He began to waver in the faith.

Menno Simons (1496-1561)

The seed of doubt fell upon promising soil. One day while Menno was perfunctorily handling the bread and wine in the celebration of a mass, the thought flashed through his mind that this bit of bread could not possibly be the flesh of Christ as he had always been taught to believe. At first he gave the suggestion but little thought, ascribing it to the work of the devil in an attempt to lure a good man away from his faith. But it came back to him again and again. He prayed, and sighed, and confessed, but all to no avail. The conviction grew. Finally he was driven to the source of help to which he should have gone in the first place—the New Testament, which up to this time, he said, had been a sealed book to him. Here, finally "without any human aid or advice," he found relief from his doubts. The bread was not the body of Christ. His conscience was relieved; and he was greatly encouraged in the belief "that no human authority can bind to eternal death."

But once he had been led to question the validity of a cardinal doctrine of the church, the way was opened to other doubts. Not long after this, Menno heard of the beheading at Leeuwarden, the capital city of the province, of one Sicke Freerks, a tailor, because of rebaptism. A second baptism seemed a strange doctrine to the troubled priest. Thus far he had never doubted the validity of infant baptism. But now he again turned to the New Testament for light and was surprised that he could find no justification there for the doctrine. He consulted his superior at Pingjum, who was also forced to admit that there was no direct scriptural authority for the practice. Menno then turned to Luther, Zwingli, and Bullinger; and finding that all these differed not only from one another in their justification of the doctrine but from the whole New Testament teaching on the question as well, he was forced to the conclusion that infant baptism too was an error without scriptural foundation.

Although convinced that his church taught erroneous views on two important religious doctrines, Menno yet had no thought of immediately withdrawing from it, or of laying down his priestly office. He had been promoted in the meantime to a more honorable and lucrative position at Witmarsum, his native village, and the future seemed promising. In view of these bright prospects, it is not difficult to understand why just at this particular time he was slow to follow his growing convictions to their logical conclusions. It was about this time, too, that Anabaptists of various types began to appear in the vicinity of Witmarsum, and soon after, disciples of Jan Matthijsz from Münster. The new parish priest, who evidently had considerable ability as a speaker and writer, now eased his conscience somewhat and exercised his talents by a vigorous attack upon the latter, gaining quite a reputation among

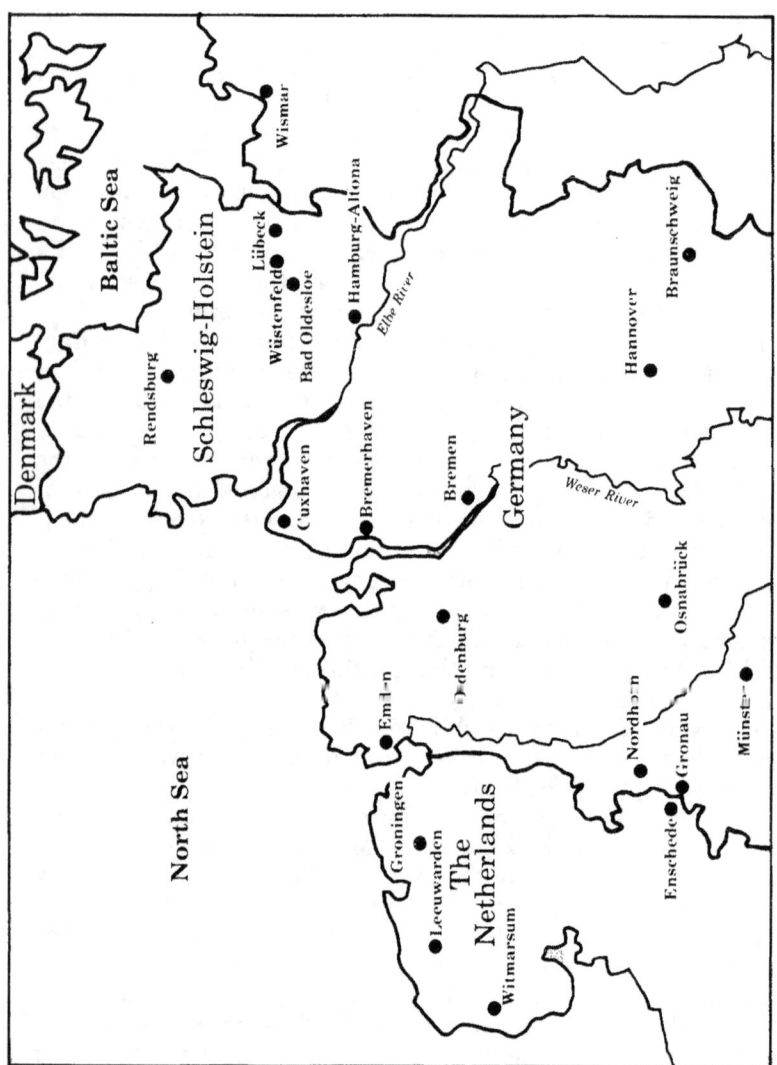

Where Menno Simons Lived
Menno Simons was born in Witmarsum. After his conversion in 1536, he fled eastward, living in Groningen, then near Emden and in Wüstenfelde, Schleswig-Holstein.

his fellow priests for his ability to successfully refute the false prophets from Münster. "The report spread far abroad that I could readily silence these persons," he said. "All looked to me."

But the troubled conscience of this sincere pastor of Witmarsum would not permit him long to live under false pretense. When he saw that his attack upon the errors of the Münsterites was interpreted by his friends as a wholehearted endorsement of the entire Catholic system, he was disturbed in spirit. Attracted by wordly success, and at the same time convicted by a tender conscience, he evidently hoped for a time to serve both God and mammon. Although not yet completely a follower of the peaceful Anabaptists, still he knew that at heart he agreed with some of their teachings, although he bitterly opposed the erroneous views of the Münsterites. His heart was sorely troubled.

Not long after this there occurred at Bolsward, not far from Witmarsum, another impressive incident—the third in the course of Menno's gradual conversion—which had a decisive influence upon his future career. A group of some three hundred Anabaptists—men, women, and children—somewhat tainted with the revolutionary theories of Münster, had taken refuge in an old cloister where they were attacked by a small force which had been sent against them by the provincial governor. These poor deluded enthusiasts took up arms in self-defense but were soon overpowered. Most of them, including Menno's own brother, were put to the sword. Only the surviving women and children were spared.

This catastrophe, occurring almost at his own door and claiming a member of his own family, made a profound impression upon the future leader of the Dutch Anabaptists. The courage of these men and women, who, although in error, dared to face death itself for their convictions, disturbed his ease-loving conscience, while the need to combat the very errors that were at the bottom of their undoing appealed strongly to his sense of responsibility for the welfare of the weak and erring. Reflecting upon these things, he wrote:

> My soul was so grieved that I could no longer endure it. I thought to myself—I, miserable man, what shall I do? If I continue in this way and live not agreeable to the Word of the Lord, according to the knowledge of the truth which I have obtained; if I do not rebuke to the best of my ability the hypocrisy, the impenitent, carnal life, the perverted baptism, the Lord's Supper, and the false worship of God which the learned teach; if I, through bodily fear, do not show them the true foundation of the truth, neither use all my powers to direct the wandering flock, who would gladly do their duty if they knew it, to the true pastures of Christ—O how shall their shed blood, though in error, rise against me in the judgment of the Almighty, and pronounce sentence against my poor miserable soul.

Renunciation of the Papacy

Menno Simons was now ready for the final step. In the month of January of 1536 he laid down his priestly office, renounced the Catholic Church, shut the door on a brilliant career and a life of ease and pleasure, and deliberately chose instead a life of uncertainty, misery, and poverty. He would be constantly threatened with imprisonment, persecution, and death; but he would lead a life of loyalty to his convictions and great service to his fellowmen, and would be at peace with his God. When comparing the choice of men like Luther and Calvin with that of Menno Simons, without in the least belittling their services to the world, we must keep in mind, nevertheless, that they made little personal sacrifice in the work they undertook. Menno Simons, on the other hand, deliberately chose the way of the cross. For the rest of his days he remained an outlaw with a reward upon his head, and with his wife and children he became a wanderer upon the face of the earth. Even those who dared give him and his family food and shelter paid for their kindness with their lives.

Referring later in life to this contrast, Menno says:

> For eighteen years now I, my poor feeble wife, and little children have endured extreme anxiety, oppression, affliction, misery, and persecution; and at the peril of my life have been compelled everywhere to live in fear and seclusion; yea, while the state ministers repose on beds of ease and of soft pillows, we generally have to hide ourselves in secluded corners; while they appear at weddings and banquets with great pomp, with pipe and lute, we must be on guard when the dogs bark lest the captors be on hand. Whilst they are saluted as doctors, lords, and teachers on every hand, we have to hear that we are ana-baptists, hedge preachers, deceivers and heretics, and must be saluted in the name of the devil. In short, while they are gloriously rewarded for their services with large incomes and easy times, our recompence and portion must be fire, sword, and death.

This converted parish priest, it will thus be observed, arrived at his conclusions and convictions through a gradual process, by his own volition, and as a result of an independent study of the Scriptures. He was not swept from his moorings by the enthusiasm of a great popular religious uprising. He seemingly had every earthly reason to remain within his church, and none to withdraw from it—except one, his conscience. In a way he typified the whole Anabaptist movement. Anabaptism, as we know, was not merely the reappearance of earlier evangelical sects, but rather a spontaneous religious movement among the common people, having its source in a widely read Bible, newly turned into the vernacular.

Menno's Baptism and Ordination

As soon as Menno Simons renounced the Catholic Church, he must have left his home village and the province of Friesland. In the neighboring province of Groningen he found a temporary refuge where he was able to study the Bible and do his first writing.

Where and when he was baptized by Obbe Philips, the leader of the peaceful Anabaptist movement, is unknown. Like Luther and other Reformation leaders who had once been priests, Menno married soon after leaving the order. Gertrude, likely from his own native village, for the rest of her days remained a faithful companion through all the vicissitudes of his precarious life, and shared with him all the dangers and hardships that were his. They had at least three children.

Hardly had Menno cast his lot with the Groningen Anabaptists when the heads of that movement, recognizing his ability as a leader, urged him to submit to ordination as an elder in the organization. But true to form, Menno refused to assume the responsibilities of leadership, hesitating, as he says, because of his "limited talents, great ignorance, weak nature, timidity of flesh, the unbounded wickedness, perversity of the world, the powerful sects, subtlety of different minds, and the heavy cross" that would oppress him if he should accept the urgent solicitations of his friends. But on the other hand, when he thought "of the miserable, starving condition, and the necessity of these pious God-fearing children, who erred as innocent sheep having no shepherd," his compassion for his misguided fellow beings overcame his natural timidity, and he finally permitted himself to be ordained an elder by the same Obbe Philips who had baptized him a short time before.

Little is known about the residence and the itinerary of Menno Simons during the next years. Together with his co-workers, Obbe and Dirk Philips, he labored earnestly in behalf of his chosen cause—preaching, baptizing, writing, ordaining other elders, and organizing the growing church. Occasionally he made a secret visit to the neighboring provinces, including his own fatherland, Friesland, where in 1542 an imperial edict, drawn up at Leeuwarden and carrying the name of Emperor Charles V, was issued against him. According to this decree, no one was to receive "Minne Symonsz" in his house or on his property; to give him shelter, food, or drink; to speak with him; or to read any of his books, under penalty of loss of property and life as a heretic. To any one who might apprehend the fugitive, a reward of one hundred *gulden* was promised, a sum equal to the annual salary of a priest at Witmarsum. In case the informant was an Anabaptist, he would be granted full pardon for having been a member of that sect, or for "lesser crimes."

Obbe's Defection

It was during this period, about 1540, that Menno experienced a great disappointment in the withdrawal of Obbe Philips from the Anabaptist cause. Just why Obbe withdrew at this time is not certain. Some say that he no longer had the courage to face the increasing dangers that threatened the lives of the leaders of the cause; others are unkind enough to suggest that he was jealous of the growing influence of his disciple Menno Simons. He himself asserted that he had been deceived in his call to the ministry; that, since the disciples of Jan Matthijsz, by whom he had been ordained, had themselves been in error, his own call, as well as that of those whom he in turn had ordained, was not apostolic nor valid.

Likely Obbe had neither the faith nor the courage of his brother Dirk or of Menno. He perhaps had shared the hopes of the Melchiorites that soon the kingdom of the elect was to be established, when the righteous would enter upon their reward. But now Hofmann was languishing in prison at Strassburg, Jan Matthijsz had met a tragic death, and the righteous everywhere were being crushed with fire and sword. The future seemed hopeless. Obbe felt himself deceived. He had neither the faith nor the heart to continue the struggle. He retired to the city of Rostock on the Baltic. His withdrawal, though by no means a deathblow to the cause, was a great disappointment to Menno, who spoke of Obbe as a Demas and as one who gave great comfort to the state churches by his defection.

In East Friesland, Menno Simons was safe from molestation for a time. Countess Anna, the ruler at this time, was well disposed toward the Reformation movement, though the exact nature of the church she hoped to establish under her rule had not yet been fully decided upon. It was during this transition stage that East Friesland became an asylum for the persecuted religious groups of northwestern Germany and Holland. Even the Batenburger and other offshoots of the Münsterites were tolerated. The outstanding event of Menno's stay here was his debate with John a Lasco, the Polish reformer, who had been responsible for Anna's religious establishment.

Debate with a Lasco

This debate, initiated by a Lasco, the outstanding Reformation leader of northern Europe, was held in Emden, the chief seaport of northwestern Germany, and incidentally the seat of the oldest

Mennonite church of this whole region. The discussion, which lasted for three days, centered about the main issue which separated the Anabaptists from the state churches—baptism and its allied doctrines—as well as several other issues, including the calling of ministers and the view of the incarnation of Christ.

On the question of baptism, Menno advanced the well-known arguments familiar to all Anabaptists, while a Lasco reviewed the common ground held by all the state churches. On the calling of the ministers, also, both covered familiar ground already so frequently advanced by earlier champions in various discussions. A Lasco favored a theologically trained, state-controlled ministry, well fed and clothed at public expense. Menno, on the other hand, advocated a ministry selected from the congregation without reference to theological training, but characterized by a regenerated life, and supported by voluntary contributions. He was especially bitter against the benefices, fat livings, and exalted positions of the state preachers of the gospel, whom he often spoke of as hirelings.

The Incarnation of Christ

On Menno's view of the incarnation it is necessary to say a few words further, for his theories on this subject were not held by his brethren in Switzerland in that day, nor by those who bear his name anywhere in the world today. His view was not original with him, but was inherited from Obbe Philips, who in turn got it from Melchior Hofmann, its first advocate as far as we know. Hofmann's peculiar doctrine needs but little elaboration here. He believed, it will be remembered, that in order to remain entirely free from sinfulness, Jesus had to receive his body elsewhere than through the flesh of Mary. Once Menno accepted this teaching, he became its consistent advocate to the end. In his attempts to justify his peculiar explanation of the doctrine, Menno often ventured into biological and philosophical arguments beyond his depth. It would no doubt have been better for him, as well as for all concerned, had he followed the advice of his South German brethren, who in a conference held at Strassburg in 1555 suggested, relative to this controversy: "The confusion of tongues has come upon the brethren in this matter because they would know more than it was intended they should know."

They should be content, so these practical Germans thought, with the statement "The Word became flesh and tabernacled among us." It should be said, however, in behalf of Menno, that he discussed the subject reluctantly and never chose it for public debate unless forced to it, and that it was just as reasonable an attempt, perhaps, to reconcile the divinity of Jesus with his humanity as was the orthodox explanation.

Cologne and Wismar

Because of the publicity attracted by the Emden debate, Menno found it expedient in 1544 to seek a new refuge. It was just at this time, too, that Anna, urged by her neighboring rulers, had agreed upon an order of exile against the various groups that had found temporary refuge within her domain. Acting upon the suggestion of a Lasco, however, she made a distinction between the peaceful followers of Menno and the revolutionary sects of Batenburg and others. The former, who for the first time were now designated as *Mennists*, were not included in the general proscription.

Menno, however, thought it best to leave East Friesland. For the next two years he found a fruitful field of labor in the archbishopric of Cologne, where, under a tolerant ruler, a spell of liberty was granted to all religious dissenters. He even challenged the theologians of the city of Bonn to a theological discussion, however without success. The restoration of a Catholic ruler in 1546 again sent him on his travels, this time to the Lutheran Hanseatic free city of Wismar on the Baltic. It was during his stay here that he again met his old friend a Lasco, though not in a personal debate this time. The latter, who had been forced to leave Emden during the period of the Interim, 1548-52, had served as the pastor of a flock of Dutch and North German refugees in London during that time. With the accession of Bloody Mary to the English throne in 1553, England ceased to be an asylum for continental Protestants; on the other hand, with the Peace of Passau a year earlier, conditions had been reversed in Germany. The Protestant exiles consequently returned to their former homes. It was while a shipload of a Lasco's followers were seeking a new refuge along the Baltic that they got caught one midwinter day in the ice in Wismar harbor a short distance from shore. But Wismar happened to be a Lutheran town, with little sympathy for the Reformed. It remained, therefore, for the little Mennonite congregation of the place, barely tolerated themselves, to play the part of the Good Samaritan to these ice-bound exiles. They visited the strangers on shipboard, brought them food and drink and needed medical supplies, and then helped them to shore and found needed work for them for the winter.

One little incident in the course of this procedure surprised and greatly pained Menno. A humble, but warmhearted, Mennonite, having compassion on the children of a Lasco, offered to take them into his home and to care for them for the winter. He was refused by their tutor, Hermes Backereel, who was one of the leaders of the party and a minister, on the ground that a Lasco, being of noble birth and having much to do with lords, could not afford to have his children cared for in the home of a humble Mennonite. "I observed," said Menno on hearing of this incident, "that we have not met with the plain, true, humble pilgrims of Christ."

Another Debate

Distressing as the situation of the London exiles was, however, it was not sufficient to cool the ardor of their leaders for a theological controversy even with their deliverers. Hardly had they been safely landed before Hermes Backereel, learning that Menno Simons was living in seclusion in the city, sought him out and invited him to a theological debate in the presence of a group of Reformed and Mennonite listeners. Menno hesitated, but finally gave his consent. Hermes, not considering himself a match for Menno, sent to Norden for Martin Micron, a renowned Dutch Reformed theologian, who had also been one of the London preachers. The debate lasted for several days, covering all the controversial points of doctrine. At times the argument became quite heated, but it ended peaceably enough with a common meal. As was usual with discussions of this sort, neither side was convinced, but both were satisfied with themselves.

Menno accused the Reformed of unfair dealing in this debate. He entered the discussion reluctantly, he said, and with the understanding that it was to be a private affair, without publicity, and that the proceedings were not to be reported to the town authorities. The Mennonites, it is understood, were merely a tolerated people in this Lutheran town, to be left in peace as long as they carried on their worship in seclusion. Publicity would jeopardize their stay in the city. Micron and his friends broke their promise. A report of the proceedings was published, with the result that soon after, the Reformed as well as the Mennonites had to leave the city. Both of the disputants later continued their arguments in print. Quite as much heat as light was generated by the uncomplimentary adjectives that were hurled back and forth in the printed pages. Neither side did itself great credit, though it must be admitted that Menno's language was much milder than was Martin's.

Menno's Literary Efforts

Menno, in fact, was a voluminous writer throughout this entire period. Most of his literary work consisted of an amplification of his arguments first presented in such debates as noted above, short treatises on the various distinctive Anabaptist doctrines, and replies to attacks made upon him by the various theologians of the day. He often found it difficult to secure publishers for his works, since to print his books was made a criminal offense by imperial edict, punishable by death. Among his most important writings are his *Testimony Against Jan van Leyden*, written while still a priest; *Renunciation of Rome*, in which he gives his reasons for leaving the Catholic church; *The Foundation Book*, written early in his ministry but revised in 1555, in which can be found a complete statement of his mature religious views; and his comments on the *Twenty-fifth Psalm*, perhaps from a purely literary point of view by far his best work. His writings were collected and published soon after his death and were published in several editions during the seventeenth century, the last time in the Netherlands in 1681. Menno's preeminence among the leaders of the Anabaptist movement in his day and his dominating influence among their later followers is due, no doubt, as much to his literary efforts as to any other cause.

Internal Dissensions

Unfortunately Menno Simons and his brethren were not only forced to defend themselves against enemies from without, but too often there was contention within. As early as 1547 Menno met Dirk Philips and a number of leading evangelists of the Baltic region for the purpose of disciplining two of their brethren—Adam Pastor, accused of antitrinitarianism, and Frans de Cuyper, charged with pro-Catholic views.

Adam Pastor, earlier known as Roelof Martens, was a Westphalian by birth, a Catholic priest, who left his order about the time Menno did. He was ordained with several others in the early forties by Menno Simons and Dirk Philips. A man of broad education and training, "of medium height and without a beard," he was inclined to independent thinking. From the first he disagreed with Menno and Dirk in his interpretation of the doctrine of the incarnation, and later developed liberal theories of the Trinity.

Of Frans de Cuyper not much is known, except that he too was one of Menno's appointees to the eldership, perhaps ordained with Pastor, and that he refused to accept the prevailing Mennonite view of the incarnation and other leading doctrines. He retained a strong leaning toward Catholicism in all his religious thinking and for that reason was placed under the ban by Menno. He returned to the Catholic church.

About the same time, 1542, Menno and Dirk, the senior elders, ordained three others to this high position—Hendrik van Vreden, Antonius von Köln, and Gillis van Aken.

Antonius von Köln began his Anabaptist career in Münster,

having been baptized by Rol in the house of Knipperdolling. He somehow survived the Münster catastrophe, but whether he left before or after the fall of the city is not certain. However, he soon cleared himself of all revolutionary taint and became one of the most energetic workers for the cause of the nonresistant type of Anabaptism in northwestern Germany. He never agreed with Menno's strict views of discipline, however, and in about 1550, he either was placed under the ban or voluntarily withdrew from the Mennonite movement.

Gillis van Aken became an Anabaptist as early as 1531. As an elder he later traveled extensively through Holland and northwestern Germany, baptizing, it is said, more martyrs than any of the other leaders of the movement. He must have been of a vacillating character, for in 1552 Menno placed him under the ban because of a moral lapse. Two years later, however, he was reinstated upon confession of guilt. While engaged in evangelistic work, he was apprehended in Antwerp in 1557. Under torture he recanted, which cost him his place in van Braght's *Martyrs Mirror*, although space was given to many of those who were baptized by him. But recantation availed Gillis nothing. His right arm was cut off at the time of execution, and his body was thrown into the flames. Some years before, he had been described as "a man of medium size, with a pale face, big eyes, and a pointed brown beard." One of his sons later became a minister in Amsterdam, and his grandson was the well-known Galenus Abrahamsz de Haan.

Co-Laborers

None of these co-laborers of Menno just mentioned, strange to say, remained faithful to the end. All at one time or another had been placed under the ban, and but one or two were reinstated. Only two of his contemporaries—Leenaert Bouwens and Dirk Philips—shared with him to the end the responsibilities of guiding the new church through the dangers of the formative years.

Leenaert Bouwens was born at Sommelsdyk in 1515 and died at Hoorn in 1582. After spending some years as an Anabaptist preacher, he was ordained an elder by Menno Simons in Emden in 1551. He was, perhaps, the most energetic and successful evangelist among the entire group of northern leaders. In the course of some thirty years as an elder, it is said that he baptized more than ten thousand converts in Friesland, Holland, Groningen, Brabant, and several other Dutch provinces. Considering the fact that this period includes the time when Duke Alva and his Council of Blood were literally combing these provinces for heretics, this is a most remarkable and courageous record. Bouwens was a strict disciplinarian and was, perhaps, largely responsible for the division that occurred within the ranks of the churches because of the strict application of the ban during this time. But even he did not escape church discipline. He was relieved of his office by Dirk Philips. But upon the death of Dirk, he resumed his office on his own initiative and retained it to the end.

Next to Menno himself, the most influential of the Anabaptist leaders was Dirk Philips. Born at Leeuwarden, trained for the priesthood, he was won for the Anabaptist cause by Pieter de Houtzager, a disciple of Jan Matthijsz. In 1536 he was ordained as an elder by his brother Obbe. Dirk was Menno's most intimate associate in all the important activities of the Mennonite movement, although he was a little more conservative than the latter on most of the religious practices common to the faith. Like Menno, he too wrote numerous treatises and tracts on fundamental doctrines, the most extensive being his *Enchiridion*, which remains perhaps the most typical treatise of the conservative Anabaptism of his day. In his later days Dirk is described as "an old man with white hair, of medium stature, dressed in black, with a round cap, and he talked the dialect of the Brabanters." He died in 1568.

These three—Menno, Dirk, and Leenaert—were the stalwart, unyielding, uncompromising defenders of a rigid Anabaptist faith, holding fast to the established doctrines to the end, banning those that strayed from the narrow path as interpreted by them. Some division of the field of labor was agreed upon among them. Dirk resided at Danzig; Menno, at Wismar and later in Wüstenfelde; while Leenaert made his headquarters at Emden, though his chief field of effort was in the northern Dutch provinces. All of them, however, found their way occasionally into the Netherlands, which remained by far the most fruitful area in results. The congregations of northern Germany remained small and few.

Church Discipline

All the above-mentioned leaders were present at the Emden meeting in 1547, where, as has already been related, Pastor and Cuyper were disciplined and finally banned for their liberal views on the Trinity and Catholic doctrine of the incarnation. It was decided to enforce Dirk's strict interpretation of the ban and avoidance.

The free use of these measures of discipline had by this time become a question of considerable controversy among the Mennonites all through the Low Countries. That the practice was driven to unjustifiable lengths there can be no doubt; but a better understanding of the conditions under which Menno worked will lead to a keener appreciation at least of the reasons for these rather harsh measures. The central doctrine of Menno's faith, as already observed, was the "new birth," a regenerated life. "Behold, worthy reader," he wrote,

> All those who are born of God with Christ who thus conform their weak life to the gospel, are thus converted and follow the example of Christ, hear and believe his holy Word, follow his commands, which He in plain words commanded us in the Holy Scriptures, for the Holy Christian Church which has the promise.

The Christian faith and life is not merely a set of dogmas and rites; it must bear fruit in a purified life. Menno's most bitter accusations were hurled not at the beliefs of his state-church opponents, but rather at their unfruitful and corrupt lives. It is a well-known fact among the historians of the Reformation that the morals of neither laity nor clergy were reformed immediately by the general Reformation movement. As the respect for the old established supports of the social order were undermined, moral standards during the transition period actually sank to a lower level. A popular couplet which went the rounds of the people clearly illustrates, Menno says, the prevailing ideals of license and liberty—*Der Strick ist entzwei*; *Und wir sind frei* (The cord is broken, and we are free).

To Menno and his followers, on the other hand, the Reformation called not for lower but for higher standards of living. He wrote:

> I know of a certainty that a proud haughty man, whoever he may be, is no Christian; neither is an avaricious, selfish man, or a drunken, intemperate man, or an unchaste, lustful man, or a wrangling envious or disobedient, idolatrous man, or a false, lying, or an unfaithful, thievish man, or a defaming, backbiting man, or a bloodthirsty, unmerciful, revengeful man a Christian, even if he were baptized a hundred times, and kept the Lord's Supper daily; for it is not the ordinances or rites, such as baptism and the supper, but a true Christian faith with its unblamable good fruits of which the ordinances testify, that makes a true Christian and has the promise of life.

The Christian church made up of—according to Menno's ideal—the regenerated and not the entire population, must be without "spot or wrinkle," pure and undefiled, not only in belief but in moral conduct as well. There must be no moral lapse. The Mennonites made the way of life straight and narrow; the state churches left it broad and open. The latter had no way of correcting gross sin. That was a function of the state, not of the church, so they said.

The only means of discipline by which a free, voluntary church could be kept up to such a high standard was the ban, through which the unworthy and unfaithful could be excluded and expelled. Against the corrupt sects of the time (as Menno calls them)—the *David Jorists, Batenburger*, and the *Münsterites*—who were trying to make inroads among the disciples of Menno, a strict application of the ban was the only adequate defense. *The Jewel of the Church* he lovingly calls this means of preserving his beloved little flock against the enemies within the gates.

This method of settling church controversies and of disciplining unruly members, which was based on Matthew 18:15-18, might be applied in three different forms, according to the seriousness of the fault—mere admonition, with hopes of a reconciliation; denial of access to the communion table; and expulsion from membership for gross sin. Several controversies soon arose among the brethren over the use of this means of discipline. Should a gross sinner be first admonished and given time for repentance before expulsion, as in the case of one guilty of a minor fault, or should he be expelled immediately after his guilt is established? Leenaert Bouwens, the strictest of the strict, favored the latter; the others favored leniency.

Avoidance

But more serious even than this difference was the controversy over another practice which followed the ban, called *avoidance*. This meant that the one excommunicated was to be "avoided" or ostracized by his former fellow members, not only in religious fellowship, but in all business and social relations as well. Scripturally this practice was based on the Pauline injunction "not to eat" with an unfaithful member (1 Cor. 5:11), in order, according to confessions of faith that advocated it, that he "may be made ashamed and thereby induced to amend his ways." The motive here was most worthy, but unfortunately it was based on poor psychology. But here, too, there were differences of opinion. What did the phrase "not to eat" mean? Did it refer to the communion table only, or to all social relations? Most of the leaders said the latter. How generally should the practice be applied? Could any exceptions be made? Should husband and wife shun one another in case one or the other should be placed under the ban? Again Bouwens said yes; the ban would even include bed and board. Dirk agreed with him. Menno, on the other hand, wavered at first, but threatened by Bouwens with the ban himself if he did not side with the rigid disciplinarians, he half-heartedly consented, a fact which in his later years he regretted. He could never quite give his hearty consent to this practice. The consciences of the parties concerned, he said, should rule in the matter.

These hard regulations of the conjugal relations seem all the more strange when we remember that among the Mennonites the institution of marriage was a sacred one. It was not quite so sacred, perhaps, as among the Catholics, who made it a sacrament, but it was certainly much more sacred than with Luther, who said, "Marriage is an outward carnal thing like other worldly matters. Just as I may eat, drink, walk, ride, buy, and talk with the heathen, Jew or Turk, and heretic, so may I also enter the married life with him and remain therein." To the Mennonites who, so to say, took a middle view, this was rank heresy. Marriage could be contracted only "in the Lord," which meant among members of the same faith, in this case, Anabaptists. Marriage with outsiders was punishable with the ban. Divorce and separation were permitted only conditionally, and on New Testament grounds. But sacred as the institution was among the Mennonites, it was not exempt among the conservatives from the blighting influences of the "avoidance."

These various questions had disturbed the brethren not a little for some years. They were discussed, as we have seen, at the Emden meeting of 1547, at later conferences, and finally at Wismar in 1554, when a number of the leaders laid down a set of rules on these as well as other subjects for the use of the churches. According to these rules, marriage with outsiders was forbidden; separation was permitted only in case one or the other party led an immoral life; marital avoidance was to be enforced in its most rigid form; business relations were to be carried on with an apostate only in cases of extreme necessity; children were advised to marry only with the consent of their parents; just debts might be collected, but no unusual pressure was to be applied in doing so; bearing arms in military service was strictly prohibited; and, finally, no one was to preach unless duly ordained by the proper church authorities.

An Unfortunate Division

The attempt to enforce these hard rules raised a storm in certain quarters. Leenaert Bouwens and Gillis van Aken decided to apply them to the letter in their jurisdictions. The trouble started when a Dutch woman by the name of Swaan Rutgers, with notions of her own, refused to deny her banned husband "bed and table" according to the regulations. Bouwens insisted. Swaan had some friends, and a division soon appeared in several of the congregations, especially Emden and Franeker. The factions appealed to Menno, who advised moderation, suggesting that the consciences of the parties concerned should govern in the matter. But his efforts were all to no avail. Bouwens and his party insisted on enforcement, banning all those who disagreed with them and even threatening Menno himself. The congregations were rent in twain, and the division was carried to other churches until the lowland region was aflame with the controversy. The strict party was sometimes called the party of the "Hard Banners," while the milder group came to be known as the "Mild Banners."

This controversy even reached the Anabaptists of South Germany. In two conferences held in Strassburg, in 1555 and 1557, the Germans and Swiss discussed both the peculiar view of the Dutch Mennonites on the incarnation, as well as their strict interpretation of the ban and avoidance. On both questions they disagreed with their Dutch brethren.

In order to learn of the true situation in the Low Countries and also to attempt a reconciliation of the two factions, the conference sent a delegation of three men to Menno's home for the purpose of learning his views on the matter; then, with this information, they were to visit the various Dutch congregations in an effort to establish harmony. But these men failed so utterly in their designs that their well-meant efforts ended only in still greater confusion, and the situation was made worse rather than better. Not only did the breach among the Dutch congregations remain, but now a new cleavage was added—between the Dutch and the German churches.

Menno's Declining Years

Menno Simons was greatly disturbed by these events in his declining years, and traveled extensively among the disaffected congregations in the interests of harmony, but to no avail. Near the close of his life, it is said, he regretted having agreed to the strict interpretation of the ban and advised his close friends not to be a "slave of men" as he had been.

In the meantime, in 1555, the Anabaptist congregation at Wismar was exiled by a general order of the Lutheran Hanseatic League of which that city was a member. Menno, weary and discouraged, chose as a final resting place the little Anabaptist village of Wüstenfelde, a few miles beyond Oldesloe, in Holstein, on an estate called Fresenburg, owned by a certain count Bartholomäus von Ahlefeld. This nobleman had learned of the economic worth of the Mennonites while in the Netherlands, and had invited them to settle on his estate. Here he defended them against all attempts of imperial and local authorities to persecute them. Menno was even permitted to set up a printing press of his own near a little building within the shadow of a magnificent linden tree which, tradition says, goes back to the days of the exiled printer himself. Why this place came to be called Wüstenfelde (waste field) is not quite certain. An old chronicler suggests that it was because the spot on which the village was built had but a short time before been cleared of a dense forest of oak.

In this village, Menno died on January 13, 1561, in the sixty-sixth year of his life. According to a custom not unknown among the Anabaptists of that day, he was buried in his own garden. The exact place of burial remained unknown for many years, because during the Thirty Years' War the village was destroyed and its site forgotten. But the memory of the traditional location was kept alive among the descendants of an old Mennonite family of Hamburg that had known Menno, and later excavations seemed to corroborate the tradition. At any rate, the church at Hamburg marked the supposed spot with an appropriate monument in 1902. Wüstenfelde is a misnomer today. The monument stands upon a little knoll in the middle of a large pasture lot, bordered by magnificent groves of oak, in which, during a midsummer visit by the author some years ago, a fine herd of sleek and well-fed Holstein cattle were browsing knee-deep upon a luxuriant growth of rich, deep, green grass. Next to the linden tree stands the little house, now a Mennonite museum, in which some of the writings of Menno were printed.

Hero Stories

The numerous hero stories that accumulated about the name of Menno in the course of time after his death are, no doubt, based not so much on fact as upon the natural tendency of humankind to worship its heroes. Some of the stories told of Menno are also told of other men. Nevertheless, some of them bear repeating.

The story is told that one time a coach in which Menno was riding as a hitchhiker was stopped by some of his enemies. Menno sat on the driver's seat, and when asked, "Is Menno Simons in this coach?" he turned and repeated the question to the interior of the coach—"Is Menno Simons within?" After satisfying themselves that Menno Simons was indeed not within, the would-be captors rode on. Another story tells of a person who was planning to betray Menno as he was passing by in a boat. At the crucial moment, however, the man was unable to utter a sound, and thus Menno was once again able to escape.

Menno's Place in History

Menno Simons deserves a high rank among the great Reformers of the sixteenth century. Although he did not play as conspicuous a role as did his contemporaries—Luther, Zwingli, and Calvin—his real greatness cannot be measured by the more humble part he seemed to play in the religious arena of his time. His task in many respects was a much more difficult one than that of the founders of the state churches. They relied upon a union of state and church, and upon the support of the strong arm of the political powers to maintain their system. Menno, on the other hand, rested his appeal upon the persuasive power of love and the simple truth of the gospel as sufficient to secure the permanency of the true church. He was centuries ahead of his day on many of the fundamentals of religious and civil liberty which today in the more enlightened parts of the world are taken for granted, such as religious toleration, separation of church and state, and the desirability of universal peace.

The Name "Mennonite"

Menno Simons, it will be observed, was not the founder of a new church, but merely the leader, perhaps the most influential leader, during a critical period of a movement already well under way. It was quite common then, as now, for religious groups to take the name of their leaders. Lutheranism itself is no exception. The Anabaptist parties followed the same rule. Among the earliest were the *Melchiorites*, the *Obbenites*, and the *Dirkites*. The term *Mennist* was first used, as noted elsewhere, by Countess Anna of East Friesland in 1544 as a term distinguishing the peaceful from the revolutionary Anabaptist parties.

The peaceful followers of Menno were especially averse to being called *Wederdoopers* (Dutch) or *Wiedertäufer* (German), the common terms applied to all who practiced adult baptism, for two reasons. First, the word implied an earlier baptism; but since the Mennonites did not recognize the validity of infant baptism, they maintained that the administering of the rite in adult years upon confession of faith was the first and only true baptism, and not a rebaptism. The odious term *Wederdooper* everywhere signified Münsterite. And so, they were glad for any name that would set them apart from the Anabaptists of the Münster variety. *Doopsgezinde* (baptism-minded) was much less odious and gained general acceptance among them. But for a time, *Mennist* (Mennonite) was quite generally used to designate the peaceful Dutch Anabaptists.

After the granting of religious toleration by William of Orange, the name Mennist might again have fallen into disuse, had it not been revived for a time as a factional name. During the controversy over the ban, the strict faction, the *Flemish* and *Frisians*, who accepted Menno's views on this question were again known as *Mennists* (Mennonites); but the *Waterlanders*, the *Upper Germans*, and the *Young Frisians*—the more liberal groups—preferred the name *Doopsgezinde*. As party strife died out during the eighteenth century, and as the Dutch churches began to depart from many of the earlier views of Menno, *Doopsgezinde* came into general use and was finally adopted as the official title in the Netherlands by the church as a whole.

There was little contact in the early days between the *Doopsgezinde* of the Netherlands and the German and Swiss *Täufer*, or *Taufgesinnte*, or *Brethren*, as they preferred to be known. The term *Mennist* (Mennonite), however, was well known and not unpopular in Germany and Switzerland during the eighteenth century when the big-hearted Dutch Mennonites so generously helped their oppressed brethren in the Palatinate and Switzerland. In France, *Anabaptist* seemingly was not unpopular.

It is obvious that the Amish received their name from Jakob Ammann among the Swiss *Taufgesinnte* when he, as a disciplinarian, tried to retain some traditions which were being given up. Coming from Switzerland to North America, the *Taufgesinnte* became Mennonites.

The name Old Order Amish originated when some of the Amish accepted innovations that others declined. The name Beachy Amish came into being when M. M. Beachy introduced some changes for which most of the Amish were not ready. Many of the Amish "rejoined" the Mennonites of Pennsylvania and other states. Among the Mennonites and Amish, there was a willingness to accept new spiritual, cultural, and economic values. Those declining this change became known as Old Order Amish or Old Order Mennonites.

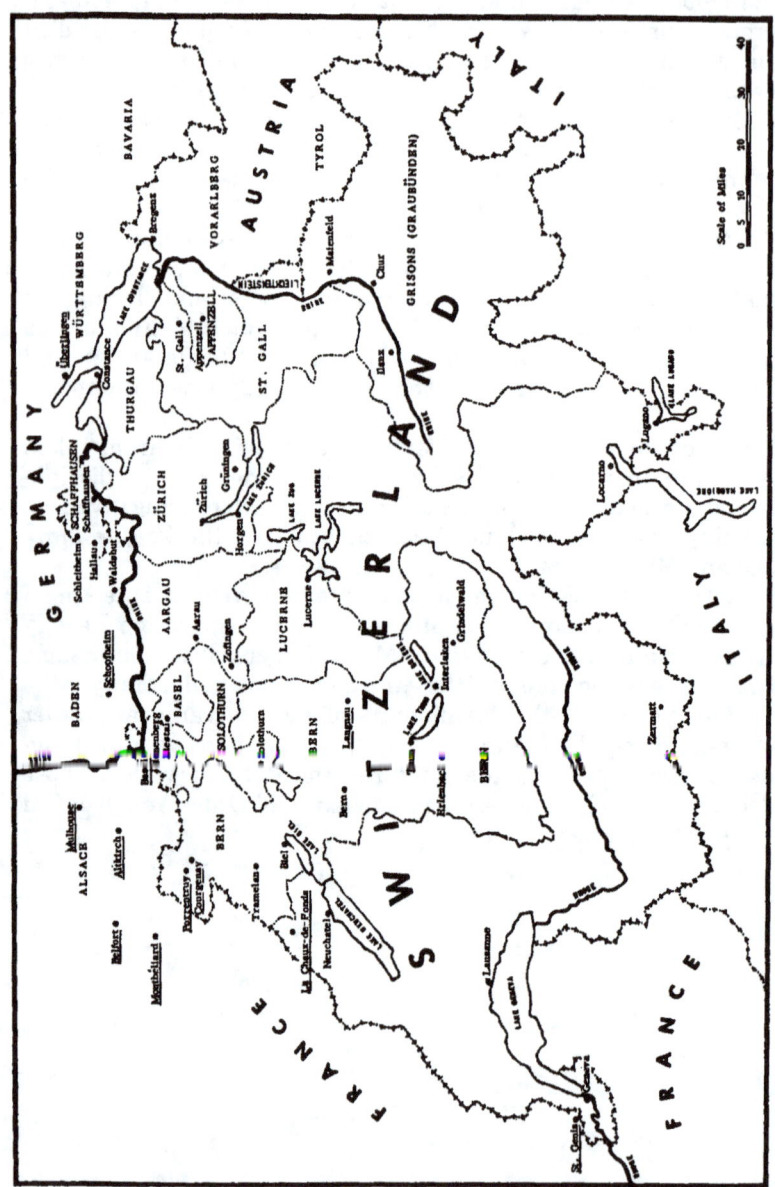

Mennonites in Switzerland
(Cities having Mennonite congregations are underlined.)

III

Switzerland

1. CONTINUED PERSECUTION

Although effectively checked as a mass movement by 1535 in Switzerland, as elsewhere, Anabaptism nevertheless lingered on in secluded corners throughout all the northern cantons—Zürich, Neuchatel, Basel, Aargau, Solothurn, Appenzell, and Bern—for several centuries longer. In course of time, however, continued and persistent persecution completely annihilated it except in a few small regions in the canton of Bern. There today one still finds a limited number of small congregations in the Emmental and the Jura regions.

The history of the Anabaptists, or Mennonites as we shall call them hereafter, in the Swiss republic, the land of their origin, is a tale of bloody persecution on the one hand, and of heroic self-sacrifice and sturdy devotion to religious conviction on the other. Swiss Mennonites were sent to the executioner's block until well into the seventeenth century. And after that throughout all the cantons mentioned above, mandate after mandate was issued by the governing authorities directed against the liberties and lives of these peaceable and God-fearing people. Mennonites were forbidden to practice their own religion and were commanded to attend the state church. They were ordered to have their children baptized and to have their marriages solemnized by the regular clergy.

To the Stake and Galleys

For refusing to comply with these demands, the Mennonites were fined, imprisoned, and occasionally sent to the galleys, although at the same time the Swiss authorities were buying the freedom of French Huguenots, condemned to the same service.

Their property was confiscated, and their children were declared illegitimate and incapable of entering into their inheritance. They were branded and whipped into exile, and if they returned, as they did sometimes, they were threatened with the death penalty. Finally, upon death, they were denied burial in the common burying grounds.

As a result of these extreme measures, a number of Mennonites died in prison; a few recanted; many of them fled to other more tolerant lands. During the latter part of the sixteenth century especially, Moravia offered them a haven of refuge, as it did also to their brethren from all parts of middle Europe. In fact, throughout the entire century, Swiss Mennonites went back and forth continually to the "promised land." It was a group of Swiss exiles on their return to their native land, it will be remembered, who while arrested and imprisoned at Passau in Bavaria in 1537, gave us the group of hymns out of which the well-known *Ausbund* later developed. Near the close of the century, both Bern and Zürich passed rigid laws against this migration on the ground that since many of the Mennonites who left Switzerland with their possessions often returned empty-handed, this caused a heavy loss to the local communities from which they originally migrated.

It is a fine tribute to the sincerity of the Swiss Mennonites that in spite of all this terrible pressure, there were but few recantations during this entire period. It is a convincing example, too, of the persistence of a strongly entrenched religious idea. The persecuting authorities had little understanding of, and less patience with, these unyielding convictions of a hard-pressed people, which they attributed to mere stubbornness of will. They called them *Hitzköpfe* (hotheads), *verdammte Irr- und Rottgeister* (damned heretical rabble-rousers), and other hard names. The refusal of the Mennonites to recant was ascribed to *Hochmut* (pride), and still worse to *kybiger Hart-näckigkeit* (stiffneckedness). Scores of the accused preferred the executioner's block to a betrayal of their innermost convictions. Van Braght, the martyrologist, is authority for the claim that by 1571 some forty Mennonites had paid the extreme price for their faith in the canton of Bern alone.

The last Bernese martyr to give his life for the cause was Hans Haslibacher of Sumiswald, whose death in 1571 is vividly recorded in the *Martyrs Mirror*, as well as in a long hymn found in the later editions of the *Ausbund*. In this hymn, somewhat colored by the pious imagination of the narrator, is found the whole story of this martyr—his imprisonment, his torture, the attempt by the state clergy to secure a recantation, the sturdy faith of the old man

("This body you may put to death/I'll give my head but not my faith"). According to the story, he prophesied that at his death three signs would prove his innocence: (1) His head would leap into his hat as soon as it was severed from his body; (2) the sun would turn red; and (3) the town pump would flow crimson. When these prophecies came true at his death, the executioner and attendants were convinced that they had shed innocent blood. This Haslibacher hymn of thirty-two long stanzas, sung in its entirety and in long meter, held a conspicuous place in the worship of the Swiss for hundreds of years.

The last Mennonite martyr in Zürich as well as in all Switzerland, so far as the *Martyrs Mirror* records show, was Hans Landis, who was beheaded in 1614. Landis was an influential minister who carried on his preaching and other ministerial duties contrary to a decree of the Zürich Council. He was arrested, imprisoned, and finally condemned to the Venetian galleys. But by filing his chains with an instrument smuggled in to him by a friend, he escaped. Returning to his native land, he was again taken into custody. Upon being ordered into exile, he refused, replying that God gave him the same right to the land as the others, and that the earth was the Lord's. At any rate, he preferred to live in his native land and did not know where to go. Besides he was now old, and no longer feared death. As a result of this refusal to leave, he was condemned to death by the Great Council. The *Martyrs Mirror* describes Landis as "a tall, stately man with a long grey and black beard, and with a strong, manly voice."

Persecution in Zürich did not end, however, with the death of the last martyr. Imprisonment and banishment continued. Especially severe was the oppression which set in again in both Zürich and Bern during and following the Thirty Years' War. All the old measures short of the death penalty were again revived. In 1657 there were 170 Mennonites in the Zürich prisons, doomed to a diet of fruit soup and bread, with a little wine and meat on Sunday. The *Martyrs Mirror* and the later editions of the *Ausbund* in an appendix give a vivid account of the suffering of numerous Mennonites between 1635 and 1645 whose names have a familiar sound to one versed in Pennsylvania history—such names as *Frick, Landes, Bauman, Strickler, Egly, Huber, Kolb, Hess, Meili, Haegi (Hege), Bachman, Schnebele,* and others from Basel. And at the same time we hear such typical later Pennsylvania Amish names as Joder (Yoder) and Troyer. A little later an order for wholesale exile was passed by the Zürich Council. Several hundred emigrated to Alsace and the Palatinate. Emigration and deportation continued, until by 1700 there were few Mennonites left anywhere in northern Switzerland except in a few isolated communities in Basel and Neuchatel, and in the present canton of Bern.

That they were not entirely driven out of Bern as they were in Zürich was not due to any lack of diligence on the part of the Bernese authorities to bring about this end; for the latter, too, had decided upon a vigorous policy of extermination of these unyielding nonconformists. In 1659, after repeated efforts to bring the Mennonites into submission to the state church, a general decree of exile was passed by the Bernese Council ordering all those who would not conform to be "utterly banished" from the country; and if they should return unconverted, they were to be "publicly scourged with rods, branded, and again expelled from the country." The property of the exiles was to be confiscated. The death penalty, however, was no longer prescribed for a third offense as it had been in earlier similar decrees.

At the same time it was decreed with equal strictness that no one, "whoever he shall be, shall lodge or give shelter to native or foreign Anabaptists, whether they be related to him or not, or help to encourage their meetings and preaching, whether by granting them the use of their barns or houses or by aiding them in any way, or to have any intercourse with them whether written or oral; or in any way lend them aid in the form of money, provisions, or the like, neither secretly or publicly." Everyone was ordered to report any known Mennonite to the magistrates, and failure to comply with this order was punishable by a fine of 100 *guilders*. This proclamation was to be read from all the pulpits in the state church.

Dutch Intercession

In the meantime, while this order for wholesale deportation was being put into effect, the Mennonites of Holland, having heard of these measures against their Swiss brethren, decided to intercede in their behalf. The Dutch Mennonites, unlike the Swiss, had by this time reached a position of great influence and power in financial and political circles in their own country. Some of the most influential merchants of the time, as well as leaders in the sciences and arts, were Mennonites. They could speak, consequently, with some degree of authority. Through their influence, the burgomasters of Amsterdam and Rotterdam, as well as the States General itself, wrote letters to both the Bernese and Zürich councils, asking for milder treatment of the persecuted Mennonites, and especially that the latter might be permitted to leave the land in peace with all their possessions and families. The Mennonites in Holland, the States General said, "are a highly respected and peaceful people, willing at all times to perform all their civil duties, and giving liberally to all worthy causes, even contributing to the benevolences of the Reformed Church itself."

Influential Dutch Mennonites sent a special representative in 1660 to investigate conditions among the Swiss prisoners, and later to bring financial aid to those in need. But their representative, Adolf de Vreede, though not himself a Mennonite, found it difficult to gain access to the prisoners, and both the Bernese and Zürich councils forbade altogether the distribution of money. In fact, some of the funds were later seized by the officials and used to carry on the work of persecution. Even the Reformed Church in Holland became interested in what they regarded as unnecessarily harsh measures adopted by their fellow believers in Switzerland. Professors in the Dutch universities, under whom many of the Swiss professors and clergymen had studied, wrote to the latter, advising more humane treatment of those whose only sin was that they desired to worship God in their own way.

None of these intercessory efforts, however, were of much avail. The Swiss autocrats in Bern and Zürich had decided to rid themselves of Mennonitism once for all without any financial loss to themselves. So they turned a deaf ear to the advice of the States General and their own Reformed brethren, as well as the the pleas of the Dutch Mennonites. The decree of 1659 was carried out to the letter. Each year the most aggressive of the Mennonites, and especially their ministers, were dispossessed of their property, torn from their families, escorted across the border, and threatened with worse treatment if they returned.

But the crucial year came in 1671 when some seven hundred men, women, and children, mostly from Bern and some from Zürich—the old and decrepit as well as the babes in arms—were driven out of their native land. Penniless and helpless, about one hundred went to Alsace, and the rest into the Palatinate. Fortunately, just at this time they had been invited to settle by Count Karl Ludwig who desired thrifty farmers to build up the deserted agricultural lands laid waste by the ravages of the Thirty Years' War. For many years, however, these immigrants remained in straitened circumstances in spite of the help received from their Dutch brethren, and the welcome from the tolerant count.

From a series of letters written to Amsterdam from the Palatinate in 1671 by the Mennonites themselves, we catch a glimpse of the suffering and hardships which were theirs during these trying times. In a letter dated April 7, 1671, it was said of the Swiss:

> They are daily hunted with constables and as many as they can get taken as prisoners to the city of Bern so that four weeks ago about

forty, men and women, were in confinement there. They have also scourged some, and banished them from the country, one of whom arrived here. They also scourged a minister of the Word, and then conducted him out of the country, into Burgundy, where, when they arrived there, they first branded him, and let him go among the Walloons. However, as he could talk with no one, he had to go about three days with his burnt body before his wounds were dressed, and he obtained some refreshments, being in such a condition that when they undressed him for binding up his wounds, the matter ran down his back, as a brother who helped dress him told me himself.

In May it was reported:

> The magistrates at Bern caused six of the prisoners, among whom was a man with nine children, to be fastened to a chain and sold for the Sea, to be used as galley slaves between Milan and Malta.

Causes of Persecution

Nowhere else did Mennonites at this time suffer such indignities as in Switzerland. In Holland and West Prussia they were enjoying a large degree of liberty. Even in the Palatinate during the eighteenth century under intolerant Catholic counts they enjoyed greater freedom, restricted though they were occasionally in their civil and religious privileges. It may not be amiss, therefore, to suggest a few reasons for this persecuting zeal on the part of the Bernese and other Swiss cantonal authorities in the land of reputed civil and religious liberty long after milder measures had been adopted in less democratic countries.

In Switzerland, the Reformed Church for a time joined the state in a combined effort to drive Mennonitism out of existence. Public debates were held with Mennonite leaders by the Reformed clergy throughout this period in an attempt to convince the Mennonites of the supposed errors of their way. Questions of theology, however, played a minor part in these debates; for both sides recognized that in fundamental theological doctrines they had much in common. Even Breitinger, the Reformed leader in Zürich in the early seventeenth century, suggested that they agreed on all points in which *die Seligkeit gelegen ist* (salvation depends).

The questions to which the clergymen always demanded answers in trial or debate were, Why did the Mennonites refuse to attend the state church, refuse to have their children baptized, insist on performing their own marriage ceremonies, and set up their own worship? In other words, why did they not conform? The charge against them was that of separatism, always a serious charge under the state-church system the world over in the days before state and church were separated. The Swiss church was not unique among the state ecclesiastical systems of the day in its attempt to stamp out nonconformity, and its measures to bring about that result perhaps not much more barbaric than those adopted by our own Puritan commonwealth during these identical years in hanging the Quakers.

One answer which the Mennonites usually gave disturbed both the clergy and state authorities not a little. They refused to attend the established church, they said, because of the worldly life of the clergy and the low moral standards of many of the members. Recognizing the charge as one of the potent causes of the continued existence of the Mennonite movement, as well as the cause of frequent dissatisfaction among the people at large, the state clergy held frequent synods to discuss means and proper remedies for raising the moral level of the whole ecclesiastical leadership. That Mennonites themselves lived on a high moral and spiritual plane is evidenced by the almost universal testimony of even their most persistent enemies during all these centuries.

From a Reformed clergyman who wrote in 1693, we have this interesting description:

> They are reputed to be true Christians, but observe strictly those practices which are peculiar to the Anabaptists, and which distinguish them from us as follows—they do not attend our church because of the presence of so many sinners among us; do not observe the Lord's Supper with us; they establish their own churches; they do not baptize their children; do not take an oath, nor go to law; they do not go to war; nor occupy positions of honor nor hold civil office; they wear simple clothes, do not wear a collar about the neck, nor adorn themselves with lace and ruffles or anything that might savor of pride or extravagance; they speak slowly, and sing in a low, soft voice, and constantly keep their eyes fixed on the ground; they have little to do with those of high station, and avoid the clergymen; they seldom visit the taverns, and do not attend baptismal or marriage feasts; they do not often attend markets, and do little trading and buying; they are willing to suffer persecution; they are industrious and appear among the people as living a simple, pure, and honest life.

After describing the virtues of the Mennonites, the writer then goes on to advise his own people to follow the example of these pious folk.

It should be remembered, too, that since the Mennonites were the only free church in the land (this was before the day of modern free churches on the Continent—Baptist, Congregationalists, Methodists), they drew down upon their heads the whole concentrated wrath of the ecclesiastical hierarchy against any attempt at separatism. They alone stood for separation of church and state. They were a very small body, but they taught a doctrine dangerous for the perpetuity of the state church.

It was not primarily to the Swiss church, however, but rather to the secular authorities to whom the Mennonites owed their bitter experiences. The causes of persecution, especially in the latter centuries, were political rather than religious. Although pastor and magistrate were usually linked together in the mandates as proper persons with whom complaints against the Mennonites might be lodged, it was the state that took the initiative in all punitive measures.

The usual excuse given by the Bernese Council, when forced by outside public opinion to justify its harsh measures, was that Mennonites refused to perform military service. When confronted with the suggestion that Mennonites in other lands held similar beliefs without serious consequences, the council replied that the Swiss cantons, unlike other countries, depended not upon mercenary armies for defense but upon a national militia. In this military policy, no doubt, is to be found an important reason for the persistent hounding of the Mennonites in Switzerland during the seventeenth and eighteenth centuries.

Refusal to Become Conscripts

Armies in Europe at this time were small and composed of professional soldiers who made soldiering a business and fought for pay, plunder, and excitement. It was not difficult usually to keep the thin army ranks filled; and conscription, consequently, was little known before the Napoleonic Wars in France. It was not difficult, therefore, for those who had scruples against war to escape military service, sometimes at the expense of other service. Especially was this true under the autocracies of the time. Thus Mennonites in the eighteenth century enjoyed military exemption not only in Holland, but also in Prussia, the Palatinate, Austria, Bavaria, Russia, and in nearly every other land in which they were found, except in Switzerland. It is only in democracies that special groups find it hard to secure unusual privileges. Democracies are inclined to show little patience with the conscientious scruples of minorities.

It must not be inferred, however, that the Swiss Mennonite policy had its roots in democratic institutions; for the Swiss cantons were democracies in name only. The number of ruling families represented in the oligarchic councils of Bern were but a few. It was not democracy, but the autocratic military system, as just indicated, that lay at the bottom of all these troubles for the Mennonites. The apologists for the Swiss policy of oppression should not have justified the course of the state authorities on the plea that the Mennonites refused to defend the fatherland, for defense of the fatherland was not the use to which conscripted

SWITZERLAND 83

soldiers were usually put. They were used to fill the pockets of ruling noblemen, rather than for common defense. Throughout all the wars of the seventeenth and eighteenth centuries, Switzerland was a favorite recruiting ground for mercenary soldiers. They served on both sides in every conflict, and Swiss were pitted against Swiss on every battlefield of Europe. The army of Louis XIV in the War of the Palatinate contained thousands of Swiss soldiers, and it was to these Swiss troops that Louis owed his overwhelming victories in that campaign of devastation.

This vicious system of furnishing troops for pay to other rulers was an old practice in Switzerland, dating far back beyond the Reformation days and extending up to the time of the French Revolution. It is needless to say that the system found much bitter opposition on economic and social grounds among all the common people, regardless of religious beliefs. Mennonites, however, opposed war because of a deep religious conviction. But since their example would encourage others to take a firmer stand against the practice, Mennonites must either give up their convictions or be driven out of the land. It is worthy of notice that persecution was most bitter during the period of European wars in the latter part of the seventeenth and the early part of the eighteenth centuries, when profits for letting out mercenary soldiers were at the maximum.

Although Mennonites believed governments to be divinely ordained and, as such, to be accorded implicit obedience in all things except where religious convictions were concerned, yet their refusal to take an oath of any sort, including the oath of allegiance on account of religious scruples, was often misinterpreted by the governing authorities as an act of civil disobedience and of disloyalty. At the same time, under the feudal system which still prevailed in Switzerland, the peasant class especially was living under considerable economic and social oppression. The charges made by the Mennonites against the prevailing order on religious grounds were often not much different from those made by peasants at large on economic grounds. And so, the ruling authorities, ever fearful of losing their positions of power and influenece, did not always stop to draw a fine distinction between the motives of the peace-loving, nonresistant Mennonites who refused to take the oath on religious grounds and the leaders of peasant revolts, whose refusal to perform the same act was a sign of armed rebellion against constituted authority. Mennonite persecution frequently followed in the wake of peasant uprisings. Mennonite ministers and rebel leaders were sometimes executed together. There is no doubt but that the peasants often sympathized with the Mennonites in their attempts to establish their own form of worship. In 1714 several *Täufer-Jäger* (Mennonite-Hunters) who attempted to arrest a number of Mennonites for refusal to attend the state church were set upon and severely beaten by a mob of some sixty peasants of Sumiswald.

The Amish

Unfortunately, the same strong spirit of individualism which inspired these men and women to face death rather than violate their religious convictions also frequently led them to hairsplitting arguments over unimportant questions of policy and practice. One such quarrel took place in Bern in 1693. Many of the church quarrels in history can be traced to the peculiar notions of some strong-willed individual who can see but one side of a controversial question. And so it was here.

Jakob Ammann was the name of a young minister whose exact local field of labor, whether in the Bernese *Oberland* or in Alsace, is not known definitely. Although Jakob himself was a resident of Alsace as early as 1696, if not earlier, a few years later his Swiss following came from the upland section of the canton of Bern. Ammann may have been one of the Swiss exiles to Alsace during the great migration of some twenty years earlier. The fact that the whole Alsatian church finally accepted his leadership, while his following in Switzerland was much smaller, would suggest that his home at the time may have been Alsace. He was a young man of decided opinions and evidently of an aggressive personality. He conceived the notion that not all was well with the Mennonites of Switzerland and proposed, according to one of the chroniclers of this controversy, "to restore the temple of God upon the old foundation." The main charge against the church seemingly was laxness of discipline—and especially the failure to apply the *Meidung* (avoidance) to excommunicated members. This practice, advocated in the Dutch Confession of Dordrecht and adopted by the Alsatians in 1660, was no doubt well known also in Switzerland, but was not followed by the Swiss church of that day.

Meidung, it will be remembered, was not a new practice, having been applied by Menno Simons and Dirk Philips and certain sections of the Dutch church, with disastrous results. Jakob Ammann now demanded its rigid observance also in the Swiss church, where evidently its practice had fallen into disuse. Together with several other ministers, who he had seemingly converted to his point of view, he set out upon a tour through the various Swiss congregations in 1693 in the interests of church discipline. The Alsatians, as well as the congregations in the *Oberland*, seemingly went over to the new camp in a body; but with those who lived in the Emmental, in the general region of Langnau, Ammann had little success. Losing patience with the ministers there because they would not agree with him on this question, he placed them all under the ban. These, in turn, under the leadership of one Hans Reist, returned the compliment and banned the Ammann party, thus starting a division that is still alive in America. The schism was carried into the Palatinate and wherever Swiss emigrants went.

A lively correspondence which was kept up between the leaders of the two factions for some years now furnishes us with our only source of information on the subject. In this we find that numerous uncomplimentary adjectives and hard names were bandied back and forth, especially by Ammann. A little later the Amish (as they were now called) also adopted foot washing as a church practice (although that was not at first an issue in dispute) and the observance of communion twice each year instead of once as had been the custom heretofore.

Ammann evidently found fault with some of the new social customs and practices that threatened to creep into the church at this time, and against which he thought the Reist party was not sufficiently on its guard; for in one of his letters there are hints of fancy clothes, shaving of the beard, wearing long hair, and attending funerals in the state church.

In fact, the whole movement was toward a strict observance of the older customs, or at least toward a crystallization of the customs and practices then current and of suspicion of all innovations in the affairs of everyday living as well as in forms of church worship. There was an ever-present fear of the dangers of "worldliness." This spirit of conservatism did not grow mellow with age. The old was seldom discarded for the new in styles of dress as these changed during the centuries. And so hooks and eyes were retained instead of buttons; shoestrings, instead of buckles; and belts, instead of suspenders. Beards and long hair, once merely a common custom, acquired a religious significance.

As already indicated, in course of time nearly all the Mennonites in Alsace and in France, as well as a small group in the Palatinate Bavaria, were Amish. The Jura *Oberland* Amish emigrated to Holland in 1711, and others emigrated to Alsace and Neuchatel so that few remained in Bern. All these congregations have since lost their old-time character and are no longer to be distinguished from other Mennonites. But in America there are a number of large settlements scattered throughout Pennsylvania and the states of the Mississippi Valley where some of the customs and practices prevailing in Switzerland in the days of Jakob Ammann are still observed.

Renewed Persecution

Unfortunately the exodus of 1671 did not end the story of persecution in Bern, though it had practically exterminated the Mennonites in Zürich and some of the other Swiss cantons. Not all of the Mennonites left the canton at that time. Some of those who did, later returned. The policy of annihilation continued. In 1688 the War Council suggested that frequent military musters take place, that all men be required to wear swords when appearing in public places, and that oaths of allegiance be taken every six years. By refusing to comply with these regulations, Mennonites could easily be identified. In 1690 the Great Council ordered that all children of Mennonite parentage be disinherited if their parents did not conform to the state church. In 1695 the fundamental law was laid down that one's usual civil obligations could not be evaded because of religious views. By 1709 the prisons of Bern were again full.

In the meantime, more efficient machinery was perfected for handling the whole Mennonite problem. A special commission called the *Täufer-Kammer* (Mennonite Commission) was organized to deal exclusively with this question. *Täufer-Jäger* (Mennonite-Hunters), usually the common rowdies of the community, were set to the task of spying out the suspects and bringing them before the magistrates. The *Täufer-Gut* (Mennonite Fund) made up from the confiscations of Mennonite property, and at first used to defray the expenses of the persecution, was later turned over to the state church for school and church. Every effort was put forth to attract the persecuting officials with alluring awards to the unpopular business of rounding up harmless Mennonites. To the "Hunters" was awarded thirty *Kreuzer* for every ordinary suspect placed under arrest. Ministers brought a higher price—one hundred *Thaler*.

But none of these drastic measures had thus far proven successful in stamping out the Mennonite movement. No matter with what harsh punishment the Mennonites were threatened, they repeatedly returned to be with their families or spend their last days on their native soil. It now occurred to the commission to try a plan which had been under consideration for some time— that of disposing of their prisoners, which included no doubt the most conscientious and thus most troublesome of the leaders, by deporting them to America or some other far-off land from which return would be extremely unlikely. The time for this experiment seemed propitious. It was the year when all South Germany and Switzerland were aflame with the Pennsylvania fever. Some ten thousand Palatines had collected in London that year, 1709, hoping to be transported at the Queen's expense to the "Paradise of America." Why not send these troublesome Mennonites along? So thought the commission; and the council agreed.

Arrangements were accordingly made with a certain Georg Ritter, a sort of colonization agent then stationed at Bern, to take charge of the proposed expedition. For every Mennonite successfully landed across the seas, Ritter was to receive the sum of forty-five *Thaler*. He started down the Rhine on March 18, 1710, with his Mennonite prisoners and a group of other unwelcome citizens whom he was to accompany to the Graffenried colony just being established in the Carolinas, at the request of the Bernese authorities.

An Emigration Project that Miscarried

In the meantime, since the Rhine flows across numerous political boundaries on its way to the sea, it was necessary for Ritter to secure a series of passports for his human cargo, usually not a difficult matter, and no trouble was anticipated here. But in their deportation schemes, the Council of Bern had not sufficiently taken into account the political influence of the Dutch Mennonites at The Hague. These latter had never ceased to interest themselves in the fate of their Swiss brethren. A special relief commission had been formed to aid the Swiss with necessary funds to carry on their struggle for existence, and to intercede for them with the Swiss governments. When the Dutch heard that a group of Swiss Mennonites were being deported down the Rhine to a foreign land against their will, they immediately used their influence successfully with the States General to prevent the passage of the Ritter expedition through Dutch territory. St. Saphorin, the Swiss representative at The Hague, was assured by the president of the States General that since Holland was a free country, the Mennonites would be at liberty to go where they pleased as soon as they reached Dutch soil, in spite of the fifteen guards which Ritter had with him. Evidently the representatives of other countries also interceded at The Hague with the Swiss ambassador for milder treatment of the Mennonites; for in a letter to his home government he said he would rather "contend against the representatives of all the combined powers, except England, than against the Mennonites alone."

Lord Townsend, the English ambassador to the Netherlands, whose interest St. Saphorin hoped to enlist, informed the Swiss representative that England wanted only voluntary immigrants, not deported prisoners, in her colonies. William Penn, who hoped that these refugees might settle on his own lands, and who had written Townsend to help Ritter to secure passage through

Holland for "fifty or sixty *Switsers* called Mennonites coming from Holland in order to go for Penn Sylvania," evidently did not know that these *Switsers* were religious exiles being deported from their native land against their will.

St. Saphorin was convinced by this time that free passage to the mouth of the Rhine was impossible, and he so informed Ritter. But Ritter was already on his way. Nothing was left for him to do but to release his prisoners along the route. Twenty-eight had already been left at Mannheim because of sickness and infirmities. When those who remained on the boat asked permission at Nijmegen, near the Dutch border, to visit their brethren in this town, Ritter did not object. They never returned to the boat. And so ended another attempt of the Bernese government to solve this troublesome religious problem.

The failure of the Bernese to rid themselves of their Mennonite prisoners as they had planned, even though they had transported them temporarily across the border, did not lighten the burden of those Mennonites who remained. The harrying process continued, and soon another set of prisoners had been accumulated, some of them undoubtedly returned exiles from the Ritter expedition. The Dutch Mennonites, in the meantime, continued their efforts to solve the problem and bring relief to their Swiss brethren. They even promised to furnish money with which to buy substitutes or make good any financial loss entailed by the refusal of the Swiss Mennonites to enter military service. But they were informed that substitutes would not be permitted where universal service was the rule. It finally became evident to all the parties concerned that there was only one permanent solution of the question—wholesale emigration of all the Mennonites (not only the prisoners) of their own accord, with their families and possessions, to a land of their own choosing. And to bring this about, the Dutch *Commission for Foreign Needs* now worked with unflagging zeal, urging both the Swiss Mennonites and the Bernese government to cooperate to this end. This should not have been a difficult task; for the authorities were anxious to rid themselves of the Mennonites, and the latter were even more concerned about finding a place of refuge. But it proved more difficult than it seemed at first.

First of all, the Bern Council wanted to be assured that none of the Mennonites, if transported elsewhere, would ever return to Swiss soil. But while they were anxious to get rid of troublesome nonconformists, they did not wish to part with the Reformed wives and husbands and children, of whom there were a number even in Mennonite circles. Military efficiency and economic well-being in those days of wars, pestilences, and famines depended upon maintaining a growing population. There was no overpopulation problem at that time. Most of the countries of middle Europe discouraged emigration with heavy emigration taxes, and some of them threatened with heavy punishment any colonization agent who tried to lure citizens from their native land. There is on record at least one case of a Swiss *Neuländer* (colonization agent) who as late as the eighteenth century was put to death for his activities in this direction. Consequently, non-Mennonite members of the family of a Mennonite exile were not permitted to accompany him. With their property confiscated, the exiles were sent out into the world empty-handed.

In this latter fact is to be found at least a partial explanation for the repeated return of Mennonite exiles to their native land even in the face of threats of dire consequences. They naturally desired to see their families and possess their property. Not to be overlooked also is the missionary zeal which dominates the life of every deeply religious people. Switzerland was the land of Mennonite origins, and many were concerned that the faith should not die out here. Benedikt Brechbill, a leading minister among the Swiss who was in exile at the time in the Palatinate, was sorry to learn in a letter from one of his brethren that "his brethren in Switzerland missed him as a shepherd of the flock of believers."

Then, too, the uncertainty of their destination made the Mennonites slow to consent to any plan of emigration. By 1711, however, the Dutch had worked out a satisfactory agreement with the government at Bern for the withdrawal of the whole Mennonite population. The prisoners were to be set free and the emigrants could settle wherever they pleased, except in the neighboring canton of Neuchatel, at that time under Prussian rule. They could sell their property and take with them the proceeds, as well as the non-Mennonite members of their families, without paying the usual emigration tax. The one condition was that all Mennonites must promise never to return. In the meantime religious meetings were to be prohibited. The Dutch Mennonites were to assume the responsibility of seeing that these provisions were fulfilled. Johann Runkel, the Dutch ambassador at Bern, was commissioned with the task of carrying out the whole program.

It seems strange that a people so despised as were the Mennonites in Switzerland should at the same time be so welcomed by nearly all the other nations of middle Europe. The reason for this is to be found, of course, in their skill as farmers and their ability to bring returns from thin soil which others less industrious often found so barren that they could not even scratch out a bare existence from it. When it became known that some five hundred peace-loving refugees were about to be driven from their native Swiss homes because of their religious beliefs, several nations vied with each other in an effort to secure them for their own sparsely populated lands. Both the prince of Nassau and the count of Neuwied wanted skilled workmen and expert craftsmen to settle in their towns; but since the Swiss were nearly all small farmers and dairymen, they could not qualify. The king of Denmark was interested in having them settle on his lands. The Palatinate, too, was open. The queen of England had a special representative in Switzerland advertising the attractions of the Crown colonies for prospective settlers, but America seemingly received slight consideration from the main body of Swiss Mennonites at this time. Ambassador Runkel, who threw himself wholeheartedly into the task of rescuing the unfortunate Mennonites from their dilemma, had a suggestion of his own. Why could not the Bernese government grant religious toleration to the Mennonites on condition that they settle as a body on the waste swamplands in the northern part of the canton? This proposal, however, received serious consideration from no one except Runkel himself. Even if Bern had perchance agreed, the cost to the Mennonites of reclaiming these swamps, according to Benedikt Brechbill, would have been prohibitive.

More plausible seemed the proposition that came from the king of Prussia, Frederick William I. This thrifty king, who took a keen interest in the whole emigration project from the first, wrote repeatedly to his ambassador at The Hague, urging that the Mennonites settle anywhere on his lands, where he promised substantial advantages "far beyond anything they could hope to gain from Holland." Especially did the king urge them to locate in East Prussia, not far from where thriving Dutch Mennonite colonies had existed for over a century, and where a recent pestilence killed off many of the inhabitants, leaving lands, houses, stock, and equipment—all of which the Mennonites might have almost for the asking. Benedikt Brechbill headed a special commission which investigated the lands in question, and had an interview with the king's representative at Potsdam. Although Brechbill himself was enthusiastic about the project, few of the Swiss took advantage of this generous offer. They feared the possibility of another plague and were displeased, too, with the institution of serfdom which still prevailed there. It was finally decided by those in charge of the emigration project to lead the expedition to Holland and to leave the matter of final destination to later consideration. A little later, however, a small group did locate in East Prussia with the help of the Hamburg and Danzig

Mennonites. But these, after some years of heavy taxation and because later Prussian kings sometimes forgot their earlier promises of military exemption, were again forced to leave their new home.

Exiled

Preparations for the voyage down the Rhine, under the direction of Ambassador Runkel, were pushed vigorously during the early months of the year of 1711. Five boats were constructed at Basel to carry the party down the river. After much effort on the part of Runkel and the Dutch committee at Amsterdam, it seemed for a time that the whole scheme would fail because of the opposition of the Swiss Mennonites themselves. The final success must be attributed almost entirely to the infinite patience and the unwearying endeavors of the Dutch ambassador. There were several reasons for the reluctance of the Swiss Mennonites to give the project their wholehearted support. First, in view of more than a century and a half of persecution suffered under the rule of the Bernese government, Mennonites were suspicious of government promises. Some hesitated to sign the agreement never to return to Switzerland. For in spite of the agreement made between the Dutch ambassador and the government of Bern, there were still several uncertainties in the way—the status of the non-Mennonite members of the families who preferred to remain behind, as well as of the children; the property rights of each in case of divided families; and the question as to whether the general amnesty promised also applied to all the ministers, some of whom were already in exile.

Especially disappointing to Runkel was the feeling of bitterness still existing between the Amish and Reist's group. The Amish in the *Oberland* seemed willing enough to emigrate and cooperate to that end, but the Reist group in the Emmental refused to comply with the demands of the Dutch ambassador until compelled to do so, after repeated delays. The fact that the Reist group contained most of the prisoners whose status was less certain than that of the others may account partly for their reluctance, but the religious bitterness still existed between the two groups who had mutually banned each other. This made a wholehearted cooperation in any common enterprise extremely difficult. But Runkel displayed infinite tact and patience, and finally rounded up most of them.

The expedition, under the leadership of the same Ritter who had led the fifty-six prisoners of the year before, left Basel on July 13, 1711. Of the five hundred expected, less than four hundred reported, and one of the five boats was left at Basel. Even the most courageous of them left their cruel, but yet beloved, native land with many a heartache. The following description of the departure of the flotilla of exiles, by the well-known historian of the Bernese Mennonites, Ernst Müller, though drawn heavily from the writer's imagination, may not be far from a true account:

> Seated upon the chests and bundles which were piled up in the middle of the vessels were the grey-headed men and women, old and weak. On the sides were the young people watching with delight and wonder the shifting scenery of the banks as they glided by. Now hopeful, now troubled, they cast questioning glances to the North, and then with longing eyes they again turned their faces to the South in the direction of their beloved homes which they were leaving forever, the homes which had so basely exiled them, and yet the homes whose green hills and silver-tipped mountains they could not forget. And, when overcome with sorrow, someone began a song which comforted them.

Most of the Reist party deserted, as they had opportunity, in the early stages of the voyage down the Rhine to seek their friends and brethren in the Palatinate. So it was mainly the Amish party, about three hundred and forty in number, that finally arrived at Amsterdam on August 3, where they were cordially received by their Dutch brethren and had all their wants provided for until they could find a permanent location.

The Dutch Mennonites were most generous in their support of these Swiss exiles with their strange customs and foreign dialect. First, the newcomers were distributed temporarily among the congregations at Deventer, Harlingen, and Groningen, and substantial sums of money were collected to help them get a new start in life on small farms. A small group of the Reist followers, who seemingly had accompanied the party unwillingly all the way to Holland, after a temporary stay at Deventer later found their way back again to the Palatinate. But the major part of the expedition, the Amish group, were gathered together in the course of a few years and located near Groningen and Kampen, where they organized several separate congregations. Within ten years these had become self-supporting and no longer needed the help of their generous Dutch brethren.

For nearly two hundred years these congregations kept up their independent existence, although in a Dutch geographical environment they had more ecclesiastical affiliation with their Swiss and Palatinate Amish brethren than with the native Dutch Mennonites. For many years they kept up their Swiss dialect, hooks and eyes, long hair and beards, broad-brimmed hats, foot washing, two witnesses to every sermon, kneeling in prayer, singing from the *Ausbund*, and other practices still in vogue today among the Old Order Amish in Pennsylvania and other states. At

first the native Dutch found these strange people with their
foreign customs of great interest. Curiosity, it is said, was so great
sometimes that local police occasionally found it necessary to
keep the crowds away from the doors of their meeting places
during the hours of worship.

We know very little of the later history of these congregations
except a few facts gleaned from a letter written in 1765 by Hans
Naffziger, an Amish bishop from the Palatinate, who had visited
them in that year. Naffziger reported to his home congregation in
the Palatinate that the churches had developed a division in their
ranks some years before, no doubt the result of an attempt to
maintain their old-time Swiss customs in a Dutch environment,
and that for six years now there had been no baptisms, no
communion, and no marriage ceremonies in the church. Many
young people had forsaken the faith; congregations lacked
competent preachers, and it was impossible to persuade young
men to accept ministerial responsibilities. For a time there was a
division into the New and the Old Swiss. Later visits from the
Palatinate evidently revived the church. It was not until the
middle of the nineteenth century, however, that the Amish gave
up their separate existence, and merged into the general Dutch
Mennonite body. No one now would suspect their Swiss Amish
origin except for their Swiss names. One would have little
difficulty in recognizing *Leutcher* as Swiss Latschar; *Ricken* as
Rich; *Root* as Ruth; *Leendertz* for Leenders; *Lutwyler* for
Litweiler; *Meihuizen* for Maihaus; and *Gauwetzy* for Gautschy—
all familiar Amish names still found in Illinois and Ohio.

But, strange to say, this weary story of persecution was even yet
not at an end. Some of the Swiss exiles returned, as already
noticed; others never left. These now again became the objects of a
most bitter attack on the part of the Bernese Council. All the old
mandates were vigorously enforced. There were still about one
hundred families left who refused either to conform or to be driven
out. Upon these, the Bernese government now turned with
renewed bitterness. All Mennonites were again ordered to be cast
into prison. Rewards were offered for their arrest—15 crowns for a
woman, 30 for a man, and 100 for a minister. Secret meetings were
prohibited, and no one was permitted to give Mennonites any
assistance. One man was fined a large sum for shielding his own
wife. Reformed parents must disinherit Mennonite children. The
installation of a minister was punishable with a heavy fine.
Returned exiles were threatened with a galley sentence. In 1715
and again in 1718, several men were condemned to that fate,
though due to protests from the Dutch States General and local
popular opinion the sentence was never carried out. At one time

there were over forty Mennonites in prison. In 1742 even an Amishman from Holland, visiting his relatives in Bern, was cast into prison for a time. In 1734 the *Täufer* council appointed several special agents to scour the community for Mennonites.

It was not until the close of the century, when the liberalizing influences of the French Revolution permeated all Europe, that democratic Switzerland reached the state of religious toleration attained by the Dutch two hundred years earlier.

2. TOLERATION GRANTED

In 1799 Switzerland passed an act of toleration granting religious liberty to every faith and permitting those who had been banished for the sake of their religious beliefs to return. But even this act of toleration, while it ended active persecution, did not place the Mennonites on an equal footing with the state church. Baptism and marriage were still regarded as civil and religious rites to be administered only by the state church. In 1810 the Emmental congregation requested that their own baptismal and marriage ceremonies be recognized as valid and final. But the authorities refused the request, and the next year all Mennonite children who had remained unbaptized since 1798, twenty-seven in all, were ordered to submit to the rite at the hands of the state church. The Mennonites could then rebaptize them if they so desired, the authorities declared, and they might repeat the marriage ceremonies according to their own customs. The spirit of the times was growing too liberal, however, for enforcing such regulations. When the Mennonites refused to bring their children to the Reformed churches for baptism, they were led unwillingly to the baptismal font by the local police. Even the state clergy, recognizing this procedure as a travesty upon religion, objected to its continuation.

Finally in 1815, after a long and bitter struggle of nearly three hundred years, the Mennonites in the canton of Bern were granted complete religious toleration with full rights of citizenship. Instead of the oath, a handclasp was permitted. In lieu of military service, they were granted the right of furnishing money for a substitute.

Just about the time the Swiss Mennonites were granted full religious toleration, many of them decided to emigrate of their own free choice to America, that land of opportunity to which their forebears had refused to be deported one hundred years earlier. Most of these came from the Jura settlements, but some also came from the Emmental.

The Jura Settlement

The Jura spoken of here consists of that part of the canton of Bern on the French side of the Jura hills, which up to 1815 had composed the bishopric of Basel, but since then had been incorporated into the canton of Bern. Along these hills, often in out-of-the-way places and on hitherto unproductive mountainsides, Mennonite exiles, at first from Alsace but later largely from Bern, had been invited all through the seventeenth and eighteenth centuries to settle as tenants on the estates of wealthy noblemen. There, because of their economic worth, they were offered protection against religious persecution by the ruling bishops. By hard work and plain living they eked out a comfortable existence, and greatly increased the income to their landlords from their meager lands.

It was perhaps only natural that their French neighbors should envy these industrious German-speaking, Mennonite farmers their greater prosperity and seemingly better reputation among the noblemen of the community. Frequent complaints were lodged against them with the ruling authorities, and demands made that they be driven from their holdings. It is interesting to note that these charges were usually economic, not religious or political. In 1731 the French peasants in one local Mennonite community complained that the Mennonites monopolized all the work of the community and, by using up the wood in the local forests for their cheesemaking, greatly raised the cost of living for all. Later it was charged that by taking care of their own poor and orphans, settling their own disputes among themselves without going to law, and helping one another in time of need, they separated themselves from the rest of society and thus formed a dangerous self-governing local unit—a state within a state.

Usually these complaints fell on deaf ears. Well-satisfied landlords and thrifty bishops were seldom willing to exchange industrious and successful German Mennonite farmers and dairymen for Frenchmen, though Catholic. With a few exceptions, the Mennonites of the Jura enjoyed comparative religious toleration under the rule of the bishops of Basel, although all through the centuries individuals and small groups migrated to America and into France mainly for economic reasons. By 1798 it was estimated by a local traveler through the bishopric that the Mennonites numbered about eight hundred souls in this region, centered largely about two large congregations—*Sonnenberg* and *Münsterberg*. It was from this region that most of the Swiss emigrants to America came in the first half of the nineteenth century.

The American Emigration

This emigration movement during the first half of the past century, not only of Swiss but also of Alsatian and South German Mennonites, was the result of several causes. Most important, perhaps, was the spirit of militarism which prevailed throughout this part of Europe during the Napoleonic Wars, and the feeling of unrest which the Mennonites feared would break out in further conflict, ultimately making it impossible for them to maintain their nonresistant principles. In some cases, equally strong were the economic motives. The Jura Swiss, especially, were decidedly poor by this time. Not being permitted to buy land of their own, they were merely tenants on long-term leases. Some did not even own a horse and were compelled to do all their labor by hand, assisted occasionally by the family cow. A goodly number were forced to practice some sort of avocation along with their farming, such as weaving, shoemaking, or cabinetmaking, in order to eke out an existence. Families were large, and the small farms could not take care of the increased population. Between 1815 and 1820 times were especially hard. As a result of the war, prices were high. Rents were increasing. Black bread and potatoes were the only food for many. Meat could be afforded only on special occasions. Even butter and eggs were scarce. But now a few crop failures had reduced some of the poorer people to actual want. These were the conditions that made the Swiss at this time turn their eyes to America—the land of milk and honey.

The Swiss pioneer who led this movement was one Benedikt Schrag, who in 1817 settled in Wayne County, Ohio. He was followed before 1860 by many from both the Jura and the Emmental, who located in large colonies in Wayne, Putnam, and Allen counties in Ohio, and in Adams County, Indiana.

Neu-Täufer

It was during the time of this emigration that another church dispute arose resulting in the creation of a new group, locally known as *Neu-Täufer*. It was organized by a Samuel Fröhlich between 1832 and 1835 in Aargau and in the Emmental. Fröhlich had been a theological student in the Reformed Church, but having been cast out of that body for some reason in 1832, he decided to organize a church of his own. It was while he was engaged in this enterprise that he visited among the Mennonites in the Emmental. His visit here was well timed for his purposes, for here, too, a quarrel was brewing under the leadership of two influential members of the congregation—Samuel Gerber and Christian Baumgartner. Gerber, who had just recently been installed as minister in the Emmental congregation by the elders of the Jura church, was ambitious to play an important role in his circle. Accusing his fellow ministers of a lack of religious zeal and of the want of all spiritual life, he introduced a series of changes in the church under his charge quite contrary to the practices then in vogue. Thus the soil was well prepared for the work of proselyting. Fröhlich, in bad repute among the clergy of the state church, was soon forced to leave his work in the Emmental due to pressure from the local police officials, but he sent a representative who was not slow to take advantage of the local quarrel, and added quite a number of the disaffected to the new following. Gerber and Baumgartner and their disciples, who had already introduced the practice of weekly communion services in their group, were somewhat reluctant at first to fellowship wholeheartedly with the Fröhlich group, because the latter insisted that all new members must submit to a rebaptism by immersion as a test of membership. Since every other faith but theirs was a dead faith and could not be recognized, no former baptism was considered as valid. This was rather humiliating to men who had all along assumed a superior piety among their fellows, but they finally swallowed their pride, and in the course of a few months the new group won over some sixty members from the Emmental congregation, as well as about an equal number from the state church.

Neu-Täufer was the name first applied to the followers of Fröhlich by his opponents. They soon developed an air of superior sanctity and a spirit of exclusiveness that set them apart from all other religious denominations. All others belonged to the "world" with whom there could be no religious fellowship whatever, and not too much social fellowship, especially with former fellow believers. Salvation was possible only by way of the new road. "Salute no man by the Way" was applied literally to those not of their own faith, and especially to those from whom they had withdrawn. They bitterly denounced the old church and ridiculed the preachers as "babblers, preachers of a dead faith" and the members of these churches as "spiritually dead." At first meetings were held every night after supposedly apostolic example. Communion was administered every Sabbath morning, while religious services were held in the afternoon. To the government they owed no allegiance except to pay their taxes. They considered it wrong to hold civil office. This was evidently the contribution of the Mennonite contingent to the new body.

The apostles of the new group carried the division to America among their relatives and friends. In 1846 several came to Ohio, where they established a small group of *Neu-Täufer* among the Mennonites of Wayne County. Later they appeared among the

Amish in New York and Illinois, where they became locally known as "New Amish."

Results of Persecution

The long-lasting persecution which the Swiss Mennonites suffered not only left its deep impress upon their souls and minds by engendering within them a spirit of submissive self-depreciation from which they never fully recovered, but it also greatly reduced their numbers. As a result of exile, emigration, defection, and withdrawal back into the state church, they have hardly held their own, and are making but slight gains. While the descendants of the seven or eight hundred exiles who crossed into the Palatinate between 1671 and 1711, part of whom later came to Pennsylvania, now number over one hundred thousand, the descendants of those who remained in Switzerland and retained the Mennonite faith number hardly more than fifteen hundred. Most of these are still found in the Jura region, with the largest congregation at Sonnenberg. The Emmental congregation numbers about three hundred members, with Langnau as its center. There are a few small settlements in Basel and Neuchatel.

At the time of the American emigration in the nineteenth century the Mennonites had no meetinghouses. Services were held in the barns, which were usually under the same roof as the houses, or in the open air in the summer season. Singing was *einstimmig* (unison), and the *Ausbund*, with its long hymns of thirty and forty stanzas, still the accepted songbook. Conservative customs and old styles of dress were still in evidence. Men wore short coats, knee breeches, hooks and eyes, and long beards, but no mustaches. The women vied with the men in the simplicity of their clothes. Adornments of all sorts were forbidden. All wordly vanities were discouraged; even looking glasses were tabooed. But according to one writer of the time, the fair young mountain maidens lost none of their charm by substituting for prohibited silk ribbons and flowers and feathers, ingeniously woven straw figures in their straw hats which they set jauntily upon their heads.

A well-known German author of the period, after a visit through the Swiss Mennonite communities, wrote of them as

> a sturdy, strong race, true-hearted, peace-loving, conscientious and benevolent, beloved by all their neighbors, Catholics and Protestants alike. They live a life of such patriarchal simplicity that one cannot help loving them. Among them are found no drunkards, no gamblers, no loafers, no liars, no jealous neighbors. If perchance strife should arise among them, it is amicably settled by their elder. They help one another in busy seasons usually without pay. Their

temperate, moderate habits assure them good health and long lives. Their conduct seems to be prompted by the one thought—"Keep God continually before your eyes."

Culture and the Spiritual Life

Many of the customs of a century ago have since been discarded, but in fundamentals the Swiss are still among the most conservative of the European Mennonites. Engaged in small farming and dairying—their Emmental cheese is famous the world over—they still lead rather a secluded life.

The Emmental settlement in recent years has perhaps been slightly less closed to outside influences than those in the Jura region. The exodus of 1711 and the persecutions which followed during the rest of the century nearly annihilated the Mennonite congregations here. For more than a hundred years after this, they were without an elder of their own, and the few scattered settlements were served in this capacity by the elders from the Jura. During the nineteenth century they were again revived, even receiving recruits from the Reformed Church. Their present meetinghouse, arranged as a combination church building and parsonage, was erected in 1887. Up to that time all the Mennonite meetings in Switzerland were held at private homes alternately in various sections of the settlements. Walking was the chief means of travel, and for that reason the owner of the home where the meeting was held served dinner to the worshipers from a distance on that particular Sunday.

The Jura congregations, being of Bernese extraction, have clung tenaciously through all these centuries to their German language, although entirely in a French environment. At their own expense they maintained their own German schools in addition to the French schools maintained by public taxation. During World War I there was friction over this language, although Switzerland herself was not directly engaged in the war.

The Swiss Mennonites were not a literary folk and wrote but few books. But their famous old hymnbook, the *Ausbund*, usually published at Zürich or Basel (the last time in 1839), went through many editions. The well-known old *Froschauer* Bible, published at Zürich contemporaneously with Luther's own, was for centuries known as the *Täufer Bibel*—a forbidden book for all the Swiss Mennonites during the years of persecution. The most recent history of the Swiss Mennonites, *Die Taufgesinnten-Gemeinden*, by Samuel Geiser, a Mennonite preacher of the Jura, was published in 1971. Their church paper, the *Zionspilger*, was founded in 1882 by Samuel Bähler. Hans Rüfenacht, the minister of the Kehr (Langnau) congregation, was the editor for many years.

Influential among the Swiss Mennonites during the past century was Ulrich Steiner, affectionately referred to in approved Swiss fashion as *Steiner Uli*. He was born in 1806 at Trachselwald, and in 1830 was elected in the Emmental congregation by lot. Five years later he was ordained as an elder. For many years he served as the spiritual adviser of the scattered members of his flock, traveling extensively—or rather continually—in the interests of the church. His work was especially arduous during the *Neu-Täufer* controversy. He died in 1877.

Another influential leader among the Jura Mennonites during the latter half of the eighteenth century was a former minister whose surname is no longer known, but who was usually spoken of among his neighbors, though perhaps not among his own people, as *Täufer-Bänz*. He was a Bernese exile driven to the Jura hills soon after the middle of the century. Without the means of support, he first settled with his family on a rented piece of ground so barren that no one expected him to extract a living from it. Through hard work and the self-sacrificing efforts of the whole family, he transformed it in the course of time into a prosperous estate that became the envy of farmers far and wide.

Täufer-Bänz was not only a good farmer, however, but he was also an inspirational religious leader among his people. He traveled unceasingly over the Jura hills, visiting the various scattered Mennonite congregations, serving their spiritual needs, and preaching, it is said, as long as three or four hours at a time. The most eloquent and self-sacrificial of all the Jura preachers, he was a man of considerable learning, unusually well versed in the Bible, though not theologically trained. He was long remembered for his eloquence, philanthropy, and worldly prosperity.

Swiss Mennonite Names

As already suggested, Switzerland was the native land, either directly or indirectly, of nearly all the Mennonites in America east of the Mississippi River—the Palatines in Pennsylvania, the Amish of Illinois and Ohio, as well as the Swiss who came directly to Ohio and Indiana in the early nineteenth century. The following family names, wherever found today in America in Amish and Mennonite communities, are all of Swiss origin—mainly from Bern and Zürich—though other cantons are also represented. In the following list no attempt is made at a consistent or correct Swiss spelling. The earlier Pennsylvania names, of course, appear considerably anglicized, as do also many names of the Amish in Illinois. The later immigrants to Ohio and Indiana who came from Switzerland directly are more likely to retain their names in their original form. Where different spellings occur—such as Guth, Gut, or Good, for instance—only one form is given although all may occur, sometimes even in the same family.

The list, which by no means pretends to be complete, follows: Ackerman, Allebach, Althaus, Amstutz, Augsburger, Bachman, Brubaker, Bertsche, Bowman, Bomberger, Baer, Brenneman, Bixel, Bechler, Bechtel, Baumgartner, Basinger, Burckey, Brand, Becker, Biery, Beidler, Buchwalter, Blosser, Boshart, Burghalter, Bucher, Brackbill, Badertscher, Dirstein, Detweiler, Diller, Eby, Ebersole, Eiman, Ellenberger, Egly, Engel, Eschbach, Eicher, Eschleman, Funk, Fahrney, Frick, Flickinger, Frey, Fellman, Gehman, Gerber, Günther, Gnaegi, Guth, Graber, Geiger, Guengrich, Gunday, Geisinger, Gochnauer, Goering, Hess, Horning, Haldeman, Hiestand, Habegger, Huber, Hostetler, Hartman, Hodel, Hauri, Herr, Hauter, Hirschler, Hilty, Hirschy, Hunsinger, Imhoff, Ingold, Kaufman, Kendig, Kratz, Krehbiel, Kennel, Kreider, Krup, Landis, Longeneker, Luginbill, Locher, Leatherman, Lehman, Litwiller, Lichty, Meili, Metzler, Maurer, Moser, Mosiman, Musselman, Newcomer, Neuenschwander, Nisley, Nussbaum, Neuhauser, Neff, Oberholtzer, Oeberli, Oesch, Plank, Ramseier, Reber, Reist, Rich, Richenbach, Risser, Roeschli, Roetlisberger, Rohrer, Roth, Rupp, Ruth, Schantz, Schellenberg(er), Schertz, Schlabach, Schlatter, Schlegel, Schmutz, Schnebele, Schneck, Schoenauer, Schope, Schowalter, Schrag, Schweitzer, Shenk, Strickler, Steiner, Stutzman, Sprunger, Steinman, Stucky, Sommer, Stalter, Stoll, Suter, Staufer, Streit, Smucker, Thierstein, Thut, Troyer, Ummel, Verkler, Welty, Wenger, Wisler, Witmer, Wuetrich, Yoder, Yordy, Zeist, Zook, Zuercher, etc.

The Swiss Mennonites Today

A depression which upset the Swiss economy between the years 1928-35 affected the Mennonite congregations considerably. Many families lost land which they had owned for generations. These either continued to live on the land as renters or moved to the industrial centers. Since that time a definite movement from the rural areas to the cities can be observed—quite a significant trend considering the fact that the Swiss Mennonites have lived in the rural areas of the Alpine and Jura valleys for over four centuries.

The Swiss Mennonites have been under pietistic influences for many decades. Gradually their lay ministers and prospective missionaries attended the *Missionsanstalt* of Chrischona and the *Missionsschule* of Basel, which they supported financially.

It should be mentioned that the final recognition of Mennonites in Switzerland as a legitimate denomination was in part due to Karl and Markus Barth who also influenced the reevaluation of the prevailing views in regard to the meaning of baptism. Both of them wrote on this subject. In matters of nonresistance, the Swiss Mennonites, like the other European Mennonites in general, gradually gave up their nonresistant stand. Only recently have young men taken the nonresistant stand for which they must serve a term in jail.

From 1946 to 1952 the Mennonite Central Committee maintained its European headquarters at Basel. In 1951 the European Mennonite Bible School was established in Basel. Moved to Bienenberg, Liestal, in 1957, it plays a significant role among Mennonites in Europe.

There are today fourteen Mennonite congregations in Switzerland with a total of twenty-seven hundred members. The Langenau Church is the largest. However, the descendants of the Mennonites of North America of Swiss background could easily reach the figure of one hundred fifty thousand, including the Mennonites (sometimes called Old Mennonites) and Amish, that originally came from Switzerland to the United States and Canada.

IV
The Netherlands

1. AFTER MENNO SIMONS

At the time of Menno Simons's death, the Anabaptists or Mennonites were still the largest evangelical movement in many sections of the Netherlands, although it was not long until they were greatly outnumbered by the Reformed, who have ever since played a dominant role in the religious life of the Netherlands. The Mennonites were found chiefly in the coast provinces—Flanders, Zeeland, Holland, Friesland, and Groningen—but small groups were also scattered throughout the interior regions. During the entire sixteenth century they were subjected to the most bitter persecution by both Charles V and his son Philip II. It is doubtful whether any other people in Europe suffered from the ravages of religious intolerance and political oppression as did the inhabitants of the Lowlands under the sway of these two Catholic rulers.

No other group in Europe can claim as many martyrs as the Mennonites. They were a relatively small group as compared with the larger Reformation groups; yet between 1531, the date of the execution of the first Anabaptist in the Netherlands, and the close of the century, more Mennonites were put to death for the sake of their religious convictions in the Netherlands alone than from all the religious groups in England during the same period. The various bloody decrees issued by Charles V were confirmed and renewed by a general edict proclaimed by Philip II in 1556. He forbade all laymen to discuss or teach the Holy Scriptures on penalty of death. The men were to be executed with the sword, and the women to be buried alive; but in case of persistence in their errors, the execution was to be by fire. Under any conditions the property of the accused was to be confiscated. Anabaptism was to be ruthlessly destroyed.

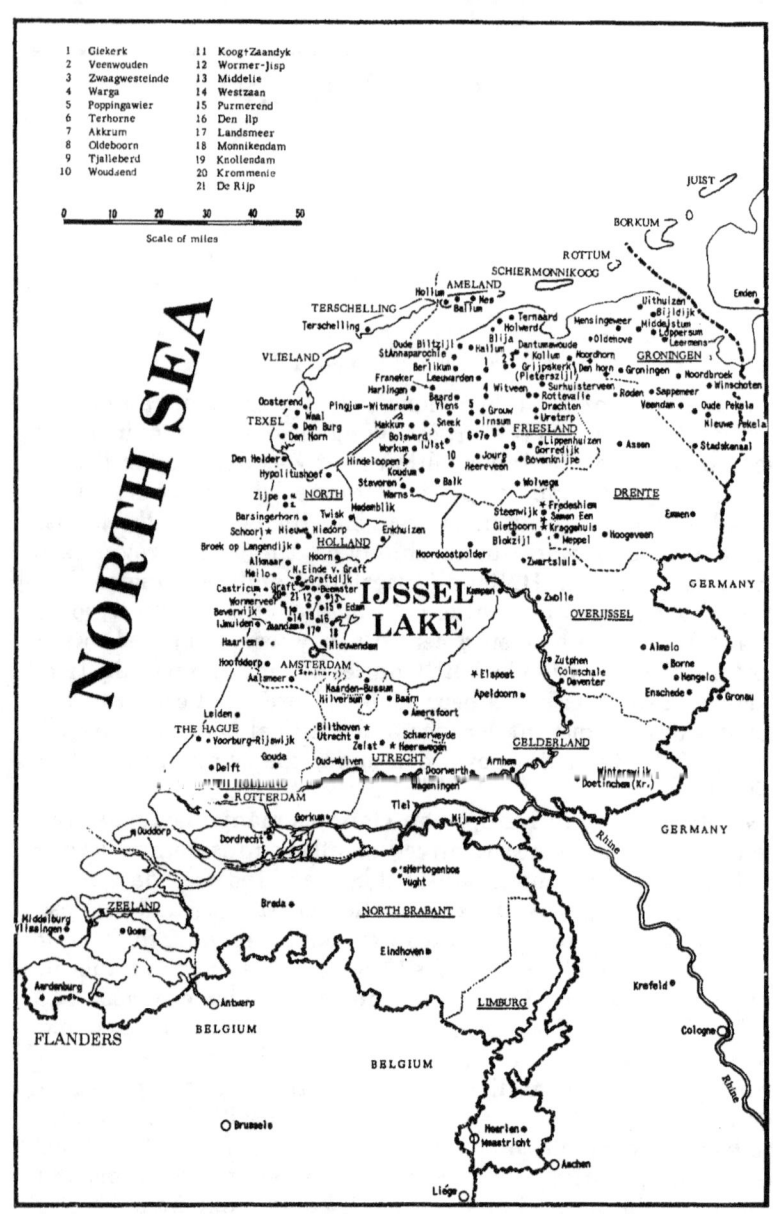

Mennonites in the Netherlands
(Towns having Mennonite congregations are shown.)

As a result of persistent persecution throughout the century, many of the Mennonite refugees found their way to more tolerant lands. In Flanders, where Catholicism prevailed and where the Inquisition consequently worked most ruthlessly, the Mennonites were practically rooted out by 1600. Many of the refugees fled to the northern provinces where opposition to Spanish rule was more determined among the people in general. But from all the provinces there was a continual stream of Mennonite refugees to neighboring countries—England, East Friesland, Poland, and West Prussia, where along the Vistula River a number of flourishing congregations were built in the course of time. This wholesale murder of innocent men and women, who asked for nothing more than the right to worship God as their consciences directed, did not cease until finally William of Orange conquered the Dutch provinces one after another, and in 1578 established a limited degree of religious toleration. The last of the Mennonite martyrs in the North to suffer the death penalty, so far as the records of van Braght reveal, was executed in Leeuwarden in 1574; the last recorded victim in the South was a woman, who was buried alive in Brussels in 1597.

As to the number of men and women who were put to death during this century for their religious faith, it is difficult to estimate. Perhaps about half of van Braght's list of fifteen hundred Anabaptist martyrs were from the Dutch provinces. Flanders alone furnished nearly four hundred. G. Brandt, the Dutch historian, lists five hundred and ninety-three. W. J. Kühler is authority for the statement that about two thousand Protestants were executed for their religious beliefs in the Netherlands during the century; of these, he thinks about three-fourths were Mennonites. This is a larger Mennonite contingent than that given by van Braght, but it is not likely, of course, that the well-known martyrologist was able to gather a complete list of all those who suffered the death penalty. It is interesting to note that the ratio of women to the entire number of executions among the Mennonites was much higher than among other groups. Of the Mennonites, more than 30 percent were women as compared with some 6 percent for the other groups.

The Witness of the Martyrs

Our best source of information of the suffering of this period is to be found in van Braght's *Martyrs Mirror*, compiled in 1660 from various court and other records. From this book we learn that the methods of execution were as cruel as fanatical ingenuity could devise. Burning at the stake, sometimes under a slow fire, was a common practice. Frequently a bag of powder tied about the neck or placed within the hat of the victim hastened his death. Women were often tied up in bags and thrown into the water to drown; occasionally they were buried alive. Men and women were stretched on the rack until their bones cracked and blood gushed forth; they had their tongues and limbs pierced with screws or pinched in vises for the purpose of forcing a recantation or a betrayal of the hiding places of their fellows. But seldom, even under the greatest pain and agony, could they be induced to implicate fellow believers. A few examples from this book of horrors will be sufficient to show the spirit of the age.

In 1539 Tjaerd Renicx was mercilessly tortured on the wheel because, out of compassion and brotherly love, he had at one time harbored Menno Simons in his house during a time of the latter's distress. In 1545 a certain Francis of Bolsward in the same province, having been charged with despising the mass and refusing to swear an oath and to observe the Eucharist according to the Roman fashion, was burned to ashes. At the time of the execution, the attendant, having stripped the victim of his clothes and fastened him to the stake, was about to strangle him with a rope when the rope broke, allowing Francis to fall to the ground. The frightened executioner then hastily tried to burn his victim with peat and wood, but under the nervous strain made such a bungling job of it that he aroused the anger of the bystanders.

Executions were especially numerous and unusually diabolical during the bloody rule of Duke Alva. In 1571 Anneken Hendriks of Amsterdam was burned at the stake for having "forsaken the mother, the holy church, and having adopted the cursed doctrines of the Menonists." When she attempted to speak to the bystanders at the time of her burning, the executioner filled her mouth with gunpowder, and then pitched her into the fire. This done, the bailiff was seen to laugh, as though, so says the chronicler, "he had done God an acceptable service."

Testifying before sympathizing bystanders at the funeral pyre was especially unacceptable to the authorities, and was not permitted if it could be prevented. In 1574 some thirty men and women in Antwerp were burned around one fire, and in order to prevent them from testifying to their faith the executioners

> filled the mouths of the pious witnesses of God with gags and balls, so that they were not able to proclaim to the bystanders their innocence, and the reason why they suffered thus. But the priests and the monks, having noticed that these pious men of God, when they came to the place of execution, freed themselves from these gags and balls and spoke to the people from the Word of God, the monks in order to prevent this had instruments made resembling vises between which they made the prisoners stick their tongues, which, when they had screwed fast, and the tip thereof touched with

THE NETHERLANDS

a red hot iron, that they should swell up and thus not slip back. And this new and abominable invention of the monks these tyrants, to their perpetual shame, used on the persons mentioned above.

The Catholic Church usually tried to secure a recantation from the victims before execution, sometimes promising them their freedom and at other times a lighter sentence in case the person would renounce the faith. To this end priests were often sent to the cells of those in prison to convince them of the errors of their ways or, if that would not succeed, to terrify them into a recantation. How well they succeeded can be seen in the following case where a friar, Cornelis, attempts the conversion of Jacob de Roore, a prisoner in Bruges, condemned to death in 1569. The following dialogue is recorded by van Braght:

> FRIAR CORNELIS: Well, I've come here to see whether I can convert you (Jacob, I believe is your name) from your false and evil belief, in which you are erring, and whether I can not bring you back to the Catholic faith of our mother, the Roman church, from which you have apostatized to this damnable Anabaptism. What do you say to this, eh?
>
> JACOB: With your permission, as regards that I have an evil, false belief, this I deny; but that through the grace of God I have apostatized from your Babylonian mother, the Roman church, to the members, or the true church, of Christ this I confess; and thank God for it, who has said: "Come out of her, my people, that ye be not partakers of her sins, and that ye receive not of her plagues." Rev. 18:4; Isa. 52:11.
>
> FR. CORNELIS: Is it true? And do you call our mother the holy Roman church, the whore of Babylon? And do you call your hellish, devilish sect of Anabaptists the members, or the true church of Christ? Eh! hear this fine fellow once. Who the devil has taught you this! your accursed Menno Simons, I suppose. . . .
>
> JACOB: With your permission, you talk very wickedly. It was not necessary that Menno Simons should have taught us as something new, that the Babylonian whore signifies your mother, the Roman church, since John teaches us enough concerning this in his Apocalypse, or Revelation, in the 14th, 16th, 17th, and 18th chapters.

Like all Anabaptists, Jacob was well versed in the Scriptures, answering all the friar's arguments with copious Bible quotations. The friar in turn relied entirely upon a citation of authority and tradition, and upon abuse. Of Scripture he knew very little. Ridiculing Jabob's profession, that of a poor weaver and candler, he was surprised nevertheless at the latter's thorough knowledge of the Bible. Referring to this characteristic of the Anabaptists, he burst out, after Jacob informed him that God often conceals His truth from the wise, and reveals it to babes:

> FR. CORNELIS: Exactly, God has revealed it to the weavers at the loom, to the cobblers on their bench, and to the bellows menders, lantern tinkers, scissors grinders, broom makers, thatchers, and all sorts of riff-raff, and poor, filthy and lousy beggars. And to us ecclesiastics who have studied from our youth, day and night, He has concealed it. Just see how we are tormented. You Anabaptists are certainly fine fellows to understand the holy Scriptures; for before you are rebaptized you can't tell A from B, but as soon as you are baptized you can read and write. If the devil and his mother have not a hand in this, I do not understand anything about you people.

Then follows a long discussion on various points of doctrine, during which the friar often loses his temper and resorts to invective and abuse. In accusing Jacob of performing the episcopal functions of baptizing and teaching without proper confirmation, the friar asks him what he thinks of confirmation.

> JACOB: I know nothing to say of episcopal authority, or of confirmation. How then should I administer it, or what should I think of it; for confirmation is a bugbear of which I know nothing.

> FR. CORNELIS: Is it possible, do you Anabaptists call the sacrament of confirmation a bugbear? Ah, accursed heretic, the devil take you into the fire of hell, to burn you forever; see!

> JACOB: Do not get so angry and excited, for I call it a strange bugbear, because it is so unknown to me. But tell me what it is, and what you hold concerning it; then I can tell you better what I think of it.

> FR. CORNELIS: Bah, this blockhead presumes to be a bishop of the Anabaptists, and does not yet know what the sacrament of confirmation is. If you are a bishop you ought to confirm yourself. My lords, see once, what a fine bishop the Anabaptists have had out there in the Gruthuysbosch, who preached so many sermons there; is it not a fine bishop, teacher, and preacher? Bah, see once with what we have been vexed and tormented.

> JACOB: I am no bishop, nor do I consider myself a teacher; but I have sometimes led the brethren and sisters and converts of our church with exhortation from the Word of God or the holy Scriptures, according to my small ability.

After several hours spent in a vain attempt to turn the poor weaver from his faith, the friar finally gives it up in despair with this parting message:

> FR. CORNELIS: Well, I have no desire to dispute any longer with you. I shall go my way, and let the executioner dispute with you, with a burning fagot . . . and afterwards the devil in hell, with burning pitch, brimstone, and tar, see.

THE NETHERLANDS

> JACOB: No; for Paul writes (2 Cor. 5:1), "If our earthly house of this tabernacle were dissolved, we have a building of God, a house not made with hands, eternal in the heavens."
>
> FR. CORNELIS: Bah! in hell, in hell. Expect nothing else than to go through this temporal fire into the eternal; hell yawns and gasps for your soul, you accursed, damned Anabaptist that you are, see.

The last Mennonite to suffer the death penalty in the Netherlands, according to van Braght, was a young woman by the name of Anneken van den Hove, who was buried alive near Brussels in 1597. After two years of imprisonment, during which every temptation had been offered her to recant without result, the court finally decided to send her to her death, in this case to be buried alive. After digging a pit into which she was cast, her executioners

> continued to throw dirt and thick sods of heath ground upon her body, up to her throat; but notwithstanding all their asking, threatening, or promising to release her and take her out of the pit if she would recant, it was all in vain and she would not hearken to it. Hence they threw much additional earth and sod upon her face and whole body, and stamped with their feet upon it that she should die the sooner. This was the end of this pious heroine of Jesus Christ.

2. INTERNAL DIVISIONS

It would seem that the common hardships which the Dutch Mennonites had to endure throughout the sixteenth century would have united them into a solid and cohesive body of believers. But such was not the case. Even in periods of the most bitter persecution they found time to argue over minor details of religious beliefs and human conduct, sometimes hardly more than the cut of a coat or the ceremonial manner of washing feet.

For this there are various explanations. First of all, Mennonites took their faith seriously. They were individualists. Members of the state churches could shift the responsibility for their religious decisions upon the shoulders of the priest or magistrate, or perhaps upon the theological doctor. Not so the Mennonites. They were their own priests, and must answer to God directly for all their spiritual shortcomings. Their church government was strictly congregational, each congregation being an independent ecclesiastical unit, with no organic connection with others except in an advisory capacity. There was no hierarchy with power to impose uniformity of doctrine or practice upon the whole body.

Mennonites, furthermore, strongly stressed right living as a corollary to right thinking. In the state church where everybody was practically born into membership, whether willing or not, not much stress could be placed on right conduct as a condition of continued membership. But to the Mennonites, the church must be a "pure church, without spot or wrinkle," and could be kept pure only by a rigid denial of spiritual fellowship to members who refused to conform to the standards of faith and practice set up by the group. This strict disciplinary use of the ban was one of the early sources of contention among the Dutch Mennonites, as we have already seen, in the days of Menno himself. Regional and linguistic differences, too, became a source of division among the brethren. It is interesting to note that most of the early factions separated more because of differences on human conduct than on points of theological opinion. Mennonites freely banned members for intemperance in drinking, extravagance in dress, evidence of dishonesty in business dealings, and infraction of the moral code.

The Flemish and Frisians

Soon after Menno's death one of the first distinct groups to be formed was the Flemish. This Flemish group consisted, as already noticed, of refugees who, because of the serious religious persecution in their own province of Flanders, had sought refuge in Friesland during the middle of the sixteenth century. They differed in some respects from the Frisians among whom they settled in racial traits, in language, and in religious customs and practices. Having had little contact with Menno Simons and with Dirk Philips, they were less rigid in the use of the ban than were their northern brethren, and less subject to the arbitrary control of the church elders in their spiritual life. In Friesland, the elders exercised considerable autocratic power, selecting the ministers, and holding all rights to baptize, while the Flemish were more democratic in their practice, allowing any preacher to baptize, and electing ministers by the entire congregation. Because of their closer contact with the French, and their occupation as weavers, the Flemish wore finer clothes than did their Frisian brethren, although it is said that the latter were more particular and scrupulous in their household arrangements. Because of these various differences, the Flemish refugees were regarded with a certain degree of suspicion by the Frisians at the time of their migration. Finding it difficult to affiliate with the native Frisians, the Flemish formed congregations of their own.

The natives of Friesland came to be known as Frisian Mennonites. After a number of vain attempts at reconciliation during the century, the Flemish and Frisians remained separate branches in many Mennonite communities for nearly two full centuries. The Flemish especially were determined to maintain their separate identity, freely banning the Frisians and rebaptizing any who wished to transfer their membership to their body. They excommunicated those who intermarried with any other branch.

Waterlanders and Upper Germans

The most influential and most tolerant of these different Mennonite groups, though perhaps at no time the most numerous, was the group popularly known as the Waterlanders. They were so named quite early in their history after the region in which they became most common, the Lowland coast along the Zuider Zee north of Amsterdam. These Waterlanders were opposed to the strict application of the rigid disciplinary rules adopted at Wismar in 1554 respecting the ban and avoidance in the case of husband and wife. They also disagreed with Menno's views on the incarnation of Christ.

At first this group was quite orthodox on the fundamentals of the Mennonite faith and practice. Their first confession of faith, published in 1577, which also happened to be the first Dutch Mennonite confession of faith, stressed all the traditional Mennonite doctrines, including the practice of foot washing. The later Hans de Ries confession, published in 1610, omitted the article on this practice, however, and specifically rejected the application of the practice of avoidance to conjugal relations. On nonresistance, the oath, *buitentrouw* (outside marriage), and the magistracy, as well as all the traditional theological issues regarding Christ, His person and purpose, the confession remains true to the general Mennonite views.

While the Waterlanders remained quite orthodox theologically during all this period, yet they very soon assumed a more tolerant attitude than the other groups toward the non-Mennonite world on such questions as outside marriage, admission of members from other branches of the church without rebaptism, participation in civil government, and general business associations. They were among the first also to adapt their church practices to the growing demands of the times, adopting audible prayer, educated and salaried ministers, and similar changes.

An outstanding leader of the Waterlander group was Hans de Ries, coauthor with Lubbert Gerritsz of the above-mentioned confession of faith, composer of a well-known hymnbook of that day, and compiler of a book of martyr stories which later developed into van Braght's famous *Martyrs Mirror*. De Ries was born of Catholic parents in Antwerp in 1553. Early in life he joined the Reformed Church, but later he joined the Waterlanders by whom he was soon elected to the ministry. Under suspicion by the authorities for his religious views, he was subjected to considerable persecution. He served a number of congregations including Amsterdam, Emden, and for forty years, Alkmaar. He took an active part in the fight against the Socinian movement in his day, and was a strong supporter of all attempts to bring about greater religious cooperation of the various Mennonite groups. He died in 1638.

Occupying somewhat of a middle position between the Waterlanders, the Frisians, and the Flemish were the Upper Germans. These consisted of some Dutch congregations but more of their neighboring German brethren. They were inclined to follow the advice of the Strassburg meeting of 1555 which advised moderation regarding the ban and avoidance. The reader will recall that the conference sent a delegation to Menno in 1556 to relay their concerns.

Further Divisions

These were the main Mennonite divisions in the Netherlands during the sixteenth century. But among both the Flemish and the Frisians there were divisions within divisions. Each developed left and right wings. Thus the former party sprouted an "Old Flemish" offshoot, and this offshoot was later subdivided into a "Groninger" Old Flemish and a "Danzig" Old Flemish wing. The Frisians in turn expanded into a "Hard" and a "Loose" or "Young" Frisian party. Most of these divisions were based on disciplinary rather than on theological considerations. Originally the terms Frisian and Flemish denoted racial as well as religious differences, but in course of time, as all these groups spread themselves throughout the country, these ethnic designations lost their significance.

All these factions spread throughout the churches of the Netherlands and in every community there were likely to be two or more Mennonite congregations side by side, but having no religious fellowship with one another. The Flemish were found for the most part in Groningen, South Holland and East Friesland; the Frisians in the northern provinces; the Waterlanders as just indicated, also in the North. All the factions, Frisian and Flemish especially, were transplanted by Dutch immigrants to daughter settlements around the Baltic; into Poland, and West Prussia in the sixteenth century, and later to Russia and even to the prairies of Kansas and Manitoba. While these factional names had almost entirely disappeared in the Netherlands by the beginning of the nineteenth century, they continued longer in the daughter colonies.

With these early divisions of the sixteenth century should be

THE NETHERLANDS 113

mentioned also several small groups that originated in the seventeenth. One of these was known as the Jan Jacobs-folk, and had its source in the Frisian church in Harlingen. There had been a discussion for some time among the Frisian congregations in general as to whether or not the ban should be strictly applied against those married outside of the church and whether candidates for membership from the Flemish should be admitted without rebaptism. It was just at this time, in 1599, that Jan Jacobs, an elder in the Frisian congregation, announced to his people that after consulting some of the ministers in his congregation, he had decided to insist upon the following rules among his brethren: no member would be permitted to sell any produce to a non-Mennonite husband of an excommunicated Mennonite woman if the woman herself could make use of the produce, but he might sell to the husband for his own direct use, or what could be used by neither; a Mennonite woman married to an unbelieving husband must prevent her children from being baptized into the state church; no Mennonite would be permitted to take passage or send freight on a vessel in which as much as one thirty-second part of the vessel was owned by an excommunicated former member, or in which any of the crew were such.

Jan Jacobs actually gained a small following for these stringent views, and established several congregations in various parts of the Netherlands, mostly in Friesland. Jan himself, getting into trouble with the Frisian government because of his strict rules, was banished from the province for a time; but wherever he went, he preached his peculiar practices and gained a few followers. The last Jan Jacobs-folk congregation merged with another congregation on the island of Ameland in 1855.

While various factions, together with numerous others not mentioned here, continued their separate existence more or less until the close of the eighteenth century, yet in the main, by that time the Mennonites in general might well be grouped together under two heads—the conservatives and liberals, or *Fine* and *Coarse*, as they were sometimes called. The more conservative included all those who held tenaciously to the old traditions—the rigorous use of the ban, marital avoidance, opposition to intermarriage, Menno's view of the incarnation, rebaptism of candidates for membership coming from other groups, lay preaching, foot washing, silent prayer, preaching from manuscript, simple clothes, and nonconformity to the world in general. Because they had departed so slightly from the ways of Menno, these regarded themselves as the real Mennonites, while the more tolerant were inclined to call themselves by the more general term *Doopsgezinde*.

The Reformed Church as Oppressor

It must not be forgotten that the toleration granted by William of Orange at the time of his conquest of the northern provinces was limited in scope. Religious toleration was still a relative term. State churches, whether Protestant or Catholic, still claimed exclusive possession of the souls of men. Complete soul liberty was not dreamed of by anyone in authority. For almost another two centuries, Mennonites were still compelled to pay taxes for the support of a state church which they did not attend, to have their marriages confirmed by that church, to build their meetinghouses on an inconspicuous back alley, without tower or bell, and to suffer humiliating restrictions of various sorts in the free exercise of their religious practices and civil privileges.

As already noted, the Mennonites were completely choked out of Flanders at an early date. But in the northern provinces, which eventually won their independence from Spanish tyranny, the Reformed Church fell heir to all the property, as well as to the ecclesiastical privileges of the former Catholic establishment. The Reformed Church was no less inclined to play the role of oppressor of nonconformists than its predecessor. In every province of the new state repeated attempts were made by the ecclesiastical authorities to completely suppress the Mennonite faith, though no longer by fire and sword. Persuasion and coercion were both tried.

Upon the insistence of the Reformed clergy, a public debate was held at Emden in 1578 between the Reformed leaders and the Mennonites, representing the brotherhood in the northern Netherlands and East Friesland. The Reformed hoped that by exposing the views of the Mennonites on such controversial questions as the oath, the incarnation, the use of the ban, baptism, freedom of the will, the magistracy, and war resistance, public opinion might be sufficiently aroused against them to justify governmental intervention.

In 1596 a similar public discussion was held at Leeuwarden for a similar purpose. This latter debate lasted several months, and ran through 150 sessions. Peter van Keulen was one of the Mennonite speakers in both of the above debates. Neither side was convinced of its errors in either of these discussions. But the Reformed clergy, having the sympathy of the ruling authorities, were declared the victors and did succeed in obtaining a government order temporarily forbidding Mennonite worship in Friesland. Several Mennonite preachers were fined for refusing to comply with the order, and some time later one of the conservative leaders, Jan Jacobs of Harlingen, was banished.

For a time, too, Mennonites were denied the right to conduct business enterprises in Leeuwarden. In Groningen preaching was prohibited, and it was decreed by the authorities that unbaptized children could not inherit property. In the city of Sneek the right of worship was denied as late as 1628. In one of their synods the Reformed clergy asked permission from the government to attend Mennonite meetings for the purpose of turning their misguided brethren from the errors of their ways, a request that was granted, to the great annoyance of those thus visited.

In 1604, at another synod, requests were made to prevent the ordination of young ministers. Later efforts would deny ministers the right of traveling from one congregation to another, and the right to baptize and preach. As late as 1664, at another synod, it was suggested that the erection of new meetinghouses be forbidden. And so throughout the entire century and beyond, synod after synod passed drastic recommendations in an attempt to completely suppress the Mennonite faith. Although they were occasionally able to influence governmental action, yet generally the Mennonites had such a good reputation for industry and integrity that the governments, both provincial and national, paid slight heed to these unreasonable demands of the state church.

The oppression of the Mennonites or *Doopsgezinden* in the Netherlands, often initiated locally by the jealous Reformed ministers and authorities, continued alike in Switzerland even into the decades when religious tolerance had been officially acknowledged. At this time it was mostly because some Mennonite ministers were suspected of teachings that were not tolerable in a country where a close tie existed between church and state.

This was the situation in the northern provinces of Friesland, Groningen, and East Friesland. It was somewhat different in the southern provinces and with the federal government of the Netherlands. Mennonites were still nonresistant, but they contributed heavily in emergency situations caused by disasters and war. As a result they enjoyed freedom and protection.

During the seventeenth century, when the Swiss Mennonites were still severely persecuted, the Dutch federal government and the mayor of Amsterdam interceded with the Swiss authorities in behalf of the persecuted Mennonites, speaking of the Dutch Mennonites in terms of highest praise.

3. THE GOLDEN AGE

The separatist tendencies of the sixteenth century were followed by numerous attempts not only to combine individual congregations of like faith and practice into more effective working organizations, but also to bring together groups that had the most in common. As early as 1566 the Mennonite congregations of four towns in Friesland—Harlingen, Franeker, Leeuwarden, and Dokkum—organized a union against "foreign" Mennonite influence, thereby starting the division into the Frisian and Flemish branches already mentioned.

Among a number of other early unification movements among various groups might be mentioned that of a number of congregations in western Friesland which, in 1639, united on a basis of a series of practical rules of living. In case of a second marriage, it is suggested in these rules that the inherited property interests of the children of the first marriage be carefully defined, so as to avoid later disagreements. Young people are advised to maintain high standards in their social relations, and to seek the advice of parents before entering the married state. Elaborate and expensive weddings are to be discouraged. Merchants, in their business dealing, are to avoid the usual visits to the taverns, thus escaping the danger of the intemperate use of strong drink. The use of tobacco, which is described as an unclean and expensive habit, is forbidden, as is part ownership of a merchant vessel which carries guns for protection. Plainness of dress and simplicity in the decoration of both ships and houses is prescribed. These regulations were read annually for nearly one hundred years before the congregations comprising this particular group.

In 1647 forty Waterlander congregations met to discuss their common problems. Thirty-two Flemish and Upper German churches did the same in 1649. Throughout the next hundred years and more, the merging and amalgamation process continued. By 1800 there was little left of the old factionalism, in spite of several new divisions. A few independent, isolated congregations remained that had somehow not kept pace with the spirit of the times. The organization in 1811 of the *Algemeene Doopsgezinde Sociëteit* completed the unification movement.

Early Confessions of Faith

It was these first attempts to find a common basis of union that called forth the first confessions of faith, nearly all of which fall well within the first quarter of the seventeenth century. One of the earliest, the *Concept of Cologne*, drawn up in 1591, represented the Frisians, Flemish, and Upper Germans along the lower Rhine. The Hans de Ries confession, written as early as 1610, became the recognized statement of faith of the Waterlanders, and was presented to the small band of the English Gainsboro exiles under

John Smyth in Amsterdam as representing the Mennonite doctrines. The *Olive Branch* drawn up in 1627 was, as its name suggests, definitely devoted to the cause of unity, that of the Flemish and Frisians. One of the best known, and later one of the most widely adopted of all the confessions, was *The Dordrecht Confession of Faith* of 1632, originally drafted by representatives of the Flemish branch of the church, but later also adopted by other groups, including the Upper German and Alsatian Mennonites. It is still today the best known statement of faith among the more conservative Mennonites in America. This statement of faith reflects the views of the conservatives on such questions as foot washing, shunning, and outside marriage; though on the doctrine of the incarnation it does not mention Menno's views, being satisfied with the declaration "which the faithful evangelists have given and left their description thereof."

It has already been mentioned that the Dutch Mennonites differed less among themselves in their doctrines than in the application of them. It seemed easier for them to think together than to live together. Their theology was decidedly biblical. Leaders of Mennonite thought were little concerned with the finespun theories and philosophical distinctions which puzzled the heads of the theologians of the day, but they expressed themselves in speech and writing on all questions of church doctrine in biblical terms, and let it go at that. It was not only much easier, but safer. Their statements, well buttressed with scriptural references, were inclined toward a literal interpretation of the Bible.

Socinians and Arminians

Among the charges made by the Reformed clergy against the Mennonites during the first half of the seventeenth century was the close affiliation between the more liberal-minded groups of the Mennonites with certain unorthodox religious movements that swept through the Netherlands at this time—Socinianism and Arminianism.

Socinianism was an anti-Calvinist, anti-trinitarian religious movement that had its origin in Poland during the latter part of the sixteenth century, and had found its way into the Netherlands during the first half of the seventeenth. The heart of Socinianism was its rejection of the doctrine of the Trinity; however, it retained a belief in the inspiration of the Scriptures, in miracles, and many other orthodox views. Jesus, according to this view, was a mere human being, though miraculously born, leading a perfect and holy life on earth, and risen from the dead. He did not atone for the sins of men, though through his teaching, and his perfect example, and by showing men a better way, he became, in a way, the Savior of men, worthy of the highest adoration and worship. Socinians were advocates of religious toleration, and, like the Mennonites, were opposed to the oath and war. They claimed to work for the restoration of the beliefs and practices of early Christianity.

Arminianism, later usually spoken of as the movement of the *Remonstrants*, was a protest against the extreme hyper-Calvinism of the Reformed Church. There was much in the teachings of the Remonstrants that appealed to the Mennonites, especially their common belief in the freedom of the will. For a time the attraction seemed mutual. In the beginning, before the Remonstrants had clearly formulated their religious views, some of them were inclined to accept the Hans de Ries confession as a satisfactory statement of their religious faith. The Mennonites, in turn, frequently worshipped with the Remonstrants; prospective ministers occasionally attended the Remonstrant seminary at Amsterdam; and Mennonites and Remonstrants sometimes exchanged ministers. During the early part of the following century one wing of the Mennonite church was called the *Remonstrant Mennonites*.

And so it was to be expected that the Mennonites would share with both the Socinians and the Remonstrants the opposition and persecution at times directed by both the state and the established church against these proscribed religious faiths.

Collegiants

There was another religious movement in the Netherlands, called the *Collegiants*, which exerted considerable influence upon the spiritual life of certain of the Dutch Mennonites. This movement, which drew rather heavily upon both Socinian and Remonstrant sources for its religious practices, had as its aim the spiritualizing of existing denominations, and represented in a way a protest against the dogmatism of both the Calvinists and the Remonstrants. There were no doctrinal tests for membership in the group. Anyone spiritually minded and baptized as an adult was welcomed to their meetings. These meetings, called *Collegia*, gave the movement its name. Because the town of Rhynsburg, near Leyden, finally became the chief headquarters of the Collegiants, they were sometimes called *Rhynsburgers*.

These Rhynsburgers were quite liberal in their religious thinking; they formulated no creeds; and like the Quakers after them, they spiritualized the sacraments and ceremonies except for baptism, which was by immersion. Like the Quakers, too, they denied the necessity of an ordained ministry. Their informal meetings for worship, frequently held during the week and open to members of any church, were often attended by the Mennonites. Collegia were also formed in many Mennonite congregations.

A War Among the Lambs *(Lammerenkrijgh)*

The affiliation with the Collegiants not only brought added oppression to certain Mennonite groups by both the state church and government, but it was also partly responsible for another far-reaching division among the Mennonites themselves. The trouble began in the Flemish congregation in Amsterdam. This congregation had two practicing physicians as ministers, serving without pay—Galenus Abrahamsz de Haan, and Samuel Apostool. Of these two, de Haan was the more progressive. He came from a long line of religious leaders. His father had been a barber and surgeon, a common combination in those days, as well as a preacher. His great-grandfather was the martyr, Gillis van Aken, mentioned elsewhere. A student of medicine, as well as of theology, he could not help being influenced by the scientific discoveries and the radical philosophical theories that were revolutionizing the thought of his day—the contributions of such men as Harvey, Descartes, and Kepler, some of whom lived in his own city of Amsterdam.

After de Haan had been elected to the ministry by his congregation in 1646, he attended the Collegiant meetings in his city, and was in sympathy with their views and practices. He was a great friend of youth, and in his later years, seeing the need among his people of a trained ministry, he gathered together a number of likely young candidates for theological instruction, thus laying the foundation for the later Mennonite Theological Seminary.

Not all the members of de Haan's congregation agreed with his views. In 1664 about seven hundred, under the leadership of the other doctor-preacher—Samuel Apostool—withdrew from the mother church and set up a new one which met in a building with the sign of the sun, for which reason they came to be known as the *Zonists*. The original church, worshipping near a house with the sign of a lamb, were distinguished as the *Lamists*. This new division soon spread beyond the borders of the local congregation into many congregations throughout the Netherlands, absorbing many of the earlier small factions, and dividing the whole brotherhood once more into two groups. Both Zonist and Lamist groups were formed throughout the land. The more conservative Zonists defended their views of the Trinity, with a trend toward Calvinism, and kept the traditional religious practices. They forbade their members to fellowship in any way with the

Collegiants, to share the communion table with them, or to follow the practices of permitting laymen to preach. It was not until the beginning of the nineteenth century that the division was finally healed.

Quakers and Mennonites

It was about this time, too, that the English Quakers, who had just started in England, tried to get a foothold among the Dutch Mennonites, from whom perhaps they may, in an earlier period, have imbibed some of their distinctive doctrines and practices, and with whom at least they had much in common. All the pioneer founders and missionaries, including Fox and Penn themselves, made repeated visits to the Mennonite congregations along the lower Rhine on proselyting tours, although usually with but slight success. As early as 1657, according to a Quaker historian,

> Ames, Stubbs, and Caton came over to Holland, they moved some of their own countrymen with their Doctrines to such a degree that they raised some disturbance in the Reformed church, and brought a few of the Country Mennonites to their side, and these made the name of Quakers first known in these Provinces.

A little later, the same writer, speaking of the work of Caton, continues,

> He goes back to Amsterdam, in which city there is a small church gathered and that principally of the Dutch Anabaptists.

The Yearly Meeting of London in 1694 reports that at Twist and Hoorn

> there is great openness among the Mennonites to hear the Friends tell the Truth.

That the Mennonites, however, were not always eager to hear the "Truth" is evident from an episode which took place in the course of the proselyting tour of an English Quaker to the Amsterdam Mennonites, who in his visit observed

> many things that he disliked among both the churches of which the whole city consisted (Reformed and Mennonite) and he wrote a letter to each. 'Twas a tart letter full of contumelious Accusations and Reproofs as if the religion of both of them was only a barren profession, and their lives the height of all manner of Hipocracie and Impiete, a denial of God, concluding with a denunciation of threats and execrations against them as if it were in the name and by the command of the Divine Being himself. The letters were sent to Harling by Cornelis Rudolf, and James Byland, the father and son, all of them citizens of Amsterdam, and former Mennonites, but now turned Quakers. So to Harling they all go.

Among the staunch defenders of the Mennonite cause against

the Quakers during this period was Galenus Abrahamsz de Haan. Croese, the Quaker historian, leaves us an interesting account of a debate held in Amsterdam in 1677 between de Haan and both George Fox and William Penn:

> William Penn and Galen Abraham, a physician and preacher among those Mennonites which we account of all, or the most part of them at least to be Socinians, at the same time almost at Amsterdam, disputed at a private house of the signs of the new church, and extraordinary call of the ministers. And after such a manner as Penn who after the manner of the nation, spake nothing but in a premeditated and set form of speech, showed upon this occasion that when he had a mind to it, he was not wanting in the faculty of answering extempore to the sudden and large Discourse of others; but the other (Galenus) so abounded in multitudes of words as he never came to the stress of the matter where the cause lay; and where he could not tell how to bring close arguments to the purpose, he either very ingeniously put off answering at all, or turned it into a Joke and Banter, and so it ended after the same rate as most Disputations commonly do.

Anabaptists and Baptists

In the meantime many Dutch Anabaptists and Mennonites had found their way across the Channel to England all through the latter part of the sixteenth century. In fact, long before the Reformation there had been more or less of commercial intercourse between the wool growers and manufacturers of the island kingdom and the skilled artisans and textile workers of the Lowland towns. But during the sixteenth century, and especially under the reign of the last two Spanish rulers, there was a steady stream of Dutch immigrants of a new type arriving on the east coast of England—political and religious refugees. Among the latter were hundreds, and perhaps thousands, of Anabaptists.

Not that Anabaptists, of course, were more welcome to Henry VIII and Elizabeth than to Philip II; but mingling with throngs of political refugees against whom there was no suspicion, speaking a foreign tongue, practicing a strange religion, and leading a quiet, unobtrusive life, these Dutch Anabaptists were able to hide their identity, and escape the persecution that would have been theirs had they been natives of the same faith.

That the English ruling authorities, however, both state and church, were as little inclined to endure the tolerant views of the Anabaptists, as were those of other countries, once they were recognized, is clearly evident. As early as 1534, Henry VIII issued a royal proclamation against them, ordering them out of the kingdom on pain of death. This decree was repeated by every English ruler during the sixteenth century. That the church, too, feared Anabaptism is shown by the fact that every confession of faith of the various churches—Anglican and Presbyterian—found it necessary, among other articles of their belief, to specifically repudiate all Anabaptist or Mennonite doctrines.

To be sure, in the early part of the century, it was undoubtedly the Münster brand of the movement that the English feared. Then too, it must be remembered that the term Anabaptist was used at that time to signify all kinds of radical beliefs and movements. But the specific mention in the confessions of the last half of the century of such distinctive subjects as the magistracy, oath, war, and even Menno's views on the incarnation, is evidence that many of the Anabaptists who came to England during that period were Mennonites.

With all their attempts to live a secluded life, however, native Anabaptists, as well as the Dutch Mennonite refugees, were occasionally sent to the block. One example was that of a group of some thirty Dutch exiles whom a contemporary writer spoke of as "Menno's" people, who were arrested on Easter day of 1575 while holding a religious service in a private home in one of the suburbs of London. Suspecting their identity, the bishop of London, before whom they were tried, asked them four test questions as to their beliefs regarding the oath, the magistracy, baptism, and the incarnation. Satisfied that they were Mennonites, the bishop sent them back to prison. The prisoners had many friends among the people. Foxe, the English martyrologist, sent a petition to Queen Elizabeth in their behalf, as did the Dutch Reformed Church in London. But all to no avail. Five of the number recanted and, after doing public penance in the courtyard of St. Paul's, were set free; a number of them escaped; and a few were released. But two of them, Jan Pieters, "a poor man upward of fifty years old, with nine children," and Hendrik Terwoort, "a handsome and respectable man about twenty-six years old, a goldsmith by trade, who had been married about eight weeks before he was apprehended," paid the extreme penalty for their beliefs. They were burned at the stake at Smithfield, according to the Mennonite martyrologist, van Braght, "without even being dispatched first by strangling or with powder according to the custom of the country."

While Anabaptism as a whole made little headway during this period among the English, yet it cannot be denied that the various separatist movements which arose during the latter part of the century in the very centers along the eastern coast of England, where Dutch artisans and political and religious refugees were most numerous, owed much of their distinctive principles to the Dutch Anabaptist leaven.

One of the earliest of the leaders for an independent church was Robert Browne of Norwich, who in 1580 was forced by religious

THE NETHERLANDS   123

persecution to take his congregation to Holland. Here at Middleburg, he established his church for a time based on congregational principles. A part of his group, it is said, later joined the Mennonites, but Browne himself returned to England where, after a period of disappointment, he gave up the struggle and lapsed back into the Anglican fold.

Not long after, another separatist congregation was formed in London under the leadership of Francis Johnson and Henry Ainsworth. These, too, were forced into exile, finally gathering together their congregation again in Amsterdam.

The most important of these independent groups, however, was the one at Gainsboro, and the neighboring village of Scrooby under the pastorate of one John Smyth. This congregation is of interest chiefly because in its membership it included a number of men who later played an important role in both English and American political and religious history—John Robinson, William Brewster, and William Bradford of the Pilgrim fathers; and Thomas Helwys and John Murton, founders of the English Baptist church. In 1606 Smyth and his Gainsboro followers found it expedient to leave for Amsterdam. John Robinson, who in the meantime had become pastor of the Scrooby contingent of the original congregation, followed with his party to the same city the following year. Smyth, refusing to join the Johnson group which had already been established in Amsterdam, set up his own independent congregation. Robinson also decided to retain his separate organization, but soon left Amsterdam for Leyden.

Although all these English groups in Holland must have come into close contact with the Dutch Mennonites, with whom they had much more in common in their religious doctrines and civic principles than with the Dutch state church, yet only a few of the laymen and but one of the leaders accepted in full the Mennonite position on complete religious toleration and a democratic and voluntary church.

John Smyth, however, and a goodly portion of his company had the courage to follow the path of religious liberty all the way to its source—Anabaptism—a voluntary, democratic church, composed of new-born men and women, entirely free from the state, granting to all complete freedom of conscience in matters of religion. Smyth came to this conclusion within two years after his arrival at Amsterdam. Convinced by this time that the New Testament church must not only be independent, but it must also be voluntary and composed of a regenerate, and necessarily adult, membership, he naturally concluded that baptism, the symbol of initiation into the church, must be administered upon confession of faith only. To think was to act. His old baptism consequently, administered in infancy, was not valid. But where could he find the baptism he desired?

Evidently the language barrier and other forbidding circumstances prevented the Gainsboro exiles at this time from cultivating a spirit of fellowship with any of the neighboring Mennonite churches. Not finding just then what he regarded as a true New Testament church anywhere, Smyth baptized himself, then Helwys and Murton and some forty of his followers.

A year later the baptist's tender conscience again troubled him. In the meantime his small congregation had been worshiping in a large bake house owned by a Waterlander Mennonite by the name of Jan Munter. Through Munter, Smyth came into closer contact with the Mennonite church, of which Lubbert Gerritsz was pastor. Satisfied now that the Mennonites were a true apostolic church, and troubled somewhat, no doubt, by his hasty act of self-baptism, the former now, with thirty-one of his members, applied to the Mennonites for admission into their church. Helwys, Murton, and a few others, however, refused to follow their leader in this step, not because they denied that the Mennonites were a true church, but rather because their pride forbade the repudiation of their earlier act of rebaptism. They in turn wrote the Mennonites requesting that Smyth's application be refused.

The Mennonites, due to internal disagreement, at first delayed action. Soon after this, Smyth died. Finally some of his followers were accepted into membership with the Mennonite congregation. In the meantime, in 1611, Helwys and his group had returned to their former home where they organized the first Baptist church in England. For a number of years Helwys and his followers kept up a friendly correspondence with the Amsterdam Mennonites, finally applying for union with them, ready even to waive the divergent views regarding the oath, magistracy, and war resistance that had thus far kept them apart. But the Amsterdam Mennonites, still true to form, delayed and flirted with the idea of union too long. With the introduction of immersion among the English Baptists in 1640, and as the native movement became more securely rooted in its own soil, all hope of a union between the two vanished. From now on, the two branches of the Anabaptist movement—the continental Mennonites and the English Baptists—each went its own separate way.

As to the direct influence of the Dutch Mennonites upon the various English separatist movements, it will thus be seen, there may be some difference of opinion. In the case of the Baptists, as just noted, the connection is direct and clear. Many Baptist historians acknowledge not only a spiritual kinship with the early continental Anabaptists but also a direct connection with the

Dutch Mennonites. They claim Menno Simons as one of the heroes of their church.

In the case of Congregationalism, the relationship is not so direct. It would seem, however, that in view of the fact that the cardinal principle of Congregationalism—an independent church—was an Anabaptist doctrine well known for nearly a century in the regions where Congregationalism had its origin, one can hardly escape the assumption of some connection. Many Congregational historians acknowledge a heavy debt to the Dutch Anabaptists and Mennonites, both in Holland and England, for substantial contributions to English Congregationalism.

Quakerism, too, must have drawn upon Mennonite sources for many of its essential doctrines and practices. It, too, first saw the light of day in those regions of southeastern England where the other separatist movements began. And it incorporated within its body of beliefs almost *in toto* the tenets of the continental Mennonites, including the whole program of nonresistance with all its implications.

A Communal Society

It may not be out of place here to briefly mention the first attempt to plant a Dutch Mennonite colony on this side of the Atlantic. Pieter Cornelisz Plockhoy of Zierikzee, seemingly a member of one of the Mennonite Collegiant groups and a dreamer of social utopias, appeared in London in 1659, petitioning parliament to establish, somewhere in England or Ireland, an experimental cooperative commonwealth in which there was to be religious toleration, the abolition of all poverty, and perfect equality of all classes—economic, social, and political.

Failing to accomplish his object in London, the Dutch reformer returned to Holland, where he actually succeeded in interesting the city of Amsterdam, which had already made several unsuccessful attempts to establish a colony on its recently purchased lands in New Netherlands along the Delaware, in his scheme. According to the agreement made with the city authorities, Amsterdam was to furnish the money for locating a colony of twenty-five Mennonite families in the new world.

Plockhoy provided an elaborate set of rules, regulating in minutest details the whole political and economic life of the colony. Like the proposed experiment in England, this colony was to be placed on a cooperative basis. All were to be equal in their rights and privileges. There was to be no slavery; free schools were to be set up for all. There was to be religious toleration; but to insure the new venture against any disturbing religious influences from the outside, "Catholics, Jews, Stiff-necked Quakers, and foolhardy believers in the Millenium" were barred from joining the settlement. In keeping, too, with the general Collegiant practice of granting laymen as well as the ordained preachers the right to conduct religious worship, there was to be no provision for gentlemen of the cloth.

Plockhoy actually succeeded in 1662 in planting his colony on the Horekill, in the present state of Delaware, but only two years later the English conquest of the Dutch settlements in New Amsterdam "plundered what belonged to the Quaking Society of Plockhoy to a naile." In 1694 Plockhoy, now grown old and blind, together with his wife, wandered into the village of Germantown one day where he found a home for his few remaining years among his fellow Mennonites, who in the meantime had been more successful than he in establishing a Mennonite settlement farther up on the Delaware.

Publications

From what has already been said, it is quite evident that the seventeenth century, and especially the latter part, marked the peak of Mennonite growth both as to numbers and as to spiritual and cultural self-consciousness. Much of the enduring literature of the denomination was written and published during this period. As already suggested, nearly all the confessions of faith originated within the first half of the century. The first attempt to collect and publish the complete works of Menno Simons was made in 1646, and the last Dutch edition appeared in 1681.

The most important Mennonite production of the time was the famous *Martyrs Mirror*, compiled in 1660 by Tieleman Jansz van Braght, a Mennonite minister at Dordrecht. This monumental collection of martyr stories of the Anabaptists and others of the defenseless faith was not entirely an original work but a revision and an enlargement of several former collections published earlier in the century. The last Dutch edition to appear was printed in 1685, after which the interest in martyr stories began to decline. The book has been printed once in England and once in Germany since, and numerous times in America in both German and English, but never again in Holland.

Not to be omitted here is mention of the well-known *Biestkens Bible*, published especially for the Mennonites by Nikolaes Biestkens, a Mennonite publisher at Emden. Published for the first time in the sixteenth century, it ran through more than fifty reprintings before the close of the seventeenth century. This edition was based on the Lutheran translation, with such minor changes as suited more nearly the Mennonite views on controversial passages. It was the first Dutch Bible to introduce paragraph divisions in the text. It was in general use among the Mennonites until well toward the close of the eighteenth century, and among the Old Flemish at Balk as late as 1837.

Among other Mennonite authors of this period must be included Tobias Govertsen van den Wyngaert, who was born in Amsterdam in 1587, and served his church as minister for fifty years. He was the author of numerous theological treatises well known in his day, and represented his congregation in 1632 at the Dordrecht convention which drew up the *Dordrecht Confession of Faith*.

Jan Philipsz Schabaelje, for a time minister at Alkmaar but later in life a bookseller in Amsterdam, also wrote a number of books including a *Life of Jesus*, published at Alkmaar in 1647 and reissued several times afterward. His best known work, however, among later Mennonite readers was a brief history of the biblical world included in *Lusthof des Gemoets*, recited by a disembodied spirit who, returning from his ethereal abode at stated intervals, received his information of what was going on in this world from the lips of Adam, Noah, and one called Simon Cleophas. The book first appeared in 1635, was reissued several times soon after, and by 1744, according to one historian, had already gone through fifty Dutch editions. It finally appeared in a German edition under the title *Die Wandelnde Seele*. It has also appeared a number of times in America. The book has also been translated into English several times. It seems to have a peculiar fascination for the Pennsylvania Germans and is still widely read by them, both Mennonites and others.

Lubbert Gerritsz and Hans de Ries published a *Brief Confession of Faith* in 1618. Lubbert Gerritsz was born at Amersfort in 1535, and was ordained as elder by Dirk Philips at Hoorn. In the Flemish-Frisian controversy in 1567, his congregation sided in with the Frisians; and thus Gerritsz remained the minister of a Frisian and Upper German congregation. Later on, because of differences between himself and the majority of his congregation on questions of the ban and other strict disciplinary measures, he took the more liberal side, and as a result was expelled by the conservatives. He then became the leader in Amsterdam of what was known as the "Loose" Frisian wing. A little later this group joined with the Upper Germans and the Waterlanders into a united congregation. Besides his coauthorship of the de Ries confession, Gerritsz wrote a number of religious treatises. He was a particular friend of the poet Joost van den Vondel, and had his portrait painted by the celebrated painter M. van Mierevelt. Both were Mennonites.

Mennonite Artists

The process of growing into the culture of the country and the acceptance of it was a gradual one that was brought about through a number of factors. When persecution was relaxed, and the piety, frugality, and industry of the Mennonites brought about prosperity, the foundation was laid for a greater participation in cultural activities. The Golden Age of the Netherlands and its prosperity and progress in culture and the fine arts speeded up this process.

After the Reformed Church had been established in the Netherlands as the state church, Mennonites enjoyed some freedom and were able to concentrate in the cities such as Amsterdam, Haarlem, Leiden, Leeuwarden, Groningen, Emden, and others. In the Dutch Golden Age of the seventeenth century the Dutch Mennonites were not only appreciating works of art but some were creators of works of art. Thus it was possible for the Dutch "Shakespeare," Joost van den Vondel, to be deacon of a Mennonite church of Amsterdam. His dramas have remained popular to this day.

The following brief summary of some early Dutch Mennonite artists is a selection from a list of twenty-three Mennonite artists of the Netherlands in the post-Reformation era.

Carel van Mander (1548-1608) was not only an artist of significance, but also an art critic and historian who wrote one of the first Dutch histories of art, *Het Schilderboek*, which was reprinted numerous times. Mander's artistic contribution was not restricted to painting and art history, however. As an active member of the Mennonite church, he wrote many hymns and published them in *De Gulden Harpe* (The Golden Harp) which first appeared in 1599. This book was used as a hymnal among the Mennonites not only in Holland but also in West Prussia.

Another outstanding Mennonite artist-poet was Jan Luiken (1649-1712). Among the wealth of poetry and etchings which made him famous are his illustrations of *Martyrs Mirror* and the Bible. His son Casper joined him as an etcher. The catalog of their etchings alone fills two large printed volumes. Of these, 3,275 etchings are known to be Jan Luiken's.

Among those who were second- or third-generation Anabaptists and became well-known artists, and who consciously made use of their talent to promote their religious convictions was Lambert Jacobsz (1598-1636). His paintings usually depict biblical scenes and show an Italian influence. Another Mennonite artist, Govert Flinck (1615-1660), was taught by Lambert Jacobsz. Like his teacher, Flinck usually painted biblical subjects.

Two famous landscape painters, Jacob van Ruisdael (1628-82)

and his uncle, Salomon van Ruisdael (1600-70), were also Mennonites. The works of the van Ruisdaels are classic in form and universally known. They can be found in all the large museums of Europe and the United States.

The question as to whether Rembrandt van Rÿn (1606-69) was a Mennonite has been raised repeatedly. Although Rembrandt was not a member of the Mennonite church in the official sense, careful investigations of his life, his contacts, and his works of art reveal that he was in close touch with outstanding Mennonite leaders of Amsterdam, through whom he received information and inspiration as an artist. Many of the art critics state that his art, not only his paintings and etchings of the Mennonite minister Anslo of Amsterdam, but also his large number of paintings and etchings of biblical subjects, reveals the spirit and atmosphere of seventeenth-century Mennonite ideals and principles more than the Calvinistic theology which was prevalent in the Netherlands of his day. It is also a fact that he belonged to a spiritual fellowship among whom Collegiant Mennonites played a significant role. If his paintings devoted primarily to biblical subjects express some basic Mennonite beliefs, we are entitled to call him a Mennonite fellow traveler in the best sense of the word.

Other Contributions

Although the Mennonites of this period were noted in the main for their achievements in the business world, yet they contributed their full share to the cultural and scientific development of their day. They took especially to medical science. There were an unusual number of doctors among them, and since their ministry was unsalaried and untrained theologically, Mennonite preachers were frequently chosen from the medical profession. Besides Samuel Apostool and his colleague Galenus Abrahamsz de Haan, doctor-preachers of the Amsterdam congregation, might be added the name of Anton van Dale, drafted into the ministry from the doctor's office in the church at Haarlem. A great linguist, but not a popular preacher, it was said that he was too prone to flaunt his erudition by the frequent use of Latin and Greek phrases which were beyond the understanding of his congregation. He devoted much of his spare time to the writing of theological treatises, especially against the Socinians, and also a book on medical healing which attained considerable popularity in his day.

The most distinguished Mennonite doctors of this century, though they were not preachers, were undoubtedly the Bidloo brothers: Nicolaas, of Zaandam, personal physician to Peter the Great of Russia during his shipbuilding student days at Holland,

and later the director of the Czar's first school of medicine in Moscow; Govert, body physician to William III; and Lambert, a well-known apothecary of the day.

Another famous minister during this time, though not a doctor, was Cornelis Claesz Anslo, a wealthy Amsterdam merchant, elected to the ministry in the Waterlander church in 1617. Anslo is best known because of his intimate friendship with the great Dutch Mennonite poet Joost van den Vondel, who was at the same time also a deacon in the same church. He is also known for his association with the great painter Rembrandt, who painted several portraits of him, including the famous picture *A Mennonite Preacher and the Widow*, now a prized possession of the National Gallery in Berlin.

Mennonite Pietism

The Mennonites of the Netherlands were open to a more individualistic, emotionally expressed spiritual life than was usually the case in the Calvinistic Dutch Reformed Church. One could trace this tradition back to the days of Menno Simons and Dirk Philips. It became particularly noticeable when Mennonite "orthodoxy" was making room for a *Vrijzinngheid* (liberal views). Jeme Deknatel (1698-1759), a well-known minister and writer of devotional works, is credited with having brought the influence of Pietism to the Dutch Mennonites. Influenced by the Moravian Brethren, he was a close friend of Zinzendorf. John Wesley, the great eighteenth-century revivalist, was a guest in his home. Deknatel was a chief promoter of a personally experienced conversion throughout his lifetime in his Amsterdam congregation. His influence, however, went far beyond his congregation.

Deknatel was a close friend of the van der Smissen family of Altona-Hamburg and Friedrichstadt. The large library of the seventeenth and eighteenth centuries of Anabaptist and Pietistic literature in Hamburg and the Mennonite Library and Archives of Bethel College are an unusual record and source of information about the type of Mennonite Pietism that existed and the contacts which the van der Smissens had with the Dutch, English, and German Pietists of their day. Balthasar Denner of Altona probably had the greatest influence in the spread of "Mennonite" Pietism at many places, and particularly through his volumes of published sermons throughout Europe and even among the early American Mennonites.

4. A PERIOD OF DECLINE

The eighteenth century witnessed a great decline among the

Dutch Mennonites both numerically and spiritually. The decrease in the entire Mennonite population, according to some writers, was from one hundred sixty thousand in 1700 to thirty thousand by 1820. In many cases whole congregations disappeared, almost one hundred it was said; and in nearly all the larger cities there were material losses. The Mennonite population in Amsterdam fell from approximately twenty-five hundred in 1743 to thirteen hundred in 1832, while in Haarlem the reduction during the same period was from three thousand to one thousand. Other cities told the same story.

The reasons for this loss in membership were many and varied. First of all, perhaps, should be mentioned the spirit of liberalism which dominated the religious life and thought of all western Europe during this period. The Mennonites in the prosperous commercial Dutch cities did not escape the blighting influences of English deism and French and German rationalism, to say nothing of the Socinianism of their own country of that day. The liberalizing influences of the French Revolution only added impetus to these tendencies among the Mennonites. Naturally the growing laxity in enforcing the old traditional regulations against mixed marriages, open communion, and worldly conformity in general contributed but little toward holding together a small religious group, the members of which were still but a tolerated people, and denied social and civil privileges which would be freely granted them if they cast their lot with the state church. One writer suggests that toleration is but a poor match for persecution in steeling the human heart against worldly temptations. Some wanted office, others social standing, and still others wanted wives or husbands of the Reformed faith. All these could be had by joining the state church. The old regulations against most of these practices had been largely abandoned among the more liberal wings of the church by the beginning of the nineteenth century.

The lack of trained ministers, in fact a dearth of ministers of any sort, is given as another reason for the decline. With no adequate facilities of their own for training their ministers, the larger city congregations were inclined to select persons trained in the Remonstrant schools, as already seen, and frequently even the Remonstrants themselves, whose liberal views contributed little to the maintenance of Mennonite unity. With little or no material support, for the *liefdepreeker* (lay minister) was still common, there was small inducement for the young men of the church to enter the ministerial profession.

To all these specific causes should be added another—more general, but nevertheless not less effective—the loosely organized congregational type of church government. Experience proves that a loosely organized religious movement cannot compete with a highly organized, strictly governed, institutionalized church. History repeated itself in the case of the Mennonites.

A New Confession of Faith

Cornelis Ris, a minister in Hoorn, North Holland, wrote a new confession of faith in 1766 in order to present a basis for the reunion of the Waterlander and Frisian Mennonites. Gradually this confession was accepted by these two groups on a local scale and also by other Mennonite groups at various places. It became even more popular abroad than in the Netherlands.

Soon the Hamburg-Altona Mennonite Church accepted the Cornelis Ris Confession, which was still in the Dutch language. In 1776 a German edition was published which spread to various parts of Germany. Carl J. van der Smissen, who came from Friedrichstadt, Germany, to the Mennonite school at Wadsworth, Ohio, revised the Cornelis Ris Confession for use in North America. His son Carl H. A. van der Smissen published the Ris Confession in 1895 as an appendix to his story of the Mennonites. Since 1902 a number of editions in the English and German language of the Cornelis Ris Confession have been published by the General Conference Mennonite Church as its recognized confession of faith.

Cornelis Ris kept in mind the need of justifying the views of the Mennonites against their attackers. The Ris statement agreed with the anti-Socinian doctrines of the state church on such controversial questions as the Trinity, the incarnation, and the redemptive functions of Jesus. It did not, however, freely endorse their hyper-Calvinistic views on the freedom of the will and predestination. Ris's attempt to satisfy both his conscience and the state church at the same time on this point is interesting. He says,

> God decreed to impart His love, His grace, and His gifts in larger measure to some than to others, and this according to His own will and pleasure, but His loving-kindness is so great and so far-reaching, and so all inclusive, that no one is excluded therefrom without just cause.

At any rate there is little need for mortal man to puzzle his brain about such matters, so thinks Ris, for "in the wisdom and ways of God, especially in this matter, there are depths which will ever be regarded beyond our ability to fathom in this life."

On such Mennonite doctrines as baptism on confession of faith, nonresistance, the oath, and opposition to the holding of civil office, the Ris Confession held the usual Mennonite views. On

THE NETHERLANDS

certain practices on which Mennonites were divided, the author was inclined to straddle the issue, attempting to satisfy all parties. On baptism he justified both forms. Baptism, he said

> we understand to be an immersing of the whole body in water, or a liberal sprinkling with water (which we in these northern latitudes consider more generally appropriate since the same blessings are signified).

On the church ban, another source of endless confusion, moderation is advised. As a final measure of discipline the unfaithful

> must finally by a decision of the whole congregation be excluded from membership, and denied all church fellowship until he is truly converted, and gives evident proof thereof. However, all must be done with true regard to position and circumstance, yet without respect to person.

The Fine and the Coarse

A good description of the various groups of the Dutch Mennonites of this period is to be found in a book written in 1743 by a German, M. S. F. Rues, who had come to the Netherlands especially to make a study of the Mennonites. According to this book, the various Mennonite factions might well be classified under two general heads—the *Fine* and the *Coarse*. Under these two general heads are represented every shade of religious practice, ranging from the extremely conservative Old Flemish, to the liberal wings of the Waterlanders, and Remonstrants. The Fine still represented fairly well at this time what all Mennonites had once been; while the Coarse pointed the way to what all would finally be in the future.

Among the practices and beliefs still common to the various groups of the Fine were rigid adherence to the old confessions of faith, a close following of the teaching of Menno, including his view of the incarnation and his strict use of the ban as a disciplinary measure. Because of this strict adherence to the teachings of Menno, these groups of the Fine wished to be known as Mennonites, in contrast with the liberals who preferred the less personal name of *Doopsgezinde*. Among the "Finest," an excommunicant was not permitted to attend meeting with his former brethren. Marriage with outsiders was still forbidden, and candidates for membership from other factions were received only upon rebaptism. Shunning of an excommunicant was still common, including in its application the conjugal relations. Among the *Danziger*, however, the practice was not carried beyond the point of forbidding the husband or wife in question to eat at the same table with the one placed under the ban.

Nonresistance was practiced to its logical limits. Suing at law was not thought of, nor holding of office. Carrying of side arms, a common social custom of the day, was prohibited, likewise the transportation of goods in an armed vessel.

Worldliness in all its varied forms was carefully guarded against. The cut of a man's coat and the style of a woman's dress were still a matter of strict regulation. Black was the acceptable color for both. Buttons, shoestrings instead of buckles, wall pictures, stained glass, and portraits were all on the proscribed list among the strictest. Men were supposed to wear beards, but the ministers complained that it was becoming increasingly common for the young men to appear with shaved faces. Of course wigs in that bewigged age were not for the chosen of God, and were allowed only occasionally when the wearer could show that he wore one not from a sense of pride but of necessity.

All this was best exhibited among the humble country folk and the more conservative Fine groups. In the cities the women, especially, were inclined to chafe somewhat under these dress restrictions. They were beginning to wear silk gowns, and carry hymnbooks with silver clasps, if they could afford such luxury. Some of them powdered their hair, and even came to church, so says Rues, with palm-leaf fans. The ministers, it is said, often looked through their fingers at these infractions of the rules among the sisters.

The ministry included three ranks—the *Oudste* (elder), the minister, and the deacon. Each congregation had its own elder who baptized, administered the communion, and performed other rites. All ministers among the Fine served without pay and were without special theological preparation.

Worship was simple and austere. Sermons were read from manuscript in a singsong fashion by the minister as he sat in a chair somewhat elevated above his fellow preachers on a platform in the forepart of the plain meetinghouse. In contrast to those of the more liberal branches, ministers wore no special garb. The worshipers prayed, kneeling, and in silence. Collections for charity were taken after the services, but the collection boxes were placed at the exit. Since absolute harmony was required as a prerequisite to the observance of the communion service, it was often irregularly celebrated. All factions among the conservatives practiced foot washing, although the ceremony was observed in two forms. The *Groninger* made it a part of every communion service; while the *Danziger*, following the teaching of Menno himself, practiced it only when receiving visiting brethren. Thus far we have described the Fine, who included perhaps not much more than one-fourth of the entire Mennonite body in the

Netherlands at that time.

The Coarse groups, although still agreeing with the more conservative on most of the Mennonite fundamentals of doctrine, such as the independent church, adult baptism, rejection of the oath, the holding of civil office, and, in the main, opposition to war, yet had discarded many of the old practices and took a more liberal attitude on many others. The Waterlanders, as well as some of the other Coarse groups, permitted their members to carry side arms as a custom, not for use; to patronize owners of armed vessels; and to hold minor civil offices. The ban was used sparingly by them only for the punishment of the grossest sins. Mixed marriages were not forbidden, nor were candidates for membership from other Mennonite factions required to be rebaptized. Worship was still simple, though somewhat more elaborate than among the Fine. Ministers were both partly salaried and educated, though not always specifically for their ministerial calling; and bore the usual title *Dominee*, like those of the state church. Hans de Ries, the Waterlander minister in Alkmaar, had introduced the practice of audible prayer among the Mennonite churches in the preceding century. Collections for various charitable purposes were regularly taken by ushers who carried small velvet bags to which were attached small bells, designed evidently for the benefit of drowsy worshipers. On the other hand, many of the old practices had been discarded—the kiss of brotherly love, practiced on baptismal occasions and at communion time; foot washing; the marriage ceremony as a religious rite; and numerous others.

The Swiss in the Netherlands

A third distinct group of Mennonites should be noted here—the *Swiss* refugees who had located in the vicinity of Groningen early in the century. For some time they were a distinct people, having little in common with the Dutch Mennonites either organically or culturally, though they shared the same Mennonite faith. The Swiss had brought with them all their customs—beards, hooks and eyes, shoestrings, Swiss dialect, and all—and kept them throughout the century. By the beginning of the nineteenth century, however, they had become totally adjusted to their new home and had become an integral part of the Dutch Mennonite brotherhood.

Contributions of the Mennonites

This description of the Dutch Mennonites of the eighteenth century would present but a very incomplete picture and distorted view of the real place they filled in the life of their times, if left to itself. There is another side to the picture that should be presented. While it must be admitted that, like many of the other independent religious groups of their day, the Mennonites had wasted a great deal of time quarreling over insignificant questions of human conduct, and had burned up an abundance of energy defending inconsequential differences in practices and customs long since discarded, yet it must not be forgotten that Mennonites of every group were still a sincere, honest folk, among the most substantial and highly respected in the land. Rues says they were "counted among the wealthiest of the country. If they were compelled to leave the land, the wealth and commerce of this country would suffer a very severe check." Their conscientious regard for genuine honesty was carried over into every detail of their daily life. Their workmanship was sincere, and their products as honest as was their insistence upon a godly life. As artisans, they never did shoddy work. So good was their reputation among their fellows for honest work that the term *Mennisten Infijn* (Mennonite fine through and through) became a sort of trademark for any goods of especially high quality in the commercial circles where Mennonites were known. Although somewhat contentious over matters of doctrine and religious practice, as we have just noticed, yet in matters of obedience to the civil law they seemingly were among the most law-abiding citizens of the land. Such misunderstandings as they had among themselves over questions of personal rights they settled in their own churches. They seldom resorted to the courts of law. The head of the police department of the city of Amsterdam, who had filled that office for over half a century, could still say in 1772 that during all that time not a single charge had ever been registered against a member of the large Mennonite congregation in that city.

They were also among the most liberal contributors to every worthy cause, especially to appeals of those in distress. During the seventeenth and eighteenth centuries they sent thousands of dollars to their oppressed brethren in West Prussia, Moravia, Switzerland, and the Palatinate. In 1790 they organized the *Commission for Foreign Needs* which functioned for many years. Originally to aid both the Swiss refugees and the Palatine Mennonites in the hour of their distress, it also indirectly aided many of them to find a new home in the newly founded colony of Pennsylvania. The work of this society has been discussed in the chapter on Switzerland.

Nor were the Dutch Mennonites of this period without their influence upon the general cultural and intellectual life of the land. Two organizations which have played a prominent role in the educational progress and scientific achievements of the

Netherlands during the nineteenth century had a Mennonite origin. The well-known *Teyler Foundation* was founded in 1778 by a Mennonite, Pieter Teyler van der Hulst, whose ancestor, an English refugee, Thomas Taylor, had come to Holland in 1580 and joined the Haarlem Mennonite Church. Pieter, who had become a wealthy manufacturer, left a large sum of money at his death for the founding of a museum of natural history and art gallery; and also a fund, the income from which was to be distributed in the form of prizes to promote scientific and philosophical research. This society did much throughout the century for the cause of genuine scholarship, and is still functioning.

The other foundation, also organized by a Mennonite, Jan Nieuwenhuyzen, in 1784, was called the *Maatschappij tot Nut van 't Algemeen* (Society for the Promotion of the Common Good). It was designed not so much for the promotion of original investigation, but rather for disseminating the general blessings of learning and culture among the common people. The first project undertaken by the society was the establishment of an elementary school system among the poorer elements of the population; for in Holland, as elsewhere, education was for the rich rather than the poor; and was regarded as a church rather than as a state function. This society must be given considerable credit for the founding of the Dutch public school system. In 1791 libraries for the poor were established, and later savings banks. True to the spirit of Mennonite toleration, the founder insisted that neither politics nor religious views were to have any influence in any of the undertakings of the organization; but Catholics have never taken any part in this work. Like the Teyler Foundation, *Het Nut*, as it is called, is still very much alive today. In 1927 the organization included 321 local affiliated societies, supporting 205 public libraries and 152 savings banks as well as many other enterprises for the benefit of the general public.

5. AT THE TURN OF THE CENTURY

As everywhere else in Europe, so Holland, too, was permeated and greatly affected in its whole social and political fabric by the spirit of the French Revolution. Nor did the Mennonites entirely escape this influence. Perhaps the most far-reaching by-product of the Revolutionary Era, so far as the Mennonites were concerned, was the complete separation of church and state in 1795. For the first time in three hundred years, Mennonites were placed on a basis of religious and civil equality with the hitherto privileged establishment. In 1809 the government offered subsidies, similar to those granted to the state church, to

Mennonite ministers who were willing to accept them. Later, help was also offered to Mennonite charitable institutions. Mennonites accepted these gifts but sparingly, however. During the French regime in Holland, Napoleon, with his passion for uniformity and system, attempted to bring all the different independent Mennonite congregations under one consolidated organization. But being congregational in their government, the Mennonites did not take kindly to this move; and later they again resumed their former system of democratic church government.

United in One Conference

The most significant event in the history of the Dutch Mennonites during the early part of the nineteenth century was the organization, in 1811, of the *Algemeene Doopsgezinde Sociëteit* (General Mennonite Association) for the purpose partly of helping weak and struggling congregations, but also of securing the united support of all for a theological seminary. Now the Mennonite Theological Seminary (*Kweekschool*), which had its origin in 1735, opened its gates to all ministerial candidates, and all congregations could extend a call to ministerial candidates or obtain financial subsidy whenever it was necessary.

By now the Mennonites, originally oppressed and persecuted, had developed certain characteristics of frugality, hard work, honesty, optimism, and even a tolerant theological liberalism which finally ended the era of the former theological quarrels, differences, and schisms. Their forebears had been oppressed because of radical Anabaptist views; now they were suspect of a theological modernism.

The Dutch Mennonites were the first among all Mennonites to start an outreach program by sending Pieter Jansz, the first Mennonite missionary, to Java. Soon most of the European Mennonites in Russia, Germany, Switzerland, and France joined in this effort which also ultimately inspired the American Mennonites to undertake similar outreach programs.

Publications and Library

The Dutch Mennonites had the first conference publication starting with the *Zondagsbode* in 1887, which is now the *Algemeen Doopsgezind Weekblad* published by the A. D. S. The oldest scholarly Mennonite publication in existence is the *Doopsgezinde Bijdragen*, started in 1861. It is now being published by the *Doopsgezinde Historische Kring*. The interest in Mennonite historical research and publications among the Dutch Mennonites has increased considerably since World War II. *The Doopsgezinde Jaarboekje* (Yearbook), published annually, contains valuable information pertaining to the ministers in service and retired, and all the activities of the brotherhood.

Throughout several centuries the Mennonite Seminary of Amsterdam acquired the richest and largest collection of rare *Mennonitica* and archival materials anywhere in the world. The books have recently been transferred from the Singel Mennonite Church Library to the University of Amsterdam Library where they are in good care and accessible to the public. The archival collection has been deposited at the City Archives.

Beyond the Dutch Borders

For centuries the Dutch Mennonites retained contact with those who had moved eastward from the Netherlands to avoid persecution or to find a livelihood. The larger congregations of Crefeld, Altona-Hamburg, Gronau, and Emden, where the Anabaptist movement had started, were the nearest Dutch Mennonite outposts in Germany. Dutch Mennonite ministers served the congregations, and at some of these places the preaching in the Dutch language continued into the eighteenth and nineteenth centuries. The Emden Mennonite Church is still affiliated with the Dutch Mennonite Conference. The Altona-Hamburg Mennonite congregation, in particular, was for a long time the channel of pietistic contacts and influences for Mennonites in West Prussia and far beyond.

Two hundred years ago when some Mennonites from West Prussia were to leave for settlement in the Ukraine, the agent of Catherine II became aware that they were divided into Flemish and Frisian groups. He was delegated to the Netherlands to meet the representatives of the *Algemeene Doopsgezinde Sociëteit* (General Mennonite Association) to appeal to them to encourage the Danzig Mennonites to unite so that the Russian government would not have to deal with splinter groups. The Dutch Mennonites sent a longer printed appeal to the departing Mennonites, encouraging them to unite, but it had little effect.

Worship and Meetinghouses

Although there has been a departure from the old standards, some of them have been retained, such as adult or believer's baptism, and rejection of the oath. Young people are given a long period of catechetical instruction before admission to church membership and are seldom baptized before their twentieth year, and often later. In some cases married couples attend church regularly, enjoy all the usual privileges of membership, and assume all the obligations without ever being baptized. There was an interesting case in one of the churches of several young men who were refused by the government the usual privilege of exemption from the oath because of the fact that they were not baptized, and thus not entitled to the exemption as Mennonites, although they were regular members of the congregation. The objection to the oath perhaps has been retained because, like adult baptism, it symbolizes religious toleration and separation of church and state, which have always remained, after all, two of the fundamental principles of Mennonites and have always distinguished them from the state churches. The Dutch Mennonites have retained also, to a marked degree, those sober virtues of moral integrity and simplicity of living which all through their history distinguished their forefathers as a distinct people.

Mennonite meetinghouses in the Netherlands, like some in America, are still inclined to be severely plain and simple in appearance, without stained glass, tower, or bell. If they are over one hundred years old, and in the city, they are likely to be located some distance back from the main street, a reminder of the days when Mennonites were still merely a tolerated people, with few civil and religious rights and not permitted to carry on their worship in public places. The Singel Mennonite Church in Amsterdam is hidden from view by a group of office buildings between it and the street. One unacquainted with Mennonite ecclesiastical architecture would hardly suspect that the modest little door opening upon the Singel was an entrance to a house of worship. In Leeuwarden, Sneek, and a number of other cities, the buildings in front of the church have since been removed, thus leaving an open court between the street and the meetinghouse.

The original meetinghouse along the Singel in Amsterdam, erected in the sixteenth century and changed but little in its general style of architecture by later remodelings, is a fair sample of the old type of church structure. On the inside, the room is large and nearly square. Along the north wall, nearly in the middle, stands an elevated pulpit reached by a short stairway, and topped by a canopy something like a sounding board, though not meant for that purpose. On each side of the pulpit extends a high bench, formerly for the use of the black-gloved, silk-hatted ruling elders, and nearby another short bench for the song leader. Around the other three sides run two balconies, and directly beneath on the first floor there are several rows of benches with long desks in front for Bibles and hymnbooks. The women were formerly seated on movable chairs which occupied the large square in the center of the floor. In front of each of these chairs one could find small perforated wooden boxes (foot warmers) filled in winter with charcoal or heated stones. The seating capacity of the house may be about fifteen hundred. Such, in brief, is the simple appearance of one of the oldest Mennonite meetinghouses in the world.

Some of the large congregations possess valuable libraries on the history and the literature of their own faith. The most comprehensive of these is the one in Amsterdam for which there is a printed catalog. Most of the larger congregations also support children's homes, sanitariums, and other charitable and philanthropic institutions for their own people, a practice carried by Dutch Mennonites to West Prussia, Russia, and later to the western prairies of North America. Taking care of their own unfortunate has always been a deeply rooted trait in the historical traditions of Mennonites everywhere.

Political and Economic Influence

The fact that the Mennonites of the Netherlands have always lived in the cities is the chief reason, no doubt, why they have been much more influential in the intellectual and commercial circles of their own nation than their brethren in other countries. Like the Quakers in England and like the Jews in America, the Mennonites of Holland have enjoyed an authority far out of proportion to their numerical strength, especially in financial and economic, as well as in political, matters. In Amsterdam nearly all the banks of the city are likely to have one or more Mennonites on their boards of directors, as well as an occasional president. During the past decades Mennonites have furnished several Cabinet members, a Governor General of the East Indies, the first president of the World Court, several members of the highest court of justice, and captains of industry, painters, professors, and doctors of the highest rank. At one time of the twenty-eight deputies in the popular house of the States General, four were Mennonites, while of the twenty-seven in the upper house, three were from the same faith. Of one hundred members of the Royal Academy of Sciences, eleven were Mennonite—a representation far out of proportion to their numbers.

First Mission Outreach

The first organized Mennonite mission work originated in Holland in 1847, when the Mennonite Association for the Spread of the Gospel in the Dutch Colonies was founded in Amsterdam. Soon the Mennonites of Germany, Russia, and Switzerland joined the Dutch in this enterprise. Thus in 1947, even though it was a dark hour, the Mennonites of Europe could look back on a century of their own organized missionary activities.

The first missionary to go out under the Mennonite Association of Amsterdam was P. Jansz, who baptized his first converts in 1854 at Japara, Java. Jansz was later joined by a number of other

Dutch Mennonite missionaries including his own son, P. A. Jansz, and some medical missionaries. P. Jansz translated the Bible into the Javanese language for the British Bible Society. The first Mennonite missionary from Russia to join the Dutch mission was Heinrich Dirks of Gnadenfeld who went in 1888. He was followed by Johann Hübert and Johann Klaassen. The mission field developed and spread but the growth was disrupted in World Wars I and II.

World War II and its aftermath had a disastrous effect in the home countries as well as on the mission field. During the war the Netherlands was cut off from the Dutch East Indies. The missionaries from Russia then serving in the field had grown old. Holland had not furnished any for some time. The German missionaries, H. Schmitt and O. Stauffer, were interned and later became war casualties leaving the Swiss missionary, D. Amstutz, and the Dutch medical doctor, K. P. C. A. Gramberg, as the main representatives on the mission fields. Fortunately, they succeeded in organizing the mission congregations into an independent mission church with its own constitution and articles of faith. During the Japanese occupation, immediately after this move, Mohammedan fanatics started a "holy war" against everything that reminded them of Western civilization. The remaining missionaries were interned and much of the fruit of the labor of a century was destroyed. After the liberation in August 1945, the Javanese began the struggle for national independence. These conditions again rendered work by European missionaries impossible.

In 1950 the Dutch Mennonites returned to the mission field that had become independent. Meanwhile the Mennonites of France, Germany, and Switzerland have joined the Dutch Mennonites and are doing their work as the European Mennonite Evangelization Committee.

In 1953 the Malay Mennonite Church had a membership of 2,410 in eleven congregations, and the Chinese Mennonite Church of Java had some 1,500 members in nine congregations in 1954. Both have been represented at the Mennonite World Conferences.

A Revival in the Brotherhood

Since World War I there has been a renewal movement among the Dutch Mennonites which was in part inspired because of the conditions in the Mennonite brotherhood in the Netherlands and above all through contacts with the Quakers in Woodbrooke, England. This led to a movement which became known as *Gemeentedag* (Congregational Day). The first meeting took place in Utrecht in 1917.

The exact purpose of this new movement was perhaps at first not quite clear, though it was hoped by the sponsors that it might somehow promote a warmer appreciation among both laity and the ministry of the practical piety of the early Mennonites and also deepen the personal, spiritual, and religious experiences of the brotherhood. As it expanded, however, its aims became more clearly defined. Its activities were grouped under the heads, called *Arbeidsgroepen* (Work groups): Bible study, missions, war resistance, and temperance. In each of these fields, increased interest has been aroused throughout the whole brotherhood. The movement promoted a practical piety and a deeper spiritual life in all its activities. In 1922 a separate youth movement was organized in connection with the parent *Gemeentedag*, and the two have worked in close harmony since that time.

At first, the meetings of the *Gemeentedag* were held at Utrecht; later for a few years, in a more or less public camping ground at Lunteren. In 1925 the first of several open camps was built by voluntary contributions on an open heath at Elspeet, with a fine assembly hall and a series of barrack-like sleeping rooms. These open camps, called *Brotherhood Houses*, became the centers of much of the spiritual and recreational life of the more progressive and youthful element of the whole denomination. Regional *Gemeentedag*, or Brotherhood meetings as they may be called, were also held in various local churches throughout the country.

Mennonite World Conference, World War II, and Beyond

The third Mennonite World Conference, devoted especially to the commemoration of the conversion of Menno Simons in 1536, took place in Holland in 1936. Representatives of Mennonites the world over had the opportunity of acquainting themselves with the land of Menno and his followers of our day in that country. The meeting took place in the Singel Church of Amsterdam, on the camping grounds of the *Gemeentedagbeweging* at Elspeet, and at Witmarsum—the place where Menno Simons was born and converted. Questions of the past and those which faced the Mennonites everywhere at that time were discussed. It was a memorable event, though the clouds of war were even then visible on the horizon.

On May 9, 1940, the German Army invaded Holland and soon this freedom-loving country was totally occupied. There were great losses and destruction of property and lives. Several of the Mennonite churches, including the one at Rotterdam, were totally destroyed. The functioning of the Mennonite Theological Seminary of Amsterdam was interrupted, and some Mennonite ministers lost their lives in concentration camps. The economic life of the Netherlands was disrupted and adjusted to the war economy of Germany. And again, as in the time of Napoleon, which gave birth to the founding of the A.D.S. (*Algemeene Doopsgezinde Sociëteit*), the Dutch Mennonites were stirred. A need and a hunger for a deeper and more meaningful spiritual life were felt.

When, after the liberation, the A.D.S. met again, new tasks and new visions confronted and beckoned the organization. When the A.D.S., during its session in 1945, listened to the message of its chairman, C. Nijdam, there was a new note in it. The meetings of the A.D.S. had, up to that time, been mostly business meetings and the organization itself a business institution. No one expected spiritual guidance from this organization. The need of spiritual reconstruction and guidance was, however, the keynote of Nijdam's message. What the *Gemeentedagbeweging* had been striving for, the revitalizing of the spiritual life of the brotherhood, now became the concern of the A.D.S. The *Gemeentedagbeweging* itself became a part of the A.D.S. Another division, newly created, was that of spiritual guidance.

Great changes have taken place in the Mennonite brotherhood of Holland since World War I and again since World War II. The former extreme individualism in religious matters and the liberal theological views have been modified considerably in the direction of a more Bible- and Christ-centered Christian life and preaching. Considerable interest is shown in relief work, nonresistance, and missionary endeavors. The war experience taught the Mennonite congregations to work in close harmony with the other Protestant churches of Holland. The A.D.S. is a member of the World Council of Churches.

Contacts with American Mennonites

Contacts with American Mennonites were established on a larger scale than ever before after World War II when relief was administered in the Netherlands through the Mennonite Central Committee. Relief units distributed food and clothing in devastated cities and helped in the rehabilitation and reconstruction of the flooded island of Walcheren. In many cases the Dutch Mennonites joined as individuals as well as officially in these enterprises. The Dutch were especially helpful in assisting and caring for the Mennonite refugees from Russia who were fortunate enough to cross the border into Holland. The Dutch Mennonites had personal and intimate contacts with the American Mennonites through relief work as well as through a large-scale student exchange program by which Dutch Mennonite students were enabled to attend Mennonite colleges in America. In 1948 numerous Mennonite delegates attended the fourth Mennonite World Conference at Goshen, Indiana, and North Newton, Kansas, traveling extensively afterwards and visiting Mennonite congregations in the United States and Canada.

Among the centers of contact between the Dutch and the American Mennonites were the Mennonite Central Committee home of Amsterdam (Koningslaan 58) and "Heerewegen" near Utrecht. The latter was operated jointly by the Dutch and American Mennonites.

Reclaiming a Vision

For some time in the Netherlands there has been a search for a revival of the Anabaptist vision in the contemporary world. It was realized that the nineteenth century through the *Algemeene Doopsgezinde Sociëteit* (General Mennonite Association) had given the Dutch Mennonites a theologically educated ministry, but now the watchword was: "Not only the ministers, but all believers are priests." The "Faith of the Fathers" on the foundation of Menno Simons in 1 Corinthians 3:11 was to be renewed. Gradually and steadfastly a change took place. Many factors and circumstances helped in the realization of some of the goals set.

After World War II, N. van der Zijpp, professor of the Mennonite Theological Seminary, related that a group of young Mennonite ministers organized an Ecclesiological Work Group and published a book criticizing the Dutch Mennonite brotherhood for its traditional liberal and individualistic theological views and stressing the importance of a confession of faith which they presented to the brotherhood. The experience during the war and the change in the theological climate caused by theologians like Karl Barth, Emil Brunner, and others, influenced the Mennonite brotherhood considerably. A generation of professors at the seminary, who have trained ministers and members of the congregations, have brought about a change in the spiritual climate. International Mennonite contacts through European Conferences and World Conferences every five years have influenced the spiritual life from which all participants benefit.

The *Doopsgezind Jaarboekje* (*Mennonite Yearbook*) of 1977 commemorated the sixtieth anniversary of the Mennonite *Gemeentedagbeweging* in a number of articles under the general heading *Een bewogen beweging* (A Moving Movement) of which the last two are entitled: "An Open Future" and "A New Perspective." This *Yearbook* also contains the commemoration of the one-hundred-fiftieth anniversary of the Conference of

Northern Provinces under the motto: "Where have we come from and where are we going?" Searching questions are being raised and challenging observations are being presented as guidelines for the future.

V
Northern Germany

By the middle of the sixteenth century the Mennonites were restricted to two well-defined areas—Switzerland and the Netherlands, to which may be added a third, Moravia, if the Hutterites are included. The present congregations of South Germany and France are mostly of Swiss origin, while those of North Germany came originally from the Netherlands, though in the course of time some native Germans and Swiss were added. By this time the fervid missionary zeal which had characterized the earlier spread of Anabaptism had been almost stamped out by relentless persecution. Only too glad to escape with their own lives, and thankful if they might hold their own, Mennonites no longer had the heart to look for new recruits.

In North Germany, along the Baltic and the North Sea, the Dutch Mennonite refugees, fleeing from the atrocities of Spanish rule, located in two well-defined areas—just across the Dutch border in northwestern Germany, and farther east along the Baltic in the delta of the Vistula River and nearby coastline.

1. NORTHWEST GERMANY

The settlements in northwest Germany may be roughly classed into three groups—East Friesland, the Lower Elbe, and the Lower German Rhine River.

East Friesland

The independent region of East Friesland, directly across the Dutch border in the extreme northwest corner of Germany, was just outside the immediate control of Charles V, the tyrant of the Netherlands, and far enough removed from his Habsburg capital as emperor of the Germans to assume somewhat of an independ-

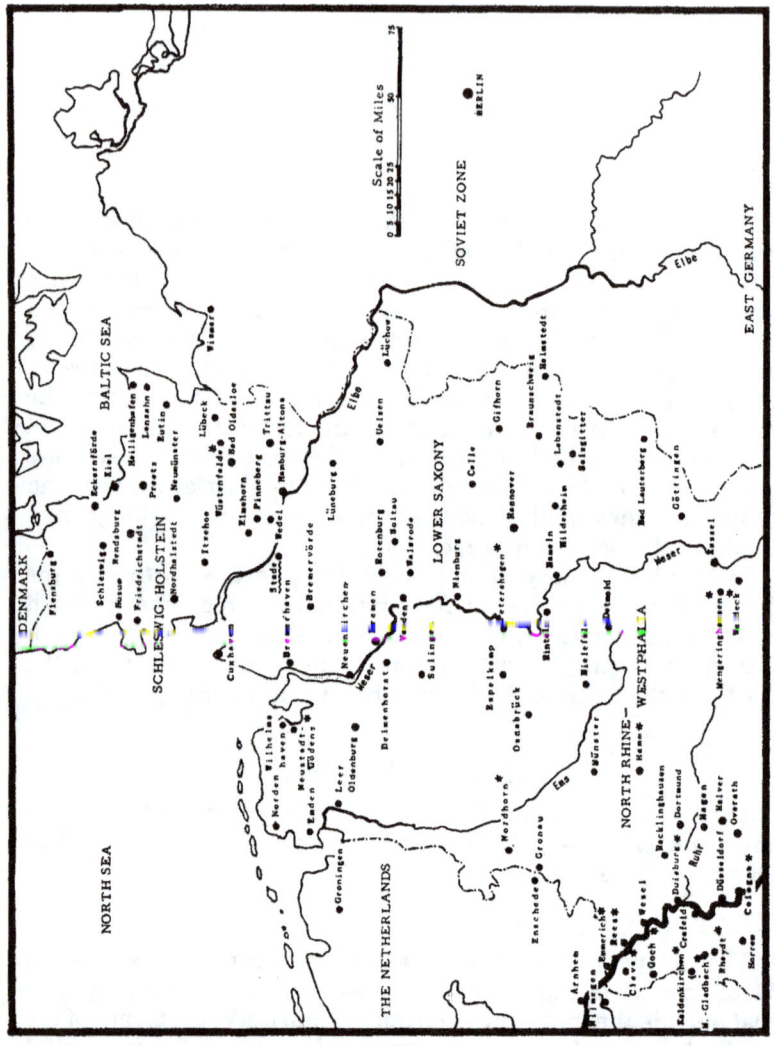

Mennonites in Northern Germany
(Only towns with Mennonite congregations or meetingplaces are shown. Extinct congregations are starred.)

ent attitude toward the great religious questions then agitating central Europe. Quite early, the local counts had turned favorably toward the Reformation movement, but for a time they remained undecided about which of the parties, Lutheran or Reformed, to follow. To John a Lasco, a Polish nobleman, was committed the task of working out a satisfactory religious system for East Friesland. In the end, a Lasco decided for the Reformed Church, which ultimately became the state church of the Netherlands.

During this transition period the local rulers assumed a somewhat tolerant attitude toward religious dissent; and East Friesland became a rallying place for religious refugees from neighboring countries, including Anabaptists from Holland. Not all the first Anabaptists here were refugees, however. In fact Anabaptism had an indigenous growth in the country. Melchior Hofmann's activities in and about Emden have already been noted. His disciple, Jan Trypmaker, first planted the banner of the new movement in Amsterdam in 1530, and the next year forfeited his life for the cause at The Hague. The execution of another of Melchior Hofmann's disciples, Sicke Freerks, a few years later at Leeuwarden started Menno Simons on his career as a reformer.

Menno himself went in and out from Emden for many years, as did his co-workers, Dirk Philips and his brother, Obbe, as well as Leenaert Bouwens and other early leaders. Here, too, many important conferences and other Anabaptist meetings of all kinds were held during the century, including the great debate with the clergy of the Reformed Church in 1578.

Emden, Leer, and Norden

With the end of persecution in the Netherlands near the close of the sixteenth century, Mennonite migration to East Friesland ceased. The settlements here from this time on remained few and small. By 1700 the congregation in and about Aurich, the official residence of the ruling counts, had died out, and only three centers remained—Emden, Leer, and Norden. The total membership of all three never exceeded several hundred.

While few, if any, Mennonites were ever put to death in East Friesland because of their faith, nevertheless they were never granted more than a limited toleration. They always remained subject to the whims and prejudices of arbitrary rulers. Some counts were worse than others. Throughout the sixteenth century, urged by neighboring Dutch regents to break up refugee settlements, or by Habsburg emperors to enforce the Edict of Speyer of 1529, or by the local clergy to root out all religious dissent, obliging East Friesland counts occasionally ordered Mennonites out of the county. But these orders seemingly were never taken seriously and seldom carried out.

In 1544 Countess Anna, although one of the most tolerant of the early rulers, issued an order for the expulsion of all Anabaptists within her jurisdiction. But, advised by John a Lasco to differentiate between the more or less fanatical groups—such as the Batenburger, Davidians, and Münsterites—and the followers of the peaceful Menno, she limited her order to the former only. Referring to the latter, the countess made use of the term *Mennist*, the name by which this group is generally known after this. Menno, however, thought it best to leave. He spent the next two years in the archbishopric of Cologne.

So *toleration* remained but a relative term. Mennonites, even under the most liberal regime, were forced to worship in secret. Even after church buildings were permitted, they had to be erected along back streets, and in out-of-the-way places without tower or bell. This latter provision, however, seemingly was not much of a hardship; for, on one occasion at least, the Reformed clergy of Norden complained to the magistrate that "the impudent Mennonites go to church to the sound of our own bells."

The toleration act of 1627, granted by the tolerant Count Rudolf Christian, guaranteed the Mennonites only the legal rights of worship and warned them especially against luring any of the faithful from the true church with "honeyed words." For this privilege each family was to pay the governing authorities the annual sum of six *Thaler*. Marriage could be performed only by the regular clergy; the full rights of citizenship were still withheld; and freedom from military service and from the oath always remained a subject for further negotiation. It was usually transmitted to a money payment.

Even as late as 1738 when Carel Edzard granted a more liberal charter, worship still had to be carried on without open display and without propaganda. By this time, however, Mennonites might be married by their own ministers and according to their own customs, but the regular Reformed pastor was still entitled to his fee of one-half *Thaler*, partly as a gift, but largely, no doubt, to insure the continuation of their privileges. A record of the marriage must be kept in the church register. The ministers from the outside were granted the right of visit. Military exemption was conceded without the payment of the usual exemption money.

In 1744 East Friesland came under the jurisdiction of the king of Prussia, at which time the combined Mennonite churches paid the new ruler one thousand *Thaler*. After this the Mennonites, with a few exceptions, enjoyed the liberties and shared the restrictions common throughout the kingdom of Prussia. During and after the Napoleonic wars, East Friesland came under the control successively of Holland, Hannover, and finally Prussia again.

Of the three congregations in East Friesland today—Leer, Norden, and Emden—the last is the most important and the oldest. In fact it is the oldest existing Mennonite congregation in the world, having had a continued existence since 1530. The congregation has never been large; however, it has given both the church and the state a long list of prominent men. In addition to the many church leaders who served the congregation in the sixteenth century, there should be added in more recent times men and women who were prominent in affairs of both church and state. From this congregation in the nineteenth century came the Brons family—Anna, author of the first comprehensive history of the Mennonites in the German language (1884); Isaac Brons, her husband, deputy to the Frankfurt Parliament in 1848, president of the East Friesland Navy League in 1861, and member of the Reichstag of the North German Confederation in 1867; and their son Bernhard, leading citizen of Emden, chief magistrate for fourteen years, Swedish consul, and for thirty years deacon in his home church.

Under the able leadership of Abraham Fast, the membership of the Emden congregation, which had dwindled down to thirty-two in 1918, had increased by 1932 to over three hundred. These accessions were primarily people of non-Mennonite background.

During World War II, Emden was almost totally destroyed by a twenty-minute air raid. Many members of the congregation lost homes and property. The old and beautiful Mennonite church, dating back to 1769, and the parsonage were totally destroyed. Gone also were the valuable archives dating back three hundred years. The industrial life, as well as the life of the congregation, suffered severely.

The destruction of property, dislocation of people, and loss of life incident to the war, as well as the greatly increased number of people requiring pastoral care, added much to the task of the minister. Since the church and parsonage at Leer remained intact, the minister at Emden moved to this location. In addition to the care of the congregation at Emden, Leer, and Norden, the pastor also became responsible for the Mennonite congregation at Gronau, at the Dutch border, in the province of Westphalia. Some of the Mennonites of Gronau such as the van Deldens were leading silk industrialists. After World War I a number of Russian Mennonite families found shelter in Gronau, and after World War II the Mennonite Central Committee maintained a large displaced-persons camp in Gronau.

Abraham Fast was succeeded as pastor by his son Heinold. Originally, it will be rememberd, these congregations were served by Dutch ministers. All of these congregations are members of both the Dutch *Algemeene Doopsgezinde Sociëteit* **and of** *Die Vereinigung der deutschen Mennonitengemeinden.*

The Lower Elbe

Throughout the latter half of the sixteenth century, Dutch Mennonite refugees also found their way to the free cities and the isolated country places along the river deltas and seacoasts of Schleswig-Holstein. The principal settlements here were along the lower Elbe, between Hamburg and Lübeck, down the Elbe from here, and up the coast as far as the marshlands of the lower Eider. Coming as they did directly from Holland where they had long known the technique of ditch digging and dike building, the Mennonites felt at home among the swamps of this region. They soon built up productive farms where there had been nothing but waste before, and brought prosperity to cities by their thrift in industry and skill in commerce. By so doing they earned the gratitude and the protection of their benefactors. Many of the Mennonites were weavers; others were fishermen; some became merchant princes, and, in course of time, became wealthy and influential.

Among the earliest of the Mennonite communities was one established in the marshlands of the lower Eider, in the southwestern corner of Schleswig and the northwestern border of Holstein. Here at first they were hardly tolerated, but by the beginning of the seventeenth century more liberal privileges of worship were granted along with the right to make their living by farming in the open country, and by trade and commerce in the cities, in spite of the opposition by the Lutheran clergy. The generous terms granted the Mennonites in Friedrichstadt a little later were also applied to the settlements along the lower Eider. In fact, these various small scattered communities in the open country never organized congregations of their own, but remained an organic part of the Friedrichstadt congregation. Winning outsiders was not allowed. Nor were they inclined to make inroads into the state church. The only accessions to Mennonitism from the outside were occasional servants who joined the church of their employers. But even these humble recruits were often made the occasion of serious attempts on the part of the Lutheran clergy to curtail the privileges of the Mennonites.

By the middle of the nineteenth century, there were no Mennonites left in the open country of the Eider lowlands. That they survived so long is an eloquent tribute to the tenacity and genuineness of their religious convictions. At best it would seem almost an impossibility for a widely scattered and isolated people—who spoke a foreign tongue and practiced a proscribed religion, and who were the object of the jealousies of a powerful state church—to maintain and perpetuate their own religious institutions. But the Mennonites here held their own for over two centuries. Among the causes given by the writers of their own history for their final dissolution as an organized religious group are the education of their children in Lutheran schools and mixed marriages, the children of which according to the law of 1751 must be regarded as members of the state church. The loss of many of the simple and pious Christian virtues of their early forefathers should also be mentioned.

Friedrichstadt

The congregation in Friedrichstadt, a little farther up the river, still exists. The city of Friedrichstadt was founded in the beginning of the seventeenth century by a group of tolerant Remonstrants with the consent of the reigning duke. In 1623 Mennonites, too, were granted full religious toleration, including a recognition of their scruples against the oath, military service, and police duty. Perhaps nowhere else in all Germany at that time did Mennonites enjoy such religious rights as here, although their status was still merely that of a tolerated people without any inherent civil or religious rights. Their privileges, however, did not include the right of expansion at the expense of the prevailing established church. When the king of Denmark fell heir to the duchy of Holstein, he confirmed all these privileges. The Mennonites here always played an important role in the commercial and industrial life of the city, although they never, with the exception of an occasional election to the city council or the office of burgomaster, took an active part in political matters.

The Friedrichstadt church was never large. It reached its greatest prosperity around 1700 when it numbered about four hundred members. One hundred years later, as a result of marriage restrictions encouraged by the Lutheran church, the scattered membership in the open country about the town, and the insistence upon the use of the Dutch language in a German environment, this number had dwindled to less than fifty. It was from the pastorate of this church that C. J. van der Smissen, the first theological professor and later the principal of the Wadsworth, Ohio, school, was called to his American field of labor in 1868.

On the right bank of the Elbe, between Hamburg and the sea, lies *Glückstadt*, once the seat of a prosperous Mennonite congregation. This town was founded in 1616 by Christian IV of

Denmark, who, desirous of attracting thrifty settlers to the new city, offered complete religious liberty to various oppressed groups of the surrounding countries. He offered many other special privileges—freedom of worship, the right to carry on trade and commerce, and exemption from military service, although for this an annual tribute had to be substituted. Mennonites came here almost from the first.

Among the prominent businessmen of this city was Gysbert van der Smissen, founder of the well-known Mennonite family of van der Smissens in northwestern Germany who had come to Glückstadt in 1643. Gysbert was a merchant prince in his day, and was responsible for making his city one of the most important seaports along the entire coast. His ships found their way to all the ports of north and south Europe, and to Greenland where he engaged extensively in the whale fisheries. When van der Smissen left for Altona and took his business with him, the Mennonite congregation here began to decline. By 1740 the last Mennonite family in Glückstadt had disappeared.

In the Hamburg-Lübeck region, Anabaptists of the Mennonite type were found soon after the middle of the sixteenth century. One of the earliest of the refugees here was Coord Roosen, ancestor of a long line of influential Mennonites who had come originally from the duchy of Jülich. He located near Lübeck; others followed him from the same duchy and from Cologne and Holland, as well as from other intolerant lands of the northwest.

By 1543 or earlier, a small group had founded the Mennonite village of *Wüstenfelde* on an estate called Fresenburg, the possession of count Bartholomeus von Ahlefeldt, not far from the present town of Oldesloe. In this village, it will be remembered, Menno himself found his final resting place, and here he lies buried in what was supposed to be his own garden. The settlement was completely destroyed in 1627 when the armies of Tilly and Wallenstein raided northern Germany in the course of the Thirty Years' War. Most of the members then left for Lübeck and Altona, but a few remained a while longer in Fresenburg. The last recorded mention of this community, in 1656, indicates that at that time there were only three members left.

Hamburg-Altona

Before the close of the sixteenth century a congregation had also been formed in the free city of Hamburg, and in the neighboring village of Altona, the latter under the political jurisdiction at the time of the counts of Schauenberg, vassals to the duke of Holstein. Refugees came here principally from Holland, Cologne, and the duchy of Jülich. At first little toleration was accorded to Anabaptists of any variety, and orders were sent out to the faithful not to harbor them nor to rent them houses or lands. But by the seventeenth century the ruling authorities had become a bit more lenient, although the usual restrictions against publicity were still in force, and in Altona an annual tax of one *Thaler* per head was collected. Somewhat later, these privileges were extended and confirmed by the king of Denmark when he assumed the title of duke of Holstein in 1741. In 1672 Emperor Leopold reminded the authorities of the Free City of Hamburg that the Mennonites were not one of the three tolerated denominations. The Senate defended them, replying that they were a peaceful, industrious, and useful people, and not at all to be confused with the fanatical Münsterites against whom the imperial edicts had originally been directed. As elsewhere, however, the Lutheran clergy were entirely out of sympathy with the tolerant policy of the magistrates. As late as 1764, they secured the passage of a regulation forbidding intermarriage between Mennonites and Lutherans.

In course of time some of the Hamburg-Altona Mennonites, engaged largely in commercial enterprises and the whale fisheries, became prosperous. When in 1674 they proposed to erect a new church building, it was agreed among the wealthier merchants that they would each contribute 5 percent of the net proceeds of the season's catch in the northern waters toward this purpose. Tradition says that the season's return was unusually large and more than enough to meet the demands of the new building. In 1713, when the city was destroyed by fire in the course of the Swedish War, the losses of Hinrich van der Smissen, one of the well-to-do members, were two breweries and eighteen houses.

The two Mennonite settlements in Hamburg and Altona formed one community, but all the divisions present in the Netherlands were transplanted here (Frisian, Flemish, and High German), to which were added several others a little later. In course of time these were united into one congregation, on the basis of the Olive Branch Confession of Faith. The united congregation, which remained in close touch with the parent communities in Holland, was classed with the Dutch Zonist group. The meetinghouse of the congregation was in Altona. When the celebrated minister Galenus Abrahamsz de Haan of Amsterdam, founder of the Lamist group in Holland, visited the Hamburg-Altona church in 1678, hoping to preach there, the local congregation decided to test his orthodoxy before permitting him to preach. He passed the examination to the satisfaction of the church council on such questions as the necessity of water baptism, the admission of the truly converted only to the communion table, the equality of the

Son with the Father, and the need of a written confession of faith. Galenus was given permission to preach, but was warned not to advocate any practices that were contrary to those of the Altona-Hamburg congregation, among others that of observing silent prayer. The local minister at the time was Gerrit Roosen.

The Roosen Family

Gerrit (or Gerhard) is the best known of a long line of distinguished members of the Roosen family. Coord, the founder of the Holstein branch, has already been mentioned. Paul, the father of Gerrit, came to Altona from Fresenburg in 1611. The last of a long line of preachers was Berend Carl, who in 1904 ended a sixty-year pastorate of the Altona church.

Gerrit, who was born in Altona in 1612, was a wealthy shipowner as well as the minister, and served his congregation for sixty-two years during a critical period in the history of the local church. Among other troublesome occasions through which he safely directed his people was an episode in 1648 when a group of applicants for membership, due to some outside influence, demanded to be baptized by immersion. At the same time they also advocated other innovations, including foot washing before communion and the observance of the Lord's Supper in the evening with unleavened bread. In spite of Roosen's tactful handling of the situation, a division could not be averted. A small group seceded and organized an immersionist, or *Dompelaar*, branch of the church which lasted for over one hundred years.

Roosen was also the author of several books. His catechism, first printed in 1702 and issued frequently afterward, was widely used for over two centuries among the Mennonites of both Germany and America. He traveled extensively in Europe and carried on a voluminous correspondence with his Mennonite brethren on both sides of the Atlantic. It was to him that the Germantown Mennonites wrote for advice concerning the installation of the first minister for the American church. He died an accidental death in 1711, having lived just four months less than a full century.

Jakob Denner

Jakob Denner, the last of the Dompelaar ministers, was another man of unusual influence. He was first a minister in the Hamburg-Altona congregation, but later joined the immersionists. He was an eloquent preacher, and his sermons were well attended even by the nobility and other men of influence. It is said that the Crown Prince of Sweden on the occasions of his visits to Hamburg often heard him. Denner was an extensive traveler, a deep student of the sciences, and a schoolteacher, as well as a preacher. Denner served in succession the congregations of Altona, Lübeck, Friedrichstadt, and Danzig. His real vocation was that of dyer.

Denner also wrote a number of books including a book of sermons first published in the Dutch in 1706, translated into German in 1730, and reprinted several times since, including the Frankenthal edition of 1792. His *Betrachtungen* (Exhortations) was extremely popular far beyond the Mennonite constituency. Two Franconia Mennonites went to Germany and purchased 500 copies of the 1792 edition of the *Betrachtungen* (1,366 pages) which were distributed in Pennsylvania in a short time. In 1860 a reprint edition appeared in Philadelphia.

The van der Smissen Family

Another family which has played a very significant role in Anabaptist-Mennonite history far beyond Hamburg-Altona is the van der Smissen family. The origin of the family has been traced to the fifteenth century in Brussels. Gysbert van der Smissen escaped to Haarlem around 1576 because of religious persecution. His son, Jan, was a Mennonite minister in Haarlem and another son, Daniel, settled in Friedrichstadt, which had become a Mennonite refuge. A third son, Gysbert II, moved via Glückstadt to Altona and established a bakery. The ninth child of Gysbert II was Hinrich I (1662-1737), who was a very successful businessman, occupied significant positions in the growing city, and became the "city builder" of Altona. The van der Smissen business reached its peak during the second generation under Hinrich II and Gysbert III. Some of the eighteenth- and nineteenth-century van der Smissen families had very strong pietistic leanings and a number of them served as ministers in Germany and in the U.S.A. They affiliated with Zinzendorf, Spener, and the Wesley brothers. Their widespread correspondence is an unusual source of information.

Hinrich van der Smissen (1851-1928) was minister of the Hamburg-Altona Mennonite Church (1882-1928), editor of the *Mennonitische Blätter* and served in numerous other positions. Carl Justus van der Smissen (1811-1890) received a theological training in Basel and Erlangen. In 1860 he became a teacher of the first theological school of the Mennonites in North America at Wadsworth, Ohio. Among his eight children was Carl H. A. van der Smissen (1851-1950), who also studied theology at various German universities and came to America where he served a number of congregations, edited Mennonite publications, and wrote one of the first Mennonite histories in North America. It was through this American branch of the family that some very valuable early documents and correspondence were brought to America. Carl and his sister Hillegonda spent the last decades of their long lives in Newton, Kansas.

After World Wars I and II

In 1700 the membership of the Hamburg-Altona congregation was approximately 700. At the beginning of this century the congregation had less than 400 members. In 1914 the church in Altona was replaced by a new elaborate large church building with a parish hall and parsonage in Hamburg. The old church building at the *Grosse Freiheit* street in Altona, which was erected in 1716, was being used for city mission purposes when it was completely destroyed in World War II.

During this war in July 1943, about 50 percent of the residences of Hamburg-Altona were destroyed in a few hours. Members of the Mennonite congregation suffered in proportion. Such Mennonite historical markers as the van der Smissen *Allee* (street), the chapel in the Mennonite cemetery, and the above-mentioned Altona church were completely destroyed. Even the new church suffered damage. Otto Schowalter served as pastor of the congregation during and after these crucial years and was succeeded by Peter J. Foth in 1968. The congregation still has some of the old family names listed as members in the church council and among its church members, but there are also many new names of West Prussian origin. Only a few of those who are coming more recently from Russia have made their way to the congregations in Emden, Hamburg, and Kiel, partly because they feel more at home in smaller towns and cities and where there is a larger number of members of similar background.

The Lower German Rhine

Mennonites were found along the Lower Rhine in the duchies of Jülich, Cleve, and Berg, the archbishopric of Cologne, and the other small principalities in this area all through the sixteenth and seventeenth centuries. The more fanatical Anabaptist groups—Batenburger, Davidians, and a few Münsterites, also lingered on for a time after the fall of Münster, though by the middle of the sixteenth century these had nearly run their course.

In all these Lower Rhine areas, and during all this time, the Mennonites enjoyed much less religious toleration than did those of the two regions already described. Here they were everywhere outlawed. Some rulers were less cruel than others and Mennonite liberties varied with the times. Catholics were usually more bitter against them than the Lutherans, and the latter more so than the Reformed.

It was during the time, it will be remembered, when Hermann von Wied, elector of Cologne, attempted to transform the Catholic archbishopric into a Lutheran principality that Menno Simons found a brief respite here from his wanderings. But with the return of the Catholics to power, persecution again set in and the Mennonites completely disappeared from the archbishopric.

Among the conspicuous victims of the executioner's axe at Cologne was Thomas von Imbroich, a young printer of twenty-five, who gave his life for his faith in 1558. While in the agonies of torture, inflicted by his accusers for the purpose of forcing him to recant, he was encouraged by his wife who was a witness of his suffering to remain steadfast. Refusing to recant, he was beheaded. The *Martyrs Mirror*, in an extended account of the trial and execution of this man of heroic mold, says that "the count would gladly have set him free, but he feared the imperial decree and the displeasure of the bishop." Thomas von Imbroich was an extensive writer. One of his devotional tracts is still printed in the American edition of the *Ausbund*, and for that reason is still read by the Amish who use the hymnal.

In 1565 fifty-six members of the Cologne congregation were apprehended with their minister, Matthias Cervaes, who was also executed. A decree issued by the ruling authorities in 1578 making Mennonitism a capital offense practically annihilated the congregation in Cologne and vicinity.

Among the other congregations along the Lower Rhine which survived the early impacts of persecution was the one at *Gladbach*, founded sometime before the middle of the sixteenth century, and by 1650 still numbering some five hundred souls. Many of the members here were prominent in the industrial and commercial circles of the city. Persistent persecution on the part of intolerant dukes finally completely scattered the church. Some went to Nijmegen, others to Crefeld. By 1720 the congregation had practically disappeared.

The *Goch* church was almost as old as the Mennonite movement itself. In 1547, it will be remembered, it was the scene of the conference at which Menno Simons, Dirk Philips, and other leaders accused Adam Pastor of anti-trinitarianism. The congregation was small, but remained intact almost up to the close of the nineteenth century.

Emmerich, on the right bank of the Rhine just a few miles from the Dutch border, was also the seat of an early congregation dating back to 1534. Tradition has it that when in 1672 the city fell into the hands of the French, Louis XIV, bent on making good Catholics out of his thrifty Mennonite subjects in this region, sent a learned theologian from the Sorbonne to instruct them in the ways of the true faith. But when the king found that the uneducated Mennonite preachers were better versed in the Scriptures than his learned theologians, he gave up the effort as hopeless. In 1740 the congregation consisted of two hundred souls, but it has steadily declined since. The last preacher retired in 1883, after which the small group was served by visiting ministers. By 1912 there were still twelve members here, but without any organized church activities.

Aachen, like Cologne, was a center of the radical reformers, including the Anabaptists, since the beginning of the Reformation. The general tendency to spiritualize theological views and sacraments often made it difficult for authorities to distinguish between the various groups. Since the test of infant baptism made it possible for authorities to check and find out who of the citizens was an Anabaptist or had leanings in that direction, it is claimed that before 1545 all reform movements in Aachen were Anabaptist. At any rate, when the Protestant majority gained control of the city in 1580, there was already a well-organized Mennonite congregation. Anabaptist refugees now came here from other places where they were persecuted.

When the Catholics returned in 1598 the Anabaptists were severely persecuted. Some found shelter in nearby towns and villages. Thus Aachen did not remain a stronghold of Anabaptism for any length of time.

The Mennonites were often ordered into exile but permitted to remain on payment of large sums of ransom money. When more drastic measures were taken, they left. A mandate issued in 1616 banished six hundred Mennonites from Aachen. In the places nearby, such as Burtscheid and Vaals, the Mennonite congregations survived and were joined by those who were exiled. During the eighteenth century the congregations were served by ministers from nearby larger churches such as Crefeld and Maastricht. These congregations are now extinct.

Neuwied near Coblenz

Unlike the Mennonites in the Lower Rhine area, those of Neuwied near Coblenz were originally primarily of Swiss background who had settled here on the estate of Count Frederick of Wied. He founded Neuwied in 1652 and offered freedom to all denominations. The Mennonites here were predominantly weavers and clockmakers. Until 1768 worship services were held in homes. In that year the Mennonites were permitted to build a church on the banks of the Rhine River just across the street from the castle of the Count Alexander, who donated a tower and bell to the congregation. The Mennonites of the Netherlands contributed to the building of the church. Goethe and Lavater visited the worship in 1774. The latter wrote in his diary: "Visited the Mennonites, Friedenreich and Kinzing—splendid faces, full of simplicity and honor, and round about them, many boys,' daughters,' and mothers' faces, equally noble, innocent, affectionate...."

In the nineteenth century great changes took place. Many members went to America and some joined the Reformed Church. In 1900 there were only eighty-eight members left and in 1940, hardly twenty-five. During the nineteenth century the Dutch Mennonites supported the congregation financially, and theologically trained ministers served the congregation.

After World War II new life came into the congregation that would have become extinct without the influx of Mennonites from West Prussia and later also from Russia. By 1956 the baptized membership was 360. Since that time a number of *Umsiedler* from Russia have joined the settlement. Immediately after World War II through Paxmen of the MCC, a number of homes were built at Torney and Niederbiber near Neuwied. In 1979 there were four Mennonite congregations in Neuwied, including the Mennonite Brethren.

In Neuwied is located the *Mennonitische Umsiedlerbetreuung* (Office for Mennonites coming from Russia to Germany) sponsored by the European agency *IMO* and the Mennonite Central Committee. The office has been managed for many years by Hans Niessen.

There was also at one time an Amish settlement near Eich not far from Neuwied. Driving from Andernach to Laach Lake, one is surprised to see a well-kept cemetery with names like Schwarzentraub. Likely most of them went to America, and those remaining joined churches nearby, including the Mennonite Church of Neuwied.

The Mennonites of Crefeld

In numerous German towns and villages bordering on the Netherlands, Dutch Anabaptist refugees established themselves as congregations. Because of severe persecution, most of them gradually disappeared. Among those congregations that survived, Crefeld is outstanding. The Mennonites made out of a little hamlet or "crow field" an industrial city of prominence. Pioneers from Crefeld were also among the founding fathers of the Germantown village in the outskirts of Philadelphia which became the first American Mennonite settlement that survived to this day.

The Crefeld congregation was established as early as 1600, if not before. One of the first Mennonites known in the city was a Herman op den Graeff, whose name appears as the Crefeld representative to the Dordrecht meeting of 1632 which drew up the well-known Dordrecht Confession of Faith. The congregation grew continuously throughout the century through the addition of refugees from the surrounding territories.

Of course, toleration here too was only relative. While the liberal Orange counts seemingly had no prejudices against religious dissenters, the Reformed Church did. It was not until 1657 that the Mennonites were granted full rights of open worship. Even then they had to gather quietly at their meeting place on *Königstrasse* one hour after the meeting time of the Reformed Church, so as in no way to interfere with the prerogatives of the established institution. In 1679 they were granted the right of citizenship, of which twenty-nine families immediately took advantage. The first meetinghouse was erected in 1695 on an inconspicuous back street, hidden from public view; and there it stood until it was destroyed in World War II.

In 1702 Crefeld came under the jurisdiction of the first king of Prussia, whose successor, Frederick William I, granted the Mennonites certain privileges, including freedom from military service upon the payment of exemption money to the amount of five hundred *Thaler*. The Reformed clergy, considering these privileges too liberal, laid their complaints before the king, who replied, "The Mennonites should not be persecuted, but should be tolerated both for reasons of state and on religious grounds since they are good Christians living peaceably according to the rules of their faith."

Influential Families

The unusual privileges enjoyed by the Crefeld Mennonites were no doubt due not only to the tolerant spirit of the Orange family, but quite as much to the conspicuous role played by many of the former in the industrial and economic life of Crefeld for nearly three centuries. In fact it was a Mennonite family—the von der Leyens, Adolf and Heinrich, coming originally as refugees from the duchy of Berg in 1665—who founded the silk and textile business for which Crefeld became noted. The institution started at that time has been managed from the beginning by descendants of the founders, and its products are known the world over.

The von der Leyen family has always been among Crefeld's most distinguished citizens—captains of industry, burgomasters, civic leaders. One was knighted by the king of Prussia, and the *Rathaus* was once his castle. Most of them remained true to their Mennonite connections. But the family name is now extinct.

NORTHERN GERMANY

During World War I a General von der Leyen fell in battle; and the last member of the Crefeld branch to bear the name was a rich coffee planter of Brazil some years ago.

Among other prominent Mennonite names must be added that of the de Greiff family. One of them, Cornelius, was honored by the city in 1865 by the erection of a statue in his honor because of liberal contributions to the charitable institutions of the city. Also to be mentioned is the Müller family, originally from the Palatinate, who established a large textile industry in Crefeld.

Not to be omitted from this list of prominent families are the von Beckeraths, of whom Hermann, born in 1801, was the most distinguished member. As a deputy to the Prussian *Landtag* in 1847 his voice was effectively heard in behalf of religious toleration, although he was no longer in sympathy with the demand for military exemption. In the following year he represented his city in the Frankfurt Parliament. For a short time he served the Prussian government as Minister of Finance, and later became recognized as the leader of the Liberal party in Prussia. The Beckeraths are still among the influential members of the Crefeld congregation.

The Crefeld Mennonites, as a whole, played a leading role in the financial and industrial affairs of the city. The best proof of this statement was their political status. Under the Prussian Constitution, before World War I, voting rights were based on tax-paying ability. The small group of wealthy citizens paying one-third of the taxes was entitled to elect one-third of the entire membership of the *Landtag*; a much larger group which paid the next third of the taxes was entitled to an equal representation; while the great mass of the population paying the lowest third of the taxes was entitled to the final third of the representation. The Mennonites were almost invariably found in the upper group, the other Protestants in the second, and the Catholics in the great mass of the population.

In spite of their high standing in financial and business circles, however, the Mennonites retained to a remarkable degree the ideals of simplicity and industry which have been a cherished tradition among the Mennonites all over Europe. Many years ago one of the wealthy von der Leyens objected to the introduction of a pulpit into their church on the ground that it savored too much of Catholicism.

Life Two Hundred Years Ago

An employee of the big silk mills back in 1760, though the husband of a Mennonite wife, was not a Mennonite himself and was not in sympathy with the rigid and austere religious practices of the day. He has left an interesting picture of the religious practices among the Crefeld Mennonites of that time. They had no organs in their churches then, he said, nor did they have specially trained ministers. They were exceptionally generous and hospitable, helping every worthy cause both within and without their own congregations. They were frugal, industrious, and frowned upon all luxuries. Their clothes were simple, usually of a somber color, and of a prescribed form. Shoestrings were prescribed instead of buckles. But the young people, this writer suggests, often broke away from these restrictions. The young men even dared to wear their hair in round curls, and to substitute the forbidden and worldly buckle for the old-fashioned shoestring. They wore blue coats instead of black, according to the prevailing fashions; but trousers and vests still had to be black.

The young women, too, began to insist on greater liberty to follow the fashions of the world. Their bonnets assumed more elaborate styles, and were more highly decorated with gay ribbons. Their dresses for workaday were of livelier colors and gayer patterns than formerly. However, on Sundays they still had to appear in brown or black. Finger rings and similar ornamental jewelry were still strictly forbidden. By the close of the century, however, most of the old restrictions had been discarded, and a salaried and educated ministry had been inaugurated.

World War II and After

Great changes have taken place in the Crefeld Mennonite Church. Like other German industrial cities, Crefeld suffered severely during World War II. The industries and monuments of culture built up by the Mennonites suffered a similar fate. The church (originally erected in 1696), parsonage, and orphanage on the Königstrasse, were completely destroyed during the air raids. This experience, however, deepened the religious life and fellowship of the congregation. Like Emden, this congregation won non-Mennonites to its fold. Many Mennonite refugees from the East found comfort and help in this city and congregation.

The congregation at Crefeld is the largest German Mennonite congregation. Because of its location so near the Dutch border and because most of its early members were Dutch, it was, for a time, a member of the A.D.S. In 1949 and 1950 the Mennonite Church on the Königstrasse, which had been destroyed in World War II, was rebuilt. During the first three decades of the century, the congregation was served by Gustav Kraemer. Its pastor after 1937 was Dirk Cattepoel who was one of the representatives of the German Mennonites at the Mennonite World Conference of 1948.

Relation to Dutch Mennonites

All Mennonite congregations of northwestern Germany remained in close cultural and spiritual relation with their Dutch brethren almost up to the present. The language of the pulpit remained Dutch until far into the nineteenth century. German was not fully introduced into religious worship in Emden until 1889, in Hamburg and Crefeld somewhat earlier. Dutch preachers, trained in the Amsterdam Seminary, served the churches even longer. The religious literature, whether written by their own pastors, or imported from Holland, was of Menno Simons's native tongue. It is not strange, therefore, that the Mennonites here would have followed the religious beliefs and practices of their brethren in Holland. In the matter of nonresistance, however, they clung to the practice a little more tenaciously and a bit longer than did the Dutch. Back in the seventeenth and eighteenth centuries the merchants of Hamburg, and other congregations along the seacoast, had occasion to make a more practical application of this doctrine than did Mennonites in other regions where military exemption could be secured by the payment of a certain sum of money. Contrary to the general practice of the times, ships owned by Mennonites carried no guns. A violation of this rule made the owner subject to church discipline—usually excommunication.

Opposition to war service, however, weakened rapidly during the exciting times of the Napoleonic period. Although the church elders kept up a running protest through the entire first half of the nineteenth century against the various attempts of the ruling authorities to establish universal service without exemptions, the number of laity to whom the maintenance of the old traditions became a matter of indifference, especially among the younger men, was constantly growing. When universal service was introduced throughout the North German Confederation in 1867, no serious attempt was made by the Mennonites of this region to secure special exemption in their behalf.

Of the essentials of the early Mennonites only two had been retained—rejection of the oath, and the practice of adult baptism—both fundamental symbols of a free church. To these may be added also a commendable emphasis in everyday life on the virtues of the simple life and aid to the needy.

Changes that have taken place in regard to basic beliefs and traditional Mennonite views and practices will be presented in the context of the developments of the Mennonites in Germany and in Europe in general.

2. WEST PRUSSIA AND POLAND

During the decades of persecution, the Dutch Mennonites fled far beyond the places thus far mentioned. Dutch merchant ships sailed not only to cities located on German shores of the North Sea, but also to the Baltic Sea, from where the passengers could easily reach Danzig, Marienburg, and other towns and cities on the Vistula River. Thus, this also became a route to escape persecution. Already in 1534 the Danzig city council wrote to the cities of Amsterdam, Antwerp, and Emden requesting that no Anabaptists be permitted to board the ships to Danzig. This would indicate that some had come to this Catholic country soon after the Dutch Anabaptists originated in Emden.

Lutherans and Reformed were more readily admitted. But gradually some Mennonites were admitted by some of the large estate owners. Often it was because they won recognition as industrious workers who converted the swamps into pastures or grain fields. Scattered Mennonite settlements must have originated in the triangle of Danzig-Elbing-Marienburg already in the early 1530s. These settlers came from various provinces of the Netherlands: Holland, Friesland, Groningen, Brabant, Flanders, and elsewhere. Persecution was mostly the reason, since the Netherlands was still occupied by the Catholic ruler, Philip II, of Spain. Some common names among them were Ens, Wiebe, Janzen, and Suderman. Even some expelled Moravian Anabaptists (Hutterites) settled in the Thorn-Graudenz-Kulm area as early as 1535.

The Anabaptist Mennonites on the banks of the Vistula River had problems of their own, just as had been the case in the Netherlands. In their homeland they had been divided into Flemish and Frisians, followed by subdivisions. Here, having come from various parts of the Netherlands, they had to adjust themselves not only to a new environment, but also to each other. It was fortunate that the Danzig Mennonite Church had Dirk Philips as the first elder or leading minister. In 1549 Menno Simons even spent some time with them, preaching and admonishing them to brotherly love and unity. This visit was followed later by a letter he wrote to the "Brethren in Prussia" encouraging them to continue in Christian love and unity.

A new phase in the migration of the Mennonites developed when in 1547 to 1550 a great drainage program was initiated in an area some forty miles wide in the Vistula Delta, east of Danzig. When the Danzig banker Loyson acquired the territory of Tiegenhof in 1547, he invited Mennonites from Holland to do the drainage work. Two Mennonites, Herman van Bommel and

Tönnis Florisson, purchased large areas of the Danzig Werder for drainage and settlement. Mennonites from the Netherlands were invited to come and help with the project. This pattern was repeated at other places, and industrious workers in the swamps often acquired land from the landlords. Thus numerous Mennonite villages originated in the Vistula Delta.

Though many of the Dutch Mennonites came from cities in the Netherlands, they were not permitted to live in cities, such as Danzig. Thus by 1550 a large congregation had been established in Schotland, just outside of the walls of Danzig. Here they worshiped and established their shops for the manufacture of textiles, lace, and other goods which were in demand. Even the *Danziger Lachs* (brandy) introduced by the Mennonites survived after their departure to West Germany.

Because of their various skills, some Mennonites were finally admitted into the city of Danzig, depending on whether the trade they pursued was welcomed in the city. These prosperous Danzig Mennonites maintained contact with their fellow believers in Amsterdam longer than those in rural areas. This was consequential for some differences that developed. Many of the sons of the Danzig Mennonites went to the Netherlands for an education in a trade. Considerable contacts were maintained, ministers were exchanged, and intermarriages took place. The Low German of West Prussia was accepted sooner among the Mennonites in the rural areas than among those in the city of Danzig, and the preaching in the Dutch language was maintained longer in Danzig than in rural congregations. In the rural churches the shift from the Dutch to the High German occurred first.

Hans van Steen (1705-1781) grew up near Danzig and received a business training in Amsterdam where he was baptized. After his return to West Prussia he joined the Flemish Mennonite Church of Danzig, married, and established a business and brewery. He was elected deacon, minister, and elder, and was very influential in defending the rights of the Mennonites who were still being constantly threatened in various ways. His sermons were popular and even attended by non-Mennonites. Throughout his lifetime he preached in the Dutch language and lamented it very much when the shift from the Dutch to the High German preaching took place in the rural congregations. He kept the Danzig Church Record in the Dutch language to the end of his life, but his successor shifted in both preaching and the entries in the Church Record to the High German (1784). This was at about the time when some of the Mennonites of West Prussia began to migrate to Russia.

Religious and Civil Liberty

Although the Mennonites of the region, with a few exceptions, had a common origin and shared a common cultural history, yet living as they did under four different and separate political divisions, their experiences in the enjoyment of religious and civil liberty were not all identical. The delta congregations were under the rule of the Catholic king of Poland; those about Königsberg and Tilsit, under the Lutheran duke and, later, the king of Prussia. Danzig was a Lutheran imperial city, and nominally under Polish domination, yet as a free city it enjoyed a great deal of local autonomy to deal with its own problems as it pleased. Elbing, too, as a former Hanseatic town, enjoyed more liberty than did the smaller settlements in the open country. By the close of the eighteenth century, however, all these separate divisions had been united under the king of Prussia. Under the feudal system of landholding which still prevailed here, the local noblemen in the lower Vistula, most of whom were of Catholic persuasion, also enjoyed more or less of local control over their large estates. This division of political authority accounts for the fact that frequently king, city, and feudal lord—Lutheran and Catholic—held conflicting views regarding the policy to be adopted toward the Mennonites and issued contradictory orders against them, each according to his own interests. In the confusion, Mennonites sometimes benefited.

However the Mennonites never enjoyed equal civil or religious privileges with those of the state churches. Toleration, at first, did not extend beyond the right of worship. Anything that might promote the growth of Mennonitism beyond their own immediate circle was strictly prohibited. There was to be no proselyting. Worship must be carried on quietly, without attracting public notice, and in private homes only. Meetinghouses were not allowed until the close of the sixteenth century, and even then they had to be held as private property in the name of some individual. Public burials were not permitted. Occasionally Mennonites benefited from the rivalries of the state churches, as when in 1612 the Reformed elector, John Sigismund of Brandenburg, became duke of Prussia. He refused to carry out against those of his own faith the restrictions passed by the Lutheran legislature against "Zwinglians, Calvinists, and Anabaptists." Mennonites shared the exemptions of the Zwinglians in this case. Usually Catholic ecclesiastical landowners were more tolerant toward Mennonites than Lutheran businessmen or clericals who had less to gain from the presence of industrious farmers than did the former.

Such popular antagonisms as occasionally manifested themselves against the Mennonites were based perhaps less on religious than upon economic grounds. At first, living in isolated groups on lands hitherto but sparsely populated, they were able to pursue the even tenor of their way without molestation. But growing prosperous in course of time, they aroused the envy of their less thrifty neighbors and fellow townsmen. The fact that they were foreigners did not help them either, and they were slow to adapt themselves to the culture of their adopted country. Segregated in large secluded groups, practicing a proscribed religion, maintaining for nearly two centuries their Dutch language, and keeping in close touch all this time with the culture of the land of their origin, the descendants of the first settlers retained many of the characteristics of a foreign people into the eighteenth century and beyond.

When in 1579 the Mennonites of East Prussia asked for permission to settle in Königsberg to earn their living there, upon the complaint of the local residents, the reigning duke replied that foreigners had never been permitted to trade in Prussian cities; and, besides, the confession of faith which the Mennonites had submitted disclosed the fact that it did not agree with the Lutheran Augsburg Confession, especially on the matter of baptism and obligations of police duty. Mennonites were consequently denied the right to engage in trade in the city, and those already there were ordered to leave.

Those who benefited from Mennonite thrift, on the other hand, were the most ardent champions of religious tolerance. In 1676, after the low delta regions had suffered heavy losses from high waters and broken dikes, the king of Pomerellen, speaking before the *Landtag* at Marienburg, accused the Mennonites of being the cause of the catastrophe. God was punishing Danzig, "the nest of the Mennonites," he said, for tolerating these people within her jurisdiction. He brought a number of deputies to his way of thinking, and these attempted to force an order for exile through the *Landtag*. However, the deputy from Marienburg, realizing the economic worth of the Mennonite farmers to the country, spoke in their behalf. "One can easily tell," he said, "whether a lazy drunken farmer tills the soil, or a sober industrious Mennonite; rather invite more of them than to drive out those already here." Other deputies from Mennonite communities who shared these views interceded for them with the king, who, by taking a personal interest in the controversy, succeeded in preventing the execution of this order.

The kings of both Poland and Prussia seemed strangely inconsistent through the centuries in their policies toward the

Mennonites. Sometimes one king would grant a charter of liberties only to have it repealed by his successor. Occasionally the same king would repeatedly reverse his own decrees. The best explanation for these inconsistencies is no doubt to be found in the fact that under absolutism, kings did not need to be consistent, but might safely follow their own caprices. Their policies were usually dictated by whatever interests at the time had influence with them. If the clergy, business interests, or city authorities desired the expulsion of the Mennonites or a curtailment of their privileges, and no other interests interposed, kings often issued the desired orders, to be as readily repealed at the request of other influences. Numerous charters of privilege, as well as orders for exile in both Poland and Prussia, were passed during the two hundred years preceding the reign of Frederick the Great. But these orders were passed merely, it seems, for effect, and never meant to be carried out. Mennonites frequently paid little attention to them.

By the middle of the seventeenth century, ruling authorities had discovered a better use here also of thrifty and prosperous Mennonites. Like the Jews, they might be made the source of considerable revenue for both local and royal treasuries. In 1642 Willibald von Haxberg, minister to the Polish King Vladislav IV, persuaded the king that inasmuch as the Mennonites had been the cause of great financial loss to the native businessmen in the cities of the delta, no doubt because of competition, their property ought to be condemned. The king authorized the confiscation, whereupon von Haxberg promised the Mennonites that if they would raise fifty thousand *Thaler* from the country churches and a small sum from Danzig and Elbing, he would intercede for them before the king and secure a repeal of the order. The Mennonites protested, but under threat of military force, they were compelled to pay. Appealing to both the provincial estates and the king, as a result of this experience they received another charter guaranteeing them against a repetition of similar extortions in the future.

As late as 1750, however, under another king who had evidently forgotten the promises of his predecessors, the merchants of Danzig were able to close Mennonite shops and other places of business. The Mennonites were given to understand, however, that they might avoid the calamity by the payment of a substantial sum of tribute money. When the Mennonites told the king that they were not financially able to meet the demands, he suggested they turn to their prosperous Dutch brethren for help. But the Dutch Mennonites, usually generous in their support of every worthy cause, refused to be blackmailed by the king in this case. Instead, they persuaded both the city of Amsterdam and the

States General to intercede with the Polish king in behalf of the Danzig church. This appeal may have had some effect, for, although the king remained obstinate and refused for some time to give back to the Mennonites their former commercial rights, yet upon payment of a smaller amount of tribute money gathered together by Mennonites from their German rather than Dutch brethren, they were permitted to reopen their places of business.

Military Exemption

Opposition to war did not seem to be a serious cause of antagonism before the days of Frederick the Great. Military exemption, as noted elsewhere, was a usual inducement offered not only to Mennonites but to other groups who would settle on sparsely populated or wastelands all over Europe during that period as well. In times of stress, of course, as in the case of the siege of Danzig by the Swedes in 1734, everyone was forced into some sort of noncombatant service. At that time Mennonites were set to the task of putting out the fires caused by incendiary shells. Frequently, too, Mennonites were forced to furnish substitutes, a privilege open to all others as well. By the middle of the eighteenth century a special exemption tax was commonly levied upon the Mennonites and paid by them for the privileges they enjoyed.

An interesting exception to the general attitude of the Prussian kings toward the Mennonite refusal to serve in the armies was an incident that occurred in East Prussia under the eccentric Frederick William I. Frederick William was noted, in addition to his other peculiarities, for his partiality for "long fellows," as his giant Potsdam guards were known. When in 1723 the king's recruiting agents in the region of Tilsit spied out some half-dozen stalwart young Mennonites as likely candidates for the king's special service, they did not hesitate to use what force was necessary to drag the unwilling recruits to Potsdam. The church elders, interceding in behalf of the young men, reminded Frederick William of the special privileges granted them under his predecessors. The king released the unwilling guards, but was determined that there should be no repetition of the incident. He ordered all the Mennonites within the Tilsit settlement to leave his kingdom, never to return. Most of them left the following year, having found a refuge among their brethren in Polish Prussia.

This order did not affect the Mennonites about Königsberg. But several years later, in 1732, after the clergy had brought a serious, though unfounded, charge of Socinianism against all the Mennonites, Frederick William was glad to include the city dwellers also in another general order for exile within three months. However, the ministers of the king, realizing that the country would lose more than it would gain by the departure of these industrious farmers and artisans, secured a revocation of the order, with this limitation: Mennonites were to remain and return only on condition that they establish textile works within the city, an industry very much desired, and in which the Mennonites were skilled. With the accession of Frederick the Great, a period of greater toleration was inaugurated.

Remaining a Dutch Community

Although divided politically, the Mennonites of East and West Prussia had a common cultural background. Like their brethren on the Vistula River, they retained the Dutch language in the pulpit for generations. High German was not introduced until about the middle of the eighteenth century. The same was true concerning the Mennonites of Dutch background living in Poland. In daily life, however, the Low German of the local population was accepted much earlier.

The large, self-sufficing settlements, especially in the Vistula Delta, made it easy for the Mennonites here to maintain and perpetuate their distinctive doctrines and customs. Since proselytizing was forbidden, they acquired little new blood during the centuries. A study of typical names as late as 1912 indicates that the West Prussian Mennonites consisted almost exclusively of the descendants of the first Dutch settlers who came there in the sixteenth century. According to this study there were, among the ten thousand Mennonites of these regions, 369 family names, of which the following are the most common: *Penner*, 527, *Wiens*, *Wienz*, 499; *Dueck, Dieck, Dyck*, 492; *Claassen, Klassen*, 409; *Wiebe*, 434; *Janzen, Jantzen*, 292; *Enns, Entz*, 275; *Janz*, 254; *Froese*, 254; *Regehr, Regier*, 253; *Harder*, 184; *Ewert*, 166; *Pauls*, 163; *Neufeld*, 161; *Fast*, 157; *Franz*, 141; *Friesen*, 140; *Reimer*, 140; *Epp*, 131; *Fieguth*, 120; *Albrecht*, 120; *Nickel*, 118; *Peters*, 107. Nearly one-half of the entire population, it will be seen, is embraced in the first twenty-one names. The other half is spread over the remaining 348 names, the vast majority of which include but one or two isolated families that came into the church since the settlements in Prussia were first made.

The author of this study says further that the entire list may be classified under four groups—

1. The merchants and artisans who first settled in Danzig and Elbing, seemingly came from the industrial classes of the larger Dutch cities. The following names are of Dutch origin, and are not found in the country congregations—*van Almonde, van Amersfort, Bachdach, van Beuningen, Conwentz, van Duehren, Dunckel, Eggerath, Engman, van Eck, Focking, van Haegen,*

Hansen, van Kampen, Kauenhoven, Krahn, Lamberts, Momber, van Roy, Rutenberg, van Steen, Utesch, de Veer. The disappearance of old as well as the appearance of new family names can be due to the fact that there was a lively migration back and forth between Danzig and the Netherlands.

2. The second group includes families of Flemish congregations in the large delta which were subject to only slight changes from migrations. The most common names are: *Claassen, Dyck, Dieck, Enz, Epp, Harder, Neufeld, Penner, Regehr, Regier, Reimer, van Riesen, Thiessen, Warkentin, Wiens,* and *Woelke.* All of these are as common today as they were two hundred years ago.

3. The third group of names of the Frisian churches of the Orlofferfelde and Thiensdorf congregations are sharply divided from the other groups. The following are the most common: *Albrecht, Allert, Bestvater, Dau, Dirksen, Friesen, Froese, Funk, Grunau, Harms, Janzen, Mekelberger, Martens, Nickel, Pauls, Quapp, Quiring,* and *Unger.*

4. The fourth group is found principally in the upper Vistula congregations: *Adrian, Balzer, Bartel, Ewert, Franz, Goerz, Kopper, Kliewer, Kerber, Schroeder, Stobbe, Unrau, Voth.*

The following names are of Polish origin: *Busenitz, Dellesky, Ratzlaff, Rogalsky, Schepanski, Suckau, Tetzlaff, Tilitzke, Utesch.*

The Flemish and Frisian, as well as other divisions among the Prussian Mennonites, kept their groups quite rigidly apart. Even intermarriage was almost impossible, except by being excommunicated by the one group and rebaptized by the other. But by the middle of the eighteenth century this relationship was gradually altered. The sharp distinction between the Flemish and Frisians was thus removed.

Philanthropy and Culture

Mennonites everywhere have always been most generous in the care of their own poor and sick. They are thoroughly committed to the belief that charity begins at home, so they never permit any of their own to become a general charge upon society at large. In each community, both in Holland and in the settlements around the Baltic, by the side of the church there was always a home for the aged, and one for homeless children, as well as a hospital for the sick. Sometimes several smaller congregations would join together to discharge this obligation. These characteristic charitable institutions have been perpetuated and transplanted ever since by the descendants of these West Prussian Mennonites wherever they have gone—to the steppes of South Russia, the plains of Manitoba and Kansas, and, in more recent times, to the high plateaus of Mexico and the wilderness of Paraguay.

The West Prussian Mennonites were as a rule not a literary people. Some of the books found among the early settlers were the Dutch *Biestkens Bible*, the writings of Menno Simons and Dirk Philips, the *Martyrs Mirror*, and perhaps a stray copy here and there of the *Wandelnde Seele*. All these were in the Dutch language. Among the books might be a confession of faith and catechism published in 1671 in the German language by Georg Hansen, elder of the Flemish church in Danzig. Hansen wrote a number of other books in Dutch and in German.

An interesting picture of the religious customs prevailing here at the time can be gathered from a series of letters written by Hans van Steen, elder of the Old Flemish congregation in Danzig, who lived during the latter half of the eighteenth century. The church buildings of the period, according to van Steen, were constructed of wood, usually with a tile roof, without paint either inside or out. Within, there was no pulpit. Instead, along the side wall, the long side, on a raised platform stood a row of chairs, the middle one of which, slightly elevated above the rest, was reserved for the speaker of the day. The preacher delivered his lengthy sermon seated, without book or notes or gesture, and in the Dutch language. Before the end of the century, however, with the introduction of the pulpit, sermons were delivered standing, and from notes, or written or printed books. Hans van Steen, lamenting the rising tide of worldliness, remarked, "The beautiful simple practices of Menno Simons are disappearing more and more." Worship was plain and simple in form. Organs were introduced in Neugarten in 1788 and in Danzig in 1806, although not without opposition. Others followed later.

The ministry, as in their original home, was still divided into three ranks: *Älteste* (elders), *Vermaaner* (ministers), and *Armendiener* (deacons). The *Vorsänger* (song leader) was also an elected official, in for life, and with a dignity just below that of the deacon. The ministry, as a whole, enjoyed the title *der Ehrsame Dienst* (the worthy ministry). All ranks were elected from among the laity, and served without pay and without special preparation. In fact, a promise to accept any call to service was one of the vows required of every male candidate for baptism at the time of admission to the church. Serving for life and without pay, the ministers exercised much more influence over their flocks than did their later salaried brethren of the cloth, who for that reason were more at the mercy of their congregations. The elders especially enjoyed a high degree of power. Although not clothed with quite the "indelible character" with which the Catholics invested their clergy, yet these elders, once elected, held life positions in their congregations, and could not be removed except for gross sin.

Church government was congregational. Frequent conferences were held by the elders from the various congregations, but resolutions that were adopted on these occasions had to be accepted by the members of each congregation separately before they became binding. It was perhaps an overemphasis upon the invalidity of infant baptism that retarded the admission of members to the church until they had reached a minimum age of at least twenty years. Often they were thirty or more, and fathers and mothers of growing families. A period of formal catechetical instruction always preceded admission.

The Prussian Mennonites at this time still observed closed communion, with the different groups—Frisian and Flemish— even discriminating against one another. Within each branch, only those who were at peace with the Lord and the brethren were admitted to the communion table. To find out the spiritual state of all the members, special visitors called *Umbitter* visited each family just before communion day in the interests of spiritual harmony.

Discipline was strictly enforced among all the groups. All social obligations had to be rigidly met. Each member must pay his taxes and tribute money. To refuse to pay the latter was to make the burden fall the more heavily upon the remainder of the membership, since such taxes were levied in a lump sum upon the membership as a whole. The ministers had much to say in their disciplinary capacities about gambling, dancing, and kindred frivolities. Corporal punishment of servants is also frequently mentioned as a cause for church discipline. In 1745 a group of applicants for baptism in one of the large churches, including several members from prominent families, was refused admission because they appeared in unbecoming clothes which had been imported from Holland—shoes with buckles instead of the traditional strings, neckscarfs, and cuffs on their coats. One had even visited a theater, the ministers said. These applicants no doubt repented of their vanities in the course of the year, for the next year they were admitted. There was much dispute over the wearing of wigs, too, but when it was found that in Holland even the preachers were wearing them, these articles of adornment could not be kept out of the Danzig church either.

Marriage was a sacred rite, though not a sacrament as among the Catholics. It must be performed, therefore, on Sunday and in church, never in a private home. Proposals were carried to the bride from the prospective bridegroom by the above-mentioned *Umbitter*, a kind of an all-around handyman, ranking just below the *Vorsänger* and deacon as a permanent church functionary. In a meeting of ministers in Danzig in 1765, one of the elders lamented the fact that the beautiful old custom of sending two men with a marriage proposal to the prospective bride, and the return in two weeks for a final answer, was passing.

Mennonites were not permitted to hold public funerals, nor were funeral sermons common before 1800. Instead of a sermon it was still customary for some friend of the deceased to write a poem in the Dutch language in commemoration of the latter. This poem, set to some well-known melody, would be sung at the funeral, and would constitute nearly the whole of the service. Since the verses were long and many, and the melody slow, the time consumed would equal that of an ordinary funeral oration. The funeral hymn of Hans van Steen, who died in 1781, was composed by his friend Hans Momber and contained twenty-four long stanzas. Funeral notices and wedding invitations were carried from house to house by the *Umbitter*, since both occasions were open to the entire membership. This practice is still being followed among some of the conservative Mennonites of Mexico and Paraguay.

Many of the old customs, like the Dutch language, were passing at the close of the eighteenth century, much to the sorrow of van Steen who saw no good in the new things that were being ushered in on the eve of the French Revolution.

A few words specifically regarding the Danzig congregation may not be out of order here. As already noted, the first settlers in the Danzig region did not locate within the city walls, but had to remain in the outside suburbs and countryside. Though a free city, Danzig was politically under the domination of the kings of Poland. Only the recognized state religions were permitted within the city walls. But in course of time Mennonites drifted into the city proper, though they were granted only limited rights of worship within their private homes. Both the Old Flemish and Old Frisian branches of the church were represented in Danzig. The Flemish built their first meetinghouse in a back alley within the city walls in 1648; the Frisians, a little later.

Both Flemish and Frisians kept in rather close contact with their Dutch brethren for many years. In fact a certain wing of the Flemish in the Netherlands came to be known as the Danzig Old Flemish as a result of this connection between the Danziger and the Dutch. Dutch remained the language of the pulpit in Danzig until well toward the close of the eighteenth century. In 1808 the two wings of the church united into one congregation. At its peak in the seventeenth century, the Mennonite population in Danzig and environs numbered over one thousand.

Under Frederick the Great

The reign of Frederick the Great, from 1740 to 1786, was in a way a turning point in the history of the West Prussian Mennonites. It was during this period and the years immediately following that the different regions in which they lived were united under one political rule. Frederick, being of a liberal turn of mind, granted the greatest freedom of religion to his subjects. One of the earliest acts, after his accession in 1740, was to invite the Mennonites who had been exiled by his predecessor several years before to return to their former homes. In 1744 he granted the Mennonites of Königsberg full rights of citizenship, more than fifty years before similar privileges were enjoyed by those in Danzig under Polish rule. Two years later he suggested to his recruiting agents that they respect the convictions of his Mennonite subjects in the Elbing district in the matter of taking part in war.

It is small wonder, therefore, that, when at the time of the first partitioning of Poland in 1772, the delta region fell to the lot of Frederick, the Mennonites here were well pleased. In order to express their loyalty to their new king as well as pleasure at his accession, the churches near Marienburg, on the occasion of a royal celebration in that city which the king attended, presented him with an appropriate gift from the products of their farms—two well-fed oxen ready for the king's table, four hundred pounds of butter, and twenty cakes of cheese, together with a large assortment of chickens and ducks.

This gift was evidently meant to be something more than a mere token of appreciation, however, for at the same time the king was handed a petition in which the churches asked for a confirmation of the liberties they had enjoyed under the Polish rulers, including exemption from military service. Frederick was glad to promise complete religious toleration, but as to military exemption, that had by this time become another matter. In the expansion of the Prussian kingdom he owed too much to a well-organized army to look with indifference to any shrinking of the supply of available troops.

The growing spirit of militarism engendered in middle Europe by the long wars of the eighteenth century boded no good for the peace-loving Mennonites. So long as the Mennonite settlements within Frederick's domain had remained small and scattered, the granting of exemption for other equally important service did not materially weaken the military strength of the nation, and Frederick, as already noted, had not been hesitant in providing for the tender consciences of his Mennonite subjects. However with the acquisition of the large compact areas within the lowlands of the Vistula, occupied almost totally with a people opposed to the use of military force, the problem took on a different aspect to a king bent on still further expansion of his possessions. With increasing warfare and growing armies, impressment was becoming more necessary, and service more unpopular among the masses. The example of a specially privileged class in the midst of a reluctant people made the task of both the recruiting officers as well as the impressment gangs more difficult.

But Frederick finally decided that money was as essential to a program of conquest as soldiers, and as hard to get; and the Mennonites, because of some peculiar twist in their logic, did not draw fine distinctions between direct and indirect service. A fairly satisfactory compromise was temporarily worked out, therefore, in the course of the negotiations during the years immediately succeeding. In 1780 Frederick granted the Mennonites a special charter in which they were guaranteed complete religious liberty with equal rights to carry on any kind of business, on conditon, however, that they pay the annual sum of five thousand *Thaler* for the support of the military academy at Culm.

In the meantime, an earlier regulation passed by the ministry in 1774 that Mennonites were not to increase by the purchasing of more land, except with the consent of the king, was full of troublesome possibilities for the future. Frederick himself evidently did not rigidly enforce this regulation, for during the next three years Mennonite holdings increased by nearly 300 percent. But the Lutheran clergy in the region of the Mennonite settlements now also became interested, along with the king's recruiting marshals, in the further expansion of these industrious nonconformists; for the support of the state church as well rested upon a substantial Lutheran landowning population.

These conditions resulted in a new edict issued in 1789 by Frederick's successor, and binding on the two Prussias, in which the same provisions for military exemptions were retained as before, but a more drastic means of preventing the further purchase of lands was stipulated. The further acquisition of land was now denied the Mennonites; nor were any more to be admitted from the outside except in case a prospective settler had money to the value of two thousand *Thaler*. Such a prospect might locate, with the consent of the king's council, upon such sparsely settled lands as were suitable to cattle raising and small dairying. Such persons and their descendants after them, of military age, were to pay a special tax of one *Thaler* to a general hospital fund however. These privileges accrued only to Mennonites. All children of mixed marriages must be regarded as members of the state churches and outside of these special concessions.

It was quite evident by this time that both church and state were determined to stop the further growth of the Mennonites. Hampered by excessive and unfair taxes, unable to provide new homes for their growing young people, and fearful of the future, the Mennonites now looked about them with heavy hearts for a new asylum where they might be free to exercise their religious convictions without fear of governmental restraint. Those most vitally concerned at first were the landless and the more conscientious.

But where were they to go? America evidently was not given serious consideration at this time. Most providential must have seemed, just now in their perplexity, the invitation from Catherine II of Russia, which had been announced in the summer of 1786. She urged them to come to southern Russia where they might enjoy all the privileges, religious and civil, that had been denied them in Prussia. Many of them accepted this invitation. During the next half century, about half of the whole delta Mennonite population migrated to the steppes of South Russia. But that story is told in a succeeding chapter.

Of the total Prussian Mennonite population at this time, only about one thousand lived in East Prussia; the remaining twelve thousand lived in the Vistula and Nogat deltas in West Prussia.

Napoleonic Wars and Revolution

Although it is fair to assume that those who remained after the exodus just described were among the better established of the Mennonite population, and perhaps the more liberal minded on the military question, yet during the troublous years that followed they continued the struggle for their traditional beliefs as valiantly as ever. During the early stages of the Napoleonic wars when the Prussian population seemed to be divided in their allegiance and the patriotic spirit ran low, the Mennonites, though nonresistant, yet remained loyal to their king and were willing to render the fatherland any aid that did not conflict with their convictions. In 1806 when Frederick William and his court, after Jena and Auerstadt, stopped at Graudenz in the course of their flight to Memel, the Mennonites of the neighboring regions gathered together some thirty thousand *Thaler* for their king as an evidence of their loyalty. Abraham Nickel, the deacon of the Schönsee congregation, was commissioned to present the gift. Nickel and his wife met the royal pair and as the deacon made the offering, his wife at the same time gave the queen a basket of butter to the great delight, so tradition says, of the grand lady.

During the so-called War of Liberation, patriotic fervor revived, and a strong spirit of nationalism swept over the land. When a universal military training law was passed in 1814 without any special consideration for Mennonite scruples, the elders found it a difficult task to maintain the faith against the popular tide, or even to curb the military ardor of some of their young people. How difficult it must have been for the young men of the time to stand for their principles in the face of this tide of patriotism and against the ridicule and taunts of their fellows can perhaps best be appreciated by the conscientious objectors in America who passed through World Wars I and II. In their appeal to the king for a recognition of their traditional views the elders said, "We will gladly suffer any loss to our property and possessions and, what is much harder, the scorn and derision of our neighbors if only our religious convictions may be spared."

Frederick William promised to observe their old privileges, but at the expense of a substantial tax instead. Just how heavy this tax was is not known, but it was extraordinarily high. During the entire period of the Napoleonic wars, the Mennonites paid special tribute above that paid to the Culm academy, a sum, it is said, mounting to thousands of dollars.

That the elders still rigidly endeavored to maintain the historic attitude of the church toward war during this period is shown in the case of a certain von Riesen, a member of the Elbing congregation, who, because he volunteered for service and fought at Waterloo, was excommunicated by his elder. After his return, von Riesen sued the elder for damages and won his suit in the local courts. But the other elders all supported their fellow minister, and appealing the case to the higher courts, secured a reversal of the decision on the grounds that the plaintiff had no cause for action.

The Revolution of 1848, followed a few years later by Prussia's first constitution, marked another turning point in the history of Mennonite nonresistance. The Frankfurt Parliament of that year laid down the fundamental principle that religious conviction could not stand in the way of performing one's civic duties. While the proposed unification attempted at Frankfurt failed to materialize, and this regulation remained merely a wish, yet it was indicative of a new danger threatening the traditional peace principles of the Mennonites.

Democracies are much less considerate of conscientious scruples, and have less patience with special privileges granted to minorities than do autocracies. It was always because of their economic worth that Mennonites were granted special privileges by autocratic rulers—in such countries as Prussia, Austria, Russia, and, in more recent times, in Mexico and Paraguay. Frederick William IV himself recognized that fact when, in the course of an interview with some of the Mennonite elders who had interceded with him in behalf of their ancient privileges, he replied that now, since Prussia had a constitution, questions of special privilege no longer rested with him but rather with the legislature which represented the people.

It was at this time that the last large migration to Russia took place. Between 1853 and 1860 some two hundred fifty families located new settlements on the Volga with the promise of military exemption, and other privileges somewhat less liberal than those granted originally to the Mennonites of South Russia.

Unfortunate for the peace testimony of the Vistula Mennonites by this time was the fact that the Mennonites in West Germany had nearly given up the peace principle. It was a Mennonite deputy from Crefeld, von Beckerath, it will be remembered, who opposed in the Frankfurt Parliament the special consideration for Mennonites which had been suggested by a non-Mennonite West Prussian deputy from Danzig.

From this time on, the special status of the Mennonites was increasingly threatened by the increasing spirit of militarism. In 1861 a Marienburg deputy proposed in the Prussian *Landtag* the repeal of the exemption clause. This again necessitated the sending of a special commission of Mennonite elders to Berlin. During the Danish and Austrian wars of 1864 to 1866 the Mennonite question was forgotten for a few years; but the growing nationalism and militarism following these overwhelmingly successful conflicts did the Mennonite cause no good in the long run.

It was during this period that Wilhelm Mannhardt, of the University of Berlin and son of the Mennonite pastor in Danzig, was commissioned by the churches to draw up a compendium of the historic Mennonite position on the question of war for submission to the authorities at Berlin. The result was the comprehensive treatise now known as *Die Wehrfreiheit der Altpreussischen Mennoniten*, (*Nonresistance of the Prussian Mennonties*), published in 1863. This book is the best collection of documents in existence pertaining to the German Mennonite stand in matters of nonresistance up to that time. Those who were not willing to accept alternative or military service migrated to Russia and North America. For those remaining, it was a monument to a heritage given up in World Wars I and II. However, in the decades after the last disastrous war, a renewal of the heritage became noticeable among the younger generation.

The Cabinet Order of 1868

The end came in 1867 with the founding of the North German

Confederation. In that year Bismarck pushed through the Confederation Parliament a new universal military service law with no exemptions. The country churches again sent a committee of five elders to Berlin in the interests of their cause. This committee was granted interviews with most of the ministers, including A. T. von Roon, the minister of war, and with both the king and the crown prince, but not with Bismarck. All of these listened to the elders with respect but refused to commit themselves as to future concessions. The crown prince, when told in the course of an interview that the Mennonites, if they could not secure some sort of guarantee of their religious liberties, might be forced to migrate en masse to Russia, replied, "In that case beware that you may not repeat the same experience in Russia that you are passing through here, for there everything is still in the making." That is just what happened to the Mennonites in Russia a few years later.

The elders returned to their congregations with no further assurances for the future than the suggestion that perhaps the new law might be modified so as to permit those having conscientious scruples to accept some sort of noncombatant service instead of regular duty. On March 3, 1868, these promises were given the force of law through a Cabinet Order according to which all members of the churches then established, and their descendants, would be granted the privilege of entering hospital, clerical, or other specified lines of noncombatant duty in the army, in case they objected to the actual use of arms.

Thus was ended for all the Mennonites of North Germany the long struggle, lasting for several centuries, to maintain what undoubtedly still remained as one of the most distinctive Mennonite doctrines. This struggle, not serious in the beginning, as already suggested, became increasingly so with the rise of the forces of democracy and militant nationalism. Perhaps a contributory factor to the loss of their old status was the growing lukewarmness of some of the Mennonites themselves, especially among the younger element. In Holland and northwest Germany the Mennonites had already, as noted above, forsaken their nonresistant principles.

However, the elders in the West Prussian churches, for the most part, especially in the country, were not inclined to surrender the old faith without further struggle. Refusing to accept even the rather liberal terms of the new Cabinet Order, they further petitioned the authorities, threatened conforming members with excommunication, and urged emigration. But all in vain. So far as the Mennonites were concerned, although the agitation was kept up for some years longer, the case was ended. The great majority of the young men after this accepted the noncombatant service offered. A few went in for full duty, for which some of them were at first excommunicated. A smaller number of those with more tender consciences refused even the terms of the Cabinet Order. For these latter, nothing was left but emigration.

As for the elders, Aron Wiebe of the *Fürstenwerder* congregation resigned his charge and left for Russia when he found that his members would accept the new order of things almost unanimously. A few years later some members of the *Heubuden* congregation and others migrated to America, settling in Kansas and Nebraska.

In the course of time Mennonite young men entering military training in times of peace found no logical reason for stepping out of the army in times of war, so they gradually lost all their antiwar scruples. In the Franco-Prussian War of 1870 many took actual service; and in World War I there were but few who insisted upon their rights under the Cabinet Order of 1868, which had been incorporated into the constitution of the empire in 1870. With the loss of their special privileges, of course, the West Prussian Mennonites were relieved of the obligation to render tribute for the benefit of the military academy at Culm, which they had paid annually up to this time.

Loss of Old Traditions

With the giving up of nonresistance, other distinctive practices and beliefs also went. Among them were the opposition to marrying outsiders, to open communion, and to an educated and salaried ministry. In the country churches, however, there were ministers who were elected from among the laity and who served without pay. In some cases the elder was an outsider with special training and serving for remuneration, while his associates in the congregation were elected according to the old method. This custom is still in practice among some of the descendants of the West Prussian and Russian Mennonites in South America and Canada.

The city churches departed from the old order more readily during this period than did those in the country. The Danzig congregation had no representative on the committee of elders which visited Berlin in the interests of military exemption in 1868, and took no part in the struggle among the elders to secure a modification of the Cabinet Order of that year. The Elbing-Ellerwald congregation, which had been made up of both city and country residents, divided into two congregations in 1852 on the basis of city and country dwellers. The questions on which they divided were mixed marriages, an educated ministry, attitude toward military service, religious instruction for children, and the enforcement of a strict discipline. Theologically all the churches of this region were more conservative than were their brethren in either Holland or northwest Germany.

The compact Prussian country churches did not produce as many men of prominence as did the smaller city churches in western Germany along the Dutch border. Among a few others, however, must be mentioned Hermann Sudermann, the German dramatist and novelist, who was the son of an East Prussian Mennonite. Among the well-known families who have served the Vistula congregations in one capacity or another, the Mannhardts occupy a conspicuous place. Jacob, the first theologically trained German Mennonite minister in Danzig in 1836, was founder of the *Mennonitische Blätter* in 1854. His son, Wilhelm, was author of the above-mentioned book on nonresistance; and Hermann Mannhardt was pastor of the Danzig Mennonite Church from 1879 to 1927.

After World Wars I and II

According to the Treaty of Versailles, almost the entire province of West Prussia became Polish territory. The Obernassau, Schönsee, and Montau-Gruppe congregations were located in this region. Two-thirds of all Prussian Mennonites were now located within the limits of the Free City of Danzig, which was attached economically to Poland by a customs union. The remaining congregations belonged to East Prussia. These congregations formed the Conference of East German Mennonites whose representatives met annually for fellowship and discussion.

The economic life of Germany after World War I, especially in the Free City of Danzig, in East Prussia, and the "Polish Corridor" region, was desperate. Poverty-stricken farmers lost land that had been in their families for generations. When Hitler came to power he took advantage of this situation, and by claiming he would save the farmers, he won many followers. Danzig was soon united with the *Reich*, but the attempt to reestablish a union with East Prussia by taking the "Polish Corridor" gave the signal for World War II.

The first Mennonite casualties were the two congregations, Deutsch-Kazun and Deutsch-Wymysle, near Warsaw, which suffered severely through mistreatment by Polish mobs during the initial stage of the war. The territory in the vicinity of Lemberg, belonging to Poland, was given to Russia, with the result that the so-called Galician Mennonites located there were evacuated to the Warthegau, a part of the former "Polish Corridor."

NORTHERN GERMANY

Even before the collapse of Germany, the loss of life among those Prussian Mennonites drafted into the army was great. The Heubuden congregation had between two hundred to two hundred fifty members in uniform. By 1944 approximately one hundred of these had been killed and an equal number were prisoners or missing. After the speedy conquests of the German Army in the West and in the East during the early part of the war, the tide turned. By Christmas 1944 the future looked gloomy for the population in Prussia. Long processions of refugees from the East had been passing through on their way westward for months. The Russian Army had broken into Poland and was approaching the Vistula Delta, reaching Elbing by the end of January 1945.

The Tragic End

The Mennonite families of Elbing and their pastor, Emil Händiges, along with other Mennonite congregations in that vicinity, joined the masses fleeing westward. Many perished through air raids, tanks, and general confusion. The refugees fled, organized and unorganized, under army supervision and without it—in private vehicles, in army trucks, by train, and on foot.

In the beginning of March 1945, it became increasingly clear to the Danzig population that the Russians were at the city gates. The civilian population was mobilized to defend the city. Among them was the pastor of the Danzig Mennonite Church, Erich Göttner, of whom nothing has been heard since. By the end of March, Danzig was taken—a heap of rubble.

All the refugees passed westward. Some were taken by ship to German cities in the West and to Danish cities then under German occupation. Among the two hundred thousand Germans who were thus stranded in Denmark were some two thousand Mennonites who lived there behind barbed wire from 1945 to 1948, when most of them were taken to West Germany. Others, pursued by the Russian Army, fled to western Germany where most of them reached the British zone. However, many were not so fortunate as to escape the onslaught of the Red Army. The fear of rape and mistreatment, of which neither women nor children were spared, drove many to commit suicide. One example of many will suffice to show the desperate situation in which some 10 million people of eastern Germany found themselves. A woman whose husband was in service hanged her children and herself when the Red Army approached. Someone stepped in and saved her life, but it was too late for the children.

No one will ever know how many German civilians, including

the Mennonites who did not manage to escape westward, were sent to Siberia for slave labor. Some have returned, but most of them never did. Of the ten thousand West Prussian Mennonites, only a few individuals have survived in their homeland. They, too, were deprived of any ownership. The beautiful farms were partly ruined by floods and other devastation and are now occupied by Poles. The church buildings are destroyed, dilapidated, and neglected, or used for Catholic services, theaters, and other purposes. The same is the case with the cemeteries.

After the War

The Berlin congregation which was founded in 1887 consisted of Mennonite families that had come to Berlin from all parts of Germany, especially Prussia. The congregation, which met in the Moravian church, had a membership of four hundred at the beginning of World War II.

During the siege of Berlin, the church, as well as the property of most members, was destroyed; many perished and others fled. But even in the ruins of Berlin a nucleus of a Mennonite brotherhood survived which, under the leadership of consecrated laymen, continued to meet for fellowship and spiritual nurture.

All the once-prosperous West Prussian Mennonites, who nearly four hundred fifty years ago started to drain and cultivate the swamps of the Vistula Delta, became homeless and shelterless. Some established new homes in western Germany and others migrated to Canada and Uruguay. The first group of nearly seven hundred reached Uruguay on October 27, 1948. Some have since returned to Germany. Numerous families established new homes in Canada. In Germany, West Prussian Mennonite settlements were established near Neuwied, Backnang, Enkenbach, and Espelkamp.

Many or most of the Mennonite congregations of West Germany have had an increase in membership since World War II, and particularly also since 1960. This was due first of all to the flight during World War II of the West Prussian Mennonites from the Vistula River and Danzig, Elbing, Marienburg, and other areas to Germany. There are now congregations in both West and East Berlin. The latter was organized in 1961 and has a membership of 300. In addition to East Berlin, some Sunday meetings take place in Rostock, Halle, Erfurt, Potsdam, and other cities of East Germany (DDR). The congregation in West Berlin (since 1887) has some 130 members and meets in the Menno-Heim.

The Mennonite Church of Bechterdissen started in 1956 and has a membership of 840 (1978). Bremen has a fellowship since 1947 with 115 members (1978). Larger congregations organized recently in various parts of West Germany are: Backnang (1951), 244 members (1978); Enkenbach (1956), 502 members (1978); and smaller congregations with over 100 members in Stuttgart (1933); Frankfurt (1948); Göttingen (1945); Hannover (1949); and Lübeck (1950). Mennonite Brethren congregations are found in Lage (Lippe) since 1966 and Neuwied since 1950. There are smaller congregations at a number of other places.

In recent years over 9,000 (1979) Mennonites have come from the USSR to West Germany. Many of these join the existing congregations. Some organize their own congregations and prefer not to affiliate with any of the Mennonite churches in Germany.

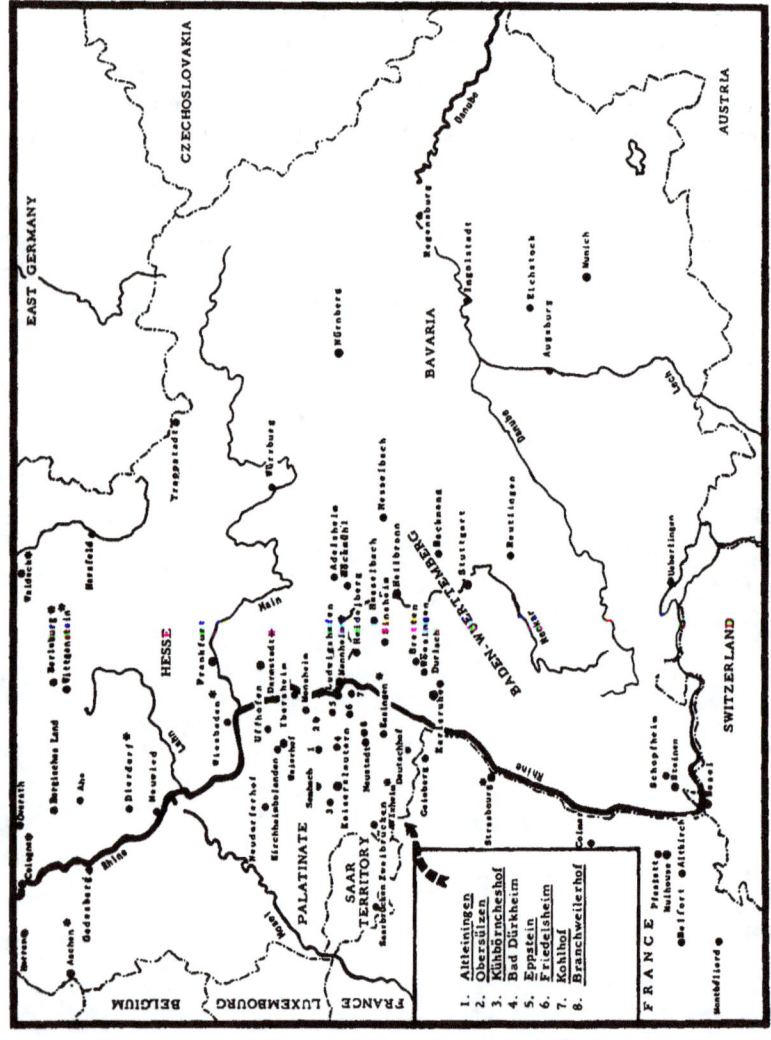

Mennonites in Southern Germany
(Only towns with Mennonite congregations or meetingplaces are shown. Extinct congregations are starred.)

VI
South Germany

1. HABSBURG CROWN LANDS

While the persecutions following the Münster catastrophe of 1535 effectually checked the further growth of Anabaptism within the empire, it did not completely annihilate the movement. For another full century, scattered Anabaptist or Mennonite communities succeeded in keeping themselves alive in mountain fastnesses and out-of-the-way places all across South Germany from the upper stretches of the Rhine to the headwaters of the Danube, from Strassburg to Vienna, never venturing far, however, beyond the confines of the German-speaking regions.

During all this time Mennonites were bitterly oppressed here. Men and women were burned at the stake and beheaded well up to the close of the sixteenth century. Persecution was most severe nearest the seat of Catholic imperial authority, the crown lands of the Habsburgs—the Austrias, Carniola, Carinthia, Salzburg, and especially in Tyrol. In all these regions the will of the Habsburgs had full sway, and the imperial edict of 1529, with its later confirmations, was executed to the letter.

In Tyrol magistrates and clergy did their utmost to completely uproot every trace of Mennonitism. Imprisonment, galley slavery, and death at the stake were the penalties prescribed for following one's conscience. Often the common people and occasionally even the jurors who were forced to pass sentence, as well as the executioners themselves, were in sympathy with their victims, and reluctantly carried out their part of the bloody program. In order to encourage the betrayal of those accused of heresy by their neighbors, and especially to thin out the ranks of the more aggressive leaders, an edict was issued at Innsbruck in 1540 promising one hundred *gulden* for the delivery of a Mennonite minister if alive; fifty if dead; and ten for an ordinary member.

Hoping that the sight of the executioner's block or the funeral pyre might serve as a deterrent to further defection from the faith, executions were usually made public spectacles. But the results were not always as expected. Mennonite martyrs often approached their fate boldly and joyfully, exhorting the sympathetic spectators to a nobler Christian life. The converts made on these occasions frequently outnumbered the victims of the executioner's torch. A slight acquaintance with the art of mental processes should have taught the ruling authorities that the blood of the martyrs is the seed of the church, and that compulsion hardly ever changed a man's religious convictions.

Among a long list of victims during the century was Hans Mändl, a Hutterite missionary from Moravia who had been apprehended in Bavaria in 1560 and brought back to Innsbruck as a prisoner. Here, with two companions, he was kept the better part of a year in a deep and damp dungeon filled with bats and mice and other vermin. After repeated attempts to turn them from their faith, all three were condemned to a public death, the two companions to be beheaded, but Mändl to be burned at the stake. Reluctant to pass judgment upon the victim against their own convictions, the jurors were themselves thrown into prison, it is said, for declaring that they "could not burden their consciences with such a case and that they would sooner endure, therefore, any punishment whatsoever."

The three were led to the place of execution together. Attempting to speak to the assembled crowd, Mändl was interrupted by one of the executioners. But the devoted martyr kept on until forced to stop from sheer exhaustion. Because the two companions were of less heroic mold, it was decided to dispose of them first. However the second victim suddenly turned about as he stepped toward the block and called in a ringing voice, "Here I leave wife and child, house and home, life and limb for the sake of the truth and my faith." Courageously facing forward again he laid his head upon the axman's block and was beheaded. In the meantime, Mändl was at the close of his exhortation. Seeing the heads of his two friends lying nearby, he exclaimed, "My brethren, he who is faithful to the end, wins everything." The executioner then tied his victim to a ladder and threw him alive upon the pile of burning fagots, where he was burned to ashes.

Throughout the century, and especially during the latter half, there was constant intercommunication between all the Austrian territories and the Moravian Hutterites by way of the Tyrolean mountain trails. The authorities were vigilant in guarding the passes and bridges along the highways over which travelers made their way back and forth. Moravian missionaries especially were summarily dealt with when caught.

2. BAVARIA

Bavaria, next-door neighbor to the Habsburg crown lands and equally devoted to the cause of Catholic domination, was no less persistent in rooting out all traces of Mennonite and other forms of religious dissent. The Passau prisoners of 1537 have already been mentioned. According to the Hutterite chroniclers, two hundred thirty-three had sacrificed their lives in Bavaria by 1581. One of the last of the martyrs was Thomas Haan who was cruelly tortured and put to death in Freiburg in 1592.

Moravian missionaries were active here, too, as elsewhere in South Germany. They passed back and forth continually between the regions of the Upper Rhine and Moravia along the Danube and its tributaries throughout the period known as the Golden Age; and were the object of special hatred and vindictive persecution on the part of the ruling authorities. In fact, it is doubtful whether the Mennonite movement could have survived through the century in South Germany without the unflagging zeal and undaunted courage of these humble followers of Menno Simons and Jakob Hutter. They braved every danger and endured every hardship to keep the faith alive beyond their own land and to carry the invitation from their own Moravian Households to their distressed and discouraged brethren throughout central Europe, offering to share with them the blessings, material and spiritual, which the Moravians themselves were enjoying in the land of milk and honey. The Hutterites seemingly were the only group of Anabaptists whose missionary zeal survived the Münster collapse and the persecuting zeal of all the Catholic rulers after that.

The promise of religious liberty and the certainty of material prosperity appealed tremendously to the harassed and oppressed Mennonites who were being hounded from one place to another at this time. Even those with property were often glad to dispose of their possessions and, having found their way to the promised land, to turn over all their money to the Households for their own and the common good.

The invitation was especially attractive to the poverty-stricken and unfortunate; for the Hutterites did not discriminate between the poor and the rich; all alike were welcome to share their blessings. An old chronicler, a contemporary but unsympathetic writer, puts this appeal into the words of an imaginary missionary in Bavaria as follows:

> Dear Uncle Liendl or perhaps Aunt Urschel, etc. Come to us in

Moravia, the Promised Land, which is ours as a gift of God. There you will fare much better than here. Neither you nor your children need suffer poverty, nor endure hard work. There you will be assured good food, comfortable shelter and clothes, your children training and schooling; you will be freed of all worry. You, Aunt Andl, since you are old, you will not be required to do anything except to spin and rest as you like the live long day. Uncle Thomas will not need to work except what and when he pleases.

Hundreds, and perhaps thousands, answered this call during the last half of the sixteenth century. The emigration movement ended only when, during the Thirty Years' War, the persecuting zeal of the Jesuits and the ravages of the invading armies, which passed back and forth across Moravia during that period, completely broke up the Hutterite Households. With their scattering the Mennonites, too, disappeared from the rest of middle Europe outside of Switzerland.

In modern Baden, Württemberg, and Hesse, Mennonites shared the experiences of their brethren to the east, except that during the latter half of the century, at least, they enjoyed milder treatment than in Bavaria and the Austrias.

3. THE PALATINATE

In the Palatinate, especially after the reigning counts had exchanged their Catholic religion for the Lutheran or Reformed faith, the Mennonites, though still limited in their religious and civil rights, yet were not hounded to death as in the Catholic countries. Here both the state and the church relied more on persuasion than on force to bring about religious conformity. Believing that religious dissent was due more to ignorance than to any well-grounded religious convictions, and that in order to win these humble Mennonite peasants and artisans into their fold it was necessary to have the well-trained theological doctors of the state church show them the way of the true faith, the state church authorities held frequent disputations throughout the country in the interests of religious uniformity. One of the best known of these occasions was the debate held at Frankenthal in 1571.

The Frankenthal Debate

This discussion lasted for nineteen days. The Elector, Count Frederick III, a Calvinist who was especially eager to win the Mennonites, appeared personally at the opening session and remained in touch with all the later proceedings through a personal representative. He had given the proposed conference wide publicity. And to encourage a liberal attendance from all the Mennonite settlements, both within and without the Palatinate, he promised a safe conduct for fourteen days before and after the meeting, and full religious toleration during the sessions to all who might attend.

In spite of these assurances, however, only fifteen Mennonites appeared, including two Hutterites, a delegate from Austria, and the remainder from other parts of South Germany. None were present from Holland, although representatives from there had been expected.

The questions under discussion were those usually debated on occasions of this sort—the Trinity, the incarnation, original sin, the ban, community of goods, separation of husband and wife, the magistracy, the oath, infant baptism, and the Lord's Supper. On many of these beliefs the Mennonites and the Calvinist theologians agreed. On the distinctive Mennonite doctrines regarding the magistracy, the oath, and infant baptism, they hopelessly differed. Respecting the incarnation, the Mennonites hesitated to express themselves except to say that they did not wholly accept Menno's peculiar views on the subject, nor did they understand all the subtle distinctions made by the Calvinist theologians.

In many ways this was an unequal contest. The Mennonite spokesmen were simple workingmen, and although in exact knowledge of the Scriptures they excelled the state-church representatives, they were no theologians. They were not able to clothe their beliefs in theological and philosophical formulas, but had to confine themselves to biblical phraseology. "We are not able to answer your questions," said one of them, "except in the simple language of the Bible. It seems strange to us that you should persist in asking us many questions that are beyond us." The Hutterites took little part in the discussions; even when the question of the community of goods, on which they differed from other Mennonites, was referred to them, they refused to commit themselves. They were present merely as observers.

Of course no one changed his mind as a result of this debate. Rather each side was more confirmed than ever in the righteousness of its own cause. The Elector, sorely disappointed in the meager results obtained by his theologians, could find relief only in calling the Mennonites bad names. He called them *Böse Buben*, a sixteenth-century German phrase rather hard to turn into twentieth-century English. "Impudent knaves" is perhaps as good a rendering as any.

Reconciliation of rival doctrinal views, of course, would not have been sufficient alone to bring the Mennonites back into the fold of the established church. They still insisted that church membership must be conditioned by righteous living. A state church, they said, from the very nature of the case, could not differentiate between saint and sinner, since both alike were entitled to membership. That the ruling authorities recognized this fact is shown by their repeated insistence upon a more consistent religious life among both the lay and official members. Godliness to them, however, was largely a matter of continual church attendance. To this end inducements were offered to officials who might set a good example in this respect. Churchgoing was to be made easy and respectable. Churches which had not already provided special seats for the dignitaries were to do so; and officials were forbidden on pain of severe punishment to go on pleasure excursions or visit the taverns during the hours of worship.

Mennonites seemingly were not converted by any of these means. Severer measures were then tried. Oppression was again renewed and became increasingly burdensome. Many of the victims, as already suggested, found their way to Moravia. But with the scattering of the Hutterite Households, this retreat too became closed to them, and Mennonitism in the Palatinate died out also. By the close of the Thirty Years' War there were no organized communities left, and only a few scattered individual families.

Strassburg

The imperial city of Strassburg remained during the entire sixteenth century, as it had been earlier, the most tolerant of all the southern regions toward Mennonite dissent. It was here, it will be remembered, that many of the Mennonite conferences were held during the century, including those of the years 1555 and 1557, where Menno's peculiar views of the incarnation and his strict interpretation of the ban were practically repudiated.

Another important Strassburg gathering was the conference of 1568 which met for the purpose of drawing up certain rules of discipline. This was attended by many ministers and elders from all over southern Germany, including several who had participated in the discussions of 1557. The rules drawn up at this meeting for both the ministry and laity must be interpreted in the light of the conditions of the times. This was still, it must be remembered, an age of persecution. Many of the small congregations were bereft of their leaders through persecution. Traveling elders, therefore, were commissioned to ordain ministers wherever necessary to visit the wives and children of evangelists who were away on dangerous missions or perhaps in prison, and to care for the orphans. These overseers were to be provided with all the means necessary for their work.

Because of the extreme hardships following the separation of families when one member was a Mennonite and the other was not, those contemplating marriage were advised to "marry in the Lord." This became a fixed practice of the church, and found its way later into most of the confessions of faith and rules of discipline. Before entering into the married state, young people were admonished to do so only with the consent of their parents and the knowledge of the ministers.

It was because Mennonites had no legal standing before the law, perhaps, and because of the nonresistant faith of which their non-Mennonite neighbors took advantage in all contractual relations, that those having money to lend were advised to place it with their own brethren rather than with the world. In case of difficulty in collecting what was due them, they might make use of the courts if necessary, but were in no way to resort to extreme compulsion.

Several of these regulations evidently were in the interest of harmonizing conflicting views among the brethren. In the breaking of bread at the communion service, there was to be no fixed rule as to whether the minister was to break the bread for all, or each was to break it for himself. The practice of avoidance, the source of so much dissension among their Dutch brethren just at this time, was to be retained, but it was to be administered in all temperance and humility. Penitents who were to be taken into the church again after confession of wrongdoing were to be received without kneeling; but this concession was in no way to apply to the practice of kneeling in prayer. The doctrine of the incarnation, also a knotty problem at the time among both the Dutch and South German Mennonites, was to be interpreted according to the simple words of the Bible; and all needless arguments and hairsplitting distinctions were to be avoided.

Brethren should greet one another with the "kiss of the Lord"; others should be saluted with the words "The Lord help you." Tailors and seamstresses were admonished not to depart from the simple customs of the land in the making of their clothes, and not to follow worldly fashions. Those seeking admission into the church from another group practicing adult baptism should be carefully examined as to their faith, and if found truly converted need not submit to rebaptism.

Respect for the ministry was commanded. Fault-finding and slandering was punishable according to the gospel manner. Those attending worship services were not at liberty to leave the meeting before the close, except for a "Godly reason," though it might last for five or six hours.

The regulation that those desiring to engage in a big business enterprise must first consult the elders and ministers was a thoroughly reasonable demand if the entire brotherhood was expected to make good any losses to outsiders that such an enterprise might entail. Mennonites were especially anxious that their reputation for business honesty and integrity should be maintained.

The Nimrods among the brethren who had a weakness for catching or shooting game were admonished not to yield to the impulse on penalty of excommunication, except in case of game for which a reward had been offered. In case a brother was set to guard duty in village, field, or forest he might hire a substitute, but if he himself served he was not to carry a deadly weapon.

These regulations, first passed in 1568, seemed to be widely followed, and were often confirmed in later years throughout South Germany and elsewhere.

Swiss Exiles in the Palatinate

Just about as the last traces of the Mennonites were being blotted out of South Germany by the ravages of the Thirty Years' War, a new immigrant movement set in from Switzerland. This was just the time, it will be noted, when a final desperate attempt was being made in both Bern and Zürich to get rid of the troublesome Mennonites forever through wholesale persecution. As for the latter, though not particularly attracted by the war-devastated and depopulated lands along the Upper Rhine and Neckar, yet they preferred even these meager prospects to the sure hardships that awaited them in their own fruitful, though inhospitable, fatherland.

Most of the exiles followed the natural course of the Rhine by way of the Vosges Mountains in Alsace to the fertile, though desolate, valley of the Upper Rhine, in what was known as the Palatinate. As early as 1650 we hear of a small group located on the right side of the river south of Heidelberg. In 1661 fifty of these were arrested near Sinsheim for worshiping secretly in the forests against the law of the land, and fined one hundred *Thaler* by the local authorities. The elector, Karl Ludwig, had, after a prolonged absence, returned some ten years previous from the English court of his uncle Charles I, where he had gotten his fill of Puritan intolerance. He ordered that the Mennonites under his jurisdiction be permitted to worship unmolested, but that they should pay an annual tribute for the privilege. Several years before, in 1654, the same elector had granted a group of Hutterites from Hungary the privilege of establishing a *Bruderhof* near Mannheim. These rights were quite liberal for that age of intolerance, for none but the three tolerated religions—Catholic, Lutheran, and Reformed—were given any recognition by the treaty of Westpha-

SOUTH GERMANY

lia. Among these concessions were those of citizenship within the city of Mannheim; exemption from judicial, police, and military duty; and commercial privileges equal to all other subjects. Religious propaganda, however, was strictly prohibited. These liberal terms were not to be regarded as rights, however, but rather as privileges. The Hutterites were still merely a tolerated people; and the symbol of their bondage was a special tax of fifty *florin*, paid annually.

Anxious to repeople his devastated farms and rebuild his ruined cities, Karl Ludwig was willing to waive religious orthodoxy in his search for thrifty farmers and industrious artisans. Liberal invitations were sent out to the persecuted people of other lands to come to the Palatinate where religious toleration would be granted them. In 1664 special inducements were offered the Mennonites also, concessions not quite so liberal as those offered the Hutterites earlier, but, in the main, not particularly burdensome. There was to be freedom of worship, but not in public meetinghouses; nor were more than twenty families to meet at any one time in a given place. No revolutionary nor heretical doctrines were to be taught; religious propaganda among the members of the state church was prohibited. Mennonites, too, must remember that they were but a tolerated people, for they were to pay as protection money an annual tribute of three *gulden* for the first year, and six after that. Failure to comply with these conditions was punishable by expulsion from the country.

This act of toleration, limited though it was, must have seemed like an act of providence to the Mennonites of Switzerland where just at this time, 1671, another drive was being made by the governments of Bern and Zürich to expel them. According to van Braght, the martyrologist, some seven hundred Mennonites were ruthlessly driven out of their homes during the year. Nearly all of them found their way to the Palatinate, though some remained in the Vosges Mountains. A letter written to the Dutch churches in 1671 asked for help to care for the Swiss refugees:

> Our Swiss friends are now coming this way in large parties, so that there have already arrived over two hundred persons, and among them are many old, gray-haired people, both men and women, that have reached seventy, eighty, yea ninety years; also a number that are lame and crippled; carrying their bundles on their backs, with their children in their arms, some of good cheer, some with tearful eyes, particularly the old and feeble persons, who now in their great age are compelled to wander about in their misery, and go to strange countries; and many of them have nothing on which to sleep by night, so that I and others with me, have now for about two weeks had to make it our regular work to provide shelter and other necessities for them.

A little later the same authority wrote that about six hundred forty had arrived, and that another hundred were to be expected soon from Alsace.

Most of these refugees finally found a welcome on the estates of noblemen in the fertile Rhine Valley on both sides of the river, and from Worms to Mannheim and Alzey to Neustadt on the left. Soon their industry and thrift had transformed what had once been a ruined land into a garden of plenty. Orchards were replanted, and villages rebuilt. Prosperity returned and few traces of the war were to be seen in the regions which they occupied.

War Devastations

Unfortunately this prosperity was of short duration. In 1688 the so-called *War of the Palatinate* began when the command of Louis XIV to "burn up the Palatinate" was almost literally carried out by his lieutenants. The rich fields of the Rhine Valley were again laid waste. Macauley's description of this event may not be much overdrawn:

> The flames went up from every market place, every country seat within the devoted province. The fields where the corn had been sown were plowed up; the orchards were hewn down. No promise of a harvest was left on the fertile plains near what had been Frankenthal. Not a vine, not an almond tree was to be seen on the slopes of the sunny hills round what had once been Heidelberg.

The Mennonites did not escape this general conflagration. Some two hundred families were driven from their homes to seek refuge further down the Rhine, and seek help from their brethren in lower Germany and Holland. Most of these returned later to try life all over again in their former homes. Others never did.

Of the fifty-odd Mennonite prisoners sent down the Rhine by the Bernese government in 1709 with a view to deportation to America, most of these, as already noted, left the prison boat en route, and remained among their co-religionists in the Palatinate; as did also some fifty of the refugees exiled from the same place two years later. Three hundred forty of these latter, mostly Amish, continued down the river to Amsterdam and later found homes near Groningen in north Holland. These exiles are described by a contemporary Mennonite writer who had seen them as they entered the Palatinate as

> a sturdy folk by nature, who could endure hardships, with long untrimmed beards, with plain clothes, and heavy shoes shod with strong iron nails. They were very zealous in serving God with prayer, reading and other ways. We could speak with them only with difficulty; for they had lived in the mountains of Switzerland far from villages and towns and had little communication with other people.

For the next quarter of a century these Swiss Mennonites in the Palatinate, in spite of wars, cold summers, crop failures, and constant emigration to America, grew and prospered. From records preserved in the government archives in Karlsruhe we learn that by 1732 there were 618 families on the two sides of the Upper Rhine, a total population of approximately three thousand. Among the congregations mentioned which still exist may be included Ibersheim, Sembach, Friedelsheim, Weierhof, Monsheim, Obersülzen, and Hasselbach. All of these were small farm communities, either on noble estates or small villages, hence the *heims* and *hofs*. Several, like Ibersheim and Weierhof, were solidly Mennonite. The latter still is.

In all the numerous wars of the eighteenth century between France and her enemies of central Europe, the rich fields of the Palatinate remained an attractive prize for the armies of both sides as they marched back and forth from one country to another. Hans Burghalter of Geroldsheim was for many years the spokesman of the Palatine Mennonites when they asked for help from the brethren in Holland. In a letter written in 1746 Burghalter complained:

> For five years the French troops have overrun our land, confiscated our property and oppressed us with heavy burdens. They consoled us by promising that everything would be paid for, but so far not a *stuiver* has been received. Besides this we were forced to work for them at hard labor for days at a time. After this the English army came, encamping only two hours distant from us for four long weeks, during which we were subjected to the same harsh treatment. After the English left us to establish their headquarters at Weyer, the Austrians encamped twice among us. So you can see what unbearable suffering we had to endure the past summer. Hardly had this great burden been lifted from us than the good Lord permitted another severe punishment to befall us. A contagious disease spread among our cattle, so that many of the brethern have not a single head left. Our poverty is so great that many of us do not know how to help ourselves any longer.

Religious and Economic Restrictions

But poverty and war were not the only burdens with which the Mennonites were afflicted during the century. To these was added a long period of religious intolerance. Under Karl Ludwig and his immediate successors they had enjoyed a fair degree of religious liberty. But with the coming into power of a new Catholic line of electors, and after the waste places of the electorate had again been repeopled, toleration ceased. In fact, under these Catholic electors, even the rights of the Reformed—who made up by far the largest part of the population, and of the Lutherans also—were greatly curtailed. According to the terms of the treaty of 1648, the religion of a country was to be determined by its ruler. Especially intolerant were the electors of the latter part of the century who had fallen under the influence of Jesuits.

The Mennonites, left without any religious rights whatsoever under the above treaty, were marked for special oppression. Throughout the eighteenth century they were forced to pay tribute money for such toleration as they enjoyed. They were denied residence in the cities, they could not engage in trade, nor were their children admitted to apprenticeship in the trade guilds. Even the Jews, then commonly despised throughout Europe, were held in higher esteem than the Mennonites; for by paying a certain amount of money the Jews could engage in trade publicly, a privilege granted Mennonites under no condition.

Beginning with 1717, under Karl Philip, a more determined effort was inaugurated to prevent the further spread of the Mennonite population throughout the Palatinate. First it was ordered that the Mennonites must be limited to 200 families, which evidently was thought to be the number at the time, though in reality there were many more. Numerous regulations were passed during the century to keep the population within this maximum. The exemption and protection money was doubled. The marriage of young people was made extremely difficult, and was permitted only with the consent of the central government.

Hans Burghalter, writing to his friend Johannes Deknatel in Amsterdam in 1747, complained that when the head of a family died it was difficult for a son to take his place, and the recognition of a new head was made possible only upon the payment of a considerable sum of money. First he must obtain permission of the local bailiff to fill the positon, then he was turned over from one official to another all the way up to the elector himself, and then back again to the church officials, all of whom must give their consent—"all the time," Burghalter wrote, "with their hands in their pockets." Often the greater part of a year passed before permission was secured. Burghalter feared that if matters could not be remedied there would be "a great falling off in the congregations of the young people."

The acquisition of land was made difficult and uncertain by the revival of an ancient right called *ius retractus* which stipulated that land which had once been in the possession of a member of one of the three tolerated religions, and in the meantime had been bought by a Mennonite, could at any time later again be reclaimed by the original owner upon the payment of the first purchase price. Frequently an industrious Mennonite, who had bought a worthless farm and then by years of toil had improved it and brought it to a high degree of productivity, was forced to turn it back at the first price to some envious neighbor of the established religion, with little or no reward for his years of effort.

Growth by propaganda, of course, was strictly out of the question. As late as 1780 two young girls of Amish-Mennonite parentage, who as orphans had been forcibly taken into a Catholic institution where they had been turned into Catholics, were declared to be worthy of death for having returned to the church of their parents. The elector, however, commuted the sentence to one year of imprisonment and exile. As for Hans Nafziger of Essingen, the elder who had baptized them, his offense was declared to be even greater than that of the two girls. But his penalty was only a fine of 500 *florin* with exile.

As a climax to these religious restrictions upon the living, there was added humiliating treatment of the dead—denial of burial rights in the public cemeteries. In 1780 a Mennonite in Kaiserslautern had been buried in the common burial ground evidently without the knowledge of the local priest, who was absent at the time. When the priest heard of the burial, he, together with the local police, dug up the body and buried it just outside the cemetery walls. This was in order to show the Mennonites, one chronicler intimates, what the public thought of those not of the tolerated churches. All this, it will be noted, took place on the very eve of the French Revolution.

Pennsylvania

In these economic privations and religious restrictions are to be found the chief source of the continued migration during the eighteenth century from the Palatinate to what was regarded as the "Paradise of Pennsylvania." The economic causes were shared by the Reformed and Lutherans also, but the religious oppression gave the Mennonites added reasons for leaving. Thousands upon thousands of Palatines of all faiths left their native land for America during the century. Of these, the Mennonites formed but a very small part; but in proportion to their relative strength at home they greatly exceeded the others in numbers. The immigrant flow continued throughout the century, broken only by the various European wars of the period. Up to 1727 the Mennonites led the way; after that they were greatly outnumbered by the other groups. All told, during the century, perhaps nearly three thousand Palatine Mennonites left for Pennsylvania. By 1800 that happened to be approximately the number of the Mennonite population remaining in the homeland also.

During all this period the Palatine Mennonites, as noted in an earlier chapter, were given liberal support by the Dutch brethren in all their needs. In 1703 a committee, *The Dutch Relief Fund for Foreign Needs*, which had been organized in the latter part of the seventeenth century to help the Swiss exiles of that time, was revived for the purpose of helping their poverty-stricken descendants in the Palatinate, as well as their persecuted brethren in Bern. This commission at first refused to sanction the migration movement, and repeatedly warned the Palatine elders to discourage the Pennsylvania fever. But when poverty-stricken Mennonites appeared at Amsterdam or Rotterdam begging to be sent to the land of promise, the commission forgot its warning and furnished the necessary means. The organization was officially closed in 1732 but continued to function unofficially long after that.

The French Revolution affected the Mennonites of South Germany as it did everyone else. The leveling spirit which brushed aside so many of the social and political class distinctions of an earlier day also put an end to religious intolerance. After the Napoleonic wars, Mennonites were no longer regarded as merely a tolerated people, subject to the whims and caprices of bigoted rulers. They were accorded the same rights as those enjoyed by the preferred churches.

The Ibersheim Conference

But their improved civil and religious status was not due altogether to the more tolerant spirit of their former persecutors, both state and church. The Mennonites, too, had changed. They met their oppressors halfway. It was perhaps for the purpose of stemming the rising tide of worldliness among the younger people and of strengthening the bonds of unity among them that two of the leading elders—Valentin Dahlem of Wiesbaden and Peter Weber of Neuwied—called a conference of the Palatine churches at Ibersheim, near Worms, in 1803. So far as the elders were concerned it was evident that at this meeting they still stood for the old faith and practices. According to the regulations passed, young men who joined the army were to be excommunicated. Mixed marriages were still forbidden, and church discipline was to be encouraged by means of the *Umfrage* (inquiry). It was customary among the early Mennonites and Amish to send out certain church officials just before the observance of communion to inquire of the various members whether they were in sufficient harmony with one another to observe the communion service in perfect unity. It will be remembered that this was also the duty of the *Umbitter* among the Mennonites of West Prussia.

Ministers were elected by lot and served without pay. The sins of drunkenness, gambling, and swearing were disciplined, as were theater attendance and dancing; vanity and pride, as shown particularly in dress and everyday conduct, were discouraged. The sisters must appear at the communion table with covered heads. Church membership was based on genuine conversion, and not as a matter of mere form; applicants for baptism must pass through a period of thorough instruction, and must have reached a minimum age of fourteen.

Among the constructive acts of this conference was the commissioning of Valentin Dahlem to write a worship manual (*Formularbuch*) for the use of the ministry. This was a very convenient help, especially for farmer-preachers, for it contained formulas for all ceremonial occasions, as well as written prayers for every contingency. It was already difficult to secure needed ministers to carry on the work of the church, and no doubt this book was designed to lighten their burden. The *Formularbuch* was printed in 1807 and went through several later editions. It was popular everywhere in the South German churches throughout the century, and was brought to America and translated into English.

Some of the above-mentioned rules, however, were more easily made than enforced. It was difficult to excommunicate the young men whom Napoleon forced against their will into the army. When the left bank of the Rhine fell to France in 1801, Mennonites gained full civil rights, but lost their military exemption. But if they had the money they might hire substitutes. It is said that in the Russian campaign of 1812 nearly every Mennonite family was represented. In Bavaria and other South German states also, substitutes were allowed at this time and for some years later. The church leaders were strenuous in their endeavors to stem the tide of militarism. At first they petitioned Napoleon for the retention of their privileges; and then, failing in this, they encouraged the practice of hiring substitutes. For a time the churches as a whole collected money for all the young men drafted into service. But this method of meeting the situation was not popular with families that had no sons liable to service. Finally each family had to look out for itself. The rich and the liberal-minded found an easy way out. The poor and conservative could only emigrate to America. Between 1830 and 1860 there was a continued migration of both the poor and the conscientious, both as individuals and as groups, from all the Mennonite settlements of South Germany, the Palatinate, Bavaria, and Hesse, principally to Ohio, Illinois, and Iowa.

In spite of conference regulations to the contrary, men unqualified for the ministry refused to serve when chosen by the lot. To remedy the lack of efficient and willing preachers, some of the more progressive congregations, beginning with Monsheim in 1819, called trained ministers from neighboring congregations and paid them a salary. Sembach followed in 1823, and Ibersheim in 1843, until most of the congregations were supplied. The first of these new ministers came from the Mennonite communities of North Germany and Holland, but later the churches were able to supply a number of young men, many of whom had taken a course of Bible study in a mission school in Basel.

Missions and Schools

At the same time, the churches became interested in the cause of foreign missions, largely through the efforts of the eloquent preaching of William Henry Angas, an English Baptist from London who had visited the various congregations in South Germany, Switzerland, and West Prussia in 1824. Tauchnitz, the famous Leipzig publisher who had become interested in the South German Mennonites, had also urged the mission cause among them. At this conference it was suggested that each congregation place a mission box beside the charity box near the church door. For a time the contributions went to an English Baptist society, but later they were diverted to various other organizations as well as to the work of the Dutch Mennonites in the East Indies.

With the coming of an educated ministry, there developed also a keener interest in the educational needs of the young people in general. The elementary village schools of the day were not of a high order. There was no religious instruction for Mennonite children except what they received in their homes. Sometimes on an estate where the population was solidly Mennonite, or in communities where a sufficient number of Mennonite children were available, an educated pastor might also become the village teacher or start a private school for the children of his own church.

One such pastor-teacher was Michael Löwenberg, who founded a school at the Weierhof in 1848. It was Löwenberg, too, who first saw the need of a training school for the new ministry if the church was to have an educated leadership. To supply this need he formed an association of fifty men who in 1867 founded the school since known as the Weierhof *Lehr- und Erziehungsanstalt*. The original purpose of the institution was never realized, although it has had a continuous growth as a Christian secondary boarding school. In 1874 at the time of the death of the founder, it had only thirty students enrolled and a heavy debt. After passing through several changes it finally assumed, in 1884 under the direction of Ernst Göbel, the character of a first-class *Realschule* with state approval. The school has a number of well-equipped buildings and laboratories. Although no longer a distinctively Mennonite institution, it maintained the wholesome religious character of its early days. Of the two hundred forty students enrolled in 1930, only twelve were Mennonites. The rest were mostly Protestants with a few Catholics. Christian Neff of the local Weierhof congregation remained for many years the religious instructor of the Mennonite contingent of the student body.

Outstanding among the educational, historical, and spiritual publications of the South German Mennonites are the *Märtyrer Spiegel* in 1780 at Pirmasens, and various catechisms, hymnbooks, and other devotional literature. *Das Gemeindeblatt* was started and edited by Ulrich Hege in 1869. It continues since World War II as *Gemeinde Unterwegs*. The *Christlicher Gemeinde-Kalender*, begun in 1892, is a valuable source of information about the life and history of the South German Mennonites. After an interruption (1942-50 inclusive), this influence has increased and the name has been changed to *Mennonitisches Jahrbuch*. It now serves all Mennonites in Germany and beyond. The *Mennonitisches Lexikon*, edited by Christian Hege and Christian Neff, was begun in 1913. The first two volumes were published before World War II. After the war, when American Mennonite scholars began the publication of *The Mennonite Encyclopedia*, they made full use of the pioneer work of the German Mennonite scholars. On the other hand, the German editors could make use of the American encyclopedia in preparing the last two volumes of the German Lexikon, of which volume IV appeared in 1967.

Rural and Religious Leaders

For a long time, South German Mennonites remained primarily rural people. They were frequently renters of small farms or even large estates, which in the long run they often purchased. The Mennonites have been very successful as farmers. In the middle of the eighteenth century, at a time when scientific agriculture was still unknown, David Möllinger of Monsheim introduced the principle of rotation of crops on his farm, the use of clovers in place of fallowing, selective stock breeding, and other improved methods of agriculture now everywhere practiced. He became known as the father of Palatine agriculture. Möllinger had many worthy followers among the Mennonite farmers of the nineteenth century, foremost of whom was Christian Dettweiler of Kindesheim.

After equal civil rights were granted, several Mennonites occupied positions of trust in their respective governments. Peter Eymann of Frankenstein was first to serve in the Bavarian Legislature in 1849. He was followed by others. Jacob Finger, a lifelong and loyal member of the Monsheim congregation, served the Grand Duchy of Hesse both in the legislature and, for some years, in various positions in the cabinet.

Among the men not already mentioned who served the Mennonite cause most effectively since 1830 should be mentioned Jacob Ellenberger, first of the new type of educated ministers to start a private Mennonite school for his congregation at Friedelsheim; Jacob Ellenberger II, a nephew of the above, pastor of numerous congregations in his day—Ibersheim, Eichstock and Friedelsheim—and author of a well-known booklet *Bilder aus dem Pilgerleben*; Johannes Mollenaar (1810-1868) of Dutch birth, but elder for many years at Monsheim, and promoter of conferences, hymnbooks, catechisms, and other good causes; and his contemporaries, Johannes Risser of Sembach, and Johannes J. Krehbiel, **member of an influential Weierhof family. Christian Schmutz,** elder for many years at Rappenau, who died in 1873, may well be called the last of the old guard. Although in the main he was favorable to all progressive movements of the new order, he retained to the end his early prejudices against an educated ministry, and especially against the missionary enterprise of the Dutch Mennonites. Matthias Pohl of Sembach was interested in historical subjects and a liberal contributor to all German Mennonite periodicals.

Originally the congregations were primarily rural, but now there are numerous congregations in towns and cities. Most of them are rather small, even after some of the West Prussian Mennonites joined them. One of the congregations located at Backnang, and founded in 1951, consists primarily of West Prussian Mennonites and has a membership of 244 (1978). Smaller congregations with a membership between 50 and 150 are located at Frankenthal, Friedelsheim, Ludwigshaven, Monsheim, Sembach, Weierhof, Worms-Ibersheim, Zweibrücken, München, Augsburg, Heilbronn, Ingolstadt, Karlsruhe-Thomashof, Regensburg, Sinsheim, and Stuttgart. Most of the ministers have had a theological training obtained at either a university or at a Bible school. In comparison to the North German and Dutch Mennonites, the South German Mennonites have, as a rule, been influenced longer and more strongly by an emotional Pietism. This is also the case with the contemporary Mennonites of Switzerland. Much depends on the many influences which the congregations undergo from generation to generation. The Mennonites of South Germany and Switzerland have been strong supporters of the Mennonite mission work, particularly in Indonesia.

The region spoken of here as the Palatinate has undergone

numerous political changes since 1648; and a number of small Mennonite groups have left the mother churches for other locations in South Germany. And so various settlements described above are now located in Rheinpfalz, Württemberg, Hesse, Baden, and Bavaria.

Bavaria

In 1802 King Max Joseph IV, somewhat liberalized by the democratic spirit of the French Revolution and desirous of finding industrious farmers for his Danubian swamp and brushlands, offered liberal terms of settlement to all prospective colonists. About one hundred Palatine farmers responded to this invitation, including eight Mennonite families, who no doubt were induced to make the change in order to improve their economic condition. These latter located along the Danube near Neuburg. Others followed, and by 1850 they numbered over twenty-five families. By dint of much hard work and at considerable sacrifice, they developed in course of time a number of prosperous farms where before there had been nothing but wasteland. Their farm homes they grouped together in a village which they called *Maxweiler*, in honor of their benefactor. In 1832, with the personal support of the reigning king, they built a combination school and church. Their private school was supplied with an efficient and approved government teacher in 1849. In the early 1850s nearly the entire congregation migrated to America, locating first in southeastern Iowa and Summerfield, Illinois, from where some went to Halstead, Kansas.

In 1818 another settlement called *Eichstock* was begun, some twenty-five miles south of Maxweiler. This congregation, which by the middle of the century had increased to some thirty-five families, migrated almost en masse to America with the Maxweiler brethren with whom they had been closely affiliated from the beginning.

About the same time, too, a number of Amish farmers from the Palatinate and Alsace had rented large estates in the general region of Munich and Donauwörth. These had little religious affiliation with the Mennonite congregations nearby, and long maintained their distinctive Amish customs and practices. They are now members of the Regensburg Mennonite Church. Prosperous farmers, they are very active in church and relief work.

Some time earlier, in the preceding century, a group of Mennonites from Baden had founded a congregation near Würzburg. Many of the early congregations have since disappeared, to be replaced by others in nearby regions and in several of the large cities of southern Bavaria—Munich, Augsburg, Regensburg, and Ingoldstadt.

The Catholic Bavarian kings were quite generous toward these industrious farmers, granting them complete religious liberty. However, while they might build their own churches, these must be without bell and tower.

4. GALICIA AND VOLHYNIA

Galicia, of course, is not a part of South Germany, but the Galician Mennonites were all South Germans. Among the thousands of Germans who answered the call of the Austrian Emperor, Joseph II, at the close of the eighteenth century for industrious colonists to settle his newly acquired Polish territory, were twenty-eight Mennonite families, mostly from the Palatinate, though a few may have come from Alsace and other neighboring regions. They had originally come from Switzerland.

These Mennonites located, beginning in 1784, near *Lemberg*. The terms offered by Joseph were quite liberal—free land, a brief period of tax exemption, a temporary loan for stocking their farms, military exemption, and religious liberty. Of course they were all poor or they would not have exchanged their well-established homes in the Palatinate for the uncertainties of a pioneer experiment. Unfortunately the group was not of one mind religiously. Assembled from various sections of the old established communities, they found themselves a mixture of both Amish and Mennonites, who did not live together in religious harmony.

The Amish contingent, about ten families, left for Russia before the close of the century, settling finally in the province of *Volhynia*. Later, in the 1870s, these latter joined the Mennonites on their trek to America, locating near Moundridge, Kansas, and Freeman, South Dakota. The Mennonites who remained in Galicia prospered, and at the close of the first hundred years had grown to nearly one hundred fifty families. About this time, in the early 1880s, approximately half of these also migrated to Kansas and Minnesota.

In the matter of military exemptions, Austria was inclined to follow the example of Prussia. After 1868 Mennonites in Galicia were permitted to accept noncombatant instead of active service. During World War I about three-fourths of the Mennonite young men in the army were thus engaged. Lemberg, being well within the fighting zone of the eastern front, suffered heavily from war ravages.

After World War I the Mennonite population in this region was about six hundred, scattered throughout 100 villages and estates which were miles apart. This made close cooperation extremely difficult. Services were held alternately throughout the territory in several different churches and private homes. In spite of its scattered membership and its different meeting places, the group formed but one congregation with its center in Lemberg. For some years before and after World War I, the congregation was served as elder by Heinrich Pauls, a progressive and forward-looking church leader. The last minister was Arnold Bachmann, who, with several assistants, looked after the pastoral needs of the widely scattered flock. The language of the pulpit was German, though on funeral occasions when Poles and Ruthenians were likely to be present, the common language of the land, Polish, was sometimes used.

As a result of World War II the Galician Mennonites were expelled from Poland, and shared the fate of millions of other Germans as refugees. They were scattered in the British and American zones of Germany, in many cases without shelter, food, and work. Sixty-five of them joined the 750 West Prussian Mennonites on the *Volendam* and arrived at Montevideo, Uruguay, October 27, 1948. Here they settled next to the West Prussian Mennonites.

5. ALSACE-LORRAINE AND FRANCE

The present Mennonite settlements within the regions of Alsace-Lorraine and France are also of Swiss origin. Religiously and culturally, even though they have not always lived under the same political jurisdictions, many have enjoyed a common heritage with their Swiss and South German brethren, including the German language. Of the early Anabaptist congregations in and about Strassburg, it is not likely that many of them survived the persecuting zeal of the sixteenth century. But Swiss refugees from both Bern and Zürich found their way into the secluded valleys of the Vosges Mountains, and especially by invitation of the prince of Rappolstein into the region of St. Marie aux Mines even earlier than into the Palatinate. By 1660 when the Alsatian Mennonites met at Ohnenheim to adopt the Dordrecht Confession of Faith as the expression of their beliefs, delegates were present from the above-mentioned settlement which had its nucleus at Markirch, and from ten other localities along the Rhine, principally between Colmar and Selestat. That these different localities, nearly all villages which lay very close together, represented as many congregations, or even settlements, is of course not likely, although the list of signers included six ministers and seven elders.

Alsace received her share of the Bernese exiles of 1671, as well as those of the early eighteenth century. Van Braght says that in 1672, 100 of the Swiss immigrants of the year before were still in Alsace. Unfortunately for the Mennonites, a little later this territory fell into the hands of the French king, Louis XIV.

Fearing, no doubt, a further influx of Swiss exiles, and urged on by jealous neighbors and intolerant priests, in 1712 Louis requested the intendant of Alsace to order all Mennonites out of his new acquisition. Those who obeyed the order left for the duchy of Zweibrücken in the Palatinate, for the county of Montbeliard, and for Lorraine, especially in the Saar Valley. Through the intervention of local princes who highly valued the industrious Mennonite renters on their estates, in 1728 Louis XV modified somewhat the harsh measures of his predecessor, demanding only that the number of Mennonites still in France should not be increased.

The French Revolution

By the time of the French Revolution both Lorraine and Montbeliard had become incorporated into the French monarchy; but by this time, too, Mennonites had been accorded most of the religious rights of other people. Religious and civil disabilities that were still in force were shortly removed by the great drive for liberty, fraternity, and equality. In 1793 they were even given special consideration for their scruples against war. In an order issued by the Committee of Public Safety, which contained among other names that of Robespierre, it was recommended that the Mennonites be treated with the same spirit of gentleness which they themselves exercised toward others, and that they be permitted to substitute for regular army service work of a noncombatant nature, or even to be exempt entirely upon the payment of a money equivalent.

Later on, under the Napoleonic levies, those opposing or desirous of avoiding military service, whether Mennonite or not, were permitted to furnish substitutes, a difficult alternative, especially near the end when almost all the available manpower of France had been used up by the long and exhaustive military campaigns. As elsewhere in middle Europe, the Mennonites of France were weaned away from their opposition to war by inability of the poor to hire substitutes, by military training in times of peace, by popular pressure against nonparticipation in a common cause, and by the growing nationalism of the period. The more conservative here, too, left for America during the early part of the century. By 1870 there were not many young men who refused service.

The French Mennonites, including those in former Alsace-Lorraine, are practically all of the Amish background. Jakob Ammann, who took up his residence in Alsace early in the history of the Amish controversy, seemingly made a clean sweep of the Alsatian church for his cause. From here, of course, it was later carried by Alsatian immigrants to other parts of France. The Dordrecht Confession, which had been officially adopted by the Alsatians, though perhaps not by all of the Swiss and the Palatines, demanded a rigid observance of the practice of shunning, which formed the chief issue, it will be remembered, of the Reist-Ammann controversy. By insisting upon the observance of this practice, Ammann was merely asking that the church conform its practice to the accepted and official Dordrecht Confession of Faith.

The Amish

The Amish division was carried into all the regions that were settled by the Swiss refugees during the latter part of the seventeenth century and the first of the eighteenth—the Palatinate, the Swiss Jura, Bavaria, and Hesse, as well as Alsace and other neighboring French areas. Both branches of the church were included in the experiences thus far mentioned. That the second generation of Amish were no less inclined to hold themselves aloof from their Mennonite brethren and neighbors than were their fathers—where the two lived in the same regions—is shown in a letter written in 1742 by Hans Burghalter of Geroldsheim, in the Palatinate, to the Dutch relief committee in Rotterdam. Burghalter reports that in the Upper Palatinate many of the "so-called Amisch" desire to go to *Pencelfania*. These, he says

> have no fellowship with us at all except when they get into trouble and have need of help, then they come to us, but never at any other time. They even try to belittle us and bring us into disrepute with the authorities. They count themselves the *Feine Manisten*....

It was about this time that many of the Amish migrated to America from all these regions, but especially from the Palatinate, in spite of the discouraging advice of Hans Burghalter and the Dutch committee. All told, perhaps about five hundred of them, children included, found their way by the middle of the century to the fertile fields and peaceful hills of southeastern Pennsylvania.

Conference at Essingen, 1779

Not much is known about the religious life of the European

Amish during this period except stray facts that have found their way into church conference records and church letters carefully preserved in manuscript and copied from one generation to another by church officials. Few of these records ever got into print.

The best known of these periodic conferences was the one held in 1779 at Essingen, near Landau. Nineteen Amish congregations and thirty-nine ministers from all the settlements in France and southwestern Germany were represented at the meeting. Among the items under consideration were the adoption of the Strassburg resolutions of 1568, and the doctrines and practices considered of special importance by the Amish since the division of 1693. The "long" confession of faith of thirty-three articles found in the *Martyrs Mirror* was specifically recommended as being in harmony with the "Word of God," largely no doubt because of its emphasis upon the practice of shunning and foot washing. Extravagance in dress continued to be denounced. Among the worldly fashions especially tabooed were four-cornered neckscarfs, high-heeled boots and shoes, shaving, and combing the hair and trimming the beard according to the prevailing fashions.

Marriage Customs

A letter written in 1781 by Hans Nafziger, an Amish bishop at Essingen, to the Amish churches in Holland, describes some of the religious practices among the South German Amish at that time. Especially interesting were the wedding customs then prevailing. Marriage must be "in the Lord," and with the consent of the parents and the knowledge of the elders of the church. Some time before the wedding the prospective bridegroom must send the deacon to the home of the bride-to-be for her answer to his proposal, an answer which both the suitor and the deacon knew beforehand would be favorable. The wedding ceremony was preceded by a sermon of several hours, in which sometimes several ministers participated, and consisted largely of a detailed recital of favorite wedding scenes from the Bible, including always the story of Apocryphal Tobias and Sara. Never omitted in the instructions to the bridal pair by the elder was the admonition to follow the example of Tobias and Sara in postponing all conjugal relations until three days after the wedding ceremony. This practice was still in vogue among the Amish of central Illinois as late as the past generation.

Amish Division Ends

These original Amish congregations retained their separate religious organization and many of their distinctive religious practices, chief of which were foot washing and the *Meidung* (shunning), until well toward the beginning of the twentieth century. It was not until the early seventies of the past century that serious suggestions were first made for a union of the Amish and Mennonites where the two existed side by side. Although these first suggestions, which seemingly came from the Mennonite side, were without result, some twenty years later various Amish congregations in South Germany began to affiliate themselves with the Conference of the South German Mennonites. In 1937 the last of the Amish congregations in this area, the *Ixheimer* church in Zweibrücken, joined the *Ernstweiler* Mennonite congregation, thus finally ending a long division begun in the days of Jakob Ammann in Switzerland and Germany. The French churches, being solidly Amish and thus forming a separate conference district, had no occasion for any organic union.

The French Amish Mennonites made little progress during the nineteenth century. A contemporary writer for a French journal in 1819, not a Mennonite himself, described how they lived just about the time they began their migration to America as follows:

> The entire number of souls may be twelve or fifteen hundred scattered about through German Lothringen, Alsace, and the neighboring areas. Their principal settlement is at Salm, near the Vosges which they occupy almost exclusively. I do not think that there is a single family living in any of the towns. They are small farmers being found especially as tenants on the estates of noblemen. Through their industry, intelligence, and experience as farmers they have become expert in all lines of agricultural industry. This circumstance as well as their reliability and punctuality in meeting all their financial obligations have made them much sought after by noblemen as farmers on their estates.
>
> They consented with reluctance to carry the tricolor cockade when that was made a duty. When they greet one they take off their hats, but like the Quakers they do not take an oath nor bear arms. When the National Convention attempted to compel them to perform military duty they refused, but suggested that they be permitted to work in the Quartermaster department instead, which was granted them by the Committee of Public Safety. Some of them served in this capacity rather than hire substitutes. To their credit be it said that, unlike many others, they pay their debts, not in worthless assignats, but in good coin. They do not use tobacco, nor play cards. To music they are strangers. They do not go to law. They take care of their poor and come to the rescue of their members who have financial reverses for which they were not responsible personally. On the whole they are rather illiterate, but honest, temperate, industrious and of good moral character.

Today, although perhaps still a bit more conservative in faith and practice than the former German Amish or Mennonites, the distinctive religious beliefs and practices that once divided them have largely disappeared. The term *Amish* as a distinct denominational name has disappeared from among the European Mennonites.

The French Remnant

From about 1830 to 1860 there was a heavy emigration of French Mennonites to America. The large Amish congregations in central Illinois and northwestern Ohio are almost of pure Alsatian and Lothringen origin. In addition to the loss to America, there was also a constant migration of individual families from Alsace and Lorraine farther into the interior of France. These latter, farmers and millers, locating on widely separated estates and mills, found it difficult to maintain an organized church life. The insistence also upon maintaining the German language in public worship against a rather hostile French Catholic opinion did not make their task any the easier. The separation of the larger and more compact Alsatian communities from the newer and more isolated French congregations in 1870 only made the existence of the latter still more precarious.

Since 1870 there have been several praiseworthy attempts to quicken the spiritual life and the social ideals of the French Mennonites. One of these was the founding of a school in 1870 at Etupes, near Montbeliard, for the special purpose of teaching the children in German, the official language of the church. The promoter was a certain Isaac Rich who had been a student for a brief period at the Wadsworth, Ohio, school then just started. It was here, no doubt, that Rich got both his inspiration and his educational ideals; for he modeled his institution quite largely after that of Wadsworth. The French Mennonites, however, were not greatly interested in the education of their young people at this time. With the exception of a little help from the Palatinate and good wishes from America, this educational venture had to be supported at first almost entirely by Rich and his immediate family. Changing his Mennonite school after a few years of struggle into a nondenominational children's home, he soon built up a rather thriving institution, well supported both by Mennonites and non-Mennonites within and without his immediate circle. But, unfortunately, the institution came to an end in 1876. It is interesting to observe that the three pioneer schools of higher learning in North America, Germany, and France were all started about the same time—Wadsworth in 1867; Weierhof in 1868; and Etupes in 1870.

French Mennonites Renewed and Reunited

After this, the French remnant seemingly continued to decline both numerically and spiritually. As late as 1905, Pierre Sommer, one of the leading preachers among the French, stated that there were eleven small and scattered congregations near the Swiss border, using the German language for the most part in their services and meeting in their own meetinghouses every two weeks. Another group of seven congregations in French Lorraine, who used the French language, were so widely scattered that they met for worship only once in every four weeks in private homes. Worship, Sommer stated, was formal; the preachers had little education. Singing, confined largely to a few of the older members, was from the *Ausbund*. Young people were admitted to church after a period of catechetical instruction and memorizing of the Dordrecht Confession, which few of them were able to understand.

Among the causes given for this numerical and spiritual decline were: the isolation of the congregations and widely scattered membership in a solidly French Catholic environment, the attempt on the part of the older people to keep up the German language in worship (which the young people did not understand), the lack of proper school facilities, mixed marriages, and the lack of organized church life.

The founding of a series of conferences among these French congregations in 1901, the issuing of a church paper, *Christ Seul*, in the French language in 1906, and a traveling evangelist or field secretary some time later all contributed toward the awakening of a renewed interest in their common religious life. In 1908 the church organized itself into the *Association des Eglises Evangeliques-Mennonites de Langue Francaise*.

The German-speaking Alsatian-Lothringen congregations, on the other hand, after the separation of 1870, were in closer contact with their more progressive South German brethren. Although they made little growth numerically, they maintained a more vigorous and healthy religious life than did their fellow believers on the French side of the boundary line. They, too, organized themselves into a conference unit in 1897. One of the leaders of these churches was Valentin Pelsy.

As a result of the restoration of Alsace-Lorraine to France in 1918 and the reunion of the two formerly separated Mennonite groups, the French language has been substituted for the former German throughout all these churches, which have now become one ecclesiastical body. This is a great advantage to the old French group, but a loss at the same time to the Alsatian, for with the adoption of the French language, the latter automatically cut themselves off from all the traditional culture and the doctrinal literature of the past which has been German, as well as from the main currents of German Mennonitism of today. The French group is hardly large enough to maintain either a literature or a culture of its own.

The French Amish-Mennonites, both in the former Alsace-Lorraine as well as in other places, are still in the main a country people, though more and more they are drifting into the cities. They are still noted, as they always have been, for their industry and sobriety and for their philanthropy and generosity. Sometimes, in fact, they are imposed upon. An observation of their kindness to the poor and needy, made some years ago by a local writer is still just as true today:

> Homeless beggars and wandering ne'er do wells knew far and wide the regions where Mennonites lived. These knights of the road always knew that here they would be assured of a warm nook in the stable for the night, and the good housewife, too, was certain not to withhold a bit of hot soup from the hungry stomach.

Although the preachers for the most part remain uneducated and unpaid, there are signs that indicate the passing of the old order. Some of the younger ministers are spending a few months or even years in the nearby Bible schools in Basel and Bienenberg for their religious work. Those without special training for the ministry are nevertheless often men of more than ordinary ability in other lines. Several years ago one of the young preachers of a congregation was the superintendent of a large textile mill, and another one, the chief government forester of that district. Hooks and eyes, of course, are gone, as are also most of the strict rules of discipline and practice once prevalent among the Amish.

In numbers, the whole reunited French church includes a total population of a little more than two thousand souls, about two-thirds of whom live in Alsace and Lorraine, and the remainder, farther in the French interior. There is also a small congregation in Luxembourg. Such names as *Roth, Lugbill, Joder, Widmer, Schmouker, Sommer, Lidwiller, Mosiman, Wagler, Neuhusser, Jordy, Pelsy, Nafziger,* and *Schertz* indicate the Swiss origin of the French Mennonites.

The French Mennonites Today

When the German Army invaded France in 1939, the Mennonite communities of Mühlhausen, Colmar, Geisberg, Belfort, and other places suffered severely. Young men were drafted into the French and German armies. Many of them were killed or spent years in prisoner-of-war camps. During the German occupation the Alsatian population, including the Mennonites, was again

SOUTH GERMANY

united with Germany as it had been from 1871 to World War I. In 1944 and 1945 this territory again became a battleground, resulting in tremendous losses of life and property. Immediately after this, the American Mennonites through the Mennonite Central Committee established contact with the war sufferers among the Alsatian and French Mennonites, assisting them and the French population in general by providing food, clothing, and spiritual nurture.

Culturally, the French Mennonites have undergone radical changes during the last decades. Little of their Amish background can be detected. They have given up the Amish practices of nonconformity, and are becoming more urbanized. In their religious life they have been influenced strongly by an emotional piety which is evangelistic and has little in common with their Amish background. They are filled with missionary and evangelistic zeal unknown to them for generations. The German language has largely been replaced by the French. Since World War II a new interest has arisen in young people's retreats, Bible study groups, choirs, student exchange, nonresistance, and cooperation with the Mennonites in other countries. The *Mennonitisches Jahrbuch* of 1978 lists 23 congregations with a membership ranging from 20 to 325 and totaling 2,000.

Between the World Wars

A few words should be said here of the Mennonites as a whole in Germany. With the exception of a few congregations in France and one in Galicia, the settlements mentioned in the last two chapters were all a part of Germany prior to World War I. In spite of a common language and common religious traditions, the four settlements—northwestern Germany, the Vistula-Nogat delta, the Palatinate and Upper Rhine, and Alsace-Lorraine—all formed separate ecclesiastical units and conference districts.

For the purpose of bringing about a closer cooperation among the different groups, several of the more progressive church leaders organized in Berlin in 1886 what became known as the *Vereinigung der Mennonitengemeinden im Deutschen Reich*, modeled largely upon the Dutch A.D.S. The objectives of this union were stated at the first meeting—to provide for traveling evangelists, to encourage worthy students for the ministry, to aid underpaid ministers, and to promote the cause of Mennonite literature. This conference has greatly promoted many common efforts among the German Mennonites.

Loss of the Nonresistant Faith

As already noted, all these groups of Mennonites had given up their nonresistant faith by 1914. Nearly all the young men accepted military service when the war broke out, although a small number in the more conservative churches in Prussia, Baden, and Alsace took advantage of the provisions of the Cabinet Order of 1868 permitting noncombatant service.

Among the reasons given by the German Mennonites themselves for the passing of their traditional peace witness are the following: first, the Cabinet Order of 1868 permitting noncombatant service was limited to the descendants of the traditional Mennonites only. Those who had become Mennonites since 1868, and were not of the original families, did not share this exemption. Secondly, universal military training in times of peace paved the way for an easy transition to universal service in times of war. Finally, not to be forgotten is the fact that the rising tide of nationalism and patriotism that pervaded German national life with increasing force after 1870 engulfed Mennonite youth as it did the rest of Germany. For some time before World War I the South German Conference supported a Soldier's Commission whose business it was to look after the spiritual interests of the Mennonite young men in the training barracks.

According to the *Mennonitische Blätter,* two thousand young Mennonites had gone into service by September 1915, one-fourth of them officers. By that time, too, one hundred fifteen had fallen in battle, ninety-five had been wounded, and twenty-three had been taken prisoner. Ninety had received the iron cross. The losses were equally heavy during the remainder of the war, but the papers ceased to publish the details. It is estimated that the total number of those who fell during the entire period was about four hundred.

At the Versailles Treaty, the German Mennonites lost nearly half their population to Poland, the Free State of Danzig, and France—a separation along national and linguistic lines that made the task of Mennonite unification in middle Europe even more precarious than it had been in the past. Those left in Germany proper counted up to a scant thirteen thousand.

Tired of War

For a time after World War I, when the whole German nation was passing through a period of great despondency and humiliation, the Mennonites seemed temporarily to be in a sympathetic mood toward their traditional views on the question of war and their relation to the state. In a meeting of the Conference of the South German Mennonites in 1923, it was unanimously agreed to petition the German government, requesting that in the proposed act providing for universal military training, proper consideration should be given to those that had conscientious scruples against entering the army.

The next year, Christian Neff, one of the best known and most highly respected leaders among the German Mennonites, in summarizing an article on the history of nonresistance among the Mennonites, wrote:

> The doctrine of nonresistance is and remains a significant religious and ethical problem. Praiseworthy have been the efforts of our churches in solving it, as is well shown in our history. The World War has revived the problem, and laid it afresh on our hearts, and challenged our consciences. May we realize the significance of this question, and above all may our young people consider it earnestly and prayerfully.

There was a revival of the principle of nonresistance especially among the young people. Leaders among them were Erich Göttner and Theo Glück. In a round-robin letter, in which Mennonite youth of all countries participated, questions pertaining to nonresistance, as well as problems confronting the young people during the rise of national socialism, were discussed.

After World War II

The South German Mennonite congregations did not suffer as severely during and after World War II as did those of the Vistula Delta and Northwest Germany. Since they are located mostly in rural areas, most of those not actively participating in the war did not experience directly the tragedy that befell those in the larger cities. However, the congregations of the cities of Ludwigshaven, Heilbronn, Munich, Zweibrücken, and others suffered severely.

The Mennonite farmers were also spared to some degree the great food shortage following World War II. They became the oasis where Mennonite refugees from the East found work, shelter, and bread. The South German Mennonites took an active part in the relief work of the Mennonite Central Committee and conducted such work independently under *Christenpflicht.*

All publications of the Mennonites of Germany were suspended either during the war or upon the collapse of the nation. Only gradually were some of them resumed. In 1948 the publication of the *Gemeindeblatt* was resumed. In 1949 the first issue of the *Mennonitische Geschichtsblätter* again appeared. A few books were published. The first conference after World War II was held in 1946. Gradually the *Vereinigung der deutschen Mennonitengemeinden, Mennonitischer Geschichtsverein,* and other organizations were again revived. The center of some activities had been shifted to South Germany. All activities were handicapped by the division of Germany into the American, French, British, and

Russian zones of occupation.

A number of outstanding leaders of the South German Mennonites died during and after the war. Among them were Christian Neff, who served the Weierhof congregation for more than five decades and was one of the most outstanding German Mennonite conference leaders and scholars, and Christian Hege, another Mennonite scholar and co-editor with Christian Neff of the *Mennonitisches Lexikon*.

The South German Mennonites were soon able to help in the reconstruction program. New congregations originated at Enkenbach and Backnang where Mennonite settlements were established. New congregations were also established in Nürnberg (1947); Frankfurt (1948); Göttingen (1945); Hannover (1949); Lübeck (1950); Berlin, DDR (1961). Some have grown, but most of them remain small.

The North American Mennonites established their headquarters for the channeling of aid to the Mennonites and those in need in general in Frankfurt, Germany. This was done primarily through the Mennonite Central Committee, the relief agent of all North American Mennonites. The German *Hilfswerk* was located in Ludwigshafen. The global effort of the Mennonites to proclaim the gospel of Christ (mission work) and to relieve the suffering "in the name of Christ" will be presented elsewhere.

6. THE MENNONITES OF GERMANY TODAY

First of all we take note of the fact that all surviving West Prussian Mennonites fled from East to West Germany empty-handed and had to be taken care of. Some went to Uruguay; others joined congregations in North and South Germany, and even established new ones such as at Backnang, Neuwied, and Espelkamp. Since 1960 a group of Mennonites is again coming from the East, this time from Russia. By 1978 nearly 8,000 Mennonites had arrived in West Germany. These have either joined congregations in Neuwied, Espelkamp, Bechterdissen, and other places in West Germany or have established independent fellowships.

Organizations and Publications

The best sources of information about the location, origin, ministers, members, and church boards of German churches today can be found in the *Mennonitisches Jahrbuch*, which appears annually. It includes not only all German congregations, but also those of Switzerland and France. The Dutch *Doopsgezind Jaarboekje* gives the same information in regard to the Netherlands. For some time, all European Mennonites have had conference sessions together and carry out some activities in a union called *Mennonitische Europäische Regional Konferenz* (MERK).

Mennonites are also organized in conferences in all countries. In the Netherlands it is the *Algemeene Doopsgezinde Sociëteit* with headquarters in Amsterdam. In Germany the major conferences are *Vereinigung der Deutschen Mennonitengemeinden* to which all congregations of North Germany and some of South Germany belong. Another conference is the *Verband deutscher Mennonitengemeinden*. The congregations of the latter are located mostly in South Germany. Some congregations hold a membership in both conferences. *Verband deutscher Mennonitengemeinden* publishes *Gemeinde Unterwegs* (The Church on the Move). The *Vereinigung* publishes *Mennonitische Blätter*. The *Mennonitische Geschichtsblätter*, published by the German Mennonite Historical Society, and *Mennonitisches Jahrbuch* always contain scholarly, informative, and challenging contributions. The latter is published by the Conference of South German Mennonites.

All these and many more sources, including recently published books, supply very valuable information about the present conditions among the German Mennonites. Only a few glimpses will be presented here.

Lost and Found

Great changes have taken place among the Mennonites in Europe. This can be illustrated by what happened at the All European Mennonite Conference (MERK) which convened at Basel in 1975. Horst Quiring, reporting about the meeting, stated that he was particularly impressed by the appearance of a young Swiss Mennonite on the platform who explained why he could not accept military service, in which all Swiss Mennonites have been involved for generations. After giving his testimony, he was taken to jail. Quiring observed: "Here at a discussion about nonresistance in the past and present, the issue emerged and the conference topic and the discussion became a *reality*" (*Mennonitisches Jahrbuch*, 1977, pp. 65-66). There is not an issue of this annual *Jahrbuch* without a serious discussion of this subject.

This is even more the case in the *Mennonitische Blätter*, which has not only an international character but also treats a wide range of theological and social issues for Christians in general. It allows considerable space to matters of war and peace, past and present. Articles dealing with the past such as "The Problem of Nonresistance Among the Mennonites of Russia" are followed by reports about the activities of the German Mennonite Peace Committee, including the article: "Ten Years of Reconciliation Work in Poland." It is impressive to read that 5,000 German young people have spent up to three weeks of work in former concentration camps, in order to restore goodwill and to establish ties of friendship between Germany and Poland. During the summer of 1978, thirty groups did this work.

Conscientious Objectors in Germany and Switzerland

In 1977 the Court of the Federal Government of West Germany decreed that a simple declaration of having conscientious scruples in regard to military service was sufficient to be exempted. It is interesting to note that West Germany had 40,634 conscientious objectors in 1976 and 62,322 in 1977. No report was given of how many of these religious objectors were Mennonites.

Hanspeter Jecker of Switzerland reported that all Swiss Mennonites who declined in decades past to serve in the army migrated to North America. Even today there is no exemption possible, and no alternative service. There are annually an increasing number of young Swiss who refuse to serve in the army. All get jail sentences.

Only a few Swiss Mennonites have thus far objected to all forms of military service. Half of them accept full service and the other half do military service without arms. The peace witness is growing, and it is being realized that neither the full military service nor the military service enlistment without arms constitutes a full peace witness.

Mennonites in Switzerland, France, Germany, and the Netherlands are very active in many other areas. There are numerous agencies active in relief at many fronts of disaster, hunger, and need. One of them is *Internationale Mennonitische Organisation* (IMO), the Mennonite relief agency of all European Mennonites. Recently a report on how Mennonites had helped West Prussian Mennonites in 1888 when dams of the Vistula River had broken and floods had destroyed hundreds of homes and fields was used to inspire donors. The *Mennonitisches Jahrbuch* lists more than two dozen agencies soliciting contributions to do their tasks in outreach programs, missions, and aid—at home and abroad.

The Mennonites under Hitler

There is still an open wound from the days of World War II. It is the question of the extent to which the Mennonites were drawn into Hitler's restoration of the German *Reich* and his military ventures.

In a chapter in a book devoted to the various aspects of

sixteenth-century Anabaptism, Hans-Jürgen Goertz pointed out that the German Mennonites had surrendered and betrayed their Anabaptist heritage in the days of Hitler. His portrayal and account stirred up a considerable reaction among the Mennonites, particularly those who were at a mature age in the crucial years of Hitler's rise, conquests, and fall.

The result was the publication of a book which was to present the story of the Mennonites during that time. It is entitled: *Die Mennoniten im Dritten Reich. Dokumentation und Deutung* (1977). The book contains significant sources and observations of what transpired in those crucial years and what the reaction of the Mennonites was. However, the interpretation of the events is not satisfactory to all, and the dialogue about the book and the actual involvement of the German Mennonites in Hitler's programs and their reactions continue.

Since the days of their origin in the Netherlands and Switzerland, the Mennonites had become a "separate" people because of their faith and status in the society wherever they went. Those that feared they would lose their identity, be this by compulsion or by gradual adjustment, moved on to countries where they would be able to retain it. Consequently, by the time Hitler came to power the Mennonites that had remained in western Europe had surrendered much of this identity. It is one task to describe this last period and another one to go back, as Goertz did, and trace all the steps of surrender of the original Anabaptist conception and testimony as well as to lift up the price that many were willing to pay to remain faithful to the Lord through the centuries. Concerning basic Christian convictions, it can be said, one can have them; one can lose them; one can, by the grace of God, even regain them.

VII
The Hutterites

The persecuting zeal which drove Jakob Hutter and his humble followers across the Moravian border in 1535 gradually spent itself. When the local noblemen, whose estates had greatly benefited from the industry and expert farming of the Hutterites, learned that there was no connection whatever between the Moravian Anabaptists and the Münsterites, they refused to carry out the cruel orders of King Ferdinand and Emperor Charles to completely annihilate the movement inaugurated by the Tyrolean hatter. Many of the exiles, of both the Hutterite and other Anabaptist groups, now returned to their former homes. Soon the households were reoccupied and others built. In a few years it was commonly reported that the number of Anabaptists in Moravia was again some four or five thousand, mostly Hutterites scattered about in some twenty households.

Where the protection of interested landlords was wanting, however, these dissenting groups were never entirely safe from attack. An illustration of what they might expect at any time is found in the experience in the year 1539 of a small group of the brethren, some hundred fifty of them, who had established themselves a short distance south of Nikolsburg in Lower Austria. Apparently, on no pretense whatever they were suddenly apprehended by order of the king and cast into prison in the castle of Falkenstein. Here they were visited by priests and theologians attempting to convince the prisoners of the errors of their ways and by representatives of the government attempting to force from them a confession as to the hiding place of their treasures, for all Hutterite communities were reported to be wealthy. "Our treasure is in the Lord Jesus Christ," the brethren replied, "not in worldly possessions." Failing in both these objectives, the authorities released the women, but held the men, some ninety of them, for galley service against the Turks. Some months later on the way to the coast, however, all but twelve of the prisoners escaped and found their way back to Moravia. The twelve who were recaptured actually served out their sentences amid great hardship and suffering.

During the Smalkald War

During the Smalkald War which ended with the treaty of Augsburg in 1555, dissenting religious groups throughout the Habsburg possessions entered another period of severe trial. It will be remembered that throughout the lifetime of Luther, Emperor Charles was so preoccupied with political worries, including a series of wars with the king of France and the constant dread of a Turkish invasion on his eastern frontier, that, though a devout Catholic, he had little time to spare for the religious questions then agitating his reign. The Lutheran movement, therefore, had a fairly free hand during this period.

With the settling of his political problems and the beginning of the religious wars in 1546, however, Charles devoted the remaining few years of his troubled reign to making his empire safe for Catholicism. The result was a bitter religious struggle which showed little sympathy for religious dissent of any sort. Although many of the local landlords were loath to part with their industrious tenants, the Catholic clergy and higher civil officials were not. Both emperor and king were agreed that Anabaptists of every sort must be completely rooted out, not only from Moravia, but from all the Habsburg possessions as well. Upon imperial request, the Moravian *Landtag* ordered all Hutterites as well as other dissenting groups to immediately renounce their faith or go into exile. Most of the Hutterites crossed the frontier into northwestern Hungary, where they established a new settlement at Sobotiste. Later in the century were added Levar, and other communities nearby in the foothills on the eastern slopes of the Little Carpathians, a region usually spoken of by later chroniclers as Upper Hungary.

In vain the persecuted Moravian brethren pled for mercy, or at least time in which to dispose of their property before leaving. They were not a menace to the country, they said, as reported; for they were less than two thousand in number in all Moravia, living in twenty-one households. But in Hungary, too, the exiles were as unwelcome as they had been in Moravia. Pressed by King Ferdinand, the local nobility ordered them back. Some, returning, escaped the clutches of their persecutors. But most of them, tolerated on neither side of the boundary line, spent their next five or six years wandering about in the highlands, finding temporary refuge in forests and waste places, hiding in caves, seeking shelter amid the rocks, finding food and clothing as best they could. "Gladly," says a chronicler of the time, "would they have shared a roof with the cattle and swine, but even that was denied them." No one dared, under severe penalty, to give them relief, sell them food and clothing, or furnish them with work. Their men, women, and children were declared outlaws, with everything that that word implies. Robbers and ruffians had the right to attack them wantonly and with impunity, rob them of their goods, ravage their women folk, and attack their men—an opportunity which the lawless elements of the region were not slow to seize.

The Golden Age in Moravia

But a better day was ahead. The treaty of Augsburg, in 1555, which inaugurated a degree of tolerance by transferring from the emperor to the local rulers the right to prescribe the religious faith of the people, and the end of the reign of the bigoted Charles, which came about the same time, marked a turning point in the history of religious liberty. The Hutterites, though not one of the tolerated parties officially recognized by the Augsburg agreement, yet in a measure shared with all non-Catholics the religious privileges of the period. There began now for these persecuted people a period called the "Golden Age" which continued throughout the greater part of the century.

The Hutterites grew in numbers and in material prosperity. At its peak it is estimated that the population reached approximately fifteen thousand, living in Moravia and Upper Hungary, and distributed throughout some fifty households. During all this period the prosperous Hutterite communities made a strong appeal to the less fortunate Anabaptists of other countries as the "promised land." A steady stream of emigrant refugees from Switzerland and South Germany kept passing in and out of Moravia, and much of the growth of the native church is to be ascribed to this migration.

The Moravian brethren, too, were ardent missionaries, desiring to share both their material and spiritual blessings with others. To this end, throughout this period, they continued to send out missionaries to other lands inviting the persecuted everywhere to come to Moravia. This was a dangerous undertaking for the missionaries, for Anabaptists were still outlawed everywhere else in Europe. The records of the time are full of the names of devoted men and women who risked their all to carry the good news throughout middle Europe. Most of them never came back. A few casual examples taken from the chroniclers of the time must suffice here as illustrations of what these devoted and courageous messengers of a new religious faith and a new social order had to suffer in behalf of their convictions.

In 1558 Hans Raiffer, a smith by trade and a minister, was apprehended on his way to the Netherlands. After being put through the most cruel torture on the rack in the hope of turning him from his faith, he was tied to a stake with a rope about his neck, and a chain around his limbs, and in this position burned to a crisp. The executioners explained that they were reluctant to carry out these orders, but if they did not the new emperor would punish them. In the year 1556 a minister was drowned at Venice, and another executed with the sword at Innsbruck. In 1571 Wolf Binder was arrested in Bavaria and stretched on the rack until it seemed that "the sun would shine through him." Refusing to forsake his faith, he was released from this cruel instrument of torture, and with a song of his own composition on his lips was mercifully beheaded. By the close of the century, hundreds of these brave men and women had given their all to promote what they believed to be their divine commission. As late as 1618 the chroniclers record the imprisonment, torture, and final execution in Tyrol of Jost Wilhelm, a well-to-do Moravian missionary.

The Way of Life

The Hutterites agreed with the peaceful Anabaptists elsewhere, later known as *Mennonites*, in all the essential Anabaptist doctrines, such as believer's baptism, rejection of the oath, nonresistance, opposition to office holding, the symbolic view of the Lord's Supper. For a time, especially during periods of special stress, they were in rather close touch with the Mennonites of Switzerland and South Germany, and occasionally with those in Holland. They frequently attended Mennonite conferences, being represented at the Strassburg meeting in 1557, where Menno Simons's Wismar rules were discussed. Although they never bore the name *Mennonite*, they must be included in any complete history of the Anabaptists.

In their later years they were more consistent followers of certain early characteristic Mennonite doctrines than the Mennonites themselves. They agreed with Menno Simons and Jakob Ammann in the rigid application of the practice of avoidance to all excommunicated members. In their practice of nonresistance, too, the Hutterites were more consistent than the Mennonites in the rest of Europe. Their cutlers in the community workshops were not permitted to make any weapons of warfare, only knives and cutlery that could be used for peaceful purposes. Nor did they manufacture gunpowder, a business engaged in occasionally with great material gain by the Mennonites of both

Holland and West Prussia. They would not pay war tax, calling it "blood money." The Swiss Brethren in Moravia at this time, Anabaptist immigrants who refused to accept the communal life of the Hutterites, had no such scruples, and drew no such fine distinctions in aiding the practice of war by this indirect method.

In one important matter, however, the Hutterites were unique and different from the Mennonites. They had all things in common, working together for a common fund, living under a common roof, and eating at a common table. Groups of families joined into households called *Bruderhof*. When a new member joined their company he turned all his private property into the common treasury; and when he left, in case that happened, it was not returned. Their communism, unlike most later similar social experiments, rested not upon an economic but a religious basis. The sharing of material as well as spiritual blessings was as much a part of their faith and as binding a divine command as any other part of their doctrinal system. It is to this religious sanction, undoubtedly, that one must turn for an explanation for the continued success, lasting now for four centuries, of this Christian utopia, while similar attempts, based mainly on economic considerations, have frequently failed. A deep religious conviction, after all, is the strongest of social forces. Written before the middle of the sixteenth century, Peter Riedemann's *Rechenschaft*, the official confession of faith of the brethren, justifies the practice with copious scriptural quotations not only from the New and Old Testaments, but from the Apocrypha as well. Rather than give up the practice, says one of their chroniclers, they would die for it; and many did.

The Bruderhof

The *Bruderhof*, as each of their households is called, was a self-sufficient economic as well as social and religious unit, consisting of from twenty to fifty or more families, all living under the roof of one or more communal houses. Land in Moravia, as elsewhere in Europe at that time, was held by feudal tenure, in the hands of great landlords. The households were established under certain stipulations, frequently including agreements to furnish labor at a specified price, or some other useful service; as well as a share of the products of the land. In turn the local landlord, if he was an influential person, would guarantee protection against religious persecution. Since the Hutterites were an industrious people, often well skilled in all sorts of craftsmanship, they were usually in demand by the feudal lords as tenants. For sobriety, skill, industry, and reliability—rare virtues in those turbulent times—there were few stewards of estates, millers, and superintendents of vineyards better than they.

In government, each *Bruderhof* was a complete economic unit. For religious control, several might unite under one elder (leading minister), but each had a "minister of the Word" to minister to their spiritual needs. By his side there was in each unit a "minister of needs," democratically elected by all the male church members, who had almost arbitrary control of the daily economic life of the community. He handled all the money, distributed the work to be done by the various members, made all the necessary purchases, sold the crops, looked after the sale of the manufactured products, and represented the business affairs of the community with the outside world. In fact he, together with his assistants, was the business manager of the community with practically unlimited powers, except the powers he shared with the elder, such as when new land was to be purchased or new buildings were to be erected.

There was no private ownership of any sort within the *Bruderhof*. No one owned anything of his own except the clothes on his back, and perhaps an heirloom or two; but even these latter reverted back to the community as a whole upon the death of the erstwhile owner. All ate at a common table and from common dishes and utensils. Unmarried boys and girls lived in separate dormitories. Married folks enjoyed a room to themselves with the bare necessities for furniture. But even this was for sleeping purposes only, and not to be regarded as a private home. All the money made on the side, such as personal tips and pay for extra labor, was turned over to the common treasury. Every detail of daily living was minutely prescribed as in a medieval monastery. The time to rise and retire, when and how much to eat, what kind of clothes to wear (and their color and cut), when to bathe, and how to pray were all decided by the community.

Since each *Bruderhof* was a self-sufficient economic unit, every occupation known to medieval agriculture and industry was practiced among the Hutterites. Besides farming, which was their major occupation, the following artisans were frequently found among them: masons, blacksmiths, sicklesmiths, dyers, shoemakers, furriers, wheelwrights, saddlers, cutlers, watchmakers, tailors, weavers, glass and rope makers, and brewers. Since milling was an important industry, they frequently located their buildings along a stream which furnished water power. Their descendants, more than three centuries later, perpetuated this practice along the James River in South Dakota. Being industrious and thrifty, they produced more than they consumed. "Beehives," their households were often called. Their surplus goods were sold in the open market, and their personal services to neighboring noblemen. They excelled especially in fine stockraising. From their stables came the finest horses and cattle in the land, while their cutlery, woolens, and linens could not be surpassed anywhere for quality. For both their services and goods there was a ready demand. Their public baths were frequented by the nobility of the region. Their doctors, in that day of simple remedies, were among the most skilled. A chronicle of the year 1581 says, "In this year emperor Rudolf sent for our doctor George Zobel. Through the grace of God he was again restored to health."

Realizing that their unusual communal life marked them as a peculiar people and lined them up with the various radical peasant movements of that day in the minds of their neighbors, the Hutterites were especially concerned about their good name among their fellow countrymen. The leaders therefore insisted that their members live exemplary lives and give their neighbors no opportunity for charging them with the vices usually ascribed to collectivism.

Great care was exercised that the material that went into the making of their goods should be of the very best quality, and that all services rendered should be the most efficient. Codes were drawn up for every industry and occupation prescribing in detail the high standards they had set for themselves. At a meeting in Sobotiste in 1654 of the "bath attendants" and the doctors, who seemingly were closely affiliated here, a number of rules were laid down to guide the profession in its conduct and to increase its efficiency. The "bath attendants" should remember that they were serving their calling for their own soul's salvation and for the common good; they should so conduct themselves, therefore, that they might bring credit to the community and the brethren. Especially should they be diligent in the reading of the Scriptures, and in the books of medicine, and the gathering of herbs and roots. The advice to go to bed early and rise upon waking was perhaps as good for others as for the doctors; as was also the suggestion that they should not gad about, either in the household or outside, indulging in idle gossip, or to frequent the drinking houses which surrounded them on all sides. They were to be friendly to all, to discriminate against no one, and to bring all their fees to the common treasury. From the brethren no fees or gifts were to be accepted for services rendered. Neither doctors nor attendants were to make their own appointments. They should also be diligent in teaching nonvitiates so that their art might not be lost to the brotherhood.

It was this meticulous regard for honest and efficient performance of every duty that created such a strong demand even among the local nobility for Hutterite service of every sort. Not only their baths and doctors, but also their midwives, were in great repute everywhere.

A Christian Lifestyle

Like the Mennonites, the Hutterites believed that a true Christian life ought to be more than merely a system of orthodox beliefs; that it should function in right living. Much was made, therefore, of leading an upright life. Occupations that offered special temptations to human frailties were tabooed. Visiting taverns was strictly forbidden the members, because of the "ungodly activities" usually associated with the life there. Wine might be offered visitors in the home, but never for money.

In their attitude toward business activities they held the prevailing economic theories common to the Christians of that day, namely, that money as such was nonproductive, and that buying and selling, therefore, was a species of gambling, neither religiously permissible nor economically sound. Consequently, merchandising was left to the Jews, who had no such scruples against the making of profits. Goods might be bought in the outside markets by the *Bruderhof*, but for use only, not for resale. In all their private and business life, the Hutterites demanded the strictest adherence to just and fair dealing, and to pure living. Even their enemies in their best moments could not forbear giving them a clean slate for upright living. A contemporary Catholic writer, who had no sympathy whatever for their religious views or social practices, nevertheless wrote, after a visit to a *Bruderhof* in Upper Hungary in the late seventeenth century, that he saw among them

> no anger, envy, passion, or malice; no vain zeal for earthly things; no gambling spirit; no vanity; in short, a most harmonious and beautiful life.

Their whole striving, he said, seemed to be to build up the kingdom of God, and promote the well-being of humankind. This writer continued,

> Would that I could introduce this kind of life among the Roman Catholics; so far as I know it even surpasses that of the monasteries. Anyone who could establish such a noble way of Christian living under the protection of the authorities would be a second saint to Saint Dominic or Francis.

But to the writer in question, the orthodox Catholic faith was even more essential than pure living. Unfortunately, he thought, one had the orthodox faith, but not the noble life; while the other, though leading a pure life, yet was heretical in faith. He concluded,

> I have said to myself if you could just convert these stubborn

Anabaptists so that they could show your Catholic brethren their art of living, what a blessed man you would be, or if you could only persuade your orthodox brethren to lead, like the Anabaptists, such an apparently Christian and noble life, what an accomplishment would be to your credit.

Of course there were other Catholic writers who could see nothing beyond their narrow orthodoxy, and who, therefore, magnified all the faults of the Hutterite system. They saw nothing in the godly lives of these honest and humble followers of the early New Testament church except wolves in sheep's clothing. The Hutterite chroniclers themselves best describe this attitude among their Catholic critics:

> As soon as we set foot out of doors we are maligned as Anabaptists, Bi-Baptists, New Baptists, Schismatics, Revolutionists, and all such sorts of blasphemous names. Everybody takes up the cry against us, and mocks us and spreads all kinds of ugly lies against us—that we eat our children, and are guilty of all sorts of unmentionable crimes even worse than that. All this because we are followers of Jesus Christ. If one goes about with only a staff in his hand, a sign that he wishes no one any harm, or if he prays before his meals, he is slandered as a heretic; but as soon as he recants and conducts himself as a heathen with a sword in his belt, and a musket on his shoulder, the world immediately welcomes him back and regards him as a good Christian. Or again, if one leaves the church and returns to evil ways, shows himself a good fellow, begins to sing filthy drinking songs in the tavern, puts a silly feather in his cap, acts a fool generally, frequents the gambling joints and dance halls, puts a big calf skin about his neck, and wears gay clothes, all embroidered with lace, and swears like a Frenchman, and blasphemes God, then he is welcomed back again and received by his own. You are a good fellow, they will say to him. You have done well to leave these schismatics. Such an one is doubly welcomed by the World, no matter how evil his ways may be.

Such is the reaction, according to this sixteenth-century chronicler, of the religious leaders of the time in the state church toward the rigid standards of conduct upheld by the Hutterites.

Schools

It speaks well for the Hutterites that in an age when illiteracy was the common lot of the average man, they had already developed a well-organized system of compulsory education. Their educational program was admirably designed to perpetuate their religious ideals and to prepare their young people for the community life they were living. First place was given to their Christian way of life. "We are concerned not with worldly, but rather with heavenly wisdom," one of their teachers said.

Children were taken from their mother's breast at less than two years of age and placed in charge of the community nursery, which was also a kind of kindergarten where they were taught little prayers, simple Bible verses, and such religious training as their little minds could absorb. At five or six the children were placed under formal school discipline, girls and boys separately. Religion, vocation, and good citizenship in the household community were the objectives of this program. All were taught reading and writing, the history of the church, the catechism, and such other religious precepts as would make them not only good Christians but good Hutterites as well. In addition, the boys were all taught some trade or prepared for some special work to which they would be assigned later in life, while the girls were instructed in spinning and general household duties. The whole course of instruction led directly to membership in the church and some allotted place in the community. All were baptized, upon confession of faith, sometimes quite young.

Since child welfare was a community concern, it was perhaps only natural that the rules and regulations governing child training should give more attention to the physical well-being of children than did the usual school systems of that time. In a code of instructions presented by Peter Walpot to a gathering of teachers of Auspitz in 1568, and later enlarged into one of the earliest treatises on teaching to be found in all Europe, numerous practical measures are suggested for the physical care of children. Long before the discovery of the communication of disease by germs, sick children here in the dormitories were to be segregated from those who were well. Teachers and nurses, when examining the mouths of diseased children, were to be careful to wash their hands before examining others, so as not to contaminate those not sick. Children coming to the schools from outside the community were to be carefully examined for contagious diseases, and segregated if necessary. Bed linen was to be changed often and always kept clean. The admonition to bathe at least once each month may seem somewhat conservative in these days of the modern bathtub, but no doubt unusually liberal in an age when the taking of a bath by even so prominent a person as Queen Elizabeth was an event worthy of special mention by the court chronicler. Each child was to have its own comb and brush.

Play was given little recognition in this school program. There were rules stipulating hours for work, and everything else was regulated, but not one hour was given for play. The value of physical exercise was recognized, however. The teachers were instructed not to send their children to bed immediately after supper, since that was against nature. Some exercise should be taken before retiring. Walking under the guidance of the teacher or some other older person was recommended. Among other regulations designed to promote the physical comfort of the children was one demanding that their boots be kept well-greased so that they might not become too stiff and thus produce corns on the feet of the wearer. The rule that girls should arise at five in the morning to begin their spinning, and boys at six, was perhaps not popular among the children, nor perhaps the stipulation that they retire at six o'clock in the summer and at sunset in the winter.

According to this Hutterite school program, children should be taught the virtues that would fit them especially to live in a closed community—patience, gentleness, modesty, self-control, and consideration for others. The teacher should inculcate these virtues by example rather than by the use of the rod. That human nature is not the same in all children was well recognized. Some are won with kind words, others by the promise of rewards, but there are those who must be ruled by a firm hand, says Walpot. All, however, must be raised "in the fear of the Lord." Such gross sins as stealing and lying must be corrected by corporal punishment, administered only by the teacher, and publicly, so that all the children may be inspired with a wholesome fear of wrongdoing. The teacher, who was the chief disciplinary officer of the household both within and without school hours, must exercise his peculiar power—not in anger, but for the good of the child. The child, on the other hand, must submit to his punishment willingly as deserving it, and must not in any way try to ward it off. The teacher, of course, must be careful not to inflict permanent physical injury. He was not to strike on the head or mouth, nor stop the mouth of his victim with a cushion or cloth to prevent an outcry.

The teachers were selected from the brotherhood for life, and with little preparation beyond what they had themselves received in their own elementary schools. They served, of course, without pay.

For higher education the Hutterites had little need, and less sympathy. In fact, they forbade their members to attend schools outside of their own where they said "only worldly wisdom and cunning is sought, while godly things are neglected." Doctors of theology and the learned men of the universities were their chief persecutors in matters of religious orthodoxy, and it was not to be expected that they would be especially drawn toward a group that was the chief cause of their troubles.

But their elementary schools, designed to fit their children for efficient everyday living in the community, were among the best of their day, and were often visited, as already suggested, by others not of their faith. During this period, Hutterite children were no doubt among the most literate, the healthiest, the most religious, highly trained, and the best behaved children of all Europe.

Das Geschichtsbuch and Other Books

Unlike the Mennonites, who were unusually modest and fearful about recording their doings, the Hutterites recorded rather completely all their experiences, both religious and economic, throughout the whole of their checkered career and wanderings across southeastern Europe. These annals—usually kept by the church leaders, and by them handed down from one generation to another—seemingly were never printed in Europe, but kept in manuscript and carried along as a priceless treasure throughout all their trekking for religious liberty. This manuscript is usually spoken of in the records as *Das Gemeinde-Geschichtsbuch* (Book of Chronicles). It contains an illuminating record of the chief activities and the deaths of their church leaders; their sufferings and persecutions at the hands of their enemies; gruesome experiences at the hands of marauding armies during the numerous wars of the seventeenth and eighteenth centuries under the Turks, Catholics, and Protestants; national calamities and unusual natural phenomena such as the appearance of comets, earthquakes, floods, and drouths; as well as numerous rules and regulations passed from time to time controlling their communal life and religious practice. Church quarrels are faithfully recorded, as well as other routine experiences that befell a humble and righteous people trying to serve their God as best they could in a cruel and unsympathetic world.

In 1883 J. von Beck published *Die Geschichtsbücher der Wiedertäufer* dealing with the Hutterite chronicles, and in 1923 Rudolph Wolkan published for the first time the *Geschichts-Buch der Hutterischen Brüder*. In 1943 this chronicle appeared again in a scholarly edition prepared by A. J. F. Zieglschmid under the title *Die älteste Chronik der Hutterischen Brüder* and published by the Carl Schurz Memorial Foundation, Philadelphia, Pennsylvania. The same editor and publisher produced *Das kleine Geschichtsbuch* in 1947. The songs of the Hutterites were published in the book *Die Lieder der Hutterischen Brüder*, Scottdale, Pennsylvania, 1914. Numerous Hutterite books have been reprinted and even more have been written about them during the last decades.

Riedemann's *Rechenschaft*

Another work highly prized by the Hutterites and the chief source of their confession of faith was a book called *Rechenschaft* written about 1545 by their chief theologian, Peter Riedemann. This volume was published several times in Europe during the sixteenth century, but in America it was known only in manuscript until 1902 when it was printed here for the first time in Berne, Indiana. Riedemann, whom the chroniclers of the day spoke of as a "God enlightened man, and a soundly evangelical minister," spent much of his time as a messenger of the Hutterite faith throughout South Germany. Like Paul he was often in jail, and, Bunyan-like, wrote most of his masterpieces in prison.

The book covers the usual views on such typical Anabaptist topics as believer's baptism, rejection of the oath, nonresistance, the magistracy, and the virtues of the simple, upright life; but it also treats the beliefs and doctrines which distinguish the Hutterites from other Anabaptists. A few random extracts may be of interest. On the question of community of goods Riedemann says, "Worldly as well as spiritual goods are the free gift of God, and must be shared." This view is corroborated by copious scriptural quotations.

Many of the later austere social practices and traditions of the brethren find a basis in this early confession of faith. Riedemann exhorts the community tailors when making clothes for outsiders to serve them faithfully. But as to gaily colored clothes that are trimmed with laces, embellished borders, and all sorts of frills—which can only encourage an arrogant and proud spirit—with such the tailors should have nothing to do, in order that they might "keep their consciences clear before their God."

When brethren meet they should greet one another with the words "Peace be with you." This should come from the heart and must be more than mere lip service. This form of greeting, however, is for Christians only. He who uses these words lightheartedly or exchanges them with a lighthearted person like a drunkard or a gambler does so at the risk of his soul's salvation. Handshaking and embracing are also symbols of unity and peace. But men and women should meet one another with a handshake only. *Zutrinken* (toasting), says Riedemann, is a bad habit, leading to drunkenness, a net devised by the devil to lead sober men astray, and so to be avoided like a serpent. Merchandising, as already indicated, is forbidden as sinful, for it increases the price for the poor and takes the bread out of their mouths.

End of the Moravian Golden Age

The Golden Age of the brethren came to an end before the close of the sixteenth century. For the next one hundred fifty years this slowly vanishing band of devoted Christians kept up a brave but losing struggle against great odds. First the marauding armies of both Catholics and Protestants swept over middle Europe during the whole first half of the seventeenth century, then the plundering Turks during the second half. Finally they faced the relentless zeal of the Jesuits, who during the first half of the eighteenth century were determined that all dissenting sects not officially tolerated by the Augsburg agreement of 1555 must be entirely exterminated from the Catholic possessions of the Habsburgs. By the middle of the eighteenth century, the humble and faithful followers of Jakob Hutter had practically been rooted out of both Moravia and Hungary. A small remnant survived by trekking to South Russia.

During the Thirty Years' War especially, the Hutterites, living in the heart of the battle-torn areas of that disastrous conflict, suffered untold horrors from both armies as they marched back and forth across this ill-fated territory. As is well known, middle Europe was so completely devastated by this cruel war that it did not recover for a full century. Cities were burned down; the armies, inadequately supported by the central governments, lived off the land, ruthlessly cutting down the men and ravishing the women. The well-filled granaries, sleek cattle, and fine-looking horses of the *Bruderhof* offered special temptation to the marauding parties of both armies.

One citation from the records must suffice as an illustration of what must have been a rather common experience of all during that troubled period. In 1619 twelve households in the Moravian settlement were completely burned to the ground; seventeen others were greatly damaged; forty men and women were cruelly killed, some under severe torture; and two hundred horses and all the cattle and sheep were dirven away. The next year the community at Pribitz was attacked by fifteen hundred troops—it is immaterial whether by Catholic or Protestant, since both alike were guilty of this inhuman treatment—and completely destroyed. In three hours, fifty-two men were killed, and seventeen other men and women so mutilated that they died within a few days. Every sort of inhuman punishment was resorted to by these murderous plunderers. For the purpose of wringing from the brethren a confession of the hiding places of their supposed wealth they

> burned them with hot irons and flaming torches, poured hot grease over their bare bodies, cut deep wounds into their flesh, which they filled with powder and then ignited, jerked off their fingers, slashed into them with their swords as though they were cabbage heads. One brother's head they completely twisted about so that he actually faced straight backward.

All this inhuman treatment of a peaceful people was unnecessary, since the Hutterites never resisted with force. It was a case of pure wantonness, perpetrated by bands of roving undisciplined troops held together by the promise of plunder.

As if this were not enough misery for a people already sorely afflicted, in September of 1622 an imperial order demanded that all Hutterites leave Moravia within four weeks, on penalty of severe punishment. The Habsburg possessions had now come under complete Catholic control. The Liechtensteins had in the meantime been succeeded by the intolerant von Dietrichsteins. The present ruler was a cardinal in the church, and was thus more than pleased to carry out the order of his emperor. In vain the poor people pled that they might at least be given until the next spring to make preparation for leaving, since it was now approaching winter. But their pleading fell on deaf ears. Several thousand of them, some twenty of the remaining households, were driven in midwinter across the border into Hungary to seek shelter wherever they might find it. Some of them finally found their way to their brethren in Sobotiste and Levar, communities established in the preceding century. Another group started a new colony at Alwinz, near Hermannstadt, in the southeastern corner of what was then Transylvania, or Siebenbürgen, now a part of Rumania. They were invited there by the famous Bethlen Gabor, Prince of Transylvania, one of the Protestant generals during the war, and favorable to the Protestant groups. By 1650 the last households had vanished from what had once been the promised land of Moravia.

Hungary and Transylvania

Here in Hungary and Transylvania the Hutterites now found a temporary home for another century, but they never recovered the prosperity of their Moravian days, nor did they entirely escape the hazards of invasions and wars that continually threatened the populations of that troubled section of the European border. Their number at best could never have exceeded several thousand, and even that was continually diminishing. Throughout the latter part of the seventeenth century their settlements were subject to the continued raids of the Turkish armies that during this period were threatening to overrun all middle Europe, culminating in the final siege of Vienna in 1683. Frequently in these raids their houses were burned down and cattle driven away, their men often carried away to the galleys, and their women to a worse fate. In 1665 they found themselves in such dire straits that they were compelled to call upon their Mennonite brethren in Holland for help; and by 1667 they had to give up their communal life for a time in some of the settlements in Hungary.

A few random extracts taken from the records will perhaps best indicate their varied experiences during the next hundred years:

1658. In this year the principality of Siebenbürgen was overrun with Turks and Tatars, robbing, murdering, and burning with great damage to all the land. Over one thousand people were murdered. An unmentionable number of people and cattle were carried away; the whole land was devastated. Alwinz was almost totally destroyed.

1659. This year in January Emperor Leopold issued to the brethren a letter of protection guarding them against all marauding parties.

1662. This year in the month of May there were two heavy earthquakes which shook the buildings, which God sent us no doubt for a good reason.

1663. On the third day of September the Turks and Tatars arrived at Dechtitz a short time before dinner. They took captive thirty-five souls, and two of the brethren were cut down and murdered. The buildings were burned down, and all the crops in the fields destroyed. The next day the community at Sobotiste was destroyed.

1678. On April 27 a sister by the name of Susanna, who had been held in captivity by the Turks for fifteen years, was released upon payment of 150 *florin* ransom money and restored to us again without the loss of her faith. God be praised.

1679. This year was one of great heat which caused a great deal of sickness, including the pest and other evils, and took many lives. It is reported that in Vienna 20,000 died, and in Pressburg over 11,000. No doubt it was a visitation of the hand of God because of the sins of the people without any sign of repentance.

1683. The year 1683 ended with great tribulation, fear, terror, misery, famine and death. It often seemed as though everything would go to ground. Many children and older people died.

1733. In this year came the terrifying mandate that we should not baptize our newborn babes, but that we must take them to the priests for baptism or suffer a heavy penalty. The elders and the superintendent together with the brethren met at Sobotiste to consult regarding this unheard-of order, and decided not without many tears and twangs of conscience, to obey this order, since there was no other way out of this tyranny. This decision caused a great deal of dissatisfaction in the church, and resulted in a division.

1748. In October, Zacharias Walter wrote to the Mennonite pastor at Amsterdam, Johann Deknatel, concerning certain points of doctrine.

1754. The entire community at Sobotiste consists of 220 souls. They refrain from making proselytes. The *Habaner* [acculturated Hutterites] among them, however, are not permitted to enter the Catholic church when they take their children there for baptism. They pay little attention to the church holidays. They bury their dead in their own church yards which they call "Garden of the

Dead." Young people among them drink only water, from twenty years on also beer; but wine, only the elder people and the sick.

1761. On March 21, Jesuit missionaries, accompanied by four guards, appeared at Sobotiste, arrested three of the leaders, Walter, Pulmon, and Cseterle, and took them away. The meetinghouse was closed, the key turned over to the Jesuit representative, and the brethren were warned that they must attend his preaching and send their children to his catechetical class. They were ordered to give up all their books, to dismiss their teachers, and send their children to the Catholic schools. The Habaner were forbidden to carry on their services. Many of the brethren vigorously protested against these measures and cried out that they would rather lay their necks on the block and lose their lives than obey the Catholic priest and send their children to his school.

1786. Old Jakob Miller died at Sobotiste a heretic. This Miller declared in his day that he joined the Catholics only to enjoy peace. In his heart he always remained true to the faith of his fathers.

And so it went. For the better part of three centuries this small band of humble Christians, clinging tenaciously to their convictions and choosing rather to suffer martyrdom than forsake their faith, wandered from one land to another in futile search of that religious toleration so well exemplified in their own peaceful lives. Now at the end of this period they seemingly were no nearer the goal of their quest than at the beginning. The world had become somewhat more humane, but not more tolerant. Ravaged by plundering bands of marauding troops, outlawed by imperial decrees, hounded by both state and church, the wonder is that they did not quit the hard struggle long before. In all history there are few finer examples of courageous faith and of extreme loyalty to Christian convictions.

As indicated in the records cited above, hardly had the Turkish dangers vanished before another peril appeared even more threatening to the Hutterite faith, the firm determination of the Jesuit clergy to thoroughly root out every religious belief not specifically protected by the religious agreements of the time. The few Anabaptist groups still left in the empire were the specific objects of their wrath. This crusade reached its peak in the reign of Maria Theresa, herself a most devoted Catholic. To Delphini, an ardent Jesuit and confirmed advocate of entire extinction, was committed the task of either converting the Hutterites or driving them out of the land. This willing agent evidently was given a free hand by the imperial authorities to use the methods he thought best to accomplish his purpose, just short of the death sentence. He made the most of his orders.

As we have seen, the Jesuits forced the brethren to give up their religious books and substitute Catholic books instead, to send their children to the priests for baptism, and to attend Catholic services. They forbade them to hold meetings of their own, and when the order was disobeyed, officials often broke up the meetings, or compelled the worshipers to remain and listen to a Jesuit sermon instead. Unwilling victims were frequently beaten into submission. Ministers especially were under suspicion, often imprisoned, sometimes dying from mistreatment. The civil authorities were in hearty sympathy with this Jesuit policy. It was the contention of the Hutterites that "they had always shown themselves true and obedient subjects; had always willingly helped support the common burdens of the land; had served their landlords well; and their peaceful, sober and honest daily life was well known"; and further that "the guarantee of the religious liberty granted them in 1635 was still in force," and thus they could not convince themselves that the recent royal mandate ordering them to send their children to the Catholic schools, and to baptize them as Catholics, represented the real intentions of the government. The authorities in turn made the countercharge that the Hutterites "would pay no war taxes, disobeyed the government, set up their own system of settling disputes, abused the sacrament of holy baptism," and finally that they "refused to accept the mercy offered them."

The Habaner

The Jesuits undermined the faith of the Hutterites through the education of their children. The religious convictions of adults could not be changed, but through the medium of Catholic schools children might easily be turned into good Catholics. But for the older people, too, they made the way easy through compromise. After a long period of futile coercion, they finally tried persuasion and temptation. The brethren might retain some of their cherished political exemptions, their distinctive economic and social institutions, and even some of their religious practices if only they would accept a few of the fundamental doctrines of the Catholic faith—infant baptism and attendance at Catholic services. They were also promised exemption from military service and certain objectionable war taxes. Most of the Hutterites finally accepted this half-Catholic, half-Hutterite compromise. *Habaner* they were later called, but nobody today knows why. But by those from whom they withdrew they were known as "stepbrothers."

The small remnant of the faithful who refused to compromise gradually drifted out of the Habsburg lands and crossed over into Russia which had, in the meantime, become the new promised land for many of the persecuted peoples of middle Europe. By 1800 the last followers of the Hutterites had vanished from Hungary and Transylvania. The remaining Habaner colonies, with their special religious and political privileges, speaking the German language, and living in closed communities, maintained their identity in Upper Hungary, now Czechoslovakia, for many years. But in course of time they lost their special status, exchanged their foreign German for the native Slovakian, forgot their traditions, and have since become absorbed into the common civil and religious life of the community. Contacts with them have been established by American Hutterites and Mennonites after World Wars I and II.

Lutherans Join Hutterites

In the meantime, the original Hutterite movement, of Moravian origin, might have completely collapsed had it not been for the acquisition of new recruits from a totally unexpected quarter. In the archduchy of Carinthia, a member of the Habsburg empire, there appeared just at this time a small band of Christians who, because of their espousal of many of the doctrines of Luther, were officially known as *Lutherans*. Influenced to a large extent by their independent reading of the Bible, and especially of the works of the pietistic Lutheran Johann Arndt, an author well known among the Mennonites everywhere, they were more like the Mennonites in their religious views than like orthodox Lutherans. Since Lutherans were not tolerated in Carinthia at this time, Maria Theresa had this small band deported at government expense in 1755 to Transylvania, another of her possessions, where both Catholics and Lutherans were free to exercise their religious views. Here the emigrants were promised new homes and lands upon their arrival.

But the exiles soon ran into further trouble. The Lutherans in Transylvania did not meet the requirements of an evangelical New Testament church as the Carinthian brethren had conceived it. Besides, by refusing to take the oath of allegiance to the empress, which was demanded of them as a prerequisite to receiving their land grants, they were denied the promised homes. Thus they were set adrift, looking for work and a resting place wherever they could find it. Some of them wandered into Alwinz, and other Hutterite colonies near Hermannstadt, where they found religious views and practices more like their own than any they had yet observed. Most of the exiles ultimately joined the households of the brethren and became an integral part of the Hutterite movement from then on. Evidence that the Carinthians remained loyal to this choice is the fact that many of the typical names found in the Hutterite households in the Dakotas and Canada today trace their origin back to Carinthia—*Hofer, Kleinsasser, Müller, Glanzer, Waldner*. This Carinthian contingent became the backbone of the Transylvania Hutterite group from this time on, and was perhaps responsible for the restoration of the Bruderhof pattern among them.

But by casting their lot with the despised Hutterites, the new recruits forfeited the toleration promised them by the empress. As Lutherans they would have been tolerated in Transylvania, but not as Hutterites. If they would not be Lutherans they must become Catholics. So they now shared the common experiences of all Hutterites. Their leaders were arrested and thrown into prison, their congregations scattered, and their religious practices proscribed.

From Transylvania to Russia

Despairing finally of finding peace in Transylvania, the whole body, both the new recruits and the faithful remnant of the older group, now decided to chance emigration across the Carpathian Mountains into Walachia, which was under Turkish rule, and where neither Catholics nor Lutherans nor Hutterites were known. All Christians looked alike to the Turk. After successfully casting the lot, upon whose favorable decision rested the determination to take this final step, a group of sixty-seven weary souls gathered at Creutz, near Alwinz, for the departure. All the villagers came out to see them off, some glad they were going, others fearful that they might be punished by the authorities for permitting their outlawed neighbors to leave in peace.

Leaving many of their leaders behind in prison and forsaking all their earthly possessions, they started out with heavy hearts. All the able-bodied men, women, and children carried packs on their backs, and some led small children as well. With staffs in their hands, they trudged along on foot. Only the feeble and sick could be loaded on the few wagons. The journey toward the mountains was made mostly by night, and the larger towns were avoided. The slow climb over the mountains was especially arduous and difficult. Finally reaching safety across the border in Walachia, they set up a temporary camp and sent a delegation to Bucharest to find a permanent location. Here the delegation met a sympathetic German who had a large estate nearby where the tired pilgrims found a temporary home. They had to begin life all over again and erect their own shelter and primitive living quarters. "It was indeed strange for us to live in the ground, but we had peace and quiet, and above all complete freedom of conscience," wrote one of their number.

Unfortunately the arrival of the Hutterites in what at first seemed a land of freedom was ill timed. Russia and Turkey soon engaged in war, and the unlucky victims of so many troubles found themselves in the heart of another battle zone, where the Turks robbed them of the property and money and sent their men into captivity and galley slavery.

After a few years of these experiences, they decided to take up the wanderer's staff once more. They had, in the meantime, won the sympathy of General Semetin, the Russian general in Moldavia, by whom they were advised to settle in South Russia where they would find not only the religious liberty they had been seeking so long but freedom from Turkish invasions as well. Acting upon the general's advice and with his help, they left their Walachian home in 1770 and founded a new settlement on the estates of Field Marshal Count Rumyantsov at *Vishenka*, one of the count's manors, on the river Desna in the province of Tchernigov. Here they were granted religious toleration, military exemption, financial aid, and such other concessions as Empress Catherine and local noblemen were offering at the time to industrious artisans and thrifty farmers upon their recently conquered lands. After a few years of pioneering, the Hutterites again settled down to a normal life. "So we began to settle down with our spinning and weaving and with the simple household necessities," writes Johannes Waldner, the chronicler of this period.

A few years later the little colony was augmented by the arrival of most of the prisoners who, in the meantime, had been released by the Habsburg authorities. Among them were Matthias Hofer, a poet, dreamer, and grumbler, who had already spent sixteen years in prison; and almost the entire Glanzer family, who had been held under examination five years in the city hall. The commanding general gave them a passport and permitted them to take their inheritance with them. They were given an escort to the border. Only three sisters remained in the land, and they had married and accepted the Lutheran faith. But, says historian Johannes Waldner,

> They had little happiness and joy, and suffered much, for they had a bad conscience all the time, and did not attend the Lutheran church, not even the Lord's Supper, and would rather have come back to the brotherhood if they had been free.

Some years later, the brethren who had remained faithful to the Hutterite teachings in Hungary or had joined the Habaner under pressure but had again come back into the fold, also found their way to Russia. By 1800, outside of the few scattered Habaner settlements in Hungary, the land of the autocratic czars became the sole home and asylum of the long persecuted followers of Jakob Hutter.

Russia-United States-Canada

Here at Vishenka the brethren now enjoyed for a time the complete religious toleration and economic freedom which they had been in search of so long. It seems a strange irony of fate that one set of Christians was hounded from one "Christian" country to another, and even burned at the stake by another set of so-called followers of the same faith, and that the victims of this intolerance finally found refuge from persecution only by fleeing across the borders into the land of the more tolerant Turks and the Orthodox Russians, neither of whom had the advantage of the spiritual enlightenment of the great Reformation.

In fact here in the land of the big Bear, they enjoyed almost too much economic and political freedom, for, like the Mennonites and other religious colonists in South Russia, they were granted economic and social liberties above those of the Russian peasants, most of whom were still serfs. So it was not altogether unexpected that upon Count Rumyantsev's death, his son and heir, forgetting the promises made by his father, tried to reduce the Hutterite colony to the status of his native tenants, that of serfdom. Unable to turn their new landlord from his determination, the brethren appealed to the Russian government in Petersburg, and in 1801 secured a grant of land on the crown properties a little farther down the Desna in the same province, and under the same liberal terms granted the Mennonites just the year before. To this place, called *Radichev*, forty-four families removed their colony the same year and reestablished a *Bruderhof* along the old traditional communistic lines.

The Radichev community grew slowly in numbers. The colonists soon built a mill along the Desna, and developed the different trades required for running a self-sufficient economic community. But they never quite reached the high degree of well-being enjoyed during their brief stay at Vishenka. The community life, too, did not seem to function as smoothly in the days of freedom as it had in the earlier days of persecution. The tradesmen especially were loath to turn over the whole of the profits they sometimes made out of their efforts. The rules of the society demanded that each trade should have its master whose duty it was to purchase the raw material necessary, to see to the manufacturing of the product, and to sell the finished goods. The profits were to be turned over into the common treasury. But each master was inclined to handle the profits himself, as one of the leaders of the time complained, and to turn over only the records to the superintendent. Quite a number seemingly preferred the greater freedom outside the community to the more restricted life within the household. Among these was Jakob Walter, assistant to the elder, who had built a house of his own for his family outside the community house. This division between the elder Johannes Waldner, who represented the old order favoring the community of goods, and his assistant Jakob Walter, who did not, divided the colony into two almost equal factions on this crucial question. Both leaders were equally insistent in maintaining their views. "I would rather go to the martyr's stake than give up the old traditions," said the grey-haired Johannes Waldner. "I would die before going back to community life again," replied his younger opponent and assistant.

Walter appealed to the government at St. Petersburg to arbitrate the matter, and especially to permit those desiring to withdraw to share the community property equally with those who remained. The government, especially interested at this time in everything that promoted the welfare and harmony of its numerous foreign colonies in South Russia, assumed the task of smoothing out the troubles. However the Petersburg representative, seemingly not favorable to the community system, sent in an unfavorable report on the economic and social conditions in the *Bruderhof*. The Hutterites were not as prosperous nor as far advanced culturally, he said, as the rest of the German colonists in South Russia. Children were not as well taken care of as under an individual system. And that is perfectly obvious, he added, because it is against nature, since neither father nor mother can do for their children what they would if they alone were responsible for their care. The general health of the people as a whole was not as good. In the whole colony of fifty families only two persons have passed the age of fifty years. The population growth has been slow. Since 1802, when the settlement was founded, there has been an increase of only fifty-eight souls. At that rate it will take them sixty or seventy years to double their number, while among the Mennonites it takes only thirty years. So reported this investigator.

All attempts to bring about unity, however, were in vain. Walter and his party withdrew from the brotherhood, taking with them their share of the community property. But in the end everything worked out well. Some of the dissenters, not finding their independence what they had expected, returned the next year. In the meantime a fire had completely destroyed the buildings of the old *Bruderhof*. Rather than rebuild, both parties now agreed to dissolve the "Brotherhood" and distribute all the property. And so in 1819 the community way of life was again given up by the

Hutterite brethren. Stouthearted old Johannes Waldner, however, did not long survive his disappointment. He died the next year.

The rest of the story of the Hutterites in Russia can be told in a few words. They gradually recovered their material prosperity and their spiritual balance. By 1842 their population had increased to such extent that they petitioned for, and were granted a new tract of land in the Molotschna region, near the Mennonite settlement. Here Johann Cornies, the well-known Mennonite educational and agricultural leader, helped them to locate a new colony which they called *Hutterthal*. A little later a daughter colony was established not far off by the name of *Johannesruh*, followed soon after by *Neu-Hutterthal*. In 1859 a number of the poorer families in the villages, deciding to revive the communal pattern under the old system, established a *Bruderhof* which they named *Hutterdorf*. When, in the early 1870s, the German colonists of South Russia lost their military exemption and other special economic and political privileges, the Hutterites living in the *Bruderhof* as well as those living in separate homes decided to follow the Mennonites to North America, a new land of freedom. The Hutterdorf settlers came first in 1874, followed by Hutterthal and Johannesruh in 1877, and finally by all the rest in 1879. All these settled in the James River Valley in the Dakotas, some establishing themselves in communal households and others settling on individual farms. The periods of severe persecution were now over, but not those of migration. World War I caused a large number of Hutterites to move to Canada.

VIII
Russia

The story of the Mennonites of Russia prior to World War I furnishes a pleasant relief from that of their brethren in the other countries heretofore mentioned. Here in the land of the most arbitrary ruler of all Europe, the Mennonites met the greatest encouragement to expand their settlements, and the widest liberty to practice their beliefs according to their convictions. The course of their unhampered development also suggests the direction Mennonitism may sometimes take when it is free to apply its principles, both economic and religious, to everyday living.

Catherine's invitation to the Danzig and West Prussian Mennonites to locate on her crown lands in South Russia came at a most opportune time. The empress had succeeded to the crown in 1762. Although unprincipled and savagely cruel as a woman, she was nevertheless shrewd and farsighted as a ruler, and did much for the political and economic development of her vast empire. Regarding agriculture as the backbone of national prosperity according to the economic theories of the time, she became very much interested in settling her unoccupied agricultural lands. She had millions of acres of these along the Black and Caspian seas, recently won from the sultan of Turkey.

Soon after her accession, the ambitious empress advertised the advantages of her crown lands far and wide throughout Europe, wherever people were hampered in their religious liberties, or were dissatisfied with their economic or political status. To prospective agricultural colonists she offered most liberal inducements such as free lands in abundance, free transportation and support until such time as the settlers should be established in their own homes, tax exemption for a limited time, exemption from military duty and certain civil obligations, religious toleration, and wide liberty

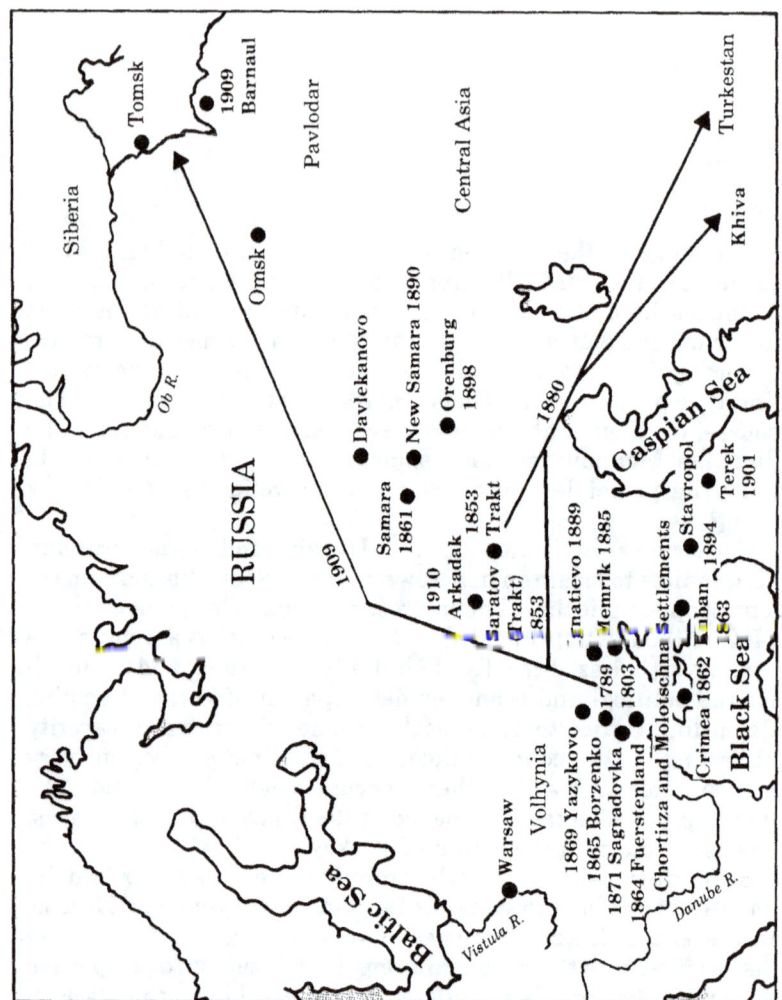

The Spread of Mennonites in Russia
Within 150 years Mennonites spread over European and Asiatic Russia establishing some fifty settlements with a population of some 120,000. They settled in 400 villages and estates in a territory of 5,816 square miles.

in establishing such educational and local political institutions as best suited their needs—privileges far beyond those enjoyed by the native Russians themselves.

Typical of a number of early colonies established on the basis of these liberal terms was a colony established by a group of Moravian Brethren, who located near the Tatar frontier along the lower Volga in 1764. They were attracted no doubt more by the prospects of a promising missionary field among the Tatars, than by the desire to better their economic condition. Few of these numerous early attempts at colonization were successful. But with the appointment, in 1774, of G. A. Potemkin as governor general of South Russia, a more vigorous and successful colonization policy began. A successful general in the Turkish wars, Potemkin was one of Catherine's favorites.

Among the various projects sponsored by the governor general during this period was the invitation extended in 1786 through Georg von Trappe, a Russian colonization agent of German extraction, to certain discontented citizens of the city of Danzig at the time of the first partitioning of Poland. In this invitation the oppressed Mennonites of Danzig and West Prussia were included. At the suggestion of von Trappe, the Mennonite churches decided to send two representatives, Jakob Höppner and Johann Bartsch, at Russian expense, to spy out the promised land.

These devoted men set out in the fall of 1786 on what their brethren at that time considered a long and perilous journey. Sailing to Riga, then crossing over to the Dnieper, they reached a station called Dubrovna in late November. From here they sailed down the river looking for a desirable settling place. At Kremenchug they met Potemkin, and in May of the following year they were presented to Catherine herself, who was on her first tour of inspection to her newly won territories. After selecting a desirable location near Berislav along the Dnieper as a promising site for their prospective settlements, the deputies started on their way homeward. Returning by way of Petersburg, they met various government officials, including Crown Prince Paul, and secured official confirmation of the promises made them by von Trappe. They reached Danzig after a year's absence without any serious mishaps except that Bartsch had frozen his toes during the winter and Höppner had delayed their return by several months because of a broken leg.

The favorable reports about the promised land brought back by the deputies, supplemented by a vigorous campaign for colonists on the part of von Trappe, who in the meantime had been appointed official director of the proposed enterprise, aroused keen interest in the emigration movement among both the Danzig and the West Prussian Mennonites. In his eagerness to serve his Russian masters, von Trappe was none too scrupulous in the methods used for winning support for his cause. To secure the aid of one of the Danzig elders, Peter Epp, he presented the elder with a personal gift. The Danzig elders had been instructed by the Danzig authorities not to permit public solicitation for emigrants. The wily von Trappe accomplished his end without violating the letter of the law by stationing himself outside the church door, handing out his circulars to the members as they passed out. The elders who were in sympathy with the emigration project could thus truthfully say to the Danzig magistrate that there was no solicitation with their consent.

1. THE CHORTITZA SETTLEMENT

A party of four families had already left for Riga before the deputies returned, and it was reported that hundreds of families were ready to depart immediately. But neither the Danzig nor the West Prussian authorities, however eager they may have been to make the further expansion of the Mennonite settlements impossible, were anxious to lose to their Russian rivals any of their prosperous farmers or industrious laborers. Passports were thus denied to all prospective emigrants who had property, and were granted only to the poor. By the fall of 1788 two hundred and twenty-eight families, nearly all from the poorer working classes of Danzig, and mostly from the Flemish branch of the church, had gathered at Dubrovna, having arrived here by the same route taken by the deputies two years before. Here they were forced, because of the lateness of the season and because of renewed warfare between Russia and Turkey along the frontier farther south, to encamp for the winter.

The enforced stay at Dubrovna was not a happy one. Homesick, largely supported at government expense, and awaiting an uncertain future during a long cold winter in temporary shelters, their prospects seemed none too bright. Added to these material discomforts, there was a certain degree of religious unrest due to the rivalry of the two religious factions represented—Flemish and Frisian. This Frisian-Flemish division had been imported from Holland to Danzig and West Prussia, and the rift between the two groups even now, in their early Russian period, was as wide as ever. Intermarriage between the two factions was forbidden on pain of excommunication.

But more disturbing still was the strange fact that among a thousand pious souls who had left their Danzig homes, largely to escape religious oppression, there was not a preacher among them. It was customary at this time among the Mennonites to choose their ministers from the laity. Since they were to serve without pay, it was usual to choose them from the class that could afford to serve, the well-to-do farmers. But the well-to-do among the Danzig Mennonites were denied passports. Even the elders of the home churches in a meeting held at Rosenort before the departure of the emigrants, could find no one suitable in the whole body to assume spiritual leadership. So this group of pioneers had to leave for their new home spiritually unorganized and shepherdless.

Worship services, of course, could be read by a layman from a book or written sermons, a practice still quite common at that time in most of the Mennonite churches. But only an elder could administer communion and baptism, and perform marriage ceremonies. Ten young couples at Dubrovna, ripe for marriage, added urgency to the demand for an ordained elder. A minister, however, could be installed only in person by another regularly ordained elder. After a meeting of elders from the home Flemish church, in which no one was found willing or able to make the long journey to Russia, it was suggested to the brethren at Dubrovna that they send a list of satisfactory candidates for the ministry from which a selection might be made by the West Prussian elders and authorized by written confirmation. This was done, and three ministers were thus selected, including Bernhard Penner, who a little later was also ordained as the first elder in Russia by the same procedure.

In the meantime, with the coming of spring, the Dubrovna group continued its journey down the river to their destination, the more prosperous on their own wagons by land, the poorer by river barge. But on the way they were faced with another crushing disappointment. The deputies were informed by Potemkin that instead of proceeding to the fertile fields chosen for them two years before at Bereslav, near which the Turkish wars were still raging, they would have to settle on lands farther up the river, near a small tributary called Chortitza, a region that seemed to be less desirable than the original site farther south.

Economic Difficulties

Great was the disappointment of the weary colonists, when upon their final arrival at Chortitza, in July of 1789, they first sighted the bare and hilly steppes that were to be their new home, their promised land. What they saw, instead of the flat fertile fields like those in their own Vistula delta, were wide, rocky barren steppes, cut through with deep gullies, filled at that season of the year with patches of dried-up grass. There was no sign of a living thing anywhere, save the wreck of a deserted palace, the remains of one of the ghost villages erected by Potemkin some time before to impress the empress with the growing prosperity of her new crown lands.

Such was the disappointment of these lonely homeseekers that a small group, the most discontented, refused to unpack their goods, hoping that at the last minute the Russian government might relent and offer them a more promising site. Others, more optimistic, pronounced the land good and immediately began the erection of their more or less temporary homes. When it finally became evident that no other location was forthcoming, even the discontented were forced to dig in for the winter, and gradually adapt themselves to their new situation.

These first temporary living quarters, of course, were mere makeshifts of real homes. While both Höppner and Bartsch were able to erect rather substantial dwellings, the rest were not so fortunate. The building material promised by the government was slow in arriving. Many of them erected crude sod shanties, partly below and partly above ground, with thatched roofs; others set up temporary tents; a few of the most dissatisfied colonists remained in their wagons for the time being. A number had to be cared for during the following winter in the nearby government barracks at Alexandrovsk.

This first fall and winter was a trying one for the pioneer settlement. The improvised huts offered but little shelter against the unexpected heavy fall rains and the winter winds. The scant food furnished by the government consisted largely of a broth made from moldy rye flour secured from distant public supply granaries. The money promised for their support, now that the colonists had safely reached their destination, was slow in coming, much of it finding its way into the pockets of greedy public officials. The country round about, which was not far removed from the frontier, abounded in thieves, who had little regard for property rights. These pilferers stole the building material meant for the colonists as it floated down the river, and appropriated their personal belongings. The baggage which had been sent down from Dubrovna on river barges was carelessly handled, and what had not been completely ruined by the rains was pillaged of its contents; trunks and boxes had been broken open, and clothing, personal effects, and precious heirlooms were taken out and exchanged for stones or other useless freight.

They held their first communion service the next spring in an old abandoned building, under the ministry of their newly selected elder, Bernhard Penner. He was sorely grieved because owning only a pair of *Bastelschuhe*, the usual footwear of the average poor Russians and also of the colonists at this time, he keenly felt the humility of officiating on this solemn occasion without shoes. Finally, several of the more prosperous members of his flock, after diligent search, gathered together a pair of boots for the elder so that he might administer this sacred duty in the proper manner. Loud were the sobs, it is said, that swept through the audience as the participants in this first communion service were reminded in their present miserable situation of the happy homes they had left behind in the Vistula lowlands.

In the meantime, becoming convinced of the fact that this was to be their permanent home under any conditions, favorable or otherwise, the settlers began the distribution of the land among the heads of the families. At first, following their West Prussian custom, each family started to live on its own farm; but the need for protection against marauders drove them to settle in small groups, some fifteen to thirty families to a village. Eight villages were thus laid out in the beginning, with *Chortitza* as the center of the settlement; and the others with such local descriptive names as *Rosenthal*, or reminders of their West Prussian homes—*Einlage, Neuenburg,* and *Schönhorst.*

The hardships of this first winter continued for some years. Many of the first colonists, being city laborers, knew little about farming; and those who came from the farms discovered that the farm methods used on the Vistula banks were not applicable to the dry and barren steppes along the Chortitza. Grasshoppers, drought, and inexperience made the first years lean ones. Material poverty, too, was matched with spiritual discontent. The disillusioned element which had never become completely reconciled to their lot, blamed especially the two deputies as the cause of most of their trouble, charging them especially with having betrayed their trust, accepting government money which was meant for all the settlers, and with erecting finer homes than the rest could afford.

So bitter was the feeling that had been worked up against these men that both were excommunicated from the Flemish church. With the connivance of corrupt Russian officials, Höppner's enemies even had him arrested and put in prison, only to see him released, however, some time later. Bartsch, after making the customary confession required by the church of its backsliders, was again reinstated into full membership in his congregation. Höppner was not so easily satisfied. He affiliated himself with the Frisian branch of the church and became a citizen of the nearby city of Alexandrovsk. Just before his death he requested that he be buried on his private estate, and not in the common cemetery by the side of his fellow colonists who had made him so much trouble in his early career. In 1889, on the hundredth anniversary of the founding of the colony, the great-grandchildren of the men who had thrown Höppner into jail erected a marble shaft to his memory on the spot of his burial. This monument is now located at the museum of Steinbach, Manitoba.

Religious Problems

The question of an ordained elder remained a matter of dispute for some time. Elder Penner, before his death in 1791, had ordained a successor in the person of one David Epp. But there were still a number of the more conservative members of the church who, because Penner had not been personally ordained according to the traditions of the church, refused to recognize either Penner or his successor as a legitimate elder. This controversy, together with the charges against the two deputies, kept the churches in a religious turmoil for several years.

The demand that the home church send an authorized elder to settle these controversies finally bore fruit. In 1794 the Flemish congregations of West Prussia at last dispatched Cornelius Regier and Cornelius Warkentin to the distracted congregation along the Dnieper. These emissaries of goodwill were accorded a hearty welcome by both the Flemish and Frisian groups. They held numerous conferences with opposing factions, received a number of young members into both churches by baptism, and did much to restore harmony among the various quarreling factions. Within a few months Elder Regier died. Before his death, however, he had installed his traveling companion, Cornelius Warkentin, as elder. Warkentin remained with the pioneer settlement for several years, doing much during that period to reconcile the colonists to their new home, and placing the religious life of the community on a safe basis.

In spite of the prospects of financial and spiritual poverty in the new homeland, emigration from the delta congregations did not abate. When Danzig was annexed to Prussia in the second partitioning of Poland, many of the Mennonites of both Danzig and West Prussia preferred the uncertainties of Russia to those of Prussia. Between 1793 and 1797, one hundred eighteen additional families, mostly farmers, and largely from the Frisian persuasion, found their way to the frontier settlement. These were more prosperous than the first party had been. Some of these remained for a time among the earlier established villages; others established two new villages, *Kronsgarten* and *Schönwiese*. In the meantime, too, a new migration had begun to the colony farther south on the Molotschna River. By 1824 some four hundred families had located in the Chortitza colony, grouped into eighteen villages, at a cost to the Russian government of several hundred thousand dollars.

Meanwhile in 1796 Catherine died, to be succeeded by her son Paul. The Chortitza colonists, concerned for their special privileges under a new ruler, sent a delegation to Petersburg for the purpose of securing a written guarantee from the new ruler that their former liberties might be continued. After an extended stay in the capital city, the delegates returned, in 1800, with the precious document in their possession, guaranteeing for both old and new settlers all the exemptions and privileges granted the original colonists, and several new ones added. The most important were 175 acres of free land to each family; religious toleration; exemption from military and certain civil services, and from the use of the oath in all judicial processes; wide liberty in establishing their own schools in their own language; political and economic institutions suitable to their own needs; the right of forbidding the erection of taverns in their midst; and the right to manufacture their own beverages, a concession usually only granted noblemen. Continued support was granted to future immigrants, though this was not a specific promise in the new charter of privileges.

All colonists during this period were placed under certain restrictions, though these were not specifically mentioned in the above charter. While religious toleration was fully granted, proselyting among members of the orthodox state church was forbidden. Since the special privileges were granted to specific groups, the privileges in question would be annulled when the privileged person left the group. Children of mixed marriages would take the status of the nonprivileged parent. Since the colonists were invited in as model farmers, the model farm of 175 acres could not be divided by inheritance, but must remain intact. Title to the land was not unlimited, and could not be sold without the consent of the village.

2. THE MOLOTSCHNA SETTLEMENT

Encouraged by these written guarantees, and at the same time driven by new restrictions upon their religious liberties and economic privileges by the king of Prussia to seek relief elsewhere, the West Prussian Mennonites again revived their interest in the migration to South Russia. Great numbers decided to leave. The movement began in the summer of 1803 with the departure of 162 families, to be followed the next year by a group of about equal size. In the meantime, the Russian government, which continued its interest in further colonization, had set apart for the

Mennonite settlers a tract of land of about three hundred thousand acres on a fertile, treeless plain southeast of Chortitza in the province of Taurida, along the Molotschna, a small stream running parallel with the Dnieper and flowing into the sea of Azov.

Most of the new colonists were from the region of Marienburg and Elbing, and were rather well-to-do farmers. After paying the 10 percent emigration tax, they still had enough capital left with which to stock up their new farms. Only a small minority had to accept the help that the Russian government still offered poor immigrants. This immigration movement continued for some years. Each year found long wagon trains loaded with household furniture and farm equipment crossing Poland and South Russia by way of their Chortitza brethren to their new settlement on the Molotschna. By 1820 some six hundred families had found their way to this settlement; and during the next twenty years, four hundred more. By 1840 forty-six villages had been established with a total population of about ten thousand. By this time, however, the Russian government had practically ceased to offer its earlier generous inducements to prospective foreign colonists.

Like those of Chortitza, the Molotschna settlers named many of their villages after their West Prussian villages. *Halbstadt* became the center of the Molotschna settlement. Other village names were *Tiegenhagen, Ladekopp, Rosenort, Tiege,* and *Ohrloff.*

Among the more important of the later villages to be founded were *Alexanderwohl*, settled in 1820, and *Gnadenfeld*, in 1835. The former was composed of a congregation which had migrated in a body from Schwetz and Culm under the leadership of their elder, Peter Wedel. In 1874 most of the congregation again migrated as a body to the plains of Kansas, where they established another Alexanderwohl.

Gnadenfeld, likewise, consisted of an organized church which found its way to South Russia by a series of treks during the centuries through West Prussia, and the Markgravate of Brandenburg. The Gnadenfeld congregation became the center, during the mid 1800s, of a vigorous missionary movement and a religious revival that spread through the Mennonite settlements of South Russia.

The Molotschna settlers, as already intimated, were better farmers, and were blessed with greater material prosperity than their fellow Mennonites in Chortitza, and were therefore spared much of the economic hardships of the latter. Taganrog, on an arm of the Azov, furnished a ready market for their dairy products during the early years until wheat growing became an important industry. Since they brought their ministers with them, they escaped the early years of religious problems which marred the peace of their fellow Mennonites of Chortitza.

Although more prosperous materially, and more peaceful spiritually, the new colonists were not spared the usual dangers of pioneer settlements. Their colony was located far out on a treeless steppe, well on the outskirts of civilization, nearer the frontier than the Chortitza colony. Just to the south were still to be found bands of nomadic Tatars, not yet reconciled to their removal by government order from the Molotschna Valley to make room for the German Mennonites. For that reason they hated these newcomers as did the Indians, the American frontiersmen. They often raided the Mennonite settlement, driving off the settlers' horses and cattle. Steppe riding to protect their property against these marauders became a thrilling adventure for many a young Mennonite during this early period. After one of these raids by the Tatars had resulted in the death of four Mennonites, the Russian government took more drastic measures against the tribesmen, forbidding them the right to carry their usual weapons—long poles, spiked and weighted at the ends, which were used on their hunting expeditions. Later on, however, natives and Mennonites lived side by side on friendly terms.

Other West Prussian Groups

In addition to the two large Mennonite settlements just described, several smaller groups had located within the czarist Russian empire during this period. These, together with several congregations which found themselves under Russian jurisdiction after the partitioning of Poland, may be roughly divided into three groups:

a. *Deutsch-Kazun*, and *Deutsch-Wymysle*, along the Vistula River near Warsaw, were daughter colonies of the Graudenz and Culm congregations in West Prussia. They were founded during the latter part of the eighteenth century, when that region was still under Polish jurisdiction, but found themselves within the czar's empire when the final partitioning took place. A number of the members of these congregations emigrated to the Molotschna settlement during the nineteenth century; and from there some of them finally found their way to America.

b. The settlement at *Deutsch-Michalin* near Machnovka, on the western border of the province of Kiev, just across from Volhynia, was composed of West Prussians, who had migrated to that region about the same time the first colony came to Chortitza. In 1802 many of these Michaliner, dissatisfied with their land contracts, moved over into Volhynia, near Ostrog, where they finally developed a number of villages including *Karolswalde, Antonovka, Waldheim,* and *Fürstlandsdorf.* They were granted small farms here on the estate of a nobleman, on terms quite similar to those offered the large colonies on the crown lands at Chortitza and Molotschna. This small group did not prosper as well, however, as those who remained at Michalin. They remained poor throughout their stay in Russia, devoting themselves largely to small farming, dairying, linen weaving, and day labor in neighboring cities. At the time of their American emigration, in the early 1870s, they were among the least prosperous, and religiously and socially less developed. Neither of these groups was located on Russian frontier territory under the special inducements offered by the Russian government.

c. *Samara.* The failure of the Prussian constitution of 1850 to provide for military exemption on religious grounds caused considerable anxiety among some Mennonites of West Prussia. After vainly petitioning the Berlin government for a reinstatement of their privileges, these decided upon emigration to Russia. But after the special inducements offered the earlier Mennonite colonists, it was extremely doubtful whether more Mennonites would be welcomed by the czar's government. Finally, however, permission was secured to locate a limited number of settlers along the Volga, in the province of Samara, on terms still quite liberal, though no longer as generous as those offered the first colonies. A large compact area of land was offered the Mennonites on easy terms. There was to be freedom from military service for twenty years, after which each colonist was to pay a special exemption tax. Each family was to deposit 350 *Thaler* with the Russian embassy at Berlin as surety that they would not prove a burden to the Russian government.

Two settlements were finally established in this region. The first was located in what was known as the *Trakt* in 1853, under the leadership of Claasz Epp. This colony east of the Volga in the province of Samara was given the name Köppenthal after one of the Russian officials who had been especially helpful in its establishment. In the course of the next twenty years it expanded into ten villages with such names as *Hahnsau, Ohrloff,* etc. The second settlement, which was begun in 1861 in the province of Samara, was known as *Alt-Samara* to distinguish it from a later settlement known as *Neu-Samara.* Among the ten villages into which this settlement expanded during the next fifteen years, *Alexandertal* is best known. The latter, however, were granted privileges less liberal than the former. The settlers had to buy their land from the crown; military exemption before the paying of the special exemption tax was to run for only three years.

RUSSIA

Several hundred families migrated to these two Volga colonies during the period, nearly all from West Prussia, and most of them fairly well-to-do when they came.

Swiss Settlements

a. Among the Mennonite settlements in Russia was a group of Swiss who had migrated to Polish Russia from Galicia before the close of the eighteenth century. They had originally come to Galicia from the Palatinate, and Montbeliard, France. They were of Amish descent, and seemingly had some difficulty in fitting in with other groups. After considerable shifting from place to place in Russia, some of them finally found a resting place at *Eduardsdorf*, near Dubno, in the province of Volhynia in 1815. By 1837 two more congregations were established—*Horodyszcze* and *Waldheim*. In 1861 the *Eduardsdorf* congregation moved to the east side of the province, near Zhitomir, and founded the new settlement of *Kutuzovka*. These were all of the same group that had originally located in Galicia, some of whom had remained in that Austrian province. Their Swiss origin is shown by such common names as *Krehbiel, Schrag, Rupp, Stucky, Kaufman, Flickinger, Miller, Graber, Goering*.

b. The *Galician* Mennonites near Lemberg have been referred to in the chapter on the South German Mennonites. They were also of Swiss background. However, they did not migrate as a body to the prairie states. Common names among them are: *Bachmann, Linscheid, Rupp, Müller, Ewy*.

c. *Hutterites.* The Russian experiences of this group have been told in an earlier chapter.

Number of Original Settlers

The number of Mennonite immigrants who came to the original colonies from West Prussia and elsewhere by 1870 is estimated to be nine thousand. Of these at least seven thousand located in the Chortitza and Molotschna colonies, and perhaps eight thousand were West Prussians. By this time the original numbers had increased to about forty-five thousand. Forty daughter colonies had been established by 1914, with a total population in all settlements of about one hundred thousand. They occupied a land area of nearly three million acres—an area three times the size of the state of Rhode Island.

3. ECONOMIC PROGRESS

Early Agricultural Life

As already suggested, these early colonists, both Danzig

artisans and West Prussian farmers, formed themselves into village groups averaging from fifteen to thirty families each. Following their style of architecture, they placed house, barn, stable, and shop all under one roof, gable end facing the front. These were located along one wide street which at first became lined with fruit trees, but in course of time with poplar or other fast-growing shade trees. The front yard became a flower garden, and the rear a fruit orchard and truck patch. The first buildings were rudely constructed of earthen walls and thatched roofs, but were later replaced by substantial structures of wood or brick.

Stretching out and away from the village over the treeless steppes were the arable farmlands and the common pastures where the village cattle were herded, or where the municipal sheep flocks were sometimes kept until such time as the common land might be turned into grainfields as the growing population demanded. While the head of each family was entitled to one hundred seventy-five acres, the land was divided for farming purposes into a number of long, narrow strips radiating from the village, so distributed among the farmers that each might share equally in the good and bad land wherever there was a difference in its fertility.

In the original contract the government forbade the sale of land to outsiders, and the division of the farm upon the death of the owner. It had to be kept intact, either in the family or by some other Mennonite. Mennonites were invited to Russia as master farmers, and a model farm supposedly needed to contain approximately one hundred seventy-five acres. This seems reasonable when we remember that originally it was thought that sheep raising might be the principal source of income rather than wheat growing. In the Volga region, where the Mennonite colonists had been granted fewer special concessions than in the earlier colonies, title rested in the village as in the Russian *mir*, instead of in the head of the family as in the South Russian colonies. In reality, it was only the use, not the ownership of land, that was granted the settler.

It was but natural that a group so closely knit together religiously and economically, as were these Mennonite colonies, should engage in a number of cooperative and communal enterprises. Neither of the two original settlements distributed all the land granted by the Russian government. Both retained a certain amount which at first was used for common pasture land, and later leased to farmers. The income was used to build up a fund with which the surplus population some time later might be helped to found a daughter colony. The daughter colonies in turn repeated the procedure. Other communal enterprises included a common granary filled in prosperous years for the use of the poor in times of emergency; for the steppes of South Russia, with an annual rainfall of less than fifteen inches, were occasionally subject to drought and crop failure. In 1820 the municipal sheep flock of the Chortitza colony consisted of a thousand fine merinos; the income from the public ferry across the Dnieper amounted to two and three thousand rubles annually; and the municipal distillery netted a substantial revenue for the common treasury.

At first these pioneer farmers, transplanted from the fertile soil and abundant rainfall of the Vistula Delta to the dry and barren steppes of South Russia, found considerable difficulty in adapting their farming methods to the requirements of their new environment. It took years of experimentation before they learned how to combat drought, grasshoppers, and occasional crop failures. They occupied themselves in the first years chiefly with stock raising, sheep breeding, and general farming to meet their home demands. The silk industry for a while assumed some importance. This accounts for the large number of mulberrry trees planted along the highways and around the fields in the first two colonies. Flax, tobacco, and bee culture in their turn all gave promise for a time of becoming substantial sources of income. Fruits and vegetables, and especially watermelons (*Arbusen*), found a ready market in the larger cities nearby. With the opening of the seaport Berdyansk on the Black Sea in the middle 1830s, wheat growing began to replace sheep raising and silk and bee culture.

Farming methods were most primitive. Farm implements were of the crudest sort. Seeding, harvesting, and threshing were all done by hand; and labor in the early years, as in all pioneer settlements, was scarce. An early sign of progress was the substitution for the flail of a large cylindrical threshing stone drawn over the threshing floor by horses. The grain was stored in the attic over the living room, while the straw was used to thatch the roof, and also for fuel in the large brick oven which served as both an oven and a furnace.

This description applies especially to the two original colonies of South Russia. Different agricultural conditions prevailed in the later settlements along the colder Ural Highlands in the North, in West Siberia, and in the arid Caucasus where irrigation was practiced.

Johann Cornies

By 1830 the experimental agricultural stage was ended. In that year some of the more farsighted and public-spirited farmers, encouraged by the *Fürsorge-Komitee* of Odessa, organized a semi-official association called *The Agricultural Improvement Society*, but which perhaps might more appropriately be named *Agricultural Commission*, since it had some government support. A board of trustees appointed by the Russian government was stationed at Odessa, supported by all the German colonists—Mennonite and non-Mennonite. Its function was to supervise the whole political and, to a certain extent, the economic life of the colonists. The first president of this agricultural commission was a prosperous farmer of the Molotschna colony by the name of Johann Cornies. Under the presidency of Cornies the organization exerted far-reaching influence during the next twenty years, not only upon the farming methods of the Mennonite colonies but, later on, upon their whole economic and social life.

Cornies was already a successful big-scale farmer at the time of his appointment. He conducted many experiments and developed many farm methods now well known to scientific agriculture. He became known far and wide as an agricultural expert, and his big Jushanlee estate became a showplace for travelers throughout South Russia. It was visited by many government officials, including both Alexander I and Alexander II, crown princes. In the course of time Cornies accumulated a large amount of property, some of which was given him by the government as a gift in return for his services. At the time of his death he held over twenty-five thousand acres of land, a flock of eight thousand merino sheep, four hundred horses, and a large herd of thoroughbred cattle.

The work of the commission later extended to other colonies, and was not confined to the Mennonites only, but included service for neighboring Jewish, Russian, and Tatar settlements. It was hoped that these backward farmers also might learn some of the better farming methods from their model Mennonite neighbors. Among some of the results secured through the efforts of Cornies and his society were: the practice of fallowing and dry farming, the use of fertilizers, the promotion of silk culture and tobacco, the four-year rotation of crops, the breeding of improved strains of livestock, the introduction of more efficient farm machinery, the erection of more practical farm buildings, and the planting of shade and fruit trees, especially the mulberry tree for the silk growers.

As the influence of the commission grew, it was granted additional governmental recognition, and authority beyond its original field of farm improvement. More and more supervision of the schools was also turned over to this body and, to a certain extent, local poor relief and child welfare. Model schoolhouses were built. The poorer colonists were induced to work for the more prosperous. Neglected children, of whom there were not many, were provided for. The organization was even influential in securing regulations compelling the lazy to seek work. Many of these arbitrary regulations, strictly enforced, aroused the animosity of those affected. But that the work of the society and its chief promoter was of enduring benefit to the Mennonite colonists there can be little doubt. After the death of Cornies, the commission continued its work, though less effectively, until well into the seventies of the century, when colonists of South Russia lost many of their special privileges, and the peculiar institutions for safeguarding them were abolished by the government.

The Land Question

Although there was little industrial development among the colonists during the early part of the century, nearly every village was a self-sufficient economic unit with smiths, carpenters, shoemakers, and countless other artisans, some of whom divided their time between farming and their avocation. Farming, however, remained the chief occupation. Industry was merely supplementary.

Aided by the agricultural commission, the colonists in both Chortitza and Molotschna enjoyed a steady economic growth, and in course of time converted the treeless plains into flourishing fields, orchards, and pastures covered with wide expanses of wheat and filled with fine herds of cattle and flocks of sheep. By the middle of the century, these colonies, as well as the private estates outside, had accumulated wealth far beyond that of their native Russian neighbors. The Volga colonies at this time were still in the pioneer stage, and had not yet reached the same degree of prosperity. The Swiss of Volhynia were also fairly well off. But the Mennonites in Polish Russia had not kept pace with their brethren elsewhere in their pursuit of either material or cultural advancement.

Even the most prosperous settlements, however, were not without their economic troubles. Population pressure by 1860 had become a serious problem in both Chortitza and Molotschna. Up to 1840 there seemed to be no dearth of tillable land for all the families that desired to enter their government allotments. But after that, rapid population increase and the government provision that the entire estate must pass intact to a single member of the family upon the death of the former owner worked a hardship upon those members of the family who did not share the land inheritance. These latter had either to purchase land elsewhere; work as farm laborers, often for a more fortunate brother; or seek labor in some village industry or other line of effort. Especially after all the available estates had been distributed among the first settlers in the two colonies, the number of landless grew rapidly with the increase of population. By 1870 it is estimated that at least two-thirds of all heads of families in both colonies were without land. Many of these were granted a small patch of ground upon which to build a house and make a living as best they could. These were spoken of as *Anwohner* (landless).

A solution of this problem was sought quite early in the purchase of daughter settlements as an outlet for the surplus population. An early example was the settling of Bergthal in 1836 by the excess population from Chortitza. Molotschna and later settlements made similar purchases all through the century. Sometimes well-to-do farmers bought estates outside the settlements. Occasionally, groups of settlers would locate as tenants on private estates of some nobleman. Up to the middle of the century, land could often be rented at a low rate from the Nogaian tribesmen nearby. Cornies sought a remedy in encouraging the manufacturing industry in the larger villages which would furnish work for the landless.

The landless had no voice in seeking a remedy for this situation. The practice of keeping the entire estate intact was a government regulation, and could not be changed. Only those who owned land had a voice in the local village assembly where all land, as well as other, policies were determined. Too often the landholders used this monopolistic privilege to their own advantage. Surplus land, which was the property of the entire colony, and which might have been divided up into small farms to meet the demands of the landless, was often leased by the village authorities to rich landlords instead, at a low rental. No help could be expected from the ministers either, for since the ministry was unsalaried, they were chosen frequently with an eye to their financial standing, rather than to their qualifications of spiritual leadership, and thus their interests were often with the landowners.

This situation naturally bred a great deal of discontent among the poorer classes, and ran a dividing line through the population on the basis of land ownership, often cutting straight through the ties of domestic kinship. The cleavage finally became so well defined that the landless party organized, and in the early sixties petitioned the Russian government for relief. Their program demanded the distribution of the remaining common land, permission to divide the full estates into smaller units with the right to vote, and the purchase by the mother colonies of new lands for the benefit of the landless. After considerable opposition on the part of the landed interests, and the usual red tape on the part of the Russian authorities, a measure of relief was finally provided by the government. It was recommended that the large estates might, where necessary, be divided into half and even quarter estates, that the surplus common land also might be distributed in the form of small farms. The broad highway leading through the settlement would be narrowed, and the income from the sale of this land would be invested in behalf of the unpropertied. All the owners of small farms were to be given equal voting rights with those owning full estates.

Daughter Settlements

These measures finally brought some relief. By 1867 there were four hundred ninety-six half estates, and fifty-one quarter estates in Chortitza and Bergthal. In the Molotschna colony there were twelve hundred full, and three hundred twenty-two half estates. This relief, together with the development of manufacturing in a number of the villages, the establishing of daughter colonies, and the exodus to America of a third of the entire population saved the situation for the time being from serious consequences.

By 1870 several new settlements were established, always aided by the mother colony, in nearby Ukrainian territory. But after that, and especially after 1890, migration of the surplus population, and occasionally of the more religiously conscientious, followed the frontier line of cheap lands southeast into the Caucasus in Kuban and Terek provinces; east toward the Urals in Ufa, Samara and Orenburg; and beyond into Tomsk, in western Siberia; and into Asiatic Turkestan. Among these daughter settlements were *Bergthal* (1836), *Crimea* (1862), *Fürstenland* (1864), *Borozenko* (1865), *Sagradovka* (1871), *Memrik* (1885), *Neu-Samara* (1890), *Orenburg* (1898), *Terek* (1901), *West Siberia* (1909), *Arkadak* (1910). (See Table 1, pages 349-352.)

Local Government

In the management of their local affairs, the Mennonites and other German settlers were granted a large degree of local autonomy, and such political institutions as best suited their needs and desires. Each village became a governing unit for the control of schools, roads, and relief of the poor; for the appointment of municipal herders, fire overseers, and village clerks; and for apportioning the arable farm lots and distributing surplus lands. At the head of each village was a magistrate called a *Schulze*, who was elected by the landowners, and had jurisdiction of petty misdemeanors. Local regulations on all these questions were passed by a town meeting composed only of those who owned land. A group of villages, at first including the whole colony, composed a district called a *Gebiet*. A superintendent, called an

Oberschulze, together with clerks and assistants elected by the village representatives made up the *Gebietsamt* with power of administering corporal punishment, the right to hold court, and to regulate other matters of local government that concerned the villages in common. Capital offenses could be tried only in the upper Russian courts. Chortitza and Molotschna each formed a separate district or *Gebiet* at first; but later Molotschna was divided into two districts—Halbstadt and Gnadenfeld.

Each *Gebiet* kept its own records, made its own fire regulations, provided for an insurance fund, took care of its own delinquents as well as the ill and handicapped, and even made its own inheritance laws. These as well as many other local regulations were provided for among their Russian neighbors by the general imperial government. In fact, the Mennonites with all their special exemptions and privileges almost constituted a democratic state within an autocratic state, enjoying local autonomy far above the native Russian communities.

The indirect supervision by the Petersburg government was exercised through a *Fürsorge-Komitee* usually headed by a German, stationed at Odessa, and directed by the Department of the Interior. This commission, which had general supervision of all the German colonies of South Russia, was organized by the Russian government in 1818, after several other forms of control had ended in failure. Later the agricultural commission in the Molotschna settlement was given a semi-official status with limited authority over agricultural and school matters. A similar institution was established in Chortitza. In the early 1870s all these peculiar institutions were either abolished throughout the German colonies, or radically changed so as to place the colonists more directly under the control of the central government at Petersburg.

Early Schools

The local autonomy granted the Mennonite colonists included control over their schools. Each village at first was free to establish schools as it pleased, or none at all if it so desired. Compulsory public school attendance was not yet required in Russia, nor anywhere else in Europe at that time. The Mennonites, however, placed an elementary school in every village from the start. However, educational interest was not on a high plane, as compared with modern standards. Teachers were ill prepared for their work, and poorly paid. Often they were workmen who converted their workshops into combination school and work rooms, with school desk and workbench side by side, and rod and plane both within easy reach. Frequently the winter teacher also functioned as the summer herdsman, thus obtaining an all-year job that enabled him to eke out a scant existence. The chief task of the schoolmaster was to hear each child recite memory work, and to keep order. This gave him ample time to ply his real trade, that of cabinetmaker, or tailor, or shoemaker perhaps.

Progress naturally was slow. Several years were required to master the elements of the alphabet and the art of writing. With this accomplished, the school days for many were ended. Those who remained longer might learn a little ciphering or ornamental writing perhaps, and memorize a few more Scripture verses. The primary aim of the whole system was to perpetuate the German language and to save the children for the faith of the fathers. The curriculum, therefore, consisted of "the three R's," with a fourth added—*religion*. Some attention was also given to singing. The dominant control of the schools was nominally placed into the hands of the elders; but there was very little effective supervision. School was originally often kept in the *Grosse Stube* (living room) of some well-to-do farmer; but later, primitive school buildings and, ultimately, model schoolhouses were erected. The distinctive school furniture consisted of a long table through the center of the room—with the boys on one side, the girls on the other, and the teacher at the head.

Secondary Schools

There were always a few far-sighted men in every community, however, who saw the need of keeping up higher education standards. Among these was a group in the Molotschna settlement who in 1820 formed a school association under the leadership of Johann Cornies for the purpose of founding at Ohrloff a sort of continuation school, the primary object of which was to train teachers for the village schools.

To the head of this *Vereinsschule*, Cornies called a trained teacher, Tobias Voth, from his old home in West Prussia. This secondary school was supported by tuition fees, and was under the control of a voluntary school association. For six years Voth enrolled an increasing number of students in his advanced classes. Evening sessions and reading circles were introduced for the benefit of those who were too busy to attend during the day. Advanced Bible study and mission courses were added to the curriculum, as well as singing classes. But Voth was ahead of his day. After seven years of teaching, this imported schoolmaster of the Ohrloff *Vereinsschule* established a private school in the Chortitza settlement, where he continued efficient work as a teacher for many years.

In the meantime, in 1829 Voth's successor at Ohrloff was found in the person of another West Prussian by the name of Heinrich Heese, a one-time clerk of the Chortitza *Gebietsamt*. A decided Russian patriot, Heese was well versed in the Russian language. But Heese, too, encountered the displeasure of the local association president. In 1842 he left Ohrloff to found an advanced school at Chortitza, called a *Zentralschule*. Several years later a third Prussian teacher, Heinrich Franz, was called to Ohrloff, where he remained until 1858. Franz was chiefly known as a strict disciplinarian and a good mathematician. He was author of a mathematical textbook long used in the schools of South Russia. He was compiler, also a composer, of the popular *Choralbuch*.

Higher Education

Thanks to the opening of the *Zentralschulen* and later secondary schools for girls, the educational level among Mennonites rose rapidly. D. H. Epp stated that during the eighty years of the existence of the Chortitza *Zentralschule*, it raised the cultural level of the Mennonites, as over three thousand pupils graduated from the school and took what they had acquired into their villages and congregations. One can estimate that between 5-8 percent of the Mennonite population attended the secondary schools.

Already during the end of the nineteenth century, a strong desire for higher education was noticeable. This came to full fruition at the beginning of the twentieth century. The *Zentralschule* and the girls' schools served as a prerequisite for entrance in the third and fourth class of the Russian *Gymnasium*, School of Commerce, and technical schools. After they graduated from these schools, many continued their study at the universities in Russia and abroad. In Halbstadt a private Mennonite *Kommerzschule* (school of commerce) was started. Fully recognized, its teaching staff consisted of Mennonites with a full graduate education. This was one of the centers of the Mennonite intellectuals. Even though there is no statistical account in regard to the number of Mennonites with a secondary and graduate training, we can conclude that these 25 *Zentralschulen* had some two thousand pupils and over one hundred fifty with a university education.

In order to attend the university, a graduation certificate from a Russian *Gymnasium* was necessary. For other graduate schools, a certificate of corresponding schools of commerce, or *Real Gymnasium*, was necessary.

For graduate studies, the Mennonite students attended mostly the universities of Odessa, Kharkov, Kiev, Moscow, and Petersburg, and the secondary schools of Ekaterinoslav, Alexandrovsk,

Halbstadt, Berdyansk, and Kharkov.

Favorite schools for the Mennonites of Russia were the University of Basel; the Evangelical Seminary of Basel; the Barmen Theological Seminary; the Hamburg Baptist Seminary; the Seminary at Neukirchen (Mörs) and other leading universities such as Berlin, Jena, Heidelberg, and Basel; and engineering schools such as Dippoldiswalde.

A list of Mennonite university graduates in Russia from 1890 to 1917 is provided in Table 2 (pages 353-357). This list illustrates that the Mennonites of Russia had a strong percentage of intellectuals qualified to furnish leadership among the Mennonites of Russia or in the countries to which they migrated. If the figure of 150 university graduates among the Mennonites is correct, this would mean that among 1,000 Mennonites in Russia, 1.5 percent graduated from a university. This was a high percentage in comparison to the Russian population.

The statistical summary that follows Table 2 provides further information about the background and subsequent careers of Mennonite university graduates in Russia. The question was raised from which social layer of the Mennonite society the students had come. The Mennonite society consisted of (1) farmers, (2) business people and large estate owners, (3) craftsmen and laborers, and (4) employees and free occupations. The largest number were children of teachers, ministers, and free occupations, after which followed farmers, businessmen, and large estate owners (see Table 2 under "Occupation of Father"). We note that those who studied came from various social groups and that they represented the various interests of the Mennonites and did not belong to any one class. It must be stated that the differences between well-to-do and less prosperous Mennonites was greater in Russia than is the case in North America. The Mennonites were in danger of developing extremes on economic levels.

To what extent did the Russian environment influence the Mennonites who received an education at Russian institutions of higher learning? Mennonites lived, generally, in isolation from the Russian environment and had little direct contact with the Russian population. As a rule, Russians did not live within the Mennonite communities, nor did the children of the Russians attend Mennonite schools. Many of the Mennonites could not communicate in the Russian language. During their studies in Russian schools, however, Mennonites made use of the Russian language; learned to know and appreciate Russian literature, history, theater, and art; and associated in Russian circles with people of like-minded interests. The ethnic and religious differences were not significant in this contact. This led to intermarriage, as is shown in the statistical report. Twenty-one percent of all students at Russian universities married Russians. The problem that arose was that the Russian partner had difficulties in adjusting to the isolated Mennonite group. In addition, it was forbidden for the children of a Russian Orthodox church member to join any other but the Russian Orthodox Church. Consequently, these families remained in, or moved to, a city and were lost to the brotherhood. The Russian government favored intermarriage in line with its Russianization policy.

4. RELIGIOUS LIFE

Early Conditions

The Mennonite colonists brought all their religious convictions with them from the mother country, but, as already seen, not their church organizations. They did not begin their religious life in either of the two settlements as a united ecclesiastical body. Being congregational in their church polity, like Mennonites everywhere, they founded independent congregational units from the start, either by villages or groups of villages, or on the basis of their West Prussian, Frisian, or Flemish affiliations. Thus in the Old Colony, Chortitza, among other villages, became almost entirely a Flemish church congregation, while nearby Kronsweide became Frisian. In the Molotschna settlement, Ohrloff, Halbstadt, and many others were Flemish, while Rudnerweide was Frisian. Sometimes whole villages came as congregational units, like Alexanderwohl in 1820 and Gnadenfeld in 1835. Alexanderwohl was of the Old Flemish faith, and a member of the Old Groningen Society of the Netherlands. Gnadenfeld was of the same background.

Not every village had a meetinghouse of its own, except where the population warranted. Thus in the Chortitza colony in 1820, there were only two meetinghouses among the nineteen villages. Where meetinghouses were lacking, the school building might be used for religious services, or occasionally private homes. In course of time, however, each congregation, whether occupying one or more or even parts of villages, aimed to have its own church building.

Church architecture, as well as religious practices, were transplanted from the mother country and underwent little change in the new home during the first fifty years. Meetinghouses were originally all alike—the plain oblong wooden building at first unpainted, each had a platform along one side for the pulpit, and a long bench for the minister and the *Vorsänger*, who intoned the long hymns that were sung without musical accompaniment. The men of the congregation sat on one side, and the women on the other. Attached to one end of the building, near the pulpit, was the little *Ohmstübchen* where the ministers gathered before the meeting to outline the program of the morning service, and transact any business that the needs of the day demanded.

Each congregation was a self-sufficient, independent ecclesiastical unit, with an elder who was authorized to fulfill all ecclesiastical functions, several ministers, and a deacon or two. All were chosen from the laity, without special training for their work, and unsalaried. As we have seen these were usually selected from among the well-to-do owners of ample-sized farms. The influence enjoyed by the ministry, therefore, was due not so much to their intellectual and moral superiority as to their economic affluence, and the reverence which Mennonites have always had for their selected spiritual leaders. Often teachers were also elected to the ministry.

Since the local civil government was also completely in the hands of the Mennonites, the ministry exerted unusual influence in the everyday affairs of the colonists, as well as in their spiritual matters. Both the local Mennonite officials and the Russian supervisory authorities at Odessa frequently consulted the elders in the administration of local affairs. This necessitated frequent meetings of the elders of every wing of the church. Out of this grew in 1850 an institution known as *Kirchen-Konvent* (Church Council), the highest church authority of the settlement.

Although the various Mennonite groups agreed on the fundamentals of the Mennonite faith, such as believer's baptism, nonresistance, and opposition to the oath, yet in matters of practice there were some minor differences. In some of the Flemish churches, sermons were read from a book of sermons, the preacher remaining seated. Among the Frisians there was less dependence on the printed sermons, and the preacher delivered his sermons standing. In some congregations, the bread in the communion service was distributed by the elder to each communicant in his seat; in others, all the participants gathered in groups around the communion table. Slight and insignificant as these differences were, however, they were often sufficiently well enough entrenched in the traditions of church practice to prevent effective cooperation in religious efforts.

The spiritual life of the colonists through the first generations was not of a high order. Frontier conditions are seldom conducive to the cultivation of high cultural or spiritual ideals. Educational opportunities for ministers were meager. The close affiliation of the church elders with the civil authorities in administering local government had its usual result. As in the state churches of both pre- and post-Reformation days, church membership was likely to become confused with the rights of citizenship. According to their special charter, in order to enjoy their privileges and exemptions in the empire, the Mennonites had to be members of the organization with which the original contract had been made. Church membership, therefore, was essential to the enjoyment of highly desirable civil privileges. Membership thus came to be regarded as a matter of course, and was no longer based on actual conversion.

To be sure, a certain amount of ecclesiastical discipline was demanded; gross sin, and in some cases slight deviations from the established rules, were punished by excommunication. Some of the more conservative groups practiced "avoidance." Denying all business and social ties, as well as religious fellowship, was almost a sure remedy for bringing a sinner to repentance. This gave the elders who exercised this power unusual control over the social well-being of the whole community, as well as over the religious faith of their members. To a person being shunned, the various church divisions were often a blessing in disguise, for the power of the elder did not extend beyond the confines of his own wing of the church.

We have here an interesting example of Mennonite self-government based on the principle of passive resistance. The experiment had its difficulties. It was not always easy to carry out the Mennonite practices of nonresistance and at the same time maintain the discipline necessary for a stable social order. To be sure, all major crimes were adjudicated by the larger Russian units of government; but to the Mennonite village magistrate fell the lot of administering local discipline. That there was a strong sentiment among the Mennonites in favor of maintaining their historic nonresistant principles is shown by the fact that although all the other local village offices were held by men of their own faith, that of local constable was sometimes turned over to a non-Mennonite Russian. Usually this was some hired man or other day laborer who happened to live in the village and who had no scruples against the use of force. In the early twenties, differences of opinion on this matter resulted in one of the first church divisions in Russia.

Kleine Gemeinde

After being ordained a minister in his church in Danzig, Klaas Reimer migrated in 1804 first to the Chortitza community, and later to Molotschna. A rather sensitive soul with a somewhat narrow religious horizon, contentious and critical in spirit, he was out of step from the beginning with the rest of his fellow ministers in the Flemish church. He found fault with the laxity of their church discipline; he criticized the entire church as being too formal in its church practices and worship; and he questioned the right of a Mennonite civil official to administer local police power over a fellow Mennonite church member. In the course of time, Reimer gained a few followers for his views and stirred up so much dissension through his preaching that the Molotschna elder, Jakob Enns, requested the local *Gebietsamt* to silence him. Reimer appealed to the Chortitza elder, Johann Wiebe, to intercede in his behalf. However, Wiebe also threatened the disturber with banishment in case he set up a separate ecclesiastical organization apart from the Mennonite body already in existence.

Paying no heed to the threats of the two elders, Reimer, with eighteen others, seceded from the main body and organized a church of their own. Although the Mennonite elders put up a strong protest against the move, the new party secured recognition from the government as a separate ecclesiastical organization with all the rights and privileges originally granted the Mennonites. Other similar groups seceded at the same time throughout the different settlements. These later united with one another to form what became known as the *Kleine Gemeinde* (little congregation).

A pamphlet, published in Ohrloff in 1838 by a member of this group, justifies Reimer's withdrawal under five heads: first, it is entirely contrary to the teaching of the Savior, and contrary to the nonresistant faith, to turn a brother over to the civil authorities for punishment in case of alleged misconduct. As this practice grew among the settlers, so says this writer, spiritual discipline grew more lax, and drinking and other vices increased. The ban was being sparingly enforced against such persons. Second, in reply to the charge that the separated group exercised too strict a church discipline for minor ecclesiastical offenses, the accusers are referred to the sixteen punishable faults recorded in 2 Timothy 3:1-5. They punish only such wrongdoing as the Word of God commands. Third, to the charge of disloyalty to the government, they replied,

> Although we do not resist evil, yet we recognize a government as divinely ordained. We have never refused to be obedient to the government, but in such matters as arresting bad people, arresting them to transport them, or to accuse some one before the

government, or to help to punish with money or corporal punishment, all such Jesus gave us no example for, but turned such over to the wordly government. We are not with those who would overthrow the government, for we know that it is ordained of God.

Fourth, the reason for warning their people against attendance at weddings, as then conducted, was due to the fact that the ancient example of young Tobit was no longer followed on these occasions; but instead

> there is lust of eye and of the flesh, and a high and proud spirit which is not from the Father but from the world. Although there is no direct word in the Scriptures forbidding attendance at weddings, yet it is said, we are to have no fellowship with the world. You know yourselves how the poor blind people act at these wedding feasts, the one proud, the other still prouder, the pipe in one hand, and the song book in the other as if the living God, and the dying Lord Jesus could be honored thereby. Warning against such practices can be found in the Georg Hansen confession of faith, and also in that of Hans von Steen.

Fifth, they did not approve of sermons and eulogies of the dead at funeral services. This practice was formerly common only among Catholics and Lutherans, but recently had been introduced among the Mennonites, the pamphlet says, and was now thoroughly entrenched among them.

On the main issue in this controversy, the use of force by the Mennonites against fellow Mennonites to bring about compliance with local temporal regulations, Reimer undoubtedly was right in his contention that this was inconsistent with the historic faith and practice of Mennonites. Never before had the Mennonites been entrusted with the task of maintaining civil order in a local community through the exercise of the police power. They could not always square their practice with their nonresistant theory when the local magistrate found it necessary to lead a fellow Mennonite to the whipping post, or lock him up in the local jail.

There was plenty of need for reform, no doubt, of the spiritual and social life in most of the churches at that time. But according to Reimer himself, the movement he inaugurated often broke the bounds of moderation, and resulted in an outbreak of fanaticism and excessive emotionalism that was even more deplorable than the conditions it sought to remedy. Reimer, himself, however, seems to have kept his head. By 1860 his small church had nearly run its course. During the 1870s the small remnant migrated in a body to Manitoba and Nebraska.

A small faction migrated from the parent body to the Crimea in the early 1860s, where under the leadership of elder Jakob Wiebe they adopted some additional practices, including baptism by immersion. In 1874 they migrated to Kansas where they were known as *Krimmer Mennonite* Brethren. They have since joined the Mennonite Brethren.

Bernhard Fast

During the early 1820s another troublesome controversy agitated some of the congregations in the Molotschna settlement. Elder Bernhard Fast of the Ohrloff congregation introduced a number of innovations in his religious practices which aroused the bitter opposition of the majority of his conservative membership. Three-fourths of his congregation, some four hundred families, withdrew and organized a congregation of their own which, because it embraced the larger part of the membership, became known as the *Grosse Gemeinde*. Among themselves they were familiarly spoken of as the "Pure Flemish." Among the innovations to which objections were raised were the ordination of Elder Fast by a neighboring Frisian elder rather than by one of his own wing of the church, the admission of a non-Mennonite missionary to the communion table, the founding of the Ohrloff *Vereinsschule*, and the organization of a Bible society, a branch of the Petersburg society whose chief function was the distribution of free Bibles. One of the charges against this Bible society was that the titles of its officers, president and secretary, had a militaristic sound; although in reality, as the chairman of the *Fürsorge-Komitee* remarked, there was no more connection between these titles and militarism than between his snuff box and the moon.

In the beginning of this controversy, Fast had the sympathy and cooperation of Elder Franz Goerz of the Frisian Rudnerweide congregation, and of Elder Peter Wedel of the Alexanderwohl group. Some years later, because of certain political activities, Elder Fast lost most of the support of these two congregations.

Mennonite Brethren Origins

There were several factors that led to the origin of the Mennonite Brethren. There were within the Mennonite brotherhood in Russia pietistic influences at work as had been the case in the Netherlands through Jan Deknatel in Amsterdam, or the van der Smissens and Jakob Denner in Hamburg-Altona. Denner, in fact, had served the Danzig Mennonite Church for a while and had started a Mennonite church in Hamburg in which he practiced baptism by immersion. Some of the Mennonites coming to Russia were influenced by this spiritual climate and transplanted it to the Molotschna settlement.

There has been a tendency to establish the origin of the

Mennonite Brethren in a direct lineage with Eduard Wüst. Wüst did indeed have a great influence on a large number of the Molotschna Mennonites, and indirectly also on the origins of the Mennonite Brethren. Wüst served in the neighborhood of the Mennonites in a congregation that had the name *Brüdergemeinde*. It had its origins in Kornthal near Stuttgart in South Germany. Wüst was a great revivalist who influenced and brought new life to his pietistic congregations as well as to the Lutherans, Mennonites, and even Catholics who lived in the neighborhood and beyond. However, Wüst died before the Mennonite Brethren came into being, and up to the end of his life he not only baptized infants in his congregation, but even used in his evangelical *Brüdergemeinde* a Lutheran baptismal ritual which implied that the water in baptism constitutes a regenerating act in the infant. In addition, Wüst did not advocate in his *Brüdergemeinde* parting of those who had accepted Christ in an act of regeneration from those who had not yet reached that point.

Among the best friends of Wüst were Leonhard Sudermann, a minister of the Berdyansk Mennonite Church and later of the Emmaus Mennonite Church in Whitewater, Kansas, and many other outstanding evangelical leaders of various Mennonite congregations, some of whom remained and others who came to the United States in 1874 and the following years. Wüst's message had made a great impression on a large number of people, and his emphasis remained consistent and unmistakable. He was, with John the Baptist, a preacher of repentance. He invited his listeners to accept Christ as a personal Savior. He said less about the invitation of Christ to take the cross and follow him.

In the midst of Wüst's *Brüdergemeinde* there was a group of *Muntere* (joyful) that had been started under the leadership of Joseph Höttmann and Matheus Prinz. Höttmann, who had been a supporter and close co-worker of Wüst at the beginning, later developed separatist tendencies and started meetings in smaller circles. The group met frequently. There was much singing and Bible study. The Bible was considered the only guide in faith and life. Some discontinued infant baptism, since the gates of the heavenly kingdom were open to children regardless. They strongly emphasized the emotional life and expressed their Christian joy in various ways but remained within the bounds of common decency.

The fact that Joseph Höttmann and Matheus Prinz performed spiritual functions led to the arrest of Höttmann. They saw these actions to be sufferings inflicted for the sake of Christ and considered their persecutors to be "spiritless Pharisees." These extremist developments by his wayward disciples negatively affected Wüst's public image. His influence and outreach beyond his *Brüdergemeinde* were now limited.

This is the situation in which the Mennonite Brethren Church had its origin: Jakob P. Bekker, a contemporary reporter on the events that took place, stated that Höttmann, "a displaced church official, called together a council of brethren at which this writer [Bekker], together with several other Mennonite brethren, was present." On the agenda was the statement that they "could no longer feel justified in observing communion with an apostate church membership... because they serve the devil in their daily walk" and consequently their "communion is no longer the Lord's table but the devil's table." Jakob Bekker stated that Pastor Wüst had "failed to teach how to differentiate between what is holy and what is unholy, how the devout should separate themselves from the wicked." He went on to state that during this meeting "the entire Mennonite Church body became the object of consideration." The conclusion was that

> If Pastor Wüst would not agree to administer communion only to those who were redeemed children of God, how much less would the elders of the Mennonite Church *Bruderschaft* do this, who, aside from Gnadenfeld, did not know who was converted or unconverted, holy or unholy.... And thus we agreed to observe communion among ourselves, in peace and quietness and also to include the Württemberg brethren,...

(the group that had withdrawn from Wüst's *Brüdergemeinde* under the leadership of Joseph Höttmann). This took place in the spring of 1859 and constituted the initial step in the founding of the Mennonite Brethren Church.

Bekker reports that "among the believing brethren in the Mennonite colonies, communion was observed several times in all quietness without being disturbed." Soon it became known and had severe consequences among the Mennonites as well as among the followers of Höttmann in Wüst's *Brüdergemeinde*. There appeared to be a clear sense of who was saved and who was not: "The converted brethren were grieved that they must take communion with those who were not part of the body of Christ.... In Wüst's church more than half of the members were unconverted." The record is silent of the applicability of the experience of Jesus with his disciples at the Last Supper when he told them that one of them would deny him and one would even betray him and yet did not ask them to leave the Lord's table.

In addition to the matter of the Lord's Supper, the question of baptism came up. Baptism of adults by immersion could not have come from Wüst who baptized children to the end of his life. In the recently published diary of Jakob P. Bekker, he refers to Menno

Simons's *Foundation Book* as a source for baptism by immersion, but this cannot be based on Menno's writings. As we have already noted, Denner had introduced baptism by immersion in Hamburg long before this matter came up in Russia. This influence came from the Collegiants in Holland and from the Baptists in England. Consequently, the practice spread throughout Europe and ultimately also reached Russian Mennonites. One should note that the Russian Orthodox Church always practiced infant baptism by immersion.

The group that had observed the Lord's Supper without the approval and presence of Mennonite ministers now proceeded to baptize each other in the open water by immersion in 1860. This was the beginning of the *Mennoniten Brüdergemeinde*. It must be taken for granted that the name was taken over from Wüst's *Brüdergemeinde* which had been transplanted from Kornthal near Stuttgart to the steppes of Russia. That they prefaced the name with *Mennoniten* implied that they wanted to remain Mennonites. There could be a number of reasons for this. A more important question is why some of the followers of Wüst maintained that those who have accepted Christ in an act of surrender should separate themselves from those whom they should lead to Christ. The reasons were given in a document which was presented to "The All-Mennonite Elders of the Molotschna Mennonite Churches" by the seceding Mennonite brethren on January 6, 1860. The statement began by saying that the undersigned have "realized through the grace of God that the total Mennonite brotherhood has decayed to the extent that we can no more be a part of it" and fear the "approach of an unavoidable judgment of God." This led to an exchange of letters involving also the *Gebietsamt* (Mennonite civil administration).

There were numerous reasons why a separation of a group from the main body would cause problems on all administrative fronts, including the possible loss of the special rights that the Mennonites enjoyed with other foreign settlers. We must take into consideration that all foreign settlements in Russia were established by an arrangement with the highest government in Petersburg. Thus a special administrative arm of the Russian government dealt with the Mennonite agencies, the secular and the religious departments. All this and many other questions complicated this parting of ways. Originally efforts were made to establish a special Mennonite Brethren settlement on the Kuban River in the foothills of the Caucasus Mountains, but ultimately they established themselves in most of the Mennonite villages, particularly in the growing number of new Mennonite daughter settlements throughout Russia.

P. M. Friesen, A. Kroeker, and others have claimed that the Mennonite Brethren returned to the foundation laid by Menno Simons (1 Cor. 3:11). Friesen says: "Menno and Wüst, in addition to the Word of God and his spirit, have made the Mennonite Brethren what the church of Christ is to be." It must be said, however, that Wüst advocated no change from the sacramental character of Lutheran infant baptism. Secondly, Wüst advocated no withdrawal of those who had been led to a personal acceptance of Christ from the main body of his congregation as the founding fathers of the Mennonite Brethren did. The Mennonite Brethren separated from the Mennonites after the death of Wüst. He grieved over the withdrawal of some of his members, including the Höttmann-led group from his church.

Contributions

The Mennonite Brethren maintained a lively contact with the Baptists and other pietistic movements of Germany, supporting their missions, reading their literature, and later even sending their young men to the Baptist Theological Seminary at Hamburg. This stimulating influence from abroad in the culturally isolated settlements of Russia resulted in the Mennonite Brethren becoming strong promoters in a number of areas including evangelism, missions, Sunday school work, publication enterprises, and the introduction of gospel songs (*Glaubensstimme*). Not that the Mennonite brotherhood as a whole did not engage in these activities, but the Molotschna Mennonite Brethren especially, considering their small number, made outstanding contributions in these fields. This was not equally true of the Chortitza Mennonite Brethren and those who came to America in 1874.

Some of the outstanding Mennonite leaders and educators of the crucial decades of the early twentieth century in Russia were of Mennonite Brethren background. Among them were men like P. M. Friesen (educator and historian), Jakob and Abraham Kroeker (writers), Heinrich Braun (publisher), Peter Braun (educator), B. H. Unruh (educator), A. H. Unruh (educator), and others. The spiritual horizon and the field of labor of some of them was widened to such a degree that they reached far beyond their original background. Nevertheless, their early stimulation was received in that group. Jakob Kroeker, who died in 1948 in Germany, was the most prolific Bible expositor that the Mennonites have produced. His fourteen volumes on the Old Testament have been published in many editions.

By way of summary it can be stated that the Mennonite Brethren made a contribution by breaking certain forms of religious and cultural life which in some cases had become a hindrance to a wholesome Christian life and by replacing these with new forms and new life. During the last decade in North America there has been a revival of interest in a recovery of the Anabaptist heritage and vision, in which the Mennonite Brethren are strongly involved. The closing chapter dealing with the Mennonites in Russia today includes the Mennonite Brethren.

Jerusalem Friends

At the same time that the Mennonite Brethren organized, another religious disturbance developed in the community of Gnadenfeld, Molotschna. *Jerusalem Friends*, or *Templer*, as they came later to be called, were a group of religious enthusiasts originally found in Württemberg, Germany. Followers of a theologian by the name of Christoph Hoffmann, who sponsored a kind of zionist movement, their chief objective was to build a new temple at Jerusalem. Theologically, the new movement was a compound of pietism, missionary zeal, and rationalistic thinking. In 1861 Johann Lange, a former student at one of their training schools in Württemberg, was installed as head of the *Bruderschule* at Gnadenfeld, by the trustees of that institution.

An ardent follower of the Jerusalem Friends, Lange soon found fault with the traditional beliefs of the Gnadenfeld Mennonites, and in special meetings for both children and adults held in the school building, taught the new doctrines. In the course of a few years he secured a small following among some of the school supporters in both Gnadenfeld and surrounding villages. But at the same time he aroused the opposition of a majority of the Gnadenfeld church membership, and especially the officials of the church. The bitter controversy lasted several years. Lange spent some time in jail and was finally forced to resign as the head of the *Bruderschule*. Together with a goodly number of his followers in 1866, he founded a settlement and church congregation called *Tempelhof*. It was not far from the Mennonite Brethren community already described. Some of the Jerusalem Friends ultimately located in Palestine.

Peters Brethren

To complete the story of Gnadenfeld's contribution to the religious life of the Russian Mennonites during this period, mention should be made of another small group, the *Peters Brethren*. These were followers of Hermann Peters, an unlettered farmer, who found the true church based on a literal interpretation of numerous apostolic injunctions, meant to meet the needs of the apostolic times. Because Christ broke the bread at the first communion service, Peters insisted that the bread must be broken, and not passed to the communicant in small pieces already cut, as was the usual Mennonite custom. For this reason his followers were sometimes called *Breadbreakers*. Minute regulations were laid down for every detail of everyday living. Men were forbidden to wear neckties, watch chains, starched shirts, and polished boots. Women were not to wear earrings, gay clothes, laces, or jewelry of any kind. Forbidden also were the reading of newspapers, discussion of political questions, and the the use of tobacco or strong drink. Children were not to attend the public schools, nor to greet strangers with the usual *Guten Tag* (good day), but were to pass silently by. When entering a home, brethren were to say "Peace be unto you"; but when entering the house of a stranger they must say, "May it be well with you." This small group had little influence upon the religious life of the Mennonite body as a whole. They disappeared from the older settlements, but some migrated to Fairview, Oklahoma.

Mennonite Alliance Church

In 1905 a new group arose which attempted to reconcile some of the divergent practices among the existing Mennonite groups. The new movement emphasized strong spiritual life with great interest in evangelism and mission activities and attempted to retain the best of the Mennonite heritage.

This movement, originating in Lichtfelde, Molotschna, in 1905 and Altona, Sagradovka, in 1907, desired to have fellowship in the Lord's Supper with Christians even beyond the Mennonite brotherhood. They also emphasized the need for stricter church discipline. They practiced immersion, but accepted members who had not been baptized according to this form. This group was known as the *Evangelische Mennoniten-Gemeinde* or *Allianz-Gemeinde*. Although not directly related historically, this group is spiritually related to the Evangelical Mennonite Brethren of the prairie states and provinces in North America. After World War I, Mennonite immigrants from Russia transplanted this group to Canada and South America.

5. MIGRATIONS TO AMERICA AND ASIA

The special privileges enjoyed by the Mennonites and the other German colonists of South Russia set them apart as a distinct group within the empire. Really a state within a state, separated from the native Russians by social and political, as well as religious, barriers, at the same time they were held together firmly as a group by ties of language, culture, religion, and ethnic awareness.

Under the conditions of the time, it was becoming increasingly difficult to grant favors to a minority above those enjoyed by the citizenry in general. The growing nationalism of middle Europe during the 1860s, evidenced specifically in the revolt of the Polish Russians in 1863, the emergence of Prussian militarism, the ambitious designs against the Turkish empire—all these conspired to convince the Russian Slavophiles that the day for the Russianizing of all foreigners had come.

The blow fell in 1870. An imperial *ukas* proclaimed that the day of special privileges had ended for the German colonists. The *Fürsorge-Komitee* at Odessa was to be abolished, and the colonists were to be governed directly from Petersburg. Russian was to be the official language in the local *Gebietsamt*, and was to be introduced as a subject of study in all the schools. All the German schools were to be supervised directly by the imperial educational authorities. And worst of all for the Mennonites, military exemption was to be abolished. The German colonists were to be given ten years in which to accommodate themselves to the new order. After that they would become full-fledged Russian citizens with no special favors.

Mennonites in Petersburg

To the Mennonites, who had every reason to believe up to this time that the promises made by Empress Catherine had been granted in perpetuity, this threat to end their exemptions from military service came as a distinct shock. They immediately took what steps they could to protect their former privileges. At a meeting held at Alexanderwohl in midwinter of 1871, delegates from the Molotschna, Chortitza, and Bergthal settlements elected a delegation to visit the imperial city and present the czar with a petition in which they stated their historic peace principles, and pled that the promises with which they were induced to settle the steppes of South Russia might not be abrogated. This delegation was under the leadership of Leonhard Sudermann of Berdyansk and Gerhard G. Dyck of the Chortitza colony, neither of whom, unfortunately, could speak Russian. Arriving in Petersburg later in the winter, they did not succeed in having a personal audience with the czar as they had hoped. But through the good offices of the president of the Odessa *Fürsorge-Komitee*, who happened to be in the city at the time, they were able to meet several ministers of the imperial council, and the chairman of the special commission that had been appointed to draft the new military laws.

Although neither the ministers nor Count Heyden of the special commission could give the Mennonites any definite or detailed information as to the exact nature of the forthcoming laws, all of them assured the elders, nevertheless, that they would not likely be granted complete exemption, but might be assigned to some sort of noncombatant service in the hospital or sanitary departments. If Mennonites were completely exempted, said Count Heyden, then all the Russians would want to be Mennonites. Assured by Leonhard Sudermann that even noncombatant services under the War Department would not be acceptable to the Mennonites, the count replied that if everybody were like Mennonites in this respect stable government would be impossible, since it would soon be overrun by its enemies. Heinrich Epp of Chortitza answered that if all were like the Mennonites there would be no enemies. The count had to agree.

In the course of the interview, one of the deputies suggested that perhaps a money payment might be substituted for noncombatant service. The minister replied that such an arrangement would not be possible. Buying military exemption with money was a common Mennonite practice running back through their West Prussian and Dutch history. It would hardly seem consistent, however, to refuse hospital service on the one hand and yet be willing to secure freedom from all military obligations by the payment of money which could be directly used for the promotion of war activities. But Mennonites were not always logical or consistent in their attempt to reconcile their heavenly with their earthly citizenship. This first attempt of the Mennonite delegation to get a favorable hearing before the Petersburg authorities was not very satisfactory. The details of the new law had not yet been worked out. The delegates returned home without any assurance as to their future, but with a growing conviction that their privileged days were numbered.

Still hoping that a personal appeal to the czar himself might ward off the threatened loss of their privileged status, the churches sent a second delegation the next year to attempt a meeting with him, but again without success. They did, however, have an audience with the Crown Prince Constantin who reminded them, in German, of the visit he had made to the Mennonite colonies some years before. But he, too, assured the delegation that while every effort would be made in the forthcoming law to meet the religious scruples of the Mennonites, yet they would be compelled to perform some sort of noncombatant service in the new arrangement. This second delegation, too, returned home greatly disappointed, more convinced than ever that emigration now was inevitable for all Mennonites who insisted upon the unconditional preservation of their former liberties. Several later delegations were sent to Petersburg during 1873, but to no avail. By 1874 the new law had been formulated, providing noncombatant service for the Mennonites—forestry service or industrial work not connected with the War Department in times of peace, and hospital service in times of war.

The Immigration Movement

In the meantime, as the hope of securing favorable consideration from the government faded, the sentiment for emigration to a foreign land increased. Various countries where there was still a demand for new settlers were considered—Russian Turkestan, and even the distant Amur region. Both of these had recently been added to Russia, but in neither would the new military laws be applied. New Zealand and North and South America were also considered. Very little was known of any of these countries. In the words of Leonhard Sudermann, one of the staunchest supporters of the emigration movement to America, "To many, America meant a country interesting for the adventurer, an asylum for convicts. How could one live in peace under his vine and fig tree amid such people." He continues, "Such a life might be possible for those who had their pockets full of revolvers, but for a nonresistant people it would be impossible to found homes amid such surroundings." The same impressions of the new world evidently prevailed among all the Mennonites and other German colonists, who were also contemplating a large emigration movement.

Among the men most active in the emigration movement were two Mennonites from the Berdyansk congregation, Elder Leonhard Sudermann, and Cornelius Jansen, a prosperous grain merchant of that growing seaport. Jansen had come to Russia from West Prussia as a young man and had never given up his Prussian citizenship. Because he had served as Prussian consul at Berdyansk for some years, he was in closer touch with world affairs than his country brethren. He saw from the start that emigration would be the inevitable fate of Mennonites who would not accept some sort of war service. As early as 1870 he wrote to Christian Krehbiel, John F. Funk (editor of the *Herald of Truth*), Jacob Y. Schantz, and others of whom he had heard, asking for detailed information about the military laws; natural resources; land laws, especially of the western states; and other matters of interest to prospective settlers. This correspondence he later printed and distributed among the Russian Mennonites.

Contacting British Officials

At the same time consul Jansen inquired of the British consul at Berdyansk about the possibility of military exemption in Canada, and also about the availability of large tracts of land suitable for large compact settlements. This inquiry led to a series of interesting letters written back and forth among various British and Canadian government officials—the British foreign office, the British ambassador at Petersburg, the governor general at Ottawa, the Canadian Department of Agriculture, and numerous lesser officials. The prospect of securing some fifty thousand industrious farmers for the unsettled prairies of western Canada aroused keen interest among the Canadian authorities, who soon began an active campaign to direct the proposed emigration to their country. The Ottawa government dispatched a special commissioner, William Hespeler, to South Russia for the purpose of interesting the Mennonites in Canada. Some of this correspondence is interesting, and is worthy of brief mention here.

The British consul at Berdyansk, writing to Earl Granville of the foreign office in London in 1872, said of the Russian Mennonites:

> Seven years residence in this country has enabled me to acquire a good knowledge of them, and I am personally acquainted with many of the elders. I feel no hesitation, therefore, in saying that these Germans would prove a valuable acquisition to any country they may select for their home. If they find difficulty in proceeding to Canada, they will seek refuge in the United States to which country their attention has already been directed, but as I have already stated their first choice falls on British soil, and though their determination to quit this country is fixed, yet from what I can learn they will do so with regret if they have to leave for any other country than Canada.

A little later the British ambassador to Russia, writing from Petersburg to the foreign office in London in answer to an inquiry whether the imperial government would object to the emigration of the Mennonites, said that Prince Gorchakov, the foreign minister in the government of Alexander II, and his greatest diplomat, suggested that the imperial government would lay no obstacle in the way of their departure if they first fulfilled all their obligations according to law. The letter further continued,

> On referring to the new military system imposed on all Russian subjects without exception which is the principal cause of these colonists emigrating from Russia, Prince Gorchakov observed that he had voted in the council of the empire against the withdrawal of the privileges and the exemption from military service formerly granted these colonists, on the principle that the promises made by the sovereign of that day should be held sacred. In this opinion the

emperor had participated, but the great majority of the council had voted in a contrary sense.

In September of 1872 John Lowe, of the Department of Agriculture at Ottawa, suggested to William Hespeler, who was touring the Mennonite settlements of South Russia, that he make arrangements with some influential Mennonite to act as an agent of Canada, to be reimbursed at the rate of two dollars per capita for all the Mennonites settling in Canada. Hespeler soon answered, insisting that the two-dollar subsidy would be a serious mistake, for,

> it would not create a very favorable effect, neither would the agency be accepted by any of the Mennonites, as according to my experience of them, I find them more conscientious than their confessionalists in Canada or the United States—it would in their eyes look too much like dealing in human beings. They are not a people like the general run of emigrants—they are a reasoning, thinking, cautious, and to a large extent an educated people.

So anxious were the Canadian authorities to secure these prospective Mennonite settlers that they authorized Hespeler to grant them all their demands—exemption from military service, free land (160 acres to each head of a family, reserved in large compact areas in Manitoba), freedom of religion, the right to maintain their own German language, control of their own schools—practically all the privileges which had been granted them by Catherine in 1787. However, because Hespeler was suspected by the Russian police of fomenting a mass emigration movement, he was forced to leave Russia. Cornelius Jansen was also exiled in 1873 for the same reason.

At the time that Jansen started his investigation of Canadian possibilities through the British consul at Berdyansk in 1871, he also made similar inquires concerning the United States from the American consul at the same port. The American government did not seem interested in the proposed migration at this time. However, in 1874, after the movement had actually begun, the United States Senate debated for over a week a bill to grant Mennonites a large compact tract of western lands. The bill was defeated, but railroad companies, together with state land departments, took a lively interest in the possibility of getting industrious farmers for their unsettled lands. The Santa Fe Company in 1875 sent a special agent, C. B. Schmidt, to South Russia to bring as many Mennonites as possible to their railroad lands in Kansas, the state which received the bulk of this immigration to the United States.

Investigating North America

Meanwhile, by this time through the efforts of Hespeler, great interest had been aroused among the Russian Mennonites in the emigration cause. It was the conviction of the leaders that nothing favorable could be expected from Petersburg. Following Hespeler's suggestion, various congregations from the different sections of the Mennonite population selected delegates to visit America on a tour of investigation. This delegation consisted of twelve men—Jakob Buller of the Alexanderwohl congregation, and Leonhard Sudermann of Berdyansk, representing the Molotschna colony; Tobias Unruh from the Volhynia settlements; Andreas Schrag, speaking for the Swiss congregations of the same province; Heinrich Wiebe, and *Oberschulze* Jakob Peters, together with Cornelius Buhr, the latter on his own expense, representing the Bergthal colony; Wilhelm Ewert, of the West Prussian Mennonites; Cornelius Toews and David Claassen, sent by the *Kleine Gemeinde*; and the Tschetter brothers, Paul and Lorenz, from the Hutterite settlements.

In the summer of 1873 this delegation visited what was then the frontier line in North America, from Winnipeg, Manitoba, through Minnesota, Dakota, Nebraska, and Kansas. They carefully investigated soil and climate and available satisfactory lands, and inquired about political conditions and military regulations. As already suggested, the Dominion of Canada had granted most liberal inducement to prospects.

Neither the federal government of the United States nor any of the states could offer terms similar to those of Canada, although later three of the western states passed legislation exempting Mennonites from militia duty. The Hutterite contingent of the delegation paid a visit to President Grant in which they asked for a guarantee of military exemption from the government. They were informed by the president that he could make no such promise, but he expressed the opinion that it was not likely that anyone in the United States would ever be called upon to serve in the army contrary to his religious convictions. The president, however, was favorably disposed toward the emigration movement, and recommended favorable land legislation in his message to Congress.

The delegation of twelve returned to Russia late in the summer—the more conservative Chortitza, Bergthal, and *Kleine Gemeinde* delegates to recommend Canada to their brethren; and the more liberal Molotschna representatives, as well as the Hutterites, to recommend the United States, in spite of the fact that the guarantees of military exemption from the government of the United States were less definite than those of the Canadian government.

Large numbers of eager Mennonites throughout all the settlements were impatiently awaiting the return of the delegates, ready if the reports were favorable, to start immediately on the big trek to the promised land. In fact, several small groups had already left for America. But the mass migration did not begin until after the prospective immigrants had heard from their deputies. The enthusiastic reports that there was plenty of good land for everybody, to be had almost for the asking, and the promise of absolute military exemption in Canada, and a fair degree of certainty that war service would never be demanded in the United States aroused great eagerness for emigration throughout all the settlements in the years 1873 and 1874. In those centers where the emigration fever ran highest, steps were immediately taken by many to dispose of their property with a view to an early departure the following spring. But it was soon found that this was not always an easy matter, especially in such compact settlements as Alexanderwohl, Bergthal, and others, where whole congregations and villages had decided to emigrate en masse.

Momentous Decisions

Everybody wanted to sell, and there was nobody to buy. To make matters worse, in many of the settlements, Mennonites were living on crown lands in which they had only a limited ownership of the soil. It was only the use of it that they had a right to sell; and even that could be transferred only to fellow Mennonites according to the original contract made with the government. Buildings and improvements, of course, belonged to the individual farmer; but without land, buildings were not of great value. The marketability of land in the Mennonite villages was therefore greatly restricted; and during the first few years of the emigration movement, well-improved farms sold for far less than their real value. Some years later the government permitted the outright sale of land, but by this time the non-Mennonite buyers frequently took advantage of the oversupply of farms for sale, and continued to purchase them at only a fraction of their real worth. In spite of these discouragements, nevertheless, throughout the spring and summer of 1874 whole villages and congregations continued their preparations for the long journey.

The next task was to secure the necessary passports permitting departure from the country. This, too, was frequently a long, drawn-out process, demanding heavy fees, and accelerated only by liberal gratuities to corrupt government officials. Sometimes it was months after requests had been sent in for passports before they were available, and every step was attended with heavy expense.

Envoy of the Czar

By this time the government officials in Petersburg, realizing that there was strong likelihood of losing some forty thousand of the czar's most industrious farmers in South Russia, began to consider means of stemming the emigration tide. To this end the czar sent Adjutant General von Totleben, himself a German Lutheran, a Crimean War hero well known among the Mennonites, through the communities offering those who would remain certain exemptions from the most objectionable features of the new military law. He met the Mennonite civil and religious leaders in May of 1874, at Halbstadt, Chortitza, and Alexanderwohl, where he informed them that he was authorized by the czar to offer them some sort of civil service as a substitute for the compulsory military duty required in the proposed conscription act. At the same time Totleben tried to discourage the emigration movement by painting America in its darkest colors. In America, he said, the pioneer settlers would be compelled to spend much of their time and labor in draining swamps and cutting down the forests before the land would be fit for cultivation. Since labor was scarce in the new country, the settlers would be under the necessity of doing all this work themselves, whereas in Russia such work was performed by cheap native labor. As for military exemption in America, the Mennonites had not been exempted in the Southern States during the Civil War; and as for the North, where they proposed to settle, it seemed likely at that time, that war was inevitable with England. In this case, no doubt, they would be called upon for service with all others.

This visit of Totleben's with his promise to substitute civil service disconnected from the army organization, no doubt influenced many of the more liberal-minded Mennonites to reconsider their earlier determination to leave Russian soil. Both in Chortitza and in Halbstadt, the majority of the leaders present at these meetings with the general, wrote him a letter of thanks after his departure, with expressions of gratitude for his kindly visit and of entire satisfaction with the substitute service offered. At the same time they uttered the hope that they might be left in entire control of their school system, which it was rumored was to be placed under government control under the new Russianization program. These promises were later enacted into law providing that the Mennonites were to be exempt from military service, in lieu of which they were to be assigned to duty in hospitals, factories, or especially in forestry service, where they were to be permitted to work in compact and exclusive groups. These concessions were to apply in times of war as well as in times of peace, but were offered only to the original Mennonite settlers in Russia and their descendants. Immigrants coming into Russia or outside accessions coming into the church after the passing of the law, were not to be included.

While the majority seemed satisfied with these rather liberal concessions, a strong minority, nevertheless, believed that any service under the guise of military law would be a violation of their peace principles. These still preferred emigration to any compromise with their consciences. In the opinion of Elder Isaac Peters, one of the staunchest defenders of this position, by keeping the substitute service under the control of the military department, and by limiting forestry service to a period of twenty years, the government was keeping the back door open for entrance later into full military service.

Many of those sharing these views, including entire villages, continued their preparations for departure. These included in the main the more conservative groups, such as the daughter colonies of the Chortitza settlement—Bergthal and Fürstenland; the Alexanderwohl congregation; the Swiss of Volhynia; the Hutterites; and the *Kleine Gemeinde* at Borozenko. These emigrated in a body; but from every settlement and almost from every village there were some additions to the mass movement.

The military question, of course, was not the only issue involved in this exodus. This is proven by the fact that not only Mennonites, but German Lutherans and Catholics had also decided to leave their adopted country for America during this time. The program of Russianization which the government had adopted would ultimately deprive all these privileged colonies of the highly favored status which they had enjoyed heretofore, such as exclusive control of their schools, the use of their German language, and a large degree of local political autonomy under the *Fürsorge-Komitee* at Odessa. This commission was now to be abolished; the schools to be placed under the direct control of the Russian government; and the Russian language to be taught side by side with the favored German. To the Mennonites, especially, there seemed to be a close relation between their distinctive Mennonitism and their *Deutschtum*. It was a matter of grave doubt to many of them whether they could maintain their traditional religious principles separated from their German tongue and culture. Then, too, in every colony, there were those who decided to cast their lot with the religious absolutists for economic reasons. In every westward movement in history there has been a large contingent of the landless. And they were not absent here. Many motives lay back of the emigration movement.

The Great Trek

Among the first of the small groups to leave in the spring of 1874 was an advance guard of ten families from the Swiss congregations in Volhynia under the leadership of Andreas Schrag, one of the delegates of the year before. Several West Prussians with Wilhelm Ewert left at about the same time. Some thirty families left from Crimea, an entire congregation under their elder, Jacob Wiebe. Breaking up their homes on May 30, and crossing over to England by way of Odessa, Lemberg, and Hamburg, they took passage at Liverpool for New York. Later in the summer they were among the first to find their way to the plains of Kansas.

Alexanderwohl had been a center of the emigration movement from the start. Here the first meetings to discuss the situation had been held in 1872 and 1873. Elder Jakob Buller was one of the delegation of twelve. And at Alexanderwohl the Mennonites had met with General von Totleben. Most of the members of the Alexanderwohl congregation had decided upon emigration even before the return of their delegate from America. Difficulty in securing their passports, however, delayed their departure until the twentieth of July 1874. On the day they left, there were few farewell scenes because only seven families remained of the whole congregation. Besides the Alexanderwohler, a number of families from various other villages attached themselves to this group so that the total number in the party that left Hamburg for Kansas was over one thousand.

About the same time, too, the remainder of the Swiss group in Volhynia—about one hundred and fifty families—left for the new world. Many of these were poor and needed help from the relief agencies in America. Poorer and more miserable still than the Swiss were the Polish congregations from the region about Ostrog. Under their leader, Tobias Unruh, and with few possessions beyond their traveling expenses, they left en masse in midwinter for the raw prairies of Kansas. They remained a serious charge upon the Mennonite relief societies for several years. Added to these were the Hutterites, who left for the Dakotas, and several hundred families from the Bergthal, Fürstenland, and *Kleine Gemeinde* groups, all of whom located on the lands selected for them the year before by their delegates in Manitoba.

The bulk of the emigrants during this first year left in large groups, consisting sometimes of entire villages and settlements. But individuals from other villages attached themselves to these large parties. The emigration fever had not struck all communities with equal fervor. Enthusiasm for the adventure varied with the conservatism of the people, the economic conditions, and especially with the zeal of the different elders. It is estimated that by the end of the year 1874 about five thousand three hundred souls had located within the United States, mostly in Kansas, and about eleven hundred in Manitoba. The mass migration continued through the following year, though with less volume. The largest number this second year located in Manitoba. By 1880, the year that ended the period of grace, the movement had about spent itself. By this time about ten thousand Russian Mennonites had left their homes in the steppes of South Russia for the United States, and about eight thousand for Manitoba.

A Refuge in Central Asia

Not all of those who had scruples against accepting the proposed forestry service joined the trek to America. There were some who, hoping that the Russian government might still relent, delayed their going to the last minute. Others, dreading the long voyage overseas to a land unfamiliar and full of uncertainties, preferred a refuge nearer home, and preferably under the emblem of their own imperial Russian eagle. This seemed possible in several small semi-independent principalities in Asiatic Turkestan. Recently conquered by Russia, and now under Russian jurisdiction, they were not yet subject to the Russian militarization laws. Among these sensitive Mennonites were two small groups—one from the Trakt settlement in Samara, largely from the village of Hahnsau, and another, consisting of the followers of Abraham Peters, from the Molotschna settlement.

This strange desire to face eastward rather than to follow their brethren to the West was strengthened by certain chiliastic ideas which infected both groups as a result of the rather widespread distribution of the prophetic writings of Jung-Stilling, a German pietistic author well known among European Mennonites of that day, and other writings of a similar nature. Among the leaders of the movement who were influenced by this literature were David Hamm in the Hahnsau church; M. Klassen, a teacher in the local school of the same congregation; and Abraham Peters of an independent congregation in Molotschna.

At the same time, Claasz Epp, Jr., son of the leader of the West Prussian emigration to Samara in 1853, added impetus to the eastward adventure through a book of his own written in 1877. Here he explained to his own satisfaction the prophecies of Daniel and the mysteries of Revelation. This book went through three editions and was widely distributed among the Trakt Mennonites at Epp's own expense. According to Epp's interpretation, Christ would appear on earth in the year 1889, and somewhere in middle Asia was to be the gathering place for the faithful. The church, "Philadelphia," mentioned in Revelation to which the open door was to be revealed was, of course, his own little flock. As the year 1880, the close of the exemption period, drew near, preparations were made not only at the Trakt, Samara, but also in Peters's congregation in Molotschna, for the most visionary adventure in all Mennonite history—an exodus to a wild, unknown, barren land, in the heart of a Mohammedan population, to meet the Lord and inaugurate the millennium. At the same time, a special delegation from the group had succeeded at Petersburg in securing from the governor general of Russian Turkestan, General Kaufmann, permission to locate near Tashkent, with a promise of military exemption. Epp's followers accordingly sold their property, and started out in their quest for utopia.

Aulie Ata in Turkestan

They left in several groups. The first group of ten families, with seventeen wagons and forty horses, set out on July 31, 1880, heading toward the east, accompanied for a short distance by relatives, prospective fellow wanderers, and friends, chanting a well-known old hymn as a fitting pilgrim song, "Our journey is through the wilderness to the promised Canaan."

For fifteen long weeks these pious pilgrims continued to drag their weary way through the Ural Mountain passes, across vast stretches of barren plains, uninhabited save by bands of roving nomads. After enduring many hardships, they finally reached Kaplan Bek, some fifteen miles from Tashkent, where they prepared to camp for the winter. Twelve children had been buried along the way. In the course of the following months many more, children and adults, died of typhoid fever and other epidemics.

A little later in the fall another group of thirteen families from the Trakt settlement, and one of fifty-six families from the Molotschna, under the leadership of Abraham Peters, had started out. Both of these groups, after enduring hardships equally as distressing as those suffered by the first party, reached their destination late in the fall. The latter remained in Tashkent for the winter; the former joined their Samara brethren. These three different groups now, having an elder among them in the person of Abraham Peters, formed a common church organization. But when Epp, who still remained in Samara, heard of this arrangement, he protested vigorously, claiming that his flock needed no human leadership, but would depend entirely in all its decisions upon the guidance of the Holy Spirit. Because of this jealousy between the Samara and Molotschna groups, and also because of their conflicting views regarding the acceptance of noncombatant military service, they decided to separate. The following spring Peters's party, with a small contingent of the more liberal element of the Epp following, all told perhaps a hundred families, finally agreed to accept the same forestry service which was demanded of their brethren back in the home settlements, and which now, since the death of Czar Alexander II, was also being required in the Asiatic possessions of the empire. They were granted a tract of land at Aulie Ata, along the Talus River, in an elevated plateau near the foothills of the Alexander Mountains, about one hundred fifty miles northeast of the city of Tashkent. Before World War I this settlement consisted of five villages, with a Mennonite population of about one thousand, approximately half of whom at that time were members of the Mennonite Brethren persuasion.

In the meantime, the last of the wagon trains from Samara, consisting of seventy wagons carrying twenty-five families, under the leadership this time of Claasz Epp himself, got off to a late start in September for the promised land. Due to the lateness of the season, the party ran into fierce snowstorms, intense cold, and icy roads in their passage through the mountains. They experienced suffering even beyond that of the other groups. The repeated breaking down of their wagons, sickness, deaths, births, and even a wedding delayed their progress so that they did not reach Turkestan until after Christmas, after a long and tedious journey of four months. Here they decided to remain for the winter.

Ak Mechet in Khiva

The following spring Claasz Epp took charge of those of the Samara group who had not already decided to remain under the somewhat saner leadership of Abraham Peters, some sixty families all told. Epp hoped for a time that he might find refuge in nearby Bukhara, where Russian jurisdiction had not yet been completely established. However, the emir of Bukhara, claiming a scarcity of food supplies for his own people, ordered the wanderers out of his country. Entering Turkestan, where Russian military laws now were in force, they were requested by the governor general of that Russian tributary to send their young men into the army. Anticipating the winding-up of all things earthly before long anyway, Epp was not in a hurry to obey the order. As a result, his party was again sent across the border into Bukhara. After having been driven back and forth across the border repeatedly, and living in their wagons for months in a sort of neutral zone between these two jurisdictions, on land owned by a rather liberal-minded nobleman in 1882, they finally received an invitation from the khan of Khiva to locate on his private estate, where the party might enjoy the religious and political liberties they desired.

Regarding this invitation as the open door spoken of in Revelation, Epp decided to lead his weary seekers after the millennium to Khiva. Leaving Bukhara, traveling north, and crossing an intervening desert by camel and horse, the small party finally reached the river Lausan. They journeyed by boat until they reached the location selected for their settlement by the khan.

But this open door only proved to be a door to further trouble. The first settlement was located in a low, disease-infested swamp along the river bank. The first mud houses with thatched roofs were neither rain nor flood proof. Finding these nonresistant settlers an easy prey, the natives soon began to steal their horses, and finally, increasing in their boldness, entered their houses in nightly raids, stealing whatever they wanted, even in several cases attempting to carry away some of the young women. In one of these raids one of the settlers was murdered by the marauders. The young men finally demanded permission from the leaders to defend themselves with effective weapons, but the only means of defense allowed them by the church authorities was permission to remain up all night armed with canes and clubs. These weapons, however, were no match for the swords and guns of the bandits. The church authorities were finally forced to strain their extreme nonresistant principles to the extent of asking protection from the khan. He sent them a group of soldiers for a time, but as soon as these were withdrawn, the depredations were renewed. Finally, the much-harassed settlers were offered a refuge by the khan near the city of Khiva, in a small place called *Ak Mechet*, where they would no longer be troubled by robbers. A traveler passing through this little colony in 1899 stated that their population statistics then included thirty-seven families, with 140 souls, living in small adobe huts, and 132 in the nearby cemetery.

A Lesson from History

Meanwhile, millennialist Epp increased in fanaticism day by day. He was now guided largely in his everyday activities by his dreams and visions. For every mystery in Revelation he now found a new explanation. He himself was to be one of the two witnesses to the ushering in of the Lord's appearance on earth. A fellow minister with whom he had quarreled, and whom he had excommunicated from his church, now became the Red Dragon of Revelation, whose expulsion was annually celebrated for some years by his small flock. Other similar holidays were added, while less and less was being made of the old holy days. Soon Epp was to meet Elijah in the skies, and with him be transported bodily to heaven. The time was actually set for this important event; and an audience of both the faithful and doubtful gathered to bid the celestial traveler farewell. An altar had been set up behind which Epp took his stand, dressed in his ascension robes, all ready for the great departure. It is said by some of those present that he actually disappeared, but no one would verify the fact of his ascension.

Finally, the great day for Christ's appearance was also set, March 8, 1889. The day came and passed, and nothing happened. The disappointed prophet who evidently had given a satisfactory explanation for his reappearance on earth after his flight to heaven some time before, now again found little difficulty in giving good reason for his failure to gauge accurately the coming of Judgment Day. He had been given his earlier clue, he said, by the dial of an old wall clock whose hands had pointed to 89. But now in a vision he had been shown that the clock had indicated the wrong number since it had been leaning to one side. Upon being set upright, the dial pointed to 91. That was to mark the end—the year 1891. Epp reached the climax of his fanatical career when he finally claimed that he was the son of Christ, as Christ was the Son of God, thus constituting the fourth person of the Godhead. After this he insisted, in all his religious ceremonies, upon the use of the formula Father, Sons, and the Holy Ghost. This was too much, of course, for even his most simple-minded followers. Many had been cured of their foolish beliefs early in their adventure. In the 1880s a group had left him and come to America; some went back to Russia to take up the same type of forestry service they might have had in the beginning; others joined the Aulie Ata group. A mere handful, as misguided as Epp himself, remained with him almost to the last, but not quite. Finding their leader's idiosyncracies and blasphemies no longer bearable, the small remnant finally had to cast him out of their fellowship. He died in 1913. Disillusioned by their false hopes, and sobered by their harrowing experiences, this small group of deluded, though sincere, religious enthusiasts finally developed into a fairly stable congregation. Before World War I, the little flock consisted of some twenty-five families, huddled together on a land complex of some fifteen acres, and devoted to small hand industry, a little gardening, and daily labor in the nearby city of Khiva.

At the turn of the century, the disillusioned followers of Claasz Epp and Abraham Peters developed a longing "for the fleshpots of Egypt." Many got in contact with friends and relatives in the United States where they had moved from the Molotschna settlement and West Prussia. Through private help and organized Mennonite relief agencies they were helped to make this trip through the desert once more back to European Russia from where they proceeded to Kansas and Nebraska to get a new start in the prairie after the failure in the Central Asian deserts.

Some of them settled in the West Prussian Mennonite communities of Beatrice, Nebraska, and Newton, Kansas. Some others found their way to Oklahoma, Idaho, California, and Saskatchewan. Of all the Mennonite migrations around 1874 to 1885, this was the longest and the most difficult journey ever undertaken in order to remain faithful to the Mennonite heritage. At the same time it also turned out to be a monument of warning that not all leaders to a "promised land" can be trusted.

Forestry Service

The forestry service, which was offered the Mennonite young men in lieu of actual army duty was inaugurated in 1880. According to government regulations this work was to consist of planting and cultivating forests on the steppes of South Russia, and the term of service was to be for four years. Almost the entire expense of the enterprise was to be met by the Mennonites themselves. They were to erect the barracks, feed and clothe the foresters, heat and care for the buildings, and assume nearly all the necessary expenses involved. The government was to pay each forester twenty *kopeks*, the equal of about ten cents, each working day, and furnish only the working tools and implements.

To the church at large also was committed the entire spiritual and cultural welfare of the young foresters. This duty was performed by a resident minister appointed by the home church for each camp. A superintendent also was appointed to look after the economic and business interests of each unit. General oversight of the whole service in behalf of the church was entrusted to a Forestry Commission. In this way the cultural solidarity, which was such a characteristic feature of every phase of life in the closed communities of the Mennonite colonies, was not threatened by the forced absence of their young men serving the state during four very impressionable years.

The heavy expenses entailed by this service had to be borne virtually by voluntary contributions from the various congregations, since the Mennonite church did not constitute a corporate, legal body with power to levy taxes. That the congregations responded so freely is a tribute to their denominational loyalty, as well as to their realization that the preservation of their special privileges demanded of all the fullest cooperation. While the contributions were more or less voluntary, yet the churches worked out a plan which aimed to distribute the burden fairly and equitably among the various congregations on the basis of ability to pay. An assessment was levied upon both individuals and corporations according to the value of their property. Persons holding property worth less than five hundred *rubles* were exempt. The whole burden was thus assumed as a common obligation of the entire church.

For some years the average enrollment of foresters remained about four hundred, at an average maintenance cost of approximately seventy thousand *rubles*, not counting the original cost of the buildings. As the Mennonite population increased, the number of men in the service did also. In 1913 the entire number of young Mennonites serving the nation in this substitute capacity numbered about one thousand, at an expense to the church of three hundred fifty thousand *rubles*. This was a peacetime year, of course; in wartime there was a heavy increase in both men and money involved. This was the price in terms of money that the Mennonites of Russia were willing to pay for the preservation of their peace principles in the empire.

6. ERA OF EXPANSION

The General Conference

These common obligations, together with others, imposed upon and assumed by the Mennonite churches of the various branches, necessitated closer cooperation among the various independent congregations, and a more united organization than had prevailed heretofore. The churches in general had maintained their traditional congregational and independent type of church government, although almost from the start necessity frequently demanded the periodic meeting of the elders to discuss common religious, as well as secular, questions. These meetings, as already noted earlier in this chapter, were spoken of as the *Church Council* of the elders, and were more or less local in their nature, dealing with local religious matters. But now with the growing importance of such nonreligious problems as forestry, schools, the preservation of the German language, and other questions more or less political in their nature, the need for a more compact working organization, and a closer cooperation among the various loosely held together congregations than had hitherto prevailed, became evident.

The *General Conference of Mennonite Congregations in Russia* was founded November 17, 1882, at Halbstadt. The following year the first session was held. These conferences were attended by elders, ministers, and lay delegates. The first sessions dealt with problems confronting the congregations in connection with the newly inaugurated forestry service, the establishment of a theological seminary, and a conference periodical. The motto of the conference was: "Unity in essentials, tolerance in nonessentials, and charity in all things." In following this policy and in its ministration to the young men in forestry service, the conference achieved great success. The proposed conference seminary, although often discussed, never materialized. A semiconference paper, *Der Botschafter (Messenger)*, was begun by J. Thiessen, D. H. Epp, and H. A. Ediger in 1905. This paper had to be discontinued during World War I. During the years 1925-28, the conference published *Unser Blatt*, which also had to be discontinued because of governmental restrictions.

Later sessions extended the scope of the conference. In 1885 steps were taken to found an institution for the deaf. In 1893 a new hymnal was published. In 1898 a new confession of faith was adopted, which had been drawn up by a special commission appointed at an earlier session. Frequently the conference busied itself with matters of church discipline and personal conduct, though only in an advisory capacity. In one of the sessions, foresters were advised not to marry while in service, very good advice under the circumstances. In another, teachers were advised to conduct their Christmas exercises in the schools in a Christian spirit, and especially to exclude objectionable dramatic performances. In still another, marriage between cousins was discouraged. The session of 1910 held at Schönsee was of special importance. For the first time the Mennonite Brethren attended the conference, although they had been invited to do so some years before. Several ministers were also appointed to visit the congregations in Siberia, and distribute such financial aid among them as they needed.

By this time, too, the Russianization program of imperial minister Stolypin had proceeded so far as to demand that all the delegates to the conference be certified to the imperial government, that the record of the proceedings be published in the Russian language, and that an official representative of the government be permitted to attend every session.

In fact, during all this period, since 1880, the czars and their reactionary ministries, fighting back the rising tide of Russian nationalism and parliamentarianism which threatened the overthrow of the Russian autocracy, were becoming more and more suspicious of special liberties and privileges. In the attempt to stamp out the growing spirit of nationalism among the Poles, Finns, Lithuanians, Germans, and other minorities on the outskirts of the empire, increasingly drastic measures were invented. It was hoped thereby that all these foreign elements might ultimately become good Russians. The Russianization program increased control of schools, use of the Russian language, censorship of the press and free speech, and curtailment of political liberties in general. The Mennonites, of course, suffered with the rest.

Although the Mennonites took no active part in the radical social and political agitation of the times, yet they were severely attacked in the press and before the government officials by many of the Slavophiles who were envious of the special privileges which the Mennonites still enjoyed, and suspicious of their German culture. In the brief revolution of 1905, the Mennonites took no active part, although since they were given the right to vote they availed themselves of this privilege in the elections of the period. Being opposed to radical socialism, they, for the most part, joined the conservative Octobrist party in their political affiliations, largely because this party guaranteed religious toleration and freedom of worship, as well as freedom of the press for the minority groups. Two Mennonites sat in the Duma in the years immediately following. Abraham Bergmann, a landlord of the Octobrist party, was a member of the third and fourth sessions. Peter Schröder, from the Crimea, member of the Cadet party which was more liberal than the Octobrists, but also favorable to concessions to subject peoples, was a member of the fourth Duma.

In 1910 the General Conference appointed a *Glaubenskommission* which in 1912 was changed into a *Kommission für Kirchenangelegenheiten (KfK)*, and which in turn practically resolved itself in the critical days that followed into a commission on church and state relations. During the years just preceding World War I this commission, among other arduous tasks, found it increasingly difficult to convince the government that Mennonites were not a sect, but one of the regularly recognized religious confessions. As a sect they would not only lose their special privileges, but would become subject to all the arbitrary and brutal treatment then being meted out to all small religious groups that were branded with the name *sect*. Both as Germans and as a still-privileged religious group, the Mennonites were becoming objects of suspicion to many in high authority. The First World War and its results only increased their troubles.

Population Expansion: 1870-1914

As already noted, the original Mennonite settlements were granted more land than was immediately taken up by the model estates first distributed to each head of a family. This surplus land area was reserved as a communal reserve possession, the income from which was set apart as a special fund to be used later in helping to purchase new homes for the surplus population that had outgrown its original land allotment. This general colonial policy was followed from time to time throughout the century by the daughter and granddaughter colonies as their numbers increased.

And so, compact Mennonite communities expanded throughout southern Russia, always following the cheaper lands on the advancing frontier, toward the southeast into Asia, northeast toward the Urals, and over into western Siberia. The landseekers were frequently of the landless class, and often of the more radical, or at least of the more emotional, religious wings of the church. The Mennonite Brethren, the Templer, and other offshoots from the main body were frequently more numerous in the new settlements than in the old. The Russian Mennonites thus remained almost exclusively a farmer class; few went to the cities. As among country people generally, who live in frontier regions where land is plentiful and labor scarce, the population growth here reached almost its biological limits. The original Mennonite population in Russia in 1820 of about nine thousand had doubled about every twenty-five years. By 1914, including the emigrants to the American prairies and their descendants, they totaled about one hundred seventy thousand—a population growth unequaled anywhere else among Mennonites.

Church membership in Russia merely equaled the population figure. The growth of the church in Russia was rather a swarming of the people than an expansion of a faith. Forbidden by their charter of privileges to make converts among the natives, and kept from leaving their own religious group by the danger of losing their special privileges, and by their sense of superior culture, Mennonites tended to stay within the fold, and the fold did not expand beyond their own flesh and blood. Absent, too, were many of the causes that in other parts of Europe continually threatened the existence of the Mennonite faith—city life, persecution, a more attractive outside cultural environment, isolation in small scattered groups which made organized church life difficult, intermarriage with non-Mennonites, and other disintegrating influences.

Although a number of small daughter settlements had been established during the first half of the century, yet the large spreading of the people for economic or conscientious reasons did not set in until the 1860s or 1870s. Although some of these daughter settlements have been mentioned earlier in this chapter, a brief mention again of the most important may not be out of place here in the way of a summary.

The first daughter community of this period was established in the *Crimea*, in 1862, by a group of Molotschna landseekers, who had first become acquainted with the fair fields about Simferopol while engaged in transporting the wounded from the battlefields to their own Molotschna homes during the Crimean War. These first settlements grew into twenty-five villages, and a number of large estates, in some cases including thousands of acres, with a combined population in 1926 of about five thousand.

Fürstenland, which was purchased from the Grand Duke Michael in 1864 by a group of Chortitza Mennonites, consisted in 1911 of five villages and a population of eighteen hundred. *Borozenko*, founded in 1865, also by a group from Chortitza, consisted in 1915 of five villages with a population of six hundred. One of the largest communities of this time was at *Sagradovka*, in the province of Kherson. Purchased in 1871 by Mennonites from the Molotschna colony, in 1918 this settlement consisted of sixteen villages and six thousand souls, not including those living on large private estates. During the sixties, too, a number of religious dissenters from the main body of Mennonites, who incidentally also belonged to the poorer classes, established a colony in the *Kuban* and the *Caucasus*.

The large migration to America relieved the population pressure for a time, but in 1885 another Molotschna daughter colony was founded at *Memrik*, which by 1910 had expanded to a land area of about twenty-five thousand acres, and a population of some three thousand. After this, population expansion began on a generous scale to the frontier lands far to the east, near the European boundaries of the empire.

Beginning with the middle nineties, some thirty villages were located beyond the Volga in the provinces of *Orenburg* and *Ufa*, near the Ural foothills. The settlement of some fifteen villages made in 1901 in *Terek*, a province in the southeastern corner of European Russia in the Caucasus near the Caspian Sea, was a mistake. Drought and (paradoxical though it may seem) floods, famine, robbery by bandits, and malaria—all these nearly liquidated the settlement by 1914. Then came the war which permitted the bandits from the foothills to drive the whole settlement back again to the mother colonies.

At the beginning of the twentieth century, a large colonization movement started from both the younger settlements along the

RUSSIA

Volga, and the older colonies farther east toward the broad unsettled steppes of western Siberia. Each family here was aided by the mother colonies to the extent of four hundred *rubles*. During the years preceding World War I, 100 villages were established near *Tomsk* and *Omsk* on cheap lands in Siberia, at first far from the Siberian railroad. But later, with better transportation and market facilities, they expanded to a land area of over one million acres, nearly one-half the size of all the land occupied by the entire Mennonite population. There was a total population, in 1914, of fifteen thousand in Siberia.

Industrial Growth

Although the Mennonites remained largely a farming people, yet they did not entirely neglect their industrial interests. For the first half century of their life in Russia, their industrial needs were supplied mainly by their own local workshops. Nearly every village had its own craftsmen. The tastes of the early settlers being simple, their imports from the outside were few. They ground their own wheat in their own mills, grew their own wool which they wove into cloth, and cut their own clothes. They made their own crude farm utensils, constructed their own simple furniture, and built their own brick ovens. The statistics for Chortitza in 1819 show that in a population of 2,888 people, distributed through eighteen villages, there were two clockmakers, nine turners, two coopers, eighty-eight joiners, twenty-six carpenters, sixteen smiths, forty-nine weavers, one dyer, twenty-five tailors, and twenty shoemakers, besides several brewers, millers, and others, not all perhaps working full time at their respective trades.

However, with the coming of large-scale wheat growing, and the demand for better farm machinery during the latter half of the century, big flour mills and large factories arose. These not only supplied all the local needs, but their products in course of time found a ready market throughout all South Russia. Halbstadt and Chortitza both became famous for their production of fine machinery. In 1911 eight of the largest of these establishments furnished 10 percent of all such machinery of South Russia, and 6 percent of all that was manufactured in the entire Russian Empire. The largest of these Mennonite firms, Lepp and Wallmann from Schönwiese, produced in one year fifty thousand mowers and three thousand threshing machines besides thousands of gangplows and other farm equipment, all sent to the remotest parts of the empire.

The first large-scale industrialist was P. H. Lepp of Chortitza, who started a foundry in 1860, with A. Koop and C. H. Hildebrand as his apprentices. Chortitza remained the industrial center of the Mennonites. Other places were Alexandrovsk, Halbstadt, and New York. In 1911 the eight largest Mennonite factories producing agricultural machinery and implements accounted for 10 percent of the total output in South Russia and 6.2 percent of the output of all Russia. The following table lists these factories, showing total annual production in terms of *rubles* and personnel employed.

Firm	Annual Production	Total Employed
Lepp and Wallmann	900,000 *rubles*	270
A. J. Koop	610,000 *rubles*	376
J. G. Niebuhr	450,000 *rubles*	350
J. J. Neufeld & Co.	350,000 *rubles*	200
J. A. & W. J. Classen	241,000 *rubles*	145
Franz and Schröder	209,190 *rubles*	153
G. A. Klassen & Neufeld	200,442 *rubles*	140
J. Jansen and K. Neufeld	200,000 *rubles*	110

The Mennonites played a considerable role in the industrial and agricultural development of the country far beyond their immediate communities. The total number of Mennonite-owned larger factories in the Ukraine was twenty-six. Smaller industries manufactured brick, cheese, sausage, soap, starch, furniture, woven goods, and clocks, brewed vinegar and beer, and distilled whisky. Other industries included print shops (*Raduga* or "Rainbow," Halbstadt; H. E. Ediger, Berdyansk; II. A. Lenzmann, Tokmak; A. P. Friesen, Davlekanovo, Ufa), and mill construction.

One of the latest industries, which finally surpassed all others, was the milling industry. Over half of all industrial enterprises of the Mennonites in the Ukraine were connected with the milling industry. The foundation for this was the windmill, which had been transplanted from Holland to West Prussia and to Russia, originally having been used mostly to regulate the water level of the Low Countries. In the steppes of the Ukraine it was used to grind feed and flour. Some horse-driven mills were also in use. The introduction of large-scale wheat production resulted in the establishment of large motor- and steam-driven mills toward the close of the nineteenth century. Soon all Mennonite settlements were dotted with large four- to five-story flour mills, in which the wheat was ground into very fine flour to be shipped into all parts of Russia and abroad. By the beginning of World War I, Mennonite-owned flour mills could also be found in many railroad centers outside the Mennonite communities. Some of the centers were Chortitza, Alexandrovsk, Halbstadt, Ekaterinoslav, Nikopol, Kharkov, and New York. Some of the largest milling industries were Niebuhr and Company of Alexandrovsk, J. J. Thiessen of Ekaterinoslav, J. Siemens of Nikopol, and Peter Unger of New York, which had a total annual production of three million *rubles*. In addition there were many flour businesses, like the one owned by Heinrich and Peter Heese, Ekaterinoslav, which had an annual turnover of 1.5 million *rubles*.

In 1908 the Chortitza and Molotschna settlements had a total of seventy-three motor- and steam-driven mills, twenty-six factories of agricultural machinery, thirty-eight brick factories, and twenty other industries, making a total of 157. In addition there were 105 flour mills and fifty-four smaller enterprises, making a total of 316 industries. In addition, there were sixty-nine industries in the other Mennonite settlements of the Ukraine and an estimated two hundred in the eastern provinces of Russia, making a total of about five hundred eighty-five industries. Of this total, nearly sixty were located in the Chortitza and Molotschna settlements. The milling industry was the largest among the large-scale industries of the Ukraine (51.8 percent). The next largest was the production of agricultural machinery. This indicates that before World War I there was a definite trend toward industrialization among the Mennonites of Russia, particularly in the older settlements. The number of industries and large farm estates on one hand and the constantly growing laboring class on the other hand were indications of a shift in process which endangered the predominant rural pattern of life among the Mennonites of Russia.

In connection with the industrial development among the Mennonites of Prussia and Russia it should be stated that many inventions were made by industrial leaders. Naturally, in most cases the industrialist used patterns of western European agricultural machinery. Their inventions were possibly more or less limited to the adaptation of these machines to their particular environment and needs. Originally many of the industries developed from smaller home industries. Later the characteristics of the modern capitalistic developments became more evident. Many of the sons of the industrialists who had started on a small scale went to schools of engineering in Germany, Switzerland, and Russia in order to be better qualified to continue the enterprise of their fathers. During the last decades, the Mennonites of Russia had numerous engineers in various branches of industry.

Benevolences and Mission Interest

Mennonites everywhere, especially when living in large compact communities, have been inclined to hold themselves aloof from the usual political and social activities of their governments. They were never a burden to their government; they always took care of their poor and unfortunate. In Russia Mennonite self-sufficiency extended through the whole field of social welfare. They established their own hospitals, orphan homes, insurance companies, homes for the aged, and a school for the deaf. In 1911 Bethania, the first Mennonite mental hospital, was established.

With the revival of their religious life in the latter part of the past century, the Russian Mennonites also developed an interest in missionary effort. In 1881 the pioneer missionary Heinrich Dirks, returning from the Dutch Mennonite mission work in Sumatra, became the elder of the Gnadenfeld congregation, and traveling secretary of the mission cause. In this capacity he aroused a growing interest in missionary effort. The work in Russia was carried on through the Dutch Society in Amsterdam, in which the Russian Mennonites were represented by a board member. At the close of the century the Russian Mennonites furnished the major portion of both the money and the workers for this society. In 1910 there were ten active Russian Mennonite missionaries in Sumatra and Java, while four had returned on furlough. The Russian Revolution stopped all active participation of the Russian Mennonites in the Dutch enterprise, with the result that the work of the society almost came to a standstill. The Mennonite Brethren were also greatly interested in the missionary cause supporting at first the efforts of the Baptist mission boards.

Cultural Life

Culturally, the Mennonites were only slightly influenced by their Russian environment. They retained their German inheritance and Mennonite traditions to the end. Many of the elders and most of the older people spoke Russian with difficulty, if at all. By 1897 the statistics indicate that of the whole Mennonite population, only 486 were designated as being Russian speaking. The younger people were of course being taught the Russian language in the schools, and were absorbing more of the Russian culture. However, the language of the pulpit and of the books generally read remained High German. The language of everyday speech was the Low German of the Vistula Delta.

Being a farmer folk, the Mennonites of Russia were not of a

RUSSIA

literary turn of mind. They wrote few books. Their reading matter was imported from Germany, and consisted in the early days of the works of Menno Simons and Dirk Philips, the *Martyrs Mirror*, the *Wandelnde Seele*, perhaps Arndt's *Wahres Christenthum*, and in some circles the writings of Jung-Stilling, a German mystic. Occasionally a family would own a Dutch Bible and *Martyrs Mirror*, some of which were even taken along to North America. The Mennonite Brethren were inclined to read the works of the German Baptists. The contemporary writings of permanent value were those of the local Mennonite historians—Peter Hildebrand, D. H. Epp, Franz Isaac, Franz Bartsch, M. Klaassen, and P. M. Friesen.

The *Botschafter*, first published in 1905 at Ekaterinoslav, though privately printed, was the semiofficial organ of the Mennonites. The *Friedensstimme* published at Halbstadt for the first time in 1903, served the same purpose for the Mennonite Brethren. The publishing firm of *Raduga*, founded in Halbstadt by several enterprising Mennonites, published during its brief existence a number of books and tracts of interest to Mennonites which were widely distributed throughout the Mennonite settlements. A number of yearbooks also were published by these privately owned firms. But the anti-German legislation, and later the revolution, put an end not only to the German printed literature, but to all religious reading matter and ultimately to the publishing houses themselves.

The Ministry

Few religious people rise higher in their cultural achievements than the intellectual level of their spiritual leadership. For the largest part of the century the ministry in Russia was selected from the farmer group, and, being unsalaried, was chosen from the wealthier landowners. Thus the ministry enjoyed unusual influence over the destinies of the whole people during the first half of the century, when the landlords, ministers, and political leaders were all from the same economic class. Even though this high calling tended later in the century to become more highly specialized, yet preaching as a profession still remained very much an avocation to farming or teaching. As late as 1910 it was estimated that among the Mennonite Brethren only 5 percent of the preachers received financial support from their congregations; and even in this small number were included the itinerant evangelists who, of necessity, had to depend on such support. In this same year, in a list of 150 ministers from both branches of the church, 110 had only finished the elementary schools; forty had had some theological or pedagogical training in the *Zentralschul-*

en; and only one had university education. This changed drastically, as has been seen in the development in education.

Just before the war there were indications of rapid changes. Teachers in both the elementary and secondary schools were increasingly being impressed into the ministry. A number of young men were abroad in religious training schools preparing for service in the home churches. Sentiment in favor of financial support of the ministry was also rapidly gaining ground throughout the churches.

7. WORLD WAR I AND AFTER

We began this chapter with the observation that the Russian Mennonites, in the beginning, enjoyed in the land of the most autocratic ruler of all Europe a degree of religious toleration and civil liberty and special privileges unparalleled in all Mennonite history. But we must close it with the disappointing observation that since World War I they have suffered a succession of tragedies—political oppression, religious persecution, destruction of property, famine, disease, slave labor, deportation, family separation, and wholesale massacre—similar to those experienced by their Dutch forefathers in the darkest days of the Inquisition.

Of course many of the Mennonite leaders had realized for some time that the enjoyment of special privileges would become increasingly difficult. As already noted, control of their schools, exclusive use of the German language, local political autonomy, and other special concessions at first freely granted to the early settlers above those enjoyed by the native Russians, were already well on the way toward liquidation even before the war. Exemption from military service especially remained a source of envy on the part of their Russian neighbors, and was severely criticized by the public press. Speaking the German language, and in close cultural contact with the fatherland, the Mennonites were suspected and openly accused of German sympathies. During the early stages of World War I, it was seriously suggested by certain authorities that young Mennonite men be removed from their home settlements and sent to work in the coal mines of western Siberia. This plan fortunately was not carried out. Instead, within a few months after the opening of hostilities, the Mennonite leaders were summoned to Petersburg to arrange for some suitable service for their young men within the limits of the special privileges they were still enjoying. It was finally agreed that the Mennonites should either remain in the forestry service or enter the sanitary department, which was largely devoted to hospital work. About twelve thousand young Mennonites entered these two departments during the course of the war.

Noncombatant Service

Those choosing forestry were assigned guard duty, largely protecting the widely scattered forests of Russia against thieves, illegal hunters, fire, and other hazards. Their duties were by no means easy. Supported entirely by the home churches, given no government support and little attention, often poorly clad, poorly sheltered, and with inadequate food, they were unarmed, and often marooned in inaccessible forests, removed from their families. The lot of the forester, especially if married, was not a happy one. Repeated petitions from the churches at home requesting the government to adequately meet the needs of the foresters, and especially to provide for their families, if married, met with little response at Petersburg. After the downfall of the czarist regime in 1917, six thousand foresters returned home, and with the Treaty of Brest-Litovsk in 1918, this special form of Mennonite service to the state came to an end.

The other young Mennonites were attached to the sanitary department, forming complete hospital units, including stretcher bearers who gathered the wounded on the battlefield, and transported them to hospitals at Ekaterinoslav and Moscow. These units were reported to be among the best in the entire army. Some one hundred twenty Mennonites lost their lives on the battlefield and from disease while on duty during the war. The entire expense of the hospital, as well as the forestry work, was met by the Mennonites themselves without government pay. It was estimated that in the year 1917, the last year of the war, the churches collected over three million *rubles* for the support of their young men in these two forms of alternative service.

Regarded as Alien Germans

The Mennonites suffered with the other German colonists all the drastic anti-German legislation passed by the government of the czar during the early stages of the war against his subjects who had a German ancestry, even though three or four generations back. These colonists were regarded almost as enemy aliens rather than as loyal subjects. Everything German was tabooed—the use of the German language in public except in formal worship, the printing and distribution of German books and periodicals, and, to a certain extent, preaching or performing wedding or funeral services in German. Violation of these regulations invited punishment.

Mennonite worship frequently took on a liturgical character, consisting largely of Scripture reading without comment, singing, and prayer in the forbidden tongue. Some of the more ingenius preachers occasionally knew how to manipulate this form of service so that it would preach as effective a lesson as if it had been a regular sermon. Naturally these German suspects were carefully watched for any sign of supposed friendliness toward the common enemy. It is reported of one zealous native superpatriot, not well versed in German, that he once charged a certain Mennonite preacher with having prayed for Kaiser Wilhelm. But the preacher's only crime turned out to be that in the course of repeating the Lord's Prayer he had uttered the petition *Dein Wille geschehe* ("Thy will be done").

Hoping to escape the consequences of this anti-German agitation by disclaiming any German ancestry, the German-speaking colonists, both Lutheran and Mennonite, insisted that they were not real Germans. The Lutherans claimed a Swiss origin, while the Mennonites maintained that their ancestors had come originally from Holland, and only indirectly through Germany. The Russian authorities insisted, however, that since they were thoroughly saturated with German culture during their stay in West Prussia, and spoke only the German language, and read German books, they thus must be regarded as Germans.

The most vicious of these anti-German regulations was the decree, issued in 1915, ordering all the German colonists to sell their land equities within a year. Obviously this could not be done within such a short period during the wartime, except at ruinous prices; and few complied with the law. The penalty for noncompliance was forcible sale by the land bank at such a price as such a sale might bring. The meager returns were then turned over to the owner, not in hard cash, but in twenty-five-year bonds, of doubtful value at a low interest rate. Fortunately for the Mennonites, the land bank, like everything else Russian, worked slowly; and the process of liquidation had hardly begun when the Revolution of 1917 afforded a temporary breathing spell from all anti-German discrimination.

The expectation of relief, however, was tempered with certain misgivings among the German colonists, and especially among the Mennonites. While the anti-German land laws were not immediately enforced, yet they were not repealed. The very fact, too, that the new government claimed to rest upon a thoroughly democratic basis was not altogether reassuring to groups which had enjoyed special privileges under the czar's regime. For, strange though it may seem, the specially privileged minority frequently fare better under an autocracy than in a democracy. The Kerensky government was avowedly socialistic, though the exact form that the socialistic state was to take had not been thoroughly worked out. But there was much talk of political and economic reorganization along local and regional lines with a large degree of local autonomy. The German colonists, hoping that perhaps they might retain most of their old privileges by forming themselves into such compact German units, called a conference early in the summer of 1917 to take what steps their interests might dictate. The Mennonites were also represented at this congress of Germans.

Mennonite Congress

But it was soon discovered that although the Mennonites had much in common with the other German colonists, yet their demand for a continuation of exemption from military service under the new regime made it impracticable to work in complete accord with the other Germans, who were not insistent on such demands. The Mennonites, consequently, withdrew from this movement, and called a congress of their own, consisting of nearly two hundred delegates representing the whole Mennonite population. This congress met at Ohrloff later in the summer to take such steps as were necessary to protect their own special interests in the new order. B. H. Unruh, teacher in the commerce school at Halbstadt and a few years later to become one of the delegates of the *Studien-Kommission* sent to America, was elected as chairman of the congress.

Among the questions discussed were the relation of the Mennonites to the state, land liquidation, military exemption, schools, and other matters that affected the cultural and religious life of the Mennonite people. The debates, which sometimes became animated and earnest, showed that there was not always unanimity on all questions discussed. Some, the landless perhaps, were not unreservedly opposed to a limited program of land redistribution, though few were out-and-out socialists. On the military question, too, there was some difference of opinion on direct and indirect service. While some were absolutists, opposed to both indirect and direct service, others maintained that they owed the state every obligation except the actual shedding of blood.

Chairman Unruh, better acquainted with the political trends of the times than the average, called attention to the fact that the Mennonites had now come to the turning of the road in their exemption privileges, as well as in their nonresistant faith, and that it was not at all certain what they might expect from the new government. They must be prepared for the worst. The support of the young men in the forestry and sanitary service was also a matter of considerable interest, for the war was still on at this time, and, as already suggested, the Mennonites had to pay all the expenses of their young men in the field out of their own pockets. It was estimated that the total amount needed for the coming year would be about three million five hundred thousand *rubles*—over one million five hundred thousand dollars. The families left at home, where married men had to serve, had to be provided for also.

The fall of the Kerensky government in October of 1917 not only shattered the hope among the Mennonites of an immediate amelioration of their lot, but also inaugurated a three-year reign of terror and suffering among both Mennonites and the whole population of southern and eastern Russia almost unequaled among any civilized people in modern history. The Red and White armies fought back and forth across the Ukraine, confiscating the people's livestock and food supplies, and spreading disease epidemics everywhere. In the interim, lawless hordes, made up of the discontented and criminal classes, marched through the country at will, plundering, raping, and killing. Even when the Bolsheviks gained control of the situation and established a certain degree of stable political order, material conditions were not immediately improved, for the new rulers nationalized all the landed estates. The period of occupation by the German army during the summer of 1918 was a pleasant interlude. Worst of all among the Germans of the Ukraine was the rule of a certain Nestor Makhno, who held sway in this region during the winter of 1919 and 1920.

The Reign of Makhno

A few random incidents here must suffice as a suggestion of the horrors the Mennonites of this region suffered at this time. A victim of the terror from the village of Münsterberg in the Sagradovka colony wrote:

> Nearly everybody in our village was struck down or murdered—old men of eighty as well as infants of a few weeks. This terror lasted from 7 to 8 o'clock, and during that time ninety-six persons were killed. After the bandits had robbed us of all our money and such personal belongings as they could carry with them they set fire to the buildings and departed for the other villages.

In another village in this same district these fiends in human form cut off the heads of eight of the men they had killed, and then placed the heads on chairs as a gruesome welcome to the absent master of the house when he would open the door on his return. In Eichenfeld of the Nikolaipol settlement, eighty-one men and four women were killed in one night. Only two men of the entire population above sixteen years of age were left.

These were a few of the extreme cases, to be sure, but in nearly every village visited by the bandits there was wanton destruction of property, murder, and especially robbery. Even worse than this was the torture inflicted on men for the purpose of extracting the last penny from the victim, though the last penny had long been spent, and the wholesale rape of the women, who at the point of a gun frequently had to sacrifice their honor to save the life of a father or husband. Hundreds of men and women were killed outright in the Mennonite villages visited during these raids. Whole villages were destroyed, and an untold amount of personal property carried away. Other German non-Mennonite villages and some Russians in the Ukraine suffered the same fate. Chortitza, Zagradovka, and Nikolaipol suffered most among the Mennonite colonies, Molotschna somewhat less, and the Crimea and Memrik very little.

Disease and Epidemics

Hard upon this trail of robbery, murder, and rapine followed disease epidemics spread by the Red and White armies as well as by the robber bandits—spotted typhus, cholera, and venereal disease. While Makhno killed his hundreds, typhus and cholera claimed its thousands. The whole population of South Russia was affected. Here again the Chortitza district was the most intense sufferer. In the village of Chortitza, with a population of a little less than seven hundred, nearly everybody was sick. One hundred fifty died. Orie Miller, who as a representative of the American Mennonite Relief committee visited the Molotschna Mennonites soon after this period, said that by March 1920, in the Chortitza district with a prewar Mennonite population of fifteen thousand, many of the nineteen villages were completely destroyed with no inhabitants left whatever; 380 persons were shot or struck down and tortured; 92 women raped; 42 houses burned; 111 homes destroyed; 113 horses taken as well as 1,073 hogs, 40,000 bushels of wheat, and 10,000 bushels of barley. Those stricken with typhus numbered eight thousand, of whom twelve hundred died. These statistics indicate the terrible conditions of the time in the Mennonite settlements. Under such distress it is needless to say that there was little economic activity or social functions or much of organized religious services. All organized life was completely paralyzed.

Selbstschutz

It was inevitable that the traditional doctrine of passive resistance should be put to a severe test when challenged by robber bands who threatened to murder their men and ravish their women. The young men of the Molotschna district, where seemingly there always had been less regard for traditions than among the Chortitza Mennonites, did not stand the test. Even before the robber bands came, the young men in this colony, influenced largely by the Germans during their brief occupation of the Ukraine in 1918, organized themselves into a *Selbstschutz*, a protective band, for the purpose of offering resistance to whatever dangers might threaten them in the future. At the time, no doubt, there was perhaps little thought that force might ever be needed or used. But when the bandits actually appeared in the region the following year, the *Selbstschutz* joined the neighboring Lutheran colony in an organized attempt to resist the invaders. For a short time they gave a good account of themselves, but in the end the invading force was too much for them. Both the Lutherans and Mennonites had to disband and leave their colonies to the mercy of the invaders. In later years, the older generation of Mennonites as represented in conferences officially condemned the *Selbstschutz* as a tactical blunder, as well as a violation of their traditional peace principles.

Feeding the Hungry

It would seem that the terrors of civil war, the ravages of banditry, the persecutions of a tyrannical and antireligious government, and the devastations caused by disease epidemics—all the result of man's greed and lust—would be enough grief for any people to bear at any one time. But more was to come. In 1921-22 followed a series of dry years which resulted in the worst famine in all Russian history. South Russia had often experienced both drought and famine before, and under normal conditions these were never serious. But conditions now were not normal. The loss of livestock and of horses, without which farming operations could not be carried on; the heavy grain requisitions demanded for export, leaving very little surplus for an emergency, and often not enough for the next year's seeding; the physical weakness of both man and beast; the careless management of many of the larger estates resulting from the replacement of industrious farmers by inefficient city-bred managers; the collapse of the whole transportation system; and above all the hopelessness of it all—all this now, together with two years of hot winds and drought, made a combination that spelled disaster for nearly a third of the whole Russian population. It took the lives of millions of native Russians and thousands of Germans and Mennonites. The Mennonites, because of their superior industry, fared better than the other Russians, though the list of those who died of starvation, and as a result of famine, was long.

It is not the intention here to present a statistical account of the famine casualties. A few pen pictures here and there must suffice to give the reader a glimpse, at least, of its terror among both the native Russians and the Mennonites. In *Feeding the Hungry* A. J. Miller, director of the American Mennonite Relief work during this period, graphically described the famine conditions in the Russian villages. Speaking of his first arrival in the starving Mennonite colonies, Miller said, "At Alexandrovsk we were received as messengers from heaven."

Famine and poverty lasted longer in the eastern settlements than among the Mennonites of South Russia. As late as 1923, after conditions had already greatly improved in the Molotschna and Chortitza areas, a report from the Siberian Mennonites stated that among the seventeen thousand Mennonites in those settlements five thousand were without food of their own.

It is small wonder that as a result of these cumulative disasters the Mennonites should again seek a way to some other promised land. The native Russians had no possibility of escape. They would have to remain and carry on as best they could. But to the Mennonites, limited in number, whose whole past history for four hundred years was characterized as a series of treks from one promised land to another, escape from the Russian terror through another mass migration seemed possible and inevitable. This movement had already gained considerable momentum before the famine of 1921. The Siberian Mennonites had already written their Mennonite brethren in Amsterdam suggesting a loan from either the Dutch Mennonites or the Dutch government, running up into the millions, sufficiently large to transport the whole Mennonite population in Siberia, some twenty-five thousand, to one of the East India islands. The amount of money involved was, of course, too large to be given serious consideration by the Dutch Mennonites.

In the meantime, in the early summer of 1920, the Molotschna Mennonites had sent a commission called a *Studien-Kommission* to America. Headed by B. H. Unruh and A. A. Friesen, both teachers in the Halbstadt schools, the purpose was to investigate the possibilities of aid for a mass migration out of Russia, preferably to America, as well as help to build up their economic life again in their native land. But to many, even before the famine, it was evident that the Mennonites were doomed in

Russia. It was this commission that first brought to America and the outside world the news of the actual condition of their Mennonite brethren.

Mennonite Central Committee

Although the plight of the Russian Mennonites had not yet reached its most acute stage by this time, yet the commission succeeded in arousing a great deal of sympathy in behalf of their brethren among the Mennonites in the various countries they visited. Before the end of 1920, committees had been organized in all of them for the purpose of rendering such help as might be needed. The Germans, hard-pressed themselves economically, could not do much except to take care of Mennonite refugees who had crossed the border; but they organized a special commission, *Deutsche Mennoniten-Hilfe (DMH)*. The Dutch Mennonites rendered very substantial aid during the famine years through an organization with the same name as the well-known commission which helped the Swiss Mennonites to migrate to Pennsylvania in the early part of the eighteenth century, namely— "Commission for Foreign Needs." A. Binnerts of Haarlem was chairman, and T. O. Hylkema of Giethoorn was secretary. In a united effort the American Mennonites, too, in the late summer of 1920, formed the "Mennonite Central Committee" with P. C. Hiebert of Hillsboro, Kansas, a member of the Mennonite Brethren Church, as chairman. Levi Mumaw of Scottdale, Pennsylvania, represented the (Old) Mennonite Church as secretary; and Maxwell Kratz, a Philadelphia attorney, represented the General Conference Mennonite Church. Later, other members were added to represent other Mennonite conferences.

The major part of the relief work fell to the North American Mennonites. The first task of the Mennonite Central Committee (MCC) logically was to find out just what was needed. In this initial work, as well as in all the preliminary stages, the (Old) Mennonite Church took a leading part, since they already had a well-organized relief work in operation in the war zones, and had just established a Near East relief station in Constantinople on the very threshold of Russia. This work was largely in the hands of a group of devoted young men and women, mostly graduates of Goshen College. Entrance into Russia at this time was both difficult and dangerous, since the country was still in the throes of a bloody civil war. The MCC naturally turned to the group at Constantinople to furnish volunteers for the attempt to reach the Mennonite settlements. Orie Miller and Clayton Kratz, both Pennsylvanians, and Arthur Slagel, of Illinois, undertook the task. They reached Halbstadt just as Wrangel's army was driven to the south by the Bolsheviks. Miller and Slagel escaped with Wrangel's army, but Kratz unfortunately remained a bit too long in Halbstadt and was never heard of again.

By this time it had become evident that South Russia was facing a serious food shortage, though the worst was not yet anticipated. All the energies of the various Mennonite organizations were now directed toward relief, and emigration for the moment was forgotten. In the spring of 1921 the MCC appointed A. J. Miller, who had spent a year with the Friends Service Unit in France, and had recently been transferred to the American Red Cross work in the Crimea and Constantinople as director of Russian Mennonite relief. Miller's first task was to get in touch with the Soviet officials in Moscow and get official permission to carry on this work of mercy among the Mennonites. This was not easy, for the Soviet government was decidedly suspicious of all foreign influence. By dint of infinite patience and consummate tact, and after repeated contacts with the Red Cross organizations, the American Friends Service Committee and the Hoover American Relief Administration at Paris, London, and Geneva, the new director was finally able, late in 1921, to sign a contract with Kamenev in Moscow, and later in the winter with the Soviet authorities in the Ukraine, permitting the Mennonites to come to the assistance of their starving brethren in Russia. Miller at the same time represented the Mennonites of Holland, who had also been negotiating through their representative Jacob Koekebakker for a similar agreement with the Soviets. Koekebakker was compelled to return home before he had accomplished his task, and so authorized the American director to sign for the Dutch. One of the conditions in this agreement with the Soviet authorities was that there should be no discrimination between Mennonites and others who might need help in the regions where relief work was to be carried on. The American and Dutch organizations chose as their fields of operation those areas in which the population was mostly Mennonite, thus most of their efforts were directed toward the helping of their own brethren. But within these areas all were equally taken care of, irrespective of creed or race.

A full year had now passed since the first efforts had been made to enter Russia for relief work. The famine by this time had assumed the proportions of a major calamity. The home organizations immediately began to collect funds and clothing, and to organize the working personnel. Following the example of the American Relief Administration (ARA) with whom the American and Dutch Mennonites had become affiliated, the American Mennonite Relief (AMR) workers on the field established feeding kitchens in the Mennonite villages and distributed food, first among the most needy. The detail work was left to local committees selected by the villages themselves. The Dutch carried on their own work separately. Actual feeding operations were started first in the Volga area and were not begun in the Ukraine until March 1922. By May the American kitchens were feeding twenty-five thousand persons daily. The peak was reached in August when forty thousand rations were issued daily. This work was continued for three years, though the need became gradually less after the fall of 1922. The kitchen feeding was discontinued after the summer of 1924, though director Miller remained in Russia for another two years to liquidate the work in the Ukraine, and also to direct further relief efforts in Siberia where famine conditions continued longer than in South Russia. Besides these feeding operations, many individual Mennonites in America sent food packets to friends and relatives and others in Russia. The AMR also sent some fifty Ford tractors into the Mennonite settlements to take the place of the large number of draft horses that had been stolen or confiscated during the period of the civil wars.

It is estimated that about one million two hundred thousand dollars were collected by the various branches of the American Mennonites during this period for this work, and several hundred thousand by the Dutch. How many Mennonites actually died of starvation and of the indirect results of famine is a matter of some difference of opinion; but proportionately fewer Mennonites died than the Russians who, as we have already noted, died by the millions. But that the help from the American and Dutch Mennonites came just in the nick of time, there can be no question. Without it, the death toll would undoubtedly have been increased by the thousands, a fact which the Russian Mennonites have repeatedly acknowledged and for which they have often expressed their profound gratitude.

The Trek to Canada

Although the famine may have delayed the emigration movement for several years, it only resulted in strengthening the determination of large groups of Mennonites to find refuge from their troubles in some more favorable land. The economic conditions, to be sure, were improving somewhat. The New Economic Policy (NEP) also gave some promise that the Soviet government would proceed more cautiously and less radically in its policy of socialization of industry and agriculture than had originally been planned. But there was enough left of the whole program and its philosophy of life that many were determined to leave. This program included complete nationalization of the land, thorough liquidation of the large landowners, and redistribution of the land of the smaller farms. It included nationalization of all church property, complete state control of the educational system, atheistic propaganda designed to root out all consciousness of God and religion from the minds and hearts of the youth of the land, and the elimination of the religious leaders.

But where were the Mennonites to go? Several countries suggested themselves. The Mennonites of Siberia inquired about the East Indies. Some thought of Mexico, but Mexico just at this time was also undergoing a revolution too much like the one in Russia to be given serious consideration. The United States, it was found, prohibited the entrance of a larger number of people. However they received financial assistance from America. Canada remained, but here, too, there were difficulties. Because the Mennonites had claimed and were granted military exemption during the war, the Canadian government, prompted by public opinion, had prohibited the further immigration of Mennonites and Hutterites. But the war was over now. The government remembered that the Mennonite immigrants of 1874 had proven themselves the best farmers in all of Canada. And the Canadian Pacific Railroad still had vast stretches of sparsely settled prairie land in need of thrifty settlers.

And so the newly formed Canadian Board of Colonization (CBC), under the presidency of David Toews, found little difficulty in securing a repeal of the Order in Council which had prohibited Mennonite immigration, as well as the order which had repealed the military exemption decree of 1873. Seemingly it was not difficult either to induce the Canadian Pacific Railway to agree to transport a limited number of Mennonites to Canada on credit, with only the assurance of the CBC that the railway company would be finally reimbursed for their outlay as security. One condition proved a bit troublesome later on. The Canadian government insisted upon a rigid health inspection of all proposed immigrants at some European port of departure. They were especially concerned about trachoma, a prevalent eye disease among south Europeans at this time.

Only one thing more was left to make the migration possible—the consent of the Russian government. But the Soviet authorities, not too willing to lose some of their best farmers in their attempt to revive Russian agriculture, and perhaps not too anxious to have the world know that some of their most peaceful and industrious citizens were eager to escape from the glorious possibilities of the Soviet paradise, were slow in granting the necessary passports to prospective emigrants. And furthermore,

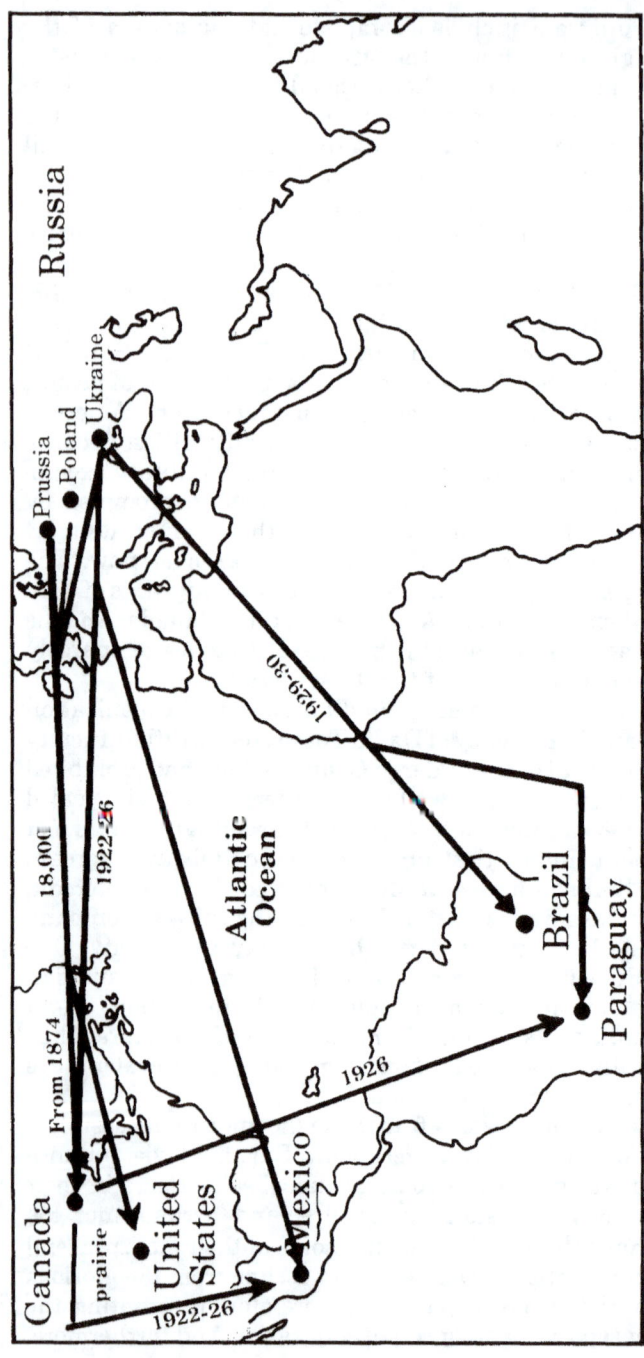

Mennonite Migration from Russia, 1874-1930. Beginning in 1874 one-third of the Mennonites in Russia (18,000) immigrated to the prairie states and provinces. Mennonites from Volhynia, Galicia, Poland, and Prussia joined them. After the Russian Revolution some 25,000 Mennonites left Russia, going mostly to Canada, Brazil, and Paraguay. Some went to Mexico and the United States.

since the Canadian government had not recognized the Soviet rule, the Soviets refused to grant the Canadian health inspectors the right of making their inspections in Russian ports. But a way out that satisfied both Russia and Canada was eventually found. Instead of going out by way of the Black Sea ports, which would have been the logical routes to be taken by the Mennonites of South Russia, they were routed by way of Riga, with the first Canadian inspection on the Latvian side of the border. Once leaving Russia, emigrants were not to be sent back in case they did not pass the rigid health inspection tests of the Canadian doctors. Germany now generously offered to provide a temporary refuge in the former military training grounds at Lechfeld, for all such Mennonite emigrants who might not be able to pass the Canadian inspection regulations, and who at the same time could not be returned to Russia. Southampton, England, became another inspection port and detention camp for rejected emigrants.

Finally, after two years of tedious negotiation with the government officials and colonization societies, and patient waiting on the part of anxious prospective refugees, the way was opened for the long-awaited escape to a better land. Among the Russian Mennonites, a leading part in the whole movement was taken by the two agricultural societies—the *Verband der Bürger holländischer Herkunft in der Ukraine (BhH)* in South Russia under the presidency of B. B. Janz; and the *Allrussischer Mennonitischer Landwirtschaftlicher Verein (AMLV)*, under the leadership of Peter Fröse and C. F. Klassen.

The first contingent of emigrants to leave Russia, in the summer of 1923, came from Chortitza and consisted of former owners of large estates, refugees of various sorts, ministers who had been disfranchised, and victims of the civil war, banditry, and the famine. Two-thirds of this first group was transported to Canada on credit of the Canadian Pacific. Coming from Chortitza, this group acted somewhat independently from the BhH, which had its headquarters in the Molotschna and which concerned itself largely with the matter of the mass migration of all the Mennonites, rather than of any individual groups.

Although the Canadian Colonization Board was unable to meet its obligations to the Canadian Pacific in 1923, yet the railroad company agreed to an even more liberal contract for the year 1924, providing for the immigration of five thousand persons. About four thousand came in this year, mostly from the Molotschna colony and other parts of the Ukraine. Some were again left at Lechfeld and Southampton.

The detention at these temporary refugee camps of those who

failed to pass the health inspection often caused real hardships. Families were separated, and the victims of trachoma and other bodily ailments often were detained for months, and perhaps years, before they were considered well enough to enter Canada. All this was at the expense of the Canadian Board of Colonization. During the emigration period, hundreds of unfortunates had to spend more or less time at these recuperation stations. However, practically all in course of time reached their objective, though some after considerable delay.

In 1925 four thousand left Russia, this time from most of the Mennonite settlements throughout the Soviet Republic, though most of them were again from the Ukraine. The peak was reached in 1926 with six thousand emigrants. By 1927 the movement had run its course. Less than nine hundred left that year, and only three hundred the year following. The later migration of 1930 was directed largely to Paraguay and Brazil, though some again went to Canada.

By 1930 it was estimated that a total of twenty-one thousand Mennonites had been transported to Canada, nearly all with the assistance of the Canadian Pacific Railway, about two-thirds of them on credit.

A Losing Struggle

Only a small portion of those desiring to emigrate were able to do so. The rest were doomed to remain and salvage as much as possible of their material possessions and their religious and cultural heritage. It was a losing fight from the start. It may be well for the reader to remember here that all Russian people—Russians, Germans, and Mennonites alike—shared the harrowing experiences recorded above, and all alike were subject to the drastic Soviet program. If Mennonites suffered more than others it was only because they were more prosperous and more consistently and unalterably religious.

The large estates of Russian noblemen and Mennonite landowners, of course, were confiscated almost from the start, as well as the communal lands of the Mennonite and other German colonies. These latter were generally distributed among the poorer peasants, often bringing into the Mennonite villages an element that later became an important factor in the liquidation of the distinctive features of Mennonite culture from these villages. The growing food shortage and the reluctance of the peasant to give up his small tract was responsible for the New Economic Policy (NEP) which tended to slow up the whole process of collectivization considerably.

There was a continual reduction by the state in the size of the individual farms, to make room for still more land-hungry peasants. The former model farms of one hundred seventy-five acres were reduced at first to sixty-five acres, and finally to thirty-five. The fear of further reductions and the claim that a farm of this size was not sufficient to support a family, together with the threat to their social and religious life, were among the important causes given by the Mennonites for their desire to emigrate.

Realizing that a radical change in the whole social order was inevitable and that a certain degree of collectivization was forthcoming, the Mennonite communities hoped at first that they might retain their solid and compact community life within the bounds of a collective management. They thought they might be able to organize themselves into Mennonite cooperatives and collectives. The best known of these attempts was the founding of a series of agricultural cooperatives including all the Mennonite colonies of the Ukraine under the presidency of B. B. Janz in 1921. This organization had the somewhat cumbersome title *Verband der Bürger holländischer Herkunft in der Ukraine* which has been already referred to as the BhH. The original purpose of this society which had been given legal status by the Soviet authorities, was to revive the agricultural prosperity of the Ukraine once more after the disastrous effects of the civil wars and famine. This mild form of cooperation, it was hoped, would satisfy the Soviet demand for collectivization. The BhH also took a leading part in the emigration movement, but finding that the government was displeased with these activities, it again gave itself over entirely to its original purpose.

But if the Mennonites thought that they might remain a collective state within a collective state, and thus retain possession and control of their compact land areas, they were doomed to bitter disappointment. Due partly to the jealousy of the German section of the Communist party because of envy of Mennonite industry, and partly to the Mennonites' refusal to admit non-Mennonites to their cooperatives, the BhH was bitterly attacked by the local and metropolitan press. The result was that finally, in 1925, the Soviet government demanded such a thorough reorganization of the BhH that, if obeyed, it would entirely lose its original purpose. In 1926 the organization was completely liquidated.

The *All Russian Mennonite Agricultural Union, (AMLV)*, representing all the Mennonite settlements, has already been mentioned. This organization concerned itself largely with improving the livestock of the Mennonites and in the selection of the best seed strains, though during the emigration period the union also gave valuable assistance to that movement. In fact

Peter Fröse and C. F. Klassen, the leaders, represented the Mennonites before the Soviet authorities in Moscow on every question that affected the Mennonites' welfare—military exemption, emigration, and excessive taxation of churches and preachers, among others. This organization also had to cease its activities in 1928 because, as the authorities said, it hindered the progress of collectivization among the Mennonites. With the introduction of the Five Year Plan under Stalin in 1928, all hope among the Mennonites of salvaging their economic institutions vanished forever.

Religious Freedom Restricted

One of the objectives of the Communist government was the complete destruction of the power of the established Russian Orthodox Church as an institution, on the ground that the church had always been one of the chief supporters of the old economic and social order under the czars. One of the first official acts of the Soviet regime, in 1918, was the complete separation of church and state. The priests and other ecclesiastical officials of the hierarchy were taken off the payroll of the state and set adrift in the world to make a living as best they could. Soon after, the vast property holdings of the church were confiscated and the buildings nationalized, rented to the church at a high rent, and taxed heavily. Many of the churches were closed as being superfluous, and turned into antireligious museums, social clubs, or public offices. Churches used for worship and congregations had to be registered. Not every Mennonite village had a meetinghouse. It was customary frequently to hold meetings in the schoolhouses. This now was forbidden. Sunday as a day of religious observance was abolished; it was no longer even a holiday. Church officials, priests, and ministers who protested too strongly against this ruthless liquidation of church property and religious freedom were arbitrarily arrested as counterrevolutionaries and imprisoned, fined, exiled, or shot.

Not only the established church but religion itself as "an opiate of the people" was to be entirely rooted out of the hearts and minds of the people as rapidly as possible. And so the antireligious crusade was not only directed against the state church but against all the other churches as well. Mennonites shared all the persecution of the rest of the churches and were equally subjected to the same antichurch and antireligous legislation.

Especially vicious was the treatment accorded priests and ministers. Disfranchised and outlawed, they were denied citizenship in the new order, and as such they were not entitled to bread cards, the right to purchase goods at the Communist stores, and other privileges that were almost essential to life during the trying times of the early years. Ministers could not be teachers, which was especially serious for many of the Mennonite ministers who earned their living by teaching. They could not join the guilds and cooperatives into which finally all industry and labor was organized. These disabilities applied to their families also. Ministers and teachers were therefore heavily represented in all the emigrations of the Mennonites during the whole period.

The churches finally were denied the right to exercise any organized charitable work, hospitals, poor relief, children's homes, insurance, or any of the various philanthropic work which was such a common part of the Mennonite churches in Russia.

The Soviet government took over entire control of the schools, liquidated private church schools, and forbade all religious instruction in the schools and of youth under eighteen in the churches. To the Mennonites, to whom religious instruction of their young people was one of their major religious concerns, this became a special ground for complaint. This refusal of the right to teach their children religion may have been one of the reasons for the increased interest during this period among the Mennonites in choral singing, which might in a way, by the use of religious chorales and other songs of a high moral content, become a substitute among the young people for the religious instruction denied them. But in the end, even attendance at these choral renditions was forbidden the young people as well as teachers in the public schools.

The whole school curriculum was changed under the new system. Instead of teaching the usual cultural subjects, teachers now were supposed to be promoting the new order, and agents for carrying out the agricultural and industrial program of the local Soviets. Church and parents lost all control of the education of their children. Mennonite teachers in the Mennonite villages were gradually replaced.

A Petition that Miscarried

Of course not all these regulations were rigidly enforced everywhere before 1928. Something was left to the local governmental authorities. In fact, during the New Economic Policy period in 1924 and 1925, it seemed for a time that the Mennonites might even recover a measure of their former religious freedom. What the Mennonites hoped for is perhaps well expressed in the following petition sent to Moscow on May 23, 1924, by the *Kommission für Kirchenangelegenheiten (KfK)*:

1. Complete freedom of religious worship and assembly for young and old.
2. The unconditional right of children and young people to assemble for religious worship and instruction and choral renditions.
3. The establishing of Mennonite children's homes under religious training.
4. Repeal of the special taxes on church buildings and ministers, and the right to erect new church buildings.
5. Permission to furnish the churches with a much-needed supply of Bible and other religious literature and periodicals.
6. Bible training courses for the ministry.
7. The schools to follow at least a neutral course, permitting neither religious nor antireligious propaganda.
8. Exemption of Mennonites from military service and military drill in lieu of some other noncombatant, constructive service; and the privilege of substituting an affirmation for the oath wherever an oath is officially required.

Even though the time seemed propitious for making these demands, only one of them was ever granted, the permission to import a certain number of Bibles.

Through the efforts of the KfK, however, permission was granted the following year to hold a session of the *Allgemeine Bundeskonferenz* in Moscow. Permission was given at the same time to publish a religious journal, *Unser Blatt*, as well as to establish a Bible school. The Bible school never materialized, however, since it had to be located in Moscow, far removed from the country communities of the Mennonites, and consequently would be of doubtful practical value. *Unser Blatt* lasted only a few years, being forced to suspend by government order with the advent of the Stalin regime (1925-1928).

This general conference, *Allgemeine Bundeskonferenz*, called with the special consent of the Soviet government, was forced to hold its sessions in the capital city, under the direct surveillance of government representatives. The first of its kind since the close of the war and, with the exception of a Ukrainian All-Mennonite Congress held the next year at Militopol, the last general meeting of the Mennonites ever to be held in Russia, the conference devoted its efforts largely to a discussion of the various problems then threatening the very existence of the Mennonite church, and to the religious freedom of its members. These problems were listed in the petition just mentioned. In addition, the need of religious instruction of the children in the home, the need of consecrated spiritual leadership, Christian marriage, visiting evangelists, religious songs in worship, the cultivation of choral societies, and the training of capable directors, Bible study among the membership, and the missionary enterprises of the church were discussed. This conference marked the peak of Mennonite hopes and expectations of rebuilding their spiritual life and religious institutions again.

During this period, however, the Mennonites lost control of their local government. The simple and economical rule of the village *Schulze* and the district *Oberschulze*, with their assistants, was replaced by inefficient foreigners who had very little knowledge of the art of government, and no sympathy for the governed. Much of the detailed work of carrying out the policies of the central Soviet authorities at Moscow was left to the local governments. But even in the Mennonite villages where the population might still be almost entirely Mennonite, the majority had little to say to questions that were submitted to the people for decision. In the first place, more or less of foreign settlers had been introduced into the villages by the land liquidations and redistributions. Former *kulaks* (wealthy landowners), ministers, teachers, and many church leaders had been denied the right to vote, with the result that the political management of the villages often fell entirely into the hands of a foreign Communist minority entirely out of sympathy with Mennonite ideals.

Military Exemption

After the Revolution of 1917, Mennonites and other nonresistant groups negotiated with the government for exemption from military service. In October 1918 Trotzky issued a decree according to which religious conscientious objectors who upon investigation were found sincere could be exempted from military service to render some form of alternative service.

In the meantime, those having religious scruples against participation in war organized the United Council of Religious Fellowships and Groups at Moscow, under the chairmanship of Vladimir Tchertkov, a follower of Leo Tolstoy. This body served as an intermediary between the government and the conscientious objectors to war. Peter Fröse of the AMLV was a Mennonite representative in this United Council. Its function was to issue certificates to the individual conscientious objector with which he appeared before the People's Courts to be examined. The council succeeded during the Russian Civil War of 1919 to 1920, in freeing some eight thousand conscientious objectors, many of whom were Mennonites, from military service. In December 1920 this procedure was discontinued, and the United Council was forced to cease its activity. However, the People's Courts continued during the NEP period to examine and exempt conscientious objectors. The KfK and the ministers assisted their men of draft age in obtaining exemption from military service.

Although the early laws provided for exemption from military service, these laws were not universally applied. Unknown hundreds of conscientious objectors suffered imprisonment during the brief period of the functioning of the United Council. It was later discovered that more than two hundred conscientious objectors had been shot because of their refusal to bear arms. These cases, however, came to the attention of the United Council too late for it to be of assistance.

Article 133 of the Stalin Constitution of 1936 states, "The defense of the Fatherland is the sacred duty of every citizen of the U.S.S.R." By this time all organized congregational activity was being dissolved, as most of the leaders were being sent to concentration camps. When the Second World War broke out, exemption from military service had ceased. The men who were still available in Mennonite settlements were drafted into military service or into labor battalions.

Those young men who were granted exemption from military service after the Revolution did not enjoy the privileges of the young men serving in hospital and forestry units prior to this time. They were now classified with the "enemies" of the people and forced to do labor in secluded areas, similar to the concentration camps. They lived and worked under the watchful eye of trained communists. The chief purpose of this arrangement was to break the resistance of the conscientious objectors and make them willing to enlist in the army.

A number of years before World War II this alternative service had been discontinued. The total impact of the witness and suffering of the Mennonite conscientious objectors under the Communist regime will probably never become known.

The Five-Year Plan

Reference has been made in the pages just preceding to the Stalin Five-Year Plan, and its important bearing on the fate of the Mennonites. This plan did not introduce a new program of social theory but rather inaugurated an extensive drive to hurry to completion the original program of socialization and collectivization of all industry and agriculture. As we have seen, collectivization of agriculture was given a breathing spell in the early 1920s because of the opposition of the peasants. But now agriculture as well as the remaining industry must come completely under the control of the state within five years.

Special attention in this program was directed to the *kulak* (fist), the more prosperous farmer. A common method of exiling these farmers was to levy upon them contributions of grain or money beyond what they could produce, and then to confiscate their property and expel them from the community. At first the term *kulak* was applied only to the larger landholders, but later it was stretched to include everybody who was in the least opposed to the collectivization program, and so expressed himself—former landowners, ministers, or teachers.

The selection of the *kulaks* to be expelled was left largely to the local village authorities; and since in the Mennonite villages the control had been seized primarily by non-Mennonite communists, it was evident that the number of *kulaks* among the industrious Mennonite farmers and devoted preachers and teachers would be unusually large. In the village of Chortitza in May of 1931, a meeting was called to vote out the remaining *kulaks* in the village. The communist contingent of the village, with a minority of the population but claiming two-thirds of the votes cast, voted to expel the remaining nine once-prosperous Mennonite farmers. Hundreds of thousands all over Russia—and hundreds, and perhaps thousands, of Mennonites—were classed as *kulaks*, arrested, and imprisoned, expelled from their homes on short notice to eke out an existence as best they could, or exiled to the forests of the far North or the vast wastes of Siberia. They were condemned to hard labor—gathering woodpulp for export, building a new Siberian railroad, or digging in the mines. They were sent from southern concentration camps by the freight trainloads, sometimes by whole families. Often men were torn from their families on a few days' notice, with insufficient food or clothing and little provision for either health or comfort. Many died of starvation, disease, or exposure.

Religious liberty was also further restricted. All the former antireligious regulations were rigidly enforced. More churches were closed. Sunday had been abolished not only as a day of worship, but as a holiday. Religious instruction of youth was prohibited. Ministers who had not already emigrated had been sent into exile, and newly elected ones hesitated to accept the dangerous obligation.

The Moscow Flight

It is not surprising then that many Mennonites under these conditions, those who suffered most and those who were most concerned for the religious fate of their children and themselves, should grasp any straw that promised the least bit of hope of escape from this unbearable situation. But there seemed little hope. By 1927 the Soviet government had practically ceased giving passports, without which emigration was impossible. But just at this time a group of some seventy Mennonites from Siberian settlements, which were again suffering famine conditions as a result of dry weather and heavy governmental requisitions, had fled to Moscow, blindly trusting that somehow they might find in the capital city the relief denied them at home. Quite unexpectedly, perhaps because of their very audacity and persistency, the Soviet authorities granted them passports with permission to leave the country.

This news, brought back to the home communities in Siberia, spread like wildfire among the Mennonites and other German colonists. Quietly, so as not to arouse too much suspicion, some Mennonites now began to dispose of their personal possessions so as to get enough money to take them to Moscow and purchase passports. They hoped that somehow the American and Dutch brethren might provide for their transportation needs beyond that. Some, in their hurry to get away, did not even sell all their personal property, leaving their furniture in their homes and turning their cattle out into the meadows. A movement on a somewhat smaller scale was also set in motion among the Mennonites at other settlements.

Before the Moscow government knew what was happening, about a thousand Mennonite families, and some hundreds of Lutherans and Catholics, had gathered together in the cheap lodging houses and temporary huts on the outskirts of the city, hoping that they, too, might find some way of escape to the New World. The first reports in the papers spoke of six thousand refugees, later of ten thousand, and finally of thirteen thousand.

This dramatic attempt of citizens of the Soviet Republic, which still boasted that it was the freest country in the world, and just at a time when the economic conditions and general dissatisfaction with the Soviet regime had reached a critical period, was given wide publicity in the world press. To the Russian government, it was as unwelcome as it was unexpected. Steps were immediately taken to stem the tide. Government agents were sent into the Mennonite settlements to discourage the movement; ticket agents were forbidden to sell tickets to Moscow to people from German settlements. At the same time, those in Moscow were requested to return to their homes. Police rounded up unwilling refugees, herded them together into freight cars, and shipped them to far-off Siberia or South Russia, without regard to food, clothing, or ordinary sanitary precautions. Families were separated in the hurry of the loading, some going to one settlement and other members to another, sometimes far removed. The cars were closed, and stops made only at long intervals. Many of the passengers were sick from exposure and neglect. Children were born all along the way. Sometimes mother and child, both without proper medical care, died. When these refugees, those who survived, did finally get back home they found themselves worse off than they had been months before. They were without household furniture, farm equipment, or livestock. Many found their homes had been occupied by strangers. Life was harder than ever, and it was only with the help of their friends and neighbors that they could start again at all. That so many of these "refugees" in Moscow were sent back to the places they had come from was due, to a large extent, to the fact that there was no country willing to accept so many people.

The plight of those remaining at Moscow was becoming increasingly desperate. After months of patient waiting, their funds were running low, and they were still not in sight of either the necessary passports or the help from abroad which would transport them to Canada. But the Western world had by this time become interested in the fate of this group of pious people seeking a new home. Germany especially was very sympathetic toward them. On November 19, 1929, the German Cabinet decided to intercede in behalf of the refugees with the Russian government. The Reichstag voted a substantial sum of money to aid an emigration project, and offered a temporary stopping place in Germany for the refugees until they could find a permanent home, perhaps somewhere in North America. The German Red Cross, as well as other philanthropic organizations, interested themselves in the project. President Hindenburg donated two hundred thousand *marks* out of his own private fortune to the cause. Even the League of Nations gave the matter some attention, though no material assistance. It was no doubt due largely to the intercession of the German government that some six thousand of these refugees, about four thousand of whom were Mennonites, came to Germany to await there their further disposition.

Of course the Mennonites of Germany took a keen interest in this whole movement. Through the efforts of B. H. Unruh, who had already so effectively represented the Mennonites from Russia in the earlier emigration, E. Händiges, editor of the *Mennonitische Blätter*, and Christian Neff of South Germany, relief work was organized. They furnished the destitute strangers from Russia much-needed clothing, food, and medical care, as well as spiritual comfort, in three former military barracks in North Germany, which the German government generously offered as a temporary resting place for the refugees.

The Mennonites in other parts of the world, too, felt a deep concern for the fate of their Russian brethren. The question was not solved permanently when the German government offered the refugees a temporary resting place. Germany itself was too hard-pressed to furnish them a satisfactory permanent home. The question still remaining for those concerned with a permanent solution was, What was to be their final destination?

In the spring of 1930 Christian Neff called the second Mennonite World Conference to Danzig to discuss the whole field of Mennonite colonization and relief the world over. Topics of discussion were: the status of the Canadian Mennonites who had recently gone to Mexico and Paraguay; the refugees still marooned at Harbin, China; the prospects of further migration from Russia; the problem of continued help for the twenty thousand Russian Mennonites who were still in need in Canada; as well as the main objective of the conference, the disposition of the Mennonites who were still guests of the German government.

Emigration to the United States was still out of the question, and was not considered by the delegates. By this time, too, largely because of an economic depression, the door had been practically closed to Canada, except for a limited number of immigrants who might have close relatives who would assume complete responsibility for the support of the newcomers. Mexico was not considered.

Only South America remained as a possibility. The German government favored Santa Catharina province in Brazil, because of the large German settlement already located there. The Hanseatic Corporation, with large land holdings in the region, warmly seconded the choice. The German government generously offered to advance the transportation costs and enough money for the first year's support to all those desiring to migrate to Brazil. There was one objection to the Brazilian adventure—Brazil did not guarantee exemption from military service to prospective Mennonite settlers as Paraguay had done. About one thousand took advantage of the German government's offer, and since these knew that they would not enjoy exemption from war service, it is reasonable to conclude that those making this choice were not among the most scrupulous on this question. At the time of the Mennonite World Conference in Amsterdam in 1936, a large part of the debt to the German government was still due. The Dutch Mennonites took a special interest in the Brazilian Mennonites as their special field of Mennonite relief work. They furnished money for the purchase of livestock at the start, and later, money for the establishing of schools.

The North American Mennonites favored Paraguay as a possible home for the refugees, partly because a few years before a Canadian colony had already been established there in the Gran Chaco, and especially because of the liberal terms offered by the Paraguayan government, including exemption from military service, and a large degree of local autonomy in matters of education and language. About two thousand colonists, including several hundred a few years later from Harbin, China, were located near the Canadian settlement, largely financed by the American Mennonites.

Perhaps about one thousand of these Moscow refugees, temporary guests of Germany, found their way to Canada, and a small number remained in Germany.

The Harbin Refugees

In the meantime some Mennonites had sought escape by way of the Pacific instead of the Atlantic. In the early 1920s a number of the victims of the famine in western Siberia, in the hope that they might better their condition in the East, started a new settlement along the Amur River in the Far East. But they were doomed to disappointment, and some of them crossed the Amur River into China. By now about one thousand, including a number of Lutherans and a few Catholics, were marooned at Harbin, China, hoping that they, too, might find their way to the promised land of Canada. Without food, clothing, or money; outlawed by the Russians; and not altogether welcomed by the Chinese, their plight was desperate. They were able to exist only by the friendly assistance of the German contingent of the city's population.

But these found entrance into Canada even more difficult than did their fellow refugees from Moscow. In addition to all the other handicaps, they had no passports, and Canada had decided in 1927 that she would accept no immigrants without passports. At this point the German government, partly through the efforts of B. H. Unruh and the German consul at Harbin, came to the rescue of these Russian Germans, promising to furnish them with passports, and assuming all the obligations involved in such guarantee. But as already seen, Canada by this time was not open to further mass immigration under any circumstances.

Through the sympathetic efforts of the American consul at Harbin, two hundred were permitted under the quota system to come to the United States. These were aided, of course, by the American Mennonites. Arriving in the spring of 1930, they were helped by the American Mennonites to a new start in life in Washington and California. It was not until several years later that the rest were able to leave China. The Nansen International Office for Refugees under the sponsorship of the League of Nations finally interested itself in their behalf, and it was under the auspices of this organization that in 1932 three hundred seventy-three Mennonites found their way to Paraguay, and three hundred ninety-seven Lutherans to Brazil. Two years later, one hundred eighty Mennonites from Harbin and one hundred

Lutherans and Catholics were located in Brazil.

Incidentally, the intervention of the League of Nations in behalf of the Mennonite emigration to Paraguay raised a question of considerable international significance. In the meeting of the Council of the League in September 1931, the Chinese delegate called attention to the plight of the Harbin refugees, requesting that the League help them to find a permanent home. The delegate from Paraguay generously offered them a home in the Chaco in Paraguay if their transportation expenses could be guaranteed. The German delegate, Count Bernstorff, whose government was already greatly interested in the whole question, thereupon thanked the Paraguayan delegate for the generous offer.

Wave of Exile 1929-1940

The cause of the flight to Moscow in 1929 was the radical collectivization, industrialization, and the liquidation of the so-called *kulaks*. This was accompanied by the merciless exiling of millions of people to Siberia, and to other almost uninhabitable places of the USSR. How this affected the Mennonite population is best illustrated in the case of the Chortitza settlement. From this settlement, with a Mennonite population of some twelve thousand, about fifteen hundred, mostly men, were exiled from 1929 to 1940. Hardly any of them returned, and most of them undoubtedly perished. This manpower was shifted from populated to unpopulated areas under the pretext of political accusations, while the real motive was usually to obtain labor to build up and develop some industries in remote areas. It was a part of the plan for which America praised Stalin, namely, that he had moved industries beyond the Ural Mountains before Hitler moved into the Ukraine. This wave of exile swept not only the Chortitza and other Mennonite settlements, but also the Russian population in general.

World War II

Immediately after the beginning of the invasion of the Ukraine by the German army in 1941, the Soviet government organized an evacuation of the population of German background beyond the Ural Mountains. In the fall of 1941 the so-called German Volga Republic, with a population of some three hundred fifty thousand, was evacuated. All people of German background were to be removed before the German army approached. The *Neu-Samara* Mennonite settlement on the Volga was also entirely evacuated. This was the fate of most Mennonite, as well as other German, settlements west of the Ural Mountains.

In the Ukraine the Soviet government did not succeed in totally evacuating the Mennonite settlements. Most of the Mennonite settlements east of the Dnieper River, however, including such large settlements as the Molotschna, Memrik, and others, were almost totally evacuated to Siberia. In the Molotschna settlement most of the men between age fifteen and sixty-five had been sent to the east in the wave of exile prior to the German invasion of the Ukraine. Now the women and children were sent east, to different places. This was still, however, the era of the German *Blitzkrieg*, and the Russians did not succeed in getting all of the trains loaded with evacuees from stations like Halbstadt. Then too, some of the remaining men of the Molotschna settlement were being used to dig trenches west of the Dnieper River. This accounts for the fact that in spite of all the precautions of the Soviet government, some of the Molotschna Mennonites remained in the German occupied Ukraine and later came to the Americas as displaced persons.

The Chortitza settlement, located west of the Dnieper River, was also to be evacuated eastward. However, because the German army moved in so swiftly and the crossing of the Dnieper River increased the difficulty of evacuation, only some thirteen hundred out of a total population of fourteen thousand were moved. This explains why most of the Mennonites who were moved to North and South America after World War II were from the Chortitza settlement.

During the German Occupation

Since the German army moved into Russia, not only as conqueror but also as "liberator" of those who were of German background, the Mennonites were treated comparatively well for the short period of occupation. This was especially true as long as the administration was in the hands of the *Wehrmacht*. When Himmler's SS (Storm Troopers) took over the administration, changes took place.

Agriculture had been collectivized long before the German army came. The German administration did not radically turn to private ownership, mainly because there was not enough machinery and horsepower to accomplish this in a short time. And yet personal initiative was immediately rewarded.

The religious life was revived—churches were opened again, ministers elected, religious instruction was given, and baptismal services took place. The schools were once more conducted more in harmony with Mennonite principles, although it gradually became noticeable that the national Socialist faith in *Blut und Boden* was to be substituted for the Mennonite heritage. One thing was certain—the German language, which had been abandoned in all schools in 1937, was once more reinstated, and the teachers were predominantly Mennonite. The Chortitza *Zentralschule* could even commemorate the one hundredth anniversary of its existence in 1942. All this proved to be only a short period of grace before the final blow. Meanwhile, the seemingly invincible German army had been defeated at Stalingrad and Moscow, and began the unprecedented retreat westward, accompanied by a mass of the civilian population who preferred an uncertain future in a defeated Germany to the conditions under Stalin.

The Trek Westward

In the fall of 1943 another evacuation of the Mennonite settlements occurred. This time the move was not eastward, where most of the husbands and sons were, but westward. In September the Molotschna settlement—whatever was left of it—was evacuated. In an endless trek beginning at Halbstadt, crossing the Dnieper River, halting for a few weeks at the Zagradovka settlement, women drove horses and wagons with what was left of their families and possessions toward the Polish border and Prussia, whence their forefathers had come nearly a hundred fifty years before. Under constant attack of the Red Army and guerrillas from the air and on the ground and with the approaching winter at hand, they suffered indescribably.

The fate of the Chortitza settlement was somewhat easier. From September 28 to October 20, 1943, some twelve thousand were taken to Germany by train. The transport usually consisted of fifty freight cars carrying approximately twelve hundred people. Most of them arrived at their destination within ten days.

The village of Chortitza itself, the oldest Mennonite village in the Ukraine, was evacuated October 1. An eyewitness gives this report about the last hours that he spent in this village:

> The village of Chortitza was evacuated October 1. I stayed there until October 16. During the night of October 14 the Dneprostroy Dam, near Einlage, was dynamited for the second time. The retreating Russians had dynamited it the first in August 1941. During the occupation the Germans had rebuilt it. The front was only five kilometers away when I left Chortitza. A deathly silence prevailed on that Saturday morning when I drove through the streets of Chortitza for the last time. During the night a rain had fallen and the sunrise was beautiful when I left that apparently sleeping village. I travelled in the direction of Dnepropetrovsk (formerly Ekaterinoslav), turned to Nikolaifeld, and continued to Nikopol. What a beautiful sight it was to see the promising fields of winter wheat put out by our people. Those who had sowed them were far, far away on an endless journey.

Most of these evacuees were scheduled to be settled not far from the region from which their forefathers had come 150 years ago, a place called Warthegau, in Upper Silesia and other places. In most cases plans failed to materialize or were of short duration. The German *Reich* was crumbling, and the Red Army was pushing westward. In January 1945 the Russians entered Germany proper, and a general mass movement of refugees further westward started.

The Refugees in Postwar Germany

The onslaught of the Red Army and the general collapse of Germany caused an indescribable panic during which all who could move pushed westward by any means available, mostly by foot. Even though it was not known that Germany would be partitioned into zones nor where these zones would run, there was definitely a subconscious urge to proceed as far west as possible, regardless of winter and the danger of attack. In spite of this, many Mennonites found themselves in the Russian zone of occupation because the Red Army had overtaken them. Their fate was sealed—Siberia. However, an unspeakable fear caused some to cross the zones into western Germany or the American sector of Berlin, bravely risking their lives in the venture.

It is estimated that the number of Mennonites evacuated to Germany could have been approximately thirty-five thousand. From the Chortitza settlement alone there must have been some twelve thousand refugees. When the Mennonite refugees in the western zones had been gathered into displaced persons camps, the total was about twelve thousand. Thus, if the above estimate is correct, more than twenty thousand had been forcibly repatriated. These were not sent to their homes in the Ukraine, not only because their homes had been destroyed but also because it was the previous intention of the Soviet government to send them beyond the Ural Mountains. The Allies did not prevent the Soviets in returning these refugees to Russia.

Toward a New Home

Almost insurmountable obstacles had to be overcome in order to gather the Mennonite refugees in camps, to obtain permission for them to leave Germany, to find a country that would be willing to take them, to arrange and finance transportation, and to handle the innumerable difficulties that presented themselves. With the cooperation of a large staff of Mennonite Central Committee relief workers, the International Refugee Organization, and the American and British occupation authorities, these seemingly impossible things were made possible. The first train with 1,125 left Berlin, passed through the Russian zone of occupation to Bremerhaven from where the *Volendam* left February 1, 1947, with 2,305 refugees destined for the Chaco, Paraguay. Later that number was more than doubled. In addition, about six thousand refugees from Russia were reunited with their relatives in Canada. Thus twelve thousand Mennonite refugees from Russia in Germany found new homes in Paraguay and Canada. They experienced hardships and missed their loved ones, but most of them faced the future with hope and faith in God who led them to a new home.

Summary

Although there are many thousands of Mennonites left in Russia, there are only a few families living in their former homes, and none that have not been broken up. Members of the once prosperous settlements are now scattered all over Russia, especially the northern and eastern parts. One member of a family may be in Siberia, one in Paraguay, one in Germany, and one in Canada. In most cases no reunion in this life can be expected. All this was the result of six particular turbulent times unleashing themselves upon the Mennonite settlements of Russia:

1. The Civil War of 1917-1920 and the famine of 1921-1922.
2. The liquidation of *kulaks* and collectivization, 1928-1933.
3. The purges and exiles of 1936-1940.
4. The evacuation eastward at the beginning of World War II, 1941.
5. Evacuation westward by the German Army, 1943.
6. The repatriation by the Red Army in 1945.

Step by step, the once-prosperous communities disintegrated. Never since the days of the martyrs have the Mennonites suffered as much as during the twentieth century in Russia.

Summarizing the migrations of the Mennonites from Russia to America we find that the first group came to the prairie states and provinces of the United States and Canada in 1874 and after, numbering some eighteen thousand. The second migration took place after World War I when from 1923 to 1927 some twenty-one thousand came to Canada, and from 1929 to 1930 some three thousand went to Paraguay and Brazil. The third migration of Mennonites from Russia took place after World War II when some twelve thousand Mennonites came to Paraguay and Canada, about half going to each country. Of the last two waves of migrations, the United States accepted only a negligible number. Around 1960 another migration of Germans, including Mennonites, from the USSR to Germany began which is still in progress.

8. THE MENNONITES IN RUSSIA TODAY

During the last decades, considerable changes have taken place in the Soviet Union in general and also in regard to religioethnic minorities. We are particularly interested in the conditions under which Christians today, including Mennonites, live and labor in a country that had attempted to eradicate any religious beliefs, be they Russian Orthodox, Baptist, Lutheran, Catholic, or Mennonite.

Church and State

The militant efforts to exterminate any religious views were softened somewhat in the days of Stalin's struggle for survival when Hitler's army had invaded Russia besieging Leningrad and Stalingrad and was approaching the gates of Moscow. In this crucial hour Stalin needed every support Russia could muster, including the basically religious peasant population. He also had to prove to his allies that he was not as antireligious as was assumed in the West.

In 1944 a book appeared in Moscow published in a number of languages entitled *The Truth About Religion in Russia*. It was heavily illustrated with pictures showing how Hitler's brigades had destroyed icons and churches during the invasion, and how this enraged the Russian believers. In a crucial moment, Stalin cleverly took advantage of the situation to win friends and support at home and abroad. Thus a certain new "church and state" relationship developed in the USSR.

First of all, it was realized that the Russian religious tradition was much stronger and more deeply ingrained than the earlier Marxists had assumed and that this situation could continue for some time. It was concluded that if it was impossible to liquidate a "superstition" through means of "enlightenment," it might be well to tolerate it for the time being and even recognize its existence legally. Official declarations and laws about the religious organizations and the mutual relationship between state and church appeared and grew in numbers which are now over three hundred pages in length. Thus the existence of religious groups in the Soviet Union is now officially acknowledged. The Russian Orthodox Church and also the recognized Baptist believers predominate. All denominations and individual congregations must be registered and acknowledged by the Department of Religious Cults. At the same time, this presupposes that these religious bodies recognize the state as the authority to be taken into consideration when believers gather, organize a congregation, build a church, and practice their Christianity in daily life.

They must be aware of what is "legal" or permissible and what is not.

Theoretically, any group of believers consisting of at least twenty members, whether Orthodox, Baptist, Mennonite, or any other group, can apply to be registered as a Christian fellowship. But it is easier to register with the Department of Religious Cults if the group identifies itself with a larger denomination. Consequently, there is an inclination among some Mennonites to affiliate with a larger Baptist denomination. As it will be seen later, this is particularly easy for the Mennonite Brethren.

On the other hand, the most "radical" believers in the Soviet Union consider it a surrender of basic Christian convictions to obtain permission to worship God from an atheistic government. These "free-lancing" Baptists, Mennonites, and other religious groups are often in trouble as "disloyal" citizens and religious "fanatics," who seem to seek martyrdom. These are called *Initiativniki*, which means "those taking the initiative."

What About the Mennonites?

With very few exceptions, all Mennonites were removed from their settlements in European Russia. As we have seen, in the days of the severe rule of Stalin, many of the males between eighteen and eighty were sent to labor camps in the northern and eastern parts of Russia where many perished. When Hitler invaded Russia in 1941, the remaining German population, including Mennonites, were sent to northern and eastern parts of the USSR, mostly beyond the Ural Mountains. Those who remained in the Ukraine were taken along by the retreating German army in 1943. At the end of World War II most of these were returned to Russia and sent to the eastern part of the country by the Soviet army occupying Germany.

Whether it was in the northern woods of European Russia or in the various republics of Central Asia beyond the Ural Mountains, groups of believers met for fellowship, Scripture reading, and prayer to strengthen their faith in the most desperate hours of their lives. Most of the time the question of whether those fellowshiping together formerly belonged to the Mennonites or the Mennonite Brethren did not seem to be of significance. Even non-Mennonites joined these fellowships. All of them found strength and courage in reading the same Bible, singing the same hymns, and calling on the same Lord for strength and endurance in those trying times. However, as conditions improved after World War II, some of the old spiritual demarcation lines were revived. In addition to this, the question came up as to whether or not a congregation should register with the government.

Mennonites and Baptists

There were some advantages in registering a fellowship like most of the urban Baptists had done. Registered groups could worship more freely and also request the right to erect a church building. An unregistered group meeting was considered illegal. Thus it was realized that a loose affiliation with a larger body of believers such as the officially recognized All-Union Council of Evangelical Christian Baptists (AUCECB), with its headquarters in Moscow, would be advantageous. However a problem soon arose. The Russian Baptists that had originally, to some extent, been inspired in their origins by Mennonites, had accepted the mode of baptism by immersion as a prerequisite for membership. This mode was traditional in the Russian Orthodox Church. For those of the Mennonite Brethren tradition this was not an obstacle in joining the Baptists. Numerous Mennonite Brethren ministers and congregations have become members of this All-Union Baptist Council.

In 1963 at the first congress of the AUCECB, Mennonites were present. In 1966 an official declaration of oneness with AUCECB was read by a Mennonite Brethren spokesman, and several Mennonite Brethren were elected to the council.

In 1974 Jakob Fast became a member of the ten-member Presidium of the AUCECB. Fast, of Mennonite Brethren background, was a leading minister of the Mennonite Brethren Church at Karaganda which merged with the Russian Baptist Church at that place. Fast is now the pastor of the Baptist-Mennonite Brethren Church. Another representative to the Council of the Moscow AUCECB is Traugott Quiring of Dushanbe in Tadzhikistan. Originally from a rural area, he came to Dushanbe where he affiliated with the Russian Baptists and became the leading minister of the large Baptist church which has since attracted many Mennonite Brethren. G. F. Goertzen, Fast, and Quiring were delegates of the Baptist-Mennonite Brethren at the Mennonite World Conference in Wichita in 1978. B. I. Sawatsky was the representative of the Mennonites.

German-speaking Mennonite Brethren quite often find an open door in Russian Baptist churches where they conduct their own German worship services in the afternoon. Naturally the younger generation that prefers the Russian language can easily attend the Russian Baptist service in the morning and sooner or later many join the Baptists. This is ultimately likely to happen to the entire Mennonite Brethren congregation that is worshiping for the time being in the afternoon in the German language. It is easy to predict that most of the Mennonite Brethren in Russia will, at places where they have this close relationship with the Baptists, lose or alter their former spiritual and cultural identity as Mennonites.

On the other hand, some Mennonite Brethren are interested in maintaining their independent identity as a Mennonite Brethren church in Russia. Willi Matthies taught in a public school in Russia for many years and then suddenly decided to devote the last decades of his life to the preaching of the gospel. He and his co-worker Heinrich Woelk found such an opportunity in Karaganda in 1960. Here they serve a Mennonite Brethren congregation that has tried to preserve its identity by placing greater emphasis on the Mennonite heritage and the German language. Ultimately the congregation was registered through direct contacts with the Department of Religious Cults in Moscow. After a few years the congregation received permission to build a church large enough for 900 members. The argument of the Russian Baptists (AUCECB) that the Mennonite Brethren must join them in order to get these privileges has lost some of its appeal.

Baptist-Mennonite Initiativniki

In 1961 the AUCECB split because the organization made some far-reaching accommodations to the imposed limitations by the Soviet government. A split-away group, called the *Initiativniki*, organized the Council of Churches of Evangelical Christian Baptists (CCECB). Most of their affiliates are unregistered. Among the leaders of this group was Georgi Vins (Wiens), whose grandfather was a Mennonite Brethren minister in Siberia. The Mennonite Brethren seem to have a large number of representatives in this more radical wing of the Russian Baptists. The official magazine of the AUCECB is *Bratskiy Vestnik* (Brotherly Messenger), while the CCECB publishes the "underground" paper *Bratskiy Listok* (Brotherly Sheet).

The *Initiativniki* are being singled out as the only true church in Russia by numerous American agencies soliciting funds to help them. A representative of one of these agencies appeared at the Mennonite World Conference in Wichita in 1978 to protest the presence of the Baptist-Mennonite delegates. He claimed the Russian delegation were collaborators with the Russian government and that the *Initiativniki* are the only faithful followers of Christ in Russia. However, that is similar to claiming one denomination in North America as truly Christian and all others as betrayers of Christ.

What About Baptism?

If the separating Brethren and the traditional Mennonites in Russia in the mid 1800s would have been less radical and better informed about the "faith of our fathers," their parting could have been prevented. Traditionally there was room and flexibility for what the parting group asked for. The crucial questions were whether the traditional acceptance of new church members could not be improved on. The separating group insisted that the candidate should have a personal assurance that Christ had saved him. Later the preference of baptism by immersion, instead of sprinkling or pouring, was added. According to the confession of faith written by Cornelis Ris (1719-1790) which has been in use among the Mennonites in Holland, West Prussia, Russia, and in North America, this option was open. Ris stated that Mennonites "baptize by dipping or an immersing of the whole body under water or by sprinkling (Rom. 6:4, Matt. 3:16)." Numerous congregations today leave it up to the candidate as to what mode is to be used.

Among the Baptists, the Mennonite Brethren, and the Mennonites in Russia today, a fundamental disagreement appears to be the mode of baptism. When the question of baptism was raised in the presence of the six delegates from Russia attending the 1978 Mennonite World Conference in Wichita, three Baptist-Mennonite Brethren stated that the only mode of baptism they practiced was immersion, and that this is the prerequisite for participation in the communion service. The fourth delegate, Bernhard Sawatzky, representing the Mennonites in Russia, reported that in his congregation the candidate for baptism is instructed, and when he has accepted Christ as his personal Savior, he is baptized by sprinkling. To this he added that even the water of an entire ocean could not add anything to salvation that had not already been given freely by Christ. This statement was applauded spontaneously by the audience which represented all branches of Mennonites from many countries around the world.

Mennonite Settlements that Survived

There were a few of the nearly sixty Mennonite settlements in Russia from which not all inhabitants were removed during the Stalin era and the German invasion during World War II. Among them was the *Orenburg* Mennonite settlement which was started in 1892 by Mennonites from the Chortitza settlement. Twenty-two villages were erected. After some hardships the settlement achieved a good status economically and culturally. During the years after the Revolution, the American Mennonites provided some help. Approximately three hundred persons left for Canada in 1926. In 1955 all religious services were forbidden, but in spite of this a spiritual revival took place. It was reported that ninety-eight persons were baptized, and ministers were ordained. Unfortunately this freedom did not last long. Orenburg still today has the reputation of being an area where people are afraid to worship.

Large Mennonite settlements were established in the early 1900s in *Siberia*. The settlers came from various places in the Ukraine and established settlements at *Omsk*, *Pavlodar*, and *Slavgorod* (Barnaul). The Slavgorod Mennonite settlement consisted of fifty-nine villages of settlers that had come from various places in the Ukraine. In 1922 there was a total population of fifteen thousand. It was at this time that the Mennonites in Siberia were in need of help because of heavy requisitions of grain following crop failures. Some help came from America. Around 1925 a considerable number of Mennonites left for Canada. Again in 1929 a large number of Slavgorod Mennonites went to Moscow asking for permission to leave the country. Some were able to leave, but the majority were returned in freight trains. In 1930 and 1931 all villages were organized as collective farms. Many farmers had been exiled and perished. Klaus Mehnert, who visited the settlement in 1955, reported about a visit on a collective farm composed of five Mennonite villages consisting of 298 families with 1,025 persons. The Slavgorod settlement had a Mennonite Church with branches in various villages as did also the Mennonite Brethren. When Klaus Mehnert visited in this region he found a very depressing religious situation. The spiritual life was being nurtured as far as possible, but ministers had been serving prison terms. Evidently no great changes have taken place since. Mennonite churches there are active but unregistered and unaffiliated.

The Mennonites in Russia were originally primarily located in the Ukraine. As we have already seen, by the end of World War II all Mennonites had been removed from here. Most of them were located in northern and Siberian labor camps. After Stalin's death in 1953 they were permitted to leave, but not to return to the Ukraine. They now gradually moved to the Siberian Mennonite settlements, but above all into an entirely new territory stretching south from Siberia to the borders of China and Afghanistan. Many Mennonites and other ethnic Germans can be found in the republics of Kazakhstan (Karaganda, Alma Ata, Dzhambul), Kirgizia (Frunze) and Tadzhikistan (Dushanbe).

Church Life and Growth

Although special activities for groups of people that might foster evangelism are forbidden, evangelical churches in the Soviet Union are experiencing growth. Mennonites, especially, have emphasized teaching the faith to the children in the home. Atheist writers have said that the distinguishing feature of Mennonites is their ability to win their young people.

Russian Mennonites, like other Soviet evangelicals, are known for their intense piety. Services are characterized by emotionalism and last for two to three hours. Recent visitors to Mennonite congregations in Russia are impressed with the emphasis on congregational singing and the choirs, which in large churches may be accompanied by instrumental music.

Some Mennonite ministers take a two-year Bible correspondence course by AUCECB. A dozen young Baptists have received theological training in Baptist colleges in England and Germany. Such training is the greatest need among all Russian Mennonites, and Christians in general.

The future of the Mennonites in the USSR is not very bright. They lack adequate leadership, particularly youthful, educated leadership. They are unable to offer as attractive a program of activity for young people as are the AUCECB and CCECB Baptists to whom they have lost many potential members. Many of their leaders have emigrated. Some Mennonites have managed, however, to obtain full registration for churches in Karaganda and Novosibirsk and have an unofficial registered status in a half-dozen other places. Each congregation is registered as an autonomous church. Although the Mennonites lack any central administrative organ, they were represented at the Mennonite World Conference held in Wichita in 1978.

Mennonites Return to Germany

In World War II, Germany was not only split in half (East and West) but in addition lost much territory by having its borders from the West and the South pushed into the interior. Many Germans remained in these areas that were taken from Germany. In addition to this, there were many Germans in neighboring countries who had been living in these countries for generations. In 1955 Germany made arrangements with various countries to give these an opportunity to return. The people returning are called *Umsiedler* (immigrants), and at times *Heimkehrer* (homecomers) or *Rückwanderer* (returnees). Between 1955 and 1975, four hundred thirty-one thousand came from Poland; sixty-nine thousand from Czechoslovakia; fifty-four thousand from Rumania; eight thousand from Hungary; and forty-four thousand from USSR. These *Umsiedler* continue to come from all countries listed. In 1978 the total number from the USSR was over sixty thousand, including eight thousand Mennonites. Many of these have lived for generations abroad and do not even speak German anymore. Not only are they invited back but their expenses are taken care of, they find employment, social security, and other benefits as if they had never left the country.

It is surprising how quickly the *Umsiedler* adjust themselves to the country of their forebears in many ways. The younger generation finds employment and gets actively involved in the educational, economic, and social program. The older generation is grateful but finds some things less to its liking. Most live in apartment houses, smaller settlements, or in their own houses financed by lower loan rates. Some face linguistic problems, particularly those who received all their education in the Russian language. Others, between the ages of thirty and fifty years, may have missed out on most of their formal education while in labor camps. All are given opportunities to get training in the field of their interest.

Mennonites emigrating from Russia usually join existing Mennonite congregations in Germany. In four of these congregations, this has meant that larger churches needed to be built. In addition, a number of new congregations have been started.

Total religious freedom does not solve all problems for those who have longed and prayed for it. Those formerly under religious pressure have developed a mold and mood and spiritual lifestyle that are very dear to them. They have also gotten accustomed to a spiritual terminology and to cultural patterns which have assumed a strong religious meaning. It is hard for them today to adjust in a number of ways. However, most of the Russian Mennonites who have not undergone too many influences from the outside find a compatible spiritual atmosphere in Mennonite churches of Germany which are of a West Prussian or North German background. An *Umsiedlerbetreuung* (spiritual ministry to emigrants) sponsored by International Mennonite Organization (IMO) and MCC serves all these groups.

Table 1   MENNONITE SETTLEMENTS IN RUSSIA
Established: 1789-1927
A. Mother Settlements

Name	Province	Founded	Villages	Acreage		Population	
1. Chortitza	Ekaterinoslav	1789 ff.	19	1789:	89,100	1819:	2,888
				1917:	405,000	1941:	13,965
2. Molotschna	Taurida	1804 ff.	60	1835:	324,000	1835:	6,000
						1926:	17,347
3. Trakt	Samara	1853 ff.	10	1897:	44,134	1897:	1,176
4. Alexandertal	Samara	1859 ff.	8	1870:	26,500		
				1917:	53,500	1913:	1,144

B. Daughter Settlements

Name	Province	Mother Settlement	Founded	Villages	Acreage	Population
1. Bergthal	Ekaterinoslav	Chortitza	1836-52	5	30,000	1874: 3,000
2. Jewish Settlement (Judenplan)	Kherson	Chortitza	1847	6	5-6 families per village	
3. Chernoglaz	Ekaterinoslav	Chortitza	1860	1	2,700	130
4. Crimea	Taurida	Molotschna	1862 ff.	c25 & estates	1929: 108,000	1926: 4,817
5. Kuban	Kuban	Chortitza and Molotschna	1862	2	17,550	1904: 2,000
6. Fürstenland	Taurida	Chortitza	1864-70	7	19,000	1874: 1,100

Name	Province	Mother Settlement	Founded	Villages	Acreage	Population
7. Borozenko	Ekaterinoslav	Chortitza	1865-66	6	18,000	1910: 600
8. Friedensfeld (Miropol)	Ekaterinoslav	Molotschna	1867	1	5,400	
9. Brazol (Schönfeld)	Ekaterinoslav	Molotschna	1868	4 & estates	1868: 14,000 1910: 187,000	1917: 2,000
10. Neu-Schönwiese (Dmitrovka)	Ekaterinoslav	Schönwiese-Chortitza	1868	1	3,788	
11. Tempelhof	Stavropol	Molotschna	1868	2		
12. Yazykovo (Nikolaifeld)	Ekaterinoslav	Chortitza	1869	6	23,315	1930: 2,200
13. Nepluyevka	Ekaterinoslav	Chortitza	1870	2	10,800	1910: 550
14. Andreasfeld	Ekaterinoslav	Chortitza	1870	3	10,620	
15. Baratov	Ekaterinoslav	Chortitza	1872	2 (4)	1872: 9,800	1905: 2,569
16. Zagradovka	Kherson	Molotschna	1871	16	57,445	1922: 5,429
17. Shlachtin	Ekaterinoslav	Chortitza	1874	2	10,800	1910: 1,000
18. Neu-Rosengart	Ekaterinoslav	Chortitza	1878	2	1,800	1910: 250
19. Wiesenfeld	Ekaterinoslav	Chortitza	1880	1	23,306	
20. Aulie-Ata	Turkestan	Molotschna	1882	6	21,600	1910: 1,000
21. Ak-Mechet	Khiva Central Asia	Trakt	1884	1	13	25 families
22. Memrik	Ekaterinoslav	Molotschna	1885	10	32,400	1,367
23. Alexandropol	Ekaterinoslav	Molotschna	1888	1	?	15 families
24. Samoylovka	Kharkov	Molotschna	1888	2	?	1905: 239

RUSSIA

#	Name	Region	Settlement	Year	Families	Population	Later
25.	Milorodovka	Ekaterinoslav	Chortitza	1889	2	5,670	1910: 200
26.	Ignatyevo	Ekaterinoslav	Chortitza	1889-90	7	38,132	1910: 1,400
27.	Naumenko	Kharkov	Chortitza	1890	4 (3)	14,350	1905: 700
28.	Neu-Samara (Pleshanovsk)	Samara	Molotschna Molotschna	1890	14	1922: 91,000	1922: 3,670
29.	Borissovo	Ekaterinoslav	Chortitza	1892	2	13,770	1910: 400
30.	Davlekanovo	Ufa	Molotschna Samara	1894	19 & estates	1926: 30,000	1926: 1,831
31.	Orenburg (Deyevka)	Orenburg	Chortitza	1894	14	63,660	1910: 1,400
32.	Suvorovka	Stavropol (Caucasus)	Zagradovka	1894	2	10,800	80 families
33.	Orenburg (Molotschna)	Orenburg	Molotschna	1898	8	29,700	1910: 1,000
34.	Olgino	Stavropol (Caucasus)	Mixed	1895	2 (4)	12,150	80 families
35.	Bezenchuk	Samara	Alexandertal	1898	3?	5,400	75
36.	Omsk	Akmolinsk & Tobolsk	Mixed	1899	29 & estates	108,000	
37.	Don (Millerovo)	Don Region	Molotschna	1900-3	*	10,800	
38.	Terek	Terek (Caucasus)	Molotschna	1901	15	66,960	1905: 1,655
39.	Rovnopol (Ebenfeld)	Samara	Molotschna	1903	1	8,250	
40.	Trubetskoye	Kherson	Molotschna	1904	2	118,800(?)	400
41.	Pavlodar	Semipalatinsk	Mixed	1906	14	37,800	

42. Sadovaya	Voronezh	Chortitza	1909	1?	16,052	
43. Slavgorod (Barnaul)	Tomsk	Mixed	1908	58	135,000	1925: 1,373
44. Zentral	Voronezh	Chortitza	1909	1	7,358	
45. Arkadak	Saratov	Chortitza	1910	7	25,500	1925: 1,500
46. Bugulma	Samara	Alexandertal	1910	1	2,700	
47. Kistyendey	Saratov	?	1910?	1		
48. Minusinsk	Yeniseysk	Ignatyevo	1913	2 (4)	10,800?	1918: 32 families
49. Amur	Eastern Siberia	Mixed	1927	20		1927: 1,300
50. Kuzmitsky (Alexandrovka)	Ekaterinoslav	Chortitza	?	1	1910: 4,860	1910: 200
51. Eugenfeld	Ekaterinoslav	Chortitza	?	1		
52. Alexeyfeld	Kherson	Molotschna	?	1		

*Millerovo, Masayevka, Nikolaipol
Source: *Mennonite Encyclopedia*, Vol. IV, pp. 386-88.

Table 2
Mennonite University Graduates
in Russia: 1890-1917

I. Theologians and Ministers
(Universities and Seminaries)
 1. Dirks, Heinrich, Gnadenfeld, Molotschna; Barmen Theological School, (1864-68). (Missionary and Minister).
 2. Ediger, Salomon S., Gnadenfeld, Molotschna; Basel Theological Seminary. (Russia).
 3. Fast, Abraham, Molotschna; University of Basel, (*Lic. theol.*). (Emden).
 4. Kröker, Jakob, Crimea; Baptist Theological Seminary, Hamburg. (Wernigerade a. II).
 5. Lenzmann, Hermann A., Gnadenfeld, Molotschna; University of Tübingen. (Russia).
 6. Martins, Heinrich, Crimea; Basel Theological Seminary. (Brazil).
 7. Quiring, Fr., Saratov; University of Dorpat. (Russia).
 8. Quiring, Jacob, Koppental, Samara: Universities of Berlin and Columbia. (Bluffton and New York).
 9. Rempel, Jakob. Schönfeld, Borzenko; University of Basel. (Russia, minister).
 10. Unruh, B. H., Timir-Bulat, Crimea; University of Basel (*Lic. theol.* 1907). (Karlsruhe).
 11. Wiens, David, Kleefeld, Molotschna; University of Dorpat, (1914). (Russia).

II. Teachers and Professors
 1. Bergmann, Cornelius, Neuhoffnung, Samara; Universities of Leipzig, Berlin, Zürich, Ph.D. (Germany).
 2. Bräul, Alexander, Ohrloff, Molotschna; University of Petersburg. (Russia).
 3. Braun, Peter J., Alexanderwohl, Molotschna; Teachers Institute, Petersburg. (Germany).
 4. Ediger, Alexander, Berdyansk; University of Petersburg. (Russia).
 5. Ediger, Heinz, Crimea; University of Petersburg. (Russia).
 6. Enns, Abram, Altona, Molotschna: Universities of Basel and München. (Lübeck).
 7. Epp, H. H., Chortitza: University of Moscow. (Chortitza).
 8. Epp, Peter G., Petershagen, Molotschna; Universities of Basel and Heidelberg, Ph.D., 1912. (Columbus, Ohio).
 9. Fast, Peter P., Münsterberg, Molotschna; University of Moscow (1890). (Russia).
 10. Friesen, Abram A., Schönau, Molotschna; University of Odessa. (Halbstadt).
 11. Friesen, P. M. Sparrau, Molotschna; Studied in Switzerland, Moscow, and Odessa. (Russia. Historian.)
 12. Fröse, Franz, Waldeck, Memrik; University of ? . (Russia).
 13. Goossen, Dietrich, Schönsee, Molotschna; University of Moscow. (Russia).
 14. Goossen, Peter, Alexandertal, Molotschna; University of Petersburg. (Russia).
 15. Günther, Viktor; Universities of Basel and Heidelberg (Winnipeg).

16. Harder, Hans, Neuhoffnung, Samara; University of Königsberg. (Germany, writer).
17. Harder, Johann G., Molotschna; University of Petersburg. (Halbstadt).
18. Heese, Peter II., Ekaterinoslav; University of Moscow. (Ohrloff).
19. Isaak, Peter; University of Petersburg. (Taught at U. of Vancouver).
20. Janzen, Johann, Ohrloff; Academy of Art. Theodosia (Feodosiya). (Ohrloff).
21. Lehn, Ekaterinoslav; University of Kharkov. (Barvenkovo).
22. Letkemann, Peter P.; University of Natural Sciences, (Halbstadt).
23. Neufeld, Abram A., Fürstenau, Molotschna; Universities of Odessa and Berlin, 1833. (Chortitza and Berdyansk).
24. Neufeld (Navall), Dietrich, Sagradovka; University of Basel. (Chortitza and U.S.A.).
25. Penner, Hans, Ekaterinoslav; University of Kharkov. (Teacher).
26. Penner, Heinrich, Gnadenfeld; University of Petersburg. (Teacher).
27. Penner, Hermann J., Molotschna; University of Petersburg. (Halbstadt).
28. Wiebe, Heinrich, Steinfeld, Molotschna; University of Petersburg. (Schönwiese).
29. Wiens, Peter J., Altona, Molotschna; University of ? . (Halbstadt).

III. Physicians
1. Dirks, Wilhelm, Waldheim, Molotschna; University of Kharkov. (Gnadenfeld).
2. Dyck, Franz, Fürstenau, Molotschna; University of Kharkov. (Molotschna).
3. Dyck, Peter, Fürstenau, Molotschna; University of Kharkov. (Ohrloff-Brasil).
4. Esau, Jakob, Ekaterinoslav; University of Kiev. (Chortitza and Ekaterinoslav).
5. Esau, Peter J., Ekaterinoslav; University of Odessa. (Ohrloff).
6. Hamm, David, Chortitza; Military Academy of Petersburg. (Chortitza and Canada).
7. Hausknecht, David, Gnadenfeld; University of Odessa. (Gnadenfeld).
8. Isaak, Johann; Military Academy of Petersburg. (Alexandrabad and Los Angeles).
9. Klassen, Rudolf, Am Trakt; University of Saratov. (Russia and Winnipeg).
10. Neufeld, Nikolai, Davlekanovo, Ufa; University of Saratov. (Winnipeg).
11. Peters, Peter, Chortitza; University of Odessa. (Ekaterinoslav and Grünfeld).
12. Thiessen, Isaak; Universities of Odessa and München. (Bethania, Russia).
13. Warkentin, Heinrich, Waldheim; University of Kharkov. (C. P. R., Winnipeg).
14. Zacharias, Dietrich, Osterwik, Chortitza; University of Odessa. (Chortitza).

IV. Science of Forestry
1. Dueck, Crimea; Petersburg Institute of Science of Forestry. (Russia).
2. Klassen, Peter, Chortitza; Petersburg Institute of Science of Forestry. (Russia and Vancouver).
3. Schmidt; Petersburg Institute of Science of Forestry. (Saratoff, Russia).

V. Lawyers
1. Funk, Peter, Neuenburg, Chortitza; University of Moscow. (Ekaterinoslav).
2. Heese, Jakob, Ekaterinoslav; University of Kharkov. (Ekaterinoslav).
3. Janzen, Peter, Schönwiese; University of ? . (Alexandrovsk).
4. v. Kampen, Julius, Chortitza; University of Moscow. (Alexandrovsk).
5. Siemens, Jakob, Schönwiese; University of ? . (Alexandrovsk).
6. Unruh, Kornelius, Ohrloff, Molotschna; University of ? . (Ekaterinoslav).
7. Wallmann, Hermann, Chortitza; University of Petersburg. (Russia).

VI. Engineers and Architects
1. Appenrodt, Heinrich, Chortitza, Institute of Technology, Karlsruhe. (Kharkov and Germany).
2. Ediger, Nikolas, Berdyansk; Institute of Mining, Petersburg. (Russia).
3. Epp, David, Ekaterinoslav; University in Germany. (Ekaterinoslav and Chortitza).
4. Esau, Alexander, Ekaterinoslav; Institute of Mining. (Ekaterinoslav).
5. Esau, Johann, Ekaterinoslav; Institute of Technology, Riga. (Manufacturer and Mayor of Ekaterinoslav).
6. Fast, Abraham, Schönsee, Molotschna; Institute of Technology, Petersburg. (Petersburg).
7. Heese, Heinrich, Ekaterinoslav; Institute of Milling Industry, Zürich and Dippoldiswalde. (Russia).
8. Heese, Peter, Ekaterinoslav; Institute of Technology, Riga. (Ekaterinoslav).
9. Hildebrand, Kornelius, Chortitza; Institute of Engineering, Germany. (Schönwiese).
10. Klassen, Johann, Chortitza; Institute of Technology, Kiev. (Russia).
11. Klassen, N. J., Chortitza; Universities of Petersburg and Kharkov. (Alexandrovsk and Vancouver. Writer of this article).
12. Klassen, Wilhelm, Melitopol; Institute of Mining, Ekaterinoslav. (Russia).
13. Klatt, Wilhelm, Melitopol; Institute of Technology, Petersburg. (Russia).
14. Lehn, Armin, Chortitza; Institute of Technology, Germany. (Moscow).
15. Lepp, Hermann, Schönwiese; Braunschweig Institute of Technology. (Schönwiese).
16. Martens, Jakob, Ekaterinoslav; Institute of Mining. (Krivoy Rog Industry).

17. Neufeld, Eugen, Chortitza-Berdyansk; Institute of Technology, Petersburg. (Russia).
18. Penner, Jakob, Rosenthal, Chortitza; Institute of Technology, Dippoldiswalde, Germany. (Berlin).
19. Penner, Wilhelm; Institute of Technology, Darmstadt, Germany. (Yevpatoriya).
20. Rempel, Gerhard, New York, Bachmut; Institute of Electrical Engineering, Petersburg. (Russia).
21. Schulz, Jakob, Schönwiese; Institute of Technology, Kiev. (Millerovo, Russia).
22. Thiessen, Heinrich, Ekaterinoslav; Institutes of Technology and Commerce, Riga. (Russia).
23. Unruh, Abram, New York, Bachmut; Institute of Mining. (Russia).
24. Willms, Heinz, Halbstadt; Institute of Architecture. (Russia).

VII. Others
1. Bock, Jakob, Schönwiese; Institute of Commerce, Germany. (Alexandrovsk and Kharkov).
2. Dyck, Arnold, Hochfeld, Chortitza; Academies of Art, München, Stuttgart, Petersburg, Moscow. (Canada).
3. Epp, Heinrich, Ekaterinoslav; Institute of Commerce, Belgium. (Russia).
4. Froese, Heinrich, Grünfeld; Academy of Agriculture, Moscow. (Chortitza).
5. Isaak, Margarete; Academy of Bestushev. (Russia).
6. Klassen, Johann, Grünfeld, Academy of Art, München. (Chortitza and U.S.A.).
7. Reimer, C. C., Wiesenfeld, Institute of Commerce, Moscow. (Russia and Canada).
8. Sudermann, Anna, Chortitza; Academy of Bestushev. (Chortitza and Winnipeg).

FOOTNOTES
[1] D. H. Epp. *Die Chortitzer Mennoniten*. Rosenthal bei Chortitz. 1888, p. 81.
[2] D. H. Epp, *op. cit.*, p. 102.

1. Occupation of Father
   a. Teacher, minister, employee 33%
   b. Farmers 32%
   c. Large estate owners 10%
   d. Businessmen, industrialists, etc. 25%
   Total = 100%

2. Field of Study and Occupation

	Practiced in Russia	Practiced in Canada
a. Physicians	18	7
b. Teachers	40	200
c. Commerce	12	1
d. Engineers	34	26
e. Lawyers	9	4
f. Theology	5 (abroad)	0

3. Home Community
   a. Chortitza Settlement 28%
   b. Molotschna Settlement 31%
   c. Daughter Settlements 25%
   d. Cities 16%
   Total = 100%

4. Denomination of Marriage Partner
   a. Mennonite 67%
   b. Evangelical 12%
   c. Russian Orthodox 21%
   Total = 100%

AMERICA

The Germantown Mennonite Meetinghouse is on the site of the earliest
Mennonite Church in North America. The first log meetinghouse, erected
in 1708 was replaced by this building. (Photo by Paul Schrock.)

IX
First Settlements and Expansions (1683-1800)

1. NEW YORK AND GERMANTOWN

The first Mennonites to come to America were stray Dutch traders and colonists who accompanied their fellow countrymen from Holland to the new world in the early days when New York was still New Netherlands. The term *Mennonite* itself is found first in a report of the religious conditions in the first Dutch settlement found among the writings of a French Jesuit traveler, Father Jogues. In a letter dated 1643, describing the *Manhate* settlement, he enumerates among the religious groups— "Calvinists, Catholics, English Puritans, Lutherans, and Anabaptists here called *Menists*." In a later document, of 1657, *Menonists* are reported at Gravesend, Long Island. Beyond these bare items, however, nothing is known concerning these first comers of the Mennonite faith.

A few years later, in 1663, we glean a few more scraps of information regarding a Dutch Mennonite settlement led by the social reformer Pieter Cornelisz Plockhoy of Zierikzee. As already noted in an earlier chapter, after a precarious existence of scarcely a year, this colony was completely destroyed by an English marauding expedition along the shores of the present state of Delaware during the war between England and the Netherlands in 1664.

Germantown

The first permanent Mennonite settlement in America was that established at Germantown, Pennsylvania, in 1683 by a group of Germans of Dutch ancestry from the town of Crefeld and the surrounding region along the Lower Rhine near the Dutch border. This colony owed its existence to two forces—religious intolerance, and Quaker missionary zeal.

At the close of the seventeenth century, Mennonites had not yet secured entire religious liberty. The day of the stake and the rack, to be sure, were past; but even in Crefeld, which was one of the most liberal of German cities toward religious dissenters, Mennonites were still compelled, as noted in an earlier chapter, to erect their house of worship on a back alley in order that they might not attract public attention. Active promotion was forbidden. Special taxes were levied against them. Frequently they were subjected to extortion at the hands of petty, but greedy, lords upon whose estates they lived. The Quakers, who by now had several congregations in the cities along the Lower Rhine, were especially abused because of their aggressive efforts in extending their faith.

It will be remembered that between 1655 and 1680, a number of Quakers from England, including both Fox and Penn, had visited northwest Germany and the Netherlands repeatedly in the interest of their cause. These were especially well received by the Mennonites, among whom the Quakers gained a number of converts in some of the Mennonite centers along the Rhine, including Crefeld and Kriegsheim, the two regions from which the first Mennonites and Mennonite-Quakers migrated to Pennsylvania. It was to these Mennonite-Quakers and their Mennonite friends and relatives that Penn first made his appeal for German immigrants to his newly inherited colony of Pennsylvania. In 1682, Jacob Telner, a Mennonite merchant of Amsterdam, together with five other Mennonites and Quakers from Crefeld and surrounding towns, purchased 18,000 acres of land in Pennsylvania for the purpose of founding a settlement. At about the same time, a group of Pietists from Frankfurt am Main, under the leadership of Francis Daniel Pastorius, established the Frankfurt Land Company which purchased 40,000 acres north and west of Philadelphia. It was from these two groups that the actual settlers purchased most of their land.

Soon after, on October 6, 1683, a group of thirteen families from Crefeld and the surrounding region, one Mennonite and twelve Mennonite-Quakers, arrived at Philadelphia on board the ship *Concord*. They immediately proceeded north several miles to a place selected for them by Pastorius, who had preceded them by several months, and founded Germantown, the first German settlement in America.

Francis Daniel Pastorius was a Pietist, not a Mennonite. As agent of the Frankfurt Land Company and founder of Germantown, he served the colony well as legal adviser, as scrivener, as the first magistrate, and finally for many years as schoolteacher. The author of many letters and treatises, he became the chief historian of the settlement.

Unlike later Mennonites who came to America, these first Mennonite and Quaker settlers were mostly mechanics and linen weavers and "not given much to agriculture." They founded a village, cultivated the soil on a small scale at first, but soon turned to weaving as their chief industry. Although they passed through a brief period of hardships, they were free from Indian dangers and disease epidemics, fatal to so many colonial experiments. These first thirteen families were soon followed by other settlers, many of whom located on the lands about the village. By 1700 the following family names, including the first comers, appear in the early records—*Telner, op den Graeff, Lensen, Streypers, Lückens, van Bebber, Jansen, Schumacher, Kassel, Keyser, Rittinghausen, Kunders, Tyson, Siemens, Keurlis, Bleikers, Tunes, van Sintern, Neus, Engel, Schlegel*, and others.

Mennonite immigrants to Germantown were not numerous. In all there were perhaps not more than fifty families. Later, many more located farther north and west along the Skippack and Pequea. After 1700, however, Germantown became the nucleus of a large settlement of non-Mennonites. Especially attractive was the colony for numerous German religious groups and denominations. In Germantown were organized not only the first Mennonite congregation and the first, and perhaps only, German Quaker congregation in America, but also the first Dunkard, German Reformed, German Lutheran, and German Moravian congregations, among others.

Soon after 1702 the available land around Germantown had largely been taken up, which necessitated the establishing of a second Mennonite settlement along Skippack Creek, a tributary of the Perkiomen, about thirty miles above Germantown. This new settlement, begun by a Germantown settler and several of his fellow immigrants a little later, became the center of a flourishing colony of Palatine Mennonites.

In Germantown, the few Mennonites at first met with the Quakers in common worship. But as new immigrants came, and as they represented different denominations, the religious groups began to separate for worship. By 1690 the Mennonites, although they were still without a minister, met in a private house for religious instruction consisting of reading by one of their number from a book of sermons. Willem Rittinghausen, who arrived in 1688, was elected in 1690 as their first minister. In 1708 the first log meetinghouse was erected on the site occupied by the present structure on Germantown Avenue. The Mennonite group did not grow rapidly, as Germantown was passed by for the newer colonies farther west. By 1712 there was a membership in the two congregations of Germantown and Skippack of ninety-nine, embracing in all, perhaps, a Mennonite population of about two hundred.

Petition Against Slavery

These Germantown Mennonites and Mennonite-Quakers not only formed the advance guard of the German immigration to America, but they were pioneers in other important respects also. In 1688 they issued the first public protest against slavery on record in America, although the institution had also been forbidden in the Plockhoy settlement in 1663. To the German Mennonites, the holding of slaves ran counter to both their racial ideals and their religious convictions. The English Quakers still held slaves. It was for the purpose of showing their disapproval of the practice, as well as for the purpose of fostering German immigration, that a group of four men—Pastorius (Lutheran Pietist), Gerrit Hendricks (Mennonite), Derick op den Graeff (Mennonite-Quaker), and Abraham, his brother (first Mennonite, but later Quaker), sent a memorial to the Quaker Monthly Meeting protesting against the holding of slaves.

"Those who hold slaves are no better than Turks," the protest declares, "for we have heard that ye most part of such Negers are brought hither against their will and consent, and that many of them are stolen." The institution was also cited in Germany evidently as an argument against further emigration. "For," the protest continued, "this makes an ill report in all those countries of Europe where they hear off, that ye Quackers do here handel men, like they handel there ye cattle and for that reason have no mind or inclination to come hither."

The English Quakers were not ready yet, however, to champion the cause of absolute freedom. The Monthly Meeting, deciding the matter too weighty for their consideration referred it to the Quarterly Meeting, which in turn avoided the subject by passing it on to the Annual Meeting where no further action was taken on the matter.

A Political Experiment

The Germantown settlement also furnishes us an interesting example of an early Mennonite political experiment. In 1691 the village was incorporated under the laws of the province, the first to receive a special charter. The form of government provided for in this first Pennsylvania borough was that of a closed corporation, the corporate members being granted the exclusive right of the franchise, of legislation, and of admitting new members into the corporation. The first corporate members were mostly Mennonites and Mennonite-Quakers, who maintained control of the village government long after they were outnumbered by residents who did not share their religious views, nor their scruples against the use of force in maintaining order. So long as village ordinances and local litigation concerned themselves only with stray pigs and line fences, there was little difficulty in securing Mennonite officials. But with the building of a jail and the introduction of stocks and the whipping post, they lost their desire for office. As early as 1701 Pastorius complained to Penn that he found it increasingly difficult to find men who would serve in the general court for "conscience' sake," and hoped for relief from the arrival of new immigrants. Several men declined to accept offices to which they had been elected. Finally in 1707 the village lost its charter, and was merged for political purposes with the township of which it was a part. The Mennonites refused to hold office; but, together with the Mennonite-Quakers who had not yet lost their former Mennonite views against office holding, they at the same time retained control of the franchise. For this reason we have here the unparalleled instance of a corporation losing its charter because no one could be found who was willing to hold the offices.

Later History

The remaining history of the Germantown church can be dismissed with a few words. Later immigrants passed it by for more favorable lands elsewhere. In 1770 the old log building was replaced by the little stone structure which is still standing. At that time the congregation numbered only twenty-five. Since 1863 the Germantown Mennonite Church has been a member of the General Conference Mennonite Church.

However insignificant its later history may have been, the Germantown settlement yet exerted no small influence upon the church at large, and indirectly upon the civil and religious history of Philadelphia and the state of Pennsylvania. In the house of van Bebber was held, in 1690, the first service of the German Lutheran church in America; and, according to N. B. Grubb, at least ten of the churches of Philadelphia—including one Evangelical, two Episcopal, and one Presbyterian—were all first organized in the little Germantown Mennonite meetinghouse. Many of these also drew heavily upon the Mennonites for their membership.

Prominent Names

In the list of names prominent in the industrial and political life of Pennsylvania can be found many of the descendants of the first Mennonite settlers. In 1690 Willem Rittinghausen built on the

Wissahickon River the first paper mill in America. His great-grandson, David Rittenhouse, born in 1732, became a celebrated astronomer of his day, and was an intimate friend of Thomas Jefferson and Benjamin Franklin. A prominent member of the Assembly during the Revolutionary War, he was appointed by Washington as the first director of the United States Mint. Among other prominent descendants of these first Mennonites, to mention only a few, were: Governor Samuel Pennypacker, who in addition to his political activities did much to create an interest, not only in Mennonite history, but also in that of all Pennsylvania Germans; Samuel Cunard, founder of the well-known *Cunard* steamship line; and William C. Gorgas, who by discovering the yellow-fever mosquito eliminated one of the most dreaded scourges of the land, and made the building of the Panama Canal possible. Gorgas was the direct descendant of both John Gorgas, a charter member of the Germantown Mennonite church, and Willem Rittinghausen, the first Mennonite minister in the Germantown congregation and in America.

2. SWISS-GERMAN PALATINES

These early Germantown Mennonites, coming largely from northwestern Germany, and for the most part of Dutch stock, constituted but the advance guard of the steady stream of Mennonite immigration which found its way into Pennsylvania throughout the first half of the century. After 1700 few came from this part of Germany. A much larger migration was that of the Swiss-Germans from the Palatinate. Although we are primarily concerned here with the Mennonites, it must be remembered that during this period tens of thousands of Germans of every faith known in Germany—Lutherans, Reformed, Catholics, Dunkards, Schwenkfelders, Moravians, and mystics—settled in southeastern Pennsylvania to form the basis of that picturesque element of the "Quaker State" population commonly known as the Pennsylvania German or "Dutch" (which they are not!).

The cause of this immigrant tide was mainly economic pressure, although in the case of some, religious oppression was a contributing factor. During the early eighteenth century there was great poverty and distress throughout the Palatinate. During the war of the Palatinate (1688-1697) the French armies completely devastated the country. Soon after, severe winters and famine added to the distress. Just at this time, too, came an urgent invitation, widely published, from Queen Anne of England to settle in the American colonies. The climax of distress seems to have been reached in the year 1709, for in that year a sudden

FIRST SETTLEMENTS AND EXPANSIONS

emigration fever seems to have seized the Palatines. Some eight or ten thousand during the year poured into England, hoping to be transported to America. The English government, surprised at this sudden inundation of Germans, was hardly prepared to care for them. Most of them were induced to return to Germany; some were settled in Ireland. About six hundred were transported to the Carolinas where Graffenried had already established a Swiss colony in New Bern. The next year a number were sent to New York. Only a few families found their way in this year to Pennsylvania. The next year, however, and the years following, Pennsylvania became the chief objective of the movement. The Mennonites, who formed only a small part of this tide, had added reason for leaving the Palatinate. While the larger portion of the settlers were Germans, the Mennonites were Swiss exiles who had been forced to find temporary homes in the Palatinate in 1671 and the years following. These were still living under annoying and oppressive religious restrictions.

Along the Skippack

The first Mennonite Palatine immigrants joined some Germantown colonists in founding the Skippack settlement on a tract of land bought by Matthias van Bebber in the year 1702, in what is now Perkiomen Township, in Montgomery County. Before 1709, however, there were only a few scattered families. According to William Penn, in that year six Palatine Mennonite families left London for Pennsylvania. Where they settled is uncertain, although it was undoubtedly along the Skippack. This initial colony expanded during the next fifty years by natural increase and by additions from Germany until it formed a Mennonite community on both sides of Skippack Creek ten miles wide extending north through the north central part of Montgomery County, the western part of Bucks County, a small section of eastern Berks and Lehigh counties, southern Northampton, and included also a few scattered settlements in Chester County. By the time of the Revolutionary War, the following congregations were already well established in this area—Skippack, Deep Run, Franconia, Salford, Swamp, Plain, Methacton, Schuylkill, Hereford, Springfield, Rockhill, Blooming Glen, Coventry, Upper Milford, Saucon, Siegfried, and others.

Among the prevailing Mennonite family names in their modern spelling are the following: *Alderfer, Allebach, Bauman, Bechtel, Beidler, Benner, Bergey, Boyer, Clemmer* or *Clymer, Detweiler, Fretz, Frey, Funk, Gehman, Geil, Geisinger, Haldeman, Hoch, Hiestand, Huffman, Hunsicker, Kratz, Longenecker, Moyer, Oberholtzer, Pennypacker, Roth, Schowalter, Shelly, Souder,*

Stauffer, Wambold, Yoder, Ziegler, and others.

An early Mennonite Palatine settlement was made in the Watauga Valley in North Carolina which was still in existence in 1773, but of which little is known since. This was likely a daughter colony of the Pennsylvania and Virginia settlements.

The Pequea Settlement

By far the largest and most important of the early Palatine settlements was the one established by the Mennonites along the Pequea Creek, a tributary of the Susquehanna in what is now Lancaster County. These pioneers who founded the first white settlement in the region of the fertile Susquehanna were mostly Swiss who had been driven into the Palatinate in 1671 and the years following. The Swiss exiles of 1709 and 1710 were not among the earliest comers, although later many of these found their way into Pennsylvania also.

This pioneer group consisted of ten men. "Switzers, lately arrived in the Province" to whom Penn gave in 1710 a warrant for ten thousand acres of land situated "on the northwesterly side of a hill twenty miles easterly from Conestoga near the head of the 'Perquin Creek.'" The consideration for the entire tract was five hundred pounds sterling money, and one shilling annually for every hundred acres. The region was "a rich limestone country, beautifully adorned with sugar maple, hickory, and black and white walnut on the border of a delightful stream abounding in the finest trout."

The first settlers were evidently well pleased with their surroundings, for early the next spring (1711) they sent one of their number, Martin Kendig, back to the Palatinate to urge their poverty-stricken and oppressed friends and relatives to join them in their new home. Kendig returned the same year with a number of new families. During the next fifty years hundreds of Mennonite families from the Palatinate—Swiss and South Germans—were added to the original Pequea settlement, for during all these years the Palatines remained poor and suffered certain religious restrictions in their native land. The distress in the Palatinate was aggravated, too, by the continual arrival of fresh exiles from Switzerland. These conditions, together with the invitation of the king of England (himself a German) to settle in Pennsylvania, as well as the repeated invitation of relatives already here, were responsible for the steady stream of immigrants who came to Pennsylvania during the next half century.

Dutch Mennonite Aid

Although a few of the pioneers were men of means, most of them were too poor to pay their passage money. The Dutch Mennonites of Amsterdam organized the "Commission for Foreign Needs" to help their needy Swiss and Palatine brethren. By 1732 over three thousand, perhaps not all Mennonites, had asked for assistance. Many of those were given aid. Among the Germans themselves, two elders, Benedikt Brechbill and Hans Burghalter, were untiring in their efforts to relieve distress and in enlisting aid through many letters to the Dutch Mennonites in behalf of those of their numbers who needed help. Both of these names are common today in Lancaster County. Burghalter was for many years a minister in the Geroldsheim church in the Palatinate, where he died at a ripe old age in 1752.

The year 1717 was one of exceptionally heavy immigration, for although the pioneer Pequea settlement remained largely Mennonite, many besides Mennonites were now coming to southeastern Pennsylvania. This settlement expanded until ultimately the Mennonites occupied nearly all of present rural Lancaster County, with some scattered settlements along the edges of the neighboring counties. By 1727 so many Germans had come to Pennsylvania that the English provincial authorities became alarmed lest the Germans completely dominate the political and social life of the province. To discourage further immigration, a law was passed levying a head tax upon every immigrant, and compelling every ship captain to submit a complete list of all new arrivals after 1727.

As to the exact number of Mennonites who came to Pennsylvania during the eighteenth century, most estimates are too large. The estimate of one hundred thousand Germans, all told, may not be much out of the way, but of these the Mennonites formed a very small part. The entire number, including children, was certainly not over twenty-five hundred.

By the time of the Revolutionary War, which marked the end of this period of German and Mennonite immigration, the following family names were common in Lancaster County—*Baer, Bamberger, Baumann (Bowman), Beyer, Boehm, Boyer, Brechbühl (Brechbill, Brackbill), Brennemann, Brubacher (Brubaker), Burghalter (Burkholder), Ebersole, Eby, Frick, Graff, Guth (Good), Herr, Hirschy (Hershey), Huber, Kaufman, Kendig, Kreider, Landes, Martin, Mellinger, Miller (Müller), Musselman, Neff, Oberholtzer (Overholt), Risser, Schantz, Schellenberg, Schenk (Shenk), Schertz, Schnebele (Snavely), Weber, Wenger,* and others.

Indian Raids

The Pequea settlement was in the heart of the Indian country.

For a time Mennonites and Indians lived on friendly terms, and their children often played together. But as the settlement grew, the Indians moved farther west, and during the later colonial wars the entire frontier, from Pennsylvania through to the Virginia settlements, often suffered from Indian raids. In 1758 a letter written by several Mennonite ministers to Holland asking for financial help stated that two hundred families in Pennsylvania had been robbed of their property by the Indians, and fifty persons had been killed. Among these were some Mennonites and Amish.

Naturalization and Redemptioners

According to the laws of Pennsylvania, only the English and naturalized non-English could bequeath and inherit property. Since naturalization could be secured only by special act of assembly upon petition, German Mennonites frequently found it difficult to become full-fledged citizens. The Germantown Mennonites were naturalized as a group in 1709. No Lancastrians were naturalized until 1729, and then only after years of petitioning. This act did not apply to the Amish, who had to petition separately in 1742. After 1742 a general act was passed covering all aliens, and special petitions were no longer necessary.

We have noted that the Palatine Mennonites were, with a few exceptions, mostly of the poorer classes. Many did not even have sufficient means to pay their passage across the Atlantic. Those who did not receive sufficient help from the Dutch relief committee were forced to seek means elsewhere. It was the practice in those days for poor emigrants to sell their services for a number of years to the ship captain in return for free passage. The captain could then dispose of this labor as he saw fit. Usually it was sold at public auction to the highest bidder when the ship arrived at Philadelphia. The term of service for an adult was usually four or five years, while a minor served until twenty-one years of age. Persons thus serving for their passage were called *redemptioners*. Many of the Pennsylvania immigrants, including Mennonites, were of this class.

Hardships of the Atlantic Voyage

The passage across the Atlantic was long and frequently hazardous. In fair weather and under normal conditions, ten or twelve weeks was sufficient for the voyage, and suffering was not great. But in case of contrary winds and storms, ships would often be driven far out of their course. The death rate, especially in cases of small children, was often high. In 1732 the *John and William*

FIRST SETTLEMENTS AND EXPANSIONS   369

left Rotterdam with 220 passengers, including a number of Mennonites. The ship was seventeen weeks on the way, and forty-four passengers died en route. In the same year another ship from Rotterdam bound for Philadelphia landed at Martha's Vineyard Island after a voyage covering twenty-four weeks. Provisions had become short. The passengers had no bread for eight weeks. So great was their hunger that they scoured the ship for vermin. A rat was rated at eighteen pence by the hungry castaways, and a mouse at six-pence. Seven died in one night. Of the 150 passengers that left Rotterdam only fifty survived, 100 having perished on the way. The next year, the ship *Experiment* left with 180 passengers and arrived at New York with only eighty on board.

These were exceptional cases, of course, but even at best a voyage across the ocean in those days was a matter requiring great courage. Added to these hazards beyond human control were others due to the greed of shipowners. Often greedy captains would overcrowd their ships, furnish poor food, and by failing to provide proper sanitation, greatly increase the death toll. In the hope of alleviating the worst conditions, Gottlieb Mittelberger, who arrived in 1750, wrote a book describing the situation on the immigrant ships. Thirty-two died on the ship on which he was a passenger. Among the breeders of disease on shipboard he mentioned "foul water full of worms, salted food, biscuits full of worms and spiders, damp, heat, hunger, lice so thick that they had to be scraped off." Warm food was furnished only three times each week, he said, and children under seven usually died from hunger, thirst, and itch. The Pennsylvania Assembly finally passed laws specifying the number of passengers that could be placed on board ship, and regulating the quality of food and sanitary conditions in general. For a long time, too, strict quarantines were maintained to prevent sick passengers from spreading contagious diseases contracted on board ship due to unsanitary conditions.

Mennonites in Lancaster

The Pequea and Skippack Mennonites were of the small farmer class in their Swiss and Palatine homes, and here too they became tillers of the soil, avoiding the towns and cities which developed later. It was the relatively few Scotch-Irish and English who organized and named the townships, cities, and other civil units. Although the Mennonites founded the first settlement in Lancaster County and later absorbed nearly the entire county, there are few names on the map outside of a number of crossroads post offices which would indicate a Germanic origin. Lancaster city was founded by the English settlers and developed into one of the most influential towns of the day. It was seriously considered by the first Congress as the permanent federal capital. A book on geography in 1816 calls it the largest inland city in America.

There was little organized ecclesiastical life among the Mennonites. Each congregation was a unit to itself. Occasionally matters of common concern, however, required united action. In 1727 a conference of all the Pennsylvania congregations was held to consider, among other matters, an English translation of their confession of faith. The following ministers and congregations were represented at that meeting:

Skippack—Jacob Gottschalk (Gaetschalck), Henry Kolb, Claes Jansen, Michael Ziegler.

Germantown—Johannes Gorgas, Jan Cunard, Klaas Rittinghuysen.

Conestoga—Hans Burghalter, Christian Herr, Benedict Hirschi, Martin Baer, Johannes Bowman.

Great Swamp—Velte Clemer.

Manatant—Daniel Longenecker, Jacob Begthley.

Frequent, but irregular conferences were held later. By 1844 Christian Herr, a local historian, wrote: "The Mennonite congregations in Pennsylvania are divided into three general circuits within each of which semiannual conferences consisting of bishops, elders or ministers and deacons are held for the purpose of consulting each other and devising means to advance the spiritual prosperity of the members."

Among the Palatines were a number of peace groups having much in common with the Mennonites. Among these were the Dunkards, who had their origin in Germany in 1708 and moved as a body to Germantown in 1719. They followed the Mennonites to their Skippack and Pequea settlements where their proselyting zeal gained a number of adherents to their faith. Conrad Beissel, one of their number, withdrew from them in 1728 and founded the Seventh Day Baptist monastic community at Ephrata. The old community house, where the brethren lived as monks in their cells, is still standing. Several of the early Mennonite pioneers were drawn into this movement.

The attempt of N. L. von Zinzendorf to unite all the Pennsylvania Palatines into one church did not seriously affect the Mennonites. Some Mennonites joined the Methodists through revival meetings during the latter quarter of the century. Among them was Martin Boehm, Mennonite bishop at Willow Street, who, as noted elsewhere, together with Ph. W. Otterbein, a Reformed minister, founded the United Brethren Church. He later also became one of the pioneer Methodist preachers in Pennsylvania. About the same time Jacob Engel, once a Mennonite, became

FIRST SETTLEMENTS AND EXPANSIONS

one of the founders of the Brethren in Christ.

The Mennonites were not a proselyting people. Consequently, although they lost large numbers of their members to other churches, they scarcely ever gained any in return. One of the reasons for the loss of membership, chiefly among the younger people, was the conservatism of the Pennsylvania Mennonites. The large, compact communities remained more conservative than did the smaller, more open settlements established in the states farther west.

3. EARLY AMISH SETTLEMENTS

Just when the first Amish came to America is not known to a certainty. Likely a few stragglers may have been included among the early Mennonite immigrants. It was not until about 1736, however, that the Amish came in sufficient numbers to establish their own settlements and form congregations. During the twenty-year period between 1735 and 1755, many Amish of Switzerland and the Palatinate arrived. There are today many descendants throughout the country. Their ancestors were Jacob Hochstetler; Jacob Beiler; Jacob Hartzler; Christian and Jacob Jotter (Yoder); Christian, Moritz, and Johannes Zug (Zook); Christian Herschberger; Christian Stutzman; and the bearers of such names as *Blauch, Detweiler, Fischer, Kaufman, Koenig, Lantz, Lapp, Mast, Miller, Peachey, Schrag, Stolzfus, Troyer, Umble*, and others. This list includes almost all of the common names of the Pennsylvania Amish and their descendants today. They have spread all over the country, and many of the bearers of these names are no longer either Amish or Mennonites.

The Northkill Settlement

The first Amish settlement and congregation was formed in 1736, some distance to the north of the Pequea Mennonite settlement, near a gap in the Blue Mountains in what is now northern Berks County, a region then spoken of as Northkill. Why these Amish established their colony so far out on the Indian frontier is not known. Perhaps it was because of the cheap lands, and perhaps partly because they did not wish to be too near to Mennonites. By 1742 the settlement was large enough to petition the general assembly for the rights of naturalization, without which they could not purchase land. Several other small settlements were located a little farther south in the same county soon after. But the entire number of Amish immigrants to Pennsylvania was not large during the eighteenth century, perhaps all told not over five hundred souls.

The Northkill location was not a happy one; it was too near the Indian frontier for safety. In the course of the French and Indian War, a series of Indian raids in 1757 resulted in the massacre of several hundred settlers all along the frontier line. Many of the Amish families were driven from their new homes. Jacob Hochstettler's home was attacked, and his wife and two children were murdered. Hochstettler and another son were carried away by the Indians. A few of the Amish came back after the war. But most of them sought safety nearer the older settlements in Lancaster and western Chester counties. The pioneer Northkill congregation eventually disappeared.

Religious Life

The Amish brought with them from their Palatine home the conservatism which had characterized their religious life in Germany and Switzerland. A report sent to Europe in 1773 by several Mennonite ministers in the Skippack settlement described the different Mennonite settlements in Pennsylvania: "As to the Amish, they are many in number but they are not here near us and we can give no further information except only this, that they hold very fast to the outward and ancient institutions."

Among the "outward and ancient" institutions which differentiated them from the Mennonites at that time were the *Meidung* (shunning) and foot washing, the latter of which the Pequea Mennonites also later adopted, though it was perhaps not practiced among them at the time of their immigration. The Amish were more conservative than the Mennonites in their dress regulations as well as in their social and religious practices in general. They retained their long hair, beards, and old styles of clothing. They met in private homes for worship, as had been their custom in Europe. In their church government they were congregational, though frequently the elders met to agree upon common rules for the guidance of their members in their social and religious practices.

These regulations were never printed, but were kept in manuscript carefully preserved by the church leaders and often copied from generation to generation. Many of these regulations are still in force among the Old Order Amish today. The Strassburg rules of 1568, drawn up before the Jakob Ammann controversy of 1693, were seemingly popular among the Amish of both Europe and America. As new conditions arose, new regulations became necessary. Although we have no record of any such new rules during the eighteenth century, yet in 1809 the Pennsylvania elders found it necessary to insist that the *Meidung* applied to eating and drinking as well as to all social and business intercourse. Shaving, trimming the beard, and jury duty were also forbidden; while high-collared coats, high trousers, high hats, combs in the hair, and other worldly customs were to be *garnicht geduldet* (not permitted).

Somewhat later, in 1857, in a meeting of the ministers of Somerset and surrounding counties, mothers were especially warned against dressing their children extravagantly. Such worldly vanities as a silk neckscarf tied in a fancy bow, high collars on the boys' shirts, and men's hats for the daughters were forbidden. Fancy house decorations, bright-colored paints, fancy glass dishes on the shelves, and mirrors on the walls were also discouraged. Jury service and voting were tabooed. Parents were warned especially against permitting their children to indulge too freely and recklessly in the pleasures of sleighing parties. Two-colored painted sleighs and vehicles were not allowed.

From this early pioneer settlement in Berks County a large Amish colony has since developed, covering the northeastern corner of what is now Lancaster County, the northwestern nook of Chester County, and the southern tip of Berks County. Many are still of the *Old Order*, with dress and customs and practices not far removed from those of their pioneer ancestors. The daughter settlements farther west will be dealt with later.

4. EXPANSION OF THE PIONEER SETTLEMENTS

Before the middle of the eighteenth century the best lands of southeastern Pennsylvania had been occupied by the German and Scotch-Irish immigrants. Consequently the children of the pioneers as well as later immigrants were forced to push the frontier line of settlements up the river valleys into the interior of Pennsylvania and Virginia. In the very front of this advancing tide were usually found a number of Mennonites, who settled in small colonies far out on the frontier where land was cheap, and where room for expansion was ample.

Maryland

Before the French and Indian War, Lancaster County Mennonites, following the advancing tide of settlements, planted colonies across the Susquehanna in York County, and then through the Cumberland Valley in Cumberland and Franklin counties, Pennsylvania, and Washington County, Maryland. Although a few stray Mennonites may have remained in the Cumberland Valley in the early rush into the Shenandoah, yet it was not until well toward the close of the century that the settlements were sufficiently large to form separate church congregations. On the Maryland side of the valley, however, they were sufficiently numerous in 1776 to demand some recognition from the state convention, which was then drafting a new constitution, when they refused to bear arms during the Revolutionary War.

The Shenandoah

As just indicated, the Cumberland Valley at first served as a convenient passageway through which the Pennsylvania Mennonites and the other Germans entered the beautiful Shenandoah. In 1729 at Massenuting along the south fork of the Shenandoah near what is now Luray, in the very first German settlement in the valley, were found some Lancaster County Mennonites. In a few years the Mennonites formed the largest contingent of the Germans in that pioneer settlement, although there were perhaps never more than several dozen families in that place. These settlements in Page County were never prosperous, and have long since become extinct.

During the French and Indian War, the Indians made raids into the valley and carried off many of the settlers. In one of these raids in 1766, John Rhodes, a Mennonite minister, his wife, three sons, and two daughters were killed by the Indians. A surviving son who was carried away returned to his friends after three years of captivity. Many families were compelled to return to Pennsylvania during these times.

This colony, too, was located in what was called the Northern Neck, a region to which Lord Fairfax for many years tried to establish a private claim. During this controversy many of the settlers, including the Mennonites, feeling themselves insecure in their land titles, moved farther up into the valley in what are now Rockingham and Augusta counties. By about 1800 the Mennonites had occupied the greater part of the Linville Valley, which embraced the region extending from Linville Creek on the east to the North Mountain on the west, and the Shenandoah on the north to Linville and Singers Glen on the south, a district about ten miles long by eight miles wide. After 1780, however, when Harrisonburg was founded as the county seat of the newly organized Rockingham County, many of the Linville settlers located west of the new town, where a large Mennonite community has since developed.

The Virginia Mennonites were the only members of their faith within the slaveholding Confederacy. To their credit it can be said that they never held slaves. Their attitude toward slavery is perhaps well illustrated in the following incident told by the

Quaker, John Woolman, in his well-known *Journal*:

> At Monalen a Friend gave me some account of a religious Society among the Dutch called Mennonists, and among other things related a passage in substance as follows: One of the Mennonists having an acquaintance with a man of another society at a considerable distance, and being with his wagon on business near the house of his said acquaintance, and night coming on, he had thoughts of putting up with him, but passing by his friend's fields, and observing the distressed appearance of his slaves, he kindled a fire in the woods hard by, and lay there for the night. His said acquaintance hearing where he lodged, and afterward meeting the Mennonist, told him of it, adding he should have been heartily welcomed at his house, and from their acquaintance in former time wondered at his conduct in that case. The Mennonist replied, Ever since I lodged by thy field I have wanted an opportunity to speak with thee. I had intended to come to thy house for entertainment, but seeing thy slaves at their work, and observing the manner of their dress, I had no liking to come to partake with thee. He then admonished him to use them with more humanity, and added, As I lay by the fire that night, I thought that as I was a man of substance thou wouldst have received me freely; but if I had been as poor as one of thy slaves and had no power to help myself, I should have received from thy hand no kinder usage than they.

As late as 1864, at a time when it took great courage in the South to oppose the institution, the Mennonites went on record in a conference resolution to the following effect:

> Decided that inasmuch as it is against our creed and discipline to own or traffic in slaves, so it is also forbidden a brother to hire a slave unless such slave be entitled to receive the pay for such labor by the consent of the owner. But where neighbors exchange labor, the labor of slaves may be received.

During the first half of the nineteenth century, the Virginia Mennonites developed considerable interest in literary and musical activities. Among the early Virginia families were the Funks. One of these, Joseph Funk, was especially active in this direction. He was a schoolteacher as well as a publisher of Mennonite books and tracts, sacred melodies, and music books. His was the first Mennonite printing press in America. In 1832 he compiled a book of sacred melodies called *Harmonia Sacra*, which had a wide circulation, not only through Virginia, but throughout the Mennonite church at large. It went through seventeen editions, the last one appearing in the latter 1870s. To the passing generation of Mennonites in the Shenandoah today, the *Harmonia Sacra* is what the McGuffey readers were to the old-timers in Ohio. Singers Glen, the original home of the publishing house, was known far and wide through the valley in its day as a center of sacred music. In 1837 Funk also translated and published the so-called "Long" Confession of Faith of thirty-three articles found in the *Martyrs Mirror*, together with *Nine Reflections* by Peter Burkholder.

Along the Juniata and Ohio Rivers

In the meantime the tide of settlement had ascended the Susquehanna and Juniata. In 1772 John Graybill from Lancaster County began a settlement on the Mahantago in Snyder County, near what is now Richfield. A little later several other small Mennonite communities were established nearby, and in neighboring counties, but these never became large, and most of them finally disappeared. The largest settlement in this general region was formed by Lancaster County and Berks County Amish near the close of the century in the picturesque valley of the Kishacoquillas, in the present Mifflin County. This picturesque valley is now almost completely occupied by Amish, mostly of the Old Order, but including also about all the varieties of Amish known.

At the same time, in 1767 Christian Blauch founded an Amish settlement near the headwaters of the Ohio River. This early settlement, made even before the Indians had been officially removed from the land, has since grown into a number of large Amish and several Mennonite congregations covering Westmoreland, Fayette, and Somerset counties. Among other early Amishmen to locate in this region was Joseph Schantz, founder of Johnstown in 1800.

5. ONTARIO

The largest and most important of the settlements of this period was the one located across the Great Lakes, in Ontario, at the very end of the century. By this time land prices in the thickly settled regions of southeastern Pennsylvania had risen extraordinarily high. But it was not population pressure alone that induced the surplus population of the older Mennonite congregations to seek a new home in Canada. The Pennsylvania Mennonites, because of their nonresistant faith, were opposed to political revolutions of any sort, including the Revolution of 1776. Consequently they were frequently accused by the revolutionary party as lukewarm toward the American cause and sometimes even as sympathetic toward the loyalists. In a few cases they were imprisoned, their property confiscated, and their lives threatened by superpatriotic mobs. The period of anarchy immediately following the war did not add to their feeling of security under the Confederation Congress. The Mennonite movement to Canada continued long

FIRST SETTLEMENTS AND EXPANSIONS

after a stable constitutional government had been established in the United States, and the young state of Pennsylvania had guaranteed both the Mennonites and the Quakers full religious toleration, including military exemption, in its fundamental law.

The Canadian government offered liberal inducements and free lands during this early period before the adoption of the United States Constitution. Thousands took advantage of these liberal terms, settling a large part of what is now Upper Ontario. This region was still the Canadian West at that time, with wide stretches of unoccupied lands awaiting industrious settlers. Being especially desirous of settlers of good reputation, the Canadian authorities offered exceptional inducements, including military exemption, to Quakers and allied groups.

The Mennonites from the crowded settlements of Pennsylvania went to Canada largely because land was cheap and fertile, and also because before the day of railroads and hard roads it was easier to follow the river valleys to the north and west into Canada than to cross the mountains over rough wagon trails into western Pennsylvania and Ohio.

The Twenty Mile Creek

By the beginning of the nineteenth century, three separate Mennonite settlements had been established across the Niagara in Ontario. The first of these was founded in 1786 near the mouth of Twenty Mile Creek where it empties into the south shore of Lake Ontario about twenty miles west of the Niagara. Five families from Bucks County, Pennsylvania—the Kulps, John, Dilman, and Stoffel; Franklin Albright; and Frederick Hahn—were the first settlers. Others followed in the years immediately succeeding until a substantial settlement was made with a total number of about one hundred souls. Soon other congregations were formed in the surrounding country, mostly from Bucks, Lancaster and other Pennsylvania counties. In the course of a short time, several small settlements had also been made to the south, on the northern shore of Lake Erie.

Waterloo County

A much larger settlement was established about the same time some sixty miles to the northwest, farther out on the frontier, where land was still cheaper in the heavily timbered valley along the Grand River. The families of Joseph Schoerg and Samuel Betzner of Franklin County, Pennsylvania, were the pioneers in this settlement, locating on the Grand River near what is now Kitchener, but was then a wilderness. This whole region had recently been vacated by the Indians, and was still unsettled except for a few wandering fur traders. Schoerg and Betzner were the first permanent white settlers, it is said, within what is now Waterloo County. Later in the same year, several more families from Lancaster County located here, to be followed each year by many others.

But in 1803 it was accidentally discovered that the farms which had thus far been purchased for several dollars per acre from a land speculator by the name of Richard Beasley were all heavily mortgaged, a fact which speculator Beasley did not mention at the time of the sale. For the time being, immigration ceased; and the colony seemingly was about to be broken up when a group of Lancaster County brethren came to the rescue. Upon the advice of Hans Eby, a group of Lancaster Mennonites formed a stock company to buy up the entire tract of sixty thousand acres, about two-thirds of entire Waterloo Township. The tract was divided into 134 parcels of 448 acres each. By paying off the first installment of the purchase price, $20,000, the mortgage was released and the title cleared. This was before the days of banking. It is said that the whole sum in silver coins was safely carried by wagon to Canada.

This effort at cooperation seemingly met with popular approval, for a few years later another stock company along similar lines was formed to purchase a tract of 45,000 acres in the neighboring township of Woolwich. This land, too, was paid for with a barrel full of gold and silver, carted without mishap all the way from Pennsylvania.

Immigration to the Waterloo settlement was now resumed again, and during the next twenty years numerous families, largely from Lancaster County but from all the other older settlements of Pennsylvania as well, were added. A little village soon developed within the settlement, at first called Ebytown. Upon the advice of Benjamin Eby it was changed in 1827 to Berlin, then during World War I, to Kitchener.

Markham

In the meantime the uncertainties caused by the Beasley fraud deflected the immigrant tide for a few years in a new direction. In this same year, 1803, Henry Wideman, a Mennonite minister from Bucks County, started a new settlement near Markham, some twenty miles north of what was then known as York, but now as Toronto. Several small congregations developed in this region.

During the War of 1812 there was no immigration for a few years, but it was resumed again soon after. The Mennonites were not forced to serve in the army, but a number were impressed with their teams into the transportation service in the Niagara region

FIRST SETTLEMENTS AND EXPANSIONS

during the battles that were fought in that area.

Among the most common names within these three original Canadian settlements are: *Bauman, Bechtel, Bergey, Betzner, Brubaker, Burkholder, Cressman, Detweiler, Eby, Erb, Gehman, Gingerich, Groff, Hagey, Horst, Hunsberger, Hoffman, Hoch, Hallman, Hoover, Kolb, Martin, Moyer, Musselman, Reist, Reichert, Shenk, Stauffer, Snyder, Shoemaker, Schantz, Wismer,* and *Witmer.*

All told, between 1786 and 1825 perhaps about two thousand Mennonites, including children, migrated to Ontario from Pennsylvania. Beginning with 1824 several hundred Amish immigrants from Europe also located near the Waterloo Mennonites.

Pioneer Hardships

These early pioneers were of hardy stock and endured the usual pioneer hardships. The journey from the Pennsylvania settlements to Waterloo covered about five hundred miles and was made sometimes on horseback but most often with the well-known Conestoga wagon. Well stocked with household utensils and bounteous eating supplies, the wagons were drawn by four or five sturdy horses, and sometimes accompanied with cows that furnished milk along the way. The route usually followed to Waterloo took the home seekers up the Susquehanna, across the Finger Lake region in New York, up the Mohawk to the Niagara, a little below Buffalo, then by way of what is now Hamilton, through the almost impassable "Beverly Swamp" to their new home on the Grand. Of course they were all genuine Pennsylvania Germans and brought with them to their Canadian homes their dialect, tastes, social customs, and religious practices.

Like Mennonites everywhere, their first task after making the first clearing for their log huts was to organize a congregation and establish a school for their children. Among the early spiritual leaders was Benjamin Eby, who came to Waterloo in 1805, and who for fifty years was a leading spirit throughout all the settlements. In 1813 the first meetinghouse was built on Eby's farm and was known as the Eby church until well into the beginning of the twentieth century. Here Eby preached and also kept school for many years. He was also interested in a printing establishment which printed many pamphlets and church tracts throughout the period, including a short history of the Mennonites written by himself in 1841.

X
The Nineteenth Century Westward Expansion

1. PENNSYLVANIA AND VIRGINIA EMIGRANTS
Ohio

During the first half of the nineteenth century, Mennonites from the original settlements beyond the Alleghenies in both Pennsylvania and Virginia moved to the states of the old Northwest Territory. In the very opening of the century, and before Ohio became a state, a small settlement had been started within the boundaries of that state. Among a group of settlers from Lancaster County, Pennsylvania, who had founded the present town of Lancaster in Fairfield County, just ten years after Marietta was settled, was a Mennonite named Martin Landis, who a few years later built a meetinghouse on his farm to be at the service of all denominations desiring to use it. Several years later a number of Mennonites came to the same region from Pennsylvania and Virginia. Among these was Henry Stemen, who settled near the present town of Bremen in 1803, and who became one of the pioneer Mennonite ministers of the state.

During the next fifty years a number of communities were established in various parts of the state, wherever cheap lands in good farming regions were to be found. Congregations were begun in Stark County in 1811; in Mahoning and Columbiana counties equally as early if not earlier; and in Wayne and Medina counties in 1825, and 1834, respectively. Before the Civil War, small groups had located throughout northwestern Ohio in Allen, Putnam, Hancock, Wood, Seneca, Williams, Ashland, Clark, and Franklin counties. With the exception of several small congregations near Elida, in Allen County, these latter have practically all become extinct. During these years, too, a large number of Europeans, both Mennonites and Amish, located in Ohio, as did also a number of Amish from Pennsylvania. In 1852 Ephraim Hunsberger of the Oberholtzer following from Montgomery County, Pennsylvania, organized a congregation at Wadsworth, in Medina County.

New York, Indiana, and Illinois

During the same period, several small settlements had been made in northwestern New York not far from the Niagara boundary. Natives from Lancaster County, Pennsylvania, had located in Niagara County in 1810, and in Erie County in 1824. In 1831 several German families from the Palatinate found their way here also.

The first Mennonites in Indiana were the Swiss, who came in 1838. The first native members of the church, however, came from Ohio under the leadership of John Smith from Medina County, who visited Elkhart County, Indiana, in 1843. Two years later he returned with others and began a community in Harrison Township in Elkhart County. Others followed, and soon several congregations were formed in the county. In 1853 a group of Mennonites from Holland joined the present Salem congregation. Several church divisions occurred in Indiana during the early 1870s, one led by Jacob Wisler and another by Daniel Brenneman. These are discussed elsewhere. Later a number of Wisler and Mennonite Brethren in Christ congregations were established in the region of the early settlement.

Mennonites reached Illinois even earlier than Indiana. The first Mennonite family to locate in Illinois was the Benjamin Kendig family from Augusta County, Virginia. The Kendigs left their home in the spring of 1833 in search of better opportunities in the Far West. Loading all their worldly possessions on three Conestoga wagons, they began their journey overland through Kentucky, Indiana, and Illinois for their western home. In October of the same year, after a journey of eight hundred miles, which was made in seven weeks, they reached what was then known as Holland's Grove in Tazewell County. Others followed from Virginia and Pennsylvania to form a Mennonite community near the Amish settlements begun two years before. But the community never grew large, and at times it was scarcely able to maintain itself as a religious organization.

Between 1833 and 1865 a number of small groups of Mennonites from the East located throughout the state, but none of them were large. Among the congregations are those at Freeport, founded in the forties; Cullom, in Livingston County, established in 1858; Sterling, founded about the same time; and Morrison, in 1865. Several other congregations were organized which have since become extinct. There was also a small congregation of Pennsylvania Reformed Mennonites, near Sterling, formed in 1847. The large Amish settlements throughout central Illinois are described elsewhere.

Beyond the Mississippi

After the Civil War small scattered groups of Mennonites from the East were located in Iowa, Missouri, Nebraska, Kansas, Idaho, Colorado, Oregon, Oklahoma, North Dakota, Texas, and several other states. These Pennsylvania German Mennonites on their westward trek were followed and accompanied by the Mennonite immigrants coming in large numbers from Russia, Poland, and West Prussia in the years 1873 to 1880.

The pioneers in the Far West had to endure all the usual hardships of frontier life. Many were homesteaders and most of them were poor. In the early 1870s the grasshopper plague, and later hot winds, drove many either back East or to other more favorable western localities. Others remained and have since become fairly prosperous.

The Amish Move West

The trans-Allegheny settlements described thus far in this chapter were from the Mennonite congregations only. The Amish also followed the lure of the cheap lands of the West during this period, and established many new settlements in all these states.

The pioneer Amish in Ohio were "Yockle" Miller and his two sons and their families from Somerset County, Pennsylvania, who located along Sugar Creek in Tuscarawas County in 1808. These were followed soon by many others from the same region. Although the further settlement was temporarily halted for a few years by the dangers of Indian raids in the War of 1812, and the early comers had been driven back East, yet soon after the war, additional arrivals flocked to the new colony in large numbers. The settlement spread across the western part of Tuscarawas County and the eastern end of Holmes County, forming one of the largest compact Amish communities in America.

Some years later, Pennsylvania Amish communities were formed in Wayne, Fairfield, Logan, and Champaign counties, and still later in Geauga County, in all of which, except in Fairfield, large compact settlements were established.

By 1840 the westward tide had reached Indiana. After visiting Iowa and walking back much of the way through Indiana, a group of landseekers from Somerset County, including Joe Miller, decided to locate in Elkhart County east of what is now Goshen. From Pennsylvania and some of the older Ohio settlements there were developed within the next twenty-five years numerous congregations in Elkhart, Noble, LaGrange, Marshall, Adams, Newton, Howard, Miami, Allen, Jasper, Davis, and Brown counties.

Between 1848 and 1852 several Mifflin County families founded the Rock Creek congregation in McLean County, Illinois. After the Civil War another large community of conservative Pennsylvanians, largely from Somerset County, established the Moultrie County and Douglas County congregations.

In Iowa the first settlement of Amish was established in 1846 in Johnson County by a number of Pennsylvanians. The lure of cheap lands called numerous pioneers from all these older states to Nebraska, Kansas, Arkansas, Oregon, Colorado, Oklahoma, the Dakotas, Montana, and Idaho.

2. THE NEW IMMIGRANT TIDE

In the meantime, a new immigration of both Mennonites and Amish had set in between 1820 and 1860. The Mennonites came from Switzerland and Bavaria and Hesse-Darmstadt, while the Amish were largely from Alsace and Lorraine. To the general causes of this mass immigration movement after the Napoleonic wars—militarism, economic distress, and political unrest in such revolutionary years as 1820, 1830, and 1848—may be added the rapid expansion and economic development of the Middle West during this period. Directly after the War of 1812, statistics show that the immigration tide from all classes from middle and western Europe rose rapidly, culminating especially in the high record of the year 1820. Enthusiastic letters to friends and relatives in Europe from those already here and systematic advertising on the part of ship companies in all the large centers of population greatly aided the immigration movement during those years.

The Mennonites were especially concerned about the military question. The Mennonites of France, South Germany, and Switzerland had all been pressed into service during the Napoleonic wars. At the same time they were trying to maintain their nonresistance. The Ibersheim Conference of 1803 threatened with excommunication all the young men who joined the army. The fear lest they might not be able to maintain their peace principles was a strong factor in determining the immigration of so many Mennonites.

The Swiss

Among the first of the immigrants of the new tide were the

Swiss from both the Jura and the Emmental settlements. The pioneer of this Swiss movement was Benedikt Schrag from Basel, who located with his family in what is now Wayne County, Ohio, as early as 1817. As a result of enthusiastic letters written back to his friends, two years later four families from the Jura congregations—Peter Lehman, Isaac Sommer, Ulrich Lehman, and David Kirchhofer—began the large settlement known as the Sonnenberg congregation near Dalton. In the years immediately following, many other families joined these early pioneers from both of the communities in the canton of Bern. Two large congregations were formed in Wayne County. In 1833 Michael Neuenschwander, who had come to Wayne County from Switzerland ten years before, began another settlement in what is now Allen County, along the banks of Riley Creek, three miles northwest of what is now Bluffton. In the years immediately following, numerous Swiss and several Alsatian families located in this region, and the community developed into four large congregations.

In the meantime, before 1838 Daniel Baumgartner and several others from Wayne County began another settlement in Adams County, Indiana. In a few years a small group of his fellow believers had settled in the same region and had formed a congregation. It was not until the years from 1852 to 1854, however, that large numbers came from Switzerland and laid the foundation of the present large Mennonite community at Berne.

From these pioneer Swiss settlements in Ohio and Indiana other small communities were established in Missouri, Oklahoma, and Oregon, with individual settlers in many localities in the West. Several small communities were founded in the western states by immigrants who came directly from Switzerland. Among these was a small group of fourteen families who located at Pulaski, Iowa, in 1873, under the leadership of Philip Roulet, who after two years in Butler County, Ohio, had come to Iowa in 1869. This group later moved to Missouri, however, and finally to Kansas. In 1883 another group of ten families came directly from the canton of Bern to Whitewater, Kansas.

The Immigrant Experience

When they left their homes, the Swiss immigrants of the earlier period packed their goods, wives, and children in one-horse wagons and started out on the first five-hundred-mile lap of their long journey through France to Havre. There they usually sold their horses, but not their wagons, and waited for the ship on which they were to take passage. A voyage across the ocean in the small sailing ships of those days was still somewhat of an uncertain and hazardous venture. One group of 175 persons in 1852 were given an entire vessel to themselves. A small cotton freighter, a three master, only one hundred twenty-three feet long and twenty-two feet wide, it had a carrying capacity of 800 tons. The captain, two steersmen, a cook, a mate, and nine sailors constituted the crew. In this frail bark they spent six weeks on the seas, a part of the time in heavy storms.

The ships usually landed at New York. Here these sturdy Swiss immigrants would again purchase a horse, which they hitched to the wagon they had brought over with them, and begin another overland journey of some five hundred miles over the mountains and across the rivers of Pennsylvania to their chosen homes in the hardwood forests of Ohio. The entire journey from Switzerland to Ohio usually lasted the better part of six months.

Since the first settlers were usually poor, they located on uncleared government land which could still be purchased at $1.25 per acre. The first years were spent in making small clearings and erecting the first log buildings. Farm products were cheap. The nearest market was one hundred miles away. Money was scarce. Local tradition has it that one Swiss in Wayne County walked fifteen miles to the home of an Amishman for a postage stamp to send a letter home. Clothing, from straw hats to wooden shoes, was all homegrown and homemade. For a long time, too, the Swiss retained their Swiss customs—hooks and eyes, and the *Schwyzer Dytsch* (Swiss German) in everyday conversation. Before 1854 baptism was always administered in private, never in public—a custom made necessary in the early days in Switzerland because of persecution.

In their church affiliations they remained for a long time independent from any of the organized American conferences. The Chippewa and a major part of the Sonnenberg congregations in Wayne County now affiliate with the Mennonite Church. The remaining communities in Ohio and Indiana joined the General Conference Mennonite Church in the early 1890s. In 1878 all the Swiss congregations in Indiana and Ohio met at Sonnenberg for a conference. The ministers present at that time were Ulrich Sommer, Christian Sommer, and Christian B. Steiner from Wayne County; John Moser from Allen County; and Christian Sprunger and Christian B. Lehman from Berne, Indiana.

The Hessian Mennonites

In the early 1830s about one hundred Hessian Mennonites from Hesse-Darmstadt, bearing such names as *Nafziger*, *Holly*, *Kennel*, *Iutze*, *Burckey*, *Jordy*, and *Kistler*, settled in Butler County, Ohio, near the Amish community there. About the same time a small group located among the Amish in Waterloo County, Ontario. A little later several Hessian families moved from here to Putnam County, Illinois, and in the early fifties a congregation was also established in McLean County, Illinois, near the Rock Creek Amish settlement. In all these places, after vain attempts to affiliate with the Amish in worship, the Hessians organized separate congregations.

From Bavaria

Between 1830 and 1855 some fifty families from southern Bavaria arrived in America. Although individuals from various Bavarian congregations were included in the different groups of both Amish and Mennonites who came to America during this period, yet most of them came from three congregations—Weierhof, Eichstock, and Maxweiler. Those from Maxweiler left as a body, as did most of Eichstock. The pioneer immigrant of this group, perhaps, was Jakob Krehbiel from Weierhof, who arrived at Clarence Center, New York, near Buffalo in 1831. A small congregation soon developed which later frequently served as a temporary stopping place for Bavarian arrivals whose destination was farther west.

In 1833 a small settlement started by the Krehbiels and Rissers was located in Ashland County, Ohio. This congregation was served some years later, among a number of earlier ministers, by Carl J. van der Smissen, former principal of the Wadsworth Mennonite School. The congregation is now extinct.

The chief Bavarian settlements were those in Lee County, Iowa, and Summerfield, Illinois, both begun in the early 1840s. Later, in the fifties, several groups from Bavaria augmented both settlements. The Lee County congregation was located near Nauvoo, Illinois, at this time the center of a large colony of Mormons, who were terrorizing the scattered settlements on both sides of the Mississippi. John Miller, the first minister of the Lee County group, was murdered in 1845 by a band of Mormons. This delayed the full organization of a congregation until 1849. Although the Ohio congregation became extinct in course of time, those in Illinois and Iowa have continued to the present day, and in the early 1860s became charter members of the General Conference Mennonite Church.

Among the common names of the Bavarian immigrants of the period may be mentioned *Baer, Dester, Ellenberger, Eyman, Haury, Hirschler, Krehbiel, Leisy, Löwenberg, Pletcher, Risser, Rupp, Ruth, Schnebele,* and *Schowalter.*

An interesting report of the means of travel to the West in that day, as well as of its hardships, is found in an account written in later years by J. E. Ruth, a member of an immigrant party of seventy-two, which arrived in Lee County in 1852. This party, which was gathered together from various congregations in Bavaria but principally from Eichstock and Maxweiler, left their Bavarian homes in early June of that year. They sailed from Havre in a sailing vessel, a three master with a tonnage of 1,500. The voyagers still carried their own provisions at this time, and had to prepare their own meals on shipboard. After a stormy passage of fifty-two days, the groups landed in New York where they had to wait for five days on a steamer that was to take them up the Hudson to Albany. From here they went by train to Buffalo, and from there by boat to Toledo. Here one of their number, father Lehman, head of a family of seven, became ill with cholera which was raging through the country at the time, and within ten hours he was dead. The boat stopped long enough to bury the body along the shore.

Reaching Toledo, the party again boarded the train on the first and only railroad then running into Chicago, then a little city of some fifteen thousand. This lap of the journey took two days, much of the time being spent on side tracks waiting for freight trains to pass. Not having brought sufficient food with them to last through the prolonged journey, the young men of the party were compelled occasionally during the long stops to scour the countryside for provisions. One morning young Wurz and Hertzler presented the hungry travelers with a fresh supply of pancakes and buttermilk coaxed from a generous housewife from a farm home nearby.

At Chicago, as everywhere else along the route, Ruth says, they were badly treated as "Green Dutchmen." Following their European practice, the women of the party took time out during their stay here to do their family washing on the shores of Lake Michigan. From Chicago the journey was continued southward by canal, the only means of travel then available in that direction to the Illinois River, thence down the river to Peoria.

The original destination of the group had been Summerfield by way of St. Louis, but hearing that the cholera also was prevalent in that direction they decided to stop off at Peoria and from there join the Lee County settlement. Here widow Lehman left the party by special carriage for Fort Madison, Iowa. On the way, her two-year-old son died. After carrying his dead body in her arms for half a day, she prevailed upon the driver to stop long enough at a lonely farm home along the way to build a coffin and bury the child under a shade tree by the roadside. The rest of the group left by stage for Burlington, and soon after arrived in Lee County, three months after they had left their homes in Bavaria.

The Amish Contingent

The largest group of immigrants of this period was the Amish, individuals here and there from Rhenish Bavaria, but largely from France—Alsace and Lorraine. The regions of the Saar and around Montbeliard and Belfort were especially well represented.

The Amishman who led the way in this general movement was Christian Augsburger, an Alsatian from the vicinity of Strassburg who, in the course of a land-seeking tour through the Ohio Valley in 1818, had occasion to come up the Miami as far as what is now Butler County. The next year he, with five other families, located the first pioneer Amish settlement of this migration near the present village of Trenton. A number of other families followed in the year succeeding and soon established a small congregation.

In 1832, as indicated earlier, a group of Hessian Mennonites located near this early Amish settlement, and at first worshiped with them. But in course of time, differences forced a separation. The Amish wore hooks and eyes, the Hessians buttons; the Amish forbade the use of musical instruments, the Hessians favored them. Other differences crept in and kept the two congregations apart for a number of years.

Being a pioneer settlement, Butler County became a convenient stopping place for a time for later Amish and Hessian immigrants who were headed for cheaper lands farther west, especially in central Illinois. Among the early ministers who made this congregation a way station for their westward trek was Joseph Goldsmith, who first settled in Waterloo, Ontario, becoming in 1824 the first Amish minister of that settlement. In 1831 he came to Butler County, where in 1838 he was ordained as a bishop in that congregation, only to move to Lee County, Iowa, in 1847 in time to help organize the first Amish congregation in that state. Another early minister was Peter Nafziger, also an immigrant to Canada in 1826; but because of the cold North, he chose in 1831 the more hospitable climate of Butler County. Here he served as bishop of the Hessian church until 1844, when he moved with his family to central Illinois. Here he died near the close of the century at the ripe old age of ninety-eight. Nafziger was sometimes called "the Apostle" because of his love of travel among the various scattered Amish settlements of his day. From New Orleans through Illinois and from Ohio to Canada he traveled, frequently on horseback and occasionally by foot. From Canada, too, for a stay of only one winter in Butler County, came the Rupp brothers, Christian, Andrew, and Jacob, who likewise preferred the cheaper lands of Illinois. Christian later became a bishop of the churches along the Mackinaw and adjacent prairies for many of the early trying years. Finally Joseph Stuckey, migrating with his parents from Alsace to Butler County in 1830, spent his young manhood here until 1850 when he too moved to the Rock Creek congregation in Illinois. There, in 1860, he was ordained to the ministry. Some years later he became the founder of the Illinois Central Conference group of Amish-Mennonites.

The Canadian settlement referred to above was the second of the European Amish settlements made during this period. The pioneer here was Christian Nafziger, a Bavarian who arrived in Waterloo County by way of New Orleans and Lancaster County in 1822 in search of homes for his brethren. After taking an option on a rather large tract of land in Wilmot Township, right next to the Mennonite colony already established here, he returned to Europe. He was not able to return until 1826, but in the meantime in 1824 several families had started a settlement on the lands selected. Many immigrants came in the years immediately following from Alsace-Lorraine, stragglers from Bavaria, and occasionally a Hessian, until a number of substantial settlements had been formed.

In the early thirties three new Amish settlements were started, one in Lewis County, New York; another in Fulton County, Ohio; and the third in central Illinois. The New York settlement was located along the Black River, one of the branches of the Mohawk in the northwestern part of the state, by settlers with such names as *Fahrni, Verkler, Nafziger,* and *Ringenberg.*

The immigrants to Fulton County came largely from the French section around Mühlhausen, with some Alsatians and a few Swiss. The first group arrived in 1834 and soon after with such names as *Koenig, Bender, Roth,* and *Gunday,* to be followed during the next twenty years by many others.

The largest of the Amish settlements of this period was that in central Illinois. The earliest arrivals here were Alsatians by way of Butler County. Peter Maurer, who in 1829 located along Rock Creek, a tributary of the Mackinaw in McLean County, was followed the next year by two others, John Strubhar and Nicholas Maurer, who made their journey from Ohio on foot. In 1831 a small group of Lorraine young people, some with their parents, arrived by way of Lancaster County, Pennsylvania, and the Ohio and Illinois rivers at what was then Ft. Clark but is now Peoria. A few miles below, at Wesley City, they established the first Amish community west of Ohio. The members of this group were Jacob Auer; Peter Beck; David Schertz and his father, Joseph Rusche, and two sisters; and Christian Roggi with three daughters.

Moving West

During the next twenty years many others came, mostly from Alsace and Lorraine, and located along the timbered belts bordering the tributaries of the Illinois east of Ft. Clark—the Mackinaw, Partridge, Ten Mile, Dillon, and Bureau creeks. In 1833 the first Amish congregation in Illinois was organized near the present village of Metamora, earlier known as Hanover, with Christian Engel, who had been ordained in Alsace as minister.

The route usually taken by the early pioneers to the Illinois country was Lancaster County, down the Ohio and up the Mississippi and Illinois rivers to Peoria. Later a more direct all-water route was found by way of New Orleans. For a time there was a small congregation at New Orleans.

These early settlements grew rapidly by additions from Europe until a number of substantial congregations had been established along the various well-timbered creek bottoms. The second and third generations, however, all moved out of their original homes to the more fertile open prairies to the east in Woodford, Livingston, Tazewell, McLean, and Bureau counties. After the Civil War there were several divisions within the original church—one resulting in the formation of the Central District Conference of the General Conference Mennonite Church and the other in the Defenseless Mennonites.

The Amish, as well as the Mennonite immigrants of this period, were of the same original Swiss stock as their Pennsylvania brethren of the preceding century. The Pennsylvanians were from the Palatinate while Amish came largely from Alsace and Lorraine, though the Mennonite group was largely from Bavaria, as just indicated. All were descendants, however, of the Swiss exiles of 1671 and 1710, and spoke Swiss-German.

Although of the same stock as their Pennsylvania brethren, yet the immigrants of the nineteenth century, and especially the Amish, introduced a number of new family names little known among the Pennsylvania Mennonites. The first fourteen are given below roughly in the order of their numerical importance: *Nafziger, Schertz, Bachman, Gerber, Stuckey, Schrock, Wagler (Wagner), Springer, Augsburger, Gascho, Oesch, Rockey, Rupp (Ropp), Ramseyer, Auer (Oyer), Albrecht, Pelsy, Burckey, Beck, Bender, Bechler, Brenneman, Egly, Fahrney, Guth, Gundy, Gingerich, Gautschy, Heiser, Holly, Imhoff, Iutzi, Jotter (Yoder), Kennel, Kinsinger, Klopfenstein, Kamp, Litwiller, Mosiman, Maurer, Neuhauser, Roth, Risser, Rüfenacht, Raber, Rediger, Ringenberg, Sommer, Smith, Slagel, Swartzentruber (Schwarzentraub), Salzman, Strubhar, Schweitzer, Staley, Steinman, Slabach, Streit, Verkler, Wise, Zehr,* and others.

All these Amish brought with them their European religious practices and social customs, most of which were decidedly traditional. Their worship was carried on in private homes for many years, the first meetinghouse in Illinois being erected by the Rock Creek congregation in 1853. Hooks and eyes, long hair, and beards for the men; and aprons, old-fashioned bonnets, and clothes severely plain for the women were rigorously prescribed until well into the last quarter of the century. *Meidung* and *Tracht* (shunning and clothing) were two favorite topics of discussion among the older brethren in all social conversation and among the ministers in church parleys. Everything new in religious and social practice was regarded with extreme suspicion. There is a tradition in the Partridge congregation in Illinois that in the late 1850s a certain Schertz, who, instead of following his immigrant brethren out to the creek bottoms east of Peoria, decided to take up business of his own in the city and had thus acquired a certain taste for city ways, was put out of the "meeting" one Sunday morning because he insisted on parting his hair and wearing a starched shirt front.

By the turn of the century, however, the children's children of the early fathers had discarded the most rigid of these regulations, and had begun increasingly to associate with the more progressive Mennonites and had begun to speak of themselves as Amish-Mennonites. They have now affiliated with other progressive groups, and the name *Amish* is no longer used by them.

The Dutch Group

Mention should be made here also in this list of immigrant groups of a party of fifty-two Dutch Mennonites who in 1853 left the congregation in Balk, the Netherlands, because of their opposition to military service, and their reluctance to follow their more liberal fellow Dutch Mennonites in discarding other traditional Mennonite practices. This little party located near Elkhart, Indiana, and their descendants today form a part of the conservative Mennonite congregation of Salem.

Judging entirely by the membership of the congregations that grew out of all these early settlements made by the Amish and Mennonites throughout the country, a rough estimate of the number of arrivals of all these various groups between 1817 and 1860 would be about as follows: Amish, 1,500; Swiss, 1,200; Bavarian Mennonites, 250; Hessians, 150; and Dutch Mennonites, 52.

Mennonites as Pioneers

The reader has already observed, no doubt, that the Mennonites and Amish have been among the pioneers in the westward march of the American frontier, and among the very first settlers in the opening up of new lands. By founding Germantown in 1683 they not only became pioneer settlers in Pennsylvania, but established the first Mennonite settlement in America. In 1710 they were the first whites to locate on the Conestoga, and followed hard on the heels of the Scotch-Irish hunters and traders who had blazed the way for the first permanent settlers. Before the mid 1700s they had joined the first Germans to venture into the beautiful Shenandoah. In 1772 they crossed the Alleghenies to establish one of the earliest communities along the Juniata. Before the Revolution they had reached the headwaters of the Ohio in the southwestern corner of Pennsylvania before that region had been vacated by the Indians.

In Ohio the Mennonites ascended the Hocking and located in what is now Fairfield County just ten years after the founding of Marietta farther down the river. In Illinois they began to clear the timber along the banks of the Illinois River in 1831, just ten years after the first log cabin had been erected in that part of the state. In 1839 they located in the southeastern part of Iowa before the raw prairies in that region had been occupied by the white man. And so, all through the West and Northwest, in Kansas, Nebraska, the Dakotas, Oregon, Oklahoma, and the Canadian Northwest, wherever new lands have been opened up for settlement, there Mennonites have been among the first to set up their log cabins and sod shanties, and always the first to establish pioneer churches.

XI
Pennsylvania German Groups

1. MENNONITE BRANCHES
Pennsylvania German Groups

A look at the American Mennonites gives the impression that they are divided into a great number of groups, and one wonders why this must be, especially since Mennonites emphasize the peace principle. There is no doubt that the Christian life should be in harmony with one's confession of faith. However, to understand why they are divided into so many groups which have so little contact with each other, the following has to be taken into account.

Not all existing separate groups originated through divisions. It must be remembered that Mennonites came to America from various countries and at different times. Settling in the United States and Canada at different places, they retained their practices, adjusting themselves to the local environment slowly and reluctantly. In many cases they did not know about each other nor did pioneer conditions permit them to fellowship together. It is only since the coming of the automobile and other more rapid means of communication and transportation, as well as the experiences which Mennonites shared during and after World Wars I and II, that large-scale opportunities to meet and get acquainted presented themselves.

It is true, however, that divisions have also occurred. These divisions occurred mostly when the Mennonites were challenged in their views and practices by some movement of influence coming from the environment in which they lived. Thus, for example, when a revival spread in their community, they were challenged to accept or reject the accompanying new and strange methods of promoting the Christian faith. Some would wholeheartedly accept the new methods while others would denounce and reject them. Often a minority broke away, accepting some of these innovations. Sometimes a group would separate from the mainstream because it considered that too many innovations had already been accepted. Thus, the more conservative group retained its identity.

The mainstream of the Mennonite congregations of the eighteenth and the nineteenth centuries in Pennsylvania shared in the Pennsylvania German culture which had developed in the state of Pennsylvania among Reformed, Lutherans, and others, all being of German background. In their religious life the Mennonites kept their old beliefs and practices, adjusting them only gradually to the demands of their day. It was taken for granted that a Mennonite was a farmer and needed no more than an elementary education. The elders, ministers, and deacons were chosen by lot and were the guardians of the heritage, invoking disciplinary action in case of deviation from the main path. Nonconformity was not much spoken of because it was still a reality. The right of the individual and the American principle of democracy were exercised only to a small degree.

Mennonites and Amish were peculiar in language, appearance, behavior, and religious practices and beliefs. As long as the adjustment to the environment was a gradual process, no great disturbance was caused. But whenever innovations were presented in too obvious ways and with impatience by their advocates, great disturbances and possible divisions were the result. Such innovations could be change from the German to the English language, the introduction of Sunday schools, greater emphasis on the need of personal conversion, missionary activities, secondary education, more democratic conference organizations, or any other method to promote the Christian cause hitherto unknown to the group.

The main Mennonite settlements of Pennsylvania, Virginia, and Ontario moved cautiously and slowly in their adjustment to the American environment during the eighteenth and nineteenth centuries, letting go those who would not consent to this rate of adjustment. Those Mennonites moving on to the frontier in the West, settling in smaller groups, were usually more ready to accept economic, cultural, and religious changes. Thus we find that the Pennsylvania Mennonites who settled in states like Indiana, Ohio, and farther west were much more progressive than those who remained.

Let us now briefly summarize the major divisions among the Mennonites of Pennsylvania German background and the causes and results for such divisions. This chapter will close with an account of the major group—the Mennonite Church, sometimes known as the Old Mennonites.

The Christian Funk Following

Because the Mennonites, with their nonresistant principles, did not actively participate in the Revolutionary War on either side, and because they refused to join the army and hesitated generally to take the oath required in the various tests of allegiance to the new state governments after 1776, they were suspected of loyalist preferences and frequently classified with the Tories. In the compact settlements where their principles were well known, they were not seriously molested by their non-Mennonite neighbors; but in isolated communities where they were in the minority, they were frequently given the same harsh treatment by local authorities and irresponsible mobs as were bonafide loyalists.

From actual military drill, which was prescribed by the Pennsylvania Assembly, the Mennonites and other peace groups were exempt, but they were to pay an extra sum of money called a *fine* for this privilege. These fines were paid with little objection, but as to whether they could consistently pay the special war tax which was levied upon all the inhabitants, there was some difference of opinion. Many of them joined the Quakers in their opposition to helping the war with their means as well as by actual bearing of arms. In 1776 a meeting was held in Indianfield Township for the purpose of choosing three men to represent the township in a general state convention which was to determine whether Pennsylvania should join the other colonies in declaring her independence from England. Most of the Mennonites who were present declared that since they were a "defenseless" people and could neither institute nor destroy any government, they could not take sides in this matter.

Among those present was a minister, Christian Funk, who though a staunch defender of the cause of Congress did not at this time seem to offer any serious objection to the above declaration. The following year, however, when some of his fellow ministers declared that their nonresistant principles forbade them to pay a special war tax of "three pounds and ten shillings," Funk protested and maintained that the tax should be paid. "Were Christ here," he said, "He would say, 'Give to Congress that which belongs to Congress and to God that which belongs to God.'" Andrew Ziegler, the spokesman for the opposite party, replied,— "I would as soon go to war as pay the three pounds and ten shillings." Funk was finally excommunicated for these views, and together with those who believed as he did, he organized several small congregations of his own throughout the county.

This small group of people, called *Funkites*, retained a separate organization until 1850, and when long after the participants in the original dispute had died, it became extinct.

The majority of the Mennonites of Pennsylvania objected not only to the payment of the special war tax but also to the new oath of allegiance which was required of all citizens after the Declaration of Independence. It was not that they did not wish to be loyal citizens of Pennsylvania, but in addition to their opposition to all oaths, they feared that this one in particular would commit them to the cause of the war. Many refused to take the oath, and some who took it were excommunicated from the church. The state authorities, however, knowing their scruples against both the oath and war, and that they were not disloyal, were inclined to treat them leniently.

That the local citizens were not always as considerate of conscientious scruples as the state authorities is shown by a handbill which was distributed among the citizens of Lancaster County by the local committee of inspection and observation in 1775. This interesting handbill, which appears among the exhibits in the museum of Independence Hall in Philadelphia is self-explanatory and reads as follows:

> The Committee having received information that divers persons, whose religious tenets forbid their forming themselves into Military Associations, have been maltreated and threatened by some violent and ill-disposed people in the County of Lancaster, not withstanding their otherwise willingness to contribute cheerfully to the common cause than by taking up arms.
>
> The Committee, duly considering the same, do most heartily recommend to the good inhabitants of the County that they use every possible means to discourage and prevent such licentious proceedings and assiduously culltivate that harmony and union so absolutely necessary in the present crisis in public affairs. At the same time they consider it to be their indispensable duty to intimate to the public their entire disapprobation of any abuse, opprobrious or insulting expressions that may be made use of by any persons whatsoever against such of the respectable inhabitants who may think proper to associate for the defense and support of their inestimable rights and privileges.
>
> The Committee will find means to bring such impudent persons to a proper sense of their misconduct. Yet they ardently wish and hope that no further violence, threats or animosities may appear, but that every member of the Community will readily use his utmost endeavors to promote peace, good order and unanimity among the inhabitants of this respectable County.

In Lehigh County an isolated group of Mennonites near Saucon, because they hesitated to take the new oath of allegiance required by law, were classed with the Tories by the local courts and treated accordingly. They were sent to jail and all their goods, including their bedding, household utensils, and even food were confiscated; and they were ordered out of the state within thirty days by order of the court.

Records are not available as to the final enforcement of the order. We know that the men were in jail, however, for we have a record of a petition sent by the wives to the court for the release of their husbands, since they were entirely destitute and without support.

There are numerous family traditions among both the Mennonites and the Amish of the period, especially in Berks and surrounding counties where Mennonite settlements were not large, of jail sentence and mistreatment by local authorities and citizens because of conscientious scruples against participating in war activities.

Although the Mennonites did not bear arms during the war, several of the engagements took place in Mennonite communities. The battle of Germantown was fought in the vicinity of the little Mennonite meetinghouse which still shows the scars of the battle to this day. The Valley Forge winter quarters were located in the Skippack region. A number of the Mennonites were forced into the service at the time, while the headquarters of a number of officers were in the homes of Mennonite farmers nearby. In Lancaster County the horses and wagons of the farmers were frequently impressed into the quartermaster service during the Pennsylvania campaigns.

Martin Boehm

Another event, the apostasy of Martin Boehm, while not a result of the war, yet occurred at this time. Boehm was a Mennonite minister at Willow Street in Lancaster County. During a visit to Virginia in 1761 he came into contact with a revival movement and was greatly influenced by it. By 1775 he had so aroused the ill will of his fellow ministers by his fiery preaching that he was expelled. In the meantime the Methodists had entered Pennsylvania, and Boehm soon cast his lot with them, becoming one of the pioneer Methodist preachers in Lancaster County. In 1800, together with Ph. W. Oterbein, a minister of the Reformed Church, he also became the founder of what was later known as the United Brethren Church. In 1805 he was elected a bishop in the United Brethren Church, but in the meantime he also had his name enrolled in the Methodist class book. Whether he was a Methodist or United Brethren was perhaps not quite clear to his friends, as the following epitaph which appears on the stone marking his last resting place by the side of Boehm Chapel in Lancaster County would indicate.

Here lie the remains of Rev. Martin Boehm, who departed this life (after a short illness) March 23, 1812, in the 87th year of his age. Fifty-four years he fully preached the Gospel to thousands, and labored in the Vineyard of the Lord Jesus in Pennsylvania, Maryland, and Virginia among many denominations, but particularly the Mennonites, United Brethren and Methodists, with the last of whom he lived and died in fellowship. He not only gave himself and his services to the church, but also fed the Lord's prophets and people by multitudes. He was an *Israelite* in whom was no guile. His end was peace.

The Reformed Mennonites

Another division occurred in Lancaster County in 1812, resulting in the organization of what is now known as the Reformed Mennonites. The founder of this branch was John Herr, never a member of the church himself but the son of Francis Herr, a Mennonite minister who had been expelled from the church on the ground of alleged irregularities arising out of a business deal. Francis Herr, together with several of his friends, also ex-Mennonites, held religious meetings in his own house for some time after that. Upon his death his son, John Herr, took up his cause, and becoming "convicted of sin," attended the meetings of his father's associates. He finally had himself baptized by one of these associates, whom he in turn rebaptized. Several others were added to the group, and John Herr was soon elected their minister. Thus was begun the group which assumed the name of Reformed Mennonites.

In numerous controversial pamphlets, the old church was charged with being dead, corrupt, and worldly. What Herr and his associates meant by these terms became clear by the practices they adopted soon after. The fundamental doctrines of the Mennonite church were retained, but in a few questions of practice they carried their principles to extreme lengths. They are still extremely exclusive in their religious affiliations. All those not of their faith are of the "world." They refuse to attend religious services of any sort if conducted by a minister of any other faith. The ban and avoidance are rigidly applied. They are severely plain in their dress, and discard all unnecessary adornment in their houses or on their persons as vain or sinful. They have no Sunday schools, do not support missions, nor evangelistic efforts. Many of the children do not join the church of their parents, and being taught that all other churches are "of the world," they frequently refuse to join any. Their largest settlement is still in Lancaster County, but they have a few scattered congregations in Ohio, Illinois, Michigan, and Ontario. Their influence has been small, although in Lancaster County there was often much bitter feeling for many years between the "old" and the "new" Mennonites. In 1958 the membership was 618 in nineteen congregations.

John H. Oberholtzer

The Eastern District Conference in Franconia, Pennsylvania, came into being in 1843 as a result of a controversy involving John H. Oberholtzer and others.

John H. Oberholtzer (1809-93) was born on a farm near Clayton, Pennsylvania. After having taught school for a number of years he became a locksmith at Milford Square, Bucks County. Soon he became known as an able writer and speaker. In 1842 at the age of thirty-three he became one of the ministers of the Swamp Mennonite Church of the Franconia Conference. Being a very fluent speaker and a popular preacher, he was frequently invited by his friends and admirers to hold meetings in neighboring schoolhouses and in the non-Mennonite churches of the community, a new and unpopular practice among the Mennonites of the time.

It was a rule among the Franconia Mennonites that the minister must wear the regulation "plain" coat, which was collarless. It was a sort of a short frock coat, and because of its rounded corners it was sometimes known among the nonclericals as a "shad belly" coat. For some years Oberholtzer refused to wear this prescribed clerical garb. This coat question remained a source of irritation among the Franconia Mennonites, and did not grow mellow with age. Oberholtzer had a number of sympathizers, especially in the Swamp and Skippack congregations, including his own bishop, John Hunsicker. Oberholtzer refused to wear the coat, and the Council, equally insistent, demanded that he must. Finally in 1844 those refusing to comply with the demands of the Council were denied the right to vote at Council meetings.

This was the situation in 1847. Influenced by some of his more moderate advisers, the young preacher had by this time decided to submit to the coat regulation; but much ill will had already been aroused by the controversy, and besides, another question too had arisen to disturb the peace of the brotherhood. The Franconia Conference was loosely organized. It had no constitution, no set rules of procedure, no commonly accepted discipline, and it kept no records of the Council proceedings. The only rule in practice was that at the Council meetings the oldest bishop, of whom there were five, should preside.

Oberholtzer, recognizing in this lack of organization the chief source perhaps of the arbitrary powers which enabled the majority bishops to deny the minority a hearing on their demands, now proposed that the Conference adopt a written constitution and discipline, with set rules of procedure and certain minimum agreements on religious practice, and that written records be kept of all Council sessions. In this demand he had the support of his own bishop, John Hunsicker. In a preliminary gathering, preceding the regular spring meeting of the Council, ministers and deacons who agreed with Oberholtzer, some thirteen in number, approved a prospective constitution prepared by him, and to be presented to the Council for their consideration.

But when the document was presented on the following day to the Council by majority vote, it was refused even a reading. The minority group then petitioned that it might be printed and presented at the next regular fall meeting of the Council. This petition, too, was arbitrarily refused, whereupon Bishop John Hunsicker, with perhaps equal arbitrary impatience, declared, "This is partisanship. It will be printed nevertheless."

And it was. Throughout the summer, no doubt, most of the ministers of the district had occasion to read the proposed constitution and familiarize themselves with its contents. But in the fall meeting the minority group, now grown to sixteen, instead of listening to the reading of their favored plan of organization, found themselves instead summarily and arbitrarily expelled by the bishops of the majority group for having subscribed to the ill-fated document. They were comforted only by the promise of reinstatement to their former status within the Conference upon confession of their errors.

Several weeks later on October 28, 1847, the minority group met again in the Skippack church with Abraham Hunsicker as chairman, and J. H. Oberholtzer as secretary, to organize what soon became the East Pennsylvania District of Mennonites.

This is the story as it is told in the controversial literature of the time. But the source of the quarrel lay deeper than in a difference of opinion about the cut of a coat, or the wisdom of adopting a written constitution. The new group did not differ from the old in its faith, in believer's baptism, nonresistance, opposition to the oath, rejection of secret societies, and in the retention of foot washing. The chief distinction lay rather in a more tolerant attitude of the *News*, as they were called by the *Olds*, toward the non-Mennonite world, both political and religious. Among the more liberal practices sanctioned by the former in the course of a few years were the use of the courts in "a just cause," and removal of some dress restrictions among both clergy and laity.

The Oberholtzer followers were among the first Mennonites also to adopt progressive methods of church work. Oberholtzer himself, as early as 1847, had gathered the young people of his church on Sunday afternoons for religious instruction, and by so doing is to be credited with starting one of the first Sunday schools among the American Mennonites. The official Sunday school among the group was organized in the Flatland church in 1853. The Swamp congregation also about this time introduced perhaps the first organ to be used in worship among the Mennonites of America. By 1865 a missionary society had been organized. In 1852 Oberholtzer founded the first American Mennonite religious paper, *Religiöser Botschafter.*

The new movement affected approximately a third of the membership of the Franconia Conference district. It claimed a majority in six of the congregations, including Skippack and both East and West Swamp, where they retained the meetinghouses. In a number of congregations the two groups worshiped in the same meetinghouse on alternate Sundays.

Oberholtzer and his group were instrumental in making contacts with other like-minded congregations and groups which culminated in the founding of the General Conference Mennonite Church of North America in 1860 at West Point, Iowa.

The Hunsicker Faction

The charter members did not all agree on the extent of the progressive movement. To Abraham Hunsicker, above mentioned, and his son Henry, the latter of whom had recently been ordained to the ministry, the views of Oberholtzer were not quite progressive enough. Together with a small group of sympathizers, the Hunsickers were especially opposed to the restriction against secret societies. For their attitude on this question, a number of persons scattered about through the different congregations were expelled from the new conference. These in turn organized several small centers of worship, which had only a temporary existence however. In course of time the Hunsicker following disintegrated, and the membership was absorbed by several other denominations.

The Evangelical Mennonites

Another disturbing question in certain Mennonite circles of the time was that of prayer meetings, and the need of a more spiritual life than that prevailing in the church at large. This resulted from pietistic revival influences spreading through the country at that time. William Gehman, a newly ordained minister in the Upper Milford congregation, began to hold private prayer meetings with an inner circle of adherents soon after his ordination. The movement soon attracted rather general attention, sufficient to merit conference notice. In 1853, after investigating the innovation and seeing no possible harm in prayer meetings, the new conference sanctioned them. But several years later, as a result of general dissatisfaction caused by an excessive emotionalism being manifested by the prayer group in their meetings and the assumption by the group of a piety superior to that of the nonparticipating group, the conference reversed its decision and declared that although it favored the spirit and practice of prayer in all religious meetings held by members and ministers in regular worship, yet it discouraged special meetings held for prayer only and the cultivation of intense emotionalism as then carried on. Gehman and his followers refused to abide by the advice, with the result that in 1858 he and twenty-two others were dismissed from the conference. Soon after, this group organized another small wing of the church, under the name of *Evangelical Mennonites*.

The Evangelical Mennonites grew rather slowly. By 1880 they numbered only 175 members. Later, however, through amalgamation with several other small similarly minded Mennonite groups from various parts of the United States and Canada, they developed in course of time into a body of substantial size. In 1978 there were 3,507 members in twenty-one congregations.

To say that Gehman and his following were expelled from the East Pennsylvania District Conference for holding prayer meetings does not tell the whole story. The East Pennsylvania District Conference did not oppose prayer, either privately or publicly, in connection with the regular service of worship, nor in special meetings if properly conducted and kept within bounds. That there was considerable unwholesome emotionalism connected with these meetings as conducted and danger of overemphasis of them as an essential adjunct to the regular forms of religious service is suggested by a letter written by Daniel Hoch of Canada to Oberholtzer about this time. Hoch, too, favored the prayer meeting movement of the time, though he evidently kept it within sane bounds. In his letter Hoch regrets the fact that Oberholtzer had not been seen in Canada for some time, and asks whether he has been detained by fear of prayer meetings, immersion, or handclapping and shouting, the latter of which, Hoch suggests, seems to him also to be the result of fanaticism.

It should be remembered here that the Mennonites as a whole were not given to much emotionalism in their worship. They took their spiritual life seriously as a normal growth, sometimes as a matter of fact perhaps. Children were taught the faith of the fathers and the ways of the church. In course of years, as a result of parental example and catechetical instruction, most of them arrived at a state of realization of the need of a personal Savior in their lives. Worship consisted of more or less formal services, and few attempts were made to stir the depths of individual religious feeling. In the main, their Christian convictions were sincere and deep and abiding. On the other hand, there were always a few who were more emotionally inclined and who longed for a more intense religious experience based on a more definite conviction of sinfulness and forgiveness than that demanded by the larger group. This was a major cause of tension in the church.

Church of God in Christ, Mennonite

In 1858 John Holdeman (1832-1900) of Pittsburg, Ohio, felt called to witness and preach without having received a call from his congregation. He was an ardent reader of the Bible and other inspirational books, including those written by Mennonite writers, such as the *Martyrs Mirror*. He first made zealous efforts to restore his home church to the image found in the Bible. Since he found little response, he decided to start a new church in 1859. Only a few in his home community joined him. To this day there are only a few congregations in the eastern states, although there are at least fifteen in Kansas and five in Manitoba. Today there is a membership of ten thousand.

It was John Holdeman's desire to reestablish the Church of God in Christ, Mennonite. He spent a lifetime in evangelism, preaching, traveling, and aiding those in need. His witness and zeal inspired others to win souls for Christ. He was most successful in Kansas among the Mennonites who had come from Poland during the migration in 1874 to 1880. They had a spiritual hunger and were also in need of help to get established, since many of them were poor. John Holdeman tried to supply their need on both levels. He found a similar situation among the *Kleine Gemeinde* members who had come from Russia to Manitoba and settled in the Steinbach area. He traveled much, preached, and organized congregations. He was the moderator of the conference he organized, and the editor of the *Botschafter der Wahrheit* which he started in 1897. This paper is still being read in English, as *Messenger of Truth*. John Holdeman not only read many books but he also saw to it that those who joined him would have spiritual nourishment in future years. Of the ten books he wrote, the *History of the Church of God* (1876), which appeared in German in 1875, is the basic book that defines the denomination to this day. In this book he featured the true church "as it was, whereby it can be recognized and how it can be perpetuated." Somehow some of the spirit of "exclusiveness" of his concept of the church prevails among his followers to this day.

The members of the Church of God in Christ, Mennonite,

commonly referred to as *Holdemans*, have today a very warm and appealing piety which makes persons feel at home in their midst. The discussions in Sunday school or around the dinner table are lively and full of spiritual vigor and warmth. The preaching is simple, warm, and Bible centered. The church discipline is possibly more rigid than in most of the conservative Mennonite groups of our day. Issues at stake are mostly of a conservative Mennonite-Amish nature. This includes rigidly enforced dress codes hailing back to the pioneer days with a strong emphasis on simplicity, particularly for women. There is a prescribed level of education; no use of musical instruments, radio, or television; and, for men, no neckties or shaving of the beard.

In the 1970s a wave of disciplinary action swept through the congregations which caused the excommunication of many and the tightening of restrictions everywhere. This seems to have been a uniform and widespread effort throughout all congregations to set standards and maintain them. It affected not only lay members but also ministers. The sincerity in this effort cannot be questioned, but it was not always matched with the love of Christ.

Old Order Mennonites

Another division occurred in the Yellow Creek congregation in Elkhart County, Indiana. Among the pioneer settlers in this community was Jacob Wisler from Ohio, a man devoted to the principles of the church, but exceedingly conservative by nature and opposed to the introduction of all new things, such as English preaching, four-part singing, Sunday schools, evening meetings, and revival meetings. In fact, every slightest departure from the ways of the fathers was banned by Wisler and a considerable part of his congregation. However, a number of the members of the congregation, under the leadership of Daniel Brenneman, a fellow minister, demanded a more progressive policy. This Wisler opposed, threatening with excommunication those who advocated the introduction of the new methods of church work. Finally, as a result of his arbitrary method of enforcing his views, Wisler was deprived of his office in 1870. He and those who believed as he did then organized a new congregation.

The same attempts to keep the church within narrow bounds were made by ultraconservative persons in other sections of the country. Finding themselves weak in number, but akin in faith, these finally affiliated themselves into one body. The first contingent to join Wisler's group was a band of conservatives in Medina County, Ohio. A little later, in 1886, several groups in Waterloo County, Ontario, who opposed English preaching, Sunday schools, evening meetings, "falling" top-buggies, and other evidences of "modernism" among the Mennonites of that community, withdrew from the church. These *Woolwichers* as they were locally called, soon allied themselves with the Indiana *Wislerites*. A second group, the *Martinites*, was led by Jonas Martin of the Weaverland congregation in Lancaster County, Pennsylvania, who withdrew from the church in 1893 because of a quarrel over a new pulpit recently installed in his church. Taking a conservative position on other questions, Martin retained one-third of his former congregation. The third group consisted of a conservative Virginia congregation in Rockingham County of about one hundred members which allied itself with the *Martinites* of Pennsylvania.

These four original groups of *Wislerites*, *Woolwichers*, and Pennsylvania and Virginia *Martinites* are a group now of about 12,800 members throughout Indiana, Pennsylvania, Virginia, Michigan, and Ontario. They are quite conservative in dress, forms of worship, and social customs, and are very slow to adopt new ideas. Although they do not wear hooks and eyes or homemade coats, they are similar to the Old Order Amish in their general spirit, and are known as the *Old Order Mennonites*.

The United Missionary Church

The *Mennonite Brethren in Christ*, now *United Missionary Church*, was the result of a series of amalgamations of four small kindred groups, three of which had seceded from the parent body for similar reasons, namely a more evangelistic and emotional spiritual life. One of these groups, the *Evangelical Mennonites*, has already been mentioned. Two of them had their origin in Canada.

New Mennonites was the name of a group of Canadian Mennonites who during the middle of the 1800s under the leadership of Daniel Hoch, an aggressive minister in the Twenty congregation, had been expelled from the church by Bishop Benjamin Eby for advocating and practicing special evangelistic and prayer meetings. Hoch himself, although at first one of the leaders of this group, did not follow the rest in the series of unions which finally ended with the Mennonite Brethren in Christ. He remained closely affiliated with the Oberholtzer group in Pennsylvania, and was one of the participants in the movement that finally resulted in the formation of the General Conference Mennonite Church of North America, of which he remained a member throughout his life.

Reformed Mennonites was the name of a group of Mennonites in Bruce County, Ontario, and in Elkhart County, Indiana. Solomon Eby had been chosen by lot to the ministry in the Port

Elgin, Ontario, congregation in 1858, but according to his own testimony had not been "happily converted" until 1869. Expelled from the main body for countenancing methods of worship unknown to the usual practice of the church, Eby had a number of followers throughout the different Canadian settlements. About the same time, Daniel Brenneman of the Yellow Creek congregation in Indiana had likewise been dismissed by the Indiana bishops for sponsoring a more aggressive evangelistic work in his community than was thought wise by his ministering brethren. After making several visits to Canada where a spirited revival movement was in progress among the Eby people, Brenneman and his following decided in 1874 to join their Canadian brethren in the formation of an organization called the *Reformed Mennonites*.

The fourth contingent of this combination was the *Brethren in Christ*, who as early as 1838 had seceded from the *River Brethren*, who in turn had originally sprung from the Mennonite body in the 1700s.

These four small groups, all with a more or less direct Mennonite origin and with similar beliefs and practices, united to form the *Mennonite Brethren in Christ Church*. The first step toward union occurred in Waterloo County, Ontario, when in 1875 the New and the Reformed Mennonites joined their forces under the name of *United Mennonites*. In 1879 the *United Mennonites* consolidated with the Pennsylvania Evangelical Mennonites to form the *Evangelical United Mennonites*. The unification movement was completed when at Jamton, Ohio, in 1883, the latter were joined by the *Brethren in Christ* to form the *Mennonite Brethren in Christ*, now *United Missionary Church*.

This church union, with a membership of about fifteen thousand, still holds to some of the characteristic Mennonite practices such as foot washing, nonconformity, and opposition to the oath and secret societies.

But in the course of time, as a result of the amalgamation of these different groups each with certain distinct practices, the United Missionary Church has also adopted a number of practices and doctrines not common among Mennonite groups—sanctification, second work of grace, second coming, holiness, and baptism by immersion.

No other group of Mennonites has reached out into non-Mennonite fields so far for its membership as has the United Missionary Church. Few of the additions since the early years have come from Mennonite sources. Many of their present congregations started as mission stations in both city and country districts. During the world wars the doctrine of nonresistance was much more difficult to maintain in Canada and Michigan where there was a large element of non-Mennonite ancestry than in Indiana and Pennsylvania where the opposite was true.

The United Missionary Church is very well organized, being semi-episcopal in its church polity. The *Gospel Banner*, founded in 1878 by Daniel Brenneman in Goshen, Indiana, is still the official church organ. Bethel College, founded in 1947 at Mishawaka, Indiana, is the conference college.

2. AMISH BRANCHES

There are two major groups in the Anabaptist-Mennonite tradition throughout the 450 years that have, like a Rock of Gibraltar, withstood many of the changes that have affected all other Mennonites—the Amish and the Hutterites. We will confine ourselves here to the Amish who differ from the Hutterites primarily in not sharing with them the tradition of the community of goods and the living together on a *Bruderhof*, that is in a "brotherly community." Both groups have in common that they aim to preserve the inner spiritual core of their faith by retaining the outer lifestyle of the "faith of their fathers."

The fear of Jakob Ammann of Switzerland some three hundred years ago was that the Mennonites were giving up their Anabaptist heritage by surrendering spiritual and cultural values in their adjustment to the "world" around them. That fear prompted the origin of the Amish who were so named after the leader of the movement. This split among the Mennonites spread from Switzerland to South Germany, and to Alsace Lorraine, and ultimately was transplanted to North America. Only the tombstones in Amish cemeteries in Europe are reminders of the places from which some came. The typically Amish names of our day were originally general Swiss Mennonite names, many of which survive in Amish as well as Mennonite families to this day.

Up to the middle of the nineteenth century, the whole Amish brotherhood, both the Pennsylvania contingent and the more recent Alsatian immigrants, felt themselves to be one body in faith and practice. On both sides of the Atlantic their common faith and traditions had been preserved so that when the Alsatians migrated to America near the middle of the century they found themselves in accord with their brethren who had come to Pennsylvania a hundred years earlier. They both still stressed particularly the faith and practices that had caused their separation from the Mennonites in Switzerland in the latter part of the seventeenth century and the practice of *Meidung* (shunning) which they still applied rigorously as a disciplinary measure. They wore the same clothes and the same cut of hair, and manifested the same spirit of suspicion toward everything new as did their Swiss and German forebears of the eighteenth century.

Services were held in their homes in the community—in the houses in winter, and in the capacious barns in the summertime. Worship lasted for several hours, and ended with a common meal at the home of the host. The preachers were elected by lot for life as long as they maintained good behavior. The hymns, long drawn out, sung to melodies never committed to print and several hundred years old, were from the *Ausbund*. Singing with more than one part or with notes was strictly forbidden. The language in use was Pennsylvania German or an Alsatian or Bavarian dialect among the more recent immigrants.

Need for Cooperation

In spite of their conservatism, which preserved the fundamentals of their faith without much change, slight differences in practice developed. These differences, which came as a result of their loose organization, their scattered settlements in the prerailroad days, and sometimes their pure personal perverseness, were taken very seriously.

By 1850 the Amish brotherhood throughout various communities began to be stirred by the general feeling of unrest then commonly prevailing throughout the religious life of the country. In Mifflin County, Pennsylvania, an Amishman, a bit more independent in his thinking than the average of his people, conceived the idea that baptism by sprinkling in a house was unscriptural, but that the rite should be administered by sprinkling in a flowing stream outside. He gained a few followers in his own congregation, and soon the movement spread into other communities. In Butler County, Ohio, the Hessian Amish had imported a piano, an unheard-of innovation among the American Amish of that day. The large ultraconservative community in Holmes County, Ohio, found their Wayne County brethren entirely too worldly. There were differences of opinion also between the communities in Elkhart and Lagrange counties in Indiana.

It was for the purpose of harmonizing these various disagreements and for bringing about a closer cooperation among various communities that a general conference was called of all the Amish congregations in the United States and Canada. The first session in this series was held in a large barn in Wayne County in 1862. Seventy-two ministers were present from Ohio, Indiana, Illinois,

Pennsylvania, and Maryland. Annual sessions were held for twelve years after that, ending in Eureka, Illinois, in 1878, without accomplishing the purpose for which the conferences were originally called.

In the meantime, the various Amish communities throughout the country had become crystallized into several permanent factions. On the one hand the congregations in McLean County and the Hessian congregation in Butler County, both of which had discarded some of their severe dress regulations and had otherwise assumed a somewhat more tolerant attitude, lost interest in the conference, ceased to attend the later sessions, and began an independent church career. On the other hand, a goodly number of the extreme conservatives also withdrew their support, and, together with those who never had favored the conference idea at the start, maintained the good old customs of the fathers without the least modification. These became known as the *Old Order Amish*. Between these two extremes were left a considerable number of congregations, including nearly all of the Alsatian immigrant communities, and the Wayne, Champaign, and Logan county Pennsylvanians. These occupied a middle position, following a fairly moderate course of religious practice, and later became known as *Amish-Mennonite*. They later merged with the (Old) Mennonite Church and ceased their separate existence.

The Central Conference of Mennonites

The *Central Conference of Mennonites*, locally known for a long time among the other groups in Illinois as the *Stuckey Amish*, had their origin in the Rock Creek congregation in McLean County. The bishop here was Joseph Stuckey, one of the most promising young leaders among the Amish. He was a man of strong personality, a writer of some ability, and talented with more than ordinary organizing power. Being more tolerant than most of his fellow ministers, he occasionally was brought into friction with other leaders even before 1870, the time his troubles began with his fellow ministers. A dispute arose between Stuckey and the Amish ministers' conference over the expulsion of a member of Stuckey's congregation by the name of Joseph Yoder. The conference ordered Yoder's excommunication on the ground that he did not believe in eternal punishment, having expressed this sentiment in a poem called *Die frohe Botschaft*. Stuckey, however, refused to carry out the order. The question was taken up at the annual sessions of 1870 to 1872 without a final agreement. Finally a committee of easterners was appointed to make a thorough investigation of the whole matter and dispose of the case. This committee, made up of ultraconservative Amish from Pennsylvania, decided against Stuckey and his congregation, and ruled that unless they complied, they would no longer be regarded as Amish.

Most of the other Illinois congregations regarded this decision as final, and it was announced in the various churches that Stuckey and his following were no longer one of them. Stuckey did not attend the later conference sessions, which ceased a few years later; however there was no further formal division. The Illinois congregations were independent of each other and each went its own way. Had it not been for the influence later of the conservative Amish ministers of the East, it is more than likely that today there would be little difference even in matters of dress between the Amish-Mennonites and the followers of Joseph Stuckey. However, when the Western District Conference of the Amish was organized in the late 1890s, Stuckey's congregations were not included. At that time they became a separate group of Amish. Stuckey not only retained control of his church during this controversy, but also of a small congregation at Meadows which he had been serving as an elder. Soon other congregations joined his in a more liberal church policy, and new ones were formed. What was for a long time known as the "Stuckey" following grew and prospered largely at the expense of the conservative Amish.

In 1899 these congregations organized a conference and assumed the name of Illinois Conference of Mennonites, then changed to *Central Conference of Mennonites*. The Central Conference maintained several city missions and, in conjunction with the Defenseless Mennonites, a mission station in the African Congo. They also maintain a home for the aged at Meadows, and a large well-equipped hospital at Bloomington. Loyal supporters of Bluffton College, they are represented on the board of trustees. The congregations have changed from a lay ministry to a trained ministry.

In 1947 the Central Conference of Mennonites officially became affiliated with the General Conference Mennonite Church, and in 1957 it united with the Middle District under the name Central District Conference.

Evangelical Mennonite Church

Another storm center developed among the Amish, first in Adams County, Indiana, and later also in Illinois and Ohio. The leader of this new movement was Henry Egli, a minister in the Amish congregation of that place. About 1864 Egli began to urge the necessity of a definite conversion experience. His charge that the spiritual life of the time was too formal and was not based on a vital experience may have had some ground, but the contention that the austere, simply dressed brethren of that day were too liberal in their dress regulations can hardly be taken seriously. In 1866 Egli withdrew from the old church and formed a new one, which soon included the larger part of his former congregation. The movement later spread to Livingston and Tazewell counties, Illinois, where several large congregations developed.

At first Egli's followers were quite strict in their dress regulations, and rather exclusive in their religious affiliations. They rebaptized all those of their members who had come from the Amish church but who could not confess that they had been truly converted before, a confession which, under the circumstances, few would make. Through the years the old ethnic barriers were gradually toppled through church extension and marriage. They are optional immersionists, and have discarded the former dress restrictions. At first spoken of as the "Egli Amish" by members of the church which they left, they later assumed the name *Defenseless Mennonites*. In 1948 the name was changed to *Evangelical Mennonite Church*. In 1978 the membership was 3,507 in twenty-one congregations. Their official church organ is called *Communique*.

The Apostolic Christian Church

Mention should be made of another disturbance among the Amish of Illinois and several other states in the early 1850s. The *Neutäufer* described in the chapter on Switzerland, sent several emissaries of their faith to their former Swiss countrymen in Wayne County, Ohio, in 1846, where they won a few converts. A little later others came to the Amish settlement in New York, from whence, together with a few recruits from the latter place, they found their way to the Amish community in Woodford County, Illinois. Here, too, they succeeded in bringing about the secession of a few of the dissatisfied members of the Amish church, and relatives of the New Yorkers. From Illinois the movement was carried to the Butler County, Ohio, Amish settlement.

This new group, which was locally known among the Amish as the *New Amish*, but among themselves as the *Gläubige* (believers), had but a slow growth. By 1877 there were only eighty-nine members in all the various communities. Their number and influence would have been insignificant and might have disappeared entirely had it not been for an additional immigration from Switzerland of recruits from their mother church. Today there are a number of large and prosperous congregations in central Illinois and Indiana, with several in other nearby states.

The *Apostolic Christian Church*, as it is officially known, is exclusive, and its members have no affiliation with other religious groups. They exercise a strict discipline among themselves, applying the practice of avoidance to all business and social relationships as well as to religious fellowship, not even excepting husband and wife in case one or the other should be expelled from their communion.

In business matters and as farmers they are among the most industrious and uniformly prosperous members of the community. Wherever they locate they have the finest farms and the best livestock; and the price of land immediately goes up.

Their present connection with the Amish and Mennonites is that both in Switzerland and in America their first converts came from the same places and they do share with them some of the fundamental beliefs such as nonresistance; avoidance; a general spirit of nonconformity to the world; insistence upon plain, though not necessarily peculiar, dress; and other traditions.

The "Beachy" Amish

In 1927 a new group of Amish emerged from the Old Order Amish. It must be remembered that the "Old Order" had been added to the name *Amish* to distinguish them from those that became Amish Mennonites and ultimately dropped the name *Amish*.

At some places among the Old Order Amish the introduction of the Sunday school for children as well as mission work caused differences and divisions. "Bishop" Moses M. Beachy of Grantsville, Maryland, favored the introduction of Sunday school and permitted the use of electricity and the automobile. He declined to excommunicate and shun members of his congregation for accepting these and other new practices traditionally forbidden by the Old Order Amish.

Other Amish districts in various states followed the practices introduced and tolerated by Moses M. Beachy, but they did not all become known as "Beachy" Amish. In Pennsylvania some were called "Stoltzfus Amish" and in Indiana, "Burkholder Amish." Some of these evangelical Amish resent being named after a leader and prefer to be called just *Amish*. They follow the evangelistic pattern and have Sunday school, Bible study, missionary outreach, and relief work for the needy. However, in most instances they retain the traditional Amish dress, unison singing, and the use of the Pennsylvania German language in worship as well as in conversation among themselves.

In 1977 the Beachy Amish had some five thousand members and two hundred twenty ordained ministers. In addition to their outreach program they have their own publications and Bible schools.

The Old Order Amish

This description of Amish divisions leaves the main body of the conservative Amish with religious beliefs and social customs almost as they were in Switzerland, the land of their origin, several centuries ago. These are now generally known as the *Old Order Amish* or *Amish*. The Old Order now have a population of approximately fifty thousand grouped together in settlements stretching almost in a straight line west from Lancaster County, Pennsylvania, through Ohio, Indiana, Illinois, Iowa, and beyond. In fundamental doctrines they do not differ from other Amish or Mennonites. But in their religious and social customs, and their general life outlook, and especially their suspicion of everything new, the Old Order Amish have remained decidedly conservative.

Their distinctive social practices and peculiar styles of dress do not have their origin in any departure from the established social order. On the contrary they have always been reminders of a usage general among the common people ages ago. Beards were generally worn in Switzerland when Jakob Ammann withdrew from the Mennonites in the latter part of the seventeenth century. When shaving became common, fear of being regarded worldly prevented the Amish from following the new custom. Hooks and eyes were also common at the time, as were long hair, homemade clothes, and broad-brimmed hats. The collarless coat was the usual style worn by everybody, but fear of pride kept the Amish and some Mennonites from adopting the "worldly" inventions.

And so social customs, styles of dress, and other traditions have remained intact until the present day among the Old Order Amish. Customs that changed did so only under bitter protest. New demands made by improved methods of agriculture, more convenient household appliances, changing styles of dress, and social customs were either ignored or were accepted only after a long and bitter church struggle in which the pioneers of change caused the origin of a new group.

Among the things still quite generally tabooed by the Old Order Amish, with a few occasional exceptions, are buttons, "store clothes," parted hair, carpets, window curtains, wall pictures, sofas, writing desks, brightly painted farm machinery or houses, power farm machinery, steam heat in homes, "falling" top buggies, telephones, automobiles, radios, high school attendance, meetinghouses, church conferences, Sunday schools, evening meetings, English preaching, four-part singing, and musical instruments except the mouth harp. Uniformity in dress and every form of personal appearance is prescribed. Children are dressed exactly like their elders.

Sometimes when new farm equipment appears that proves to be

especially useful, and especially if its ownership and use cannot be accredited to a spirit of pride, there is a tendency to be a bit more liberal in accepting it. Thus the tractor has been a strong temptation to many an Amish farmer. In Indiana tractors were permitted for a time for belt uses only, that is for running machinery, threshing, and grinding, but not for field work; in Iowa it was allowed for field work but not with rubber tires. This attempt to satisfy both his sensitive conscience and his social urge, as well as his material interests at the same time, frequently leads the Amishman to inconsistent compromises.

At times their consciences get the Amish into trouble with the authorities when government regulations conflict with what in their minds are the laws of God. In Pennsylvania they refused to accept the government farm bonus for curtailing their crops, although they voluntarily reduced their acreage. At various places they have encountered serious difficulty when they refused to send their children to the centralized high schools for the period of years prescribed by state law.

Rigidly prescribed though their daily lives may be by church regulations, yet there is room for slight differences among the Old Order Amish. The large compact settlement in the Kishacoquillas Valley in Pennsylvania may serve as a good example of this diversification. There are seven grades of Amish in this beautiful valley, including the Amish-Mennonites, and five of these at least might be classed as Old Order.

This description of the Old Order thus far given would not be fair to them without an additional word on the other side. The press notices occasionally given them and their treatment by modern writers of fiction often fail to render them justice. They are a devout, honest people, devoted to their families, generous to all human needs, law-abiding, industrious, mindful of their own business, and usually highly successful as farmers. Their less prosperous neighbors may smile at their broad-brimmed hats and long hair, but they can have nothing but admiration for their fine farms and well-fed cattle and comfortable bank accounts.

The Old Order Amish survive best in the older and larger communities and more readily give up some features of their identity in newer and small communities. This is because the Amish in new western communities can more readily alter some traditions by introducing Sunday school or more modern agricultural machinery which have not been approved of officially. This can ultimately lead to a break with the Old Order Amish and an affiliation with the Beachy Amish or another more progressive group.

An Amish preacher from another state proceeded according to

tradition in his preaching in an Old Order Amish congregation in Kansas using the traditional Pennsylvania German until he came to the climax of his message. Then he exclaimed: *"Manche Leit sind* chuck-full of religion, *aber haben kein* salvation." ("Many people are chuck-full of religion but are not saved.") What he had experienced through revivalistic influences, he could not express in Pennsylvania German. The results soon became noticeable. Not long after this, a group left the Old Order Amish to join the Beachy Amish and start Sunday school, an outreach program, and preaching in English. Soon electricity was introduced into homes and barns; and cars, trucks, and more modern agricultural machinery were being used.

According to J. A. Hostetler in *Amish Society*, (3d ed., 1980, Johns Hopkins Press), there were 85,783 Amish in 526 church districts in 1979. Each district has a "bishop" and a number of ministers elected by lot. The largest centers of population are Holmes County, Ohio, with 103 church districts; Lancaster County, Pennsylvania, with 60; and Elkhart County, Indiana, with 47.

3. THE (OLD) MENNONITE CHURCH

The largest body of the Mennonites of Swiss background in North America is composed of many streams of immigrants that came to the United States and Canada from Switzerland, Alsace-Lorraine, and South and Central Germany. The individual congregations and districts vary greatly in their background, as well as in their religious traditions and practices, depending in part on where they came from and when. Many of them were originally Amish who gradually affiliated with the (Old) Mennonite Church as congregations, groups, or individuals in a process that has continued since the beginning of this century. All have a Swiss Mennonite background in common as well as a gradual, often reluctant, adjustment to the prevailing general American spiritual and cultural atmosphere.

Among the Mennonites of Pennsylvania-German background, the acceptance of the English language in worship services began at the turn of this century. Thus a gradual accommodation to the prevailing lifestyle of the country took place. This included in the early days first of all the acceptance of some farming practices and other adjustments.

Nonconformity and Other Issues

There was an era in the larger Mennonite settlements of Pennsylvania, Ontario, and Virginia when the Mennonites were to some extent immune to outside influences in a constantly changing environment. They retained and developed the lifestyles of their European background in their own way, whether they were Amish or Mennonites. They had their own Pennsylvania-German language or dialect, and maintained a rigid and exclusive way of life by always being slightly "behind the times" in dress and in religious and cultural practices. On the other hand, they were very hard-working and successful farmers. Since few were engaged in any other occupation it was easy for them to preserve their religiocultural identity. Among the practices still forbidden around 1940 to 1950 were life insurance, belonging to labor unions, membership in secret societies, marriage outside the membership of the church, and the attendance of commercial amusements, such as movies. There was not always a uniformity among all congregations and conferences, and these practices were subject to alteration, during a longer period of time. Many congregational and conference meetings were devoted to resolving problems which originated through these rules of "nonconformity to the world."

At one time the Lancaster Mennonite Conference discipline prohibited the following activities: membership in literary societies; choral quartet, duet, or solo singing in churches; the performing of wedding ceremonies by someone other than the bishop; and wedding marches and flower girls. Dress regulations were at times very specific. Here is a sample:

> A plain dress is made of plain goods, full to the neck, the sleeves long to the wrist, the skirts to be long enough to be modest in every way, the waistline to be properly observed and maintained. The cape must not be omitted, transparent goods cannot be used in making plain dresses. Fancy colored stockings must not be worn.

It is striking that these regulations listed were mostly made by men and were designed for women. However, the men similarly were expected to observe rules and regulations pertaining to them.

The emphasis for both sexes was on "plainness," and the Mennonites and Amish consequently became known as the "Plain People." These regulations were not agreed upon in congregational meetings, but were established by the *Bench*. The term *Bench* was used to designate the bishops and ministers of various congregations that met regularly to agree upon rules of behavior and enforce them. Naturally they could also gradually alter some and introduce new ones.

Bishops and Ministers

The traditional practice among the Pennsylvania-German Mennonites was that the ministers were elected by lot. Each congregation as a rule had more than one minister. In addition to the ministers there were deacons. It proved to be practical to designate one of the ministers as the "leading" minister. In German he had the title *Ältester* ("elder"). Evidently under the influence of the Episcopalians and Methodists, the title *Ältester* in America was translated as "bishop." That the bishop was the only one who could perform baptismal services, marriages, and conduct the communion service was a definite deviation from the earliest Anabaptist-Mennonite brotherhood tradition, although the term *Ältester* (German) and *Oudste* (Dutch) came into being rather early.

There seems to be a considerable inconsistency in this practice within a 'plain' Mennonite tradition of giving the leading ministers not only the title *bishop* but also the authority to exercise severe discipline without congregational action. This is an unusual development among Mennonites, although it was common in authoritarian Catholic, Lutheran, and Episcopalian churches where the title and office of bishop was a tradition. It can be explained only as an emergency measure at a time when there were great difficulties that could not be settled in a brotherhood meeting. These were consequently left to be taken care of by the strong arm of a leading minister who was given the authority of a bishop in a fraternal setting. The title *bishop* and his office are disappearing gradually in the twentieth century.

The original brotherhood concept is being revived in a more democratic setting in North America. With the introduction of the trained ministry, the practice of the multilay-ministry is bound to disappear gradually, and with this development, also the office of the bishop. There may even in some ways be more of a loss than a gain in this development, but that has been the trend everywhere else among the Mennonites.

There were many channels and needs of a spiritual and general nature that brought Mennonites closer together during the difficult years of pioneering on the American frontier. Thus bridges were built among those who had previously had no fellowship with each other. But on the other hand, the challenges of the new environment and the reactions to them were not always the same. These challenges could be alterations in the daily lifestyle, in dressing, in obtaining agricultural machinery, and in many other areas. They could also be caused through the public schools that the children attended.

The greatest challenge, however, came gradually through the frontier methods of evangelization and the promotion of the spiritual life by free-lancing evangelists, or through a more emotional and evangelistic neighborhood in which the tradition-bound Mennonites and Amish found themselves. The acceptance or rejection of these influences disturbed the Mennonites at various places and caused new splinter groups. Quite often it so happened that what caused a departure of a group or individuals today would sooner or later gradually be accepted by all. How this happened, who some of the leaders were, and what the ultimate results were is to follow.

Pioneers of Renewal

An early outstanding leader in a renewal effort of the Anabaptist vision, calling, and mission among the Swiss and Pennsylvania Mennonites was John F. Funk (1835-1930) who was born in Bucks County, Pennsylvania. Funk's early youth and aspirations could easily have led him on a path into the world at large so that we would have never heard of him, as has happened with many others and which continues to be the case to this day. First of all he attended Freeland Seminary (now Ursinus College), taught school, and went to Chicago, Illinois, where he started a lumber business. In Chicago he experienced a renewal of his spiritual life among the Presbyterians, and in contact with D. L. Moody. After having started a printshop in Chicago, he transferred it to Elkhart, Indiana, in 1864. There he spent the rest of his life.

His greatest contribution to the Mennonites started with his publishing enterprise. Jointly operated with his brother, it later became the Mennonite Publishing Company. For decades he published the *Herold der Wahrheit* and the English counterpart *Herald of Truth* which had an unusual influence far beyond the Mennonites of Swiss background. Personally and through his publications, Funk played a very significant role in the migration of the Mennonites from Russia and West Prussia to the United States and Canada. He hosted and advised the delegates and printed valuable information for and about them in his periodicals.

Beyond this he published many widely read books which led to a renewal of the spiritual life and gave direction to the Mennonites for decades. He published Menno Simons' *Complete Writings* and the *Martyrs Mirror*, not only in English but also in German. For the Mennonites from Russia who were settling in the prairie states and Manitoba, he published the *Mennonitische Rundschau*, a periodical which is still being read in Canada over one hundred years later. Funk promoted sound evangelism, mission work, and Sunday schools, and published materials for this purpose. He gave guidance to the major body of the Mennonites of Swiss background and promoted the deepening of their spiritual life on the basis of the Anabaptist-Mennonite foundation. This was rare in his day and was an inspiration even for future generations. What John H. Oberholtzer had introduced several decades before him, Funk successfully continued on a much larger scale. By now the constituency was ready to accept new ways and means to achieve and promote a spiritual renewal.

John S. Coffman (1848-99), a young schoolteacher from Virginia, followed the invitation of Funk to come to Elkhart to become the editor of the *Herald of Truth*. He was a young man of unusual charm and attractive personality, an able speaker, and better educated than most of the ministers of his day, many of whom had not yet mastered the English language. Young people were greatly attracted by the winning personality of this unusual preacher. Coffman aroused a great interest in more progressive church work, evangelism, and mission work so that talented young men were inspired to dedicate their lives to teaching, the ministry, and mission work.

Among the younger generation who continued the work and the efforts of these pioneers were a number of schoolteachers. Teaching was almost the only vocation open to the young Mennonite men at that time, outside of farming. Among these teachers, who made significant contributions to the church were Daniel D. Miller and Jonas S. Hartzler of Northern Indiana; C. Z. Yoder, John Blosser, M. S. Steiner, C. K. Hostetler, and Abram B. Kolb of Ohio; G. H. Ressler and D. H. Bender of Pennsylvania; G. S. Shoemaker of Illinois; and Daniel Kauffman of Missouri.

Daniel Kauffman (1865-1944) was born in Iowa, but grew up in Indiana and Missouri. He studied at the Missouri State University, taught school from 1883 to 1897, and served for a time as county superintendent. Converted under the preaching of John S. Coffman, he was ordained minister in 1892 and bishop in 1896. Kauffman exerted a great influence through his numerous books which he published in rapid succession between the years 1898 and 1943. In addition to this he was editor of the *Gospel Herald* (successor to the *Herald of Truth*) during the period of 1908 to 1943. In this position he was able to mold the spiritual life and give direction to the church. He was also strongly involved in the development of the Sunday school publications. Kauffman combined vigorous evangelicalism with a predominantly conservative tradition of the (Old) Mennonite Church as he called it. A gifted speaker, leader, and writer, he exerted a lasting influence on Mennonites during the over forty years of his ministry.

The Mennonite General Conference

The first significant organizational effort among the large

body of Swiss-Pennsylvania Mennonites was made in 1898 in the establishment of the Mennonite General Conference. Most of the Mennonites of Swiss background ultimately identified with the Mennonite General Conference now called the Mennonite General Assembly. However, some of the early and larger local conferences (Lancaster, Franconia, and Franklin, Pennsylvania, and Washington County, Maryland) have not joined. These conferences do, however, cooperate in many projects. The best source of information about the many conferences, be they independent or a part of the Mennonite General Conference, is found in the annual *Mennonite Yearbook*.

H. S. Bender

This is the place to briefly mention H. S. Bender as an outstanding educator and scholar who contributed greatly to research and publications and inspired many to follow in his footsteps. He was instrumental, in cooperation with Mennonite scholars and publishers in Europe and North America, in producing in a few years (1955-59) the four-volume *Mennonite Encyclopedia*, which is a standard source of information pertaining to the Anabaptist-Mennonites everywhere. Bender also contributed much through the inter-Mennonite channels of the Mennonite Central Committee which have operated on a global scale in relief work since World War II.

Among the Mennonites of Swiss-Pennsylvania background, a great variety of groups existed that differed considerably in numerous ways, and consequently did not have full spiritual fellowship with each other. To bridge the gap, Bender promoted the common bonds with them. This was done not only in cooperating in common tasks in global relief work but also by establishing a strong self-identity within his constituency by promoting a new understanding of the spiritual roots of Anabaptism.

From Old Mennonites to Mennonite Church

As early as the eighteenth century there were, in addition to the Amish, the *Old* Mennonites and the *New* Mennonites. The first wanted to remain faithful to their Mennonite heritage by practicing nonconformity, while the latter were willing to accept some of the spiritual and cultural practices of their environment. This was particularly the case in the large Mennonite communities of Franconia and Lancaster in Pennsylvania. Even to this day one finds the engraving *Alt-Mennoniten* on tombstones and cornerstones to verify this fact. According to J. C. Wenger, John F. Funk loved to speak of the "Old Mennonite Church," while Daniel

Kauffman preferred the name as follows: (Old) Mennonite Church. On the other hand, Harold S. Bender contributed more than anyone else to its being replaced by the name *Mennonite Church*. In his numerous writings, and particularly in the *Mennonite Encyclopedia*, all congregations and places of Swiss background, past and present, were considered to belong to the Mennonite Church.

H. S. Bender claimed that the Mennonite Church can trace its origin to the earliest settlers in Germantown in 1683. This claim can be made by all other Mennonites of North America. We have no information that the New York Mennonites ever had a congregation. The Germantown Mennonites coming from Crefeld, Germany, were of Dutch background, and the present congregation belongs to the General Conference Mennonite Church as much as to the Mennonite Church. In fact, it was saved from extinction through the efforts of the General Conference Mennonite Church.

John Oberholtzer of Franconia, the founder of the Eastern District Conference and one of the founders of the General Conference Mennonite Church, constitutes another link with Mennonite origins in North America. But this merely calls attention to the common roots that all sons and daughters of Menno Simons and Conrad Grebel in North America have, regardless of present affiliations.

Contributions

Among the many agencies of service and outreach of the Mennonite Church, the Mennonite Publishing House, which originated in 1908, must be mentioned. It has become the largest and most successful publishing establishment among Mennonites anywhere. Located in Scottdale, Pennsylvania, it operates under the Mennonite Publication Board. It publishes periodicals, Sunday school materials, and books in various fields. Among the scholarly publications in the field of Anabaptist-Mennonite theology and history printed at the Mennonite Publishing House, one of the most outstanding accomplishments has been the four-volume *Mennonite Encyclopedia* which was jointly produced and edited by representatives of the Mennonite Church, General Conference Mennonite Church, and Mennonite Brethren Church. Among the numerous periodicals of the Mennonite Church are the *Gospel Herald* and *Christian Living*, published by the Mennonite Publishing House, and *The Mennonite Quarterly Review*, published by the Mennonite Historical Society at Goshen College, Goshen, Indiana, since 1924.

Colleges operated under the Mennonite Board of Education are

Goshen College, Goshen, Indiana, begun in 1895; Hesston College, Hesston, Kansas, in 1909; and Eastern Mennonite College, Harrisonburg, Virginia, in 1927. Numerous other schools on secondary and college levels have come into being in the United States and Canada since World Wars I and II. The theological training of ministerial students takes place at the Associated Mennonite Biblical Seminaries at Elkhart, Indiana, which is jointly operated by the Mennonite Church and the General Conference Mennonite Church.

A good source of information about the Mennonite Church is the annual *Mennonite Yearbook*. It outlines the present structure of the district conferences, the General Assembly, and the General Board under which function the Board of Congregational Ministries, the Mennonite Board of Education, the Mennonite Board of Missions, the Mennonite Board of Mutual Aid, and the Mennonite Publication Board.

XII
Russo-German Groups

1. THE PRAIRIE STATES AND PROVINCES
(1874-1884)

Kansas has a larger Mennonite population than any other state west of the Mississippi. Although most of these came to America during the great Mennonite migration of the 1870s from Russia, Poland, and West Prussia, the first Mennonites to settle in Kansas came from the eastern states at an earlier date.

M. W. Keim and his friends from Pennsylvania purchased from Case and Billings 5,000 acres near Marion Center in 1869 to 1870. Attracted by the Homestead Act of 1862, Daniel, Christian, and Margaret Kilmer of Elkhart County, Indiana, settled in the southeastern part of McPherson County in 1871. This became the nucleus of the Spring Valley Mennonite Church. A "twenty-three-mile furrow" was plowed across the prairie to connect the scattered farms of the Pennsylvania-German Mennonites of this area. The east end of the twenty-three-mile furrow bordered on the Brunk farm and cemetery located on Highway 50 between Hillsboro and Marion. Here R. J. Heatwole and Henry G. Brunk from Virginia located. Soon others followed from Ohio, Indiana, Illinois, and Missouri. The beginnings of this settlement preceded the great Mennonite migration to the prairie states and provinces from Russia by two years. Later, Pennsylvania Mennonites established additional congregations.

Russian Mennonites Come to Kansas

It has already been related how when the Mennonites settled in Russia in 1789 and the following years, they were given written guarantees by the czars that they could settle in solid communities, conduct their own schools, have their own administration,

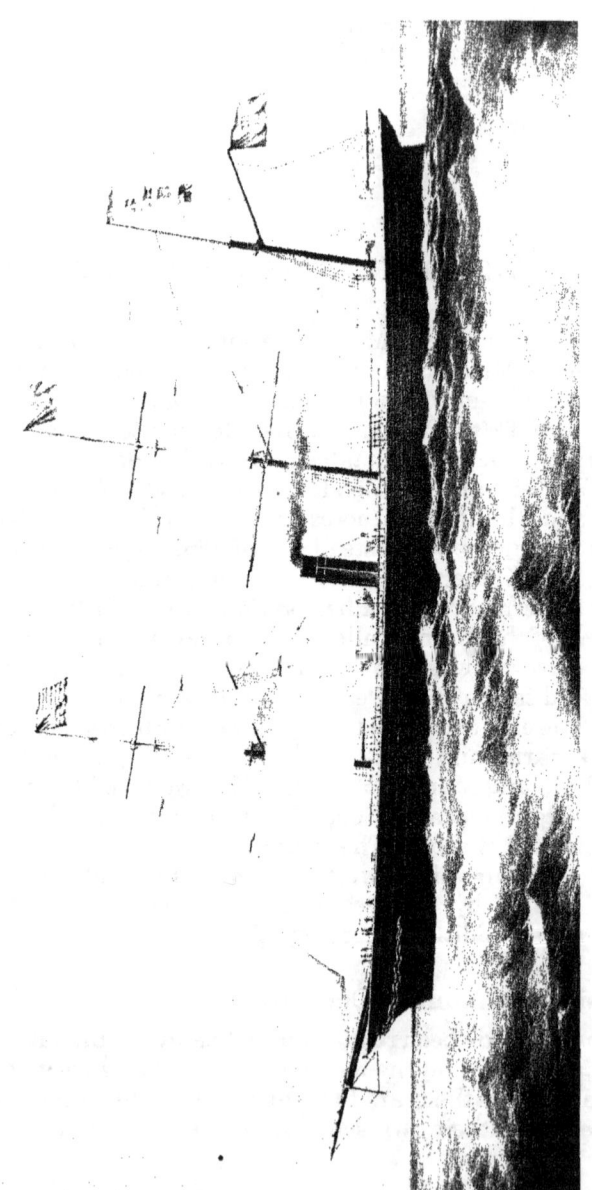

The Teutonia on which members of the Hoffnungsau congregation near Inman, Kansas, came to America.

and be exempted from any form of military service. When rumors regarding a general conscription law came into circulation among the Mennonites in Russia around 1870, they were alarmed. For some individuals of deep-rooted convictions, immigration to America appeared to be a solution. Among them was Cornelius Jansen who was in touch with Russian and foreign authorities at Berdyansk. From them he received information regarding Canada and the United States.

In 1872 Bernhard Warkentin and three friends came to the United States, making their headquarters at Summerfield, Illinois, in the home of Christian Krehbiel. Railroad agents tried to interest Warkentin in various settlement possibilities. Faithfully he reported all his experiences and findings to David Goerz of Berdyansk, who circularized the information among the Mennonites of the Molotschna settlement and beyond.

The first settlement by Mennonites from Russia in Kansas took place in 1873 when Peter and Jacob Funk bought land from the Santa Fe Railroad near present Hillsboro for $2.50 per acre. Christian Krehbiel, who was present at the time of the purchase, reported: "With this land purchase the die was cast for Kansas." This was the beginning of the Brudertal Mennonite Church.

Meanwhile the Summerfield (Illinois) Mennonites also became interested in the land of the prairies. As a result of investigative trips they chose land near Halstead, Kansas. The first Summerfield Mennonites moved to Kansas in the spring of 1875.

Although not all official delegates favored Kansas, and even Cornelius Jansen who initiated the immigration to America chose Nebraska, Kansas became the preferred state by most of the immigrants. Some Mennonites preferred Canada because they were offered large compact areas such as the East Reserve and the West Reserve on the Red River in Manitoba. Here they could live just as they had in Russia, with their own schools and self-government. The United States Congress, however, felt that the Mennonites would have to be satisfied with settling on alternate sections of land offered by the railroads. Then, too, the Canadian promises regarding nonresistance were more specific than those of the United States.

While Congress was still debating their petitions, the movement of the Mennonites from Russia, Poland, and West Prussia to the United States set in. Wilhelm Ewert, the West Prussian Mennonite delegate, arrived in Peabody May 16, 1874, accompanied by a number of West Prussian Mennonites. He joined the Funk brothers of Brudertal near Marion Center. Elder Jacob A. Wiebe and Johann Harder, crossing the Atlantic with the Krimmer Mennonite Brethren on *The City of Brooklyn*, arrived in New

York on July 15, 1874. They settled on twelve sections of land in Marion County, establishing Gnadenau village and the Gnadenau Krimmer Mennonite Brethren Church.

Delegates, Agents, Ships

The large Alexanderwohl group arrived in New York aboard the *Cimbria* on August 27, 1874, and the *Teutonia* on September 3, 1874. They were met by David Goerz, Wilhelm Ewert, and C. B. Schmidt of the Santa Fe, all boosters for Kansas. The *Teutonia* group, with Dietrich Gaeddert and Peter Balzer as leaders, followed them to Kansas, while Jacob Buller and his group proceeded to Nebraska. As a delegate, Jacob Buller had refused to see Kansas. Now he and his group soon went from Lincoln, Nebraska, to Kansas, where they bought land in Marion and McPherson counties north of Newton. This became the large Alexanderwohl settlement and church at Goessel. These immigrants settled in villages similar to those they had left behind in Russia. The settlers who had come on the *Teutonia* under the leadership of Dietrich Gaeddert chose to settle twenty miles west of the Alexanderwohl settlement, purchasing about thirty-five thousand acres of railroad land in the adjoining corners of Reno, McPherson, and Harvey counties. This settlement and church became known as Hoffnungsau. The town of Buhler was founded in the heart of the settlement.

Places and Numbers

Another group of some 109 families from Russian Poland arrived in Topeka about the same time. During the middle of the winters of 1874 and 1875, 265 more families followed. These were Swiss Volhynian Mennonites under the leadership of Jacob Stucky, who settled along Turkey Creek in McPherson County in the vicinity of present Moundridge. They organized the Hoffnungsfeld Church, the mother church of the Eden and other congregations.

The Mennonites led by Tobias Unruh from Ostrog, Poland, left Antwerpen in November on three ships, *Nederland*, *Vaderland*, and *Abbotsford*. The group consisted of 265 families. The poorest 50 families remained in Pennsylvania for the winter while the others continued their trip to Kansas. The Mennonite Board of Guardians gave them aid and distributed them for the winter in the vicinity of Newton, Florence, and Great Bend. Most of them were settled on small farms in the spring in the vicinity of Canton, Kansas. The Emmanuel Church and the Pawnee Rock Bergtal Mennonite Church also belong to this group. Later, others moved to Oklahoma. Still others settled in Dakota. Some later joined the

Church of God in Christ, Mennonite, founded by John Holdeman.

One thousand two hundred seventy-five families arrived in the United States and Canada during 1874. Of these, 150 families temporarily remained in the East, some in Pennsylvania, some in Ontario. About half of the total number of immigrants of 1874 came to Kansas. The next largest group went to Manitoba, after which followed the group to the Dakotas. The passengers used the *Inman, Allen, Red Star, Hamburg-America,* and *Adler* lines. Some arrived in New York and others in Philadelphia. Only some one thousand four hundred persons came to Kansas during 1875, the migration to Manitoba being much greater during this year.

C. B. Schmidt, the most enthusiastic agent, who secured some letters of introduction from Mennonites who had arrived in Kansas, left New York on February 1, 1875, and went to Russia to win more immigrants for Kansas. Yet 1874 remained the peak year for Mennonite immigration to Kansas.

The West Prussian Mennonites, who founded the Emmaus Mennonite Church, the First Mennonite Church of Newton, and Zion Mennonite Church at Elbing, began to come to Kansas in 1876 and the following years. Among them was Leonhard Sudermann of Berdyansk. Only smaller numbers reached Kansas after this. The steamer *Strassburg*, arriving in New York on July 1, 1878, carried thirty-five families headed for Kansas. A large number of the West Prussian Mennonites settled near Beatrice, Nebraska. The steamer *Switzerland*, arriving in June 1879, brought forty-two additional families to Kansas. Of the Swiss Galician Mennonites, twenty-two families came to Kansas, settling near Arlington and Hanston. By 1880 the immigration had dwindled down to a few families per year. Again in 1884 some Central Asian Mennonite families reached Newton. Abraham Schellenberg arrived in Kansas in 1879 with some Mennonite Brethren and settled at Buhler and Hillsboro.

Of the approximately eighteen thousand Mennonites who came to North America from Russia between 1873 and 1884, about ten thousand came to the United States, of whom possibly five thousand settled in Kansas. Kansas received a large portion of the Molotschna, the West Prussian, the Swiss Volhynian, the Swiss Galician, and the Polish Mennonites. No Old Colony Mennonites from Chortitza came to Kansas, except for those few who had joined the Mennonite Brethren.

There were a number of factors influencing the decision of so many Mennonites from Russia to settle in Kansas. The Kansas railroads were active recruiters from the beginning. Through Bernhard Warkentin and David Goerz (who was still in Russia), they advertised and spread information about Kansas. Goerz continued this promotion after his immigration to Halstead in his paper *Zur Heimath*, and in his booklet *Die Mennoniten-Niederlassung auf den Ländereien der Atchison, Topeka und Santa Fe Eisenbahn* ("The Mennonite Settlement on the Santa Fe Railroad"). Most important, however, was very likely the fact that Kansas was located geographically very much the same as the Ukraine whence the Mennonites came. The weather, the crops, and the general conditions were very similar to those of the Molotschna settlement. Winter wheat, and even watermelons, could be expected to grow here just as in Russia. The water level could easily be reached. Many feared the severe winters of Manitoba, Minnesota, and Dakota.

Lending a Helping Hand

In the meantime the American Mennonites were busy organizing emergency committees to provide for the temporary needs of the new arrivals, and to help them to their new western homes. Some of the immigrants were rich, others well-to-do, but many were poor and some extremely so. Many had to be temporarily supported and provided with means to begin their life on the raw prairies.

In 1873 the Western (later Middle) District Conference, largely through the influence of Christian Krehbiel of Summerfield, had appointed a committee to collect money for the immigrants who needed help, and to direct them to their new settlements. About the same time John F. Funk of Elkhart, Indiana, secured a similar organization among the Pennsylvania-German Mennonites of the Middle West. These two organizations were soon consolidated into the *Mennonite Board of Guardians*, with Christian Krehbiel as president; David Goerz as secretary; John F. Funk, treasurer; and Bernhard Warkentin, agent. The Mennonites of eastern Pennsylvania organized a special committee, as did also the Canadian churches under the leadership of J. Y. Schantz of Berlin, Ontario. These organizations all did valuable service in providing for the needs and conveniences of the immigrants while they were becoming settled. It is estimated that about $100,000 was collected and spent for this work, some of which was tendered as a loan and later repaid. In addition to this sum, there were many individual loans. In Manitoba the Canadian government advanced a loan of approximately $100,000 at 6 percent to prospective settlers upon security furnished by Ontario Mennonites. All of this, in due time, was paid back.

Railroad companies and state immigration departments that had vast stretches of unoccupied lands still awaiting settlement took a lively interest in the coming of thousands of industrious

European farmers. The Canadian government passed an Order in Council offering each settler of twenty-one years of age and over a free homestead of 160 acres, with an option on another three-quarters of a section at one dollar per acre in the province of Manitoba. Full religious rights were granted with exclusive control over their schools and entire military exemption. Some twenty-six townships of land were finally reserved for the exclusive use of the Mennonites.

In Kansas, the Atchison, Topeka, and Santa Fe Railroad Company, aided by the state immigration department, secured the passage of a similar law exempting the future colonists from the state militia service. A similar concession was also made later by the state legislatures of Nebraska and Minnesota, in an attempt to attract some of the immigrants to their cheap lands. Vast stretches of railroad land were offered at from $2.50 to $5.00 per acre. So active was the Santa Fe company in directing the immigrants to Kansas that they sent their agent, C. B. Schmidt, to the Russian Mennonite settlements for the purpose of presenting early the claims of Kansas. The company even chartered a *Red Star* ocean steamer which was sent to the Black Sea for a shipload of Mennonite household goods and farm implements. These goods were brought to New York and thence by rail to Kansas, all free of charge to the colonists. Influential men among the immigrants and members of the various committees were granted free tickets for their travel. Groups of immigrants as they arrived at the Atlantic ports were carried West in special trains. The Chicago, Burlington, and Quincy Railroad Company was equally active in Nebraska, but the Santa Fe secured the largest number of settlers for Kansas.

Economic Life

The economic status and background of the Kansas Mennonite farmers differed greatly. Some had been successful and prosperous farmers and brought a considerable amount of money; others were poor and needed the aid of the Mennonite Board of Guardians and others. Generally speaking, the Mennonites of West Prussia and the Molotschna were more prosperous and advanced in culture. The economic status and the educational level of the Mennonites coming from Poland was considerably lower. All intended to preserve their lifestyle and language as they had in their respective countries.

Noble L. Prentis has given us a vivid portrayal of Mennonite life in the villages of the Alexanderwohl immigrants from 1874 to 1877 in *From the Steppes to the Prairies*. He describes their life at home, their dress, their food, how they farmed, and their qualities as farmers, such as patience, endurance, skill, and success, in spite of pioneer difficulties and grasshopper plagues.

Against the advice of Bernhard Warkentin, the settlers brought with them all kinds of furniture, tools, and implements, even wagons and plows. If they had forgotten anything they wrote to relatives to bring it along, from gooseberry sprouts to tulip bulbs. They transformed the prairie by erecting their homes on their quarter section or in villages surrounded by rows of shade trees, mulberry trees, and fields of waving grain. The mulberry hedges were planted to provide food for the silkworm, since they intended to continue the silk industry which they had developed in the Ukraine. A silk mill was established in Peabody, Kansas, but it did not prosper. Mulberry hedges, Russian olive trees, and watermelons are still very much in evidence in Kansas today. Threshing stones and other implements used in early days can be seen today in museums.

The most important economic contribution of the Mennonites was the introduction of hard winter wheat. In 1874 the Mennonites from Russia sowed the first winter wheat seed which they had brought with them. After experimenting with different varieties they found that the Turkey Winter Wheat was best suited to the soil and the climatic conditions in the prairie states. Bernhard Warkentin, whose father had been a miller in the Ukraine, had established a mill in Halstead. He ordered a large shipment of wheat from the Crimea in 1885 to 1886 for distribution among the farmers of Kansas and established the Newton Milling and Elevator Company, using steel rollers instead of stone burrs to grind the hard wheat. In 1896 Mark A. Carleton of the United States Department of Agriculture came to Warkentin to inquire about his experiments with wheat. Carleton went to the Ukraine in 1898 to study the Turkey wheat in its native country. Warkentin located a plot for him near Halstead where he could experiment with some three hundred varieties of wheat from Russia. Numerous varieties of wheat have been developed since. In 1900 the Kansas State Millers' Association and the Kansas Grain Dealers' Association asked Warkentin to import a large shipment of seed wheat from the Ukraine. As a result fifteen thousand bushels were imported and distributed to farmers the next year. Thus the Mennonites were pioneers in transforming the prairies into wheat fields and making them a breadbasket for the world.

Cultural and Religious Life

One of the reasons why the Mennonites came to North America was their insistence on maintaining their religious and cultural life as they had inherited it. To promote this, schools and churches were immediately erected everywhere. In these, the use of the Bible and the German language prevailed for many years. Gradually the parochial schools were replaced by public schools, but some of them continued, supplementing the education of the public schools with instruction in Bible and the German language. Some of these schools became secondary schools patterned after the traditional Russian Mennonite *Zentralschule*. Halstead Seminary, founded in 1882, was the first step toward collegiate education. Bethel College was established at its present location in 1887 as the successor to the Halstead Seminary. Preparatory schools for teachers were established in all larger Mennonite communities such as Hillsboro, Goessel, and Moundridge. A Kansas Conference was organized in the interest of education. The Teachers' Association (*Lehrerverein*) played a very significant role in the promotion of education. Soon a belt of elementary and secondary schools operated by the Mennonites flourished in all Mennonite communities between Newton, Kansas, and Winnipeg, Manitoba. In many instances these communities also developed hospitals and homes for the aged. All of this was a heritage transplanted from the steppes to the prairies.

Kansas Mennonites Today

The pattern of the cultural life of the Mennonites of Kansas has changed considerably. The walls which separated the various ethnic and cultural groups, such as the Swiss Volhynian, Low German, West Prussian, and Polish background Mennonites have been torn down, as have the walls between all groups and their environment. The former practice of nonconformity has either received an entirely new interpretation or has been nearly forgotten. The barrier of language and customs has been almost completely removed, with the exception of some of the more conservative groups. As a rule, Mennonites fulfill their obligations as citizens in voting. Some of them even choose the legal profession as a vocation. It was formerly said that Mennonites stay out of court and that there are no divorces in Mennonite communities. This is no longer completely true.

Out of the Kansas Conference came the Western District Conference of the General Conference Mennonite Church. Of the seventy-three congregations of the Western District, forty-six are located in Kansas, which is by far the largest number of General Conference congregations in the United States. The Mennonite Brethren have seventeen congregations in Kansas; the Mennonite Church, sixteen; and the Church of God in Christ Mennonite, seventeen (1974).

Regarding the more conservative groups not listed, it can be said that through the contact with other Mennonite groups in Civilian Public Service and in relief projects, their spiritual life and their forms of worship have been revitalized, and as a rule, they have developed an active program of missionary and evangelistic outreach.

Interest in education is growing. Kansas, with its three Mennonite colleges (Bethel College, Tabor College, and Hesston College) is not only the center for the Mennonites of the prairie states as far as education is concerned, but also a center for conference organizations and publications. The headquarters of the General Conference Mennonite Church are located in Newton. The General Conference maintains a bookstore in Newton, and together with Bethel College, owns the Mennonite Press in North Newton. In North Newton there is also a clothing center of the MCC for the prairie states.

Hillsboro, located some twenty-eight miles north of Newton in Marion County, has become the headquarters for the Mennonite Brethren. It is the location of the largest Mennonite Brethren congregation east of California, the Mission Board of the Mennonite Brethren, the Mennonite Brethren Publishing House and bookstore, and Tabor College.

Hesston and Hesston College, six miles northwest of Newton, has become a center for the Mennonite Church in Kansas. All three college campuses are being used extensively by their constituencies for conferences and religious and cultural programs sponsored by the respective colleges. Bethel Deaconess Home and Hospital at Newton, Bethesda Hospital at Goessel, and Salem Hospital at Hillsboro, as well as the Mercy Hospital at Moundridge and a number of homes for the aged, are Mennonite sponsored and supported by the Mennonites. Prairie View Mental Health Center, which originated during World War II, is also located in Newton.

2. MENNONITES MOVE WESTWARD

The Rocky Mountains did not stop the Mennonites of the plains from moving to the West Coast, be this in California or British Columbia. The first Mennonite on record to have reached California was Johannes D. Dyck who explored the gold mines of California already in 1850 when the American West was hardly being considered for settlement by any of the Mennonites. Henry Rees from Ashland, Ohio, could have been the first to settle in Pomona, California, in 1887.

The first Mennonite congregation was established in 1897 near Paso Robles by West Prussian Mennonites. By 1903 another congregation was established in Paso Robles and also in Upland. The Mennonite Brethren established a congregation in Reedley in 1905 followed by Bakersfield, Shafter, and other places. Since 1942 a large number of Mennonite Brethren have been attracted to Fresno, where the Pacific Bible Institute was established in 1944. Of the thirty Mennonite congregations in California, twelve belong to the Mennonite Brethren, six to the General Conference Mennonite Church, and three to the Mennonite Church.

In 1960 there were some six thousand Mennonites in California. Most of them were farmers in the San Joaquin Valley between Los Angeles and San Francisco. However many are moving to towns and cities, especially Fresno and Reedley. They have several homes for the aged and an MCC mental hospital.

There are hardly any states between the prairies and the Pacific Coast where Mennonites coming from the eastern and prairie states have not settled. In some of the states, like Oklahoma, Arizona, and Montana, Mennonites started a missionary outreach program soon after their settlement in Kansas. Mennonites from the eastern and prairie states established themselves in Texas, Colorado, Idaho, Oregon, and Washington. Efforts have been made and are being made to establish fellowships and congregational centers in larger and smaller cities including Phoenix, Dallas, Denver, Los Angeles, and in other cities.

In 1978 the General Conference Mennonite Church had twenty-five congregations in the states of Arizona, California, Washington, Oregon, and Idaho, and the Mennonite Church had approximately the same number. There are also a number of congregations of the Mennonite Brethren, the Evangelical Mennonite Brethren, and the Amish.

3. MENNONITES IN MANITOBA

Beginning in 1874 Mennonites from Russia settled in the province of Manitoba on both the east and west banks of the Red River, between Winnipeg and the United States boundary. This area still constitutes the main concentration of Mennonites in the province, as well as in all of Canada. Originally confined to the rural areas, Mennonites are found today in all the surrounding towns and cities, and particularly in Winnipeg.

In contrast with the immigrants settling in the prairie states of the United States in 1874 to 1880 who were primarily from the Molotschna settlement of Russia, West Prussia, and Poland, the Manitoba settlers of the same period were, with a few exceptions, from the Chortitza or Old Colony settlement and its daughter settlements Bergthal and Fürstenland. That this group and some of the *Kleine Gemeinde* Mennonites chose Manitoba is not accidental. The delegates of these groups were interested in the most liberal guarantees which would safeguard the future of their traditional economic, cultural, and religious life in a foreign environment as they had known it in Russia. Most of the Mennonites settling in the United States, particularly those of Molotschna and West Prussia, were willing to adjust themselves to a much greater degree to the environment of the chosen land. They had already adjusted themselves to the economic and cultural life of their Prusso-Russian homelands to a larger degree than the conservative Old Colony groups had.

Delegates Inspect Manitoba

After delegates from the Chortitza and Molotschna settlements had repeatedly tried in vain to obtain from the Russian government a guarantee that they would continue to be exempt from any form of governmental service to the country, some of the leaders listened to voices stating that the only alternative would be emigration to a country which would offer them the *Privilegium* (privileges) which the Russian government had given them and was now withdrawing.

Many meetings took place in the Chortitza and Molotschna settlements. The Bergthal and Fürstenland Mennonites took an active part in these meetings and watched the development with apprehension. Under the influence of Cornelius Jansen, Elder Gerhard Wiebe of Bergthal became interested in an emigration to North America. When a delegation of twelve was sent to North America in 1873 to investigate settlement possibilities, the Bergthal group sent Jacob Peters and Heinrich Wiebe. The Old Colony (Chortitza) itself and Fürstenland had no official representatives in the delegation. The *Kleine Gemeinde* was represented by David Classen and Cornelius Toews. Meanwhile John Lowe, secretary of the Canadian Department of Agriculture, had sent William Hespeler to Russia. Hespeler met Cornelius Jansen at Berdyansk on July 25, 1872, and promised the Mennonites "fullest assurance as to freedom from military service."

The Bergthal delegates, Peters and Wiebe, arrived in Berlin, Ontario, in March 1873, where they were guests of Jacob Y. Schantz, who was a strong promoter of Manitoba. Together they investigated Kansas, Texas, Colorado, and Nebraska, finally proceeding to the Red River Valley of Manitoba to meet the other delegates. Here the twelve delegates were introduced to the governor by Hespeler. A group of twenty-four persons on five wagons drove forty miles southeast of Winnipeg to inspect the land which became known as East Reserve. Before the group had seen all the eight townships of the East Reserve they returned to Winnipeg. Disappointed, most of them went to the United States. Hespeler accompanied the four Bergthal and the *Kleine Gemeinde* delegates to the West Reserve located north of the boundary and west of the Red River extending toward the Pembina Mountains.

After this inspection, the delegates proceeded to Ottawa, where they received on July 26, 1873, a statement regarding the conditions under which the Canadian government would accept and settle the Mennonites who desired to come to Manitoba. These "privileges" were briefly the following: (1) complete exemption from military service; (2) a free grant of land in Manitoba; (3) the right to conduct their own traditional schools (with German and Bible as the main subjects); (4) the privilege of affirming instead of taking the oath in court; (5) a cash grant for passage from Hamburg to Fort Garry (Winnipeg) of thirty dollars per adult, fifteen dollars per child under eight years, and three dollars per infant.

After the delegation returned to Russia, the Bergthal group, consisting of five villages, immigrated as a body to the East Reserve of Manitoba. Elder Gerhard Wiebe reported about the choice as follows:

> The congregation chose Canada because it is under the protection of the Queen of England and, therefore, we believe that the principle of nonresistance will be maintained there for a longer period of time and also that the school and the church will be under our own administration.

The last point was made possible because the Canadian government set aside the East Reserve and West Reserve tracts for the Mennonites to establish compact settlements with their own schools and local administration. Although the Mennonites probably misunderstood the extent and duration of some of these "privileges," the United States could not match this offer.

The First Arrival

The first Bergthal immigrants arrived in Winnipeg on July 31, 1874, on the steamer *International* by way of Chicago, St. Paul, and the Red River. Immigrant houses had been erected for them at the place where Niverville is located today. During 1874, 780 Bergthal Mennonites arrived. They were joined by members of the *Kleine Gemeinde*. The largest number of Bergthal immigrants came in 1875, followed by the last group in 1876, making a total of about five hundred families consisting of nearly three thousand persons who were transplanted from Bergthal in Russia to the East Reserve in Manitoba.

The *Kleine Gemeinde*, which also came to North America as a group, was the conservative wing of the Molotschna Mennonites, organized by Klaas Reimer. About half of the members of the group went to Jansen, Nebraska, and the other half to Manitoba, where they established Steinbach on the East Reserve and Rosenhof and Rosenort on the West Reserve. The total number of this group that went to Manitoba was about eight hundred persons. They were the only Molotschna Mennonites to settle in Manitoba.

In 1877 the East Reserve consisted of thirty-eight villages occupied by seven hundred families with some three thousand five hundred people. The majority had come from Bergthal and had been joined by families from the Chortitza settlement and the small *Kleine Gemeinde* group. Some of the original thirty-eight villages still in existence today are Steinbach, Grünthal, Chortitza, and Schönsee. The villages were patterned after those which the Mennonites had left in Russia and received the same names. The advisers and sponsors of the settlements on the East Reserve were William Hespeler of the Department of Agriculture and the Ontario Mennonite Jacob Y. Schantz. When Lord Dufferin visited the East Reserve on August 21, 1877, he praised very highly the progress made by the settlers. In Winnipeg he reported that he had seen "village after village, homestead after homestead, furnished with all conveniences and incidents of European comfort," and he had seen "cornfields already ripe for harvest and pasture populated with herds of cattle stretching away to the horizon." The Canadian government loaned the Mennonite immigrants nearly $100,000 guaranteed by the Mennonite Aid Committee of Ontario, to which the Mennonite Aid Committee added some of its own funds.

The Bergthal Mennonites reserved for themselves the East Reserve, leaving the West Reserve for the Mennonites from the Old Colony and Fürstenland. Fürstenland, the daughter colony of Chortitza, had its own elder in Johann Wiebe, but did not have its own *Oberschulze* (superintendent). Administratively it was a part of the Chortitza settlement at the time of migration. The leadership of the Chortitza or Old Colony settlement was more progressive than Fürstenland. Elder Gerhard Dyck and his co-minister Heinrich Epp of Chortitza had been in Petersburg repeatedly but they did not favor emigration to America. Elder Gerhard Dyck and Elder Gerhard Wiebe of Fürstenland and Elder

Johann Wiebe of Bergthal were related and in contact with each other.

In spite of the fact that the Chortitza settlement had no intellectual leaders and delegates as promoters of the emigration, a great number of the Mennonites from this settlement were ready to go to Canada. They attached themselves to the spiritual leadership of Johann Wiebe of Fürstenland. Some three hundred families or one thousand six hundred persons settled on the West Reserve in Manitoba during 1875. The West Reserve, consisting of seventeen townships comprising an area of 612 square miles, was located west of the national border between the Red River and the Pembina Mountains and reaching to the United States border. During the summer of 1875 the first arrivals lived in immigration houses while villages were laid out and homes constructed.

Jacob Y. Schantz kept a list of all Mennonites passing through Ontario. D. H. Epp reported that 3,240 of them came from the Chortitza and Fürstenland settlements. Schantz listed a total of 799 persons from the *Kleine Gemeinde*. Adding these two lists we have 4,039. Sixteen thousand had come from Fürstenland, which leaves about three thousand four hundred as coming from the Bergthal settlement. It can thus be concluded that the Bergthal group was slightly larger than the Chortitza-Fürstenland group together, and that of the Chortitza-Fürstenland group about one-third came from Fürstenland while the other two-thirds came from Chortitza. The term "Old Colony" Mennonites, referring to the conservative group of the West Reserve, is therefore appropriate.

Villages in the Prairie

By 1877 twenty-five villages had been established on the West Reserve. Most of their names are repetitions of those in use in the Chortitza or Old Colony settlement in Russia: Rosengart, Neuendorf, Blumengart, Kronsthal, Chortitza, Osterwick, Schönwiese. In the two reserves together some one hundred ten villages were established in the first decade. Some of these gradually disintegrated, others were transplanted to other localities. When the East and West Reserves were finally set aside "for the exclusive use of the Mennonites from Russia" by Order-in-Council of April 25, 1876, they included twenty-five townships, or over a half million acres, which was about 6 percent of the total area of Manitoba at that time.

The Chortitza-Fürstenland people had scarcely all arrived when a shift of the Bergthal people from the East Reserve to the West Reserve set in. Around 1880 Hespeler reported that some three hundred families of the East Reserve had moved to the West

Reserve, leaving four hundred families in the East Reserve. The reason given for this was that the East Reserve suffered more during the wet years since it lay lower than the West Reserve. Already at this time, departure from the traditional village settlement pattern was becoming common among the Bergthal people; a similar departure soon became apparent in other areas of life. Thus the Bergthal Mennonites of the East Reserve introduced a disrupting element into the fixed pattern of the Old Colony Mennonites of the West Reserve. However, innovations introduced by Bergthal Mennonites were, as a rule, followed and accepted by some of the Old Colony Mennonites.

The Bergthal Mennonites of the East Reserve continued as an ecclesiastical unit under the name Bergthal Mennonite Church, while the Chortitza-Fürstenland group on the West Reserve was organized as the Rheinland Mennonite Church, later known as the Old Colony Mennonite Church. They had all come from the same background, but had developed slight differences which increased from year to year. After the large group of the Bergthal Mennonites had moved from the East Reserve into the heart of the Old Colony Mennonite settlement, the differences were accentuated by innovations and personality clashes. The Chortitza-Fürstenland group of the West Reserve became the custodian of tradition, while the newcomers from the East Reserve, the Bergthal Mennonites, became champions of progress and adjustment to the new environment. For the Old Colony Mennonites of the West Reserve, the village pattern was the only way of life permissible and deviation was punishable. There was also disagreement regarding singing and the use of songbooks. The Bergthal Mennonites from the East Reserve who had located in the West Reserve could not worship and have fellowship with the Old Colony group of the West Reserve. Thus differences between Old Colony and Bergthal Mennonite groups were in various respects intensified.

Administration and Schools

In 1880 the provincial government intended to replace the Mennonite self-government of the *Schulze* and *Oberschulze* with the regular Canadian civic government. In the East Reserve the change met little opposition. The Bergthal Mennonites of the West Reserve were also ready to accept this change, particularly since the Mennonite government was in the hands of the previously established Old Colony Mennonite authority. For the Old Colony Mennonites to give up their self-government with the *Schulze* and *Oberschulze* and to yield to the Canadian municipality system meant not only forfeiting a practical and cherished tradition, but also the infiltration of practices and directives coming from a government beyond the jurisdiction of the elders and the discipline of the congregation. In spite of this opposition the municipality of Reinland was organized in 1883. The Old Colony Mennonites approved of the *Waisenamt* (a mutual aid system centering around the care of orphans), but refused to cooperate in the *Brandordnung* (a mutual fire insurance) of the Bergthal Mennonites. Excommunication and the ban were used for those who adjusted themselves by wearing the clothing of the Canadian environment and by introducing other innovations such as bicycles.

One of the greatest problems arose from the school question. The Old Colony Mennonites of the West Reserve wanted to have their own teacher (without special preparation) teaching the children for a shorter term and for fewer years than public schools and according to their own curriculum. The *Kleine Gemeinde* and the Bergthal Mennonites were more progressive and willing to avail themselves of government aid to improve teaching. They established district schools in a number of Mennonite villages. The first inspector of the Mennonite district schools was Jacob Friesen. H. H. Ewert, principal of the Gretna Mennonite School, did much to improve the educational system and practices of his day, particularly after he was appointed government inspector. But this only antagonized the conservative Old Colony Mennonites, and it was to become the basic reason for their migration to Mexico.

Economic Life

The tendency to abandon the traditional village and to settle on one's own land increased after 1880. First it was noticeable in the outskirts of the Reserve, from Winkler south to the international boundary and from there east to Gretna. By 1898 the West Reserve had only twenty-four villages left. This involved changes regarding the traditional community land which had to be parceled out to those who left the village.

The traditional three-year rotation of crops gradually gave way to the Canadian practices. Great changes came about through the purchase of modern machinery. The Mennonites are credited with the introduction of the mulberry tree, flax, and sunflowers to Manitoba. Grain was brought along in bags by the immigrants, especially wheat. But the hard winter wheat, which made Kansas famous, proved to be a failure in Manitoba. Spring wheat, oats, and barley became staple crops. Vegetables and fruits were cultivated. Jacob Y. Schantz helped the Mennonites along these lines. Windmills were located in a number of villages. Feed mills were found in Blumenort, Altona, and Gretna. Cheese making became important among the Mennonites, who generally operated on a cooperative basis. By 1907 the West Reserve was encircled by a network of railroads, supplied with grain elevators and business places. Winnipeg became an accessible market for butter, cheese, cream, poultry, eggs, and livestock.

On the favorable soil of the West Reserve, wheat and cash crop farming soon became prevalent, while most of the East Reserve, with its inferior soil, was for many decades limited to dairy farming. Because of the rapid increase of the Mennonite population it became necessary to subdivide standard-size farms. The Mennonites later extended their landholdings in other directions beyond the limits of the reserves. The Old Colony Mennonites took the initiative in creating a new reserve in the Rosthern-Hague district of Saskatchewan, where by 1897 two hundred Mennonite families from Manitoba were residing in villages just as they had been in Manitoba. Another settlement was made in Swift Current, Saskatchewan, in 1904, also by the Old Colony Mennonites. Other settlements were established in Didsbury, Alberta; Drake, Saskatchewan; and other places. According to the church record of the Old Colony Mennonite Church, the total number of the Old Colony Mennonites in Canada in 1912 was 8,166, of whom 4,358 lived in Saskatchewan. In 1911 the number of Mennonites in Manitoba was 14,498 and for Saskatchewan, 6,542, which makes a total of 21,040. The Old Colony group was thus about 40 percent of the entire Mennonite population.

Problems of Adjustment

The religious and cultural life of the Manitoba Mennonites was marked by very conservative attitudes. Gradually, however, the *Schulze* and *Oberschulze* were replaced by the reeve, and Mennonite church schools by district schools. All this was alarming for the Mennonites, who remembered that they had come to Manitoba not only because of their objections to military service but also out of opposition to the Russianization program and the introduction of the Russian language into their schools. Now they faced a similar problem in Canada.

In 1880 Elder Johann Wiebe, through a brotherhood meeting, reorganized the Reinland Mennonite Church of the West Reserve, making adherence to the old principles and practices a test of church membership. Many of the Old Colony Mennonites at this time joined the Bergthal group of the West Reserve, which had moved in from the East Reserve and had organized, under the leadership of Elder Gerhard Wiebe, an independent church with

Johann Funk as elder. However, Johann Funk was too progressive for some of the Bergthal Mennonites of the West Reserve. In 1890 most of the group rejected his leadership and organized what became known as the *Sommerfeld Church*, since its elder, Abraham Dörksen, lived in the village of Sommerfeld. Elder Johann Funk and his following continued under the name *Bergthal Mennonite Church*. In the East Reserve the Bergthal church became known as the *Chortitza Mennonite Church*, since its elder resided in the village of Chortitza. Thus by the turn of the century the descendants of the original Chortitza settlement in Russia had divided into the large Old Colony Mennonite Church of the West Reserve, with a less conservative Sommerfeld Church and a rather progressive Bergthal Mennonite Church nearby, and a Chortitza Mennonite Church of the East Reserve, which was spiritually and culturally most closely related to the Sommerfeld group. In addition to this there was the *Kleine Gemeinde* of Molotschna background represented in both East and West Reserve as a minority group. Although conservative in comparison to the Molotschna Mennonites in their attitude toward education and other questions which confronted the Manitoba Mennonites, they could be compared with the progressive Bergthal group led by Johann Funk.

In addition to the divisions caused by internal differences, new divisions occurred also because of new religious ideas and practices brought in from the outside. In 1882 representatives of the Church of God in Christ, Mennonite (Holdeman group), caused a break among the *Kleine Gemeinde* of the East Reserve. The *Kleine Gemeinde* elder, Peter Toews, and nearly half of the total group joined the Church of God in Christ, Mennonite. By 1890 the Mennonite Brethren had started a fellowship in the West Reserve at Winkler which became the nucleus of the various Mennonite Brethren congregations in Manitoba. The Evangelical Mennonite Brethren, originating at Henderson, Nebraska, and Mountain Lake, Minnesota, won followers at Steinbach among the *Kleine Gemeinde* and others, which led to the organization of a congregation at the turn of the century. By now the *Kleine Gemeinde* survives only in Mexico.

The Bergthal Mennonite Church, with the help of H. H. Ewert from Halstead, Kansas, spearheaded an educational progress which led to the establishment of the Mennonite Collegiate Institute at Gretna and the organization in 1902 of the Canadian Mennonite Conference, which most of the immigrants coming from Russia to Canada after World War I and World War II have joined. Most of the congregations of this conference are also members of the General Conference Mennonite Church.

Western Canada

Scarcity of land and internal differences among the early Manitoba Mennonites made many move to the neighboring province of Saskatchewan. Some settled north of Saskatoon in 1891 to 1892, establishing traditional villages at Rosthern, Hague, and Osler. After the Russian Revolution a large number of Mennonites from Russia came directly to the province of Saskatchewan, establishing new settlements at numerous places.

The city of Saskatoon attracted a large number of Mennonites, especially among those that came from Russia. This was also the headquarters of the Canadian Mennonite Board of Colonization, chaired by David Toews, and later by J. J. Thiessen. This board did much to help the Mennonites from Russia arriving empty-handed during the decade between 1920 to 1930. Not all remained in Saskatchewan and Manitoba. Many went to Alberta and, above all, to British Columbia.

The Mennonites started coming to British Columbia in 1928, settling in Yarrow, which had a Mennonite population of two thousand by 1955. Mennonites also settled around the town of Abbotsford, conquering the land for farming by clearing it of trees and stumps. Others went to the nearby city of Vancouver where a number of Mennonite congregations were established. From here they spread into the Lower Frazer Valley. By 1951 the Mennonite population in British Columbia had reached the fifteen thousand mark, of whom two thousand had come from Russia after World War II.

In addition to the General Conference Mennonites and the Mennonite Brethren, there are also some Evangelical Mennonite Brethren and the Church of God in Christ, Mennonite living there. The Mennonites have a number of Bible schools and a Mennonite high school. As in Manitoba, many have their worship services in the German language or use both the English and the German.

Migration to Mexico

During World War I the school question and the resistance of the Old Colony Mennonites and other conservative groups of Manitoba to adjustment to the Canadian environment came to a showdown. The School Attendance Act passed in 1916 did not prohibit the attending of private schools, provided they conformed to the standard set up by the school administration, but once a private school was condemned, a public school was established with compulsory attendance. C. B. Sissons summarized the situation as follows: "When the war spirit got hold of the West, and to poor equipment were added the dual sins of pacifism and German speech, . . . recourse was had to compulsion." Repeated delegations were sent to the provincial and Canadian governments without success. The government was determined to break the resistance of the conservative Mennonites. Public schools were established in all Old Colony districts, and teachers were hired to hoist the flag each morning and lower it again each evening, but not a single child attended the schools. Thereupon attendance at public schools was made compulsory, and punishment was administered when children did not attend the school. When repeated petitions to give the Mennonites the right to conduct their own schools were of no avail, a decision was reached to look for another country.

In 1919 two delegations went to South America, visiting Brazil, Argentina, and Uruguay. Even Alabama and Mississippi were considered as places to settle. In 1920 the Old Colony Mennonites sent a delegation to Mexico. They obtained a *Privilegium* very similar to that which they had once received from the Canadian government.

On March 1, 1922, the first trainload of immigrants left Plum Coulee, Manitoba, followed by three from Haskett. Two more trains left Swift Current, Saskatchewan. All of these settled near Cuauhtemoc, Chihuahua, Mexico. By 1926, of the 4,926 Old Colony Mennonites of Manitoba, 3,340 had moved to Cuauhtemoc; and some one thousand of the Old Colony Mennonites of Swift Current, Saskatchewan, and 946 of Hague, Saskatchewan, had immigrated. *Kleine Gemeinde* Mennonites from Manitoba established a settlement near the Old Colony settlement at Cuauhtemoc in 1948, called *Quellenkolonie*.

From 1926 to 1927, 1,744 Sommerfeld and Chortitza Mennonites from Manitoba went to the Chaco in Paraguay where they established the Menno settlement, the first one of a number of settlements established by Mennonites in that country (later settlements were made by Mennonites from Russia).

Thus the most conservative element of the North American Mennonites in Manitoba and Saskatchewan became trailblazers of Mennonite settlements in a wholly new cultural environment. In Latin America they sought out an environment to which it would not be tempting to adjust themselves. Altogether five to six thousand Mennonites left Manitoba after World Wars I and II for the new settlements. In the case of the Old Colony Mennonites, only a minority was left in Manitoba.

From Village to City

That the most conservative element of Mennonites was thus removed from Manitoba is, in itself, significant for the later development of the Mennonites in the provinces. However, the most important fact was that an almost equal number of Mennonites from Russia settled in Manitoba after World Wars I and II. Thus far Mennonites of Manitoba had been rural; many believed that to give up rural life for city life would mean to give up the Mennonite faith. With the coming of the Mennonites from Russia after World War I and the Great Depression, this idea was completely altered. Of the two thousand Mennonite families which came to Manitoba from 1922 to 1930, about four-fifths settled on farms, some of which had been left behind by the Mennonites moving to South America and Mexico, while about one-fifth located in Winnipeg. After World War II about three thousand Mennonites from Russia came to Manitoba, mainly to Winnipeg. In the city the Mennonites were employed as laborers, and established businesses and factories.

In the rural areas Manitoba had been significant for the spread of the cooperative movement. By 1946 the Federation of Southern Manitoba Cooperatives, with twenty-six affiliated organizations, covered territory with a total population of about twenty thousand, which was almost exclusively Mennonite. The cooperative tended to replace the old institution of mutual aid which had served the Mennonites in decades past. Altona in the West Reserve became the center of numerous cooperative enterprises. In 1944 the Cooperative Vegetable Oils Limited was organized by some eight hundred farmers and businessmen in the Altona area. Other towns with a predominant Mennonite population in the East Reserve are Steinbach, Niverville, Grünthal; and in the West Reserve, Winkler, Altona, Gretna, Plum Coulee, Rosenfeld, and Lowe Farm.

During World War II approximately 2,453 Manitoba Mennonites served their country in Alternative Service as conscientious objectors. Almost an equal number served in the regular army. In addition to this a great number of men were exempted from service because they were farmers or teachers. During this time the Mennonites in Manitoba organized the Mennonite Peace Committee. The elders of the Sommerfeld, Chortitza, Bergthal, Rudnerweide, *Kleine Gemeinde*, Church of God in Christ, Mennonite, Evangelical Mennonite Brethren, and the Old Colony Mennonites organized their own council. The executive committee of this council had authority to negotiate with the government pertaining to all conscientious objector matters.

Mennonites in Winnipeg

The flow of Mennonites from the country to the city increased rapidly with the coming of the Mennonites from Russia after

World War I. During the days of the Great Depression many of the daughters went to the city to do housework. They had to make a living and to pay off debts for their transportation from Russia to Canada.

North Kildonan on the outskirts of Winnipeg, one of the Mennonite settlements, has grown to a modern suburb, with numerous enterprises as well as churches. Winnipeg has factories established by J. Klassen, the C. A. Defehr and Son's Importing and Sales Company, and numerous other enterprises. There is also the fifty-bed Concordia Hospital, and the Bethania Old People's Home operated by the Mennonite Benevolent Society. Winnipeg is also the home of the Mennonite Brethren Bible College and the Canadian Mennonite Bible College, established in 1944 and 1947, respectively.

Winnipeg has the largest concentration and number of Mennonites in the world. In 1978 there were thirty Mennonite congregations representing the various backgrounds of those who were the pioneers of the prairie, and of those that came to Winnipeg in large numbers after World Wars I and II. All branches of Mennonites that originated in Manitoba or were transplanted there can be found here. Some have been totally anglicized while others continue all Sunday services in High German, with the members of the congregations speaking Low German or High German at home. The once "world-shy" young people study in any of the departments of the two universities of Winnipeg, and a large number of Mennonite professors are teaching there. The two Mennonite colleges attract young people from far beyond the city limits and also from other provinces. Winnipeg, the "village" that greeted and welcomed the Mennonites over a century ago, has still retained some of the village flavor in spite of its multiethnic and metropolitan development. It is estimated that sixty thousand Mennonites live in Winnipeg (1978).

4. WESTERN UNITED STATES

Mennonite settlements were also established along the western frontier line through Minnesota, Dakota, Nebraska, and Kansas. Most of the Mennonites here came from the Molotschna settlement and some other communities. Like their Manitoba brethren, they too asked for land reservations large enough to form compact and closed Mennonite communities. This demand was debated in the United States Senate for several weeks, at the time of their planning to immigrate to the United States. At that time Senator Pratt of Indiana, speaking of the native Mennonites in his state, said, "There is no worthier class of people upon the face of the globe"; and Senator Cameron of Pennsylvania, in behalf of his own state, added, "They are among our best citizens." But the bill embodying these demands did not pass. The Homestead Act did not permit the granting or reserving the public domain in areas larger than 160 acres to any one person; and the railroad companies owned only every alternate section along their right-of-way. In a few cases, an attempt was made to reproduce the Russian village type of life in the prairies. Virgin land was bought by the settlers from the railroad companies, or from former homesteaders who, for a few dollars profit, were glad to pull up stakes and move farther west. Some of the poorer immigrants took up land set aside by Congress. All the settlements, however, in course of time developed into rather compact communities.

Transforming the Prairies

Over half of the newcomers to the United States located in the state of Kansas along the frontier line through the central part of the state in Harvey, McPherson, and Reno counties, north of Wichita, on lands owned by the Santa Fe Railroad Company. The Santa Fe aided the settlers and built immigration barracks to house them temporarily while they were selecting their prospective homes and erecting their first crude living quarters.

Most of the settlements consisted of selected groups or congregations that had lived together in Russia. One of the largest of these was the *Alexanderwohl* congregation consisting of about six hundred members.

Halstead, a little hamlet along the Santa Fe in Harvey County, named after a well-known journalist of the day, formed the nucleus of a settlement made by a group of Palatines from Summerfield, Illinois. It became the cultural and administrative center of the whole emigration movement for a time. Here lived Bernhard Warkentin, who established a prosperous milling business and introduced from Russia the well-known hard red winter wheat, now known all over the West. David Goerz, another resident, directed many of the early Mennonite enterprises, and was editor of *Zur Heimat*, a weekly devoted to the interests of the Russian Mennonites of both Russia and America. A paper quite cosmopolitan in character, not at all like the ordinary run of country weeklies published in a village of two hundred, it carried in its advertising pages more notices of ship and railroad companies, with dates of sailing, than the great New York dailies. Christian Krehbiel of Summerfield, founder of an Indian school and president of the Mennonite Board of Guardians, was also a resident of Halstead. Halstead also became the seat of the first school of higher learning among the western Mennonites—Halstead Seminary.

Other western states, too, got a smaller share of the new settlers. Cornelius Jansen joined a group of the *Kleine Gemeinde* in Jefferson County, Nebraska, where he purchased several sections of land from the Burlington and Missouri Railroad Company. Later the town of *Jansen* was named in his honor. Jansen was the first town in Nebraska, so it is said, to have written into every deed for a lot the stipulation that no saloon could be established on the premises. Several congregations were also established in York and Hamilton counties. The settlement near Beatrice was of West Prussian origin.

In Minnesota the beautiful, rich region around *Mountain Lake* in the southwestern part of the state became the center of a number of substantial Mennonite congregations.

The Hutterites and some Mennonites from Poland and some of the Swiss Volhynians located in the southeastern part of what was then the territory of Dakota, not far from Yankton.

Transplanting a Bit of Russia

These foreigners with their strange customs and foreign clothes, coming in large groups, often aroused a good deal of interest in the small frontier towns when they first arrived. In the fall of 1874 the Santa Fe company was obliged to find temporary quarters for a few weeks in their railroad shops at Topeka for several hundred families en route to their homes on the prairies. Here the newcomers were visited by large and curious crowds of Topeka citizens who sometimes regarded their future possibilities with some misgivings. Speaking of the appearance of the men of the party, the Topeka *Commonwealth* observed:

> The men appear to have conscientious scruples against wearing clothes that fit them, the idea appearing to be to get all the cloth you can for the money. The men's vests therefore descend toward the knees, and their pants possess an alarming amount of slack. Their favorite headgear is a flat cloth cap which they pull off in saluting any person. This habit they will soon drop now that they have arrived in Kansas where "nobody respects nothing."

But when these strange Mennonites began to spend large sums of money freely in Topeka stores for farm utensils and household necessities for their western homes, idle curiosity turned to admiration, and the *Commonwealth* forgot all about the "alarming amount of slack" in their pants, and thought instead only of their future economic worth to Topekans. "These people" the *Commonwealth* reported, are making extensive purchases from our neighbors, creating quite a demand for articles necessary to opening homes. This is creating quite a trade which, considering the dull times, is very acceptable to our merchants. The people will be large buyers for some time to come, and the acquaintances formed by their temporary location here will give our merchants a strong hold on their trade which it only needs their exercise to retain.

It was for the purpose, no doubt, of cultivating this good feeling that the merchants and public officials of Topeka planned a public reception and a procession through the city, which all the citizens were urged to join. The reason for this public recognition of the Mennonites, according to promoters of the plan, was to show "our friends from Russia that we recognize and appreciate their presence among us and are anxious to cultivate neighborly relations with them."

Not all the Mennonite immigrants were as well supplied with means to buy utensils and implements for their farms. Many were poor and needed all the help so generously granted them by the relief societies of the American Mennonites. Among the poorest was the Polish contingent under Tobias Unruh which landed almost unannounced in Florence, Kansas, one cold winter morning, with the thermometer twelve below zero, lacking food, shelter, clothing, and the means with which they might supply themselves with these elemental necessities. This emergency taxed the ingenuity of the Mennonite Board of Guardians almost to the limit. After an emergency session, the Board supplied the new arrivals with temporary winter quarters in the surrounding towns; and the next spring they helped them each to a forty-acre farm with a limited amount of equipment, all with money lent them by eastern Mennonites.

The Mennonites tried to transplant as much as possible of their Russian way of life to their new homes. Villages proved to be impracticable and were soon abandoned. But the German language, the parochial school, interest in the mission cause, their own hospitals, children's homes, and fire insurance companies all were encouraged as they had been in their old home. Favorite articles of diet, too, were continued—watermelons, sorghum, sunflower seeds, cucumbers, various fruits, *Borscht*, and *Zwieback*. Occasionally they attempted to adapt some of their German farm equipment to American conditions. The Manitobans early ordered from Russia a supply of their farm wagons, but when it was found that the narrow gauge of the foreign vehicle would not fit the wider track of the Canadian wagon, the order was not repeated. In Kansas several farmers manufactured for their fellow Mennonites a number of their familiar threshing stones, but here too the American power thresher soon rendered this primitive method of threshing obsolete.

Wheat growing, of course, was as well adapted to the American western prairies as to the Russian steppes, and flour milling became an important industry in all the Russian Mennonite communities. For a time the Mennonites around Peabody, Kansas, tried to introduce silk culture. After an experiment for several years, however, the attempt had to be given up.

But there was one Russian institution that was well adapted to the needs of the American prairies with their lack of wood and coal, and which elicited nothing but the highest praise from the natives—the big, straw-burning Russian brick oven and stove. This oven was so built into the walls of the three main rooms of the typical Mennonite home as to heat the entire house, and at the same time serve for cooking. The big fireplace was fed with straw for an hour or so each morning, and the brick, retaining the heat, kept the building warm for the remainder of the day. Mennonites also made an excellent fuel from rotten straw and manure in the form of sun-dried brick.

Cultural Groups and Conferences

With the exception of the *Krimmer Mennonite Brethren*, the *Kleine Gemeinde*, the *Mennonite Brethren*, and one or two other independent bodies, the Mennonites early united their forces in promoting their common religious and educational interests. Schools and missions were the chief concern for a time, and it was for the purpose of advancing their common school cause that they met in 1877 to organize what became known as the *Kansas Conference*. Active and leading in these efforts were the Mennonites at Halstead and the West Prussians near Newton. When the West Prussian congregation at Beatrice, Nebraska, joined them some years later, the name was changed to the *Western District Conference*. Daughter colonies from Oklahoma and other nearby states later joined this conference.

The Dakota and Minnesota congregations later organized themselves for similar purposes into the *Northern District Conference*. Still later, as states farther west were settled by Mennonites from these older colonies, the *Pacific Conference* was founded. In the course of years, these various conferences assimilated the West Prussian, Swiss, and Galician congregations which grew up in the meantime in these regions. Practically all the congregations included in these three district organizations now also hold membership in the *General Conference Mennonite Church*.

At the time of the Russian Mennonite immigration, both the

(Old) Mennonites and those of the General Conference were generous in their support of the new arrivals with money and other forms of service; and both invited them into membership in their bodies. The (Old) Mennonites, however, because of their conservative dress regulations and other practices, were more hesitant to assimilate the new arrivals than were the General Conference Mennonites. The latter, too, at the time were more sympathetic than the former to foreign missions, a cause of considerable interest among the Mennonites from Russia even before their migration. The different congregations joined the General Conference Mennonite Church independently and at different times. The Alexanderwohl Church was first in 1876; the Dakota Swiss followed in 1881; Minnesota sent her first delegates in 1890; and Nebraska, in 1893. Each succeeding conference session found new additions.

The Mennonite Brethren

Small scattered groups and individuals here and there of the *Mennonite Brethren* were found in most of the first settlements of the Russian Mennonites in the United States. Although these groups occasionally found one another and held religious worship in the homes, in general there was little of organized church activity among them. With the coming of Elder Abraham Schellenberg in 1879, however, the church was organized, and more aggressive work began in the interests of church extension. Scattered members were gathered into congregations, revival meetings were held, and considerable numbers from other Mennonite groups joined them. By 1887 the membership had reached 1,266, all through the various Mennonite communities.

Conferences, held annually and well attended by both laymen and ministers, played an important role in the religious life of the membership. In a session held in 1900 the following practices were discouraged: writing foolish articles and jokes for the newspapers, attending weddings of members with unconverted partners, and participation in lawsuits. Later sessions went on record against life insurance, marriage of cousins, and Fourth of July celebrations. As a substitute for the latter it was suggested that "something better" be offered the young people for that day, missionary festivals for example.

For several years, beginning in 1898, the educational interests were served by a "German Department" in McPherson College, a Church of the Brethren institution. In 1908, however, a separate school was founded—Tabor College at Hillsboro, Kansas. Since that time colleges have been founded in Fresno, California, and Winnipeg, Manitoba, as well as a number of Bible schools.

A statistical summary shows that the Mennonite Brethren had a membership in 1978 of 35,563, which was distributed almost equally in the United States and Canada. The Mennonite Brethren conduct a very active program in missions (both foreign and domestic), relief, and education. In 1978 they had 189 missionaries in foreign fields (on furlough and on duty), in addition to mission workers in home-mission fields. The total contributions for all causes amounted to $13,971,142.00.

Evangelical Mennonite Churches

The name *Evangelical Mennonite Church* became very popular among some Mennonite groups that had preserved a nonconformist traditional piety and became sparked by an evangelical revivalist spirit. At times a strong leader who was not fully accepted would cause a departure of a group from the main church. Such was the case with John Holdeman who found no followers among the Ohio Mennonites but was very successful in Kansas among Mennonites from Poland, and among the *Kleine Gemeinde* Mennonites of Manitoba.

The Jansen, Nebraska, *Kleine Gemeinde* moved almost totally to Meade, Kansas, where it soon split into two congregations under the influence of evangelistic Mennonite ministers. Although basically similar, they are now the Evangelical Mennonite Brethren Church and the Emmanuel Mennonite Church. The influence and inspiration for the name and basic beliefs came from a number of sources. Isaac Peters of the Henderson Mennonite Church of Nebraska exerted a considerable influence on the *Kleine Gemeinde* of Jansen before the major part moved to Meade, Kansas. Peters separated from the Henderson Mennonite Church by establishing an "Evangelical Mennonite Brethren Church." A similar congregation was organized by Aaron Wall in Mountain Lake, Minnesota.

Another Evangelical Mennonite Conference originated in the *Kleine Gemeinde* in Steinbach, Manitoba, and spread locally. They place a strong emphasis on revivalism, missions, and at times a support of Mennonite Central Committee and Disaster Service. The interest in education is increasing, particularly in Bible school. The current issues faced by the conference are, among others, marriage and divorce, social drinking, the role of women in the church, the preferable Bible translations, and plural ministry. In 1978 the total membership was 4,690 in forty-five congregations. English is given as the official language, but German is also being used. The conference headquarters are in Steinbach, Manitoba.

An *Evangelical Mennonite Mission Church* originated in the conservative Sommerfeld Church of Manitoba in 1936 (organized in 1959) with headquarters in Winnipeg. In 1978 it had a membership of 2,240 worshiping in twenty-seven congregations. There is a strong emphasis on Sunday school, the training of the young people, and mission work. This effort finds expression in going out to the very conservative Mennonites of Manitoba who have not yet been touched by the spirit of evangelism and missionary outreach. These evangelistic Mennonites easily find a field of outreach right in their neighborhood among the more conservative Old Colony, Chortitza, and Sommerfelder Mennonites. Although there are only some five thousand of them left in Canada since their immigration to Mexico and South America, in recent years a number of them have returned to Canada, particularly to Ontario.

The attractiveness of the name *Evangelical Mennonite Church* was already strong in the days when the prominent Mennonite historian P. M. Friesen introduced it among the Mennonites in Russia. Friesen became disappointed in the developments between the Mennonites and the Mennonite Brethren that took place during the turn of the century. Although basically in agreement with the Mennonite Brethren principles, he was strongly opposed to any exclusiveness in matters of the kingdom of God. He promoted an *Allianz* that provided for a fellowship of all children of God, particularly among Mennonites. He stressed an inter-Mennonite fellowship combining the warmth of Pietism with the Anabaptist concept of discipleship.

The Hutterites in North America

To these various groups of Mennonite immigrants should be added another, which shared many of their religious experiences through the centuries, including the immigration from Russia—namely the Hutterites. Strongly nonresistant, the Hutterites decided to cast their lot with that of the Mennonites in the American venture. They came in three groups—nearly one hundred families all told—and settled in Dakota. Two groups came in 1874, the one located at *Bon Homme* west of Yankton on the Missouri; and the other at *Wolf Creek*, on the lower James. The third group, at *Elm Spring*, arrived in 1876 and established its settlement farther up the James River.

These three groups each bought several thousand acres of land in as secluded a region as possible along the river and established *Bruderhofs* (households). In Europe the Hutterites had mixed agriculture with industry, but in Dakota, since there were no markets for industrial products, they confined themselves almost entirely to farming, for which they needed large land areas. They preferred to locate along a riverside because milling was always an important sideline with them. Population increase among them has been rapid. The original three *Bruderhofs* had increased by 1942 to more than fifty, with a total population of six thousand. Of this number there were five households in South Dakota, fourteen in Manitoba, thirty in Alberta, one in Montana, and one in Ontario. The number has since considerably increased. Early expansion was up the James River, with only one *Bruderhof* of twelve families following the traditional westward course, locating in Montana.

Each *Bruderhof* is a complete, independent, economic, and social unit, consisting of from fifteen to thirty families living together in a large house built dormitory-like, and substantially of stone if possible. All eat in a common dining room, which is also used as an assembly room each evening for devotional services and business meetings before they retire. There is no private property or income or choice of occupation. The whole economic life is directed by a superintendent, generally locally known now as the "boss," who is elected for good behavior by the men of the colony. He directs the work of each member, has charge of all the income, and makes all the disbursements. All earnings go into the common treasury. The main boss is assisted by a number of department heads such as the farm boss, pig boss, duck boss, and cow boss.

There is no idleness. Everybody works at something. The teacher, miller, tanner, and other highly specialized occupations are permanent appointments, but the common workers periodically rotate their tasks. The main occupation has been farming, though each *Bruderhof* specializes in some sideline.

Small children are taken care of in a common nursery; the older ones are sent to school until age fourteen, after which they take their place in the economic order of the community. Until the state and provincial laws set up certain standards, the school program was simple, consisting of reading, writing, a little arithmetic, Bible, and instruction in some of the practical arts. Teachers were selected from the colony and were usually poorly trained. The language was Tyrolean German. Now, however, teachers must teach in English and must meet the state requirements. In case no one from the colony meets these requirements, some outside teacher must be employed. Since this has frequently occurred since World War I, some young men of the colony are preparing themselves for this task.

In their religious practices the Hutterites are still conservative. Preachers are selected by lot and have no special training.

Sermons are read from a book of sermons in manuscript form in the German language. Peter Riedemann's *Confession of Faith*, printed in Germany in 1562, and published for the first time in America in 1902, is the basis of their church doctrine. Their hymns, largely martyr stories dating back to the sixteenth century, are sung without notes, with the melody only, to tunes centuries old. The old hymnbook rivals the Amish *Ausbund* as the oldest hymnbook still in use by any Christian church in the world.

The social contacts of the Hutterites with the outside world have been meager, and their knowledge of what is going on is very limited. Many of their social customs have been perpetuated from Middle Europe, common centuries ago. Clothes are very plain, often still homemade, of a style outdated, and always of a somber color. The great social event of the year is the wedding, which lasts for several days and is usually staged in the fall after the harvest has been gathered. Courtship is not permitted officially until after the engagement has been announced from the pulpit. Formerly matches were made by the elders, but today each young man is permitted to select his own bride. There are no bachelors or spinsters, and few widowers in these households.

In its ecclesiastical government the *Bruderhof* is not quite as independent as in its economic arrangements. Each colony has its own minister, and a group of them a common elder. These various elders from all the colonies frequently meet to discuss their common problems. And their decisions have considerable weight in each *Bruderhof* as is always the case in a deeply religious society.

The North American Hutterites have not only preserved much of their middle European religious and traditional culture, but in all their wanderings have retained their original racial strains with practically little addition. All told, the entire Hutterite population today is the offspring of some fifteen European families running back several hundred years—*Decker, Entz, Glänzer, Gross, Hofer, Kleinsasser, Knels, Mändel, Stahl, Tschetter, Waldner, Walter, Wipf, Wollmann, Würz*. Only one of these families comes originally from Moravia. The families *Decker, Entz, Knels (Cornelsen)*, and *Wollmann (Wallmann)* were of West Prussian-Russian background. No new family names have been added in America.

Economically the Hutterites have been successful. Life is simple. No money is wasted on luxuries. There has never been any unemployment; relief is never needed; and there is no social security problem for old age. Surplus profits are large and are always invested in additional households for the rapidly expanding population.

During World War I the golden era of the Hutterites in the United States seemed to have come to an end. A great number of young Hutterite conscientious objectors went through great hardships in prisons. Two died because of mistreatment. As a result, most of the Hutterites moved to Canada where exemption from military service was granted and they were welcome. They located in Manitoba and Alberta. Only the Bon Homme colony on the James River remained intact. Since that time some have returned to South Dakota and Montana.

There seems to be a considerable difference in the modern operation of a *Bruderhof* in comparison to the early years, or even a few decades ago. The *Bruderhof* has now often more or less assumed the character of a well-organized corporation, producing hogs, poultry, and cattle according to the latest methods whereby man exploits creatures. Modern machinery also contributes to great changes. Changes of rules and regulations from year to year are noticeable. Nevertheless some young people, particularly boys, leave the *Bruderhof* to find greater "freedom."

In spite of these developments the *Bruderhof* demonstrates that a sincere Christian brotherhood can be maintained in a chain of generations and through centuries. No wonder that Eberhard Arnold (1883-1935) was inspired to establish such a *Bruderhof* in a contemporary setting. After World War I a Society of Brothers was established in Germany, inspired by the Hutterian example and as a direct result of the longing of some Christians in the disturbed postwar era for a true Christian brotherhood. Its leader, Eberhard Arnold, was ordained by an elder of the American Hutterites. In the days of Hitler's rise the German Hutterites migrated to England where they established the Cotswold and the Oaksey *Bruderhofs*. In 1940 these colonies migrated to Primavera, Paraguay. In 1961 the Society of Brothers was transplanted to Rifton, New York. It now consists of English, Dutch, Swiss, and other nationalities. It should be borne in mind that the new Hutterite colonies are composed mainly of members of high cultural interests and appreciations. In many instances the members were professors, ministers, doctors, and other intellectuals. These Hutterites are filled with a zeal for testifying for their newly adopted way of life. The Society of Brothers, located at Rifton, New York, operates the Plough Publishing House, and maintains a woodcraft industry and other related activities.

West Prussian and Swiss Groups

Several other small groups of European Mennonites settled in the western prairies. Among these was a group from the West Prussian congregation of Heubuden. Although the new German

Imperial Constitution of 1871 respected the noncombatant privileges granted the Mennonites in the Cabinet Order of 1868, yet there were still some German Mennonites, especially in the conservative Heubuden congregation, who objected to any sort of service under military control, even noncombatant service, as being contrary to their religious convictions. It was this group that was represented by Wilhelm Ewert in the deputation trip of 1873. Ewert himself and several others came to America to stay in 1874. In 1876 a score or more of families, under the leadership of Elder Johann Andreas, left for America, spending the winter at Mt. Pleasant, Iowa, where their elder died. The group divided the next spring, part of them locating in Kansas near Newton, and the others along the Blue River near Beatrice, Nebraska. In the early 1880s about a dozen families from the ill-fated Asiatic Khiva adventure joined this group.

Mention should be made here, too, of the settlement made by about seventy-five families from Galicia in the late 1880s in Kansas and Minnesota. These *Galicians* were originally South Germans who had migrated to Galicia from Bavaria, Alsace, and Switzerland upon invitation by the Austrian Emperor, Joseph. This was near the close of the eighteenth century soon after the emperor fell heir to Galicia on the occasion of the first partitioning of Poland. About one-third of them came to Kansas and two-thirds to Butterfield, Minnesota. About the same time, a number of families coming directly from Switzerland located near the West Prussian settlement at Whitewater, Kansas. All of these joined the Western District as well as the General Conference Mennonite Church.

Growth and Adjustment

The Russian Mennonites on the plains of North America, like their brethren on the steppes of Russia, increased rapidly in numbers. Land was plentiful and cheap, labor was in demand, marriages were early and frequent, and families were large. The eighteen thousand who arrived between 1873 and 1883, not counting the more recent immigrants since 1923, have since grown to some eighty-five thousand. The growth of church membership likewise was almost identical with that of the population. Their large, compact, closed, farm communities, with their German language and foreign customs, kept their own children from leaving them and others from joining. They held their own better than any other group in all Mennonite history, save their own brethren in Russia before them who lived under the same pioneer conditions.

Although they lived a life apart from the rest of the world at first, many of the younger element among the Russian Mennonites, particularly of the second and third generations, have played a creditable part in the political and cultural development of the country. Peter Jansen of Beatrice, Nebraska, son of Cornelius, became a prominent rancher, and early entered the public life of his adopted state, having been several times elected to the state legislature and serving for a time as state senator. A son of H. H. Ewert, founder of the Gretna, Canada, school, was a Rhodes scholar at Oxford, England, where he was professor at that venerable university.

All through the West men and women of Russo-German Mennonite parentage are holding positions of usefulness and influence in business and as public officials, school superintendents, college and university professors, doctors, and other roles of public trust.

5. THE GENERAL CONFERENCE MENNONITE CHURCH

The General Conference Mennonite Church, although having its origin in congregations of Pennsylvania German and more recent South German background, is composed of congregations with a predominantly Russo-German background. This mixture of cultural background has been characteristic of the General Conference ever since it began as a unification movement in 1860. Unlike the Mennonites and Amish who are mostly of a Pennsylvania German background, it is composed of congregations with a Swiss, South German, Swiss Galician, Swiss Volhynian, Hutterite, Amish, Polish German, West Prussian, but above all, of Russo-German background, making it the most heterogenous union of all Mennonite conferences in North America.

John H. Oberholtzer

After their parting from the Franconia Conference in 1847, J. H. Oberholtzer and his followers immediately organized themselves into a new religious body. Oberholtzer began a vigorous campaign for the spread of his cause. For the advancement of the religious interests of the congregations which had cast their lot with his, he founded in his hometown, Milford Square, the first Mennonite church paper in America called *Religiöser Botschafter*, later changed into *Das Christliche Volksblatt*. These papers he used to good advantage in advocating a closer union among a number of isolated Mennonite communities.

Although Oberholtzer was active in promoting the interests of the new movement, he had not entirely abandoned the hope of effecting a reconciliation with the Franconia Conference. He sincerely desired a union, and as late as 1860 he suggested in a pamphlet called *Verantwortung und Erläuterung* the terms upon which the two groups might come together. These terms, however, were rejected by the Franconia Conference, and so no reconciliation was possible. At the same time he was also advocating through his church paper a union of all the Mennonite congregations of America.

In the meantime a movement, similar in many respects to the one in Franconia, had been making headway among a few of the scattered churches near Niagara Falls in Lincoln County, Ontario. Favoring more aggressive church work, especially of greater evangelistic efforts, in 1853 the group appointed Daniel Hoch as a visiting minister to various scattered congregations in the region. Hoch also had evidently come into contact with a small congregation at Wadsworth, Ohio, composed of a few families who had recently come there from Pennsylvania under the leadership of Ephraim Hunsberger. In 1855 these two groups organized themselves into the *Conference Council of the Mennonite Communities of Canada-West and Ohio*. The purpose of the organization seems to have been to promote greater evangelistic and missionary zeal among the churches.

Oberholtzer had taken a deep interest in the Canadian movement from the very beginning, for here might be an opportunity perhaps of enlarging the circle of congregations that favored a revised church policy, and the beginning of the realization of a dream which he already began to cherish, namely the unification of all the Mennonite churches of North America. Consequently in the *Volksblatt*, in 1856, he advocated the union of the Canada-Ohio conference with his own Pennsylvania conference in the interests of the mission cause, and suggested a general council of the two conferences. This plan was favorably received by the Canada churches, and resolutions were passed by the conference in its session of 1857 urging that steps be taken in this direction. But no further results followed at this time.

Initial Meetings

While this subject was being agitated in the East, a similar movement had begun in the West. In Lee County, Iowa, there were two small congregations composed largely of Bavarian and Palatinate immigrants who had come to the United States a few years before. They were located near the Amish settlement which had been made some time earlier. But having come more recently from Europe than the Amish, and differing from them in customs and practices, they never worked in harmony with them.

Consequently these two congregations found themselves somewhat isolated from the other Iowa churches. Feeling the need of united effort, especially in evangelistic work among members of the church who had settled some distance from the main body, a joint meeting of the West Point and Zion congregations was brought about at West Point, Iowa, in 1859, largely through the influence of Daniel Krehbiel. He continued for the rest of his days a most enthusiastic advocate of the unification cause. Another leader of the union movement for the Iowa churches was Christian Schowalter, also a South German immigrant, and at this time a teacher in the parochial school at the Zion congregation. According to the resolutions passed at this meeting, its purpose was to "devise ways on the one hand for the centralization of the Mennonite churches, but chiefly on the other for supplying isolated families with the Gospel blessings." The ideal of the union of all Mennonite churches seems to have captured the imagination of the leaders of the Lee County congregations also. Near the close of the meeting, after an urgent plea by Daniel Krehbiel, it was decided to extend a general invitation to other Mennonite churches to meet with them in another conference at West Point the following year. The report of the initial meeting, together with the invitation for the coming year, were published in *Das Christliche Volksblatt*.

Oberholtzer naturally was also interested in the Iowa movement. During the year he repeatedly urged through the columns of his paper that both the Pennsylvania and the Canada congregations send representatives to the meeting in Lee County. Neither, however, seemed enthusiastic in responding to the invitation for several reasons. In the first place, Iowa at that time was on the frontier line of American civilization, and why should the eastern churches go so far west to attend a meeting, the purpose of which was to form a union of congregations almost all of which were in the East? Secondly, the Iowans were recent European immigrants in whom the easterners, whose ancestors had been in this country for more than a century, felt little personal interest. Neither of the eastern conferences appointed delegates to the western meeting. Hoch and Oberholtzer appeared to be the only individuals interested in the enterprise, and it seemed doubtful whether they would be able to attend because of financial considerations. But finally at the last moment, through the generosity of a friend, it was made possible for Oberholtzer and one companion to be present.

The General Conference Founded

The conference, if indeed it may be called such, was held May

28-29, 1860, near West Point, Iowa, and was composed of the two congregations already named, another minister from a nearby settlement, and the two representatives from Pennsylvania. Oberholtzer was chosen chairman, and Christian Schowalter of the neighboring congregation, secretary. Although unpretentious and local in character, this meeting was not deterred by that fact from discussing a lofty and ambitious ideal, namely the unification of all the Mennonites of America under one working organization. Deploring the fact that there was so much factionalism among the Mennonites, and that the brotherhood "has never since its existence in America constituted an ecclesiastical organization," and further that because of this factionalism there is "a corresponding decline in spiritual life," the assembly drew up a set of resolutions which it was hoped would serve as a common platform upon which all might unite for the extension of the mission and other interests of the church. These resolutions are as follows:

> 1. That all branches of the Mennonite denomination in North America, regardless of minor differences, should extend to each other the hand of fellowship.
>
> 2. That fraternal relations shall be severed only when a person or church abandons the fundamental doctrines of the denomination; namely, those concerning baptism, the oath, etc., as indeed all the principles of the faith which we with Menno base solely upon the Gospel as received from Jesus Christ and His apostles.
>
> 3. That no brother shall be found guilty of heresy unless his error can be established on unequivocal scripture evidence.
>
> 4. That the General Conference shall consider no excommunication as scripturally valid unless a real transgression or neglect conflicting with the demands of Scripture exists.
>
> 5. That every church or district shall be entitled to continue without molestation or hindrance and amenable only to their own conscience any rules or regulations they may have adopted for their own government; provided they do not conflict with the tenets of our general confession.
>
> 6. That if a member of a church, because of existing customs or ordinances in his church, shall desire to sever his connection and unite with some other church of the General Conference such action shall not be interfered with.

Although the motive for this united action was to provide for more effective evangelistic efforts, two other subjects were also discussed during the meeting—the establishing of a publishing house and an institution for theological training. Both of these measures had been advocated for several years by such men as Oberholtzer, Hoch, and Daniel Krehbiel, and these men were undoubtedly responsible for introducing them into the discussions at this time. After a two-day session, the assembly adjourned, but not before it was decided to meet again the following year at Wadsworth, Ohio.

Thus was launched the *General Conference Mennonite Church.* The aim of the movement was an ambitious but worthy one. Just how seriously the leaders of the cause at this time entertained the thought of a union of all the Mennonites is not easy to say. It may be safely inferred, however, that none were so sanguine as to expect the fulfillment of the work in their own day, for such a task would have been an impossible one. The gap between the extremes of Mennonite custom and practice of that time was too wide to be bridged over easily. But a union of some of the more concerned of the older American Mennonite churches and a number of the recent immigrant congregations was entirely feasible. The dozen or so of the Pennsylvania congregations, of course, would likely come into the union, as would also a number of the South German churches in Summerfield, Illinois, and Hayesville and Cleveland, Ohio, all of whom were bound to the Lee County people by ties of kinship. The Wadsworth congregation would also be likely to join the movement. And so would the two or three Canadian congregations under the influence of Daniel Hoch. But beyond these scattered congregations there was not a strong probability that many others could be secured for the cause in the immediate future. And yet this time was more opportune, perhaps, than any later period would have been for attempting such a program. None of the Alsatian Amish churches nor the older Mennonite churches in Ohio, Illinois, and Iowa had as yet formed themselves into conference districts. Each congregation was independent of all others, and some had already departed somewhat from the older traditions and customs. Although a few of these in more recent years have affiliated themselves with the movement, its growth has been confined largely to congregations of Mennonites from Russia, West Prussia, Switzerland, and other scattered congregations.

The General Conference, however, was hardly a fact as yet in 1860. Neither the Canada-Ohio Council nor the few other independent congregations which it was hoped might be brought into the conference had accepted the first invitation. It remained to be seen what action these would take at the next meeting at Wadsworth.

This session, the second to be held, met at Wadsworth in Medina. County, Ohio, on May 20, 1861, in the very days of the opening of the Civil War. It was soon found that the unification movement was taking root, for now eight congregations were represented, including in addition to those present the year before, those at Waterloo, Ontario; Summerfield, Illinois; and several of the Oberholtzer following in Pennsylvania. Daniel Hoch of Canada and Daniel Hege of Summerfield were elected chairman and secretary, respectively. Two new subjects were discussed at this meeting. An article discouraging secret societies was added to the platform adopted the year before, and the first steps were taken toward the establishing of a theological school. Daniel Hege, a well-educated minister of the Summerfield congregation, was appointed as home evangelist and was authorized to visit all the churches in the interest of missions and the new school. After signing a formal unification agreement, the assembly adjourned to meet again, the time and place to be decided by the chairman and secretary. The conference was now a fact.

Continued Growth

The third meeting was held in Summerfield in 1863. The chief discussion at this time concerned the proposed school, and further steps were taken toward its organization. Triennial meetings were agreed upon and also a method of representation according to the size of the affiliated congregation. From this time on the General Conference maintained a steady growth. Nearly every succeeding meeting showed a gain in the number of affiliating congregations. At first the new additions came from the Eastern District Conference, founded in 1847 in Pennsylvania. But in 1875 the Swiss congregation at Berne, Indiana, was represented for the first time by S. F. Sprunger. And the following year at a special session the first immigrant church, the Alexanderwohl congregation, was represented by Heinrich Richert and Heinrich Goertz. Twenty congregations were present by delegates at this session. After this, most of the additions came from the Mennonites that had come from Russia and West Prussia, whose sympathies had been won to the leaders of the General Conference movement both because of the help they had received in settling in their new home and also because of their common interest in the cause of missions. The meeting of 1893 was held at Bluffton, Ohio. For the first time, the Swiss churches at Bluffton and Dalton, Ohio, and the Amish congregations at Trenton, Ohio, and Noble, Iowa, sent delegates. Fifty congregations were represented at this meeting, eighteen coming from Kansas. Each succeeding session now recorded some new additions, either from immigrant or some other isolated congregations which for various reasons had not become identified with any of the other Mennonite conferences which were being formed in the meantime.

In 1978 a total of 321 congregations were affiliated with the General Conference Mennonite Church, with a total membership of 60,397. The above includes the Conference of Mennonites in Canada, but not the mission churches on the various continents.

Among the persons, in addition to those already mentioned, who played an important part in the early formative period of the movement must be mentioned A. B. Shelly of Pennsylvania, president of the General Conference continuously from 1872 to 1896 and interested in all its various lines of work; Christian Krehbiel of Summerfield, Illinois, but later from Halstead, Kansas, a South German immigrant interested in the Russian immigration and one of the leaders in the Indian mission cause; David Goerz, one of the leaders of the Mennonites from Russia; Heinrich Richert from the Alexanderwohl congregation; J. C. Krehbiel, chairman of the first meeting in 1859 at West Point and a member of many important committees later; S. F. Sprunger of Berne, Indiana; Ben Eicher, leader among the Amish churches in Henry County, Iowa; Daniel Hege, the first home evangelist and collector of funds for the Wadsworth school; C. J. van der Smissen, theological professor at Wadsworth and later secretary of the mission board; J. S. Moyer of Pennsylvania; John S. Hirschler of Kansas; A. S. Shelly, prominent in the Eastern Pennsylvania District Conference and editor for many years of *The Mennonite*; J. B. Baer, promoter of the mission cause and early evangelist; and N. B. Grubb, pioneer pastor of the First Mennonite Church of Philadelphia and the first editor of *The Mennonite*. Among other leaders active in conference work were P. R. Schroeder, P. H. Richert, C. E. Krehbiel, David Toews, and A. Warkentin.

The Wadsworth School

The two questions that occupied much of the time and thought of the General Conference during its first twenty years were education and missions. The school at Wadsworth held the center of interest from 1863 when the first committee was appointed until 1878 when it was forced to close its doors. It took six years after Daniel Hege began to collect funds in 1862 before the school was opened. The institution which was known as *The Christian Educational Institute of the Mennonite Denomination* was located at Wadsworth, Ohio, which was thought to be the most centrally located between the East and the West. It opened its doors on January 2, 1868, with Christian Schowalter of Iowa as principal, one other teacher, and twenty-four students. Its purpose was primarily to train young men for Christian work, although secular subjects were also taught. During the same year C. J. van der Smissen from Friedrichstadt, Germany, was called to the chair of theology with the assurance that the position was to last the rest of his life.

The course of study covered three years. Prospective students were admitted by examination, and no qualifications were prescribed other than a good character and an age between eighteen and thirty.

The instruction was to be principally in the High German language, since even the Pennsylvanians at this time used that language exclusively in their religious worship, and Pennsylvania German in their social intercourse. The school was for boys only. Early in its history the Pennsylvania churches suggested that it be made coeducational, but the Germans from the West, and especially the German-bred theological professor van der Smissen and his wife, opposed the suggestion so strongly that women were only reluctantly admitted.

Each student was to spend three hours each day in some sort of manual labor for the sake of his mental and physical health and for the benefit of the institution. That this program was carried out is evidenced by glancing through a random list of assignments by the steward for one day. On this particular day one person was to do stable work; two were to peel potatoes; two were to carry wood to the kitchen, and another was to take a wagon to the village blacksmith; still another was to fasten the washline; three were to work at carpentering, and two at shoemaking; two persons were to saw wood, and one to borrow the saw from one of the townsmen; one was to go for the mail and another to take meat to Hunsbergers to be smoked, while all the rest were to cut wood. This was one day's assignment. Thus it was hoped that expenses might be kept down. But the cost of getting an education was not high at its best. For the sum of $100 per year the student was entitled to "instruction, board, lodging, washing, fuel and light."

The school never prospered. The attendance hardly ever went beyond that of the opening day. It began with a deficit in the building fund, and poor financing handicapped its work throughout its entire career. Although there were only three teachers, expenses could hardly be met. Besides financial difficulties there were personal differences within the faculty. Schowalter and van der Smissen did not agree upon matters of policy, and the former finally resigned, leaving to the latter the entire management of the educational policy of the institution. In 1878 the churches of the West and those of Pennsylvania disagreed as to certain questions of management, with the result that the school had to close in 1878 with a heavy debt and but few students. This experiment in higher education, however, was not a complete failure. Many of the later leaders of the church received their initial training in this pioneer Mennonite theological seminary.

The Mission Interest

In its other major objective, the mission cause, the General Conference was more successful, though equally slow in getting started. Although founding of a missionary society was one of the first official acts of the conference, it was some time before any actual missionary work was undertaken. S. S. Haury, a graduate of the Wadsworth school, became the first volunteer, but the General Conference remained undecided for a number of years both as to the location of a mission station and the best means of establishing the work. Mennonites in Russia were involved in the Dutch Mennonite mission work in Indonesia. After some communication with the Mennonite Mission Society in Amsterdam with a view to supporting their work in the East Indies, it was finally decided to form an independent mission enterprise and to begin the work among the American Indians. S. S. Haury and J. B. Baer were sent on an extended trip through Alaska looking for a desirable field for Indian mission work, but after a preliminary survey and finding the Alaskan field already well occupied by the Presbyterians, they returned still undecided as to a definite location. Finally by 1880 Haury and his wife established the first American Mennonite mission, then called a foreign mission, among the Arapahoe Indians in what was then Indian Territory, but now Oklahoma.

The General Conference was the first among the American Mennonites to carry on missionary effort among the American Indians. It played an important part in their missionary enterprise. Later on, stations were established among the Cheyennes in the old Indian Territory and in Manitoba, as well as among the Hopis in Arizona.

In addition to S. S. Haury as the pioneer missionary, special mention should be made of H. R. Voth and Rodolphe Petter who were outstanding not only as missionaries but also as researchers into the folklore and languages of the Arapahoe and Cheyenne tribes. The results of Voth's ethnological studies among the Arapahoes were published in a number of volumes, and together with a rare collection of relics, are now to be found in the Chicago Natural History Museum. Voth and several other missionaries in this field reduced the Arapahoe language to writing and made many translations. For nearly fifty years Rodolphe Petter worked on a dictionary of the Cheyenne language, and also translated nearly the entire Bible into that tongue. He was regarded by the officials of the Smithsonian Institution as the best authority on the Cheyenne language in America. His archives and library are now in the Mennonite Library and Archives of Bethel College.

Mission work abroad was begun in India in 1900, and grew out of relief work carried on under General Conference direction in the famine-stricken districts several years before. The first missionaries were P. A. and Elizabeth Penner and J. F. and Susie Kroeker. At first missionary effort was limited largely to evangelism and to taking care of the children left orphans by the famine; but later increased attention was given to both educational and industrial work, and especially to the care of lepers. P. A. Penner, who was in continual service for nearly forty years, established the second largest, and one of the finest, leper asylums in all India, for which he was given generous government support and the highest praise by the British inspectors. Somewhat later a mission station was established in China. The General Conference also sponsored several home missions in the cities, though these are now the direct responsibility of the local district conferences.

The General Conference today supports about 140 missionaries in fourteen countries with an annual budget of approximately two million dollars.

Objectives

The General Conference Mennonite Church has never forsaken the objectives of its original sponsors—a union of the various Mennonite groups into a common working organization for the promotion of common church interests, missions, aid to needy, education, and publication. To make the attainment of this goal possible, the slight differences which separated the groups had to be minimized, and only the fundamentals of Mennonitism upon which all could still agree, emphasized. The sessions of the General Conference have remained almost entirely advisory, with discipline left to the local districts.

These objectives are well stated by H. P. Krehbiel:

> The churches constituting the General Conference have by their union not become something different from what they were before. Each church remains just what it was, and retains all the peculiarities she had if she chooses. Each church retains her individuality as well as her independence. It is not a separate class or division of Mennonites which may be distinguished from others by special doctrines or customs. It is impossible to class the Conference as such a division because her membership list contains churches which differ very much in customs and special views, and which to this day retain these differences precisely as they did previously to uniting with the Conference.

And yet, although the General Conference Mennonite Church aims to be an advisory body and a convenient means for furthering common spiritual efforts, the fact that it must necessarily set up definite qualifications for admission to membership gives it the character of a separate ecclesiastical body. The revised constitution of 1929 prescribed as a test of membership that the congregations which unite with the Conference "hold fast to the doctrine of salvation by grace through faith in the Lord Jesus Christ, baptism on confession of faith, the avoidance of oaths, the biblical doctrine of nonresistance, and the practice of a scriptural church discipline."

From time to time there have been tendencies on the part of the more conservative elements to transform the loose confederation of 1860 into a firmer union with more definite doctrinal commitments and disciplinary powers over individual congregations. In 1902 the Cornelis Ris Confession of Faith was officially published and recommended for general use among the churches. A standing committee on doctrine and conduct occupied itself for some time with the question of lodge membership.

Conference Organization

The conference meets every three years and is composed of delegates elected by the participating congregations which are given voting power according to the size of their individual membership. The sessions are devoted largely to the discussion of reports from the various standing commissions—overseas missions, home ministries, and education—and temporary committees that have been appointed for special purposes. The congregations composing the General Conference Mennonite Church are grouped into six district conferences—the Canadian, Eastern, Central, Northern, Pacific, and the Western Districts. The church government is congregational, each minister usually being an elder; that is, having full power to administer all the religious rites and practices by the church. The support of the mission cause has remained one of the chief concerns of the General Conference.

Peace Testimony

The congregations of the General Conference together with the other Mennonite groups were most generous in the support of their famine-stricken and persecuted brethren in Russia after World War I; but most of this work was carried on through cooperative organizations such as the Mennonite Central Committee, the Canadian Colonization Board, and other Mennonite relief agencies. The special Emergency Relief Board of the General Conference did not do much individual work except to urge the support of these larger and more general committees.

The General Conference, and especially the Mennonites from Russia, has always been vitally interested in the preservation of the traditional Mennonite peace principles, although the subsidiary district conferences, especially the Western District, have been more active in promoting the cause. During World War I when hundreds of Mennonite young men were drafted into the army, the General Conference Mennonite Church in its session held at Reedley, California, in 1917 appointed a committee of seven to cooperate with the district committees and similar organizations of other branches of the church. They were to present to the government a united statement of Mennonite peace principles, as well as to aid the young men in the service to adapt themselves to the demands of the exemption law, and to appear in their behalf before the military authorities both in Washington and the various camps.

The war experiences convinced the leaders that more positive teaching of peace doctrines was necessary than had prevailed before. A special peace committee was added to the other committees of the General Conference Mennonite Church which has since done effective service for the cause by publishing peace tracts, holding peace meetings, furnishing peace lessons for the Sunday school curriculum, and cooperating with other Mennonite conferences and nonresistant groups, especially the Quakers and Brethren, in peace conventions and institutes. As a result of the alternative service program of World War II, the General Conference Mennonite Church began a program of voluntary service which carries out projects in the United States and Canada.

The Federal Council of Churches

For a short period, from 1908 to 1917, the General Conference Mennonite Church was affiliated with the Federal Council of Churches. But after 1914 the growing militarism developing in the Federal Council aroused a good deal of opposition among some of the peace-loving Mennonites to the continuance of the connection. A special committee was appointed to study the question. This committee, reporting to the 1917 session and disagreeing on its findings, gave a majority and minority report, the majority favoring the continuation of the affiliation. But a vote before the conference favored the minority report, and the connection with the Federal Council was discontinued. Among other charges brought against the Federal Council at that time was a liberal attitude of some of the members of the organization to "higher criticism, secret societies, and modernism in theology."

Shift to the West and North

During the early years the whole General Conference movement was dominated by the influence of the eastern Pennsylvania Mennonites, but in the course of time with the addition of a large number of congregations of Mennonites from Russia the control gradually shifted to the West. According to the General Conference report of 1978 a total of 311 congregations were affiliated with the General Conference Mennonite Church and its districts. Of these, 29 congregations belonged to the Eastern District, 63 to the Western District, and 110 to the Canadian Mennonite Conference. The Central Conference of Mennonites with its 20 congregations officially joined the General Conference in 1946. However, the greatest growth of the conference during the last decades took place in Canada because of the large number of Russian Mennonite immigrants after World Wars I and II. Thus there can be observed a shift of population and strength from the East to the West and more recently to Canada. Between World Wars I and II the publications were transferred from Berne, Indiana, to Newton, Kansas, where in 1943 the General Conference Mennonite Church established its headquarters and publishing office, Faith and Life Press. This shift to the more recent European arrivals from both Russia and Germany accounts largely for the fact that the German language and culture has been retained longer in the General Conference than among other Mennonite groups. Fortunately this shift has not weakened but rather strengthened the cause of peace among the American Mennonites; for the Mennonites from Russia (with the possible exception of some of the more recent arrivals), having migrated to America largely because of their scruples against war, seem to be more peace minded than many of the older groups.

Toward a United Witness

More than a century ago Mennonite congregations united to strengthen their efforts in mission work, education, and publication, which led to the founding of the General Conference Mennonite Church. Under the motto "Unity in essentials, tolerance in nonessentials, and charity in all things," the conference experienced a steady growth. Through its various boards and committees, such as the unity committee, the conference keeps in touch with congregations and groups that seek affiliation.

The General Conference whole-heartedly cooperated in such enterprises as the All-Mennonite Convention, the Conference on Mennonite Cultural Problems, Civilian Public Service work, and the relief projects of the Mennonite Central Committee. The channels of inter-Mennonite contacts and cooperation increase continually in many areas. In Mennonite Disaster Service (MDS) on a local scale, and in global efforts in feeding the hungry, providing shelter, assisting in agricultural efforts, and in numerous other services, the concept of missions and aid has been widened.

XIII
In Search of Freedom of Conscience

1. CANADA

After visiting the United States, Mexico, and Canada, the Russian *Studien-Kommission* (Land Commission) of 1920 finally decided that under existing conditions, Canada held out the best prospects as a refuge for their persecuted brethren. A. A. Friesen, a member of the commission, remained in Canada, and later played an important role in all the early phases of the immigration movement. But even here there were difficulties in the way, the most formidable, seemingly, being the Order in Council of 1919, still in force at the time, forbidding the immigration of Mennonites into Canada. But the Canadian Mennonites, determined to help their suffering Russian brethren escape from their hard lot at any cost, were not dismayed by seemingly impossible barriers.

From Russia to Canada

The Canadian General Conference, in its annual session at Herbert, Saskatchewan, in 1921, appointed H. H. Ewert as a delegate to cooperate with H. A. Neufeld, representing the Mennonite Brethren; S. F. Coffman, of the Mennonite Church; and A. A. Friesen to visit the Canadian capital at Ottawa and attempt to secure a repeal of the Order in Council. Fortunate for the immigration cause just at this time was the victory in the general elections of this year of the Liberal party, and the election as prime minister of the Canadian government of William Lyon Mackenzie King. Having lived in Kitchener, Ontario, as a young man, King was well acquainted with the Mennonites of that region and had a high regard for them.

With the aid of the new prime minister, the objectionable Order in Council was soon rescinded, and the door was thrown wide open for the admission of the Russian Mennonites. There were several conditions, however. The immigrants must settle on the land; they must not become a burden to the state; and they must pass a rigorous health test at the European port of embarkation.

Mennonite Board of Colonization

In the meantime, for the purpose of aiding the proposed immigration movement, the different branches of the Canadian Mennonites formed an organization which they called the *Canadian Mennonite Board of Colonization*, with David Toews of Rosthern, Saskatchewan, as its president and chief promoter.

But permission to enter the country was only the first step in the movement to bring over the thousands of Russian Mennonites who were eager to exchange their native homes for the promised land of Canada. Nearly all of the prospective immigrants had scarcely enough money left with which to buy their passports, to say nothing about the means for covering the expenses of their ocean transportation.

After considering various financial schemes, none of which seemed promising at first, the Colonization Board finally turned to the Canadian Pacific Railway Company, with its extensive railway system, its fleet of ocean steamers, and its vast stretches of uncultivated prairie lands as offering the most likely source of help for carrying out an extended immigration and settlement project. Here again the board was fortunate in finding a sympathetic friend in C. S. Dennis, chief commissioner of the railroad company's department of immigration and development. As a young man, Dennis had been officially connected with that other migration of Russian Mennonites to Manitoba some fifty years before, and remembered the valuable service rendered by these pioneers in the settling of the raw prairies of that province.

Through the efforts of C. S. Dennis and President Beatty, who was likewise friendly to the project, the Canadian Pacific Railway Company agreed to finance the whole enterprise on the condition that the Colonization Board enter a contract promising to repay the railroad company the whole transportation expense within eighteen months after the arrival of the immigrants. The first contract called for the transportation of three thousand persons from the Black Sea to Winnipeg at $140.00 per person, counting up, all told, to nearly half a million dollars.

The officers of the board did not see where this amount of money was to come from; and Mennonites who feared that the action of the board might obligate all Mennonites, were opposed to the whole scheme. But the Canadian Pacific insisted on the signing of the contract before a single Mennonite could be brought across. As president of the board, David Toews, fully aware that the contract could not be carried out within the specified time, signed the agreement on his own initiative, trusting God for the results. It appeared a little later that the railroad company could not fulfill its part of the contract either, especially that part which called for the embarkation of the Mennonites from a Black Sea port, due to certain disease epidemics then prevalent in that area. The Canadian Pacific, therefore, did not demand that the board live up to the letter of the bond, postponing from time to time the due date for the repayment of the transportation expenses; and at the same time even entering into new contracts for further immigration quotas.

Just how to provide for the temporary needs of these large groups of penniless refugees, and start them out on the road of self-support even after they did arrive here, was another problem that taxed the faith and ingenuity of David Toews and his coworkers to the uttermost. How would the Canadian Mennonites, many of whom (as was just indicated) were lukewarm on the whole enterprise, react to the assumption of this added burden? These were matters of grave concern to the leaders of the movement.

Great was the satisfaction of these men, therefore, when upon the arrival at Rosthern on July 22, 1923, of the first trainload of some six hundred immigrants, more than enough automobiles, buggies, and wagons from the large Mennonite settlements nearby were on hand to welcome these exiles to their prairie homes until such time as permanent quarters could be found for them. Before the year was up nearly three thousand penniless refugees had found their way to the promised land, and were temporarily distributed among the various Mennonite settlements throughout Saskatchewan, Alberta, Manitoba, and Ontario.

In the years immediately following, they came by the thousands. In the peak year of 1926 the number of arrivals reached the figure of 5,940. But by this time the movement had nearly exhausted itself, not because the Canadian government and the Canadian Pacific Railway company opposed the continuation of the stream of arrivals, nor because there was a lack of desire on the part of the Russian Mennonites to leave their native land, but rather because by this time the Soviet authorities had decided not to let their best farmers and most industrious citizens leave the country. By raising the price of passports to impossible levels after they had already dispossessed the well-to-do Mennonites of most of their property, and by putting other hindrances in their way, the Russian governmental authorities made emigration practically impossible. In 1927, 847 Mennonites left Russia, and the next year only 511. Mennonite immigration to Canada had just about come to a close.

But soon after this, in 1929, a new group of Russian refugees, some thirteen thousand (not all Mennonites), had gathered at Moscow seeking escape. The plight of these refugees desiring entrance to Canada was first learned by the Canadians from the metropolitan press. But both the economic and political conditions in Canada had changed materially in the meantime. The western provinces especially had been struck by an economic depression that had brought in its wake a great deal of unemployment, financial stringency, and hard times in general. Political control had been reversed, too, in most of the provinces, as well as in the Canadian government. In the general election of this year the Liberal party had lost to its Conservative rivals, who had never been sympathetic toward the generous immigration policies of the Liberals.

The newly elected Conservative premier of Saskatchewan, reading in the papers soon after his election to office that some five thousand stranded Mennonite refugees in Moscow hoped to find their way to western Canada, immediately announced to the public that they would not be received in Saskatchewan.

The president of the colonization board made strenuous efforts, both in the provincial capitals and in Ottawa, in behalf of the Moscow unfortunates, but without success. The Canadian government would not have offered any serious objection to the admission of the immigrants, but hesitated to oppose the wishes of the western provinces. Manitoba finally agreed to accept two hundred families on condition that their friends and relatives guarantee their support if necessary. The Canadian Pacific also was willing to finance their transportation. But Saskatchewan and Alberta were determined in their opposition. And so only about one thousand were admitted during the year. A few hundred more the following year practically ended the Mennonite migration to Canada. By this time about twenty-one thousand Mennonites had entered Canada since the Russian Revolution and had been distributed throughout the various parts of Canada.

Transportation Difficulties

That the transportation of these thousands of immigrants from Russia to Canada and their final settlement in permanent country homes of their own was beset with many hardships goes without saying. The Canadian quarantine regulations were strict. Hundreds of refugees were held up for periods of indefinite lengths at Riga, Southampton, Hamburg, Quebec, and other detention camps because of sore eyes or other physical ailments, all at the expense of the colonization board. Even after their arrival in Canada the sick had to be cared for at considerable cost in local hospitals.

The rapid accumulation of the transportation debt to the railroad company also became a cause of increasing anxiety, though it must be said to the credit of the Canadian Pacific that, even as the debt piled up, the company seemed willing at all times to enter into new contracts for bringing over more colonists, convinced that in the end Mennonite integrity and honesty would ultimately liquidate all their obligations.

The vast majority of these refugees took their obligations seriously, and in spite of hard times and lean years did all that could be expected of them toward the liquidation of their debts. But there were some who too soon forgot the debt of gratitude they owed their Canadian brethren, the Canadian government, and the railroad company. In nearly all the meetings held by the immigrant groups in which they discussed their common problems, this transportation debt question had an important place on the program. C. F. Klassen, himself an immigrant, was finally appointed as the special representative to collect money from the immigrants to repay this obligation. When David Toews died in 1947 he had lived to witness the entire repayment to the Canadian Pacific Railway of the debt amounting to nearly $2 million.

After the Mennonites found that the contract made by the colonization board did not legally bind them to assume the financial burden of the enterprise, the opposition of many gradually melted away; and before the immigration movement had gotten well under way, nearly all of these churches, including all the branches of the denomination on both sides of the international boundary line, supported the work wholeheartedly and generously with money, clothing, and supplies.

Settling on Land Again

What to do with these refugees permanently after their arrival here was an equally perplexing problem. The original agreement with the Canadian government was that the newcomers should settle on the land. Since nearly all of them had been farmers in Russia, this seemed a logical arrangement. Canada, still having plenty of available land for settlement, presented many possibilities.

One of these possibilities seemingly was to be found in the large selection of well-improved farms of the Old Colonists and Sommerfelder of Saskatchewan and Manitoba, who just at this time were finding their way to Mexico and Paraguay in large numbers. These farms were for sale at fairly reasonable prices, and on rather easy terms of payment. At the same time, too, a number of wealthy farmers along the western frontiers, finding large-scale farming decidedly unprofitable during the depression years, were willing to turn over their farms, fully equipped with livestock and farm tools, to any group of industrious Mennonites who would agree to repay the owners over a course of years with an annual share of the crops raised. Here and there homestead lands and some railroad lands were still available also, though rather far removed from the railroads and markets along the fringes of civilization.

Unfortunately, most of these first fine promises ended in disappointment. Only a small part of the new immigrants were able to locate on the lands of the Old Colonists. The experiment of farming the large estates as a community enterprise usually ended in failure. A few of the farmers continued as individual operators on small portions of these estates, but community farming for which they had neither experience nor inclination was entirely abandoned. Most of the land had been contracted for at too high a price, from thirty to forty dollars per acre. The prolonged period of crop failures and the low prices caused many of the settlers in a few years to give up their contracts. Some succeeded in having their agreements modified; others left farming entirely and found their way, for the time being, into the various cities nearby in the hope of finding some other means of making a living. Ultimately most of them found their way onto the land again on more favorable terms.

To protect the newcomers from the land speculators who might prey upon unsuspecting foreigners, a special board was organized, consisting of several members appointed by the Canadian Pacific Railway Company and others representing the Mennonite group. This board was called the *Mennonite Land Settlement Board*, and worked in close cooperation with the colonization board. This organization supervised most of the settlements made by the immigrants, helping them to nearly a million acres of land, all told. Practically all of this was on long-term credit, of course, to be paid from a share of the crops raised.

Most of the immigrants located in the western provinces, though a number also remained in Ontario near the settlements of the Pennsylvania Mennonites. Many of these latter at first found work in the factories of Kitchener, Waterloo, and surrounding towns. About one thousand located, in the course of time, on small farms as tenants or purchasers, on credit. In the southwestern corner of Essex County, where the native farmers lacked farm labor because of their close proximity to Detroit, they were gladly welcomed. A small colony was also established on homesteads in the woodpulp regions of northern Ontario, some miles beyond North Bay.

Many of the young women, about one thousand at one time, found work in domestic service in the western cities, thus greatly helping out the family budget and making possible the liquidation of the transportation debt.

Although the newcomers tried as much as possible to locate in compact settlements, as had been their custom in Russia, that was not always possible in Canada. Today the original twenty-one thousand immigrants and their children are distributed throughout three hundred different settlements ranging all the way from half a dozen families to large settlements, such as that near Coaldale in the southwestern corner of Alberta, and in the Fraser Valley of British Columbia.

Religious and Cultural Life

Being a devoutly religious people, these later Russian immigrants were deeply concerned that their children should be brought up in their traditional beliefs and practices, both in the home and school. In every settlement, wherever possible, the first institution to be established after the home was the church, and then the school. For the Mennonites in Russia had always been firmly convinced that the school was a vital agency in the cultivation of their religious principles. Religion was not a mere theory among them, but a very vital part of the whole of life. God was very near to them, and worship an essential experience. One of the immigrant trains, on its way west, stopped for ten minutes at a small way station in Ontario one Sunday morning in 1923 for a change of engines; the leader of the immigrant group asked permission to conduct a brief worship service on the station platform during the interval. There was a short Scripture reading, a brief prayer, several familiar German hymns by the large concourse of devout worshipers, and the train moved on westward. But the brief scene was not without its effect on the small crowd of native Canadians who had come down to the station to witness this unusual spectacle. "If that is the kind of immigrants they are bringing over here," said one of the bystanders, the local Presbyterian pastor, "we have nothing to fear. We need more like them."

About three-fifths of the Mennonites coming from Russia were Mennonites, and about two-fifths were Mennonite Brethren and Evangelical Mennonite Brethren. The latter two joined the General Conference of the Mennonite Brethren Church of North America, while the Mennonites (in Russia *Allgemeine Bundes-*

Konferenz der Mennoniten) joined the Conference of Mennonites of Canada, which is affiliated with the General Conference Mennonite Church.

Since the new arrivals included an unusually large number of both preachers and teachers, churches and schools were rapidly organized. Up to 1949 nearly two hundred church buildings had been erected. Bible schools seemed especially popular. In 1948 there were twenty-two, in addition to ten high schools. The growth of these schools was the result, no doubt, of the desire to give young people the religious training which the public schools dared not offer. Both of the Mennonite schools at Gretna and Rosthern were greatly revived, if not altogether saved, by a large influx of immigrant students. In the Mennonite settlements of the Fraser Valley in British Columbia, numerous elementary and secondary Mennonite schools were established. In 1944 the Mennonite Brethren established a Mennonite Brethren Bible College at Winnipeg, while the Conference of Mennonites of Canada founded the Canadian Mennonite Bible College in 1947, also in Winnipeg. The interest in higher education among the Mennonites of Canada is increasing continually.

In 1924 D. H. Epp founded *Der Bote*, a weekly paper which in 1948 was merged with *Christlicher Bundesbote* and is now the official German publication of the General Conference Mennonite Church. The *Mennonitische Rundschau*, formerly published by the Mennonite Publishing House, Scottdale, is now published by the Christian Press, Winnipeg. This establishment has become the official publishing house of the Mennonite Brethren. Among the numerous periodical publications of the Canadian Mennonites the *Mennonitische Warte* (1935-38), published and edited by Arnold Dyck, should be mentioned. The *Echo Verlag* published a series of books pertaining to the Russo-Canadian culture and history. Nowhere, with the possible exception of Holland, have Mennonites ever been as productive in the field of literature and art as the Mennonites who settled in Canada after World War I. Arnold Dyck, J. H. Janzen, P. J. Klassen, Peter Epp, J. P. Klassen, and others made outstanding contributions in cultural areas. Some of the intellectual leaders have found their way into institutions of learning, both in the United States and Canada.

Hospitals and Homes

In Russia, as we have seen, the Mennonite settlements formed not only independent religious bodies, but independent economic and social units as well. The Mennonites took care of their own sick, aged, and poor, and their own dependents and delinquents. They desired as far as possible to do the same here. In Canada a number of hospitals were erected in the larger settlements. For the purpose of furnishing a wholesome social atmosphere for the thousand or more girls who were engaged in domestic service in the larger cities, a number of girls' homes or social centers were established in Winnipeg, Calgary, Vancouver, Saskatoon, and several other cities. These homes not only greatly added to the social life of the girls but also were vital factors in the preservation of their religious faith during these trying transitional stages. Several itinerant ministers were also supported in their visits to the various scattered settlements.

The German Language

Linguistically and culturally, of course, the Russian Mennonites were German, in spite of the fact that they had lived in Russia for nearly one hundred fifty years. German is still the language of worship and social intercourse for many. Living as they do in compact areas, they have been able to perpetuate their German culture for some years, and perhaps retard somewhat the trend that set in toward the use of English among the earlier Russian immigrants. Unlike the Old Colonists who had left Canada for Mexico and Paraguay, however, these later immigrants were anxious and perfectly willing to learn the language of their adopted country. They seemed to have no scruples against sending their children to the public schools, though they were still committed to the necessity of adding religion as a subject of instruction somewhere in the system. Some retain the use of the Low German in daily conversation and the use of the High German in polite conversation and in worship.

Nonresistance

In their attitude toward war service, the later immigrants were inclined to assume a somewhat more liberal policy than did their brethren of the earlier period in the 1870s. The latter, it will be remembered, left Russia because they could take no part whatsoever in war, or war preparation, not even in such noncombatant services as Red Cross in times of war or forestry work in times of peace. The former, the descendants of those who remained in Russia at that time, were satisfied with the substitute service offered by the Russian government. They were therefore more liberal than the early immigrants toward all forms of so-called noncombatant war activities. During the First World War the Mennonites of Russia did valuable service as complete Red Cross units under their own control, though under government supervision, and in the war department. The descendants of the immigrants to Canada, on the other hand, were granted complete military exemption during World War I by the Canadian government.

When the National Resources Mobilization Act was passed in 1940, representatives of all Canadian Mennonite groups approached the government in the interest of the conscientious objectors. First they were told that the only alternative for the Mennonites would be noncombatant service. The conservative Manitoba Mennonites asked for complete exemption, basing their appeal on the Order in Council of 1873. They were offered a choice between noncombatant or hospital service in the army, and work in parks or on roads under civilian supervison.

In 1941 the government informed the conscientious objectors that they were to serve for four months in alternative service camps operated by the Department of Mines and Resources. This period of service was later extended for the duration of the war. During this year the first camp was opened in Ontario. In 1942 forestry camps were opened in British Columbia. In 1943 there were nineteen camps in British Columbia, five in Alberta, two in Saskatchewan, two in Ontario, and one in Manitoba. The Canadian government paid $2.50 per day per man, of which amount the camper received fifty cents and the rest was used for maintenance (board, lodging, medical attention).

In 1943 the Alternative Service System was transferred to the Ministry of Labor which opened the way for the use of conscientious objectors on farms and factories, thus gradually decreasing the number of forestry camps. In these individual assignments current wages were paid of which a large proportion was turned over to the Canadian Red Cross. At the end of the war over five thousand Mennonite young men of Canada had served in camps or in other areas of service. Some preferred to serve in the medical corps as noncombatants, as well as in regular service.

Helping Hands

The migration of some twenty thousand Mennonite refugees from Russia to the Canadian prairies, where at first an Order in Council still barred their entrance, is an epic in Mennonite history. The successful accomplishment of this task under trying conditions required the most skillful leadership; the closest cooperation of thousands of kind-hearted Mennonites on both sides of the international boundary line; the most sympathetic support of liberal-minded Canadian public officials; and the generous assistance of the Canadian Pacific Railroad Company, without whose timely help the project would have been impossible.

Space permits here the mention of only a few of the outstanding men of the large number who gave unstintingly of their time and talents in this long and tedious rescue work. Among these should be mentioned H. H. Ewert of Gretna, educational leader of the Canadian Mennonites and one of the first to urge that the task of rescuing their Russian brethren be undertaken. He died before the work had been finished. H. A. Neufeld of Herbert, Saskatchewan, an original member of the committee sent to Ottawa in the interests of the repeal of the Order in Council barring the entrance of Mennonites; P. H. Wiebe of Steinbach, Manitoba, of the Church of God in Christ, Mennonite; and three members of the Mennonite Church, S. F. Coffman of Vineland, Ontario, and E. S. Hallman and A. S. Bowman, both of Guernsey, Saskatchewan, must be mentioned. The Mennonite Central Committee and other relief agencies of the United States were organized in response to the call of their brethren in Russia. As they had been active in feeding the hungry in Russia so they also helped in the migration and resettlement of the Russian Mennonites in Canada.

But special credit must be given to David Toews of Rosthern, Saskatchewan, who remained the chief promoter of the movement throughout the entire period, and was the guiding spirit in every phase of the work. He was president of the Canadian Mennonite Board of Colonization, later also president of the Mennonite Land Settlement Board, and in the course of time an official member of nearly every organization that had anything to do with the welfare of the Russian immigrants. For a full twenty years David Toews spent the best part of his life and gave generously of his time and energies without remuneration above his meager expenses, in behalf of the welfare of his Russian brethren. Toews was a quiet, patient, determined, and deeply religious man. A victim in his childhood of the ill-fated Asiatic Khiva expedition in the 1880s, and soon after an immigrant to Kansas, he was well qualified by experience as well as temperament to head up what at first seemed a lost cause, and to most men would have seemed an impossible task. His heart went out to his suffering Mennonite brethren, and he let nothing stand in the way of bringing them effective help. When the Mennonite churches in western Canada and some of the Mennonite periodicals openly discouraged the whole immigration movement, he almost singlehandedly carried on the enterprise, patiently hoping that those opposing would soon change their minds. When the Canadian Pacific again later complained that the immigrants that had been brought over were in arrears in their payments of their passage money, he entreated the delinquents at every opportunity to do their best to meet these obligations. At the same time he entered into further agreements with the company to bring over still larger contingents and assume larger obligations. He traveled extensively in both Canada and the United States, collecting money and clothing for the sick and the needy, and repeatedly visited Ottawa as well as the provincial capitals as new needs demanded.

2. MEXICO

It seems rather strange that while Canada seemed a promised land to the Russian Mennonites, to another group of Canadian Mennonites it was regarded as a land of oppression. Regarding the German language as an integral part of their religious faith, they immigrated to Mexico when the Canadian government insisted that all the Mennonite children attend the English public schools where German was not to be taught.

The delegation of Old Colony Mennonites from Manitoba which visited Mexico in 1921 in the interests of a mass migration arrived in Mexico at a rather opportune time. The request for such special privileges as exemption from military service, complete religious toleration, control of their own schools conducted in a foreign language, and land available for large and compact closed settlements could be obtained only from a country that was unusually anxious to secure industrious farmers, and at the same time had sufficient uncultivated soil on which to locate them. The Mexican government at this particular time was in a position to meet all these demands.

While no special laws were passed to meet the requirements of the prospective colonists, the delegation was assured by President Obregon that all their requests were fully covered in the Constitution of 1917 and the prevailing laws of the country. The Mennonites, he said, need have no fear whatever that they would be restricted in their religious freedom. This assurance of President Obregon's might have been received with a little less faith had the delegation been a bit better versed in Mexican current history. For at this very time the government of Mexico was engaged in bitter struggle against the Catholic church, and had closed all the church doors, forbidden the priests to perform their clerical functions, and had banned all foreign clergy. It was understood, of course, that this crusade was against the state church and would not seriously affect the non-Catholic free churches. But it was not a hopeful sign for the future at the best.

Military service, the delegation was told, was on a voluntary basis; and the laws respecting local government and schools, with the exception of the Catholic schools, were quite liberal. Neither was there any restriction against the use of any foreign language, either in the church or schools. Court procedure did not demand an oath. Mere affirmation was sufficient. In other words, the constitution and the liberal laws of Mexico already provided all the guarantees they desired without the necessity of special legislation.

Land, either government land or private estates, could be had at reasonable prices and in unlimited quantities. Much of the land in Mexico at this time was still held by speculators, both native and foreign, in the form of large estates. The actual farmers, called peons, were mostly Indians and half-breeds. They lived in a state of serfdom, huddled together in small villages in crude adobe huts, completely at the mercy of the absentee landlord and with little hope of bettering their condition. Much of the soil was still uncultivated.

The new land policy of the government called for the liquidation of all these large estates and their redistribution among the actual tillers of the soil. For this reason the government was anxious to settle the waste areas with industrious farmers like the Mennonites who might serve in a way as model farmers to the less thrifty and efficient native peons. Many of these estates had already fallen into the hands of the government; and the remaining private owners of large haciendas were eager to unload.

Two large Mennonite colonies were established in Mexico—the largest one, about fifty miles west of the city of Chihuahua, the other near the city of Durango. From 1922, when the first Canadians arrived, until 1926, about five thousand Old Colonists and nearly another thousand Sommerfelder from Manitoba and Saskatchewan had located in these two colonies. During this time some forty long trainloads of passengers, with livestock, farm equipment, and household utensils, crossed the Rio Grande from the north into the land of the cactus and the eagle. Here the colonists purchased a number of large estates, counting up well toward a half million acres of land at a price of nearly four million dollars, mostly in cash, though the colonists had some difficulty in disposing of their Canadian farms for ready cash during the depression years.

Both of these groups brought with them and transplanted on Mexican soil all their traditional, conservative, social, and economic institutions and religious practices. They reproduced as nearly as possible the kind of life they had left in Canada. They formed themselves into some forty village groups of from twenty to forty families each, as their forefathers had done on the steppes of South Russia and on the prairies of Manitoba. Even the village names were reproduced—*Rosenort, Steinbach, Schönwiese—*

although the names once descriptive of the beautiful meadows or flower gardens of South Russia did not quite fit the sandy cactus fields of central Mexico. In both colonies the land consisted of a high plateau, more than a mile above sea level, almost within the tropics. Semiarid, only a small fraction of the land was under cultivation. The remainder was grazing land or still the haunt of the rattlesnake and desert vegetation.

The beginning was, of course, hard. But in a remarkably short time, what had once been an uninhabited and desolate stretch of sand and cactus had been transformed into a series of prosperous villages, surrounded by fields of wheat and corn and green pastures dotted with fine herds of Canadian livestock. The natives marveled at the superior products from the Mennonite farms and herds, and soon learned to discriminate between native and Mennonite stock in the marketplaces. A scrawny Arkansas razorback could easily be recognized as a native, but the sleek, well-fed porkers that found their way to the markets in Durango and Chihuahua were soon designated as "Mennonite" hogs, and the healthy-looking cows as "Mennonite" cows. In their tours of inspection, the government officials expressed themselves well pleased with what the Mennonites had accomplished in so short a time. However they were somewhat disappointed at what they called the exclusiveness of the Old Colonists who, living in large compact settlements and refusing to mingle socially or economically with the natives, did not have the influence as model farmers which the governmental officials had hoped for. The native Mexican villages near the Mennonite settlement all greatly benefited, however, from the prosperity of the Mennonites. The little village of Cuauhtemoc, just at the edge of the Mennonite colony in Chihuahua, consisted of only a few poor families in 1921. By 1949 it had grown into a prosperous, up-to-date city of nearly eight thousand.

Arrivals from Russia

Meanwhile, there seemed to be a fair possibility about this time of securing the influx of a large body of Mennonites from Russia. Although the Russian delegation of 1920 had bypassed Mexico as a possible home for prospective Mennonite refugees, yet a certain amount of interest remained among the Mennonites of Russia, as well as certain Mennonite groups in the United States. The telegram of B. B. Janz to Newton, Kansas, requesting that arrangements be made with the Canadian Pacific Steamship Company for the transportation of ten thousand Russians to Mexico has already been mentioned. In the meantime, in 1921 another Mennonite Colonization Society had been formed among a number of men, of whom H. P. Krehbiel of Newton, Kansas, was the chief promoter. Its objective was to further the Mexican project.

The Mexican government, especially the officials in the land and railway departments, were greatly interested in the proposed migration, and the officials of the Mennonite Colonization Society were given liberal passes over the railroad company lines for inspecting suitable sites for settlement. At a meeting in 1924 of officials of the Mexican government, the colonization society, and certain New York financiers, a rather elaborate scheme was worked out for financing a mass immigration movement. According to this proposed scheme the New York financiers were to finance the enterprise by issuing 6 percent bonds, endorsed by reliable American Mennonite individuals and then countersigned by the prospective Russian immigrants. The Mexican government was to furnish transportation from the Mexican seacoast at Vera Cruz to the homes selected in the interior. For a number of reasons this ambitious plan was never carried out. It was chiefly, no doubt, because of the difficulty of finding the Mennonite endorsers. Between 1924 and 1926 several hundred stragglers arrived in small groups at Vera Cruz, usually penniless and sometimes unheralded, and found their way into the interior where they formed several settlements on available haciendas which they purchased on long-term contracts.

The largest of these settlements was located near the city of Irapuato in the state of Guanajuato. All these small Mennonite colonies from Russia had to be supported by the Mennonite Colonization Society during their stay in Mexico. Unable to meet their payments and dissatisfied with their prospects here, most of them finally found their way to Canada. A few remained, however. These latter drifted for the most part into the city of Cuauhtemoc, on the outskirts of the Old Colony settlement, where in 1938 H. P. Krehbiel organized them into a small congregation which affiliated with the General Conference Mennonite Church. Among the leaders in this small group were David Redekop and his sons who succeeded in building industries and stores through which they purchased the produce of the Mennonite settlements, and in turn supplied them with groceries, dry goods, machinery, and whatever a Mennonite farmer in Mexico might need.

Neither the Kansas aid society nor any of the other American Mennonite relief agencies took much interest in the affairs of the Canadian Old Colonist enterprise in Mexico. They were able to finance themselves and needed no outside help. Religiously, too, they were well organized, and too conservative in their beliefs and practices to accept any spiritual ministration outside their own group. Although they suffered considerable economic hardship during the early years, their church and school privileges were fairly well respected during these years of political disturbance.

The Old Colony Mennonites established new villages for the second generation of their group in Mexico. The members of the *Kleine Gemeinde*, who migrated to Mexico from Manitoba during the years 1948 and 1949, also established a settlement north of the Old Colony area. They built churches and schools and established themselves in Los Jagueyes, renamed Quellen-Kolonie (Spring Colony) because of the number of springs found in the area.

Anxious Days

During the early 1930s the new socialist government, forgetting the promises of Obregon to the delegation of 1921, began to apply their socialization program to the Mennonite schools as well as to those of the natives, and demanded that native Mexican teachers replace those of the Mennonite faith. For some months the Mennonite schools were closed. It was just for this that the colonists had left Canada—loss of control over their own schools. Once more there was talk of another trek, even back to Canada if no other place opened up. Several hundred did return between 1936 and 1938.

At the same time, Mexican bandits, taking advantage of the pacificism of the Mennonites, frequently broke into their homes and even attacked them in their homes or on their way to the markets. Several Mennonites had already been killed in these encounters. When the Mexican government learned that the Mennonites were seriously considering leaving the country, they decided to intervene in their behalf. After all, the government did not wish to see the flourishing villages and well-cultivated fields of some ten thousand Mennonites revert back to the barren deserts they once had been. And so in 1936 President Cardenas promised the Mennonites all their school privileges again and added police protection against banditry. The schools were reopened, robbery and banditry ceased for a time, and the plans for a wholesale exodus were given up.

At the close of World War II the MCC established a public health service in the city of Cuauhtemoc, while the home mission board of the General Conference supported the work of the General Conference Mennonite Church in Cuauhtemoc. In 1978 the population of the Old Colony Mennonites was thirty-four thousand and of the General Conference Mennonite Church, five hundred. There were also one thousand members of the *Kleine Gemeinde* in Mexico.

During the last decades, numerous Old Colony Mennonites

IN SEARCH OF FREEDOM OF CONSCIENCE

have left Mexico and returned to Canada or migrated to South America and to the United States.

3. PARAGUAY

The Menno Settlement

Not all of the conservative Canadian Mennonites favored Mexico as a future home. Some Bergthal, Sommerfeld, and Chortitza Mennonites considered South America and made contacts with Paraguay.

Paraguay is divided into two halves. East Paraguay, with a subtropical climate, has regular rainfall and good vegetation. West Paraguay, known as Gran-Chaco, has a hot and dry climate and an occasional frost in wintertime. The rainy season is not the same every year. The Chaco has a stony soil, hardwoods, thorny bushes, various cactus plants, and other vegetation which gives it a uniqueness. The Gran-Chaco reaches also into Argentina and Bolivia. It was in this territory where the Menno Colony was begun in 1927 and 1928.

In 1921 a delegation sent to the Chaco obtained from the Paraguayan government the assurance of religious freedom and the promise that they could have their own school system and their own administration if they would settle in the Chaco. Without a thorough investigation of the Chaco, a considerable number of the Sommerfeld, Chortitza, and Bergthal Mennonites decided to migrate to Paraguay. This migration materialized five years later. A total of 284 families, or 1,742 persons, left Canada in seven groups between November 1926 and November 1927. The land, consisting of 1,875 hectares or 4,500 acres, was sold to them by the *Corporacion Paraguaya* for twelve dollars per hectare, which was much too high a price.

The first group arrived in Puerto Casado, a small airport on the Paraguay River, on December 30, 1926. Since the land was not yet surveyed, the group remained here for sixteen months, an extremely disappointing beginning for the settlers. Much of the money to be used for the settlement was spent during this time without any progress. Health conditions were extremely difficult, and an epidemic of typhoid fever broke out, resulting in 171 deaths. Three hundred persons returned to Canada, disappointed by what they had experienced.

Once the settlement began, the pioneers had first of all to develop roads through the wilderness, following the trails of the military posts established in the Chaco. Until this time the Chaco had been occupied only by nomadic Indians. This isolation had its advantages and disadvantages. It was a protective wall against the "world" from which the Mennonites escaped. As far as the economic development was concerned, however, it seemed an insurmountable disadvantage.

The Beginning of the Settlement

At last, in the middle of 1928, the settlement of the exhausted pilgrims could begin. The land was surveyed, and the sites for the buildings of the village were distributed by lots. Thus the indescribably difficult task of taming the Chaco began. The settlement consisted of 1,300 persons in fourteen villages, all but one of which continue to this day. The climatic conditions are extremely severe. The Chaco is located between 57 and 63 degrees latitude and 19 and 25 degrees longitude. The subtropical climate of the Chaco caused many diseases and hardships, which had to be endured without hospitals, medicine, medical doctors, or nurses. The economic crisis in Canada and other parts of the world delayed help and made a return to Canada, for those who would have liked to do so, nearly impossible. Thus there was no alternative but to stay and try to survive.

In view of the fact that most of the capital had been used up before the settlement started, great hardships had to be overcome. Those who had some money left loaned it to those who had none. Much experimentation and much time was needed to produce crops for a livelihood. The land agency that had sold this land gave some help. An agricultural experiment station was established, and the sponsoring agent provided some credit for seeds and food. Cows and oxen were obtained.

Self-government entailed new responsibilities in administrative matters. The Mennonites had "privileges" and responsibilities which they had enjoyed in Canada, and before in Russia. However, they had to develop a tradition and practice to start to administer all social and economic institutions, including the building of hospitals, acquiring of medical personnel, finding a market, and keeping order in the household of Menno. Everything, including the building of roads, depended entirely on their own efforts.

The major solution to the problems that the brotherhood faced was the establishment of a Cooperative Administration in 1936. This body became the economic agent that bought and sold products, and built the roads, the hospitals, and the traditional Mennonite schools. The spiritual level of the community had to be raised. The notion that the migration to the Chaco had been motivated by the desire to maintain the status quo on all levels had to be overcome. The conservative elements, who had sacrificed so much for this cause, were slow in accepting changes.

Progress in the Chaco

Fortunately the colony had men who with vision and much patience untiringly introduced the needed and feared changes. Step by step, progress had to be made by convincing and proving with every move that it was necessary, and Christian, and in the Mennonite tradition. This was particularly difficult in regard to raising the level of education. The Cooperative Administrative Office established the hospital, an industrial center, a business office, and even a secondary school with a dormitory. The training of teachers and more progressive farmers contributed considerably to the progress of the settlement.

Another significant step was the purchase of a considerable amount of land adjacent to what had originally been bought. This time it was obtained for twenty-five cents per acre instead of five dollars as had been the case. Much of the land had to be cleared of shrubs and trees so that the younger farmers could settle. Roads had to be built, and first-aid stations and stores had to be established.

In 1958 the Menno settlement received a long-term loan from the Mennonite Central Committee. It was used to purchase agricultural machinery such as tractors and bulldozers, and to establish a modern dairy, an oil press, and many other projects. As a result, the milk and cattle industry has been considerably improved. This branch of the economy of the settlement produces 55 percent of all income.

In October 1972 the total population of the settlement was 5,384 persons in 938 families. Of these, 562 families were involved in agriculture. In addition, 2,300 Indians are located in the territory occupied by the Mennonites, and the colony is responsible for them.

During the first years there were only several hundred Indians. Through the influence of the Mennonite missionaries, the Indians have stopped killing infants, thus increasing their number considerably. Through medical care, the health conditions have been improved. However, the hunting territory has been decreased through the purchase of the land by white settlers. This has increased the responsibility of the Mennonites toward the Indians. About 260 Indian families have been settled on land and taught farming skills by the Menno colony. Many more will be settled as soon as there is an opportunity. The Indians had to get used to an entirely new way of life when they turned from hunting to agriculture.

Cooperative

Every family is a member of the cooperative. The surplus

income of the organization is used for projects such as the construction of roads and support of the hospital. The remaining income is added to the capital. The following establishments are of particular significance for economic progress: a cotton gin, a dairy, an oil press, an electric plant, a communal pasture, and a tannin factory, which uses an extraction from Quebracho wood. Since the trans-Chaco highway from Asuncion to the border of Bolivia has been finished, the cooperative has taken over the freight transport of the colony. This has solved many of the transportation problems of the settlement.

Menno has an administrative house as well as a business center in the city of Asuncion. This includes a store and a cold storage unit for such products as cheese and butter which are marketed in the capital. These arrangements have reduced the cost of the freight by 50 percent. Formerly butter, cheese, and eggs had to be transported to Asuncion by plane. Through German economic help, it has been made possible to improve the industrialization of the settlement. Air-conditioned trucks have added to the efficiency and the economic life considerably.

Since the seventy-one villages and places of the settlement are scattered over a large area, the cooperative has established a business center in Loma Plata and three branches in remote villages. The central office has radio contact with the office in Asuncion and the branches. Telephone service is also being introduced.

Since the income from the cooperative enterprise is taking care of most of the settlement expenses, there are hardly any taxes. Life in Menno without the cooperative business structure is unthinkable. It is not only the basis and the core of the Mennonite settlement, but it also greatly benefits other Paraguayans, including the Indians.

Fernheim

A second settlement, *Fernheim*, consisting of some forty thousand acres bordering the northwestern boundaries of the Menno tract, was settled by Moscow refugees, who were unable for one reason or another to gain admission to Canada and did not volunteer for Brazil. The Mennonite Central Committee took special interest in the plight of these Moscow refugees from the start. The committee preferred Paraguay to Brazil as a possible home for several reasons—a successful Canadian Mennonite colony had already been established here, and the Paraguayan government had guaranteed prospective Mennonite immigrants military exemption and other special terms.

The first contingent of this Moscow group which left their

temporary barracks in Germany on March 15, 1930, were welcomed at Asuncion by the Paraguayan president as their Canadian brethren had been before them. Finally they reached the terminus of the Puerto Casado railway where they were met by their Canadian brethren from Menno. They were then transported in big two-wheeled ox carts to the corporation camp which had been prepared for them on the outskirts of their proposed colony. Here they soon established themselves into villages of from fifteen to twenty families each. Other groups during the year brought the total number of arrivals up to fifteen hundred. In 1932 a group which left Russia crossing the Amur River into Harbin, China, joined the colony. These, together with a small company of Mennonites from Poland who had also found their way here, brought the whole number of immigrants to this settlement to about two thousand. Perhaps because they were homesick the first settlers called their colony *Fernheim*; and their individual villages, too, repeated familiar names from the homeland—*Lichtfelde, Orloff, Rosenort. Hiebertsheim* commemorated one of their American benefactors, and *Auhagen*, the German representative who had helped them in Moscow.

Hardships

Both the *Menno* and *Fernheim* settlements experienced almost unbearable hardships from the start. Hundreds of miles from markets and sources of supplies, with no transportation facilities other than the ox cart, with insufficient money or tools, and heavily in debt for all their land, the Fernheim colony, especially, had to start from scratch. They received some tools and farm equipment from Germany. Their first makeshift houses were without floors or ceiling, with thatched roofs made of the native bitter grass, or perhaps of discarded galvanized sheet metal. Windows without glass admitted an invasion of flies, mosquitoes, and all the pestiferous insects that infest a hot, swampy wilderness. The furniture was all homemade from the hardwoods nearby. Almost the first concern of the settlers was the search for fresh water. Numerous wells were dug, but most of them contained only salt and bitter water. The finding of a fresh, or "sweet" water well was the source of great rejoicing. Some of the villages were forced to carry the water for both their stock and themselves for miles, from the supply of more fortunate neighboring villages.

The intense summer heat, with occasional dust storms from the Argentinian north, and periodical droughts just when the growing crops needed moisture, bore heavily on the physical stamina of the settlers.

Familiar crops like wheat and certain highly prized garden vegetables refused to grow in the tropical Chaco. The lack of white bread remained a major complaint for some years among the more particular. Sorghum bread, they said, made good chicken feed, but was not particularly palatable for humans, especially those from the Canadian and Russian wheat fields. It was some years before it was found that such crops as sorghum, peanuts, beans, cotton, and even watermelons could be grown with some success and fair profit. Too often, even when growing crops gave promise of a good harvest, either a prolonged drought, or a sudden swarm of grasshoppers in a few days would blast all the cherished hopes of better times ahead.

It was to be expected, of course, that under these conditions, all of which tended to undermine the physical stamina of the early settlers, disease should make its inroad among them. Like their neighbors at Menno, the Fernheimers also had their period of mourning. Eighty-eight new graves, scattered throughout the village cemeteries, gave mute evidence of the disease ravages during the first year.

Naturally these disappointments and hardships caused a good deal of homesickness and developed a desire among them to seek a better location, if possible. Unlike the Canadian brethren, the Fernheimers could not return home, for they had no homeland to go to. But they might seek a more suitable place in Paraguay, and some of them did. For a time it seemed that the entire Fernheim colony might leave. By 1939 about one-third of the colony had left for other locations, some for the larger cities, but most of them for a new settlement in eastern Paraguay which they called *Friesland*, after the native land of the founder of their faith, Menno Simons.

Gradually the situation improved somewhat, and living conditions became more tolerable. Year by year a little more land was cleared, and living quarters became a little more comfortable. Kiln-dried brick replaced the original adobe huts in a few places; fresh water wells were discovered in increasing numbers. Cotton, it was discovered, could be cultivated with considerable success and became the chief cash crop, though the inflation and the distance to market made the net profits still disappointingly small. Labor-saving machinery, though crude and homemade, lightened somewhat the burdens of the farmer. A crude threshing machine run by a gasoline engine replaced the old hand flail. A cotton gin, an oil press, a sorghum flour mill, and other machinery were gradually introduced. Horses and mules gradually replaced the slow-moving and stubborn oxen as the chief beasts of burden. The breeding of cattle and hogs and raising of chickens have increased both the quality and quantity of food, and health conditions have improved as a result.

The destructive forces of nature, however, unfortunately have not shown a similar trend. The ravenous grasshoppers, the ubiquitous ants and fleas, the tropical sun, droughts, and dust storms have continued their devastating visits unabated. In fact, it is extremely doubtful whether any other people than these pious and industrious Mennonites, overjoyed at their escape from Russia, and with no other prospect for a future home than the Chaco wilderness, would have been able or willing to endure these hardships. They were willing to face any trial and undergo any distress if only their religious faith and the spiritual welfare of their children could be spared. So great was their gratitude that they set apart November 25, the day they left Moscow, as a special annual day of thanksgiving for their deliverance.

Indians and the Chaco War

The small bands of Indians that roved around the underbrush of the Chaco were not a threat to the Mennonite colonists. They were peaceful and harmless; and in the early days, before they knew the value of money, they were of great help in clearing the underbrush from the first farms. The Fernheim Mennonites, supported by their Canadian brethren, especially the Mennonite Brethren, conducted mission work among the Indians almost from the beginning of the settlement. When they started their mission work in 1935, the Presbyterians had already translated parts of the Bible into Lengua. B. W. Toews learned the language from the Indians while teaching them Bible stories. At the first baptismal service of thirty-four Indians in 1957, the number of Mennonites witnessing it was one thousand, matched by an equal number of Indians.

The Bolivian-Paraguayan War, known as the Chaco War (1932-35), was fought during this period, sometimes not far from the Mennonite settlements. The roar of cannon was often heard in the villages, and soldiers frequently passed through the streets. With the exception of a few tragedies, however, the colonists were not seriously molested.

In fact, paradoxically, there was more benefit than hardship derived from the Chaco War. The army considered itself as a protector of the settlement. The military hospital was made available to the Mennonite settlers. Here those that suffered from trachoma and other diseases caused by the change of climate got help. The military became the first to buy produce from the settlers.

Help from Mennonite Central Committee

The Mennonite Central Committee (MCC) took a special interest in the Fernheim colony. Though it had little part in the promotion of the Menno settlement or of the Brazilian venture, these settlements too were visited by different members of the committee at various times in the interest of their general welfare.

The financial arrangements between Fernheim and the Corporation Paraguay during most of this time were especially unsatisfactory. In the early years much of the local equipment and supplies needed by the settlers were bought through the corporation at rather exorbitant prices. The price paid for the land was also too high, and payments could not be met. For a time foreclosure threatened the colony. Finally, in 1938 the MCC bought out the interests of the corporation at a greatly reduced price and made new contracts with the farmers at a figure which they could meet. Thus the financial future of the colony was assured again for a time.

Government Insurance

The charter granted the Mennonites by the Paraguayan government, as we have seen, permitted a wide degree of freedom in the selection of forms of local government and educational programs. The Fernheim group adopted a form of local control that was based upon that known to their early forefathers in Russia. At the head of the colony is a superintendent called *Oberschulze,* elected by a general assembly of all the villages. He is aided by several assistants and a clerk. This superintendent is granted considerable power. Each village also has a local magistrate called a *Schulze,* as well as a village clerk and a peace officer.

There is also an independent court system, consisting of a central peace office located at the headquarters of the colony and local justices of peace in each village. Village peace officials are selected by the *Oberschulze* from a list prepared by the local village town meeting. This type of government is a compromise between a pure democracy and rule by a centralized superintendent.

This independent and privileged position of the Mennonites within the framework of the Paraguayan government accords them almost the status of a state within a state, and so long as they remain isolated in the Chaco they likely will not be molested by the Paraguayan authorities in the control of their local domestic affairs.

Both settlements, Menno and Fernheim, continue the practices of their ancestors in Russia and Canada and supply their own fire and livestock insurance companies, children's homes, and hospitals. The primitive conditions of their settlements and their common needs demanded for a time a number of cooperative business enterprises. Fernheim early established a cooperative store, cooperative mills, and other necessary undertakings. The cooperative spirit pervading the whole life of the colony is well expressed in a large wall motto hanging above the front stage of the town hall: *Gemeinnutz vor Eigennutz* (Public Welfare above Self-interest).

In the Fernheim settlement all these enterprises, together with the local government offices, the high school, industrial plants, mills, cotton gins, and the printing press, were centrally located in a town especially built to be the headquarters for the entire settlement. This town, built on a tract of land consisting of 250 acres specially donated for that purpose by the Corporation Paraguay, was called *Philadelphia*.

Schools

In both settlements, control of their schools continued to be a major interest. In the Fernheim colony, especially, the reeducation of their children was a matter of grave concern, since they had already been subjected in Russia to ten years of influence by communist teachers.

Fortunately, there were a number of efficient teachers among the Russian immigrants. The first crude building to be erected in every village after living quarters had been provided for was the primitive little school hut, without furniture or school equipment, and for a time without schoolbooks. The curriculum, however, was up-to-date and varied, stressing especially the German language, with some history, nature study, and mathematics, as well as singing and religion. The native tongue was not neglected. The second year a number of teachers spent some time, at government expense, at Asuncion to learn the language of the land.

After 1935 a *Zentralschule* was erected at Philadelphia. Fritz Kliewer was sent to Germany, with some support from the overseas German Institute at Stuttgart, for a three-year course of study to prepare for the principalship of this high school. A general school board has supervision of the educational system of the colony. In the course of time, teachers' associations and teachers' institutes were established.

Today in both the Menno settlement and the Fernheim settlement, the educational level is maintained as it was in Russia prior to the Revolution in 1917. In fact, all South American Mennonites get most of their educational materials from Germany. Not only do some of the South American young men and women go to Germany to prepare themselves for teaching and for other professions, but German teachers spend a number of years in their schools as teachers and advisers.

Religious Life

In Fernheim three branches of Mennonites are represented—Mennonites, Mennonite Brethren, and Evangelical Mennonites, though the latter compose only a small contingent. Realizing the need of cooperation in their religious, as well as in their economic, life in the midst of their primitive surrounding, these three groups have united their forces through a *Kommission für Kirchenangelegenheiten* in all their religious efforts except in their baptismal and communion exercises.

Mission festivals, choral singing, Bible conferences, evangelistic meetings, and observance of the various church holy days play an important role in the religious life of the Chaco Mennonites as they did in Russia.

The youth problem gave the Fernheim leaders no little concern at times. Under the guidance of Fritz Kliewer, the high school teacher, and other progressive leaders, a youth organization was formed, with branches in various villages; this, by sponsoring music festivals, Bible study, and dramatic performances, gradually directed the activities of some of the unruly youth into higher levels of social life.

Arrivals after World War II

The plight of the Russian Mennonites who found themselves in western Europe at the close of World War II will be recalled from the chapter on Russia. Some twelve thousand Mennonites from Russia found themselves as displaced persons in the British and American zones of occupied Germany and in Berlin. It was most urgent to rescue the refugees in Berlin since they were in danger of being forcibly repatriated to Russia. After careful preparation, the Russian authorities finally agreed to permit 1,125 Mennonite refugees to proceed from Berlin to Bremerhaven by train. Peter and Elfrieda Dyck, representatives of the Mennonite Central Committee, were instrumental in taking this group to Bremerhaven where the *Volendam* received other Mennonite refugee passengers, making a total of 2,305. On February 1, 1947, they departed for Paraguay, arriving in Buenos Aires on February 22. The transportation of this group to Paraguay was delayed because of a revolution in that land. About half of this group settled in the new colony *Volendam*, west of the Friesland colony and bordering the Paraguay River. The next largest group established a new colony south of the Fernheim colony in the

Chaco. The total cost to the MCC of moving these immigrants was $494,807, of which the International Refugee Organization contributed $160,000. This was the first of a number of shiploads of Mennonite refugees transported to Paraguay.

On March 13, 1948, the *General Stuart Heintzelman* arrived in Buenos Aires with 860 refugees aboard, and on May 16, 1948, the *SS Charlton Monarch* left Bremerhaven with 758 refugee passengers. The *Volendam* again left Bremerhaven on October 7, 1948, with 827 refugees destined for Paraguay. This ship stopped in Montevideo, October 22, disembarking 751 West Prussian Mennonite refugees for their destination in Uruguay.

In 1946 the Menno colony, founded by Mennonites coming from Canada, had a population of about two thousand nine hundred; Fernheim, about two thousand one hundred; and Friesland, one thousand. With the arrival of nearly five thousand Mennonite refugees, the total population of the colonies in Paraguay almost reached twelve thousand in 1949. After the establishment of the new colony, Volendam, the later refugees were directed mostly to the Fernheim-Menno colonies where they settled on newly purchased land. In 1978 the Menno settlement had a population of six thousand living in eighty villages. Approximately four hundred fifty had left for Bolivia and fifteen hundred had returned to Canada.

Approximately sixteen thousand Mennonites of German descent and language live in Paraguay today. This number includes not only baptized members, but also children, youth, and adults who have not been baptized but belong to the fellowship because of their ethnic origin. The following list gives a clearer picture of all groups:

Name of Settlement	Year Founded	Population (1976)
Menno	1927	6,100
Fernheim	1930	2,700
Friesland	1937	742
Neuland	1947	970
Volendam	1947	638
Bergtal	1948	1,300
Sommerfeld	1948	1,300
Reinfeld	1966	70
Luz y Esperanza*	1967	125
Agua Azul*	1969	79
Rio Verde	1969	1,100
Tres Palmas	1970	250
Santa Clara	1972	140

Rio Corrientes*	1975	28
Asuncion		400

*In Luz y Esperanza are the English-speaking Amish; in Agua Azul and Rio Corrientes the English-speaking conservative Mennonites from the USA and Canada.

The following Mennonite groups live in the different colonies: Sommerfelder Mennonites (from Canada) in Menno, Sommerfeld, Bergtal, and Reinfeld; Old Colony Mennonites (from Mexico and British Honduras) in Rio Verde and Santa Clara; General Conference Mennonites (from Russia) in Fernheim, Friesland, Neuland, Volendam, and Asuncion; Evangelical Mennonite Brethren Church (from Russia) in Fernheim; Mennonite Brethren (from Russia) in Fernheim, Friesland, Neuland, Volendam, and Asuncion; *Kleine Gemeinde* (Evangelical Mennonite Conference/Canada) at Tres Palmas; Mennonite Christian Brotherhood (from the USA) at Agua Azul and Rio Corrientes; and Beachy Amish (from the USA) at Luz y Esperanza.

Source: *Mennonite World Conference Handbook*, page 252.

4. BRAZIL

From Moscow to Brazil

About one-fourth of the Moscow refugees who had been temporarily housed in the German military barracks decided to accept the German offer of free transportation to Santa Catharina in southern Brazil. There, near Blumenau, a flourishing German city of some five thousand, a large German colony had been established some hundred years earlier. Near here the Hanseatic Colonization Society, founded some years before to promote German colonization in Brazil, still had a large area of unoccupied primitive forest land for which it desired settlers. It was with this society that the Mennonites contracted for their land, at a rather high price, but on the installment plan.

The land selected was located just below the tropics in the foothills along the *Alto Rio Krauel*, a tributary of the Itajahi, which in turn flows eastward into the Atlantic. Although only one hundred fifty miles from the coast, and forty miles from the nearest railway, it was still a primeval forest of subtropical hardwoods and a tangled mass of underbrush. The nearest town of any size, *Blumenau*, was one hundred miles distant seaward.

The first group of Mennonite colonists, consisting of 180 persons, was aided by the German government with transportation expenses on credit, and by the German Red Cross with necessary household utensils. Under the leadership of Heinrich Martens they left Hamburg on a German liner in midwinter of 1930 and reached their Brazilian destination in southern midsummer, about a month later. Other transports followed during the succeeding months, until by the end of the year nearly one thousand Mennonite refugees had reached the wilderness along the Krauel, eager to begin life all over again with practically nothing of this world's goods except a financial obligation that would doom them to a life of toil for many years to come. In 1934 several hundred of the refugees who had left Russia by way of Harbin, China, found their way to the Brazil settlement.

Two separate settlements were established. The first comers located along the Krauel, but later arrivals, finding the Krauel Valley already well filled, were forced rather reluctantly to move some miles inland upon an elevated plateau about twenty-five hundred feet above sea level, called *Stoltz-Plateau*. The Krauel settlement was divided into three districts—*Witmarsum* (which ultimately became the headquarters for the whole group), *Waldheim*, and *Gnadenthal*. The Stoltz-Plateau group named their settlement *Auhagen*, after the German official who was of great service to the Moscow refugees in the flight from Russia to Germany.

Unlike the Russian Mennonites elsewhere, these Brazilians did not congregate in villages, but each family located on its own farm tract of one hundred acres, more or less. This was due perhaps partly to the difficulty of clearing enough of the woodland immediately for village sites. They kept the usual form of local government, however, with the *Schulze*, the *Oberschulze*, and other local officials, as had been their custom in Russia.

Early Hardships

As in Paraguay, the Mennonites along the Krauel passed through a period of great disappointment and disillusionment, and they almost despaired at times. Coming as they did from the broad wheat fields of Russia, where their labor was lightened by the use of immense horse-drawn harvesters, they found that in the Brazilian jungles their first task was to clear by axe and saw enough of a lot on which to erect their first rude log huts. Then, by further hand labor, they had to extend the clearing for sufficient room in which to plant the beans, sweet potatoes, or sorghum with which to feed themselves. It would take years of hard work before sufficient land would be cleared to even raise enough food for a modest living, and a full generation before they could pay off their debts. There seemed to be no marketable product except *aipim*, a root plant strong in starch content; but so long as they were far from market, and without a starch factory, *aipim* could not be grown with profit. In the course of time, however, it became the chief cash crop. The excess of moisture and the tropical sun encouraged the growth of rank weeds and underbrush almost as fast as it could be cleared, greatly adding to the farmer's labor. Farming thus by hand with spade and hoe, instead of horse-drawn machinery, was of the most primitive nature.

There were several encouraging factors in the situation, however. The climate, though tropical, was not unbearable, especially on the plateau; and health conditions remained fairly good. There was no period of high death rate as in Paraguay.

The colonists received substantial financial aid, too, from their Dutch brethren, who made the Brazilian venture their special charge. Through S. H. N. Gorter, chairman of the Dutch Emigration Bureau, substantial sums of money were sent to the settlers for the purchase of livestock, for the establishing of schools, for the erection of a starch factory, which made possible the marketing of the *aipim* products, and for other needed purposes. In the course of time, more land was cleared, better houses were built, and more roads opened. Cooperative stores, mills, factories, and creameries were established. During the first year the Mennonites from Witmarsum organized a cooperative to include every family. This cooperative grew to a creditable business concern and greatly helped the settlement in its early trying years.

From Witmarsum to Curitiba

Naturally the hard living conditions in the original settlements drove a number of the settlers to look for more favorable locations elsewhere in which to establish permanent homes. Many of the younger people soon found their way into the larger coastal cities, into domestic service, or into factory work and clerical positions. Parents frequently followed their children. By 1935 a mass movement had begun, especially from the Auhagen settlement, for a new location near *Curitiba*. This movement threatened for a time to depopulate all Auhagen. As it was, only some thirty families remained.

In 1946 the population of the Curitiba group numbered some two hundred fifty families, living mostly in the suburbs of the city and outlying districts. The milk industry, especially, had become popular among the Mennonites. Three-fourths of all the milk for the city of Curitiba, which has a population of one hundred twenty-five thousand, was supplied by the Mennonites. Other Mennonites were employed in factories and business places.

Gradually the milk industry of the Mennonites in the outskirts of Curitiba reached its climax. Some sold their property, since the city was expanding, and started their own businesses and workshops for woodworking or worked in factories and other businesses. Where Mennonites had had their large cow barns and open fields pursuing dairying, there are now flourishing suburbs. Occasionally there is still a trace of a farm and cow barn. Even though the owner is pursuing another occupation, he milks the cow and, above all, waits for a higher price for his land.

Some Mennonites have gone into plywood manufacturing, originally on a small scale. Although some failed, several ultimately succeeded in building large factories employing hundreds of workers. Among these are Heinrich Löwen and Wilhelm Berg. Curitiba is a striving, prosperous, industrial center with some fifty new international industries that have come there during the last ten years. Among them is the van Delden fabric factory, a Mennonite industry of Gronau, Westphalia. It is a long way from the time that the first Mennonite refugees were dumped into the primeval forest of the Krauel, where they struggled for a number of years to eke out a meager living, and finally moved to Curitiba.

Church and School

In Brazil, three branches of Mennonites were represented, with the Mennonite Brethren in the lead numerically. Although retaining their separate divisional organization and church fellowship, yet the three groups have united under a *Kommission für Kirchenangelegenheiten* (KfK) for safeguarding their common religious and cultural interests, and frequently for common worship. Each settlement showed the usual concern for maintaining an efficient school system. In 1933 a *Zentralschule* was established at Witmarsum, the so-called county seat.

Unlike the Paraguayan and Mexican settlements, the Brazilian Mennonites were not offered any special concessions by the Brazilian government as an inducement to their settlement here—neither military exemption nor local self-administration nor a private school system. At first they were permitted considerable liberty in conducting their own schools in the German language; but during World War II a governmental decree demanded that in all schools the language of instruction was to be Portuguese and the teachers to be native born. This handicapped the Mennonite educational system very much. They had many well-trained teachers who were born in Russia and who now had to stop teaching. The children had to be sent to the public school or minority schools, such as a Catholic private school in Curitiba. Even the worship services in the German language were prohibited. This was a special hardship for the Mennonites from Russia who did not know Portuguese. Somehow the Mennonites convinced the government officials that Low German was not the German language, and they were granted the permission to conduct their worship services in the Low German language. Songs and other means of worship had to be translated into the Low German, a unique chapter in Mennonite history.

In 1932 Peter Klassen founded a German paper called *Die Brücke*, devoted to the religious and cultural interests of the colony. Owing to lack of support, and especially to the governmental demand that translations of the paper be also made in the Portuguese language, the venture unfortunately had to suspend in 1938. Since 1954 *Bibel und Pflug* has been published in Brazil for the Mennonites of South America. The first editor was Fritz Kliewer.

At first the Mennonites and Mennonite Brethren held their services together at both Curitiba and Witmarsum. Only the monthly meetings for communion and business were held separately. However, new church buildings have gradually been erected as congregations develop and become independent. The Mennonites of Brazil were represented at the Mennonite World Conference held in the United States in 1948. Two congregations of Witmarsum and one congregation from Curitiba joined the General Conference Mennonite Church in 1947. In 1972 the Mennonite World Conference was held in Curitiba.

What About the Future?

The Mennonites in Brazil are confronting great problems. They are small groups surrounded by a Latin-Catholic environment. They long for more fellowship with their like-minded brethren abroad. This need has been partly met through contacts with the Mennonites in Paraguay and Uruguay and representatives from North America.

On the other hand, the Mennonites have contact with pietistic-evangelistic groups of Brazil and Germany. However, at times a sense of discrimination is lacking in regard to what is in line with their Anabaptist-Mennonite heritage. This is very common also among North American Mennonites, but more dangerous for Mennonites in an isolation where often a corrective counterbalance is missing. The sound judgment and spiritual leadership of the first generation that brought them from Russia to Brazil cannot easily be replaced.

The contact with the Mennonites in Paraguay and Uruguay is helpful but is bound to decrease as the linguistic developments lead the Mennonites in Spanish-speaking countries to a full acceptance of Spanish, while the Mennonites in Brazil are already strongly exposed to the acceptance of the Portuguese language, leading to intermarriages with Portuguese-speaking, Catholic-Brazilian partners. The witness of a warm pietistic Mennonite faith, combined with successful hard work, makes them attractive in numerous ways. But is their Christian-Mennonite witness strong enough to be transplanted on a large scale? That goes, however, not only for a minority group of Mennonites in Brazil but also for all others in a Latin American environment and beyond.

Mennonites in South America

XIV
Theological and Cultural Developments

Neither the early Anabaptists between Zürich and Strassburg, nor those between Emden and Amsterdam, were totally unanimous on all details of the faith and Christian discipleship, nor was there ever a time later where this could be claimed to have been the case. Nevertheless, many meetings took place to express the generally accepted doctrines and, above all, the Christian life. In their defense of their Christian faith they had many occasions to formulate their views in regard to doctrines and their way of life. With Menno Simons they emphasized 1 Corinthians 3:11, "For no other foundation can any one lay, than that which is laid, which is Jesus Christ." They accepted the confessions which were in use in the early Christian church and were aware of those produced by the Lutherans and the Reformed in the days of the Reformation. Under the pressure of persecution and in their study of the Bible, they formulated some generally acceptable expressions of their Christian *faith* and *life*. Both always remained inseparable, and often led to differences of opinion and application. One of the oldest confessions of faith, consisting of thirty-three articles, was published in the *Martyrs Mirror* (1660). Most of the writings and Mennonite publications in general had their origin in the Netherlands. There were more Mennonites in the "Golden Age" of the Netherlands that were able to write and publish devotional and doctrinal books than was the case in other countries.

Anabaptist-Mennonites in general, even the leaders, were not always of a theological-doctrinal mold as were their opponents, the Lutherans, Calvinists, and Catholics. First of all, the Anabaptist-Mennonites reacted to what seemed to them "empty" theological claims of the medieval theologians and those of the Reformation, observing that they had little, if any, bearing on the practical Christian life of their followers. Secondly, the Mennonite leaders were soon exterminated everywhere, leaving the "sheep without a shepherd" who did as well as they could. They were more biblically than theologically oriented. For them the *Nachfolge* (following) of Christ was more important than to be in line with the theology of the Middle Ages or the Reformers. In their dialogue with the theologians of the Reformation they, who had just learned to read and write, quoted the Bible profusely, with a strong emphasis on a practical Christianity emanating from a faith in Christ and the fellowship of believers.

Whatever they produced in writing in regard to doctrinal and ethical statements was of a more practical nature and for the purpose of being a guide for "faith and life" for those who needed this guidance and inspiration in addition to the Bible, as well as for use when they were apprehended and had to give account of their faith and practices. This led to formulations of credal statements and guides for those who had to defend themselves.

However, soon there was another reason for the confessions of faith and the production of devotional and catechetical books. Because of the dispersion of the Mennonites into various parts of Europe, and later in North America, guides were needed to prevent deviations from the "faith of the fathers." More important, however, were the outside influences that penetrated the congregations wherever they were, in spite of their isolation, which was often forced on them or even sought in order to find a place of freedom and land to make a living. There were at times influences of a doctrinal nature such as the questions of the Trinity of God or the divinity of Christ.

The Mennonites were often referred to by their opponents as *Himmelsstürmer* (invaders of heaven) in attempting to establish the kingdom of God on earth or to achieve the purity of the church on earth. It was this effort to present the "Body of Christ without Spot and Wrinkle" (Eph. 5:27) that caused many disciplinary actions and divisons among the Mennonites throughout the centuries, both in the early days in Switzerland and the Netherlands, and later in West Prussia, Russia, Pennsylvania, and wherever they went. This is happening to this day among the nonconforming groups. It includes an aloofness toward the environment and the population by which they are surrounded. Intentionally these groups and congregations practice a "nonconformity" and "simplicity" which sets them apart from the rest of society in lifestyle, practices in daily life, school, and social life.

In the numerous migrations of the Mennonites from country to country, this unwillingness to adjust to the practices of the chosen country made some move to another country where they would be free to live according to their tradition. Among the most important reasons were, as a rule, exemption from military service, the right to have their own schools and, if possible, their own administration. These were means to preserve their spiritual identity, their lifestyle, their heritage, and their faithfulness to Christ. Thus Mennonites attempting to escape problems by leaving a country and migrating to another soon faced the same or similar conditions that they had left behind. That was in many instances also the case in North America.

Confessions of Faith

The essential doctrinal unity of the American Mennonites is evidenced by the adoption of common confessions of faith. All the conservative groups and some of the moderates agree with the Dordrecht Confession of Faith which, in addition to the commonly accepted Mennonite doctrines, includes the practice of *shunning*, or avoiding all those who have been excommunicated from the church in "eating or drinking or other such like social matters" in order "not to become defiled by intercourse with him and become partakers of his sin," and also "that he may be made ashamed" and be drawn back into the fold. This confession also prescribes foot washing and marriage only "in the Lord," which is interpreted to mean only with another member of the same group.

The Dordrecht Confession of Faith had been officially approved by the Alsatian and Palatine Mennonites in 1660 before the Amish separation, was printed by the Pennsylvania Mennonites in Philadelphia as early as 1727, and was the very first Mennonite book to be printed in America and, strange to say, in English. It has been frequently reprinted since, and universally accepted by the groups above mentioned.

The Cornelis Ris Confession of Faith, translated into German from the Dutch in 1849 by C. J. van der Smissen, was published in English in 1902 by the General Conference Mennonite Church and became the accepted statement of the more progressive group. The Cornelis Ris statement agrees with that of Dordrecht in the fundamentals, though differing somewhat in details. It is slightly more tolerant than the latter. It is silent on foot washing and shunning. Marriage with "unbelievers" is forbidden, as is divorce, except on scriptural grounds.

Church Government

In their church government the Mennonites are congregational, with a decided inclination, however, among the large, compact settlements of the Mennonites in southeastern Pennsylvania to group a number of congregations into districts under a bishop who assumes considerable ecclesiastical authority within his district. Among all branches, and most completely in the case of the General Conference Mennonite Church, the congregations are entirely independent, choose their own ministers, and regulate their own affairs. Conferences have only advisory powers, with no disciplinary control over either members or congregations, except to exclude them from conference membership in case of serious disagreement. In the General Conference Mennonite Church a two-thirds vote of all the membership is required for an action by the congregation.

Among the conservatives and most of the moderates, the ministers are chosen from the congregation, usually by lot for life and without material remuneration. The method of selection varies in different congregations. In the Franconia Conference, until recently, on the appointed day of the selection candidates who were thought worthy of the ministry by a vote of the congregation stood before the pulpit desk upon which were placed as many hymnbooks as there were candidates. Into each book a slip of paper had been placed, one of which contained the passage from Proverbs "The lot is cast into the lap; but the whole disposal thereof is of the Lord." The recipient of this paper slip would then preach for the rest of his days. If perchance it is impossible for the minister thus chosen to serve his people in preaching, he must retain his office and perform such minor duties as his capacities afford. The lot may be cast again among a new set of candidates. The use of the lot was never practiced among the Mennonites of Dutch-Russo-German background.

An increasing number of young men, and some women, now prepare for the ministry by attending one of the numerous Mennonite colleges and seminaries, and are then chosen by a congregation for a term of service. Some of the larger congregations have more than one minister. The term of service lasts from five to ten years or more, but the contract is usually for a term of three years.

Sense of Otherworldliness

The first Mennonite immigrants to America, both the Pennsylvanians as well as the early Swiss and the Russo-German Mennonites in Kansas and Manitoba, brought with them from their ancestors the traditional Mennonite sense of "otherworldliness" or "nonconformity." Although no longer persecuted here as in Europe, yet their life in compact isolated communities, as well as their nonresistant principles which forbade their taking of human life in maintaining a stable social order, tended to keep them out of politics here, for the time being. With the exception of an unsuccessful experiment among the Crefelders in Germantown, the early Mennonites never held office nor participated in political affairs even where they were in the majority.

The Mennonites in the West tried to retain at first as much as possible of the local political freedom which they had enjoyed in Russia. In Manitoba they were allowed for a good many years the control of their schools, and considerable leeway in the handling of their local civil affairs.

To this day the more conservative groups oppose the holding of public office, with the exception of such local positions as school director or road overseer. Most of them, however, make free use of the right to vote. Moderate groups have little objection to holding of office except where it might compel them to enforce capital punishment.

The Mennonites in America have retained to a large extent the traditional emphasis of the early Mennonites on right living as an essential part of their faith. They emphasize the virtues of honesty, integrity, simplicity, truthfulness, genuine trustworthiness, and a high moral standard of family life.

Nonconformity and Acculturation

Wherever the Mennonites settled throughout the centuries, even if it was in total isolation where no human foot had trod, they could not preserve a status quo nor remain totally unchanged. In building houses, tilling the soil, choosing seeds and plants to sustain their life and animals to assist them, and marketing their products, they had to acquire the linguistic skills of their neighbors and get acquainted with new habits and ways of doing things. Without intending to do so, and often without fully realizing it, they underwent changes. They accepted into their Swiss or South German language half-germanized foreign words and phrases and partook with other German neighbors in the "creation" of the Pennsylvania German dialect (by mistake called Pennsylvania "Dutch"). Pennsylvania German is basically the Palatine dialect of the early eighteenth century, with the admixture of an occasional English word that for one reason or another was drafted into the vernacular. Pastorius himself was one of the first to yield to the temptation of mixing the two tongues. In a letter written to the Frankfort Land Company in Germany, he attributed his inability to protect the interests of his company against rival claimants with these words, *Ich fand das alle Lawyers "gefeed" waren* (I found that all the lawyers had been bribed.) Similar linguistic infiltrations occurred in the Low German from Kansas to Manitoba, as it had also happened in Russia.

For generations many remained farmers living in concentrated communities in Pennsylvania or in the prairie states and provinces. Today, with few exceptions—such as those who have recently come from Europe and a few conservative groups like the Amish, Holdemans, and Hutterites—they can hardly be recognized on the streets as being "nonconformists" either in the clothing they wear or in any linguistic peculiarities they retained. World Wars I and II contributed considerably to the liquidation of the remnant of the German culture and language that most of the Mennonites still had considered an integral part of their heritage. Now they had to justify this "loss" by an emphasis on other issues—issues for which past generations had paid a high price from the days of martyrdom, exile, and migrations.

There has never been any question but that the emphasis on peace, although not always noticeable within the Mennonite community, was one of the strongest principles surviving the centuries of persecution, hardships, migrations, and even prosperity. The peace heritage played a very significant role in setting the group apart, and it became for all branches of the descendants of the Anabaptists the common symbol for unity, even if there was at times not much else left of the faith and practices among the sons and daughters of Conrad Grebel and Menno Simons.

Russo-Mennonite Culture

As we have seen, the largest number of Mennonites living in the plains from Oklahoma to Manitoba came from Russia over a century ago. Their forebears had come from the Danzig-Elbing-Marienburg area and, before them, from the Dutch provinces of Flanders, Holland, and Friesland. They used the same Dutch Bible, hymnaries, and devotional literature as their Dutch brethren. Their sermons were in the Dutch language. However, in their daily conversations with each other, they had fully accepted the Low German language that was spoken by their neighbors in West Prussia. By the end of the eighteenth century when some of them started to pack their bags for a voyage to the shores of the Dnieper River in the Ukraine, the High German language that they had been exposed to in the schools was now also conquering the last surviving fortress, the pulpits of their churches. However, some included in their baggage copies of the Dutch Bible, the Dutch *Martyrs Mirror*, and hymnaries and took them along to Russia.

Now the isolation and the insulation of the Russian environment they had chosen to escape to became an issue. They were by now gradually but surely accepting the High German language,

THEOLOGICAL AND CULTURAL DEVELOPMENTS

thus the acculturation to the environment that they had come from continued. Ultimately this also resulted in a willingness by some to accept some features of the Russian environment in matters of lifestyle, food, and language.

Thus when the Mennonites left Russia for North America, they spoke primarily Low German in their daily life (except for those of Swiss or Hutterite background). In the United States they continued their germanization process, strengthened through their schools, publications, and contacts with others of the same ethnic background. But when, during World War I, signs were posted in public places and stores, "American Spoken Only!" things started to change. High German was soon replaced by English. However, the Low German and Swiss dialects survived to some extent beyond World War II. In Canada especially, the Low German and High German Mennonite literature, which had its origin in Russia, reached its climax.

Literary Fruits of Acculturation

The literary efforts among the Mennonites in Russia had their beginning a century ago. Bernhard Harder, a well-known leader, teacher, and minister wrote over one thousand poems and songs which were published in 1888. With the improvement of the economic and educational conditions and contact with Germany, the situation changed rapidly. The giant in this development was Johann Cornies (1789-1884) who in his life exerted an unusual influence on all levels, the economic, educational, and cultural. Teachers came from Germany, and Mennonite students began to study abroad, as well as at the various Russian educational institutions and universities. Secondary schools were found in all larger settlements.

By 1890 students began to study at universities such as Basel, Zürich, Tübingen, München, Dorpat, Petersburg, Moscow, Odessa, and Kharkov. Between 1890 and 1917 about one hundred Mennonites of Russia had received a university training in the various branches of knowledge, including education, medicine, industry, and the fine arts.

It was this unique situation in which the Mennonites found themselves that inspired interest in the fine arts and creativity on various levels. They produced their own textbooks and songbooks. The contact with the outside world, their homeland in West Prussia; attending universities at home and abroad; the improved educational aids, books, school buildings, and preparation of the teachers; and the many cultural and religious influences from abroad aroused curiosity and inspired active involvement in the fine arts.

Jacob H. Janzen (1878-1950)

Jacob H. Janzen was an outstanding educator who lived in a period among the Mennonites in Russia when it was common and acceptable to elect good teachers to the ministry. He received his education in the Molotschna elementary and secondary schools as well as at the universities of Kharkov, Melitopol, Greifswald, and Jena. He was a very popular teacher-minister and began his writing early in his life. The first volume of short stories (383 pp.) appeared in 1910.

The acceptance of these short stories in the High German language inspired Janzen to continue his writing. In 1912 he published the Low German one-act play *De Bildung* (Education), and a year later *De Enbildung*. They have been presented and reprinted many times, not only in Russia but particularly in North America. They were designed to promote education when it was not yet generally accepted. Janzen's sense of humor was accepted by all, even if they did not always follow him in all conclusions.

Plautdietsch
by J. H. Janzen

Maunch eena kaun keen Plautdietsch mea en schämt sich nich emaol. Em Geagindeel: he meent sich sea met siene hoage School, red't hoogdietsch, english, rusch—so väl, daut eenim dieslich woat. Weat es de gaunze Klätamähl nich eene Schinkeschwoat.

Auls eck noch kleen wea, saut eck oft bi Mutt're oppim Schoot, en plautdietsch säd se,—o so oft;—"Mein Jung, eck sie die goot."

Waut Mutta Plautdietsch to mi säd, daut klung so woarm en tru, daut eck daut nimmamea vegät bat to de latzte Ruh.

Low German
Translated by Elmer F. Suderman

Few know Low German anymore and aren't even ashamed of it. On the other hand, they take pride in their prodigious learning, speak High German, English, Russian until I get dizzy. But the whole rabble isn't worth the rind of a ham.

When I was a child, I often sat on Mother's lap and not infrequently she'd tell me in Low German: "My son, I love you."

So sincere and affectionate were Mother's Low German words that I will never forget them until my dying day.

Transplanted to Canada

The upheaval of the Revolution and the civil war that followed in the Ukraine exposed all Mennonites and the whole German population to unparalleled sufferings. It can be assumed that among those who left Russia for Canada between 1922 and 1930, there were more highly educated than among those who remained. Those who stayed have had only limited opportunity to have anything appear in print. And yet some Mennonite writers contributed to the Soviet papers published for the Germans in Russia such as *Die Freundschaft, Neues Leben*, and others.

But there were more writers among those that went to Germany or to North America. Among them we will name only a few—G. A. Peters (narration and poetry), Gerhard Loewen (poet), Peter J. Klassen (narration), and Johann P. Klassen (poetry). Most of them arrived in Canada in the days of the depression. They had little time for writing and no money to publish what they wrote. Those who went to the United States were mostly better off. Peter Epp, author of *Eine Mutter*, taught at the University of Ohio; Gerhard Wiens (linguist and writer) taught at the University of Oklahoma; and Dietrich Neufeld (Navall), who wrote *Der Totentanz* (The Russian Dance of Death) which has been translated into English, taught in a number of American universities.

Arnold B. Dyck: Artist, Poet, Narrator

The best known and most gifted among the writers transplanted from the Russian steppes to the Canadian prairie was Arnold B. Dyck (1889-1970). Jacob H. Janzen had opened the dream gate to him beyond the confines of the village, but on the other hand, he began to see the village they were confined to in a new light.

Arnold Dyck studied art and literature at the universities of München, Stuttgart, Petersburg, and Moscow. He returned to the Chortitza area where he taught art in secondary schools until he left Russia and went to Canada in 1923.

In 1947 he published a comedy in the Low German language entitled *De Fria* (The Marriage Proposal). To this day, one performance of this play at one place is never enough; it must always be given at least two to three times. In 1950 Dyck published another Low German drama entitled *Wellkaom op'e Forstei!* followed by a sequence *De Opnoam* (1951), both dealing with the Mennonite forestry service which young men did in Russia in lieu of military service. Both have been popular presentations in communities and on college campuses.

In *Verloren in der Steppe* (five volumes, 1944-48) Dyck returns to his childhood days and relates in High German what he experienced in the village on the banks of the Dnieper River. It is a masterpiece in narrating a boy's life in such detail as no one had done. This is the only book by Dyck that has been translated and published in English, titled *Lost in the Steppes*.

No other Mennonite writer-artist of the twentieth century has received as much attention and honor as Arnold Dyck. Numerous articles have been written about his life, his works of art, and above all, about his writings.

A Heritage Survives

It has been pointed out that the Mennonites of Russia developed a considerable interest in the fine arts and that they had some poets, writers of fiction, and artists. This era ended during the Russian Revolution and caused the migration of many Mennonites to Canada. Here very few of the writers and artists could devote time to their artistic skills. It was surprising, nevertheless, how much was written and even published.

The Mennonite Mirror, published in Winnipeg, Manitoba, reflects the development of the arts among Mennonites in Canada today. Every issue contains quality articles in both English and German, and even some in Low German. Some deal with contemporary questions pertaining to religious issues; the fine arts, such as drama, music, fiction, and poetry; and Mennonite history, life, and thought. Some Mennonite writings have been published in anthologies. Perhaps the most outstanding Mennonite writer of the modern period is Rudy Wiebe, whose novels, which have won top awards in Canadian fiction, include *Peace Shall Destroy Many*, *The Blue Mountains of China*, and *The Temptations of Big Bear*.

There is an unusual interest, especially among the Mennonites of Winnipeg, in the fine arts. Dramas and music festivals are held annually. Numerous adult and children's choirs give regular concerts in Winnipeg, as well as in other places. Soon one may be tempted to compare Winnipeg with Amsterdam and Haarlem of the eighteenth and nineteenth centuries when the role of the Mennonites in the fine arts, social work, government, law, medicine, and business was outstanding in comparison to their number.

The Arts in Pennsylvania and Beyond

Great changes have taken place also among Mennonites of Pennsylvania German background with respect to the arts. There was a time when the arts were frowned upon, if not actually forbidden. Today there are an increasing number of Mennonite artists and writers. Among the authors of fiction dealing with Mennonite subjects are J. W. Yoder (*Rosanna of the Amish*, 1940), and more recently, Kenneth Reed (*Mennonite Soldier*); Merle Good (*Happy as the Grass Was Green, People Pieces*); and Myron Augusburger (*The Broken Chalice, Pilgrim Aflame*). The Herald

Press catalog lists ten pages of fiction by Mennonite writers. Outstanding among them is John L. Ruth's *Conrad Grebel, Son of Zürich*, and *'Twas Seeding Time*, the Mennonite view of the American Revolution. John Ruth has also been involved in film production.

The Festival Quarterly, published by Merle and Phyllis Good at Lancaster, Pennsylvania, seeks to promote Mennonite art and artists. The magazine contains a wide range of interviews, articles, and reviews which are of interest to Mennonites. In addition, the Goods sponsor People's Place, a center which produces dramas, films, and other programs featuring Mennonites and Amish.

Music

Ulrich Zwingli, who guided the first steps of the founding fathers of Anabaptism, abolished all media from his worship service except the Bible and preaching. In contrast, the early Anabaptists not only used singing, but they had many members who composed hymns. The *Ausbund*, the hymnbook which was first published in 1564, contained many of these hymns. It is still in use today among the Old Order Amish. The Anabaptists did not seem to object to the use of melodies selected from the popular folk tunes of their day. Anabaptist singing became one of the strongest attractions for outsiders who attended their worship services. Thus singing was from the beginning an integral part of the Anabaptist-Mennonite worship and witness.

Originally, singing was primarily done in one part, but in the nineteenth century, some Mennonite groups and congregations, especially in their choirs, began four-part singing. Originally, choirs did not sing during the worship service in the congregation, but during special performances at various occasions. However, during the present century, choirs and other special music became an integral part of worship services among most of the Mennonites of Russo-German background, with the exception of the very conservative groups such as the Old Colony Mennonites in Manitoba and Mexico.

The revival movements that swept through the United States in the nineteenth century and European Pietism also greatly influenced the musical tradition of the Mennonites. The lighter English and Methodist gospel songs were translated into the German language and accepted by Mennonites in general, and especially by those who formed Mennonite splinter groups under the influence of the revival movements.

The first pipe organs were introduced in Mennonite churches in Hamburg-Altona (1764) and Utrecht (1765), and other Dutch

Mennonite churches followed in rapid succession. Some West Prussian Mennonite churches introduced organs at the turn of the century. The introduction of musical instruments in Russia followed later. In the General Conference Mennonite congregations in the United States, the first pipe organ was installed in the West Swamp Church at Quakertown, Pennsylvania, in 1874. The reed organ often paved the way for the pipe organ.

Musical instruments were not in use in worship services among the Swiss-German Mennonites of North America until recent times. They have, as a consequence, developed a very strong choral musical tradition. Although some congregations now have pipe organs, their use is not universally accepted.

All Mennonite colleges have strong departments of music, and Mennonites are generally known as good singers who perform well in public presentations. This is not surprising, since in the history of the Mennonites, music was often the first and only legitimate contact with the world around them.

Education

The leaders among the early Anabaptists and Mennonites were usually learned men—former priests, university trained men, and sometimes university professors. In the course of a few years, however, the leaders were all killed off by persecution, and the rank and file driven under cover. Persons educated in theology were usually hand in glove with the magistrates in driving the Mennonites to a martyr's stake, or hounding them out of the country. Under such conditions higher training was neither possible nor popular. In lieu of theologians and priests, Mennonites depended upon direct access to the Bible for their religious instruction and guidance. But to know the Bible it was necessary to read. Sufficient schooling to enable their children to read was consequently universal among the Mennonites. There was far less illiteracy among them than among the average common folk of their day. Their opponents marvelled at their knowledge of the Bible.

This interest in elementary schooling the Mennonites brought with them to Pennsylvania. In Germantown they started a school even before they had a church building. When Francis D. Pastorius began his subscription school several years later, the Mennonites became its chief supporters. Every community in colonial Pennsylvania had its local institution of learning, usually supported by the congregation, and kept sometimes by a pious Mennonite, but frequently by a not-so-pious wandering schoolmaster. The school was kept in a church building, or occasionally in a home or a special school building.

THEOLOGICAL AND CULTURAL DEVELOPMENTS

The best known among the Mennonite pioneer schoolmasters was Christopher Dock. Because he was found dead one evening after school hours, kneeling at his desk in the attitude of prayer, he has been called the "pious schoolmaster of the Skippack" by his admirers.

A successful teacher, Dock was invited by Christopher Saur, the well-known Germantown publisher, to write out his method of teaching for the benefit of other teachers. The modest schoolmaster consented, but with the request that the work was not to be published until after his death. This request was honored by the publisher and so the *Schulordnung*, which is regarded today as the first work on the art of teaching to be published in America, did not appear in print until 1770, after both Dock and the elder Saur had died.

Like all the Mennonite schools of that day, and perhaps other similar institutions of learning as well, Dock's school paid much attention to religion. The New and Old Testaments were used as texts, and as a basis for the reading and writing exercises. It was the usual "blab" school, that is, all the studying was done audibly; and silence during the study period became a misdemeanor. Dock described in the *Schulordnung* how he maintained silence during the recitation period—

> I walk up and down the room, and when I think they have learned their lesson I order them to be quiet and then appoint a monitor, who has been detailed for this duty. He stands on a bench or other high place where he can see all, and reports the Christian and surname of each one who talks, studies loud, or does anything else that is forbidden.

Dock was a born teacher. Discussing the need of winning the respect of the pupils rather than their fear, he says, "I have a great love for children, a grace from God, otherwise it would be a great burden among the scholars."

This *Schulordnung* (school regulation) went through later editions, but is known today only among the antiquarians and students of the history of colonial education. Dock also wrote a number of poems and *A Hundred Rules for Children*. Among the rules is this one on table manners: *Rule 34*. "The bones, or what remains over, do not throw under the table, do not put them under the tablecloth, but let them lie on the edge of the plate."

When the public school system was introduced into Pennsylvania, the Mennonites, as well as the other religious denominations, fought the movement out of fear that religion would be barred from the curriculum. In the course of time, however, the Mennonites in the East became reconciled to the public school system. Prior to World War II a parochial school movement was launched among the eastern Mennonites. This movement made rapid progress during the war, and in 1948 there were thirty-five parochial schools sponsored by the Amish and the Mennonites and attended by more than two thousand pupils.

This movement has continued to grow so that the *Mennonite Yearbook* of 1977 listed fourteen Mennonite high schools and seventy-four elementary schools located in seventeen states. Of this number more than half were located in Pennsylvania. There are also some in Canada. This would indicate that a larger number prefer the Mennonite schools, and possibly also that the number of conservative parents sending their children to these high schools is increasing.

Kansas and Manitoba

The later immigrants from South Germany and Russia during the nineteenth century were much concerned about keeping control of the education of their children; and most of them were supplementing the regular public system with additional parochial schools where religion and German are given a place in the curriculum.

In the pioneer settlements along the western frontier where the Mennonites lived in compact school districts, and when the school laws were still quite lenient, they had little difficulty in maintaining schools that met their needs, giving ample time to both religion and German. But where the Mennonites constituted only a part of the school population, and when the educational requirements demanded by the state became more rigid, the demand for the favorite subjects was satisfied by special church or private schools held during the summer months after the close of the regular public school year, which for some time was rather short. The demand for German is still strong among the Canadian Mennonites. The religious interests are being satisfied by the establishing of a number of Bible schools in various localities.

In Manitoba the Mennonites were granted almost complete control over their schools by the provincial and Canadian governments at the time of their settlement. But their school experiences are told in another chapter, and no further reference is needed here except to remember that after the war the provincial authorities in both Saskatchewan and Manitoba insisted on the establishing of public schools in all the Mennonite settlements to replace the former church-controlled schools, and also upon the exclusive use of the English language as a means of instruction. German, even as a subject of study, was to be barred. As already noticed, some six or seven thousand of the more conservative Mennonites from the Old Colony and Sommerfelder preferred to immigrate to Mexico and Paraguay rather than to give up the use of their German. After World War II another wave of emigrants from the prairie provinces followed their conservative brethren to Mexico and Paraguay.

Higher Education

The first steps toward a full liberal arts college training were taken in Kansas, where the largest number of Mennonites coming from Russia had settled between 1874 and 1882. Already in Russia the Molotschna Mennonites had raised their educational level. Back of the developments that followed was the founding of the General Conference Mennonite Church in 1860 which led to the establishment of the Wadsworth Mennonite School in Ohio in 1868, which however was closed in 1878. With the arrival of the Mennonites from Russia and their joining the General Conference Mennonite Church, the need for an advanced educational institution was again strongly felt.

Step by step the plans were materialized. A *Vorbereitungsschule* (preparatory school) began in the Alexanderwohl congregation near Newton, Kansas, in 1882 was followed by the establishment of a *Fortbildungsschule* (preparatory school) in Halstead, which in 1893 was transferred to Newton and was named *Bethel College*. Under the leadership of David Goerz and C. H. Wedel it grew and developed into the first Mennonite college. Bethel College has made its influence felt strongly throughout the western churches from the beginning, furnishing many of the church leaders and missionaries. Under the efficient presidency of Ed. G. Kaufman the college made rapid progress and in 1938 was admitted into membership of the North Central Association of Colleges, the first of the Mennonite institutions to achieve this recognition. The plant facilities of the college were considerably increased in the 1940s and again in the 1970s. The size of faculty and student body has also grown, particularly in the years immediately following World War II.

In addition to a number of dormitories, a library, a fine arts center, a student center, and gymnasium have been constructed during the last decades. In the tradition of the first president, C. H. Wedel, who wrote the first textbooks for use in teaching Mennonite history and faith, the college has established one of the leading Mennonite libraries, which is being used far beyond those attending the school.

The eastern Mennonites of Swiss German background did not awaken to the need of a church school of higher learning until the beginning of the twentieth century, and even then there was very little sentiment in favor of such an institution. *Goshen College* owes its existence to the foresight of a small group of progressive men who realized that young and efficient leadership could be secured and maintained only through an educational institution initiated by the church. In 1895 this group of men formed an association and secured funds for a building at Elkhart, Indiana, for a preparatory and Bible school. This institution called *Elkhart Institute* was the outgrowth of a private, normal, and business school founded several years earlier. In 1902 the school was moved to Goshen and enlarged into a college under the name of *Goshen College*. This college trained most of the foreign missionaries and many of the younger leaders of the church. First in the long list of early leaders in the history of this pioneer institution was John S. Coffman, pioneer evangelist, who took a leading part in the founding of the Elkhart school and was the president of the board of trustees until his death in 1899. Jonas S. Hartzler was secretary and treasurer for over twenty years, and bore the chief financial burden of both schools. Noah E. Byers, first as principal of the Elkhart school and later as president of Goshen College, molded the early educational policy of the institution. Under the presidency of E. E. Miller, Goshen College was admitted to the North Central Association of Colleges.

Goshen College has become the largest of the Mennonite colleges. Its Bible department has developed into a theological seminary which in turn has become affiliated with the biblical seminary of the General Conference Mennonite Church at Elkhart, Indiana. *Eastern Mennonite College*, a sister college in Harrisonburg, Virginia, was founded in 1927.

The Mennonite Brethren founded *Tabor College* in Hillsboro, Kansas, in 1908. A fire in 1918 destroyed the entire plant, but a vigorous campaign for funds secured $100,000 for new buildings. Among the leaders in the founding and early management of Tabor College were H. W. Lohrenz, an early president, and D. E. Harder, secretary, a member of the *Krimmer Mennonite Brethren*, who were affiliated with the *Mennonite Brethren* in their educational work. Under the presidency of P. E. Schellenberg, the college experienced a continuous growth.

The *Pacific Bible Institute* of the Mennonite Brethren was established at Fresno, California, in 1944. It has since grown considerably. In 1956 the *Mennonite Brethren Biblical Seminary* was added to the campus.

The *Mennonite Brethren Bible College* at Winnipeg, Manitoba, was begun in 1944. The *Canadian Mennonite Bible College* was established in 1947.

Numerous Bible schools were established in the various

Canadian provinces, some of which continue to the present.

The Mennonite Brethren in Christ, now United Missionary Church, attempted to found a Bible training school at Elkhart in 1902. A small group of Indiana members secured the Elkhart Institute building in which a school was held for several years, but owing to opposition and lack of support the work had to be abandoned. In 1947 they opened a school under the name of *Bethel College* at Mishawaka, Indiana.

Bluffton College was founded by the Middle District of the General Conference Mennonite Church in 1898. It was first an academy but later a junior college, and was originally known as *Central Mennonite College*. Ultimately, the school was enlarged into a full-fledged senior college and seminary through the cooperation of members from three district conferences of the General Conference Mennonite Church (the Eastern, Central, and Middle districts). They are officially represented on the board of trustees, although members are unofficially selected from several other groups. The enlarged institution became known as *Bluffton College and Mennonite Seminary*.

This first attempt at a union educational enterprise was largely the result of the efforts, among others, of two college presidents, S. K. Mosiman of the Central Mennonite College, and N. E. Byers of Goshen College. The former was retained as the first president of the new college, and the latter became the first dean. J. H. Langenwalter, a former president of Bethel College, became the first dean of the seminary.

In 1921 the seminary separated from Bluffton College and organized an independent board of trustees drawn from different branches of the church under the name of *Witmarsum Theological Seminary*. This institution remained located at Bluffton, with J. E. Hartzler as president and P. E. Whitmer as dean. Like Wadsworth, Witmarsum survived a scant ten years, justifying its brief existence, however, by training many influential missionaries and ministers.

In September 1945 the *Mennonite Biblical Seminary* was opened in affiliation with the Bethany Biblical Seminary (Church of the Brethren) in Chicago, Illinois. Abraham Warkentin served as president until his death in 1947. In 1958 the seminary moved to its own campus in Elkhart, Indiana, and began an association with *Goshen Biblical Seminary*. Since 1969 the two seminaries have shared one campus in Elkhart and are cooperating in some educational programs.

Besides the institutions mentioned above, there are a number of junior colleges and special Bible and preparatory schools; among others, *Hesston College* at Hesston, Kansas, sponsored by the

Mennonite Board of Education of the Mennonite Church; and *Freeman Junior College*, Freeman, South Dakota, which is supported largely by the local congregations of South Dakota and surrounding churches of the Northern District of the General Conference Mennonite Church; and numerous Bible and secondary schools sponsored by local congregations among the western Canadian provinces. In 1943 the *Grace Bible Institute* was founded in Omaha, Nebraska.

From a study of attendance in 1938 of twenty Mennonite schools, three of which were senior colleges, four junior colleges, and the rest secondary and Bible schools, it was found that in that year there was a total attendance in all these institutions of about three thousand, of which about one-half were found in the senior and junior colleges. By 1948 the total number attending Mennonite schools and colleges had doubled. In 1967 in twenty-four Mennonite schools and colleges, including three seminaries, eleven four-year and three junior colleges, two nursing schools and five Bible schools, there were 7,032 students. The number has not changed significantly since that time.

Early Publications

The first comers to America brought few books with them, perhaps a well-worn Bible, a copy of their confession of faith, and a prayer book. Occasionally one might find a family owning an old Dutch copy of the *Martyrs Mirror*, a family heirloom, likely, and soon unreadable by the younger generation. An occasional copy of the works of Menno Simons in Dutch could also be found. The first meager supply of necessary books evidently was soon exhausted, for in 1708 the Germantown church wrote to Germany for a supply of Bibles, prayer books, and catechisms.

The first book translated and printed expressly for the American Mennonites was an English edition of *The Christian Confession of Faith*... issued at Amsterdam in 1712 and reprinted in Philadelphia in 1727. With one or two exceptions this was the only English edition of a standard Mennonite book for over a century and a half. The demand among the Mennonites at this particular time, according to the preface of the first edition, was for the purpose of setting themselves right with their fellow English colonists, for

> the greatest part of the people doth not know what they (Mennonites) confess of the Word of God and by reason of that ignorance can't speak and judge rightly of their confession nor of the confessors themselves, nay through prejudice as a strange and unheard of thing do abhor them so as not to speak well but oftimes ill of them.

The most highly prized book among the early Mennonites, next to the Bible, was the *Martyrs Mirror*. This book was highly regarded because it not only told of the trials and sufferings of those of their own and kindred faiths, but often of those of their own blood; for many of the martyrs bore names still familiar among the Pennsylvania Mennonites and their descendants. The book was a voluminous work, as large as the old family Bible, and was available only in the Dutch language. The first European German edition did not appear until 1790.

There seemed little demand among the first generation of pioneers for more than the occasional copies of the book which the first settlers brought with them. But by the mid 1700s the dangers which threatened the doctrine of nonresistance among their young people because of the colonial wars created a demand for their book of martyrs, written in a language that could be read by all. After attempting in vain to have the work published in Germany, the Pennsylvania churches contracted with the brethren of the Ephrata cloister for an edition of thirteen hundred copies. The undertaking was an arduous one, and it took three years to finish it.

The Ephrata Brethren were obliged to manufacture their own paper, make the translation from the Dutch into the German, and do all the printing and binding. The book, which appeared in 1748, was the most ambitious publication undertaking in Pennsylvania up to that time. The *Martyrs Mirror* has gone through many editions since then. In 1886 it was translated into English. Numerous reprints have appeared.

The writings of Menno Simons were also familiar, but these were printed only in fragments. Among Menno's treatises the most important is the *Foundation Book*, which contains the most complete statement of his views. This was printed at Lancaster in 1794 and was the first of his works to appear in an American edition. Other treatises were published through the nineteenth century, but the first complete edition was issued in German at Elkhart in 1876 and in English on the same press in 1871.

Dirk Philips, a co-laborer of Menno's, also wrote several books, the best known of which was *Enchiridion* or Handbook, a treatise on the characteristic Anabaptist doctrines, first published at Haarlem in 1578. The first American edition was published at Lancaster in 1811. Two later German editions appeared, and in 1910 it was translated into English by A. B. Kolb and published at Elkhart.

Among other books found occasionally on the bookshelves of the Mennonite pioneers were several books of sermons written for the most part by Dutch and North German ministers of the seventeenth and early eighteenth centuries. Among these compilations were those of Jakob Denner (1659-1746), for many years a minister at Altona, and those written by Johann Deknatel, originally printed in Dutch but later, in 1757, in German. The latter was never published in America, but Denner's collection was printed in 1792 in Germany. Two Pennsylvania Mennonites went to Germany and brought along 500 copies of the 1500-page volume. In 1830 a book of sermons by Wilhelm Wynantz, also a minister at Altona, was translated from the Dutch by David Zug, an Amishman of Belleville, Pennsylvania, and published at Lancaster.

Among other old books (all in German) popular in Mennonite homes for years were *Güldene Aepffel in Silbernen Schalen* printed at Ephrata in 1745, at the request of the Mennonites; *Geistliches Blumengärtlein*, published for the eighth time in America in 1800; and *Die Wandelnde Seele (The Wandering Soul)*, written by J. P. Schabaelje, a minister in the Alkmaar Mennonite Church. First published in the Dutch language in 1638, it turned out to be the most popular Mennonite book ever published. In all, at least eighty-four editions have appeared—forty-eight Dutch, nine German (in Germany), and eighteen German and nine English in the United States.

The first book written by an American author was *Ein Spiegel der Taufe, mit Geist, mit Wasser, und mit Blut (A Mirror of Baptism, With the Spirit, the Water, and With Blood)*. Published in 1744 on the Christopher Saur press, it was reprinted many times. The author, Heinrich Funck, migrated to America in 1717 and became the founder of a long line of Funks, many of them prominent publishers, including J. F. Funk, founder of the Mennonite Publishing Company of Elkhart; and Joseph Funk, pioneer Virginia printer. Heinrich Funck also wrote a more extended work, *Restitution*, a treatise on a number of the principal points of the law, their fulfillment and significance. The book was published by his children after his death, was reprinted at Lancaster in 1863, and was put through an English edition at Elkhart as late as 1915.

Not to be forgotten among eighteenth-century writings was Christopher Dock's *Schulordnung*, published after his death in 1770 by Christopher Saur, Jr.

During the early and middle nineteenth century the books of Mennonite authorship were for the most part controversial in character and were written by the founders of various church divisions in defense of their views and activities. Among these men were John Herr, Daniel Hoch, Daniel Musser, John H. Oberholtzer (1809-1895), John Holdeman (1832-1900), and Jacob

Stauffer.

The most enduring literary work done in the last hundred years has been that in the realm of church history. The earliest work in this field was Benjamin Eby's *Short History of the Mennonites*, which appeared first in 1841 in Berlin, Canada, and whose chief merit is that it appeared first. Daniel Musser's *History of the Reformed Mennonite Church* was published at Lancaster in 1873. *Abriss der Geschichte der Mennoniten* by C. H. Wedel of Bethel College, in four volumes (1901-1904), was the best and most readable work on the subject that had appeared to that time. Wedel also wrote a number of other books on general church history, as well as on the Mennonites, including *Sketches from Church History for Mennonite Schools* which appeared first in a German edition and was reprinted many times. In a short life span he wrote numerous other books including a commentary for young people on the German catechism. C. H. Wedel was not only a pioneer educator among the Mennonites of North America but also a pioneer in writing Mennonite history on a popular level for Mennonite schools and homes. He was in personal contact with and strongly influenced by the pioneer European Mennonite scholars, particularly Samuel Cramer of Amsterdam and Ludwig Keller, archivist in Münster and later in Berlin.

C. H. A. van der Smissen, pastor at Summerfield at the time, published in 1895 a treatise on the history and the doctrines of the Mennonites, which also included his father's translation of the Cornelis Ris *Confession of Faith*. D. K. Cassel's *Geschichte der Mennoniten*, published in German in 1890 and in English two years earlier, is largely a compilation of historical articles appearing in earlier publications, and written by other authors. Many of them were from the pen of Governor S. W. Pennypacker. Pennypacker, himself of direct Mennonite descent, was greatly interested in Mennonite affairs and was one of the pioneer writers to arouse general attention to the importance of early American Mennonite history.

At the beginning of this century the number of Mennonite writers dealing with Mennonite history, life, and thought increased steadily. This paralleled the beginning of Mennonite higher education on a college and graduate level. Contact with European scholars increased the interest. J. S. Hartzler and D. Kauffman published *Mennonite Church History* in 1905. At the same time H. P. Krehbiel and John Horsch began their writings on the various aspects of Mennonite history. Most of the books were now being published in the English language.

Hymnology: Amish, Hutterite, Mennonite

In the field of Mennonite hymnology the old *Ausbund* easily holds the center of interest. The *Ausbund*, which is undoubtedly the oldest hymnbook still in use anywhere in America, consists of a collection of 140 hymns from various sources, including a nucleus of 51 originally composed for the most part by a group of Swiss Mennonite captives driven out of Austria and imprisoned in the castle of Passau on the Bavarian frontier between 1535 and 1537. This collection was first printed during the middle of the sixteenth century. Since that time twelve editions appeared in South Germany and Switzerland, the last issue being printed at Basel in 1838. The *Ausbund* became the adopted hymnal of the Swiss and South German Mennonites for several hundred years. When the first Palatines came to Pennsylvania they brought this book with them, as did also the Swiss Mennonites and the Alsatian Amish in Ohio and Illinois in the early nineteenth century. The first American edition was printed at Germantown in 1742. It has been frequently reprinted, and is still being used by the Amish of America.

This old book was never revised, but merely reprinted, thus perpetuating its original quaint colloquial Swiss-German. Many of the hymns are detailed narratives of the trials and the sufferings of the early martyrs; others consist of lengthy discourses upon some points of doctrine. Few of them possess anything of a lyrical quality. Most of them are long, several of them consisting of some scores of stanzas. (To sing one song often required the better part of an hour.) They were printed without music. The melodies to which they were sung were transmitted orally from one generation to another, and in this process the original melodies were often altered. Basically, the old tunes of the hymns go back to the sixteenth century when they were used with folk songs.

Another collection of hymns, almost equally as venerable as those of the *Ausbund*, is the collection used in worship by the Hutterites. Many of these hymns are also martyr stories first told in the sixteenth century. The collection was preserved in manuscripts in the archives of the various *Bruderhofs* and were not put in print until 1916, when the Dakota Hutterites had them published at Scottdale, Pennsylvania.

Although the *Ausbund* is still in use among the Old Order Amish, it was early discarded by the Pennsylvania Mennonites as well as by the Ohio Swiss, who also brought the old hymnal with them in the early part of the nineteenth century. Some of the successors of the venerable hymnbook in Pennsylvania were the *Die kleine Geistliche Harfe* published in Franconia, in 1803; the

Unpartheyisches Gesangbuch, in Lancaster in 1804; the *Unparteiische Liedersammlung* in 1870. The first English hymnal, *The Harmonia Sacra*, was printed on the press of Joseph Funk at Singers Glen in Virginia in 1847. The General Conference Mennonite Church published the *Gesangbuch zum gottesdienstlichen und häuslichen Gebrauch* in 1873, which originated in Worms in 1856. The Mennonites from Russia brought with them the hymnbooks that were in use in their home churches, but later adopted those of the conferences they affiliated with. The General Conference *Mennonite Hymnary*, first published in 1940, found general acceptance even beyond the conference. In 1942 the *Gesangbuch der Mennoniten* was published by the General Conference Mennonite Church, primarily for the use of the Canadian churches. In 1969 *The Mennonite Hymnal* appeared as the successor to two Mennonite hymnbooks, *The Church Hymnal* (1927) of the Mennonite Church and *The Mennonite Hymnary* (1940) of the General Conference Mennonite Church. This was a joint publication of the Faith and Life Press, Newton, Kansas, and the Herald Press, Scottdale, Pennsylvania.

Publishing Houses and Periodicals

All Mennonite conferences publish one or more church papers. Some were started as a private enterprise by some aggressive member who was concerned for the welfare of his church, then were later taken over officially by the various conferences. Among the early Mennonite literary centers was Singers Glen in Virginia, where in 1847 Joseph Funk established a small printing press on which he published the *Harmonia Sacra* and various other early books on song and religion. Milford Square in Bucks County, Pennsylvania, was the home for a time of the literary productions of John H. Oberholtzer, and later of the Eastern Mennonite Conference, including (beginning in 1852) the *Religiöser Botschafter* and (in 1881) *The Mennonite*, as well as numerous pamphlets and books by Mennonite writers, mostly of the General Conference Mennonite Church. Berlin, Ontario, was the home of Benjamin Eby whose son Heinrich operated a printing establishment in which were printed a number of pamphlets and books of Mennonite interest, including Benjamin's brief history of the Mennonites in 1841. The largest, and by far the most influential, early private Mennonite publishing house was the Mennonite Publishing Company established by John F. Funk in 1864, first in Chicago but soon removed to Elkhart, Indiana. There he published for many years the *Herald of Truth* and its German companion, *Herold der Wahrheit*; *The Complete Writings of Menno Simons*; the *Martyrs Mirror*; and numerous other Mennonite periodicals and books. Here he also began, in 1877, the publication of the *Mennonitische Rundschau* which has changed little in the hundred years of its existence. Present publisher is *Rundschau* Publishing House, Winnipeg, Manitoba.

The Mennonite Publishing House located at Scottdale, Pennsylvania, is the successor to the Elkhart Publishing House, and publishes all the periodicals and other books and supplies of the Mennonite Church. The General Conference Mennonite Church, in cooperation with Bethel College, established The Mennonite Press at North Newton, Kansas, in 1949. The General Conference Mennonite Church offices and the Faith and Life Bookstore are located on 722 Main Street, Newton, Kansas 67114. Publication is done by Faith and Life Press, Newton, Kansas. The Mennonite Brethren offices and Publishing House are located in Hillsboro, Kansas.

The following are the major conference papers: General Conference, *The Mennonite* and *Der Bote*; Mennonite Church, the *Gospel Herald*; Mennonite Brethren, *Mennonite Brethren Herald*, *The Christian Leader*; United Missionary Church, the *Gospel Banner*; Evangelical Mennonite Church, *Zion's Tidings*; Reformed Mennonites, *Good Tidings*; Old Order Amish, *Herold der Wahrheit*. Among private papers with a large Mennonite circulation and of general interest are the *Mennonite Weekly Review* of Newton, Kansas; *The Altona Echo*, Altona, Manitoba; *Die Mennonitische Rundschau*, Winnipeg, Manitoba; *Mennonite Mirror*, Winnipeg; and *Mennonite Reporter*, Waterloo, Ontario.

The *Mennonite Quarterly Review* is devoted to Anabaptist-Mennonite history, thought, and life published for Goshen College. *Mennonite Life*, published by Bethel College, is an illustrated quarterly magazine. Since 1946 it has featured the religious, economic, and social phases of Mennonite culture. It carries an annual bibliography of all major publications dealing with the Mennonites.

Farming and Other Vocations

With the exception of the first colonists in Germantown, the American Mennonites have been almost exclusively a farmer folk. They were farmers in Europe, and they became farmers in America, as did their children and children's children for generations after them. The city always seemed to these country-bred people more or less a center of worldly influence. Gradually a great change has come about. In cities like Winnipeg, Vancouver, Abbotsford, Clearbrook, Wichita, Saskatoon, Waterloo, and Souderton, we find that active and large congregations have emerged. City missions are developing into self-supporting congregations.

Increasingly, Mennonites are moving from nearby large compact farm communities into small towns. In some of them the Mennonite population forms a dominant influence. This is especially true near the large settlements in Mountain Lake, Minnesota; Newton, Halstead, Moundridge, Hillsboro, and Buhler, Kansas; Henderson and Beatrice, Nebraska; Reedley and Fresno, California; Freeman, South Dakota; Rosthern, Saskatchewan; Winkler, Altona, and Steinbach, Manitoba; and similarly in British Columbia; the Swiss settlements in Pandora and Bluffton, Ohio, and Berne, Indiana; the Mennonite settlements in Lancaster County, Pennsylvania, and others.

Mennonites have always been good farmers, among the best in the land. They are seldom found on poor soil, having somehow developed a keen sense of discrimination for good land in all pioneer settlements. If perchance they made a poor choice, they moved out as soon as an occasion was presented. The Amish first settled in the early part of the century, before the prairies were opened up, in Woodford County, Illinois, on the washed-out, clay timberlands in the western end of the county. With the opening up of the rich prairie lands in the eastern end of the county after the Civil War, the Amish Mennonites were the first to leave their clay knobs; and today there is hardly a single Mennonite left on the original farms. The poorest section of Lancaster County is the southern tip; but not a single Mennonite farmer, among over the twenty-five thousand Mennonites, is found in this area.

Several years ago the United States Department of Agriculture designated Lancaster County, Pennsylvania, and McLean County, Illinois, as the two wealthiest farming counties in the nation. Both of these counties have a large Mennonite population.

Anyone acquainted with the favorite farming sections of the country will easily recognize the truth of the above claims that Mennonites are good farmers—Wayne County, Ohio; Lancaster County, Pennsylvania; McLean and Livingston counties, Illinois; Johnson and Washington counties, Iowa; Harvey County, Kansas; the Mennonite Reserve, Manitoba. Land prices are highest in Mennonite communities. In 1978 it was reported that two farms were sold in Pennsylvania at an auction ranging between four and five thousand dollars per acre. This was not considered to be a record price. The combined amount for nearly two hundred acres was one million dollars.

Of course while Mennonites in the main remained on the farm, yet there were always young men here and there a bit more ambitious than their fellows who found their way into the cities, and entering business or professional life, made good. Such prominent American names as *Rittenhouse, Pennypacker, Landes, Frick, Cunard, Herr, Hershey,* and many others are plain evidence of the fact that not all the Mennonite boys stayed down on the farm. But they were not followed up by their home congregations to organize them in the city. They seldom came back to either the farm or the church. The number of young men and women leaving their home place for education and locating jobs has increased steadily. However, efforts are being made by conferences, and individually, to establish centers for fellowship and congregations near campuses and other suitable places.

Among the other lines of occupation and professions that were open to Mennonites of conservative leaning, the least objectionable was that of the teacher. An unusual number of Mennonites are found in this profession, both in the public schools and in colleges and universities. There is hardly a large college or university in the land today that does not have on its faculty one or more professors of immediate or indirect Mennonite origin.

Medicine as well as nursing has a strong appeal for many who see in it a fruitful field for serving their fellowmen. Law was formerly not popular or acceptable among Mennonites but is now steadily increasing as a profession. In recent years several congressmen, members of state legislatures, a United States senator, an attorney general in a Middle West state, numerous mayors of small towns and cities and a few also in larger cities, several judges, and other public officials have been Mennonites.

Adventure in Fellowship

During World War I and thereafter, the youth of all groups experienced a new fellowship as they confronted draft boards, prisons, and camps together. The needs of a war-torn world challenged many to work together in foreign countries.

Another avenue of cooperation and exchange of thought, although on a smaller scale, was the All-Mennonite Convention meeting triennially from 1913 to 1936. The sessions, held in various parts of the country, were attended by leading representatives of various conferences. The lectures presented were published.

In 1942 the Mennonite colleges organized into a Council of Mennonite and Affiliated Colleges. At the annual meetings the educators discuss their common problems, arrange foreign-student exchanges, and they sponsored the Conference on Mennonite Cultural Problems (1942-67). The latter met annually to discuss social, educational, and religious issues in connection with Mennonite culture. All papers presented at the sixteen sessions have been published. The last session took place in 1967.

The Mennonite Research Fellowship, begun during World War II, presents possibilities of exchange of thought in fields of Mennonite research. It was this fellowship that conceived and promoted the plan to publish an American *Mennonite Encyclopedia*. The encyclopedia was completed in four volumes in 1957 and was reprinted in 1971-74.

Research pertaining to Mennonite history, theology, and other phases has been conducted during the last decades on a larger scale than ever before in America. Goshen, Bethel, and Bluffton colleges have been the center of these activities. However, many other graduate schools have also given opportunity for students to do special research in these fields. Numerous books published, and magazines such as *Mennonite Quarterly Review* and *Mennonite Life* give evidence of an unprecedented activity and interest in this field. The larger colleges have established Mennonite historical libraries, and some of the conferences have active historical committees charged with the responsibility of preserving material pertaining to our Mennonite heritage and making it available for public use. A large collection of items in this area of interest can also be found in the Kauffman Museum on the campus of Bethel College, North Newton, Kansas.

XV
Witnessing in War and Peace

1. CHURCH AND STATE IN EARLY AMERICA

The Oath

On no other points of their faith have the American Mennonites been so often misunderstood as on their attitude toward the oath and warfare. Their objection to the oath and their refusal to bear arms have been repeatedly misconstrued, both in Europe and in America, as indicating a spirit of disloyalty to their country. In Pennsylvania the Mennonites were welcomed by the Quakers, who held similar views on these questions, but the law passed by the English Parliament permitting the affirmation instead of the oath applied to the Quakers only. Mennonites and others who had similar scruples against the taking of the oath were compelled to petition for the privilege of affirming. The Mennonites, in 1717, and the Amish, in 1742, were granted the rights of affirmation.

In Maryland the constitution of 1776 specifically mentions "Quakers, Tunkers, and Menonists," to whom the right of affirmation is guaranteed wherever an oath would otherwise be required. Today this right is guaranteed by the United States Constitution and by the constitutions of practically every state, and even those not belonging to a nonresistant tradition avail themselves of the privilege.

The refusal to take the oath did not seem to involve the Pennsylvania Mennonites in any serious consequences before the Revolutionary War; but the Declaration of Independence, which severed the political ties between Pennsylvania and the British Empire, introduced a new sovereign state. According to this act all male inhabitants above the age of eighteen were to take the oath before the following July, renouncing their allegiance to the king of Great Britain, and promising loyalty to Pennsylvania as an independent state. Later amendments to the act provided that all those refusing to take the oath were to be sent to jail for thirty days or pay a heavy fine. The third refusal was to be followed by an order of exile from the state within thirty days, and the confiscation of all the personal property of the one expelled.

The act was aimed at the Tories, of course, but also involved some Mennonites who had a tender conscience on the matter of oaths in general. In the large, compact areas like Lancaster County, where the principles of the Mennonites were well known, and where their numbers served as a restraining influence against hasty action, there was probably little difficulty in convincing the authorities that the hesitancy of the Mennonites to take the prescribed oath was not due to their political principles, but rather to their religious convictions. In the smaller isolated communities, however, the Mennonites occasionally encountered serious difficulty. We have on record the experiences of at least one community at Saucon, in Lehigh County, where they paid the extreme penalty for their convictions. The whole adult male population of the congregation was sent to jail. All their personal belongings, including bedding, stoves, furniture, dishes, food supplies, and even their Bibles, were confiscated; and their wives and children, deprived of all the necessities of life, were ordered to leave the state within thirty days. A petition to the General Assembly on September 10, 1778, by the wives of several of the prisoners, accompanied by a similar petition from some of the non-Mennonite neighbors attesting to the good reputation of the Mennonites, and ascribing their reluctance to take the oath and their "present blindness to their own essential interests" to an "unhappy bias in their education and not from any disaffection to the present government," may have brought some relief. We have no further record of what disposition was made of these victims of the war spirit. It is likely, however, that the men were released and the order for exile repealed, though it is entirely likely that their property, classed with that of the Tories, may have remained in the possession of the state.

Military Service

Exemption from military service was also generally recognized, and conscientious scruples were always given careful consideration by those in authority. The only colonies in which Mennonites were located at the time of the Revolutionary War were Pennsylvania, Maryland, and Virginia. In each of these, Mennonites were exempted from military musters. This seemed to be generally provided for by the local county authorities, upon the payment of a sum of money usually called a *fine*. In Virginia, however, in 1777, where provisions were made for conscription, it was possible for Mennonites who were drafted for service to be discharged upon furnishing a substitute, who was to be paid by a levy upon the membership of the entire church.

After the war, in 1790, the constitution of Pennsylvania declared that "those who conscientiously scruple to bear arms shall not be compelled to bear arms, but shall pay an equivalent." A law of Maryland, in 1793, provided that "Quakers, Mennonites, and Tunkers and all others who are conscientiously scrupulous of bearing arms, and who refuse to do military duty shall pay a sum of three dollars annually." The Virginia code of laws in force in 1860 provided that all citizens refusing to attend military musters must pay a fine of seventy-five cents, which of course the Mennonites freely paid. The wars of 1812 and of 1848 as well as the war of 1898 were all fought by volunteers, and consequently there was no occasion to test the faith of the nonresistant churches.

In the Civil War both the North and the South finally resorted to conscription. The federal act of February 24, 1864, exempted those having conscientious scruples, permitting them to accept hospital service when drafted, or to pay $300 exemption money. No person, however, was to be entitled to the benefit of this clause unless his declaration of conscientious scruples "shall be supported by satisfactory evidence that his deportment had been uniformly consistent with such declaration." This exemption clause, it will be observed, differed from the provision permitting substitutes, by which one could secure exemption by furnishing a substitute at such price, of course, as the substitute demanded. Under this law Mennonites were able, with but few exceptions, to live their life of nonresistance undisturbed in their various communities.

In the South, Virginia resorted to universal service almost from the beginning, and no exceptions were made on account of religious scruples. A number of Mennonites from Rockingham County were called into the army in 1861. These refused to fight. Others were captured attempting to escape through the lines into the North. These were imprisoned in *Libby Prison* for a time and tried, but because of their religious convictions were permitted to go home. Early in 1862 Virginia passed a law exempting members of a church forbidding the bearing of arms upon the payment of $500, and the further sum of 2 percent of the assessed valuation of all taxable property. In case of the refusal of such members to comply with this law, or the inability to do so, they were to be taken into some form of noncombatant service.

This law, however, was superseded in the same year by the general conscription act of the Confederate government, which also provided for the exemption of members of the "Society of Friends, Association of Dunkards, Nazarenes, and Menonists," upon the payment of $500. All these religious denominations, being opposed to both slavery and war, were bitterly denounced in their communities by those not of their faith, but they were not compelled to take up arms by the government until the summer of 1864 when, because of the great need of men, the Confederate Congress repealed all exemptions. A number of the young men escaped through the lines into western Virginia and into the North. The Mennonite communities, located in the heart of the Shenandoah Valley, also suffered heavily from the numerous raids made through the valley.

Canadian Laws

The Canadian government has been even more considerate of conscientious scruples than the United States. As early as 1808 Ontario passed a law exempting "Quakers, Menonists and Tunkers" from militia service, upon an annual payment of twenty shillings in time of peace, and five pounds when the militia should be called out for defense. Refusal to comply with this law was to be punished by a jail sentence of not more than a month. In 1839 the fine was raised to ten pounds, and later several minor changes were made in the law, but its general purport remained the same. In 1863, after the formation of the Dominion of Canada, an act was passed exempting Quakers, Mennonites, Dunkards, and members of other religious denominations opposed to war from militia service under such conditions as the Governor-in-Council might prescribe. This law, although perhaps not generally known, was still in force at the time World War I broke out. The Conscription Act of 1917 exempted from combatant service all religious bodies opposed to war in principle.

The clause in this act which exempts only from combatant service differs from the act of 1868, which exempts from all service. The act of 1868 was the basis on which the Canadian government promised the Russian Mennonites who settled in Manitoba in 1873 complete military exemption as a condition of their migration to that province. The state of Kansas also guaranteed exemption from military musters to all those conscientiously opposed to bearing arms in behalf of the Russian Mennonites in 1874. This guarantee was confirmed as late as 1915, but was of no value since it is subservient to the federal law on the subject. Nebraska followed a few years later with a similar law.

2. WORLD WAR I

In Canada

When the Canadian Conscription Act of 1917 was passed, the government, upon being reminded of this early regulation and promise by a committee of Mennonites from the western provinces, graciously agreed to abide by the promises made to the early Mennonite settlers in 1873, and granted entire exemption to all the descendants, both baptized and unbaptized, of these settlers. Whether this liberal provision would apply also to the Mennonites of Ontario, who were not a party to the agreement of 1873 but were included under the act of 1868, at first seemed doubtful. A number of young Ontario Mennonites were taken into the army at first, and upon refusing to serve were court-martialed and given two-year prison terms which were later changed to farm furloughs. As just indicated, the laws of 1868 and 1917 were not quite the same, but the Canadian government finally decided to abide by the more liberal provisions of 1868 and the promises of 1873, and thus granted the Ontario Mennonites the same generous consideration as that given to members of the church in Manitoba and the western provinces.

The Canadian churches also took a stand in the beginning of World War I against contributing to war loans. But upon the promise of the government, at the time of the last loan, that Mennonite money was to be used only for relief purposes and not for direct war purposes, the Mennonites endorsed the loans, and it is estimated that they raised about a half-million dollars in the western provinces. They supported heartily Red Cross and YMCA campaigns. In the last drive each farmer was expected to contribute fifty dollars for each quarter section of land, and business and professional men accordingly. It is estimated that some $200,000 was raised for this work, an average of over six dollars for every man, woman, and child among them.

Few of the young men enlisted in the service, and those who did were usually considered as being under church censure. The price paid by the Mennonites, however, for their exemptions was disfranchisement for the period of the war. The Canadian government was considerate of Mennonite scruples throughout the war, but in some localities, especially in the western provinces, considerable bitterness began to develop near the close of the war over a new problem. The question as to whether the exemption applied to Mennonites who should enter Canada after the passing of the Conscription Act was precipitated by the migration of a number of Mennonites from the United States, especially the Hutterites from South Dakota, who bought large tracts of land in

Saskatchewan and Alberta for the purpose of escaping military service and intimidation in the United States. Appeals were made to the government by numerous local organizations, not only to prevent the settlement but even to repeal the original exemption clause. The government took no formal action on the matter, but it seemed the opinion of many of those in authority that such immigrants were not entitled to the exemption; and had the war continued much longer, measures would perhaps have been taken to restrict the privileges of the new arrivals. As it was, much bitter feeling developed throughout the Northwest, especially against the Hutterites.

In the United States

Within the United States, World War I tried the faith of the Mennonites as no other American war had. The struggle was on such an enormous scale and demanded such a complete mobilization of the nation's resources that every single individual was called upon to bear his share of the burden. The Universal Service Law, the popular liberty bond campaigns, and Red Cross and YMCA fund drives immediately singled out and marked as "slackers" those who would not participate, no matter what their motives may have been.

However, Congress, influenced by numerous petitions from the nonresistant churches, by influential Quakers, by the example of the English Conscription Act, and by our own former precedents, included an exemption clause in the conscription law passed May 18, 1917. This clause was found in the bill as it came from the hands of the Committee on Military Affairs. It was debated, several attempts were made to amend it, and one vote was taken in the Senate to repeal it. But it remained practically as it came from the hands of the committee. The clause exempted on religious grounds:

> members of any well organized religious sect or organization at present organized and existing whose creed or principles forbid its members to participate in war in any form and whose religious convictions are against war of participation therein in accordance with the creed or principles of the said organization. But no person shall be exempted from service in any capacity that the President shall declare non-combatant.

Under this law a number of young Mennonites were drafted and taken to various camps during the summer and fall of 1917. In the meantime, the church leaders were formulating the policy for the church at large toward the war problem. The view became quite general during the summer that in order to maintain their nonresistant principles they could not even accept noncombatant service if it was to be conducted under the military department of the government. The *Gospel Herald* opposed the acceptance of noncombatant service, and declared it inconsistent to participate in Red Cross, YMCA and liberty loan campaigns, and all other campaigns for direct war purposes. Several of the other papers reflected the same opinion, but none of them were so outspoken. *The Mennonite*, organ of the General Conference Mennonite Church, while thoroughly in sympathy with the nonresistant attitude, advocated participation in auxiliary war-fund drives. A meeting held at Goshen, Indiana, July 9-10, 1918, of representatives from nearly all Mennonite branches, declared against entering noncombatant service under the military arm of the government, and sent a petition to the president stating this decision. During all this time, too, a number of special committees from the various branches of the church were in communication with the War Department, working in behalf of some sort of service not under the military organization.

The Conscientious Objector

The War Department, in the meantime, found the problem of the conscientious objector a difficult one. Many of the young men from all branches of the church refused to put on the uniform and to perform work of any sort. These were frequently roughly handled by petty officers who had little sympathy for their scruples, nor for the law under which they were permitted to enter noncombatant service. In all the camps they were subjected to ridicule and were considered fair game for any army officer or YMCA secretary who cared to take a hand in converting them. Even some of the higher officers in some of the camps, being entirely out of sympathy with the liberal policy of the War Department, permitted unnecessary abuse of the conscientious objectors.

In Camp Funston near Manhattan, Kansas, the worst abuses prevailed, and two officers, a major, and a captain were removed for negligence in permitting rough treatment of the conscientious objectors. Some of the conscientious objectors were brutally handled in the guard house; they were bayonetted, beaten, and tortured. Eighteen men one night were aroused from their sleep and held under cold showers until one became hysterical. Another objector had the hose played upon his head until he became unconscious. A short time before the armistice was signed, the War Department finally was forced to interfere.

In other camps similar abuse prevailed, carried on usually by under officers for the purpose of breaking down the morale of the conscientious objector, or perhaps to retaliate for his refusal to obey peremptory military orders. Men were forced to stand at attention, sometimes with outstretched arms for hours and days at a time on the sunny or cold side of their barracks, exposed to the inclemencies of the weather as well as to the jeers and taunts of their fellows until they could stand no longer. Some were chased across the fields at top speed by their guards on motorcycles until they fell down exhausted. Occasionally they were tortured by mock trials, in which the victim was left under the impression to the very last that unless he submitted to the regulations the penalty would be death. Every conceivable device—ridicule, torture, offer of promotion, and other tempting inducements were resorted to in order to get them to give up their convictions; but with only few exceptions the religious objectors refused to compromise.

Fortunately for the Mennonites, both President Wilson and Secretary of War Baker displayed consideration for the scruples of the sincere objectors. These abuses were not perpetrated with the consent of the War Department, and those guilty of them were usually punished as soon as discovered. Secretary Baker stretched the Conscription Act to the limit to meet the situation. The government was rather slow in working out a satisfactory policy, but by the spring of 1918 a fairly satisfactory system of taking care of the conscientious objector was evolved. The abuses above described continued in some of the camps, however, throughout the period of the war, due to the inability of the War Department to keep in close touch with all the details of the work of the vast military machine in charge of organizing the army.

On March 18, 1918, upon the suggestion of the Secretary of War, Congress passed a law permitting the department to furlough out certain men in camp for agricultural purposes whenever it was deemed advisable. On March 20, the president for the first time defined noncombatant service. On April 22, the War Department completed its program for the conscientious objector who refused all work. First of all, a special Board of Inquiry, consisting of Julian W. Mack of the Supreme Court, Dean H. F. Stone of the Columbia Law School, and Major Richard C. Stoddard of the United States Army, was appointed to visit the various camps in which conscientious objectors had been segregated and weed out those who were insincere. Those who were found to be sincere were to be sent to a detention camp at Fort Leavenworth, Kansas, from whence they were to be furloughed out for farm work. Court-martial was provided for three classes—the insincere, the defiant, and those who were engaged in active propaganda, among others. The first class was to be sent into the ranks, while the other two were to be given prison sentence. This program was carried out only in part. Those classed as sincere were not sent to the Fort Leavenworth detention camp, but were furloughed out for farm work directly from the camps to which they had been sent originally. Those who went to Fort Leavenworth did so under prison sentence.

In the meantime, the young men in whose behalf the church was formulating its advice, and the government its war policy, were compelled to work out their own line of action. Not all followed the recommendations of the Goshen meeting already referred to. The exact number who accepted some form of noncombatant service is not quite certain. But since many had a deferred classification because of occupational or dependency reasons, the number was less than the general average of other classes. Perhaps fifteen hundred to two thousand, all told, were in camp and overseas during the war.

Of these it would seem that a majority, taking the denomination as a whole, refused service of any sort; a strong minority accepted noncombatant service with the uniform; and a very few entered the regular service. The church as a whole, and especially the leadership, stood quite unitedly in favor of maintaining the nonresistant doctrine. Among the young men in different sections and in isolated congregations, however, there was some difference of practice. The following random observations have come to the casual notice of the writer. The Hutterites were the only group whose young men stood as a unit against service of any sort. The Krimmer Mennonite Brethren had fifty young men in camp—twenty-eight of these were conscientious objectors; twenty took noncombatant service; and two entered the regular service, one of whom was killed on the battlefield. The Central Illinois Conference with a membership of twenty-six hundred reported seventy-two men in the service in August 1918. Of these, twenty-six had enlisted; thirty-eight were in the regular service; twenty-seven were noncombatants, and only five were classed as conscientious objectors, who refused all work. Of the Mennonites and Amish a large majority were conscientious objectors, though some of these accepted camp work. Among the General Conference and Mennonite Brethren, perhaps three-fourths of those in Kansas and Oklahoma were conscientious objectors, while the remainder took noncombatant service. Barely a dozen among them throughout the West took regular service. On the Pacific Coast and in Minnesota there were a larger number of noncombatants and fewer conscientious objectors. The Eastern District General Conference Mennonites generally accepted noncombatant service. The Mennonite Brethren in Christ (now United Missionary Church) were largely conscientious objectors. The large Swiss community of Bluffton, Ohio, had a few men in the regular service, but all the rest were noncombatants. None were conscientious objectors. The Swiss congregation at Berne, on the other hand, had a number of conscientious objectors, several of whom were sent to Fort Leavenworth. One congregation in Iowa was outstanding, perhaps, in having practically all of its young men in the regular service.

Mennonites were by no means the only people who refused to enter the army. Friends, Brethren, and other peace churches, totaling perhaps an entire population of one million, all came under the exemption clause of the Conscription Act. Both the Friends and the Brethren, however, accepted the noncombatant service prescribed by the law far more generally than did the Mennonites. This circumstance, together with the fact that many of the Mennonites were of more recent German origin, explains why the Mennonites were given more unfavorable publicity during the war than the other nonresistant denominations.

Major Kellogg, a later member of the Board of Inquiry, in his book entitled *The Conscientious Objector*, stated that 2,100 objectors were examined by the board, half of whom he estimated were Mennonites. Of these, 1,500 were recommended for farm or industrial furloughs; 80 for work in the Friends' Reconstruction Unit; 390 for noncombatant service; and 120 were sent back into the regular service as insincere. The above number does not include 1,300 who took noncombatant service nor 400 who were sent to Fort Leavenworth.

Of the 100 conscientious objectors confined in the disciplinary barracks at Fort Leavenworth at the close of the war, only about one-third were Mennonites. So far as the Mennonites and other religious objectors were concerned, these were practically all there because of the willful misrepresentation of local courts-martial. The law provided that only the insincere and defiant be given prison sentence. The "willful disobedience of orders of officers," which constituted the charge against practically all of these, meant in reality the refusal of sincere objectors to obey orders which ran counter to their religious convictions.

The Testimony of the Conscientious Objector

Some of the prisoners at Fort Leavenworth, including a few Mennonites, suffered extreme tortures at the hands of prison guards and officials for refusing to perform certain service which they regarded as inconsistent with their religious convictions. They were regarded by the prison authorities as ordinary criminals, and not as political prisoners. Some refused to work on the ground that the prison was a part of the military system;

others, for various reasons, refused to put on the uniform; still others refused to work because of sympathy for those who were unjustly disciplined. Some of these men may have carried their logic to unnecessary lengths, but no matter what the provocation, there was no justification for the harsh measures adopted in breaking the spirit of these men whose only crime was a tender conscience. Among the methods resorted to were

> continuous solitary confinement in cells in a hole under the basement of the prison, sleeping on a cement floor between foul blankets full of vermin, fed every alternate two weeks on bread and water, forbidden to read and write or talk, manacled in a standing posture for nine hours a day to the bars of the cell. In addition they were frequently beaten and tortured by the guards.

Among those given this treatment were several Mennonites. Two Hutterite young men, who had been removed to Fort Leavenworth from Alcatraz where they had been submitted to the most brutal treatment for refusing to put on the uniform and perform the work assigned them, died as a result of exposure and torture received at the hands of prison guards. Two young Amishmen sent here from Camp Sherman refused to don the prison uniform because their creed forbade them to wear clothes with buttons. Both were forcibly disrobed by guards and held under cold showers until they were thoroughly chilled. One of them was dragged across the cell room by the hair, knocked down upon the cement floor, and then pulled up by the ears and otherwise roughly handled. As a result of this treatment both of them submitted to prison labor contrary to their religious convictions.

The national Civil Liberties Bureau, together with such journals as the *Survey*, *Nation*, and the *New Republic*, gave these abuses of the conscientious objectors in the Leavenworth prison wide publicity with the result that a short time afterwards the War Department ordered the abolition of manacling and other severe methods of punishment. Still later, January 25, 1919, 113 of the conscientious objectors, mostly Mennonites, were honorably discharged from the army and released from prison. These Mennonites were principally from the western states.

It is only fair to add that the large majority of the Mennonites at Fort Leavenworth had little cause to complain of their treatment as prisoners. It was only those who, because of their tender consciences, refused to perform the prison work assigned them and to put on the prison garb who were given the drastic treatment described above.

Those imprisoned at Ft. Leavenworth, of course, constituted only a small portion of the Mennonite conscientious objectors.

Many were furloughed out for farm work directly from their local camps. A number were permitted to enter the reconstruction work carried on by the Friends' Reconstruction Unit. The furlough system worked fairly well, but in some localities the non-Mennonite population objected to the presence of farmhands from the camps, and they had to be sent back.

It is not out of place here to say a few words regarding the attitude of the conscientious objectors toward war service. Not only were they subjected to these gross abuses in camp, but they were also most bitterly reviled and denounced by almost the entire press of the country. The *Kansas City Star* and the *Chicago Tribune* were especially severe in their criticism. There were few voices raised in their behalf either from pulpit or platform. Everywhere they were denounced as slackers, cowards, parasites, and draft-dodgers. The most charitable epithet applied to them was that of religious fanatic. Theodore Roosevelt, always intolerant of any views contrary to his own, was most vindictive in his utterance against them. He suggested that all men who had conscientious scruples against war service should be sent to the most dangerous points of the front line with shovels to dig trenches, or be placed on mine sweepers. They were not fit to live in America, he said, and ought to be denied all political rights. It was only such liberal journals as the *Nation*, and others as already noted, that dared raise a voice in behalf of freedom of speech and liberty of conscience.

While much of this bitterness must be ascribed to war madness, yet some of it was due, no doubt, to the failure of the people in general to understand the character and appreciate the point of view of the men who refused war service on the ground of conscientious convictions. The average citizen is thoroughly indoctrinated all through his life in the schoolroom, from the pulpit and the platform, and by the press with the idea that it is his most sacred duty to come to the defense of his country with gun and sword whenever called upon. Many regarded the conscientious objector as an ordinary draft-dodger, trying to shirk his honest duty, or as endowed with a yellow streak that made him cringe from danger. Undoubtedly even under the most favorable circumstances there would have been considerable opposition to the granting of special privileges and exemptions even on grounds of religious scruples. Yet a better understanding of the real spirit of the conscientious objector might have disarmed his more intelligent critics, at least, of some of their bitter antagonism.

A coward he certainly was not. The Conscription Act offered an easy way out for those who had scruples against war. A strong minority of the Mennonites, and most of the Brethren and the Friends, accepted this easy escape. But the other half of the Mennonite contingent in the camps, refusing to compromise with their consciences, took the hard way. Neither was the conscientious objector a slacker; he was willing to do any kind of work, in the danger zone or out, if its purpose was to save life rather than to destroy it, and if it was not connected with the military establishment. He was neither a coward nor a slacker; he chose the hard road of loyalty to his convictions rather than the easy one of compromise. He was made of the same stuff as that of his forefathers, who some hundreds of years earlier went to the martyr's stake by the thousands rather than to surrender religious beliefs which they thought to be right.

But even the warmest friends of the conscientious objector sometimes wondered whether he did not carry his logic to unnecessary lengths, and whether he at times did not strain at a gnat to swallow a camel. Why did he refuse to sow grass seed on the lawn in front of his barracks, or join the kitchen force at the mess hall? For two reasons—to cook for the soldiers under military order and as a part of the military machine committed him as much to the killing process as if he actually carried a gun to shoot his fellows; and secondly, the whole purpose of the camp officials was to break down the objector's morale, to find a flaw somewhere in his logic, by setting a trap for him to inveigle him into active service. If he could be induced to take one form of service, he might be led by easy steps into any other form. The objector knew the purposes of the officers, and drew the line at the only logical place possible, namely to refuse work of any sort connected with the military machine. That this was the situation, at least in Camp Funston, is shown in the following letter:

November 18, 1917

Hon. Arthur Capper
Governor of the State of Kansas
Dear Sir:

Your letter of November 10, accompanied by a petition from various Mennonites, addressed to General Wood, has been referred to this office. I have carefully gone over these petitions and wish to advise you that in every way we are carrying out the War Department's instructions in regard to the Mennonites and Conscientious Objectors. Further there is nothing that we can do in the matter. If these Conscientious Objectors under the care and treatment they receive at this camp can be talked into rendering any kind of work that is connected with the military service by their fellow soldiers it does not appear that their belief can be very solidly grounded.

Very respectfully,
N. C. Shiverick,
Major Ad. Gen., U.S.A.

Unable to appreciate the views of the conscientious objector against war, and failing to convict him of cowardice, many tried to explain him on the basis of low mentality. Accordingly, the War Department, as already mentioned, appointed a special psychological board to study this strange phenomenon from a psychological point of view. The investigations were no doubt honestly and intelligently made, but the results were hardly what those responsible for the appointment of the board had expected. The conclusions of the special board were that the conscientious objectors were above the average of all enlisted men in intelligence.

War Drives

Regarding participation in the various campaigns for war and relief work, there was considerable diversity of opinion and practice during the war. Except among the more liberal congregations, the leadership at first was quite generally agreed against any participation. But the pressure from local committees in most localities became so great that in almost every community a large number supported the various campaigns for funds. The Mennonites, Amish, Defenseless, Reformed Mennonites, and the Mennonite Brethren opposed all participation, but most of them under compulsion made some contribution to the various funds and bought bonds. Several attempts were made to escape the purchase of bonds directly by depositing money in local banks for a stipulated number of years, but which it was understood was not to be used for buying bonds, although it might release other money to be thus invested. In several localities scruples against supporting the war with money were satisfied by promising that money contributed would be used for the purchase of food, and not for ammunition and other means of warfare.

The Mennonites in the West as a rule contributed quite freely to YMCA and Red Cross funds but hesitated to buy bonds, although under compulsion, many did so. The Middle and Eastern districts of the General Conference Mennonite Church and the Central District Conference bought quite freely and contributed liberally to all funds.

Besides these funds, the Mennonites and the Amish, assisted by the Central District Conference and the Defenseless Mennonites, contributed heavily toward reconstruction work in France. Later relief work was also taken up in Armenia. In 1919 when famine and pestilence spread among the Mennonites of South Russia, most of the relief work of the various branches of Mennonites, including the General Conference, the Mennonite Brethren, and other Mennonite groups from Russia, was directed toward the assistance of their afflicted brethren.

In spite of these efforts, however, and in striking contrast to the considerate treatment accorded them by the federal government, Mennonites in most communities were harshly criticized and frequently abused by the non-Mennonite population. Throughout central Illinois and also in many other sections of the country, a number of church buildings were painted yellow. In Kansas several men were tarred and feathered. The most serious attacks were made upon the German-speaking Mennonites in Oklahoma. One minister who was seized by a mob and strung up a telegraph pole was rescued by local officials. Two other men were attacked and driven out of their community for promoting nonresistance. Two Mennonite church buildings were burned down, as was also a barn which was being used as a temporary meeting place. In Ohio one prominent minister was called from a prayer meeting and had his hair shorn because his donation to the Red Cross was not considered large enough by the mob which attacked him. Everywhere men were intimidated and abused by local committees for hesitating to purchase bonds or contribute to the various war funds, although Mennonites as a whole gave a great deal more to general relief work than did those who abused them. In South Dakota the Hutterites, after having been robbed of forty thousand dollars' worth of livestock by an irresponsible hoodlum mob with the connivance of an official Liberty Loan Committee, were forced to flee to Canada to escape further persecution at the hands of super-patriots.

Comparatively few communities escaped some form of intimidation or abuse. The newspapers, both local and metropolitan throughout the entire country, were most bitter against the nonresistant churches, and especially the Mennonites; and many were unscrupulous in their attempts to stir up feeling against them. Few of the papers and few of the local communities were in sympathy with the liberal policy the government followed toward the conscientious objectors.

The government authorities were quite lenient toward Mennonite publications and church leaders, who, under the guarantee of religious liberty, were permitted considerable freedom in advising their constituencies against participating in war activities. One editor of a Mennonite paper, however, was fined $500 for printing an objectionable article. Most of the editors were wise enough in their papers to merely state the position of the church on all war questions, which under the guarantee of religious liberty they had a perfect right to do, but not to urge any opposition to the policies of the government for which under the Espionage Act they could have been prosecuted. A number of Mennonite ministers who signed the Yellow Creek Conference resolutions advising the Mennonite young men against accepting noncombatant service were interviewed by federal officials and warned not to interfere too seriously with war measures. Had the war continued much longer, several of the church leaders who were most outspoken against participating in the various war-work campaigns would perhaps have been placed under certain restrictions for the period of the war.

Relief Work

In the meantime, Mennonites who had scruples against participating in the various war drives but who at the same time were anxious to serve their fellowmen during this time of crisis, and desirous as well of convincing the non-Mennonite world that their refusal to take any part in the destructive processes of war was not due to any lack of loyalty to their country, sought other ways to be of help to the civilian victims in the warring countries. They were willing to assume any burdens or make any sacrifices necessary to restore and preserve human life, but refused to be any part of the killing process.

In December 1917 the Mennonite Relief Commission for War Sufferers was organized which in the course of a few following years collected some three hundred thousand dollars to be distributed through the American Friends' Service Committee among the civilian war victims in France. A number of young men, mostly conscientious objectors, volunteered their services for this work, but none were admitted until after the signing of the peace treaty.

Immediately after World War I, however, some fifty young Mennonites joined the American Friends Service Committee in reconstruction work in the war-stricken lands of Europe. A little later twenty-six young men and two young women enlisted with the American Committee for Relief in the Near East for relief work among the refugees in that region. Over $360,000 was collected for this service among the American Mennonites.

The General Conference Mennonite Church revived an earlier committee of some years' standing, the Emergency Relief Committee, for the purpose of aiding war sufferers wherever they might be found. Early in 1920 the Mennonite Brethren and the Krimmer Mennonite Brethren joined the western contingent of the General Conference Mennonite Church in sending clothing and other supplies to their suffering fellow Mennonites in Siberia. But this project hardly got started before it had to be abandoned because the door to Siberia had been closed by the civil wars in that region. The efforts of these branches of the church were then directed, for a few years, to relief for the needy people of central Europe, Germany, Austria, and Poland.

By 1920 the American Mennonites had heard of the suffering and distress of their brethren in South Russia. From this time on relief work among all Mennonites was turned in that direction. On July 27, 1920, a new organization representing all Mennonites came into being under the name of the *Mennonite Central Committee* (MCC). Cooperating in this effort were the *Emergency Relief Committee* of the General Conference, the *Mennonite Relief Commission for War Sufferers* of the Mennonite Church, and similar committees from the Central Conference of Mennonites, the Mennonite Brethren, and the Krimmer Mennonite Brethren. Other smaller groups also liberally supported the work of this committee, though not always through any subsidiary organizations of their own. But the splendid service rendered by the American Mennonites to their suffering brethren in Russia during this critical period is described elsewhere, and needs no further reference here. All told it is estimated that during the war and the period immediately following, the entire brotherhood collected and distributed over $2,500,000 among the various war sufferers through all the different relief agencies above mentioned, all outside of any of the official YMCA, Red Cross, or other war drives of the period.

Profiting by Their Experiences

The Conscription Act of 1917 had found the Mennonites ill prepared to meet the demands made upon them by the exigencies of war. For over two hundred years, with but few exceptions, they had enjoyed almost complete exemption from military service, even in wartime; and they had little reason to expect anything else for the future. Respect for religious conscience, they thought, had been won forever in America. It was generally believed that wars would be fought by volunteers as they had been in the past. Their nonresistant doctrines had never been seriously challenged, and therefore had given them little concern. Like the other tenets of their faith, it had been taken for granted and its practice no more to be challenged.

Profiting by their experiences in the late war, many Mennonites were constrained to reexamine and reappraise these principles in the light of the new demands that would likely be again made on them in the case of another war. To clarify their thought and fortify their resolution to remain firm in the faith if the worst should happen, several of the larger Mennonite branches, especially the General Conference Mennonite Church, the Mennonite Church, the Mennonite Brethren, and the Central

Conference of Mennonites appointed standing peace committees. By holding peace institutes and by printing peace literature and through various activities, these committees greatly strengthened the peace convictions among their members and gave them a new realization of the soundness of their faith as a solution for the troubles of a warring world.

Realizing also that the cause would be greatly strengthened by cooperation with other historic peace churches, the Mennonites joined in numerous peace meetings with the Friends and Brethren.

Alongside of these efforts to clarify their own thinking, and to fortify their own convictions on the question of peace, the Mennonites were assiduous in acquainting the general public, and especially the governing authorities, with their peace principles and the grounds upon which they refused war service. From time to time at proper intervals, petitions were sent to congressmen and to the president commending legislation or executive action which in their minds would promote the peace of the country. Protests against measures that would have the contrary effect were also sent, informing the recipients of these petitions of the Mennonite stand on the war question. Noteworthy among the incidents in this campaign of education was a personal interview with President Roosevelt in February 1937, by a committee composed of members of the three historic peace denominations—Friends, Brethren, and Mennonites. In the course of the visit, the president was presented with a statement of the peace principles held in common by the three churches, supplemented by special documents from each of the groups. The Mennonite representatives were A. J. Neuenschwander and C. L. Graber.

3. WORLD WAR II AND AFTER

At the time of Mussolini's conquests, the Spanish-Civil War, Hitler's rise to power, and the consequent international armament race, it became increasingly clear that another world struggle was at hand. Being opposed to participation in armed violence, the American Mennonites prepared to meet the emergency. The various conferences had experienced leadership and organized machinery to deal with the approaching crisis. More and more these efforts became centralized and, by delegated action, represented in the Mennonite Central Committee.

Not only did the Mennonites have more adequate machinery than in previous crises, but they were also doing some positive educational work and restudying of the whole issue of nonresistance to make it a more meaningful and positive witness. Through congregations, publications, special peace committees, and educational institutions this program was promoted.

When World War II broke out in September 1939, the Peace Committee of the Mennonite Central Committee formulated definite plans to meet the situation in case the United States should become involved in the war. On September 16, 1939, the officers of this committee met with representatives of the Church of the Brethren and of the Friends to outline a plan of action. This plan proposed that members of the *historical peace churches* should register, indicating their conscientious objection to military service and willingness to render useful service of a nonmilitary character. It was also agreed to see the president and other government officials to propose definite plans of alternative service; this was done January 10, 1940.

In September 1940, Congress passed the Selective Training and Service Act providing that all persons who "by reason of religious training and belief" were opposed to military service should "be assigned to work of national importance under civilian direction."

On October 5, 1940, the historic peace churches organized what later was known as the National Service Board for Religious Objectors (NSBRO). The NSBRO became the agency through which the peace churches worked in dealing with Selective Service. The peace churches now presented a plan to Selective Service for setting up Civilian Public Service camps in which the work would be under the direction of government technical men and the social and religious life under the supervision of the peace churches. This plan was accepted by Selective Service and approved in a modified form by President Roosevelt on December 20, 1940. The peace churches had recommended that the government provide the cost of maintenance and pay the men the approximate wages that drafted men in the army received. This proposal, however, was turned down by the president. It was agreed that the government would

> provide work camps, bedding, other equipment, technical equipment for soil conservation and pay the men's transportation costs to the camps while the peace churches agreed to supply subsistence, hospital care, and generally all things necessary for the care and maintenance of the men.

Civilian Public Service

In May 1941 the first Civilian Public Service (CPS) camps were opened. By the end of the year there were 25 camps. Most of them were concerned with soil conservation and forestry service.

During 1942 a total of 52 additional units were organized, and by the end of the war 151 had been authorized. These units were scattered over thirty-four states, Puerto Rico, and the Virgin Islands. Some eighteen different kinds of agencies were organized, each performing a different kind of service. Among these services, besides forestry and soil conservation, were experiments in technical fields such as biology, meteorology, and agriculture; community education, recreational, and health programs; public health work; mental hospital work; "guinea pig" projects; dairy programs; fire fighting in trained parachute-corps; and processing food.

As the war progressed, more and more of the units were assigned to mental hospitals. Of the fifty-one such units, the Mennonites administered twenty-five. Nearly three thousand CPS men engaged in this kind of work. They worked in forty-six of the nation's three hundred fifty public mental hospitals. Among the results of the mental hospital work of the Mennonites and other peace churches was the establishment of the National Mental Health Foundation. The nation was shocked after World War II to learn of the terrible conditions existing in mental hospitals as this discovery found expression in revealing books, stirring magazine articles, and the book and film *The Snake Pit*. This interest resulted in drastic reforms in our mental institutions. Since World War II the Mennonites have established their own mental hospitals.

The Directory of Civilian Public Service of May 1941 to March 1947, listing all names and addresses of CPS men, gives a total of 11,996. They came not only from the three historic peace churches but also from 226 other religious groups. In addition, 449 were nonaffiliated and 709 unclassified as to denomination. There were 107 groups that furnished only one representative each. The fourteen churches which had a hundred or more members in CPS came in this order: Mennonite, 4,665; Church of the Brethren, 1,353; Society of Friends, 951; Methodist, 673; Jehovah's Witness, 409; Congregational Christian, 209; Church of Christ, 199; Presbyterian, 192; Roman Catholic, 149; Christadelphian, 127; Lutheran, 108; Evangelical and Reformed, 101. Thus we see that the Mennonites with their active teaching of nonresistance furnished more than a third of all men in Civilian Public Service.

Not nearly all Mennonite young men chose to serve in Civilian Public Service, however. Many served in the army as noncombatants in the medical corps, and others entered regular service. Among the most conservative Mennonite groups, the young men were almost 100 percent conscientious objectors, while among the more liberal groups who had adjusted themselves more completely to the American environment, many took up service in the army.

Cost and Administration

According to Melvin Gingerich in *Service for Peace* (1949), the total contribution of all Mennonite churches to the Civilian Public Service fund from 1941 to 1947 amounted to $3,386,254 in cash and gifts in kind. With a constituency of approximately 120,000 members, this amounted to about $25.00 per member. This sum is almost half the total spent by the three peace churches in support of CPS. The above total also includes a considerable amount spent for the support of nonpeace church men in CPS. The amount needed for the operation of CPS was raised through voluntary offerings from the entire constituency of the MCC by a quota system which at first suggested contributions of fifty cents per member. But with the rising cost of CPS, this figure was later set at $6.00 per member per year. Unlike the men in alternative service camps in Canada, the CPS men received no pay, but at various times were given a monthly allowance from the MCC amounting to $1.50 to $5.00.

In line with the original agreement between the peace churches and Selective Service System, the administration of CPS was shared by the government and the churches. The churches supervised the in-camp social, educational, and religious life while the government was responsible for living quarters and supervision of the work program. Induction, discharges, transfers, and all matters of camp discipline remained the responsibility of the Selective Service System under Major General Lewis B. Hershey. To fulfill its responsibility the MCC appointed camp directors for each camp who administered camp life in its religious and social phases. In all larger areas, camps were supervised by a regional director who was responsible to the general director at Akron, Pennsylvania. For the early period of CPS the director was H. A. Fast. He was succeeded by Albert Gaeddert, who in turn was succeeded by Erwin Goering.

The Mennonite Central Committee also created the office of Educational Director of CPS. This position was filled for most of the CPS period by Elmer Ediger. The purpose of an educational program was, broadly speaking, to build morale among the men, to supply outlets for various talents and interests, to secure a better understanding of the principle of nonresistance, and to inculcate an appreciation of the Mennonite heritage in its various aspects. To help achieve these aims the MCC published a series of six booklets under the general title *Mennonites and their Heritage*. The educational division at Akron arranged for educational programs in all camps directly supervised by a camp educational director. Many outside people—college instructors, ministers, professional men, and government technical men—participated as lecturers and camp visitors. The contact with home communities was maintained by visiting ministers and relatives.

Even though the actual work performed by men assigned to "work of national importance" did not always seem important to them, the educational results for the men coming from all parts of the United States and from all Mennonite and many other religious groups were of positive value in challenging them to become more conscious of their heritage and their peace contribution. The churches at home, challenged to cooperate and present a united witness, benefitted from the spiritual impact the CPS program made upon them. To quote from the statement of policy on CPS approved by the Mennonite Central Committee meeting, September 16, 1943:

> They (Mennonites) desire to transform the compulsion of CPS into the free service of a Christian who seeks to establish the Kingdom of God among men by the preaching of the Gospel and the practice of Christian discipleship.

"In the Name of Christ"

The CPS program of the Mennonite churches of the United States does not present a complete picture of their activities during and after World War II. The following table shows some figures of relief expenditures, gifts in kind dispensed, and the number of relief workers for three representative years.

	1946	1947	1948
Total Relief Expenditures (US and Canada)	$ 898,500.40	$ 936,786.33	$ 868,604.05
Gifts in Kind Dispensed	$1,948,285.02	$2,136,153.59	$1,777,585.03
Workers on the Field	237	288	217

The rehabilitation program of some ten thousand Mennonite refugees is not included in these expenditures. It is true, the International Refugee Organization contributed to this cost, but the major contributions to this program came from the Mennonites in Canada and the United States.

The number of relief workers on the foreign field rose to a peak of 317 in July 1947, so that by the end of 1948 some 600 men and women had been out to serve "in the name of Christ." Most of them went for a two-year period. Material compensation was maintenance plus $10 per month. Among these workers were more than a hundred young men who had already served from one to four years in Civilian Public Service. While yet in CPS the young men, even though they had no income, began to contribute financially for the relief program and to prepare themselves for this task. Many of them would have preferred to do relief work in war devastated areas rather than spend their time in CPS camps. One unit actually proceeded as far as Capetown, South Africa, but had to return because Congress did not approve of conscientious objectors doing relief work.

Clothing, food, and gifts in kind were collected in the Mennonite Central Committee collection centers and warehouses such as: Silver Springs and Ephrata, Pennsylvania; North Newton, Kansas; Reedley, California; Kitchener, Ontario; and Winnipeg, Manitoba. Between December 1946 and November 30, 1947, some 5,073 tons of food, clothing, soap, and other commodities were collected, having a value of $1,878,000. Twenty-seven carloads of food were attached to the Friendship Train. Furthermore, tools, garden seeds, religious literature, Christmas bundles, school bags, toys, and implements were shipped to Europe and to the Mennonite settlements in Paraguay. Germany received the major portion of the MCC relief contributions.

Besides the testimony which Mennonites gave through Civilian Public Service and relief and rehabilitation abroad they made other efforts at presenting a consistent peace witness in time of war and peace. They were confronted with the challenge of buying war bonds to finance the war. For many, a Christian solution of this problem presented itself when the government offered "civilian" bonds, the proceeds of which were designated for civilian operations of the government. Under the Canadian plan the proceeds of civilian bonds were used for the relief of war sufferers. Another area in which Mennonites tried to give a positive witness was in refusing to work in munitions factories and to do "defense work" in general. It was generally felt that participation in such work was inconsistent and contrary to the faith of nonresistant Christians.

A new field of activity for Mennonites during and after World War II was that of race relations. Beginning as CPS public health units in Florida and Mississippi, work with black people has continued in these states through voluntary service units. In these units all people, regardless of race, are given the benefit of health and recreational services, as well as spiritual fellowship.

Postwar Services

Wars end, but the need for Christian service never ends. The awakened sensitiveness to the spiritual and economic needs of the world cannot find rest, but must continue to serve wherever a need arises. Through the channels of the Mennonite Central Committee, North American Mennonites continued their service at home and abroad. The 1-W program gave young men of military age an opportunity to do work similar to that which the Civilian Public Service provided. Many young men of military age chose to serve in Pax units abroad. Voluntary Service continues to provide opportunity for young people to serve at home and abroad for longer or for shorter terms. Disaster units—regularly organized or spontaneously called to serve—help in floods, tornadoes, fires, and other emergencies.

A direct result of Civilian Public Service during World War II was the establishment of a number of mental hospitals. During the war many of the young men served in mental hospitals. The need for a service in this field on a consecrated Christian basis led to the establishment of Brook Lane Farm, Maryland, 1949; Kings View Homes, Reedley, California, 1951; Philhaven, Lancaster, Pennsylvania, 1952; and Prairie View Hospital, Newton, Kansas, 1954. In addition to this, many 1-W men served in hospitals throughout the country.

Mennonite World Conference

Among the many other areas of Mennonite cooperation is the Mennonite World Conference which began in Switzerland in 1925 by observing the four hundreth anniversary of Mennonite origins. The initiator of this observation was Christian Neff, a German Mennonite minister, leader, and scholar. Only one North American Mennonite, H. J. Krehbiel, was in attendance. It was again Christian Neff who arranged for the second Mennonite World Conference which convened in Danzig in 1930. The program and the discussion focused primarily on relief work, particularly in connection with the Mennonites that had come to Canada and South America from Russia and those that had just come out of Russia and waited for a country that would be willing to accept them. This was still on the agenda at the next conference, convening in 1936 in the Netherlands.

The 1936 conference was, however, primarily devoted to the commemoration of the conversion of Menno Simons and the beginning of the Dutch Anabaptists in 1536. The attendance had grown considerably, and there was a strong feeling of a global Mennonite brotherhood. This was, however, still primarily a European Mennonite oriented conference.

World War II brought about unprecedented changes affecting the Mennonite brotherhood in all countries including those in which, through missionary efforts, congregations and schools had come into being. An entirely new field of outreach and aid for the suffering and starving in European countries and beyond came into being through the channels of the Mennonite Central Committee. Consequently, North American Mennonites became the primary sponsors of the fourth Mennonite World Conference which convened in 1948 in Goshen, Indiana, and at Bethel College in North Newton, Kansas. Christian Neff, the convener of the preceding conferences, had died in 1946. The Mennonite Central Committee of Akron, Pennsylvania, initiated this conference. Several thousand attended this conference, of whom only twenty-seven were from overseas.

The fifth Mennonite World Conference again took place in Switzerland in 1952 in the country of Anabaptist origins. The daily attendance was approximately 600 persons. A climax was the visit in Zürich where the Swiss Brethren had their beginnings and where their bold witness led to the martyrdom of many. The topic at this conference was: "The Church of Christ and Her Commission." The sixth conference convened in Karlsruhe, Germany, in 1957. This was followed by the seventh in Kitchener, Ontario, in 1962, which had an attendance exceeding all previous conferences.

The eighth Mennonite World Conference took place in Amsterdam in 1967. Representatives from thirty countries coming from five continents were present. For the first time there was a greater awareness that not all Mennonites have a white skin. It was learned that there were some forty thousand Mennonites in Africa. There was for the first time a stronger representation from the newer Mennonite congregations in Asia, Africa, and South America.

The voices of the younger generation were heard. There were reminders that present-day Mennonites did not have the bold and radical witness of the early Anabaptists. Some claimed that the hope of early Anabaptists for great changes had been lost. And yet there were moments like in the days of the outpouring of the Spirit in Jerusalem. Ethnic differences were not noticed, and linguistic problems were solved by means of modern techniques. The worship of the last day, led by Henk Bremer and Vincent Harding, pointed out that the message of the gospel must today have the same effect that it had in the days of old. Vincent Harding became very popular among the Dutch.

When the ninth Mennonite World Conference convened in Curitiba, Brazil, in 1972, it was the first Mennonite World Conference in the Third World. It had a much stronger representation from South American countries and fewer from North America and Europe.

The tenth Mennonite World Conference, by far the largest, convened in Wichita, Kansas, in 1978. The attendance from Third

World countries and their participation in the programs was predominant. It was the first time that a Baptist and Mennonite delegation from the USSR was present and participated in the program. The present complex Mennonite brotherhood, which has spread during the past century from the western countries into the Asiatic, African, and South American countries, was well represented at the conference in Wichita.

In addition to lectures on various subjects, there were Bible discussions and musical and dramatic performances by many groups from various countries. Book displays invited the guests to get acquainted with the Mennonite books available.

Numerous printed books and guides in addition to the *Mennonite World Conference Handbook* were available to help the participants to orient themselves, and to take them home for further study. Provisions had been made to break up into smaller groups after major presentations for discussion of various topics of biblical nature or other subjects.

In spite of the great variety of ethnic, national, and linguistic backgrounds of those participating in the tenth Mennonite World Conference, all had enough in common to make it a Pentecost in our day based on the biblical foundation of Anabaptism: "For no other foundation can anyone lay than that which is laid, which is Jesus Christ" (1 Corinthians 3:11, RSV).

Bibliography

A. GENERAL

The following list of books is divided into two parts. The first list includes periodicals, brief histories covering the story of the Mennonites in general, and the *Mennonite Encyclopedia*. The list is a guide to general sources dealing with the Mennonites. After this follows a list of bibliographies.

BOOKS AND PERIODICALS

Mennonite Encyclopedia. 4 vols., Scottdale, Pa.; Newton, Kans.; Hillsboro, Kans.: 1955-1958.

Mennonite Quarterly Review. Published by Goshen College, Goshen, Ind.: since 1927.

Mennonite Life. Published by Bethel College, North Newton, Kans.: since 1946.

Proceedings of the Annual Conference on Mennonite Cultural Problems. Published 1942-1967.

Proceedings of the Mennonite World Conference, since 1925.

Bender, H. S. and Smith, C. Henry. *Mennonites and Their Heritage.* Scottdale, Pa.: Herald Press, 1964, 150 pp.

Cummings, Mary Lou, ed. *Full Circle: Stories of Mennonite Women,* Newton, Kans.: Faith and Life Press, 1978, 204 pp.

Dyck, Anni. *Mennonites Around the World.* Basel: Agape Verlag, 1967, 126 pp.

Dyck, C. J., ed. *An Introduction to Mennonite History.* Scottdale, Pa.: Herald Press, 1967, 324 pp.

Hostetler, John A. *Amish Life.* Scottdale, Pa.: Herald Press, 1959, 39 pp.

Hostetler, John A. *Hutterite Life.* Scottdale, Pa.: Herald Press, 1969, 40 pp.

Krahn, Cornelius. *The Witness of the Martyr's Mirror for Our Day.* North Newton, Kans.: Bethel College, 1974, 47 pp., Illustrated. (Digest of the *Martyrs Mirror.*)

Warkentin, A. and Gingerich, Melvin. *Who's Who Among the Mennonites.* Newton, Kans.: 1943.

BIBLIOGRAPHIES

Bender, H. S. *Two Centuries of American Mennonite Literature.* Scottdale, Pa.: Herald Press, 1929.

Giesbrecht, Herbert. *The Mennonite Brethren:* a Bibliography Guide to Information. Winnipeg, Man.: General Conference of Mennonite Brethren Churches, 1971, 17 pp.

Hillerbrand, Hans. *Bibliography of Anabaptism 1520-1630.* Gütersloh: Gerd Mohn Verlag, 1962, 261 pp., 4665 entries.

Hostetler, John A. *Annotated Bibliography on the Amish.* Scottdale, Pa.: Herald Press, 1951, 100 pp.

Krahn, Cornelius. "The Historiography of the Mennonites of the Netherlands," *Mennonite Quarterly Review.* Goshen, Ind.: October 1944.

Krahn, Cornelius. *The Mennonites: A Brief Guide to Information.* Newton, Kans.: Faith and Life Press, 1976, 32 pp.

Krahn, Cornelius. *Menno Simons Research* (1910-1960). 12 pp.

Springer, Nelson P. and Klassen, A. J. *Mennonite Bibliography, 1631-1961.* Scottdale, Pa.: Herald Press, 1977.

In addition, annual bibliographies have been published in *Mennonite Life* since 1947, usually in the April issue.

B. CHAPTER REFERENCES

I. THE ANABAPTISTS, SWITZERLAND, SOUTH GERMANY, THE HUTTERITES: CHAPTER I, pp. 3-52; CHAPTER III, pp. 75-102; CHAPTER VI, pp. 189-223; CHAPTER VII, pp. 225-248.

Armour, Rolin S. *Anabaptist Baptism: A Representative Study.* Scottdale, Pa.: Herald Press, 1966, 214 pp.

Augsburger, Myron S. *The Broken Chalice.* Scottdale, Pa.: Herald Press, 1971, 136 pp.

Augsburger, Myron S. *Pilgrim Aflame* (Michael Sattler). Scottdale, Pa.: Herald Press, 1967, 288 pp.

Beachy, Alvin J. *The Concept of Grace in the Radical Reformation.* Nieuwkoop: B. De Graff, 1977, 238 pp.

Bender, Harold S. *Conrad Grebel: Founder of the Swiss Brethren.* Scottdale, Pa.: Herald Press, 1950, 343 pp.

Bennet, John W. *Hutterian Brethren.* Stanford University Press, 1967, 298 pp.

Blanke, Fritz. *Brother in Christ.* Scottdale, Pa.: Herald Press, 1961, 78 pp.

Braght, Thieleman J. van. *The Martyrs Mirror.* Scottdale, Pa.: Herald Press, 1951, 1,157 pp.

Clasen, Claus-Peter. *Anabaptism: A Social History, 1525-1618*: Switzerland, Austria, Moravia, and South and Central Germany. Ithaca: Cornell University, 1972, 523 pp.

Davis, Kenneth Ronald. *Anabaptism and Asceticism,* a Study in Intellectual Origins. Scottdale, Pa.: Herald Press, 1974, 384 pp.

Ehrenpreis, Andreas. *Brotherly Community, the Highest Command of Love: Two Anabaptist Documents of 1650 and 1560.* Rifton: Plough, 1978, 133 pp.

Estep, Wm. R., Jr., ed. *Anabaptist Beginnings 1523-1533.* A Source Book. Niewkoop: B. De Graaf, 1976, 172 pp.

Estep, Wm. R., Jr. *The Anabaptist Story.* Grand Rapids, Mich.: Wm. B.

Eerdmans, 1975, 250 pp.
Flint, David. *The Hutterites: A Study in Prejudice.* Toronto: Oxford University Press, 1975, 193 pp.
Friedman, Robert. *Hutterite Studies.* Goshen, Ind.: 1961, 338 pp.
Gratz, Delbert. *Bernese Anabaptists.* Scottdale, Pa.: Herald Press, 1953, 219 pp.
Grebel, Conrad; Transcribed and translated by J. C. Wenger. *Conrad Grebel's Programmatic Letters of 1524, with facsimilies of the original German script of Grebel's letters.* Scottdale, Pa.: Herald Press, 1970, 71 pp.
Gross, Paul S. *The Hutterite Way.* Published by author, 216 pp.
Hofer, Arnold M. and Walter, Kenneth J. *History of the Hutterite-Mennonites.* Published in connection with the Centennial Observance of the coming of Hutterites to Dakota. Freeman, S.Dak.: Pine Hill Press, 1974, 172 pp.
Horsch, John. *Mennonites in Europe.* Scottdale, Pa.: Herald Press, 1950, 414 pp.
Horsch, John. *The Hutterian Brethren, 1528-1931.* Goshen, Ind.: 1931, 184 pp.
Hostetler, John A. *Amish Society.* Baltimore, Md.: Johns Hopkins Press, 3rd ed., 1980, 403 pp.
Hostetler, John A. and Huntington, Gertrude Enders. *Children in Amish Society: Socialization and Community Education.* New York: Holt, Rinehart, and Winston, 1971, 119 pp.
Hostetler, John A. *Hutterite Society.* Baltimore, Md.: Johns Hopkins Press, 1974, plus 403 pp.
Hutter, Jakob. *Brotherly Faithfulness: Epistles from a Time of Persecution.* Rifton, N.Y.: Plough Publishing House, 1979, 232 pp.
Keim, Albert N., ed. *Compulsory Education and the Amish; the Right Not to Be Modern.* Boston: Beacon Press, 1975, 211 pp.
Klaassen, Walter. *Anabaptism: Neither Catholic nor Protestant.* Waterloo, Ont.: Conrad Press, 1973, 92 pp.
Klaassen, Walter and Klassen, William, eds. *The Writings of Pilgram Marbeck.* Kitchener: 1978.
Klassen, William. *Covenant and Community.* The Life, Writings and Hermeneutics of Pilgram Marbeck. Grand Rapids, Mich.: Wm. B. Eerdmans, 1968, 211 pp.
Krahn, Cornelius. *The Mennonites. A Brief Guide to Information.* Newton, Kans.: Faith and Life Press, 1976, 36 pp.
Lienhard, Marc, ed. *Origins and Characteristics of Anabaptism.* The Hague: Martinus Nijhoff, 1976, 272 pp.
Menno Simons. *The Complete Writings of Menno Simons.* Scottdale, Pa.: Herald Press, 1956, 1,092 pp.
Oyer, John S. *Lutheran Reformers Against Anabaptists.* The Hague: Martinus Hijhoff, 1964, 269 pp.
Packull, Werner O. *Mysticism and the Early South German-Austrian Anabaptist Movement, 1525-1531.* Scottdale, Pa.: Herald Press, 1977, 252 pp.
Peters, Victor. *All Things Common.* The Hutterian Way of Life. Minneapolis: The University of Minnesota Press, 1966, 233 pp.
Rideman, Peter. *Account of Our Religion, Doctrine and Faith.* Transl. by the Society of Brothers. Rifton, N.Y.: Plough, 1970, 295 pp.
Rideman, Peter. *Confessions of Faith.* Rifton, N.Y.: Plough Publ. House, 1970, 298 pp.

Ruth, John L. *Conrad Grebel, Son of Zürich.* Scottdale, Pa.: Herald Press, 1975, 156 pp.
Ruth, John L. *'Twas Seeding Time: A Mennonite View of the American Revolution.* Scottdale, Pa.: Herald Press, 1976, 224 pp.
Verduin, Leonard. *The Reformers and Their Stepchildren.* Grand Rapids, Mich.: Wm. B. Eerdmans, 1964.
Wenger, John C. *Even Unto Death.* Richmond, Va.: John Knox Press, 1961, 127 pp.
Williams, George H. *Spiritual and Anabaptist Writers.* Philadelphia: Westminster Press, 1957, 421 pp.
Williams, George H. *The Radical Reformation.* Philadelphia, Pa.: Westminster Press, 1962, 924 pp.
Yoder, John H., translator and editor. *The Legacy of Michael Sattler.* Scottdale, Pa.: Herald Press, 1973, 183 pp.

II. MENNO SIMONS: THE NETHERLANDS: CHAPTER II, pp. 53-73; CHAPTER IV, pp. 103-146.

Armour, Rollin S. *Anabaptist Baptism.* Scottdale, Pa.: Herald Press, 1966, 214 pp.
The Believers' Church: Proceedings of the Study Conference, August 23-25, 1955. Newton, Kans.: Faith and Life Press, 246 pp.
Bender, Ross. *The People of God: A Theological Study of the Free Church Tradition.* Scottdale, Pa.: Herald Press, 1971, 208 pp.
Dirk, Philips. *Enchiridion or Handbook of the Christian Doctrine and Religion.* Aylmer, Ont.: Pathway Publishing Corporation, 1966, 539 pp.
Dosker, Henry E. *The Dutch Anabaptists.* Philadelphia, Pa.: Judson Press, 1921, 310 pp.
Durnbaugh, Donald F. *The Believers' Church: The History and Character of Radical Protestantism.* New York: Macmillan Company, 1970, 315 pp.
Dyck, C. J., ed. *A Legacy of Faith. The Heritage of Menno Simons.* Newton, Kans.: Faith and Life Press, 1962, 260 pp.
Friedmann, Robert. *The Theology of Anabaptism.* Scottdale, Pa.: Herald Press, 1973, 183 pp.
Gleysteen, Jan, compiler-editor. *The Drama of the Martyrs.* From the death of Jesus Christ up to the recent times. Engravings by Jan Luyken (1649-1712). Lancaster, Pa.: Mennonite Historical Associates, 1975, 141 pp.
Horsch, John. *Menno Simons. His Life, Labors, and Teachings.* Scottdale, Pa.: Mennonite Publishing House, 1916.
Horst, Irvin B. *The Radical Brethren, Anabaptism and the English Reformation to 1558.* Nieuwkoop: B. de Graaf, 1972, 211 pp.
Keeney, William E. *The Development of Dutch Anabaptist Thought.* Neiuwkoop: B. de Graaf, 1968, 247 pp.
Klaassen, Walter; Keeney, William; Mast, Russell; Neufeld, Vernon; and Krahn, Cornelius. *No Other Foundation. Commemorative Essays on Menno Simons.* North Newton, Kans.: Bethel College, 1962, 76 pp.
Krahn, Cornelius. *Dutch Anabaptism. Origin, Spread, Life and Thought.* (1450-1600). The Hague: Martinus Nijhoff, 1968, 303 pp.
Krahn, Cornelius, *Menno Simons.* Ein Beitrag zur Geschichte und Theologie der Taufgesinnten. Karlsruhe, 1936, 190 pp.
Littell, Franklin H. *The Anabaptist View of the Church.* Boston: Starr King Press, 1958, 229 pp.

Littell, Franklin H. *A Tribute to Menno Simons.* Scottdale, Pa.: Herald Press, 1956, 72 pp.
Menno Simons. *The Complete Writings.* Scottdale, Pa.: Herald Press, 1956, 1,104 pp.
Shelly, Maynard, ed. *Studies in Church Discipline.* Newton, Kans.: Mennonite Publication Office, 1958.
Verheyden, A. L. E. *Anabaptism in Flanders,* 1530-1650. Scottdale, Pa.: Herald Press, 1961.

III. NORTHERN GERMANY: CHAPTER V, pp. 147-187.

Bachmann, P. *Mennoniten in Kleinpolen.* Lemberg, 1934. 404 pp.
Dollinger, R. *Geschichte der Mennoniten in Schleswig-Holstein, Hamburg und Lübeck.* Neumünster i.H., 1930. 219 pp.
Mannhardt, H. G. *Die Danziger Mennonitengemeinden, ihre Entstehung und ihre Geschichte von 1596-1919.* Danzig, 1919.
Mannhardt, Johann Wilhelm. *Die Wehrfreiheit der altpreussischen Mennoniten.* Marienburg, 1863.
Mezinski, K. *From the History of the Mennonites in Poland.* Warsaw: Akademia Rolniza, 1975. 83 pp.
Müller, J. P. *Die Mennoniten in Ostfriesland vom 16. bis zum 18. Jahrhundert.* Emden, 1887.
Münte, Heinz. *Das Altonaer Handelshaus van der Smissen 1682-1824. Ein Beitrag zur Wirtschaftesgeschichte der Stadt Altona.* Altona, 1932. 172 pp.
Penner, Horst. *Ansiedlung mennonitischer Niederländer im Weichselmündungsgebiet...* Weierhof, 1940.
Penner, Horst. *Die ost-und westpreussischen Mennoniten in ihrem religiösen und sozialen Leben in ihren kulturellen und wirtschaftlichen Leistungen. Teil I. 1526 bis 1772.* Weierhof, 1978. 500 pp.
Penner, Horst. "The West Prussian Mennonites Through Four Centuries," *Mennonite Quarterly Review.* Goshen, Ind.: vol. XXIII, October 1949.
Postma, J. S. *Das niederländische Erbe der preussisch-russländischen Mennoniten in Europa, Asien und Amerika.* Marburg, 1958. 187 pp.
Reimer, Gustav. *Die Familiennamen der westpreussischen Mennoniten.* Weierhof, 1940.
Roosen, Berend Carl. *History of the Mennonite Community of Hamburg and Altona.* Salt Lake City, Utah: 1974. p. 76.
Schreiber, William I. *The Fate of the Prussian Mennonites.* Göttingen, 1955.
Unruh, B. H. *Die niederländisch-niederdeutschen Hintergründe der mennonitischen Ostwanderungen.* Karlsruhe, 1955.
Wiebe, Herbert. *Das Siedlungswerk niederländischer Mennoniten im Weichseltal zwischen Fordon und Weissenberg bis zum Ausgang des 18. Jahrhunderts.* 213 pp.

IV. RUSSIA: CHAPTER VIII, pp. 249-356

Bekker, Jacob P. *Origin of the Mennonite Brethren Church.* Hillsboro, Kans.: Mennonite Brethren Publishing House, 1973, 215 pp.
Belk, Fred R. *The Great Trek of the Russian Mennonites to Central Asia 1880-1884.* Scottdale, Pa.: Herald Press, 1976, 251 pp.
De Fehr, Cornelius A. *Memories of My Life.* Altona, Man.: D. W. Friesen &

Sons, 1967, 231 pp.
Duerksen, Martin. *Die Krim war unsere Heimat*. Winnipeg, Man.: 1977, 323 pp.
Dyck, Arnold. *Lost in the Steppes*. Steinbach, Man.: Derksen Publisher, 1974, 354 pp.
Dyck, Peter P. *Orenburg am Ural*. Die Geschichte einer mennonitischen Ansiedlung in Russland. Clearbrook, B.C.: 1951, 160 pp.
Ehrt, Adolf. *Das Mennonitentum in Russland von seiner Einwanderung bis zur Gegenwart*. Langensalza: 1932.
Epp, D. H. *Die Chortitzer Mennoniten*. Odessa, 1889.
Epp, D. H. *Sketches from the Pioneer Years of the Industry in the Mennonite Settlements of South Russia*. Leamington, Ont.: 1972, 80 pp.
Epp, D. H. *Johann Cornies*. Züge aus seinem Leben und Wirken. 1909, 223 pp.
Fast, Gerhard. *Das Ende von Chortitza*. Winnipeg, Man.: Selbstverlag, 1973, 151 pp.
Friesen, P. M. *The Mennonite Brotherhood in Russia* (1789-1910). Translated from the German. Fresno, Calif.: 1978, 1,065 pp.
Froese, L. *Das pädagogische Kultursystem* der mennonitischen Siedlergruppe in Russland. Göttingen, 1949.
Görz, H. *Die Molotschnaer Ansiedlung, Entstehung, Entwicklung und Untergang*. Steinbach, Man.: Echo-Verlag, 1951, 211 pp.
Hein, Gerhard, ed. *Ufa: The Mennonite Settlements in Ufa, 1894-1938*. Winnipeg, Man.: 1977, 176 pp.
Hiebert, P. C. and Miller, Orie. *Feeding the Hungry*. Russia Famine, 1919-1925. Scottdale, Pa.: 1929.
Isaac, Franz. *Die Molotschnaer Mennoniten*. Halbstadt, 1908.
Klassen, Elizabeth Suderman. *Trailblazer for the Brethren, the Story of Johann Claassen, a Leader in the Early Mennonite Brethren Church*. Scottdale, Pa.: Herald Press, 1978, 309 pp.
Neufeld, D. *The Russian Dance of Death*. Revolution and Civil War in the Ukraine. Translated from German by Al Reimer. Winnipeg, Man.; 142 pp.
Nickel, Katherine. *Seed from the Ukraine*. New York: Pageant Press, 1952, 113 pp.
Peters, Victor. *Nestor Makhno*. The Life of an Anarchist. Winnipeg, Man.: Echo Books, 133 pp.
Priess, Anita. *Exiled to Siberia*. Steinbach, Man.: Derksen Printers, 1972, 82 pp.
Quiring, Walter and Bartel, Helen. *In the Fullness of Time*. 150 Years of Mennonite Sojourn in Russia. Waterloo, Ont.: 212 pp. (Illustrated).
Rempel, David G. *The Mennonite Commonwealth in Russia:* A Sketch of its Founding and Endurance, 1789-1919. Reprint from *Mennonite Quarterly Review*, October 1973, and January 1974, 99 pp.
Rimland, Ingrid. *The Wanderers: The Saga of Three Women Who Survived*. St. Louis: Concordia, 1977, 323 pp.
Schrag, Martin. *The European History of the Swiss Mennonites from Volhynia*. North Newton, Kans.: 128 pp.
Smith, C. H. *The Coming of the Russian Mennonites*. Berne, Ind.: 1927.
Stumpp, Karl. *The Emigration from Germany to Russia in the Years 1768 to 1862*. Tübingen: Stumpp, 1978, 1,018 pp.
Sudermann, L. *From Russia to America: In Search of Freedom*. Tr. by E. F. Suderman. Steinbach, Man.: 1974, 47 pp.
Toews, John B. *Lost Fatherland:* The Story of the Mennonite Emigration

from Soviet Russia, 1921-1927. Scottdale, Pa.: Herald Press, 1967, 262 pp.
Toews, John B., ed. *The Mennonites in Russia from 1917 to 1930;* Selected Documents. Winnipeg, Man.: The Christian Press, 1975, 503 pp.
Toews, J. C. and Klippenstein, L. *Manitoba Mennonite Memories.* Altona, Man.: Manitoba Centennial Committee, 1974, 254 pp.
Willms, H. J., ed. *At the Gates of Moscow.* Translated by George Thielman. Yarrow, B.C.: 1964, 215 pp.

AMERICA

V. FIRST SETTLEMENTS AND EXPANSION, THE NINETEENTH CENTURY WESTWARD EXPANSION, PENNSYLVANIA GERMAN GROUPS, CHAPTER IX, pp. 359-379; CHAPTER X, pp. 381-393; CHAPTER XI, pp. 395-424

Bachman, C. G. *The Old Order Amish of Lancaster County.* Norristown, Pa.: 1942.
Brumbaugh, M. G. *The Life and Works of Christopher Dock.* Philadelphia, Pa.: 1908.
Brunk, A. *History of Mennonites in Virginia,* 1727-1900. Park View, Harrisonburg, Va.: H. A. Brunk, 1959. vol. I, 1972, vol. II.
Burkholder, L. J. *A Brief History of the Mennonites in Ontario.* Markham, Ont.: 1933.
Coffman, Barbara F. *His Name Was John* (Coffman). The Life Story of an Early Mennonite Leader. Scottdale, Pa.: Herald Press, 353 pp.
Diffenderfer, Frank Ried. *The German Immigration into Pennsylvania.* Baltimore: Genealogical Pub., 1977, 328 pp.
Erb, Paul. *South Central Frontiers.* A History of the South Central Conference. Scottdale, Pa.: Herald Press, 1974, 448 pp.
Gingerich, Melvin. *The Mennonites in Iowa.* Iowa City, Iowa: State Historical Society, 1939.
Gingerich, Orland. *The Amish of Canada.* Waterloo, Ont.: Conrad Press, 1972, 244 pp.
Horst, Samuel L. *Mennonites in the Confederacy;* A Study in Civil Pacifism. Scottdale, Pa.: Herald Press, 1967, 148 pp.
Hostetler, John A. *Hutterite Society.* Baltimore, Md.: Johns Hopkins Press, 1963, 347 pp.
Hostetler, John A. and Huntington, Gertrude Enders. *Children in Amish Society;* Socialization and Community Education. New York: Holt, Rinehart and Winston, Inc., 1971, 119 pp.
Smith, C. Henry. *The Mennonites of America.* Goshen, Ind.: 1909, 484 pp.
Smith, C. Henry. *The Mennonites.* Berne, Ind. 1920, 340 pp.
Smith, C. Henry. *The Mennonite Immigration to Pennsylvania in the Eighteenth Century.* Norristown, Pa.: 1929.
Stoltzfus, Grant M. *Mennonites of the Ohio and Eastern Conference. From the Colonial Period in Pennsylvania to 1968.* Scottdale, Pa.: Herald Press, 1969, 459 pp.
Studer, Gerald C. *Christopher Dock: Colonial Schoolmaster.* Scottdale, Pa.: Herald Press, 1967, 445 pp.
Umble, John. *Mennonite Pioneers.* Scottdale, Pa.: 1940.
Weaver, M. G. *Mennonites of Lancaster Conference.* Scottdale, Pa.: 1931.
Weber, H. F. *Centennial History of the Mennonites of Illinois.* Goshen, Ind.: 1931.

Wenger, John C. *History of the Mennonites of the Franconia Conference.* Telford, Pa.: 1937.
Wenger, John C. *The Mennonites in Indiana-Michigan Conference.* Scottdale, Pa.: Herald Press, 1961.
Wenger, John C. *The Mennonite Church in America;* Sometimes known as the Old Mennonite Church. Scottdale, Pa.: Herald Press, 1967, 384 pp.

VI. RUSSO-GERMAN GROUPS, IN SEARCH OF FREEDOM OF CONSCIENCE: CHAPTER XII, pp. 425-472; CHAPTER XIII, pp. 473-506

Baerg, Justina, ed. *History of Manitoba Mennonite Women in Mission, 1942-1977: Commemorating 35 Years of Caring and Sharing.* Winnipeg, Man.: 1977, 96 pp.
Epp, Frank H. *Mennonite Exodus.* Altona, Man.: D. W. Friesen & Sons, 1962, 571 pp.
Epp, Frank H. *Mennonites in Canada*, 1786-1920. vol. I. Toronto: Macmillan of Canada, 1974, 480 pp.
Fast, Karl and Unruh, G. G., eds. *Fiftieth Anniversary of the Mennonite Settlement in North Kildonan, 1928-1978.* Winnipeg, Man.: 1978, 128 pp.
Francis, E. K. *In Search of Utopia: The Mennonites in Manitoba.* Altona, Man.: D. W. Friesen & Sons, 1955, 294 pp.
Fretz, J. Winfield. *Immigrant Group Settlements in Paraguay.* North Newton, Kans.: Bethel College, 1962, 194 pp.
Gaeddert, Albert M. *Hoffnungsau Mennonite Church.* 1874-1974. Centennial History, 1974, 143 pp.
Gerbrandt, Henry J. *Adventure in Faith: The Background and Development of the Bergthal Mennonite Church of Manitoba.* Altona, Man.: D. W. Friesen & Sons Ltd., 1970, 379 pp.
Hack, Hendrik. *Indianer und Mennoniten im Paraguayischen Chaco.* Amsterdam: 1976, 161 pp.
Harvest. Anthology of Mennonite Writing in Canada, 1874-1974. Gretna, Man.: Centennial Committee, 1974, 182 pp.
Hiebert, Clarence. *The Holdeman People: The Church of God in Christ, Mennonite*, 1859-1969. 1973, 663 pp.
Kaufman, Edmund C. *General Conference Mennonite Pioneers.* North Newton, Kans.: Bethel College, 1973, 438 pp.
Klippenstein, Lawrence and Toews, Julius G., ed. *Manitoba Mennonite Memories, Settling in Western Canada.* Winnipeg, Man.: 1977, 342 pp.
Krahn, Cornelius. *From the Steppes to the Prairies.* Newton, Kans.: 1949.
Krahn, Cornelius and Schmidt, John F., ed. *A Century of Witness.* Newton, Kans.: Mennonite Publication Office, 1959.
Krause, Annemarie Elisabeth. *Mennonite Settlement in the Paraguayan Chaco.* Chicago: 1952, 143 pp.
Krehbiel, Christian. *Prairie Pioneer.* The Christian Krehbiel Story. Newton, Kans.: Faith and Life Press, 1962.
Krehbiel, H. P. *History of the General Conference of the Mennonite Church of North America.* vol. I. St. Louis, Mo.: 1898, and vol. II, Newton, Kans.: 1938.
Lohrenz, Gerhard. *Heritage Remembered.* Winnipeg, Man.: CMBC (Canadian Mennonite Bible College) Publications, 1974, 232 pp.
Lohrenz, Gerhard. *The Mennonites in Western Canada.* Steinbach,

Man.: 1974, 52 pp.

Minnich, R. H. *The Mennonite Immigrant Communities in Parana, Brazil.* Cuernavaca, Mex.: Centro Intercultural de Documentacion, 1970, 384 pp.

Minnich, R. H.; Smith, W. H.; Stahl, W. *Mennonites in Latin America.* An Annotated Bibliography: 1912-1971. Reprint M.Q.R., April, 1972, pp. 177-235.

Pannabecker, S. F. *Faith in Ferment.* A History of the Central District Conference. Newton, Kans.: Faith and Life Press, 1968, 385 pp.

Pannabecker, S. F. *Open Doors: The History of the General Conference Mennonite Church.* Newton, Kans.: Faith and Life Press, 1975, 462 pp.

Poettcker, Henry and Regehr, Rudy A. *Call to Faithfulness: Essays in Canadian Mennonite Studies.* Winnipeg, Man.: CMBC, 1972, 222 pp.

Quiring, Walter. *Mennonites in Canada.* A Pictorial Review. Altona, Man.: D. W. Friesen & Sons, Ltd., 1961, 207 pp.

Quiring, W. *Russlanddeutsche suchen eine Heimat.* Karlsruhe, 1938.

Redekop, Calvin Wall. *The Old Colony Mennonites: Dilemmas of Ethnic Minority Life.* Baltimore, Md.: Johns Hopkins Press, 1969, 302 pp.

Reimer, David P., ed. *Experiences of the Mennonites of Canada During the Second World War: 1939-1945,* 142 pp.

Reimer, Gustav G. and Gaeddert, G. R. *Exiled by the Czar.* Newton, Kans.: Mennonite Publication Office, 1956. (Cornelius Jansen)

Sawatzky, Harry L. *They Sought a Country: Mennonite Colonization in Mexico.* Berkeley: University of California, 1971, 387 pp.

Schrag, Martin. *The European History of the Swiss Mennonites from Volhynia.* North Newton, Kans.: 128 pp.

Smith, C. Henry. *The Coming of the Russian Mennonites.* Berne, Ind.: 1927, 298 pp.

Smith, Willard. *Paraguayan Interlude.* Scottdale, Pa.: Herald Press, 1945, 184 pp.

Stucky, Harley J. *A Century of Russian Mennonite History in America.* North Newton, Kans.: 127 pp.

Suderman, Leonard. *From Russia to America: In Search of Freedom.* Translated by Elmer R. Suderman. Steinbach, Man.: Derksen Printers, 1974, 47 pp.

The Swiss-Germans in South Dakota (From Volhynia to Dakota Territory), 1874-1974. Freeman, S.D.: Pine Hill Press, 1974, 220 pp.

Tiessen, Paul, ed. *People Apart, Portrait of a Mennonite World in Waterloo County.* St. Jacobs, Ont.: 1977, 110 pp.

Toews, J. A. *A History of the Mennonite Brethren Church.* Hillsboro, Kans.: M.B. Publishing House, 1975, 151 pp.

Toews, John B. *Lost Fatherland.* Scottdale, Pa.: Herald Press, 1967, 262 pp.

Toews, Paul, ed. *Pilgrims and Strangers: Essays in Mennonite Brethren History.* Fresno: Center for Mennonite Brethren Studies, 1977, 183 pp.

Unruh, John D. *A Century of Mennonites in Dakota.* 1972, 151 pp.

Warkentin, Abe. *Reflections on Our Heritage.* Steinbach, Man.: Derksen Printers, Ltd., 1971, 371 pp.

Wedel, David C. *The Story of Alexanderwohl.* Goessel, Kans.: 1974, 194 pp.

Wiebe, David V. *They Seek a Country.* Hillsboro, Kans.: Mennonite Brethren Publishing House, 2d ed., 228 pp.

Zacharias, Peter D. *Reinland: An Experience in Community.* Altona, Man.: 1976, 350 pp.

VIII. CULTURAL DEVELOPMENTS, WITNESSING IN WAR AND PEACE: CHAPTER XIV, pp. 507-533; CHAPTER XV, pp. 535-560

Bluffton College. An Adventure in Faith, 1900-1950, 268 pp.
Brumbaugh, M. G. *The Life and Works of Christopher Dock.* Philadelphia: 1908. (1969 Repr. of 1908 edition, New York: Arno Press.)
Brunk, Gerald R. and Lehman, James O. *A Guide to Select Revolutionary War Records Pertaining to Mennonites and Other Pacifist Groups in Southeastern Pennsylvania and Maryland, 1775-1800.* Harrisonburg, Va.: Eastern Mennonite College, 1974, 28 pp.
Burkholder, John R. and Redekop, Calvin, eds. *Kingdom, Cross, and Community.* Scottdale, Pa.: Herald Press, 1976, 323 pp.
Durnbaugh, Donald F., ed. *Every Need Supplied.* Mutual Aid and Christian Community in the Free Churches, 1525-1675. Philadelphia: Temple University Press, 1975, 242 pp.
Durnbaugh, Donald F. *To Serve the Present Age: The Brethren Service Story.* Elgin: Brethren Press, 1975, 224 pp.
Epp, Frank. *Mennonite Peoplehood: A Plea for New Initiatives.* Waterloo: Conrad Press, 1977, 120 pp.
Epp, Frank H. *Education with a Plus. The Story of Rosthern Junior College.* Waterloo, Ont.: Conrad Press, 1975, 450 pp.
Epp, Gerhard K., ed. *Harvest.* An Anthology of Mennonite Writings in Canada, 1874-1974. Winnipeg, Man.: Mennonite Centennial Committee, 1974, 186 pp.
Gingerich, Melvin. *Mennonite Attire Through Four Centuries.* Breinigsville, Pa.: Pennsylvania German Society, 1980, 192 pp.
Gingerich, Melvin. *Service for Peace.* A History of Mennonite Civilian Public Service. Akron, Pa.: Mennonite Central Committee, 1949, 508 pp.
Hartzler, John E. *Education Among the Mennonites of America.* Danvers, Ill.: 1925, 195 pp.
Hernley, H. Ralph. *The Compassionate Community.* Scottdale, Pa.: Association of Mennonite Aid, 1970, 573 pp.
Hershberger, Guy F. *The Mennonite Church in the Second World War.* Scottdale, Pa.: Herald Press, 1952.
Hershberger, Guy F. *War, Peace and Nonresistance.* Scottdale, Pa.: Herald Press, 1969, 382 pp.
Hiebert, Clarence, ed. *Brothers in Deed to Brothers in Need.* A Scrapbook about Mennonite Immigrants from Russia, 1870-1885. Newton, Kans.: Faith and Life Press, 1974, 469 pp.
Hiebert, P. C. and Miller, Orie O. *Feeding the Hungry* (in Russia). Scottdale, Pa.: Herald Press, 1929.
Horst, Samuel L. *Mennonites in the Confederacy: A Study in Civil War Pacifism.* Scottdale, Pa.: Herald Press, 1967, 148 pp.
Janzen, A. E. *A History of Tabor College.* Hillsboro, Kans.: Mennonite Brethren Publishing House, 1956, 40 pp.
Juhnke, James C. *A People of Mission.* A History of the General Conference Mennonite Overseas Missions. Newton, Kans.: Faith and Life Press, 1979, 280 pp.
Juhnke, James C. *A People of Two Kingdoms.* The Political Acculturation of the Kansas Mennonites. Newton, Kans.: Faith and Life Press, 1975, 215 pp.
Kadelbach, Ada. *Die Hymnodie der Mennoniten in Nordamerika* (1742-

1860). Eine Studie zur Verpflanzung, Bewahrung und Umformung europäischer Kirchenliedertradition. Published by author, Mainz, 1971, 175 pp.

Kauffman, J. Howard and Harder, Leland. *Anabaptists Four Centuries Later. A Profile of Five Mennonite and Brethren in Christ Denominations.* Scottdale, Pa.: Herald Press, 1975.

Kaufman, Edna Ramseyer and the Bethel College Women's Association. *Melting Pot of Mennonite Cookery, 1874-1974.* Newton, Kans.: Bethel College Women's Association, 1974, 372 pp.

Kaufman, E. G. *The Development of the Missionary and Philanthropic Interest Among the Mennonites of North America.* Berne, Ind.: 1931, 416 pp.

Kaufman, Donald D. *What Belongs to Caesar? A Discussion on the Christian's Response to Payment of War Taxes.* Scottdale, Pa.: Herald Press, 1969, 128 pp.

Kaufman, Donald D. *The Tax Dilemma: Praying for Peace, Paying for War.* Scottdale, Pa.: Herald Press, 1978, 104 pp.

Klassen, A. J., ed. *The Seminary Story: Twenty Years of Education in Mission, 1955-1975.* Fresno, Calif.: Mennonite Brethren Biblical Seminary, 1975.

Kollmorgen, W. M. *Culture of a Contemporary Rural Community: The Old Order Amish of Lancaster County.* Pennsylvania, Washington, D.C., 1942.

Kraybill, Donald B. *Mennonite Education: Issues, Facts and Changes.* Scottdale, Pa.: Herald Press, 1978, 77 pp.

Lapp, John Allen. *The Mennonite Church in India, 1897-1962.* Scottdale, Pa.: Herald Press, 1972, 278 pp.

Lapp, John A., ed. *Peacemakers in a Broken World.* Scottdale, Pa.: Herald Press, 1969, 159 pp.

Lehman, James O. *Creative Congregationalism: Oak Grove Mennonite Church.* Smithville, Ohio: Oak Grove, 1978, 320 pp.

Lohrenz, Gerhard. *The Fateful Years, 1913-1923.* Winnipeg: 1978, 142 pp.

Miller, Mary. *A Pillar of Cloud. The Story of Hesston College, 1909-1959.* 260 pp.

Minnich, Reynolds Herbert. *The Mennonite Immigrant Communities in Parana, Brazil.* Cuernavaca, Mex.: Centro Intercultural de Documentacion, 1970, 384 pp.

Peachey, Paul. *The Church in the City.* Newton, Kans.: Faith and Life Press, 1963, 115 pp.

Pellman, H. R. *Eastern Mennonite College, 1917-1967.* Harrisonburg, Va.: Eastern Mennonite College.

Ratzlaff, Harold. *Fellowship in the Gospel: India, 1900-1950.* Newton, Kans.: Mennonite Publishing Office, 1950, 164 pp.

Showalter, Mary E. *Mennonite Community Cookbook.* Philadelphia: Winston, 1957, 494 pp.

Smucker, Donovan E., ed. *The Sociology of Canadian Mennonites, Hutterites, and Amish, A Bibliography with Annotations.* Waterloo, Ont.: 1977, 506 pp.

Sprunger, Keith L.; Juhnke, James C.; and Waltner, John D. *Voices Against War. A Guide to the Schowalter Oral History Collection on World War I. Conscientious Objection.* North Newton, Kans.: Bethel College, 1973, 190 pp.

Studer, Gerald C. *Christopher Dock: Colonial Schoolmaster.* Scottdale, Pa.: Herald Press, 1967, 445 pp.

Toews, J. A. *A History of the Mennonite Brethren Church*. Pilgrims and Pioneers. Hillsboro, Kans.: Mennonite Brethren Publishing House, 1975, 540 pp.

Toews, J. J. *The Mennonite Brethren Mission in Latin America*. General Conference of the Mennonite Brethren Church of North America, 1975, 255 pp.

Toews, J. B. *The Mennonite Brethren Church in Zaire*. Fresno: Mennonite Brethren Board of Christian Literature, 1978, 255 pp.

Unruh, John C. *In the Name of Christ*. A History of the Mennonite Central Committee and its Service, 1920-1951. Scottdale, Pa.: Herald Press, 1952.

Weaver, Edwin and Irene. *From Kuku Hill: Among Indigenous Churches in West Africa*. Elkhart: Institute of Mennonite Studies, 1975, 128 pp.

Wedel, David C. *The Story of Alexanderwohl*. Goessel, Kans.: Goessel Centennial Committee, 1974, 194 pp.

Wedel, P. J. *The Story of Bethel College*. North Newton, Kans.: Bethel College, 1954, 632 pp.

Wedel, Walter. *Nur zwanzig Kilometer*. Eine Jugend in den russischen Wäldern. R. Brockhaus. Wuppertal, 1979, 221 pp.

Weissman, Benjamin M. *Herbert Hoover and Famine Relief to Soviet Russia: 1921-1923*. Stanford, Calif.: Hoover Institution Press, 1974, 255 pp.

Wellenreuther, Hermann. *Glaube und Politik in Pennsylvania, 1681-1776*. Wien: Böhlau Verlag, 1972, 475 pp.

Wiebe, David V. *They Seek a Country*. A Survey of Mennonite Migrations. Hillsboro, Kans.: Mennonite Brethren Publishing House, 1974, 228 pp.

Yoder, John Howard. *The Christian Witness to the State*. Newton, Kans.: Faith and Life Press, 1964.

Yoder, John Howard. *The Original Revolution;* Essays on Christian Pacifism. Scottdale, Pa.: Herald Press, 1971, 189 pp.

Yoder, John Howard. *The Politics of Jesus*. Grand Rapids, Mich.: Wm. B. Eerdmans, 1972, 260 pp.

Yoder, S. C. *For Conscience' Sake*. A Study of Mennonite Migrations Resulting from the World War. Scottdale, Pa.: Herald Press, 1945, 300 pp.

Index

A

Aachen, 160
Aargau, Switzerland, 75
Abbotsford, B.C., 530
Abraham, Galen, 121
Acculturation, 511, 513
Afghanistan Border, 346
Agricultural Machinery, 307
Agriculture, 261, 415. *See also* Farming
Ahleheld, Bartholomäus von, 70, 154
Ainsworth, Henry, 123
Aken, Gillis van, 64, 69
Ak Mechet, Asia, 296-97
Alberta, 455, 475
Alexander, Czar, 264, 296
Alexandertal, 260
Alexanderwohl, Russia, 258, 272, 289, 291, 293, 428, 464
Alexandrovsk, Russia, 307
Algemeene Doopsgezinde Sociëteit, 116, 138, 139, 152
Allgemeine Bundeskonferenz, 328, 479
Allianz, 454
Allianz-Gemeinde, 283
All-Mennonite Convention, 471, 532
All-Union Council of Evangelical Christian Baptists (AUCECB), 343
Alma Ata, 346
Alsace-Lorraine, 18, 77, 79, 84, 196, 209-211, 215, 384, 409
Alternative Service System, 446, 482
Ältester (Elder), 419
Alt-Mennoniten, 422
Altona, 139, 154, 156, 283
Alt-Samara, 260
Alva, Duke, 106
America, 359ff.; North, 283; South, 283
American Friends Service Committee, 550
American Mennonite Relief (AMR), 319
American Red Cross, 319
American Relief Administration (ARA), 319
Amish, 73, 84, 91-92, 161, 207, 208, 211, 212, 214, 261, 371, 376, 382, 383, 389, 392, 409, 422, 459; Names, 371, 390, 391; Old Order, 406
Amish-Mennonite, 411
Ammann, Jakob, 73, 84, 211, 213, 228, 409, 415
Amsterdam, 43, 78, 79, 91, 92, 123, 125, 129, 131, 136, 166, 170, 202, 317, 367, 559
Amstutz, D., 142
Amur River, 335, 493
Anabaptism, 12, 17, 123; Essentials of, 14; High Standards, 18
Anabaptists, 3-6, 10, 16-19, 21, 24, 30, 43, 50, 55, 59, 73, 121, 228; Doctrines, 63
Andreas, Johann, 458

Anna, Countess, 52, 60, 150
Anslo, Cornelis Claesz, 130
Antonovka, Russia, 260
Antwerp, 65, 106, 166
Anwohner (Landless), 266
Apostolic Christian Church, 413
Apostolic Church, 14
Apostool, Samuel, 119, 129
Appenzell, Switzerland, 12, 75
Arapahoe Indians, 467
Argentina, 445
Arizona, 435, 467
Arkadak, Russia, 267
Armendiener, 174
Arminianism, 118
Arndt, Johann, 243
Arnold, Eberhard, 457
Artists, 128-29
Ascherham, Gabriel, 37
Associated Mennonite Biblical Seminaries, 424
Asuncion, Paraguay, 492
Atchison, Topeka, and Santa Fe Railroad, 431
Augsburg, 19-21, 23, 28, 227
Augsburger, Christian, 389; Myron, 516
Auhagen, 493
Aulie Ata, 295, 296, 298
Ausbund, 32, 40, 76, 77, 92, 98, 99, 159, 215, 410, 517, 528
Auspitz, 38, 234
Austerlitz, 36
Austria, 10, 12, 13, 21, 27, 31, 193, 208
Avoidance, 50, 66, 68, 70, 111, 195, 274. See also Ban

B

Bachman, 261; Arnold, 209
Backnang, 186, 187, 206, 220
Backereel, Hermes, 62, 63
Baer, J. B., 467
Bakersfield, 435
Ban, 65, 66, 68, 69, 113, 133. See also Avoidance
Baptism, Adult, 9, 14, 22, 23, 29, 34, 45, 55, 61, 94, 102, 133, 135, 139, 279, 344, 386, 410; **Immersion**, 14, 276, 283, 343, 408; Infant, 34, 193
Baptists, 121, 123, 342, 345

Barth, Karl and Marcus, 102
Bartsch, Franz, 309; Johann, 251, 254
Basel, Switzerland, 4, 19, 20, 75, 95, 98, 216, 271
Batenburg, Jan van, 51
Batenburger, 52, 60, 62, 68, 150, 158
Baumgartner, Christian, 96; Daniel, 385
Bavaria, 18, 19, 37, 191, 203, 207, 384, 387, 458
Beachy, Amish, 73, 414, 416
Beachy, Moses M., 414
Beards, 98, 373, 415
Beatrice, Nebr., 299, 449, 458
Bebber, Matthias van, 365
Bechterdissen, 186, 220
Beckeraths, 163
Beissel, Conrad, 370
Bekker, Jakob P., 279
Belfort, 216
Believer's Baptism, 24, 139
Bench, 418
Bender, H. S., 422, 423
Berdyansk, 263, 278, 286
Bergmann, Abraham, 302
Bergthal, 267, 289, 292, 293, 436, 440
Bergthal Mennonites, 438, 440, 443, 489
Bergzabern, 20
Berlin, 181, 186, 220, 271
Bern, Switzerland, 75-79, 95
Berne, Ind., 385
Bernese Council, 82, 87, 88, 93
Bethania Old People's Home, 308, 447
Bethel College, 434, 521, 559
Bethel Deaconess Home and Hospital, 434
Bethesda Hospital, Goessel, 434
Betzner, Samuel, 377
Bible, 3, 5, 14, 15, 193, 277, 507, 508, 522
Bibra, Hans von, 26
Bidloo, Lambert, 130
Bidloo, Nicolaas, 129
Bienenberg, 216
Biestkens Bible, 126, 174
Bildung, De, 514
Binnerts, A., 318
Bishop, 419, 509
Bismarck, 182

INDEX 575

Black Sea, 263
Blauärmel, Philip, 37
Blaurock, Georg, 7, 9, 13, 14, 31, 35
Bluffton, Ohio, 385, 464, 523
Blumenau, 500
Board of Colonization, *See* Canadian Mennonite Board of Colonization
Bocholt, 51
Boeckbinder, Bartel de, 44
Boehm, Martin, 370, 399
Bohemia, 33
Bolivia, 492
Bolsward, 57
Bommel, Herman van, 166
Borozenko, Russia, 267, 292
Bote, Der, 480
Botschafter, Der, 301, 309
Botschafter der Wahrheit, 405
Bouwens, Leenaert, 65, 66, 68, 69
Brabant, 166
Bradford, William, 123
Brandordnung, 441
Braght, Tieleman Jansz van, 76, 126, 210
Brandt, G., 105
Braun, Heinrich, 281; Peter, 281
Brazil, 334, 445, 492, 500, 559
Breadbreakers, 283
Brechbill, Benedikt, 89, 367
Breitinger, 80
Bremer, Henk, 559
Brenneman, Daniel, 406, 408, 409
Brethren, 9-11, 17, 73
Brethren in Christ, 408
Brewster, William, 123
Brief Confession of Faith, 127
British Columbia, 479, 480
Brons, Anna, 151; Isaac, 151
Brook Lane Farm, 558
Brötli, Hans, 6, 8, 9, 11, 14
Browne, Robert, 122
Brubacher, Hans, 14
Brücke, Die, 504
Brüdergemeinde, 278
Bruderhof, 37, 196, 229, 230, 232, 238, 247, 455, 457
Brudertal Mennonite Church, 427
Brunk, Henry G., 425
Brünn, 37
Bucer, Martin, 19, 22
Bucharest, 244
Bucks County, Pa., 365

Buhr, Cornelius, 289
Bukhara, 296
Buller, Jakob, 289, 293, 428
Bullinger, Heinrich, 5, 50, 55
Burghalter, Hans, 199, 200, 367, 370
Burkholder Amish, 414
Buttons, 134, 415

C

Cabinet Order, 181, 183
Calgary, Alberta, 481
Calvin, John, 72, 507
Camp Funston, 541, 547
Canada, 186, 248, 290, 335, 340, 345, 346, 376, 427, 460, 473, 488, 539, 549
Canadian Laws, 538
Canadian Mennonite Bible College, 447, 480, 522
Canadian Mennonite Board of Colonization, 321, 323, 444, 469, 474, 483
Canadian Pacific Railway, 321, 474, 477, 483
Capito, Wolfgang, 19, 22
Capper, Arthur, 547
Cardenas, President, 488
Carinthia, 31, 189, 244
Carleton, Mark A., 432
Cassel, D. K., 527
Castelberger, Andreas, 8
Catherine II of Russia, 179, 249, 257, 288
Catholics, 3, 10, 12, 15, 17, 25, 29, 42, 107, 226, 332, 419, 507
Cattepoel, Dirk, 164
Caucasus Mountains, 280, 304
Central Asia, 294, 342
Central Conference of Mennonites, 411, 412
Chaco, 334, 340, 489, 495
Charles, Emperor, 27, 31, 59, 103
Cheyenne Indians, 467
Chihuahua, Mexico, 485
Chiliasm, 24, 28, 42
Chortitza, Russia, 252, 258, 263, 268, 291, 305, 307, 316, 323, 331, 336-39, 436, 438, 442, 454; Manitoba, 436-443
Chortitza *Gebietsamt*, 270
Chortitza Mennonite Church, 443

Chortitza *Zentralschule*, 270, 338
Chrischona, 101
Christenpflicht, 219
Christian Living, 423
Christlicher Bundesbote, 480
Christ Seul, 215
Church and State, 137, 341, 535
Church Council, 300
Church Discipline, 66. *See also* Ban, Avoidance
Church of God in Christ, Mennonite, 405, 429, 433, 443
City Missions, 531
Civilian Public Service (CPS), 434, 471, 553-58
Civil Office, 135
Civil Order, 276
Civil War, Russian, 340; U.S., 537
Claassen, David, 289
Clarence Center, N.Y., 387
Clemer, Velte, 370
Cleve, 158
Clothing, 386, 415. *See also* Dress
Coaldale, 479
"Coarse" Mennonites, 113, 133
Coffman, John S., 421; S. F., 473, 483
Collection Boxes, 134
Collectivization Program, 331, 340, 346
Collegiants, 118
Cologne, 62, 158, 160
Commission for Foreign Needs, 88, 136, 367
Communal, Enterprises, 262; Living, 38; Society, 125
Communion, 68, 85, 134, 277, 279
Complete Writings of Menno Simons, 126, 420
Concept of Cologne, 116
Concord, 360
Concordia Hospital, 447
Conestoga, 366
Conference Papers, 530
Confession of Faith, 17, 22, 23, 111, 116, 132, 155, 236, 376, 507, 509
Congregationalism, 125
Congress, 313, 540, 542
Conscientious Objector, The, 544
Conscientious Objectors, 399, 446, 541-48
Conscription, 82; Act, 538, 539, 540, 546, 551; General Law, 427

Constance, 13, 21
Constantin of Russia, 285
Constitution, Written, 402
Conversion, 14, 396, 413
Cooperative, 262, 490, 491, 492
Cooperative Vegetable Oils Limited, 446
Cornelis, Friar, 107
Cornies, Johann, 248, 264, 269, 513
Corporation Paraguay, 496
Council of Churches of Evangelical Christian Baptists (CCECB), 344
Cramer, Samuel, 527
Crefeld, Germany, 139, 161, 163, 359, 360
Crimea, Russia, 293, 304, 315
Cuauhtemoc, Mexico, 486
Culm, Germany, 183, 258, 259
Cultural Life, 308, 479, 512
Cumberland Valley, 373
Cunard, 532; Samuel, 364
Cuper, Dirck, 44
Curitiba, Brazil, 502, 559
Cuyper, Frans de, 64
Czechoslovakia, 243

D

Dahlem, Valentin, 202
Dakotas, 248, 289, 447, 454
Dale, Anton van, 129
Daniel, Book of, 26, 42
Danube, 12
Danzig, 66, 134, 166, 167, 170, 171, 176, 184, 185, 218, 256, 277
Daughter Settlements, Russia, 267
Davidians, 52, 150
Declaration of Independence, 398
Defenseless Mennonites, 413
Deknatel, Jan, 277; Jeme, 130; Johann, 200, 240, 526
Delden Fabric Factory, 503
Delegation of Twelve, Russia to North America, 436
Denk, Hans, 12, 19, 20, 22, 27, 34, 35, 43, 46, 48
Denmark, 41, 155
Denner, Balthasar, 130; Jakob, 156, 277, 526
Dennis, C. S., 474

INDEX

Deutsch-Kazun, Poland, 184, 259
Deutsch-Michalin, Poland, 259
Deutsch-Wymysle, Poland, 184, 259
Deventer, 92
Diet of Speyer, 13, 30
Dirkites, 72
Dirks, Heinrich, 142, 308
Discipline, Church, 68, 84, 175, 274, 396. *See also* Ban, Excommunication
Divisions, 69, 109, 112, 395
Divorce, 69
Dnieper, 251
Dock, Christopher, 519, 526
Dominee, 135
Dompelaar, 156
Doopsgezinde (Mennonites), 9, 51, 72, 113, 115, 133
Dordrecht Confession of Faith, 117, 127, 162
Dress, 386, 415, 418. *See also* Nonconformity, "Plain" Coat
Drinking, 17, 18, 29
Dubrovna, 252, 254
Duma, 302
Dunkards, 361, 370, 538
Durango, 486
Dürer, Albrecht, 24
Dushanbe, 343, 346
Dutch Bible, 512; Colonies, 141; Community, 172; Group, 392; Language, 167, 172, 512
Dyck, Arnold B., 480, 515
Dyck, Gerhard O., 284, 438; Johannes D., 434; Peter and Elfrieda, 498
Dzhambul, 346

E

East Berlin, 186
East Friesland, 43, 52, 60, 105, 147, 150
East Indies, 204
East Prussia, 90, 169
East Reserve, Manitoba, 427, 437, 438, 439
Eastern District Conference, Pa., 401
Eastern Mennonite College, 424, 522
Eby, Benjamin, 379, 407; Hans, 378; Solomon, 407
Ecclesiastical Discipline, 274
Ecclesiological Work Group, 145
Echo Verlag, 480
Ediger, Elmer, 555; H. A., 301; H. E., 306
Eduardsdorf, 261
Education, 396, 434, 443, 514, 518, 521. *See also* Schools, Higher Education
Edzard, Carel, 150
"Egli Amish," 413
Egli, Henry, 412
Eibenschitz, 37
Eichenfeld, 314
Eichstock, Germany, 207, 387
Einlage, Russia, 255
Ekaterinoslav, 307, 311
Elbing, 170, 185, 258
Elbing-Ellerwald, 183
Elder, 134, 140, 181, 419
Elijah, 42, 298
Elkhart, Indiana, 420
Ellenberger, Jacob II, 206
Emden, 43, 44, 66, 69, 139, 149, 166
Emergency Relief Committee, 550
Emigration, 87, 96. *See also* Migrations, Immigrant
Emmaus Mennonite Church, 429
Emmental, Switzerland, 75, 85, 91, 94, 96, 98, 99, 100, 385
Emmerich, 159
Emotionalism, 404. *See also* Pietism, Revival, Evangelism
Enbildung, De, 514
Enchiridion, 66, 525
England, 105, 124
English Baptists, 124
English Language, 396; Preaching, 406
Enkenbach, 186, 187
Enns, Jakob, 275
Enoch, 42, 45
Ephrata, Pa., 370, 557
Epp, Claasz, 260, 296; Claasz, Jr., 294; D. H., 270, 301, 309, 439, 480; David, 256; Heinrich, 285, 438; Peter, 252, 480, 515
Erfurt, Germany, 24
Erhard, Christoph, 51
Ernstweiler, 213
Espelkamp, 186, 220
Essingen, 211

Evangelical Christian Baptists, 343
Evangelical Cups, 21
Evangelical Mennonite Brethren, 283, 500
Evangelical Mennonite Church, 413, 453, 454
Evangelical Mennonites, 404, 407
Evangelism, 283, 419, 421
Ewert, H. H., 441, 459, 473, 483; Wilhelm, 289, 427, 458
Ewy, 261
Excommunication, 113, 274, 406. *See also* Discipline, Church
Exile to Siberia, 1929-40, 336

F

Faith and Life Press, Newton, 471, 529
Family Names, *See* Names
Farming, 95, 264, 271, 530. *See also* Agriculture
Fast, Abraham, 151; Bernhard, 277; H. A., 555; Jakob, 343
Federal Council of Churches, 470
Feeding the Hungry, 317
Ferdinand of Austria, 31, 33, 39
Fernheim, Paraguay, 492, 493, 495, 496
Festival Quarterly, 517
"Fine" Mennonites, 113, 133
Finns, 302
Five Year Plan, 326, 330
Flanders, Netherlands, 103, 110, 114, 166
Flemish, 72, 110, 112, 116, 127, 139, 166, 173, 175, 252, 256, 272, 275; Old, 112
Flickinger, 261
Flinck, Govert, 128
Florisson, Tönnis, 167
Flour Mills, 306, 307
Foot Warmers, 140
Foot Washing, 85, 113, 134, 372
Forestry Service, 299, 310, 481
Formularbuch, 203
Fortbildungsschule, 521
Fort Leavenworth, Kansas, 542-545
Foth, Peter J., 158
Foundation Book, 64, 525
Fox, George, 121, 360

France, 142, 209, 216, 222, 226
Francis of Bolsward, 106
Franck, Sebastian, 12, 19, 24, 43
Franconia, Germany, 24
Franconia Conference, Pa., 422, 460, 510
Franconia Mennonites, 157
Franeker, 69, 116
Frankenhausen, 26
Frankenthal, 157, 192
Frankfurt, Germany, 187, 220; Land Company, 360
Franklin, Benjamin, 364
Franklin Conference (MC), 422
Fraser Valley, B.C., 479, 480
Frederick the Great, 171, 177
Frederick William I, 90, 171, 180
Freeman Junior College, 524
Freerks, Sicke, 43, 55, 149
French Revolution, 94, 201, 202, 210
Fresenburg, 70, 154, 156
Fresno, Calif., 435
Fria, De, 515
Frick, 532
Friedelsheim, Germany, 199, 206
Friedensstimme, 309
Friedrichstadt, Germany, 152, 153
Friesen, A. A., 473; A. P., 306; P. M., 281, 309, 454
Friesland, 103, 110, 166, 494, 498
Frisians, 72, 110, 112, 116, 127, 139, 166, 173, 175, 252, 256, 272, 273; Young, 73
Fröhlich, Samuel, 96
Froschauer Bible, 34, 99
Froschauer, Christoph, 34
Fröse, Peter, 323, 326, 329
Frunze, 346
Fulda, Germany, 24
Funck, Heinrich, 526
Funk, Christian, 397; John F., 286, 420, 422, 430, 526; Joseph, 375
Funkites, 398
Fürsorge-Komitee, 263, 268, 277, 284, 292
Fürstenland, Russia, 292, 293, 304, 436, 438
Fürstenwerder, Prussia, 183

G

Gabor, Bethlen, 239

INDEX

Gabrielists, 38, 40
Gaeddert, Albert, 555; Dietrich, 428
Gainsboro, 124
Galicia, 184, 208, 261, 429, 458
Gebietsamt, 268, 275, 280
Gehman, William, 403
Geiser, Samuel, 99
Gemeentedag, 142
Gemeindeblatt, Das, 205
Gemeinde-Kalender, 205
Gemeinde Unterwegs, 205
General Conference (of Amish), 410
General Conference Mennonite Church, 132, 412, 423, 434, 451, 459, 463, 465, 468, 471, 487, 488, 500, 510, 550; of North America, Founding, 403; in Russia, 300, 302
Gerber, Samuel, 96
German Army, 342; Invasion, 337; Occupation, 337
German Language, 337, 396, 433, 481, 504, 520; High, 167, 447, 512, 513; Low, 447, 504, 512, 513
German Schools, 99; Speaking, 95; Red Cross, 333
Germans, 302; Upper, 73, 112, 127
Germantown, 126, 156, 359, 360, 363, 368, 423
Germany, 12, 24, 28, 142, 147, 220, 222; Northern, 147, 165; South, 10, 12-14, 18, 19, 21, 24, 189, 409; West, 186-187
Gerritsz, Lubbert, 111, 124, 127
Gertrude, Menno Simons's Wife, 59
Gesangbuch, 529
Geschichtsbuch, Hutterite, 236
Gingerich, Melvin, 555
Gladbach, Germany, 159
Glaidt, Oswald, 34
Glückstadt, 153
Gnadenau, Kansas, 428
Gnadenfeld, Russia, 258, 268, 272, 279, 282
Göbel, Ernst, 204
Goch, 159
Goering, 261; Erwin, 555
Goertz, Hans-Jürgen, 223
Goertz, Heinrich, 464
Goerz, David, 427, 448, 465, 521; Franz, 277

Goessel, Kansas, 428
Golden Age, Netherlands, 115, 128, 507; Moravia, 227-37
Goldsmith, Joseph, 389
Gorchakov, Prince, 287
Gorgas, Johannes, 370; William C., 364
Gorter, S. H. N., 502
Goshen College, 424, 522
Gospel Banner, 409
Gospel Herald, 423, 541
Göttingen, 187, 220
Göttner, Erich, 185, 219
Gottschalk, Jacob, 370
Graber, 261
Graffenried, 87
Gramberg, K. P. C. A., 142
Grant, Ulysses S., 289
Graudenz, 259
Grebel, Conrad, 5-9, 11, 13, 17, 35, 48, 423; Jacob, 6
Gretna Mennonite School, 441, 480
Gronau, 139, 151, 503
Groningen, Netherlands, 59, 92, 103, 134, 166
Grubb, N. B. 363, 465
Guanajuato, 487

H

Haan, Galenus Abrahamsz de, 65, 119, 129, 155
Haarlem, 43, 131
Habaner, 241, 243, 245
Habsburg, 31, 189, 226
Haetzer, Ludwig, 4, 6, 8, 12, 13, 17, 19, 20, 22, 43
Hague, The Netherlands, 43, 87
Hague, Saskatchewan, 444
Hahnsau, Russia, 260
Halbstadt, Russia, 258, 268, 291, 301, 307
Halstead, Kansas, 427, 432, 448; Seminary, 433, 449
Hamburg, 71, 139, 152, 153, 154, 165, 271, 277
Hamm, David, 294
Händiges, Emil, 185, 333
Hanseatic Corporation, 334
Hansen, Georg, 276
Harbin, China, 334, 493; Refugees, 334, 335
"Hard Banners," 70

Harder, Bernhard, 513; D. E., 522; Johann, 427
Harding, Vincent, 559
Harlingen, Holland, 92, 113, 116
Harmonia Sacra, 375, 529
Harrisonburg, Virginia, 374
Hartzler, J. S., 527
Haslibacher, Hans, 76
Haury, S. S., 467
Haxberg, Willibald von, 170
Heatwole, R. J., 425
Hege, Christian, 205
Helwys, Thomas, 123
Hendriks, Anneken, 106
Herald of Truth, 420, 421
Herald Press, Scottdale, Pa., 529
Heritage, 396, 509
Hermannstadt, 239, 243
Herold der Wahrheit, 420
Herr, 532; Christian, 370; John, 400, 526
Hershey, 532; Lewis B., 555
Hespeler, William, 287, 289, 436, 438
Hesse, Germany, 24, 37
Hesse-Darmstadt, 384
Hesston College, 424, 434, 523
Het Nut, 137
Heubuden, Germany, 183, 185
Heyden, Count, 285
Hiebert, P. C., 318
Higher Education, 270. See also Education, Schools
Hildebrand, C. H., 305; Peter, 309
Hilfswerk, 220
Hillsboro, Kansas, 434
Himmelsstürmer, 508
Hindenburg, Paul von, 333
History of the Church of God, 405
Hitler, 223
Hoch, Daniel, 404, 407, 460, 526
Hochrütiner, Lorenz, 8, 12
Hochstettler, Jacob, 372
Hofer, 244; Matthias, 245
Hoffmann, Christoph, 282
Hoffnungsau, Kansas, 428
Hoffnungsfeld Church, 428
Hofmann, Melchior, 22, 24, 41, 46, 49, 61, 149
Holdeman, John, 405, 429, 526
Holdemans, 406
Holland, 43, 78, 90, 103, 166, 199, 312, 382
Holstein, 152, 153
Homestead Act, 448
Hooks and Eyes, 98, 386, 415. *See also* Dress, Nonconformity
Hoover, 319
Hopi Indians, 467
Hoeppner, Jakob, 251, 254
Horb, 23
Horodyszcze, 261
Horsch, John, 527
Hospital, 178, 311, 481; at Ekaterinoslav, 311; at Moscow, 311
Hostetler, J. A., 417
Hottinger, Hans, 14
Houtzager, Pieter de, 66
Hubmaier, Balthasar, 4, 5, 8, 11, 13, 14, 19, 22, 25, 27, 33, 34, 48
Huguenots, French, 75
Hungary, 39, 226, 239, 243; Upper, 232
Hunsberger, Ephraim, 382, 460
Hunsicker, Abraham, 403; John, 401, 402
Hut, Hans, 20, 21, 25, 26, 35, 42, 49
Hutter, Jakob, 31, 38, 40, 191, 246
Hutterdorf, 248
Hutterites, 18, 40, 51, 190, 191, 193, 194, 225-28, 232, 233, 235, 239, 242, 245, 247, 261, 289, 409, 454, 456, 459, 528, 539, 549
Hutterthal, 248
Hylkema, T. O., 318
Hymns, 14, 40, 410, 512, 528

I

Ibersheim, Germany, 199, 202; Conference, 202
Idaho, 299, 383
Illinois, 203, 382; Conference of Mennonites, 412
Imbroich, Thomas von, 159
Immigration, 286, 385. *See also* Emigration, Migrations
Imperial Edicts, 22, 30
Incarnation of Christ, 42, 61, 70, 194, 195
Indiana, 382, 383, 412
Indians, 491; Raids, 367; Territory, 467
Indonesia, 206
Industries, 305, 307, 492
Ingoldstadt, 33

INDEX

Initiativniki, 342, 344
Innsbruck, 31, 41, 228
Inquisition, 105
Intermarriage, 271
Internationale Mennonitische Organisation (IMO), 222
"In the Name of Christ," 556
Iowa, 203, 383
Isaac, Franz, 309
Italy, 31

J

Jacobs, Jan, 113-14; Folk, 113
Jacobsz, Lambert, 128
James River, S.D., 230, 248, 454
Jansen, Cornelius, 286, 427, 436, 449; Peter, 459
Jansz, P. A., 142; Pieter, 138, 141
Janz, B. B., 323, 486
Janzen, Jacob H., 480, 514
Java, 142, 308
Jefferson, Thomas, 364
Jena, 271
Jerusalem, 282
Jerusalem Friends, 282
Jesuits, 192, 200, 241
Jews, 200
Johannesruh, 248
John the Steadfast, 30
Joris, David, 51, 68
Judgment Day, 298
Jülich, Germany, 158
Jung-Stilling, 294
Jura, Switzerland, 75, 95, 96, 99, 385
Jushanlee, Russia, 264

K

Kaiserslautern, Germany, 201
Kampen, Holland, 92
Kansas, 289, 299, 383, 385, 405, 425, 427, 429, 447, 448, 520; Conference, 451
Kaplan Bek, Asia, 295
Karaganda, 343, 344, 346
Karlstadt, Andreas, 41
Karolswalde, Volhynia, 260
Kauffman, Daniel, 421, 422, 423
Kauffman Museum, 533

Kaufman, 261; Ed. G., 521
Kaunitz, Barons von, 36
Kazakhstan, 346
Keim, M. W., 425
Keller, Ludwig, 527
Kellogg, Major, 544
Kendig, Benjamin, 382; Martin, 366
Kerensky, 312, 314
Kessler, Johannes, 12, 17
Keulen, Peter van, 114
Kharkov, 270, 307
Khiva, 296, 297, 298
Kingdom of God, 16, 508
Kings View Homes, 558
Kirchen-Konvent, 273
"Kiss of the Lord," 195
Kitchener, Ontario, 377, 478, 557
Kitzbühel, 31, 32
Klaassen, Johann, 142; M., 309
Klassen, C. F., 323, 326, 477; J. P., 480; M., 294; P. J., 480
Kleine Gemeinde Mennonites, 274, 275, 289, 292, 293, 405, 436-39, 441, 443, 445, 451, 453, 488
Kliewer, Fritz, 497, 498, 504
Knipperdolling, Bernhard, 45
Koekebakker, Jacob, 319
Kommerzschule, 270
Kommission für Kirchenangelegenheiten (KfK), 327
Königsberg, 168, 169, 177
Koop, A., 305
Köppenthal, Russia, 260
Kornthal, 278, 280
Kraemer, Gustav, 164
Kratz, Clayton, 318; Maxwell, 318
Krauel, Brazil, 501
Krehbiel, 261; C. E., 465; Christian, 286, 427, 430, 448, 465; Daniel, 461; H. J., 558; H. P., 468, 487, 527; Jakob, 387
Kremenchug, 251
Krimmer Mennonite Brethren, 277, 428, 451
Kroeker, Abraham, 281; Jakob, 281
Kronsgarten, Russia, 256
Kuban, Russia, 267, 280, 304
Kühler, W. J., 105
Kulaks, 329, 331, 336
Kürschner, Christopher, 28
Kutuzovka, Volhynia, 261

L

Labor camps, 342, 346; Unions, 418
Ladekopp, Russia, 258
Lamists, 119
Lancaster Conference, 422
Lancaster County, 366, 367, 369, 373, 378, 381, 382
Landis, Hans, 77
Lange, Johann, 282
Langenmantel, Eitelhans, 19, 21
Langer, Matthias, 31
Langnau, Switzerland, 85
Language, English, 396, 520; See also Dutch, German
Language Barrier, 433
'Lasco, John a, 60, 62, 149
Lausan, 297
League of Nations, 336
Lechfeld, Germany, 323
Lee County, Iowa, 460
Leer, Germany, 149
Leeuwarden, 43, 55, 116
Lemberg, 184, 208, 261
Leningrad, 341
Lenzmann, H. A., 306
Lepp, P. H., 305
Leyden, Jan van, 46, 49, 64
Leyen, von der, 162
Liberalism, 131
Liberty Loan Committee, 549
Library, 138
Liechtenstein, Leonhard von, 28, 33-35, 239
Lohrenz, H. W., 522
Loma Plata, 492
London, 62, 125
Longenecker, Daniel, 370
Lord's Supper, 18, 23, 193, 279
Lorraine, See Alsace-Lorraine
Los Jagueyes, 488
Lot, 203, 410, 418, 510
Lothringen, 213
Low Countries, 43, 46
Low German, See German Language
Lowe, John, 288
Löwen, Heinrich, 503
Löwenberg, Michael, 204
Lübeck, 152, 187
Ludwig, Karl, 79, 197, 199
Ludwigshaven, 206
Luiken, Jan, 128

Luther, Martin, 3, 10, 27, 29, 41, 53, 55, 69, 72
Lutherans, 10, 11, 15, 17, 19, 22, 44, 332, 361, 419, 507

M

Maatschappij tot Nut van't Algemeen, 137
Magistracy, 16, 23, 35, 43, 274, 276
Makhno, Nestor, 314, 315
Malay Mennonite Church, 142
Mander, Carel van, 128
Mändl, Hans, 190
Manitoba, 405, 429, 435, 436, 453, 455, 475, 520
Mannhardt, Hermann, 184; Wilhelm, 181
Manz, Felix, 5, 7, 8, 9, 13
Marbeck, Pilgram, 22, 23, 31
Marienburg, 166, 169, 177, 181, 258
Marriage, 11, 69, 94, 175, 202; Customs, 212; Mixed, 178, 202
Martens, Heinrich, 501; Roelof, 64
Martinites, 407
Martyrs, 105, 190; First, 9
Martyrs Mirror, 23 76, 105, 111, 126, 159, 174, 212, 309, 405, 420, 507, 512, 524, 525, 529
Martyrs' Synod, 20, 21, 28
Matthies, Willi, 344
Matthijsz, Jan, 43, 45, 49, 60
Maxweiler, Germany, 207, 387
Meetinghouses, 14, 98, 114, 115, 134, 140, 272, 415
Mehnert, Klaus, 346
Meidung, 84, 372, 392, 409. See also Avoidance
Melchiorites, 44, 51, 52, 60, 72
Memrick, Russia, 267, 304, 315
Mennisten Infijn, 136
Mennists, 62, 72
Menno Colony, Paraguay, 489, 491, 493, 496
Menno Simons, General, 43, 48, 52-73, 107, 110, 143, 150, 159, 165, 166, 423, 558; Conversion, 44, 55-58; Ordination, 59; Writings, 63-64, 126, 525, 529
Mennonite, Name, 72, 73, 359
Mennonite Aid Committee, 438
Mennonite Biblical Seminary, 523

INDEX

Mennonite Board of Colonization,
See Canadian Mennonite Board
of Colonization
Mennonite Board of Guardians,
428, 430, 448, 450
Mennonite Brethren, 279, 296,
301, 303, 342, 343, 345, 443, 451,
452, 500
Mennonite Brethren Bible
College, 447, 480, 522
Mennonite Brethren Biblical
Seminary, 522
Mennonite Brethren in Christ
Church, 408
Mennonite Central Committee
(MCC), 102, 144, 151, 220, 318,
339, 422, 469, 471, 488, 491, 492,
496, 498, 551, 552, 557, 559
Mennonite Church, 397, 423. See
also Old Mennonite Church
Mennonite Collegiate Institute,
443
Mennonite Congress, 313
Mennonite Cultural Problems
Conference, 532
Mennonite Encyclopedia, The,
205, 422, 423, 533
Mennonite Family Names, See
Names
Mennonite Hymnary, The, 529
Mennonite *Initiativniki*, 344
Mennonite Land Settlement
Board, 478
Mennonite Life, 533
Mennonite Literature, 513, 516,
517
Mennonite Mission Society, 467
Mennonite Press, 434, 530
Mennonite Publishing House, 423,
530
Mennonite Quarterly Review, 423,
533
Mennonite, The, 541
Mennonite Theological Seminary,
(*Kweekschool*), 119, 138
Mennonite World Conference, 142,
143, 334, 343, 345, 558
Mennonites, 52, 73, 133, 196, 379,
538; as Alien Germans, 311; and
Baptists, 343; Canadian, 520; in
Oklahoma, 549; Palatine, 361;
in Siberia, 550; South German,
459
Mennonites, "New," 401, 402, 407,
422; "Old," 402, 417, 422, 423,
452
Mennonitische Blätter, 184, 218
Mennonitische Rundschau, 480
Mennonitische Warte, 480
Mennonitisches Jahrbuch, 205,
217, 221
Mennonitisches Lexikon, 205
Mental Hospitals, 558
Messenger of Truth, 405
Methodists, 370
Mexico, 334, 444, 454, 481, 484
Micron, Martin, 63
Migrations, America, 283, 508;
Asia, 283; Mexico, 444
"Mild Banners," 70
Milford Square, Pa., 401
Military Exemption, 82, 329, 377;
Service, 16, 82, 330, 334, 509;
Training, 218; Question, 384
Millennium, 24, 26, 35, 45
Miller, 261; A. J., 319; Orie, 315,
318
Ministers, 15, 61, 131, 174, 203,
204, 271, 309, 418, 510; Lay, 131;
"Leading," 419; Salaried, 111;
Training, 347
Minnesota, 208, 289, 447
Missions, 15, 138, 141, 204, 283,
308, 396, 403, 421, 435, 467; City,
531
Mollenaar, Johannes, 206
Molotschna, 248, 257, 265, 268,
427, 436, 514, 521
Momber, Hans, 176
Montbeliard, 210, 261
Moody, D. L., 420
Moravia, 7-10, 12, 13, 19, 27, 31,
33, 38, 76, 136, 191, 226, 238, 361
Moscow, 270, 311, 343, 346; Flight,
331; Refugees, 500
Moundridge, Kansas, 208, 428
Mountain Lake, Minn., 449
Mulberry Hedges, 432
Mühlhausen, Germany, 24, 25, 216
Müller, 261; Ernst, 92
Mumaw, Levi, 318
Munich, South Germany, 24
Münster, 44, 45, 46, 57, 68, 150,
155, 191
Münsterberg, 95, 312
Müntzer, Thomas, 25
Musser, Daniel, 526
Mysticism, 20, 23

N

Naffziger, Hans, 93, 201
Nafziger, Peter, 389
Names, 77, 101, 172, 216, 261, 361, 365, 367, 379, 387; Amish, 93, 371, 390, 391; Hutterite, 456
Napoleon, 165, 203
Napoleonic Wars, 179, 202, 384
Naturalization, 368
Nebraska, 289, 299, 383, 447
Neff, Christian, 205, 219, 334, 558
Netherlands, 12, 43, 103, 135, 166
Neuchatel, Switzerland, 75, 98
Neuenschwander, Michael, 385
Neufeld, Dietrich, 515; H. A., 473, 483
Neu-Samara, 260, 267
Neu-Täufer, 96, 97, 413
Neuwied, 90, 160, 186, 202, 220
"New Amish," 98, 413
New Economic Policy (NEP), 320, 327
New Jerusalem, 42, 44, 46, 51
"New" Mennonites, *See* Mennonites, New
New Netherlands, 359
Newton, Kansas, 299
New York, 382, 386, 387
New Zealand, 286
Nickel, Abraham, 179
Niessen, Hans, 161
Nijdam, C., 144
Nikolaipol, 314, 315
Nikolsburg, 33, 34, 35
Noncombatant Service, 182, 311. *See also* Military Service, Nonresistance
Nonconformity, 113, 396, 418, 508, 511
Nonresistance, 15, 16, 24, 29, 35, 82, 96, 102, 134, 217, 276, 481
North Dakota, 383
Northern District Conference, 451
North Kildonan, 447
Northkill, 371
Nürnberg, 19, 21, 24, 26, 28

O

Oath, 11, 13, 16, 43, 135, 139, 140, 397, 398, 535
Obbenites, 50, 51, 52, 72
Oberholtzer, John H., 401, 407, 421, 423, 459, 462, 526, 529
Oberschulze, 268, 329, 440, 442, 496, 501
Obregon, 484, 488
Odessa, 270, 273
Oecolampadius, 19, 20
Ohio, 203, 214, 381, 386, 396
Ohmstübchen, 273
Ohrloff, Russia, 258, 260, 313
Oklahoma, 299, 383, 435
Old Colony, 436, 440, 443, 444, 454, 477, 478, 481, 484, 487, 500. *See also* Mexico
Oldesloe, 70
Old Flemish, 112, 133, 176, 272
Old Frisian, 176
Old Groningen Society, 272
"Old" Mennonites, *See* Mennonites, "Old"
Old Order Amish, 73, 407, 411, 415, 416, 528
Old Order Mennonites, 407
Omsk, 305, 346
Ontario, 376, 387, 396, 475
Order in Council, 473, 482
Orenburg, Russia, 267, 304, 345
Organ, 403
Orthodox Church, 341, 343
Osiander, 19
Ostrog, 293
Oterbein, Ph. W., 399
Ottawa, 287, 476, 484
Oudste (Elder), 134, 419

P

Pacific District Conference, 451
Palatinate, 18, 30, 37, 77, 79, 85, 90, 136, 192, 196, 198, 203, 209, 261, 366
Palestine, 282
Paraguay, 334, 340, 481, 489, 494; Government, 496; River, 498
Parochial Schools, 433, 519; *See also* Schools
Paso Robles, Calif., 435
Passau, South Germany, 24, 40, 76, 528
Pastor, Adam, 64, 159
Pastorius, Francis Daniel, 360
Paul, Prince, 251
Pauls, Heinrich, 209
Pavlodar, 346

INDEX

Peace, 535; Heritage, 512; Testimony, 469
Peasants' Revolts, 11, 24, 26
Penn, William, 87, 121, 360, 365
Penner, Bernhard, 254; P. A., 468
Pennsylvania, 201, 382, 395, 409, 463, 512, 516, 528; German, 511; German Culture, 396; Germans 364, 396
Pennypacker, 532; Pennypacker, Samuel W., 364, 527
Persecution, 10, 16, 80, 86, 98, 105, 189. See also Martyrs
Peter the Great, 129
Peters, Abraham, 294, 295; Hermann, 282; Jakob, 289
Petersburg, 247, 251, 257, 270, 284, 438
Petter, Rodolphe, 467
Philadelphia, Pa., 157, 497
Philip of Hesse, 30, Philip II, 103
Philipists, 38, 40
Philips, Dirk and Obbe, 44, 50, 59; Dirk, 65, 66, 68, 159, 166, 525; Obbe, 59, 60, 61
Pietism, 130, 360, 403
Pilgrim Fathers, 123
Pingjum, Friesland, 53
"Plain" Coat, 401. See also Dress
Plain People, 418
Plockhoy, Pieter Cornelisz, 125, 359
Poland, 105, 166, 169, 184, 218, 258, 302, 425, 428, 459, 493. See also Prussia, Danzig
Potemkin, G. A., 251, 254
Prairie View, 434, 558
Prayer, 111, 195; Meetings, 403; Silent, 113
Prentis, Noble L., 431
Prinz, Matheus, 278
Prohibition, 17, 21
Prussia, 168, 169; West, 105, 136, 166, 167, 186, 229, 251, 256, 259, 425, 457, 459, 464. See also Danzig, Poland
Publications, 126, 138, 220, 524
Publishing Houses, 529
Puerto Casado, 489, 493
Puster, 31

Q

Quakers, 81, 120, 125, 126, 142, 213, 360, 361, 397, 535, 538
Quiring, Horst, 221; Traugott, 343

R

Radichev, Russia, 246
Raduga, 309
Raiffer, Hans, 228
Rappolstein, 209
Rebaptism, 9. See also Baptism, Anabaptism
Rechenschaft, 236
Red Armies, 314
Red Cross, 319, 481, 482, 539, 548, 549, 551
Redekop, David, 487
Redemptioners, 368
Reedley, California, 435
Reformation, 12, 15, 19, 24, 67
Reformed Church, 10, 11, 15, 79, 80, 99, 114, 130, 161, 361; as Oppressor, 114
Reformed Mennonites, 400, 407, 408
Refugees, 318; Harbin, China, 334, 335; Moscow, 500
Regensburg, Germany, 24, 33, 207
Reichstag, 333
Reimer, Klaas, 274, 438
Reist-Amman, 211
Reist, Hans, 85, 91, 92
Relief Commission, 550; Fund, 202; Work, 550; Global, 422. See also MCC
Religiöser Botschafter, 403
Religious Dissent, 16; Freedom, 326, 331; Instruction, 327, 520; Life, 272, 337, 372, 498.
Rembrandt, 129, 130
Remonstrants, 118, 131, 133, 153
Renicx, Tjaerd, 106
Reublin, Wilhelm, 3, 5, 6, 7, 11, 12, 22, 33, 37
Revival, 142, 399, 406
Revolutionary War, 397
Rich, 93; Isaac, 214
Richert, Heinrich, 464
Riedemann, Peter, 229, 236, 456
Ries, Hans de, 111, 127, 135
Riesen, von, 180
Rink, Melchior, 12, 28, 41
Ris, Cornelis, 345, 509, 527; Confession of Faith, 132
Rittenhouse, 532; David, 364

Ritter, Georg, 87
Rittinghausen, Willem, 361, 364
Robinson, John, 123
Rol, Henric, 45
Romer, Hans, 28
Roore, Jacob de, 107
Roosen, Gerrit, 156
Roosevelt, Theodore, 546
Rosenthal, Russia, 255
Rosthern, Sask., 444
Rothmann, Bernhard, 44, 48
Rottenburg on the Neckar, 13, 23, 32
Rotterdam, 78, 143, 202
Rues, M. S. F., 133
Ruisdael, Jacob van, 128; Solomon van, 129
Rumyantsev, Count, 246
Runkel, Johann, 89, 91
Rupp, 261
Russia, 39, 249, 262, 329, 425, 449, 464; South, 249, 251, 258, 291, 338
Russianization, 272, 291, 301, 302
Russo-German, 459; Mennonite Culture, 512
Rutgers, Swaan, 69

S

"Sacramentarian" Movement, 41
Sagradovka, Russia, 267, 283, 304, 314
Salzburg, 31, 32, 189
Samara, Russia, 260, 294, 295
Santa Catharina, Brazil, 500
Santa Fe Railroad Company, 288, 431, 448
Saskatchewan, 299, 442, 444, 475
Saskatoon, Sask., 444, 481, 530
Sattler, Michael, 13, 19, 20, 22, 35, 46, 48
Saur, Christopher, 526
Sawatsky, B. I., 343
Saxony, Germany, 18, 24, 25
Schabaelje, Jan Philipsz, 127, 526
Schantz, Jacob Y., 286, 430, 436, 439, 441; Joseph, 376
Schellenberg, Abraham, 429, 452; P. E., 522
Schiemer, Leonhard, 32
Schleitheim Confession, 17, 23
Schleswig, 152. *See also* Holstein

Schmidt, C. B., 288, 429, 431
Schmitt, H., 142
Schoerg, Joseph, 377
Schönwiese, Russia, 256
Schools, 204, 233, 235, 268, 433, 440, 497, 509, 511; Elementary, 309; Secondary, 269, 270, 415, 513
Schowalter, Christian, 461, 462; Otto, 158
Schrag, 261; Andreas, 289, 293; Benedikt, 96, 385
Schröder, Peter, 302
Schroeder, P. R., 465
Schulordnung, 519
Schulze, 267, 329, 440, 442, 496, 501
Schumacher, Fridli, 14
Schwenckfeld, Casper, 19, 23
Schwertler, 36, 40
Schwetz, Germany, 258
Scriptures, 16, 42. *See also* Bible
Secret Societies, 418
Selbstschutz, 316
Selective Service, 553
Sembach, Germany, 199, 206
Sermons, 113, 134. *See also* Ministers
Service for Peace, 555
Shafter, California, 435
Shaving, 373. *See also* Beards
Shelly, A. B., 465
Shenandoah Valley, Va., 374
Shunning, 133, 372, 409. *See also* Avoidance
Siberia, 186, 267, 301, 303, 305, 317, 336, 346
Silk Industry, 263, 264, 432, 451
Simplicity, 29, 508. *See also* Plain, Nonconformity
Singel, Amsterdam, 140
Skippack, Pa., 361, 365, 403
Slagel, Arthur, 318
Slavery, 362, 374
Slavgorod, 346
Slavophiles, 302
Smissen, van der, Family, 130, 157, 277, 465; Carl H. A., 157, 527; Carl J., 132, 387, 465, 466, 509; Gysbert, 154, 157; Hinrich, 155, 157
Smith, John, 382
Smyth, John, 123
Sobotiste, 226, 241

INDEX

Society of Brothers, 457
Socinians, 117, 131, 171
Sommer, Pierre, 215
Sommerfeld Church, 443
Sommerfeld Mennonites, 454, 477, 489, 500
Sonnenberg, Switzerland, 95, 98, 385
Souderton, Pa., 530
South America, 286, 334, 445, 454
South Dakota, 230, 539
Spittelmaier, Hans, 34, 36
Sprunger, S. F., 464, 465
St. Gall, Switzerland, 6, 8, 12
Stäbler, 36, 40
Stalin, 330, 336, 342
Stalingrad, 341
State and Church, 16. See Church and State
State Church, 8, 10, 17, 18
Stauffer, O., 142
Steen, Hans van, 167, 174, 176, 276
Steinbach, Manitoba, 405, 438, 453
Steiner, Ulrich, 100
Steinmaur, 17
Stemen, Henry, 381
Steyr, 31
Stoltz-Plateau, Brazil, 501
Storch, Nickolaus, 25
Strasburg, 19-24, 42-45, 60, 61, 70, 189, 194; Rules, 372
Stuckey, Joseph, 390, 411, 412
Stucky, 261; Jacob, 428
Studien-Kommission, 313, 317, 473
Stumpf, Simon, 5, 8
Stuttgart, 24, 187, 206, 278, 280
Styria, 31
Sudermann, Hermann, 184; Leonhard, 278, 285, 286, 289, 429
Sumatra, 308
Summerfield, Illinois, 387, 388, 427, 463
Sunday Schools, 396, 403, 406, 414, 415, 421
Swabia, 30, 37
Swamp Mennonite Church, Pa., 401
Swiss Brethren, 3, 9, 17, 19, 29, 33, 559; Swiss Amish, 93; Swiss Galicians, 459; Swiss-German Palatines, 364; Swiss Refugees, 135-36; Swiss Volhynians, 449, 459
Switzerland, 18, 19, 25, 31, 75, 80, 136, 142, 197, 222, 384, 409, 458, 559

T

Tabor College, 434, 452, 522
Tadzhikistan, 346
Taganrog, 258
Tashkent, 295
Tatar, 251, 259
Täufer-Bänz, 100
Täufer Bibel, 99
Täufer-Jäger, 84
Taufgesinnte, 9, 73
Tauler, Johann, 20
Tchertkov, Vladimir, 329
Teachers, 273, 310, 433, 513
Telner, Jacob, 360
Templer, 282, 303
Terek, Russia, 267, 304
Texas, 383
Teyler Foundation, 137
Theological Seminary, 301
Theresa, Maria, 241
Thiessen, J., 301; J. J., 444
Thirty Years' War, 77, 192
Thomashof, 206
Thuringia, Germany, 18, 24, 30
Tiege, Russia, 258
Tilsit, Prussia, 168, 171
Tobacco, 263
Toews, Cornelius, 289; David, 321, 444, 465, 474, 475, 483
Toleration, Religious, 10, 94, 150, 168
Tolstoy, Leo, 329
Tomsk, Siberia, 305
Topeka, Kansas, 449
Topeka Commonwealth, 449
Tories, 397, 398
Totleben, General von, 291
Tracht (Clothing), 392. See Clothing, Dress
Trakt, Samara, Russia, 260
Trakt, Mennonites, 294
Transylvania, 239, 243, 244
Trappe, Georg von, 251
Trinity, 64, 132
Trotzky, 329

Trypmaker, Jan Volkertsz, 43, 149
Turkestan, 267, 295, 296
Turkey Winter Wheat, 432
Turks, 27, 28, 31, 42, 249
Twenty Mile Creek, 377
Tyrol, 7, 12, 13, 23, 27, 31, 37, 189, 228

Vorsänger, 176, 272
Voth, H. R., 467; Tobias, 269
Vreden, Hendrik van, 64
Vreede, Adolf de, 79

U

Ufa, Russia, 304
Ukraine, 306, 316, 319, 346
Ukranian All-Mennonite Congress, 328
Ulm, South Germany, 23, 24
Umbitter, 175, 202
Umfrage, 202
Umsiedler, 161, 347, 348
United Brethren Church, 370, 399
United Missionary Church, 407, 408
United States, 290, 540; Senate, 288
United Witness, 471
University Graduates, 271, 513. See Table 2, 353-56
Unruh, A. H., 281; B. H., 281, 313, 333, 335; Tobias, 289, 293, 428, 450
Unser Blatt, 301, 328
Ural Mountains, 295
Uruguay, 186, 445

V

Vadian of St. Gall, 6, 20
Vancouver, B. C., 481, 530
Vera Cruz, 487
Vereinsschule, 269, 277
Vermaaner, 174
Vienna, 12, 13, 27, 31, 189
Villages, 439; Traditional 441, 445
Virginia, 373, 396
Vishenka, 245, 246
Vistula Delta, 166; River, 105, 166, 172, 178, 259; See also Danzig, Prussia
Vladislav IV, 170
Volendam, 340, 498
Volhynia, 208, 259, 261, 265, 289, 292, 293, 428
Voluntary Service, 558
Vondel, Joost van den, 127, 128

W

Wadsworth, 214, 382, 460; School, 465, 521
Wahres Christenthum, 309
Waisenamt, 441
Walachia, 39, 244
Waldenses, 12
Waldheim, 260, 261
Waldner, 244; Johannes, 245, 247
Waldshut, 11, 33
Walpot, Peter, 234
Walter, Jakob, 247; Zacharias, 240
Wandelnde Seele, 174, 309
War, 11, 535; Bonds, 548; Department of, 286, 541; Taxes, 35, 397. See also World Wars I, II
Warkentin, A., 465; Bernhard, 427, 432; Cornelius, 256
Warthegau, 184, 339
Waterlanders, 73, 111, 112, 116, 127, 133, 135
Waterloo, 379, 478, 530; County, 378
Watermelons, 263, 432, 450
Wayne County, 385
Wedding Attendance, 276; Customs, 212
Wedel, C. H., 521; Peter, 258
Weierhof, 199, 204, 214, 387
Wesley Brothers, 157
Western District Conference, 451
Westphalia, 44
West Point, Iowa, 461
West Reserve, Manitoba, 427, 437-439, 442, 443
Wheat Growing, 451; Turkey Winter, 432. See also Agriculture
Whitewater, Kansas, 458
Wichita, Kansas, 530, 559
Wideman, Henry, 378; Jakob, 35
Wiebe, Aron, 183; Gerhard, 436-438, 442
Wiebe, Jacob A., 427; Jakob, 276; Johann, 275, 442; P. H., 483
Wied, Hermann von, 159

INDEX

Wiedertäufer, 9, 51, 72
Wilhelm, Jost, 228
William of Orange, 72, 105, 114
Wilson, President, 542
Winkler, Manitoba, 441
Winnipeg, Manitoba, 289, 435, 437, 446, 447, 480, 481, 516, 530, 557
Wisler, Jacob, 406
Wislerites, 407
Wismar, Germany, 62, 66, 70
Witmarsum, Friesland, 43, 53, 55, 143, 501, 502
Woelk, Heinrich, 344
Woolman, John, 375
Woolwichers, 407
World Council of Churches, 144
World War I, 142, 208, 217, 218, 310, 481, 539; II, 143, 219, 330, 336, 342, 345, 553, 556
Worldliness, 134, 415. *See also* Nonconformity
Worms, 20
Worship, 114, 134, 139, 311, 405, 410
Württemberg, 18
Wüst, Eduard, 278, 279
Wüstenfelde, 66, 70, 154
Wyngaert, Tobias Govertsen van den, 127
Wytekon, 3

Y

YMCA, 539, 548, 551
Yoder, J. W. 516; Joseph, 411

Z

Zaandam, 129
Zagradovka, 315, 338
Zaunring, Georg, 31, 37
Zeeland, Netherlands, 103
Zentralschule, 270, 309, 497
Zhitomir, 261
Ziegler, Andrew, 397
Zierikzee, Holland, 125
Zijpp, N. van der, 145
Zinzendorf, 130, 157; N. L. von, 370
Zionspilger, 99
Zondagsbode, 138
Zonists, 119
Zur Heimat, 448
Zürich, Switzerland, 3, 5, 10, 11, 17, 18, 33, 34, 75, 77-80
Zweibrücken, Germany, 210
Zwickau Prophets, 24, 26
Zwieback, 450
Zwingli, Ulrich, 3-10, 17, 19, 22, 55, 72